Skill Acquisition and

Skill Acquisition and Training: Achieving Expertise in Simple and Complex Tasks describes the building blocks of cognitive, motor, and teamwork skills, and the factors to take into account in training them. The basic processes of perception, cognition, and action that provide the foundation for understanding skilled performance are discussed in the context of complex task requirements, individual differences, and extreme environmental demands. The role of attention in perceiving, selecting, and becoming aware of information, in learning new information, and in performance is described in the context of specific skills.

A theme throughout this book is that much learning is implicit; the types of knowledge and relations that can profitably be learned implicitly and the conditions under which this learning benefits performance are discussed. The question of whether skill acquisition in cognitive domains shares underlying mechanisms with the acquisition of perceptual and motor skills is also addressed with a view to identifying commonalities that allow for widely applicable, general theories of skill acquisition. Because the complexity of real-world environments puts demands on the individual to adapt to new circumstances, the question of how skills research can be applied to organizational training contexts is an important one. To address this, this book dedicates much of its content to practical applications, covering such issues as how training needs can be captured with task and job analyses, and how to maximize training transfer by taking trainee self-efficacy and goal orientation into account.

This comprehensive yet readable textbook is optimized for students of cognitive psychology looking to understand the intricacies of skill acquisition, while being accessible to a range of students and practitioners.

Addie Johnson is Professor of Human Performance and Ergonomics at the University of Groningen. She is co-author, with Robert Proctor, of *Attention: Theory and Practice*, and *Neuroergonomics: A Cognitive Neuroscience Approach to Human Factors and Ergonomics*. Her research focuses on the intersection of memory and attention.

Robert W. Proctor is Distinguished Professor of Psychological Sciences at Purdue University. In addition to the books with Addie Johnson, he is co-author, with Trisha Van Zandt, of *Human Factors in Simple and Complex Systems* (2nd ed.) and, with Kim-Phuong L. Vu, of *Stimulus-Response Compatibility Principles: Data, Theory, and Application*. His research focuses on basic and applied aspects of human performance.

Skill Acquisition and Training

Achieving Expertise in Simple and Complex Tasks

Addie Johnson and Robert W. Proctor

Routledge
Taylor & Francis Group
NEW YORK AND LONDON

First published 2017
by Routledge
711 Third Avenue, New York, NY 10017

and by Routledge
2 Park Square, Milton Park, Abingdon, Oxon, OX14 4RN

Routledge is an imprint of the Taylor & Francis Group, an informa business

© 2017 Taylor & Francis

The right of Addie Johnson and Robert W. Proctor to be identified as authors of this work has been asserted by them in accordance with sections 77 and 78 of the Copyright, Designs and Patents Act 1988.

All rights reserved. No part of this book may be reprinted or reproduced or utilised in any form or by any electronic, mechanical, or other means, now known or hereafter invented, including photocopying and recording, or in any information storage or retrieval system, without permission in writing from the publishers.

Trademark notice: Product or corporate names may be trademarks or registered trademarks, and are used only for identification and explanation without intent to infringe.

Library of Congress Cataloging-in-Publication Data
Names: Johnson, Addie, author. | Proctor, Robert W., author.
Title: Skill acquisition and training / by Addie Johnson and
    Robert W. Proctor.
Description: 1st Edition. | New York : Routledge, 2016. |
    Includes bibliographical references and index.
Identifiers: LCCN 2016008665 | ISBN 9781138640153 (hb : alk. paper) |
    ISBN 9781138640160 (pb : alk. paper) | ISBN 9781315531656 (e)
Subjects: LCSH: Ability. | Attention. | Cognitive learning.
Classification: LCC BF431 .J594 2016 | DDC 153.9—dc23
LC record available at https://lccn.loc.gov/2016008665

ISBN: 978-1-138-64015-3 (hbk)
ISBN: 978-1-138-64016-0 (pbk)
ISBN: 978-1-315-53165-6 (ebk)

Typeset in Palatino
by Apex CoVantage, LLC

Printed at CPI on sustainably sourced paper

Contents

Preface viii

1 Skill Acquisition and Training in Context 1
   Historical Overview of Skills Research 4
   Information-Processing Approach to Skill Acquisition..............12
   Phases of Skill Acquisition......................................13
   Quantifying Performance Changes 14
   Modeling Skill 20
   Applications of Skills Research 25
   Summary..27

2 Perceptual Learning..29
   Mechanisms of Perceptual Learning 30
   Facilitating the Development of Perceptual Skill 43
   Visual Search 49
   Procedural Learning 52
   Adaptive Perception 53
   Summary..56

3 Response Selection and Motor Skill...........................58
   Response-Selection Skill...60
   Motor Learning 70
   Factors Influencing Motor Skill Acquisition 78
   Summary..85

4 Attention and Skill 87
   Conceptualizing Attention..88
   Attention and Automaticity.......................................96
   Attentional Skill...100
   Implicit Learning 107
   Summary...112

5 Cognitive Skill and Instruction 113
   Problem-Solving Skill...114
   Learning and Remembering 122

    Learning by Analogy 128
    Facilitating the Acquisition of Cognitive Skill......................133
    User Models and Intelligent Tutors 141
    Summary..142

6 Expertise..144
    The Investigation of Expertise......................................145
    Understanding Expert Knowledge...................................146
    Acquisition of Expert Performance..................................150
    General Characteristics of Experts 153
    Expertise in Three Specific Domains 155
    Skilled Memory Theory 168
    Summary..171

7 Why Errors Occur and Their Contributions to Learning...........173
    Errors and Action Control 174
    Effects of Making Errors on Learning...............................178
    Performance Monitoring 184
    Prediction Error and Learning......................................187
    Repeating Errors Made during Training 190
    Error Orientation 199
    Summary..200

8 Individual Differences in Skill Acquisition and Maintenance 202
    Intelligence and Aptitudes..204
    Task Analysis Based on Individual Difference Variables.............212
    Dynamic Accounts of Abilities and Skill 215
    Problems of Interpretation in Understanding the Relation
        between Abilities and Skill Level 222
    Individual Differences in Reading Skill.............................225
    Skill and Aging 231
    Summary..235

9 Situational Influences on Skilled Performance 237
    Arousal and Performance..239
    Theories Based on General Arousal and the Yerkes-Dodson Law.......240
    Arguments against "General Arousal" and the
        Yerkes-Dodson Law 243
    Circadian Rhythms 245
    Sleep Deprivation and Fatigue 252
    Stressful Physical Environments...................................256

Drug Use and Performance 259
Summary..266

10 Designing Effective Training Systems 268
Assessing Training Requirements...............................269
Structuring Training 274
Team Training..277
Implementing and Evaluating Training in Organizations 281
Trainee Characteristics 283
Evaluating Training Effectiveness................................287
Maximizing the Benefits of Training.............................289
National Culture and Training 290
Summary..293

References..295
Author Index 354
Subject Index 374

Preface

Skilled behavior is fundamental to all human activities. Skills such as driving, reading, and typing are so common that we sometimes take them for granted. However, most skills are a marvel of coordination. The same basic processes of perception, cognition, and action that underlie basic skills go into the development and performance of more specialized skills, such as electronic troubleshooting, operating heavy machinery, playing tennis, and managing an organization. The way in which skill is acquired and maintained, as well as the factors that affect skilled performance, is of major concern to individuals, educators, professional trainers, and human resource specialists in industry. Training programs are devised that are intended to maximize acquisition, retention, and transfer of the acquired skills to the situations in which they must be executed. These programs must take into account how people learn, but also their motivation to learn and organizational barriers to change. The goal of the present text is to describe the basic components of skilled performance and the way that these components can be integrated through practice and training to produce the high-level skill required in various aspects of life.

Historically, a primary focus of skills research has been on perceptual-motor performance. This research, both basic and applied, has produced a better understanding of such issues as the way in which actions are selected and coordinated, levels of skilled performance, and the conditions of practice and training that facilitate the acquisition and transfer of skill. Over the years, however, skills research has expanded to encompass higher-level cognitive skills, such as those involved in expert problem solving and decision making. This expanding research base, coupled with the development of sophisticated methods for modeling performance, has resulted in major advances in the investigation and understanding of skill. It is our intent to present these advances in a unified way that provides researchers, designers, and managers with the knowledge they need to evaluate new research and assess and develop training programs and selection criteria.

Basic processes of perception, cognition, and action provide the foundation for understanding skilled performance, but an understanding of complex skills requires an integrative, interdisciplinary view of human performance. Thus, in addition to reviewing skills research in the perceptual, cognitive, and motor domains, we consider individual differences in basic cognitive abilities and goal orientation and the limitations they place on what can be learned or performed, as well the influence of situational factors on the learning and expression of skills. Where appropriate, we use models of skilled performance and skill acquisition within the various domains of skill, as well as real-life examples, to frame research findings. Importantly, we do not simply describe skilled performance; we also discuss how to achieve it. Chapters on training and instruction describe in detail how basic research can be applied to practical problems.

This book was originally intended as the second edition of the book *Skill Acquisition and Human Performance* that we published in 1995. However, much has occurred in the field since publication of that book, and we ourselves have expanded our knowledge and interests into more applied domains of skill and training. Consequently, this book is considerably different from the previous one, although some of the material in this book has been adapted from that of the prior one. Because we take a more applied thrust in the current volume and have completely restructured and updated the writing, we have decided that it warrants the new title of *Skill Acquisition and Training: Achieving Expertise in Simple and Complex Tasks*. It is our sincere hope that students, trainers, and researchers will find the material covered in this book to be both interesting and informative.

Addie Johnson
Robert W. Proctor

1

Skill Acquisition and Training in Context

All learning from experience, all thinking, all inference, is transfer: there are only differences in degree.

C. K. Lyans (1914, p. 384)

When Asiana Airlines flight 214 crash-landed in fair weather at the San Francisco International Airport on July 6, 2013, fatally injuring three passengers and severely injuring many more, one question raised was how the flight crew could have allowed the flight speed to become dangerously slow in their final landing approach without reacting and correcting it. In fact, the U.S. National Transportation Safety Board's (2014) report on the crash identified pilot mismanagement of the descent as well as the complexity of the aircraft's autoflight system as contributing factors in the incident. Among the Board's recommendations were improved training for the pilots on the autoflight system and increased time flying the aircraft manually during training.

In contrast to the apparent failure of the pilots, the skill with which the flight attendants carried out their duties to evacuate the aircraft to minimize casualties was praised in the news media. The cabin manager for the flight, Lee Yoon-hye, told journalists, "I wasn't really thinking, but my body started carrying out the steps needed for an evacuation. I was only thinking about rescuing the next passenger" (quoted by Briggs, 2013). Candace Kolander, head of air safety, health, and security for the Association of Flight Attendants, commented,

> She reacted automatically. When that happens your brain says: "OK, it's time to do what I'm trained to do." And your body just does it because through training you build those motor skills, the motions you're supposed to do, the voice commands you're supposed to do . . . You become a robot. That's why I can open that (aircraft) door in my sleep because in training you get that adrenaline going and you do it the same way every year. So when it does happen you know what adrenaline feels like and you know you can do it.
> (Quoted by Briggs, 2013)

These quotes capture many of the characteristics of highly practiced skills: They are automatized as a consequence of extensive practice in contexts similar to those under which the skills will ultimately have to be performed. Such incidents emphasize the importance of designing training programs to ensure that necessary skills are acquired.

Although the flight attendants operated under an emergency situation, skilled behavior is fundamental to virtually all human activities. Some skills, such as driving, reading, and typing, are so common that they can be taken for granted. Other skills, such as serving tennis balls, playing bridge, or baking bread, are more specialized, yet most of us can, with some practice, master them. Skills may have large perceptual (e.g., reading a medical image), cognitive (e.g., reading or remembering large amounts of information), or motor (e.g., typing or skiing) components. A basic question regarding skill acquisition is whether skills in perceptual, cognitive, and motor domains share common mechanisms. Some researchers emphasize commonalities across the different domains, whereas others point to differences (see, e.g., A. Johnson, 2013). Almost all skills, however, require coordinated processes of perception, cognition, and action. In acquiring skill we learn to select relevant information and link it to actions in a smooth, integrated fashion. Skill can thus be defined as *goal-directed, well-organized behavior that is acquired through practice and performed with economy of effort.*

One skill that illustrates how the processes of perception and cognition, as well as the ability to react and to interact with others, jointly determine performance is air traffic control (ATC). ATC can be considered a dominantly cognitive task (Corver & Aneziris, 2015; Vu, Kiken, Chiappe, Strybel, & Battiste, 2013). The air traffic controller must keep track of large amounts of information (weather conditions, the registration numbers and types of aircraft under the controlled space, as well as the speeds at which they are traveling, the positions of the aircraft in the air and on the runway, etc.) and make complex decisions. The controller must also communicate and coordinate actions with pilots and other controllers in the ATC system, as well as learn and follow rules but still be flexible when necessary. Even though ATC is predominantly a cognitive task, understanding how skill in the task develops and predicting who will excel at the task require a broad approach. Research in this field has shown that training for ATC should be perceptual (e.g., learning to make a quick scan across aircraft in the airspace), cognitive (e.g., developing decision-making skills), and social (e.g., focusing on communication and teamwork skills) in nature (Durso & Manning, 2008).

Although understanding and training complex skills such as ATC can be considered an essential goal of skills research, much of the research on skill acquisition has been carried out in laboratory settings. Laboratory settings offer convenience, but more importantly allow the researcher to control the environment so that operative variables can be identified. It can be argued that the basic processes involved in the execution of controlled laboratory tasks are required in more complex tasks (e.g., Raymond, Healy, & Bourne, 2012). However, it remains essential to question whether principles derived from studying skill in simple laboratory tasks are applicable to the more complex real-world tasks. Complex tasks, by definition, consist of a number of processes, and it is necessary to understand how these processes compete and are coordinated. Performing complex tasks will likely require processes of attention and cognitive control that are not required when component tasks are performed in isolation. Moreover, real-world task performance is affected by a wide range of variables and subject to fewer constraints than laboratory task performance (Beier & Oswald, 2012). The competing desires to impose experimental control and to consider a wide range of factors thus trade off in using laboratory versus real-world tasks.

Because of the need to balance experimental control with applicability to complex tasks, it is often necessary to use a range of tasks to study skill acquisition in any particular domain. A good example of how laboratory and more naturalistic tasks have been combined to understand skill is reading radiological images for medical diagnosis. Reading medical images is a skill that develops over many years (van der Gijp et al., 2014). Due to its importance in diagnosing serious medical conditions, this skill has received considerable investigation, much of which is discussed in Chapter 6. Diagnostic processes have been studied naturalistically by comparing the performance of medical students, residents, and practicing radiologists. To gain a fuller understanding of particular factors influencing diagnostic skill, such as prior knowledge of patient anatomy, more detailed analyses have been performed using constrained diagnostic tasks with people of varying levels of skill and training. Because diagnosis from medical images depends on basic skills such as visual inspection and decision on an interpretation (Krupinski, 2010), findings from laboratory studies of these basic abilities have also been applied to the specific problem of medical diagnosis to develop a better picture of how skill in this domain develops.

Historical Overview of Skills Research

Research relating to skill began in the early years of experimental psychology with the publication by Ebbinghaus (1885/1964) of a monograph on learning and memory that, although not directly concerned with skill acquisition, set the stage for the research on skill that would follow. In Ebbinghaus's time, the generally accepted view was that higher mental processes such as thinking and memory could not be studied experimentally. Given this prevailing atmosphere in early scientific psychology, the breadth and depth of Ebbinghaus's investigations are remarkable. Using himself as the subject, Ebbinghaus demonstrated beyond question that it in fact was possible to obtain objective, quantifiable measures of the mental processes underlying memory.

Ebbinghaus introduced a set of materials, consonant-vowel-consonant nonsense symbols, that provided him with many different items from which lists of varying length could be composed. He used serial recall, learning the lists to a criterion of one or two completely correct recalls in correct order. One fairly unsurprising finding resulting from Ebbinghaus's explorations was that the number of repetitions of a list required for learning increased with the length of the list.

More important, rather than relying on recall of the lists at a later time to measure retention, Ebbinghaus developed the method of relearning the list to a criterion of correct recall and measuring a savings score relative to the initial learning. This *savings* paradigm provides a measure of the benefit of prior learning when something is learned again at a later time, even when the original list could not be consciously recalled. Hilgard (1964) emphasizes the significance of this contribution in his introduction to a republication of Ebbinghaus's monograph, stating, "Ebbinghaus took the ease of relearning something once known—a fact so plausible that it must have been often observed—and made it a part of science by developing the quantitative saving score, in which the saving in relearning is scored as a per cent of the time (or trials) in original learning" (p. viii). Formally,

$$\% \text{ savings} = \frac{P_{\text{original}} - P_{\text{relearning}}}{P_{\text{original}}} \times 100,$$

where P is some measure of performance.

For Ebbinghaus, performance was usually the number of trials to learn series of nonsense syllables to a criterion of correct recall as a function of variables such as retention interval and number of successive days on which learning was repeated. He demonstrated that much forgetting occurred over the first hour after initial learning and that forgetting continued to occur in decreasing amounts as the retention interval increased over hours and days (Wixted & Carpenter, 2007). In one study, Ebbinghaus memorized stanzas of Byron's *Don Juan* and found that savings increased over 3 successive days of relearning. Most remarkably, when he relearned the same stanzas 17 years later, long after they could no longer be recalled, those stanzas showed savings of approximately 20% compared to learning of stanzas that had not been learned previously (Verhave & van Hoorn, 1987).

One of Ebbinghaus's most theoretically important findings was that items could act as retrieval cues for other items in learned lists even when the cued and retrieved syllables were separated by other elements in the original list. He demonstrated this by showing savings for lists composed of the same syllables as the originally learned lists but with adjacent syllables in the new lists having been separated by 1, 2, 3, or 7 intervening syllables in the original lists. Assumptions about how associations are formed between elements that are relatively remote from each other distinguish many models of learning and memory (e.g., Cleeremans, 1993). The problem of how associations between items that occur together are formed, as well as remote associations linking items that are separated by others, is treated in more detail in Chapter 4.

Early Studies of Skill Acquisition

The advent of the study of skill acquisition, per se, can be dated to the work of Bryan and Harter (1897, 1899) on the acquisition of skill at telegraphy. Telegraphy was a major form of communication at the turn of the century, when the broadcast of news and other current events depended on the accurate transmission and reception of telegraphic messages. In telegraphy, a skill that can take up to 2.5 years to master, a sender must transcribe a written message into Morse code and rapidly tap a telegraph key, in taps of long and short durations, separated by pauses. The receiver of the code must re-transcribe the message, typically using a typewriter. Receiving high-speed Morse code depends on the (a) perceptual ability to parse the "dits" and "dahs" that make up the message and to group these symbols into conceptual units, (b) motor ability to quickly type the message, and (c) strategic ability to "copy behind"—that is, to allow the typing of the message to lag behind the decoding of the message (Wisher, Sabol, & Kern, 1995). The speed with which messages are transmitted is limited by the skill of the operators at translating the messages and executing the required physical actions.

Bryan and Harter's initial work focused on differences in performance as a function of level of experience. They found that (a) rates of receiving varied greatly across operators, (b) external disturbances had less impact on experts than on novices, and (c) variability in sending time decreased with increasing skill level. Bryan and Harter also examined the individual learning curves of several operators. Measures of operator performance were taken weekly, starting with the operators' initial experiences as telegraphers and continuing for up to as many as 40 weeks (see Figure 1.1).

As shown in Figure 1.1, Bryan and Harter found that the sending rate improved more rapidly than the receiving rate but also reached asymptote sooner. Eventually, the receiving rate approached or even exceeded the sending rate, so that a skilled receiver could easily handle the most rapid incoming message. Moreover, the sending curves showed continuous improvement with practice up until the point that the asymptote was reached, whereas the receiving curves for some operators showed distinct *plateaus*, or periods during which there was relatively little change in performance. These plateaus led Bryan and Harter to characterize skill acquisition as the development of a *hierarchy of habits*. For telegraphic skill, this hierarchy was proposed to involve letters, words, and higher-language units. According to Bryan and Harter, receivers are concerned with identifying individual letters during their first few days as telegraphers. Over this period they begin to identify words, and it is words that then become the primary units for the next few months. Only after the letter and word "habits" have been acquired does the operator fully benefit from the higher-level organization of the language. Thus, the plateaus represent periods where a lower-level habit is at asymptote but the next higher habit is not yet affecting performance. Bryan and Harter emphasized that automatizing lower-level habits in the hierarchy is necessary for skill to be acquired, due to the freeing up of attention, and that "in learning to interpret the telegraphic language, *it is intense effort which educates*" (1897, p. 50), a sentiment that is mirrored in contemporary studies of acquisition of expertise in other domains.

Just as Ebbinghaus's research set the stage for the investigation of skill by establishing paradigms for measuring learning and demonstrating fundamental learning phenomena, Bryan and Harter's work provided a direct impetus for the systematic investigation of skilled performance. Their seminal papers can be directly linked to three major areas of investigation: (a) variability in

Figure 1.1 Sending and receiving curves for two telegraphers studied by Bryan and Harter.

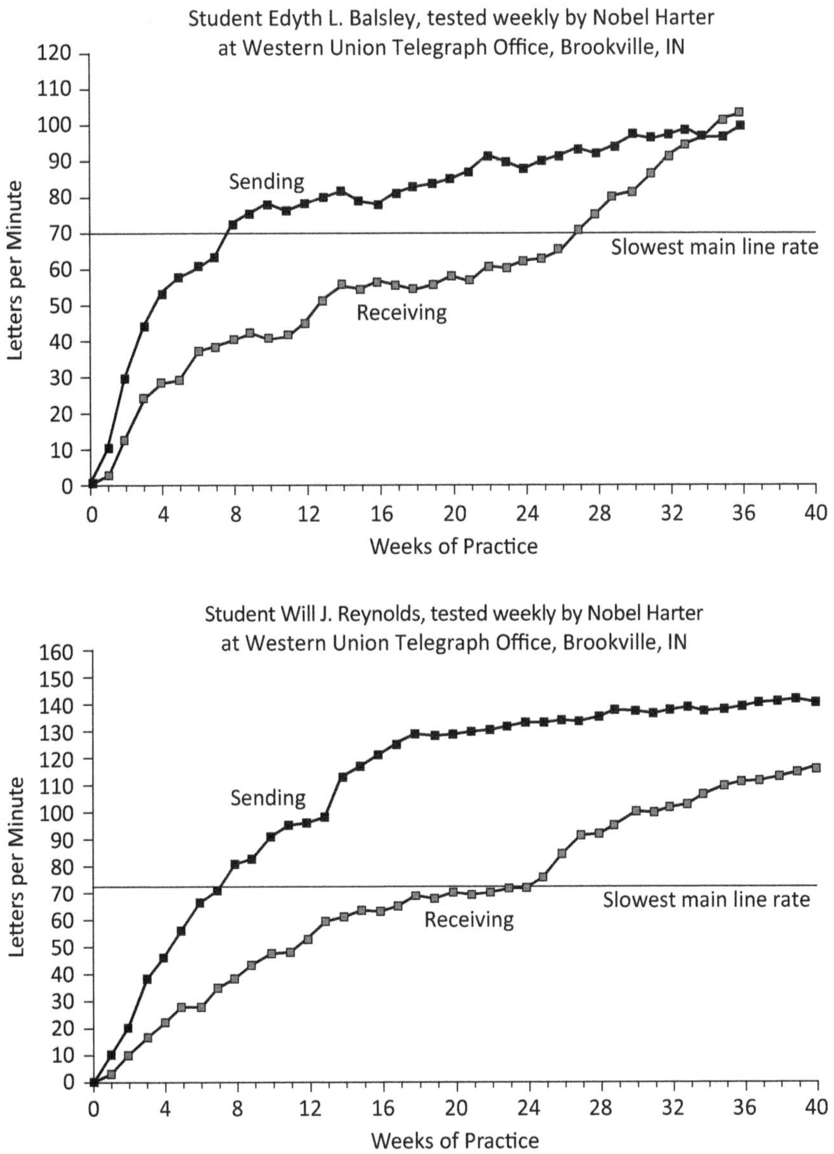
Student Edyth L. Balsley, tested weekly by Nobel Harter
at Western Union Telegraph Office, Brookville, IN
Letters per Minute
Sending
Receiving
Slowest main line rate
Weeks of Practice
Student Will J. Reynolds, tested weekly by Nobel Harter
at Western Union Telegraph Office, Brookville, IN
Letters per Minute
Sending
Receiving
Slowest main line rate
Weeks of Practice

Source: Bryan and Harter (1897).

performance, (b) whether the changes underlying the acquisition of expertise are qualitative or quantitative in nature, and (c) the nature and development of automaticity (T. D. Lee & Swinnen, 1993).

The most visible effect of practice documented by Bryan and Harter, the learning curve, has achieved the status of a psychological law. Performance of most tasks seemingly improves continually, with the greatest changes occurring early in practice. This improvement with practice tends to follow a power function (see Figure 1.2):

$$\text{Performance Time} = a + bN^{-c},$$

where a and b are constants representing asymptotic performance and the difference between initial and asymptotic performance, respectively, N represents the number of practice trials, and c is the learning rate. Note that this implies that the logarithm of response time plotted as a function of the logarithm of the number of trials performed will be a straight line. Snoddy (1926) was the first to conclude that learning could be described as a linear function of the logarithms of time and trials and thus conformed to a power function. This relation is referred to as the *power law of practice* and has become a benchmark for models of skill acquisition (A. Newell & Rosenbloom, 1981). Although the power law provides a good description of group learning curves, it may not do so for the curves of individuals (Haider & Frensch, 2002; Heathcote, Brown, & Mewhort, 2000). Specifically, Heathcote

Figure 1.2 A learning series for a single participant in an experiment in which a participant had to respond as quickly as possible whether a spelled out number matched the number of dots in a display. The best fitting power function is illustrated by the dashed line, and the best fitting exponential function with the solid line.

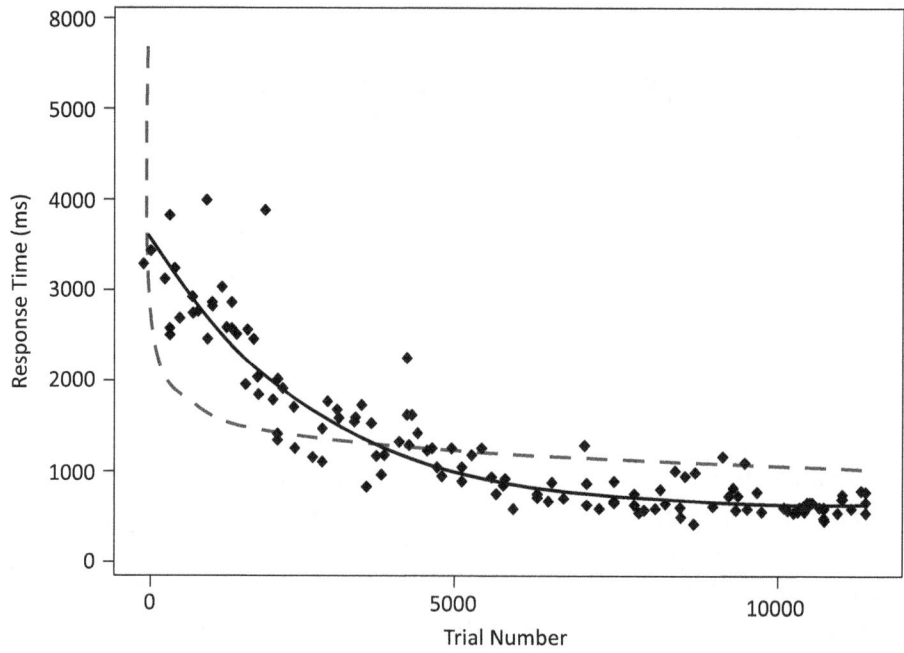

Source: Heathcote et al. (2000).

et al. showed that for many tasks individual learning curves are described better by an exponential function,

$$\text{Performance Time} = a + b\ exp(-cN),$$

for which the terms are defined as above (see Figure 1.2). Both power and exponential functions show the greatest learning early in practice, although they differ in the precise shape of the learning curve.

Transfer of Learning

The criterion for successful learning is not always performance on the task at hand. In many cases, the critical issue is whether practice of one task will lead to improved performance of another one. For example, practice on the driving range (a facility for golfers to practice long shots) must transfer to the golf course, and practice in a flight simulator must transfer to the airplane cockpit. In the *transfer* research paradigm, practice on a task is followed by a later test that differs in some way from the original task, and performance on this test is compared to that of a control group. The most commonly used index is

$$\%\ \text{transfer} = \frac{P_{control} - P_{tranfer}}{P_{control}} \times 100,$$

where P is a performance measure. By varying the relation between original and transfer tasks, tests of transfer provide evidence about the nature of the learning that has occurred.

Alternative theories of skill or learning differ in the breadth of transferability that they predict. Broad transferability was the key feature of the view called the *doctrine of formal discipline* (see Lyans, 1914), which was popular at the close of the 19th century. According to this doctrine, training in classical disciplines, such as mathematics and Latin, should foster the acquisition of general reasoning abilities that are of use in virtually all mental endeavors, rather than establishing a collection of specific associations between particular stimuli and actions to be taken. The idea that specific learning can lead to general improvements in behavior is an attractive one. However, this view has been challenged virtually since it was first proposed.

Thorndike and Woodworth (1901a, 1901b, 1901c) were the first to present data challenging the doctrine of formal discipline. In their tasks, participants were given a pretraining test on their ability to perform a simple task, such as estimating the area of a rectangle, and then were given training on a related task, such as estimating the area of a triangle. Following training, the participants received a transfer test on the original task. In every case, Thorndike and Woodworth looked for evidence of transfer from the training experience to the subsequent performance of the original task. Their general finding was that there was relatively little transfer from one task variation to another. In fact, in many cases performance was worse in the transfer test than in the pretraining test.

A more recent challenge to the doctrine of formal discipline has to do with the "use it and keep it" movement that sells "brain training" products as a means of preserving cognitive functioning in the face of age-related declines in cognitive ability. The general idea behind brain training is that the benefits of engaging in tasks requiring problem solving, memorizing, and other cognitive activities should yield improvements in cognitive functioning that transfer to other tasks and slow age-related decline in these functions. A large industry has developed promoting brain training and, as a consequence, people tend to believe that it is effective (Rabipour & Davidson, 2015). However, although the jury is still out (see, e.g., Rabipour & Raz, 2012; C. Schooler, 2007), the effects of practice with puzzles seem to be restricted to the type of puzzle practiced (Salthouse, 2006). In one of the most thorough studies to date, Owen et al. (2010) had more than 11,000 participants in an online study train for 6 weeks on tasks designed to improve basic cognitive skills. They concluded, "Although improvements were observed in every one of the cognitive tasks that were trained, no evidence was found for transfer effects to untrained tasks, even when those tasks were cognitively closely related" (p. 775). Likewise, although working-memory training (tasks intended to improve working-memory capacity) may encourage use of strategies that transfer to closely related tasks (Dunning & Holmes, 2014), there is little compelling evidence that such training provides an increase in working-memory capacity that generalizes more broadly (Harrison et al., 2013; Redick, Shipstead, Wiemers, Melby-Lervåg, & Hulme, 2015).

Thorndike and Woodworth interpreted their findings as evidence against the view that practice at one task develops a general ability that enhances performance of most other tasks. Instead, they theorized that practice strengthens particular associations between elements within a task. This *theory of identical elements* predicts transfer of training only when two tasks have particular elements in common. For example, transfer is expected, and found, between the addition task 2 + 6 and the addition task 6 + 2, because the operand is identical, but not between the addition task 2 + 6 and the subtraction task 8 − 2 because the operator and one of the operands are different (J.I.D. Campbell, Fuchs-Lacelle, & Phenix, 2006). The theory of identical elements marked a turn away from the doctrine of formal discipline and its emphasis on general faculties such as attention, memory, and reasoning, toward consideration of "habits" and "associations" particular to individual tasks. Although research within the tradition of identical elements continues to flourish (e.g., J.I.D. Campbell et al., 2006; Rickard, 2005), the formal discipline view has been largely discredited (Leberman, McDonald, & Doyle, 2006).

Skilled Action

"Man is not merely perceptive and intellectual, but distinctly active or reactive" (Woodworth, 1899, p. 1). These words heralded the early study of the initiation and execution of voluntary movement, and emphasized its role in skilled performance. In his most extensive study within this skilled action perspective, Woodworth had people draw series of ruled lines of a specified length. He examined the accuracy and variability of the movements executed to make these lines under different conditions of speed stress, practice, fatigue, and sensory control. By comparing performance under these conditions, Woodworth was able to reach conclusions about the relative influence of each factor.

Two major findings that continue to receive investigation stand out. First, when people were required to make the same movement but at different rates (as governed by a metronome), accuracy decreased as the speed of the movement increased. Woodworth noted that equal increments of speed did not produce equal increments in the error rate; rather, the function was S-shaped such that when movements were very slow or very fast, increments in movement time had little effect on error rate. Second, Woodworth found that, although being able to see one's limb and the line while drawing was usually beneficial, the benefit of vision depended on the duration of the movement performed. For movement durations of less than 450 ms, accuracy was no better with the eyes open than with the eyes shut. However, for slower movements, accuracy was better when the eyes were open. These results suggested to Woodworth that visual feedback can be used to guide movements, but only if the movements exceed some critical duration so that guidance is possible.

Not only were Woodworth's empirical contributions important, but so were his theoretical ones. He distinguished between two phases of movement control, which he called *initial impulse* and *current control*. Foreshadowing more recent ideas on the initiation and control of movement (see D. Elliott, Helsen, & Chua, 2001), Woodworth believed that "the first impulse of a movement contains, in some way, the entire movement" (p. 55). This idea implies that a representation or plan (often called a *motor program*) underlies the intended movement and that the current control phase consists only of adjustments based primarily on visual feedback.

Information-Processing Approach to Skill Acquisition

In an *information-processing approach* to cognition, the human is considered to be an element in a system and described much as any other system component would be in terms of inputs, transformations, and outputs. Craik (1948) referred to the human "operator" as a chain composed of links by which the sensory signal (e.g., the perception of error in the control of a process) is converted into a motor response (in this case, a corrective action). The approach of conceiving of the human being as an information processor actively operating on environmental information to produce an observable response has been taken by many skills researchers (and psychologists in general) over the past 60 years.

Most information-processing approaches to studying human performance divide performance into the constituent components of perception, cognition, and action, as did Craik (1948). In such an approach, it is assumed that the activities taking place within a person between the presentation of an external stimulus and the observation of an overt response can be studied with behavioral and psychophysiological methods. Typically, distinct stages of processing are assumed, and experimental methods are applied to isolate and study the stages of interest. The simplest framework of information processing, shown in Figure 1.3, distinguishes just three stages: perceptual processes, decision making and response selection, and response programming and execution. This framework typically is supplemented with an attentional system that selects some sources of information for processing over others and a memory system that stores the vast knowledge that we possess (*long-term memory*) and maintains in an active state a limited amount of the information of immediate relevance to the task at hand (*short-term* or *working memory*).

Specific models differ in the proposed properties of the stages, such as the role of task preparation, whether attention is required for processing, whether particular processes can be carried out concurrently or must be

Figure 1.3 Three-stage model of human information processing.

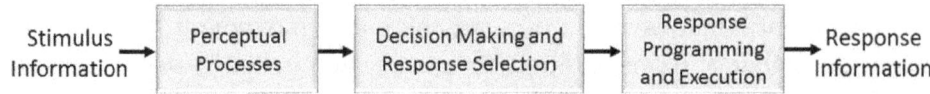

performed sequentially, and the extent to which one process affects another. Because the goal of most skills researchers is to determine the contributions of perceptual, cognitive, or motoric processes to skilled performance and the nature of changes within these processes as skill develops, the simple information-processing framework consisting of just the three primary stages described earlier serves well as an organizing framework for research on skill.

The information-processing approach was further developed and formalized by A. Newell and Simon (1972). In their classic book, *Human Problem Solving*, they presented new methods for describing problem-solving behavior and developed a comprehensive theory of problem solving. Newell and Simon employed modeling concepts and notation systems from the field of artificial intelligence to show that the human problem solver can be described as an information-processing system. Although Newell and Simon were concerned primarily with problem-solving performance and not the acquisition of problem-solving skill, research directed toward understanding the differences in problem solving across levels of expertise has followed directly from their work.

Phases of Skill Acquisition

Skill is acquired through practice or training. A defining characteristic of skills is thus that they are not innate but must be learned. Moreover, skilled behavior is goal-directed. Skill develops in response to some demand imposed by the task environment on the organism, although some learning may occur solely as a function of performing a task, with no explicit intention to learn. Skill is said to have been acquired when the behavior is highly integrated and well-organized such that, through experience, the components of behavior are structured into coherent patterns. Often, information-processing demands are reduced as skill is acquired, freeing limited resources for other activities.

Since the work of Bryan and Harter on acquisition of skill at telegraphy, it has often been proposed that skill acquisition proceeds through phases characterized by qualitative differences in performance. Although the plateaus from which Bryan and Harter initially deduced different phases of skill acquisition do not seem to be general characteristics of learning, much evidence suggests skill acquisition progresses in qualitatively different phases.

A very useful and influential framework for skill acquisition was proposed by Fitts (1962/1990, 1964; Fitts & Posner, 1967). Based on his observations that different cognitive processes are involved at different stages of learning,

Fitts distinguished three phases: the *cognitive*, *associative*, and *autonomous* phases. Early in the learning of complex skills, cognitive processes are used by the learner to understand the nature of the task and how it should be performed (in other words, to institute a mental set to perform the task). The learner must attend to outside cues, the instructions that are provided, and feedback about performance. Because of the heavy involvement of conscious cognitive processes early in learning, Fitts called this the cognitive phase.

After the instructions have been learned and task expectations are understood, the learner enters the associative phase. In this phase, inputs are linked more directly to appropriate actions, and the need for verbal mediation is diminished. Thus, error rates decrease, as does performance time. The transition from the associative phase to the autonomous phase is marked by reduced interference from outside demands and the lessening of attentional requirements. When task performance has reached the autonomous phase it is said to be automatic, no longer requiring conscious control. According to Fitts, this automaticity may take months or years to develop, and will allow the automated task to be performed concurrently with many other activities.

Even though Fitts distinguished three distinct phases of skill through which the learner passes, he regarded the progression through the phases as continuous. Transition from one phase to the next was predicted to be gradual and not marked by an abrupt shift. Moreover, Fitts acknowledged that the learner may not make the transition to later stages. In his work extending this theoretical framework to training methods, Fitts found that the efficacy of a particular method depended on the current phase of skill acquisition and that appropriate training methods could reduce acquisition time dramatically. For example, with regard to the cognitive phase of skill acquisition, Fitts (1962/1990) summarized research showing that the number of hours of training preceding a student pilot's first solo flight could be reduced markedly by use of practice procedures designed to provide an intellectual understanding of flight problems and processes. Similar ideas for training have been pursued more recently, as is discussed in Chapters 8 and 10.

Quantifying Performance Changes

It cannot be taken for granted that skill will be acquired just because a task has been practiced. Some activities are more likely to lead to improvements in skill than are others, and performance improvements observed under some conditions may not hold up when the situation is changed. To be able to determine the factors that facilitate skill acquisition and transfer, techniques are needed to quantify the changes in performance that occur. The most obvious of performance measures are increases in the speed and accuracy with which a task is performed. However, these increases may reflect a number of things, including changes in mental representations or operations involved in task performance, the choice of strategies used to perform the task, or the degree of attentional involvement. In addition to the question of how we can best detect performance improvements, a major question is "What differences in information processing underlie these measurable changes in performance?"

Performance Measures

Most of the experimental tasks used to study skill focus on the speed and/or accuracy of performance. For example, the speed and accuracy with which problems can be solved under different conditions would be of interest to investigators of cognitive skill. A motor skills researcher might measure the time to initiate a movement, as well as the time to execute the movement and its accuracy, and a researcher investigating a predominantly perceptual skill would measure accuracy of classification or perceptual thresholds.

When reaction time is the primary measure of skill, means or medians are obtained for different groups or conditions, and differences between the conditions are used to make inferences about the complexity of the required processing. However, it is not enough to know only that two conditions differ in reaction time. We want to be able to characterize more specifically the nature of the differences in information processing that lead to the observed reaction-time differences. Consequently, methods have been developed that allow inferences to be made about the stages or processes that contribute to the overall reaction time.

The earliest of these chronometric methods, the *subtractive method*, can be attributed to Donders (1868/1969). To use this method, two experimental tasks are created that are presumed to differ by exactly one information-processing stage or process. According to the subtractive logic, then, the difference in reaction times between these conditions is taken as the time to complete that stage or process. For example, Posner and Mitchell (1967) had people classify pairs of letters as "same" or "different." Reactions to classify a pair as "same" were approximately 75 ms faster if the letters were identical in form (e.g., AA) than if they were identical only in name (e.g., Aa). Posner and Mitchell proposed that this difference in response times occurred because the former judgments could be made on the basis of the visual information, whereas the latter judgments required in addition that the name of each form be determined. Applying the subtractive logic, they concluded that this additional naming process took approximately 75 ms. Note that application of the subtractive logic, as in this example, depends on the assumptions that the processing stages are distinct and independent and that the insertion of the additional process does not alter the basic task structure.

A more recent technique, the *additive factors method*, developed by S. Sternberg (1969), allows determination of the processing stages involved in task performance. To use this method, the researcher manipulates several factors (i.e., independent variables) and determines whether the factors have additive or interactive effects on reaction time. If two factors have additive effects, they are assumed to affect different stages. If the factors interact, they are assumed to affect the same stage. Usually at least one of the factors manipulated can be logically assumed to affect a particular processing stage (e.g., stimulus clarity most likely affects perceptual processing time). By examining the patterns of interaction contrasts, the underlying processing stages can be inferred (e.g., if the frequency with which a stimulus occurs interacts with stimulus clarity, the effect of frequency can be localized at the perceptual stage).

Both the subtractive method and the additive factors method require the assumption that the stages of information processing are serial and that the processing associated with one stage must be completed before that associated with the next stage begins. These assumptions will not always be met, because many processes likely operate concurrently, and a given process may output partial rather than complete information (e.g., McClelland, 1979; Townsend, 1974). Despite these limitations, a consistent picture emerges when a set of findings of additivity and interaction is interpreted in terms of processing stages (Sanders, 1998).

Accuracy of response is typically used as a primary measure of skill in situations in which there is no speed stress for responding, and the task is sufficiently difficult that accuracy is less than perfect. This difficulty may be inherent in the nature of the task (e.g., a problem may be sufficiently difficult that not all people will solve it), or it may be induced by presenting stimuli briefly or under degraded conditions (e.g., an array of letters may be exposed for just 50 ms, followed by a masking stimulus). As with reaction times, factors are manipulated and their influences on accuracy are compared to determine the nature of the processing involved.

Another informative approach is to manipulate experimental factors at different points along the learning curve to see whether the processing characteristics of the task have changed with experience. For example, Logie, Baddeley, Mané, Donchin, and Sheptak (1989) had people play a complex computer game that relies on both perceptual-motor and cognitive skills for many sessions, and evaluated the way in which processing changed as skill at the game was acquired by adding the requirement to perform various secondary tasks (e.g., tasks requiring paced rhythmic tapping, spatial visualization, or verbal cognitive processing) at different points during practice. The secondary task "paced tapping" was found to have only a small effect on game performance early in practice, but a larger effect later in practice, which Logie et al. interpreted as indicating that response timing is more crucial to expert performance than to novice performance. Also, whereas both visuospatial and verbal secondary tasks interfered with game performance at low levels of practice, the disruption produced by the visuospatial task was reduced greatly at higher levels of practice. Logie et al. interpreted this aspect of their results as suggesting that perceptual-motor tracking control is a demanding part of the computer game initially, but that it becomes an automated skill for expert performers.

Verbal Protocol Analysis

In some tasks, particularly those requiring complex problem solving, a more complete picture than that provided by performance measures alone can be gained by asking participants to verbalize the steps taken to perform the task. The goal of such *verbal protocol analyses* is to provide insight into the strategies and hypotheses of the performer (Ericsson & Simon, 1993; T. G. Gordon, Coovert, & Elliott, 2012). To perform protocol analyses, reports consisting of verbalizations made by the person either during (*concurrent protocols*) or after (*retrospective protocols*) solving a problem or performing some other task are collected and analyzed.

A framework proposed by Ericsson and Simon (1980) provides a theoretical rationale for the use and interpretation of verbal protocols. According to this framework, the necessary conditions for valid protocols are that (a) participants report the contents of working memory (i.e., what they are thinking about) without interpretation or elaboration and (b) the contents of working memory be verbal, as opposed to spatial or pictorial. Only concurrent protocols satisfy the first of these conditions, which cautions against the use of retrospective protocols. Even with concurrent protocols, however, several potential problems exist. First, the requirement to verbalize may interfere with, or otherwise alter, primary task performance. For example, if the task is to determine whether two complex geometric forms shown in different views are the same or different, the requirement to verbalize the actions being performed may interfere with performance of the task. Second, some crucial aspects of performance likely occur without the person's awareness and so would not be verbalized. Third, interpreting verbal protocols is not only time-consuming but also problematic, requiring a systematic description of the task, a theory of task performance, and consideration of the goal the participant is trying to achieve.

Psychophysiological and Neuropsychological Measures

The measures of human information processing described earlier are increasingly being supplemented by measures of the physiological processes that underlie such processing (see, e.g., A. Johnson & Proctor, 2013). The most widely used of these psychophysiological measures is the *event-related potential*, or ERP, which is the electrical activity recorded at the scalp that is time-locked to an external stimulus event (see Lagopoulos, 2007, for an overview). To compute an ERP, the electrical activity at several scalp sites is recorded for many trials and then averaged to eliminate the electrical activity unrelated to stimulus processing.

A number of components of the ERP have been associated with specific cognitive events (see Figure 1.4), and changes in the latency and magnitude of these components can provide insight into how tasks are performed. Most of these components are designated by the letter N or P, to indicate whether the component is negative-going or positive-going, and a number indicating the serial order in the event sequence. For example, N1 is the first negative-going component. Sometimes timing in milliseconds, rather than serial order, is used to designate the components (e.g., N1 is also called N100 because it occurs approximately 100 ms after stimulus onset). Both the N1 and the P1 are related to perceptual processing. The N2 appears to reflect object recognition and categorization (Folstein & Van Petten, 2008). The N2pc (pc stands for posterior-contralateral, or the visual cortex opposite to the location of the attended object), which is computed by subtracting right- from left-side activation (or vice versa), appears to be related to target differentiation (Eimer,

Figure 1.4 The early cognitive event-related potential components and an illustration of the enhanced P3 component to an unexpected target stimulus (the letter *T*; right panel) relative to an expected, repeated stimulus (left panel) in the oddball paradigm.

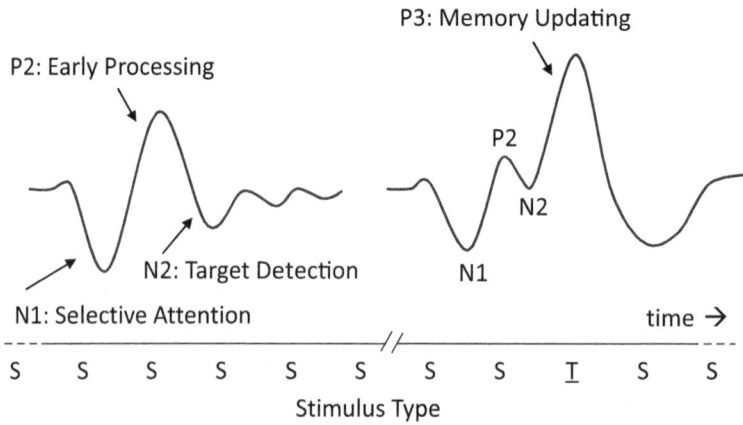

Adapted from Polich (1993).

1996). Finally, the P3 (Polich, 2007; Polich & Kok, 1995) appears to reflect memory updating and cognitive load.

As an illustration of how components are identified and linked to cognitive processing, consider the P3. The P3 has been clearly linked to one aspect of performance in the so-called oddball paradigm. In this paradigm, one standard stimulus is repeated in a series. Occasionally, a different stimulus (the oddball) is presented, and the participant is either to make an overt response to or to covertly count the occurrences of the oddball stimulus. A large P3 component is elicited to the oddball stimulus (see Figure 1.4, right side) that is not elicited by the repeated stimulus (see Figure 1.4, left side). Since only when the oddball stimulus appears does memory need to be updated, the P3 component has been interpreted as reflecting processes involved in memory updating (Donchin & Coles, 1988). P3 amplitude has been found to be affected by cognitive variables, such as whether attentional resources are allocated to the task, and P3 latency is considered to reflect the time devoted to stimulus evaluation. Increasingly, analysis of the ERP and other aspects of the electroencephalogram is providing evidence about information processing that is not obtainable from performance measures.

The information provided by ERP analyses may become useful even before the stimulus is presented and remain useful after a response is made. So-called contingent negative variation (CNV) reflects anticipation or preparation for an upcoming stimulus (Zaepffel & Brochier, 2012). Recently, an aspect of the ERP, referred to as SPCN (sustained posterior contralateral negativity) or CDA (contralateral delay activity), has been associated with maintenance of information in visual working memory (a memory store that is assumed to be nonverbal in nature and that can hold a limited number of visual items; Gao, Yin, Xu, Shui, & Shen, 2011). The lateralized readiness potential (LRP) has been linked to response preparation (Smulders & Miller, 2011), and, when a response made is in error (providing negative feedback), feedback-related negativity (FRN), a negative component that has a fronto-central distribution, occurs (Luque, López, Marco-Pallares, Càmara, & Rodríguez-Fornells, 2012).

Brain imaging techniques based on the measurement of blood flow to brain regions are also used to study the correlates of skill. These techniques generally assume that blood flow increases to brain regions of increased neural activity, and the measurements of blood flow are used to construct images of activity in the brain. Often, subtractive logic of the type described for reaction time is applied to interpretation of the brain images: Two tasks are performed, and the process unique to the more complex task is attributed to regions of the brain that show greater activity for that task than for the simpler one. Cabeza and Nyberg (2000) reviewed 275 PET (positron emission tomography) and fMRI (functional magnetic resonance imaging) studies and found, among other things, that perception and imagery activated regions in the dorsal and ventral visual pathways, attention and working memory produced activation in prefrontal and parietal regions, and long-term memory encoding and retrieval produced activation in prefrontal and other regions. One example of applying fMRI to skill acquisition is a study by Poldrack, Prabhakaran, Seger, and Gabrieli (1999). They compared fMRI while participants learned a probabilistic classification task (for which the relation between cues and categories is probabilistic) to that measured while the participants performed a perceptual-motor task. Their results showed that the frontal cortices and the caudate nucleus of the striatum (a subcortical part of the forebrain) were active during the probabilistic classification task, thus showing that the striatal system is involved in cognitive skill acquisition as well as in perceptual-motor skills.

Additional insight into the composition of skills and the nature of learning processes can be gained by the use of neuropsychological studies with brain-damaged patients (see, e.g., Shallice, 1988). Such studies typically compare performance of patients with specific neurological impairments to that of unimpaired people on a battery of tasks. The basic assumption of these studies is that the information-processing system of the patient has been damaged in some specific way. To the extent that the specific nature of the damage can be determined, evidence about what the impaired person can and cannot do becomes relevant for evaluating models of the intact information-processing system.

Modeling Skill

Theories of skill range from general frameworks to verbally stated accounts of specific phenomena, to formalized models. Cognitive architectures provide a powerful framework for creating models of skill. A *cognitive architecture* is a simulation environment that incorporates a theory of cognition. Models of particular tasks are created by adding task-specific knowledge to the rules embedded in the architecture. Only architectures that contain mechanisms for learning can be used for modeling skill acquisition. Two of these are SOAR (States, Operators, and Results; Laird, 2012; A. Newell, 1990) and ACT-R (Adaptive Control of Thought – Rational; J. R. Anderson, 1993, 2007; J. R. Anderson & Lebiere, 1998; J. R. Anderson et al., 2004).

Within SOAR, intelligent behavior is viewed as a form of problem solving in which new knowledge is learned when impasses are met. Impasses are moments in task performance in which several possible actions are available and no clear decision rule for selecting the appropriate one is known.

When SOAR reaches an impasse, it evaluates each of the possible actions and selects the most optimal one, and creates a new rule that can be applied when the same circumstances are encountered again. In SOAR, knowledge was originally conceived as all-or-none in that new rules are learned all at once and remembered indefinitely. Obviously, human learning and memory are often more gradual and fraught with errors, and Derbinsky and Laird (2013) have explored how forgetting can be incorporated into SOAR.

One way of overcoming the shortcomings of all-or-none knowledge representation is to attach numeric quantities, or "activation," to the knowledge elements in the architecture. This approach is called subsymbolic representation, and architectures that combine symbolic and subsymbolic representations are referred to as hybrid architectures. The best-known hybrid architecture is ACT-R (J. R. Anderson, 1993, 2007; J. R. Anderson & Lebiere, 1998; J. R. Anderson et al., 2004), which is a *production system* accompanied by a set of modules (see Figure 1.5).

Production rules consist of sets of conditions that are tested against the current internal state and states of the modules, and a set of actions that is carried out once all conditions are satisfied. Productions are basically if-then rules: *If* the condition specified in the production is satisfied, *then* the action

Figure 1.5 The ACT-R architecture, showing visual, procedural memory, declarative memory, and motor modules.

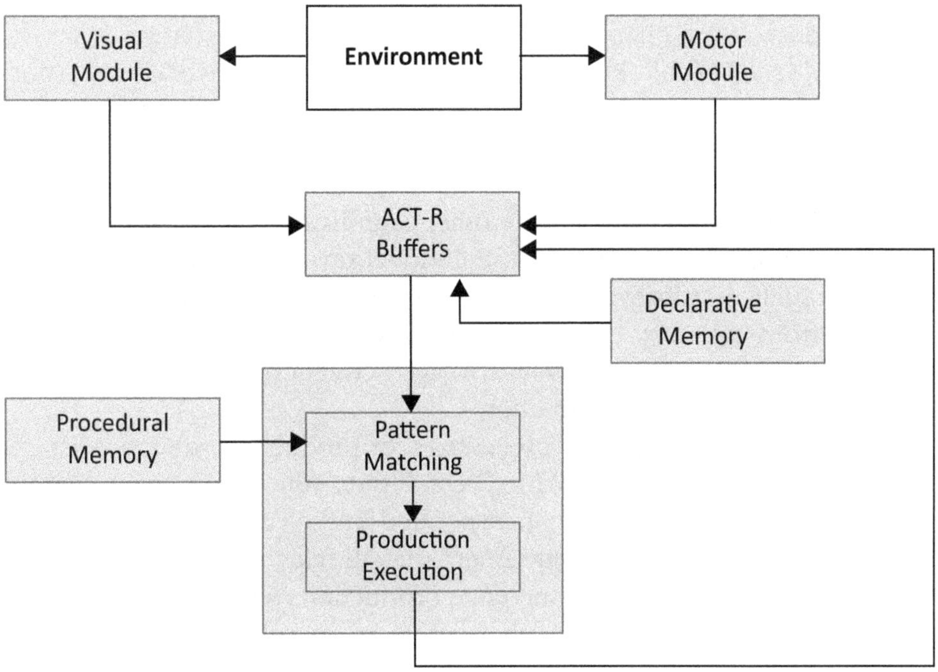

Source: ACT-R, http://act-r.psy.cmu.edu/about/.

is carried out. A production may specify something other than an overt action, as when a number is carried when performing mental arithmetic.

The modules of ACT-R include a declarative memory module that stores facts and perceptual and motor modules that serve as the interface between ACT-R and the external world via buffers containing currently attended or recently retrieved information (Byrne & Anderson, 2001). A so-called goal buffer holds the current goal, and a problem-state module stores the current state of the system, including partial approximations to the current goal. The facts stored in the memory module have activation values (i.e., subsymbolic representation) that reflect how often they have been used in the past and their association with the current context. These activation levels determine how long it will take to retrieve a fact from memory (and whether it can be retrieved at all).

The distinction between declarative and procedural knowledge is fundamental to the ACT-R framework. Roughly speaking, declarative knowledge is the body of facts and information that a person knows, whereas procedural knowledge is the set of skills a person knows how to perform. Anderson and colleagues' account of skill acquisition consists of an early declarative phase (corresponding to Fitts's cognitive phase) and a later procedural phase (corresponding to Fitts's autonomous phase), with an intermediary process of knowledge compilation. Knowledge compilation allows the learner to move from the declarative to the procedural phase by converting declarative knowledge to a procedural form.

In the declarative phase of skill acquisition verbal mediation is needed to maintain task-specific knowledge and instructions in working memory. Performance at early stages of skill acquisition thus depends heavily on declarative memory. The need to interpret instructions results in behavior that is much slower than that of experts: Retrieving the instructions takes time, and this forms a bottleneck for other cognitive processes. If the instructions are incomplete or insufficient, the model reverts to even more general strategies, such as retrieving the past experiences that have the highest activation from memory. This experience-based retrieval strategy works on the assumption that experiences with a high activation have the most potential relevance in the current situation.

More efficient, task-specific procedures, or production rules, are learned in the process of acquiring a skill. These if-then rules allow even complex environmental conditions (once incorporated in the rules) to trigger mental or overt actions without the requirement that all relevant aspects of the situation be kept active in working memory. Production rules have an associated learned utility value that reflects the success of the rule in the past (i.e., the "reward" resulting from past applications of the production rule). On each cycle of the production system, the rule with the highest utility is chosen from the rules that match the current contents of the buffers.

In many task models, the transition from novice to expert is modeled by a mechanism for learning new production rules, *production compilation* (Taatgen & Lee, 2003; see also A. Newell & Rosenbloom, 1981). This mechanism takes two existing rules that have been used in sequence and, if there are no buffer conflicts (as would be the case when, e.g., both rules specify using the right hand), combines them into one rule. Declarative memory has a special role in learning. According to the process of substitution, if a first rule requests a fact from declarative memory, and a second rule uses it, the retrieved fact is substituted into the new rule. This process is key to learning task-specific rules.

Another significant class of models is connectionist (neural network) models, which consist of some number of neuron-like processing units and connections between them (see Figure 1.6). Generally, one subset of units, called an input layer, represents input from the environment to the system, and another subset, called an output layer, represents output from the system to the environment. There also may be one or more layers of hidden units,

Figure 1.6 A multilayer network in which information from the input units is recoded by hidden units, which then activate output units.

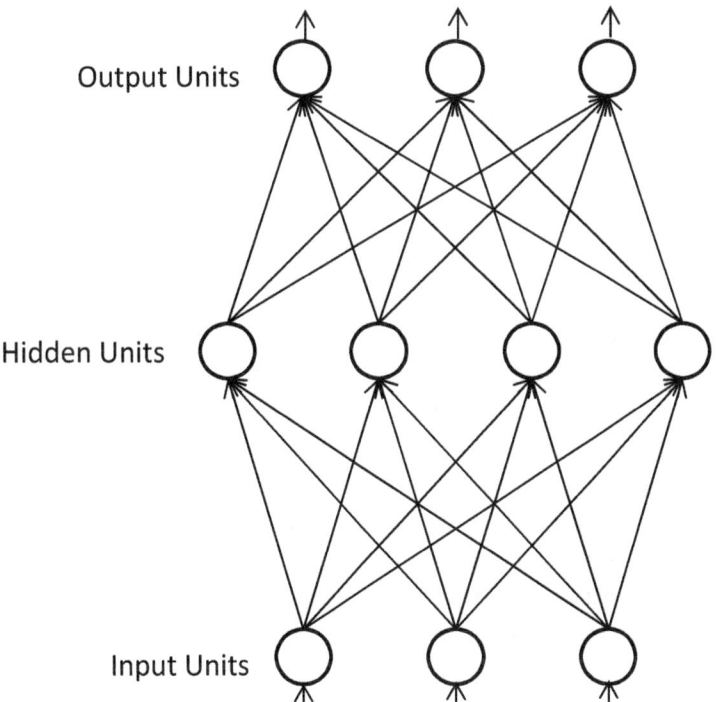

which have neither direct input from nor output to the environment. These hidden units can be conceptualized as representations of presented inputs. The knowledge or behavior of the model is contained in the connections between the units (see, e.g., Houghton, 2005; McClelland, Rumelhart, & the PDP Research Group, 1986). Each connection has an associated weight that can be zero (i.e., input has no effect), positive (i.e., input has an excitatory effect), or negative (i.e., input has an inhibitory effect). When input from the environment is received, patterns of activity are set up in the respective layers of the network. One consequence of this distributed representation is that connectionist models can continue to function effectively when some of the units are damaged, a property that is called *graceful degradation*, which is also found for brain function (e.g., Rolls, 2008). Another useful property of network models is *soft constraint satisfaction*. Specifically, connectionist models can generate a stable global pattern of activity when there are several soft constraints (which are not necessary but are desired), some of which may be in conflict, operating together.

Many connectionist models have learning mechanisms for modifying the weights assigned to the connections between units. Although different specific learning rules have been used, modifications in the weights typically are based on the reduction of error between the actual output of the system and desired output. Because these models with learning mechanisms allow performance to change as a function of experience, they have been applied in a number of domains of skill acquisition, including word reading (Seidenberg, 2005) and complex reasoning (Leech, Mareschal, & Cooper, 2008).

The growth of activation in a network in response to a stimulus can be characterized as a cascade process: Input is presented as a pattern of activation at the input nodes, and this activation propagates through the system, with the activation of each node being a running average of its net input over time (e.g., J. D. Cohen, Dunbar, & McClelland, 1990). This process continues until a response unit reaches a threshold level of activation and the response is executed. Often, a logistic, S-shaped activation function, in which the units are more responsive when they are in the middle, more linear part of their dynamic ranges, rather than at either extreme of activation, is used. One result of using an S-shaped function is that inputs may not only increase the resting-level activations for the units in the proper pathways but also put them into a more responsive state (i.e., from low activation into the middle, more response range).

The learning mechanism/rule in many networks is backpropagation, according to which connection strengths are adjusted incrementally after each trial, with the sizes of the changes made being proportional to the difference between the output pattern produced by the network and that desired in response to the input pattern. The algorithm is "supervised" in the sense that feedback must be provided for learning to occur. The changes in connection strengths will be larger early in learning than later, because as the output pattern becomes closer to that desired, due to an appropriate set of connection strengths being developed, the computed difference between the target and output patterns will be smaller. Moreover, as the units approach the target positive or negative values, they enter less responsive regions on the activation function (i.e., one or the other extremes of the S-shaped function). These two properties produce the power-law relation between reaction time and practice (J. D. Cohen et al., 1990). Automaticity is not all-or-none, but is a function of the relative strengths of the competing pathways.

Rule-based and network models are not mutually exclusive: Some models contain aspects of both and some researchers have translated one type of model to the other. Moreover, many task models do not rely on either of these frameworks, but are based on sets of equations, often embedded in computer simulations (Busemeyer & Diederich, 2010). Symbolic connectionist models have been created that implement symbolic representation in connectionist models (Hummel & Holyoak, 2003). The basic idea behind symbolic connectionist models is that the units do not have to be restricted to subsymbolic "microfeatures" but can represent complex, symbolic information. The symbolic information represented by the units can be connected in networks that allow this information to be processed in the manner of connectionist models. The existence of symbolic connectionist models and cognitive architectures with subsymbolic representation, as in recent versions of ACT-R, suggests that the two modeling approaches are increasingly coming together.

Applications of Skills Research

Just as skilled behavior is integral to nearly any human endeavor, skills research is applicable to a wide variety of work, sport, rehabilitation, and other contexts. Much training emphasizes the technical skills necessary to perform one's tasks or jobs competently in a specific profession or domain. More recently, though, awareness has developed of the need for training the "soft" skills required to interact effectively with other people—for example, crew members, fellow employees, and customers (Bancino & Zevalkink, 2007; R. E. Riggio & Tan, 2014)—and to deal with stress. Soft skills include leadership, effective communication with others, and stress recognition.

Much of the research on skill and human performance has been motivated by potential performance breakdowns in high-risk environments, such as the military command center or the medical operating room. Thus, in addition to issues in how best to train basic perceptual, decision-making, or motor skills, topics such as the robustness of skill under conditions of time pressure or stress need to be considered to ensure optimal performance. Roscoe (1980) described the range of skills that need to be considered in training aircrews as *procedures, decision making,* and *perception.* The procedural skills mentioned by Roscoe include communication, navigation, aircraft operation, and emergency skills, and, for military crews, weapons and battle management. Decision-making activities include route planning and crew management, and, for military crews, hazard assessment and the setting of target and mission priorities. Perceptual tasks include geographic orientation, processing aircraft control and indicator information, communication, and, for military crews, threat and target identification and weapons systems control. This example illustrates that many real-world tasks consist of a range of competing demands. A high level of skill in component tasks will be necessary in order to cope with these demands, and a careful analysis of task requirements will be necessary in order to design appropriate training of these skills.

Another contemporary application area for skills research is training in the medical field and health care. It is clear that many aspects of medicine (e.g., surgery, radiology, dentistry) require high levels of perceptual-motor ability, and cognitive processes and skills are also critical in medical practice. Problem solving, in particular, forms the cornerstone of many medical curricula (e.g., Barrows & Tamblyn, 1980; Elstein, Shulman, & Sprafka, 1978; G. R. Norman & Schmidt, 1992). However, the medical environment can be very stressful, making soft skills such as recognizing and dealing with anxiety and high arousal levels, communication, and leadership important issues. In fact, it is increasingly being recognized that the medical operating room shares characteristics with the aircraft cockpit and an important training method, *crew resource management* (Helmreich, Merritt, & Wilhelm, 1999), has been borrowed from aviation contexts and adapted for the operating room. More generally, healthcare providers need to be trained in effective communication with the patient (Burns, Baylor, Morris, McNalley, & Yorkston, 2012).

New developments in medical technology and treatments require that medical education extend over the lifetime of the individual. Health professionals are often required to be self-directed in their learning activities and need to be able to relate new information to their own practices and experiences. Theories of adult learning (e.g., those of Cross, 1981; Knowles, 1984; Rogers & Freiberg, 1994) that emphasize self-directed and experiential learning seek to provide a basis for understanding and structuring learning opportunities, and new media and simulation environments provide the means for implementing self-directed learning based on these theories.

Another area in which skills research is increasingly being applied is management education (Wankel & Stachowicz-Stanusch, 2011). The goal of management education is to provide managers numerous techniques, approaches, and philosophies that will enable them to perform their jobs more effectively. Management education includes specific skills such as developing a budget and negotiating with employees, general abilities such as organizational planning and communication with employees, and personal development skills such as providing effective leadership and strategies for handling stress. Knowledge of skill acquisition, transfer, and retention is applicable to all of these areas.

Sport training is yet another field that stands to benefit from advances in our understanding of skill acquisition, retention, and transfer. Recent studies have focused on the effects of training basic abilities on sport performance and on the effects of sports training on basic abilities. For example, perceptual training has been shown to enhance anticipation in specific sports (Abernethy, Schorer, Jackson, & Hagemann, 2012) and training in a sport that requires mental rotation (wrestling) has been shown to affect performance on tests of basic mental rotation ability (Moreau, Clerc, Mansy-Dannay, & Guerrien, 2012). Soft skills, including personal development, arousal regulation, and motivational skills, are also considered to be important for enhancing sport performance (Birrer & Morgan, 2010).

Summary

Systematic research on skill acquisition and skilled performance began late in the 19th century. This initial activity, which encompassed such topics as the description of learning curves, transfer of training, and motor performance, lasted approximately 30 years. A revival of interest in skill occurred around 1945. Since that time, there has been increasing emphasis on the mechanisms underlying skill and on cognitive skill. Many contemporary developments within a variety of disciplines have contributed to the growth of skills-related research in the recent past.

A defining property of skill is that it develops over time, with practice. Initial performance is usually a tentative, rough approximation of the desired action and requires considerable conscious effort. With practice, this initial, halting performance gives way to relatively effortless, smooth, integrated patterns of behavior. These modes of performance and the transitions between them are captured by several frameworks. The frameworks can be applied to the acquisition of a specific skill, as well as to the performances exhibited by a skilled individual in different task environments.

Much insight into skill acquisition and skilled performance can be gained by examining performance measures, typically response time and accuracy, and several methods have been developed to refine the inferences that can be drawn from such data. Verbal protocol analyses have been used as additional sources of data, and psychophysiological and neuropsychological techniques have been developed that provide new insight into the processes and brain structures underlying skilled behavior. Quantitative models of skill can be used to generate predictions and test assumptions regarding the mechanisms and knowledge structures underlying the acquisition of skill. The knowledge gained from skills research can be applied to training in a variety of fields where acquisition, retention, and transfer of skills are essential.

2

Perceptual Learning

Perceptual learning is a powerful way for an individual to become tuned to frequently recurring patterns in its specific local environment that are pertinent to its goals without requiring costly executive control resources to be deployed.

R. L. Goldstone, J. R. de Leeuw, and D. H. Landy (2015, p. 24)

Our perception of the world seems to occur automatically, without attention or effort. However, many of the discriminations that we take for granted are the result of repeated exposure or deliberate attempts to learn. The illusion of effortlessness results from the interaction of the intention of the observer and the environment. As long as we do not try to distinguish stimuli with which we are unfamiliar, we will not be aware of the effort associated with doing so. For example, nearly everyone can easily tell the difference between a crow and a sparrow, but many cannot tell the difference between different varieties of sparrows, or even between male and female sparrows. Most people would argue that this does not matter to them. When previously indistinguishable stimuli become important, as when a novice cricket player becomes aware of the importance of picking out a full toss from a yorker or a googly from a leg break, concentrated effort is needed.

The enhanced ability to discriminate between and to classify stimuli based on perceivable properties is a hallmark of perceptual skill. We are equipped with, as Kellman and Massey (2013, p. 121) put it, "perceptual systems that change—that attune, adapt, and discover to optimize learning, problem solving, and complex task performance." Perceptual skill develops in everyday life (e.g., recognizing ripe melons at the grocery store) and in the work environment (e.g., recognizing suspicious luggage). *Perceptual learning* has been defined as "an increase in the ability to extract information from the environment, as a result of experience and practice with stimulation coming from it" (E. J. Gibson, 1969, p. 3). This view implies that perceptual learning consists of extracting information that was previously unused and emphasizes the identification of environmental properties that have the potential to be learned. Perceptual learning has also been defined as learning that "involves relatively long-lasting changes to an organism's perceptual system that improve its ability to respond to its environment and are caused by this environment" (Goldstone, 1998, p. 586). This view focuses on the mechanisms of perceptual learning and how early stages of information processing relate to later ones.

Mechanisms of Perceptual Learning

Before addressing the question of how perceptual learning occurs, it is valuable to consider what might be learned. Any stimulus can be described in terms of features that vary along a number of dimensions. For example, a simple visual stimulus such as a red square has the feature "red," which is a particular value of the dimension "hue," and the square itself has a particular value on the dimension "size." Both features and dimensions can be learned, as can complex stimuli. Training on visual tasks has been shown to be beneficial to older adults whose visual abilities have decreased and to persons in other age groups who have visual abnormalities (Watanabe & Sasaki, 2015).

Different classifications of mechanisms of perceptual learning have been proposed (e.g., Dosher & Lu, 1999; Goldstone, Schyns, & Medin, 1997). One useful scheme distinguishes between attention weighting, stimulus imprinting, differentiation, and unitization (Goldstone, 1998). Goldstone emphasizes the adaptive nature of perceptual learning, in which learning is driven by the degree to which features or dimensions have been associated with successful performance in the past.

Attention Weighting

Attention can be thought of as a limited resource that is necessary for selecting information (Kahneman, 1973). Because it is not possible to attend to everything at once, it is necessary to focus attention on some information while ignoring other information. *Attention weighting* is a proposed mechanism for increasing the attention paid to perceptual features and dimensions that are relevant to the task at hand and, in some contexts, decreasing attention to irrelevant features or dimensions. For example, when letter strings include extra letters that are consistently irrelevant to the decision that participants are to make, they learn to give these extra letters little weight in the decision process even if they are not told that they are irrelevant to the task (Haider & Frensch, 1996).

Attention weighting has been proposed to play a major role in learning to categorize stimuli. Many influential models of category learning include parameters that reflect allocation of attention to diagnostic stimulus features (e.g., Kruschke, 1992; Love, Medin, & Gureckis, 2004; Nosofsky, 1986; but see Matsuka & Corter, 2008, for results that are difficult to explain with attention weighting). If the categorization rule is simple, learning can be said to have occurred when the attention weights have been set to 1 for the relevant dimension and 0 for any irrelevant dimensions (i.e., categorization is based solely on the dimension relevant to the rule). This is what a neurological patient being tested with the Wisconsin card-sorting task must do. The psychologist has a rule in mind, such as "sort by color," and the patient must discover this rule as she sorts cards containing pictures of varying numbers of colored shapes, using "yes" or "no" feedback from the experimenter. When the categorization task is more complex than just values of a single feature (e.g., color), attention must be spread across multiple features or devoted to compounds of features (e.g., number and color).

The difficulty associated with attending to multiple features is what makes the game *Set* (Set Enterprises; www.setgame.com) so challenging. Like the Wisconsin card-sorting task, this game requires the classification of cards on which different numbers (one, two, or three) of colored shapes (red, green, or purple; diamond, oval, squiggle) are printed (in outline or as filled forms). Because a "set" is defined according to whether all the values on the dimensions (number, symbol, shading, color) are the same or different for any three cards (see Figure 2.1), players must be flexible in classifying the shapes. In the figure, one set can be formed with the cards containing one, two, and three dark gray solid ovals. The example contains at least four more sets, and trying to find those will illustrate the difficulty of attending to multiple features.

The effects of attention to features relevant for categorization can be seen in a phenomenon called *categorical perception*: People can better tell two stimuli apart when they come from different categories than when they come from the same category—even when the physical differences between the pairs of stimuli to be distinguished are carefully equated for the two types

Figure 2.1 A configuration of cards similar to those found in the game *Set*.

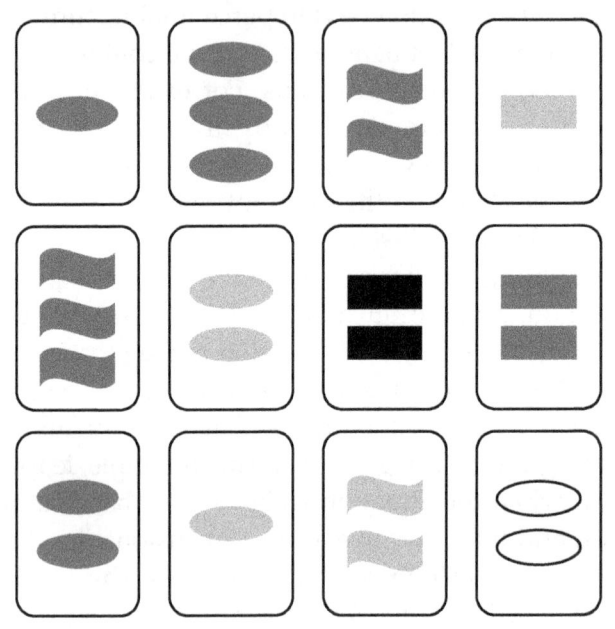

Adapted from Taatgen, van Oploo, Braaksma, and Niemantsverdriet (2003).

of judgments (Goldstone & Hendrickson, 2010). The effect is especially robust with auditory stimuli. Liberman, Harris, Hoffman, and Griffith (1957) demonstrated categorical perception using artificial speech approximations to consonant-vowel syllables that varied in the extent and direction of the transition from onset of the speech signal to steady-state vowel sound. Although the stimuli differed along a continuum of transitions, participants classified the stimuli into three categories, with sharp boundaries, corresponding to the sounds of the letters *b*, *d*, and *g*. Also, participants were able to discriminate much better between two speech sounds from different phonemic categories than between ones within the same category, indicating that different physical stimuli within the same category were heard as being the same. Recent research using fMRI analyses showed that the two perceptual categories /ba/ vs. /da/ evoked distinct patterns of neural activity in Broca's area, a region in the inferior frontal gyrus of the cortex (Y. Lee, Turkeltaub, Granger, & Raizada, 2012). These results and others imply that Broca's area is involved in categorical speech perception. Because Broca's area is also associated with speech production, its role in speech perception may be to translate speech signals into categories in terms of articulatory codes.

Categorical perception is not restricted to speech stimuli. It also occurs for stimuli such as emotional facial expressions (e.g., Sauter, LeGuen, &

Haun, 2011) and familiar faces (e.g., Roberson & Davidoff, 2000). For example, for two familiar faces, those of U.S. presidents John Kennedy and Bill Clinton, morphed along a continuum, people were more accurate at distinguishing two faces that straddled the category boundary (i.e., to the Kennedy side or the Clinton side) than two morphed faces from within the same category (e.g., both to the Kennedy side; Beale & Keil, 1995). Similar results are obtained when the morphed faces are of oneself and a friend or two friends (Keyes, 2012). Although there may be some contribution of innate mechanisms to categorical perception (e.g., Eimas, Siqueland, Jusczyk, & Vigorito, 1971), there is general agreement that for the most part categorical perception is a consequence of learning.

Consistent with the view that categorical perception is learned, learning to classify unfamiliar items has been shown to affect the way we see (or hear) those items. Such effects show us that category members may effectively become more similar to each other (Goldstone, Lippa, & Shiffrin, 2001) and members of different categories may become more distinct (Livingston, Andrews, & Harnad, 1998). Learned categorical perception has been demonstrated for previously unfamiliar faces: The familiarity acquired in the context of a laboratory experiment is sufficient to produce categorical perception (Kikutani, Roberson, & Hanley, 2010). In general, compression of the dimensional space within categories and expansion of the space between them seem to be an important way that we make sense of the world.

Stimulus Imprinting

Imprinting differs from attention weighting in that new, specialized detectors that are tuned to specific stimuli or parts of them are developed (Goldstone, 1998). Simple repeated exposure to stimuli is enough to sensitize the perceptual system—if those stimuli are deemed to be important. Although in some cases the areas of the brain that represent stimulus information may change as a function of experience, stimulus imprinting refers to any process that produces a benefit to perception due to repetition of stimuli or features.

The concept of stimulus imprinting is most clearly illustrated through models that develop representations based on specific instances. These include *exemplar* models, in which stimuli are categorized by comparison to prior exemplars (e.g., Nosofsky, 1986, 2011). They also include *template* models in which objects are classified by comparing them to a stored, idealized image (e.g., Ullman, 1989). Such models are used in industrial applications to classify information, and several learning algorithms have been developed to allow the classifiers to move from particular instances to template representations (e.g., Poggio & Edelman, 1990).

When a stimulus part or feature is identified as being important, people may imprint on just that part. Imprinting in this sense is assumed to produce a specialized feature detector for the critical part and result in sensitivity to that part of the stimulus when it is present in novel stimuli. Schyns and Rodet (1997) illustrated just this in a study in which two groups of participants were pre-exposed to ensembles of novel stimuli ("Martian cells"; see Figure 2.2) that they were told to observe with the intent of answering questions about them later. One group saw instances of A cells that were defined by the elementary feature *a* and *BC* cells defined by the conjunctive feature *bc*, whereas another group saw *C* cells with the elementary feature *c* and *AB* cells with the conjunctive feature *ab*. After this pre-exposure phase in which they viewed cells characterized by either one single feature

Figure 2.2 The top left picture depicts a "Martian cell" used by Schyns and Rodet (1997). The abstract shape next to it is the part of the cell that was manipulated in the study; the other parts of the cell were varied randomly. The numbered arrows indicate the possible points of perceptual segmentation. The labels *a*, *b*, and *c* designate the basic shapes present in each stimulus. The shapes labeled *bc* and *ab* are combinations of two basic shapes. In the experiment, each basic shape was seen equally often in the pre-exposure phase, but different observers saw different mixtures of one basic shape and one combination shape (e.g., *a* and *bc*).

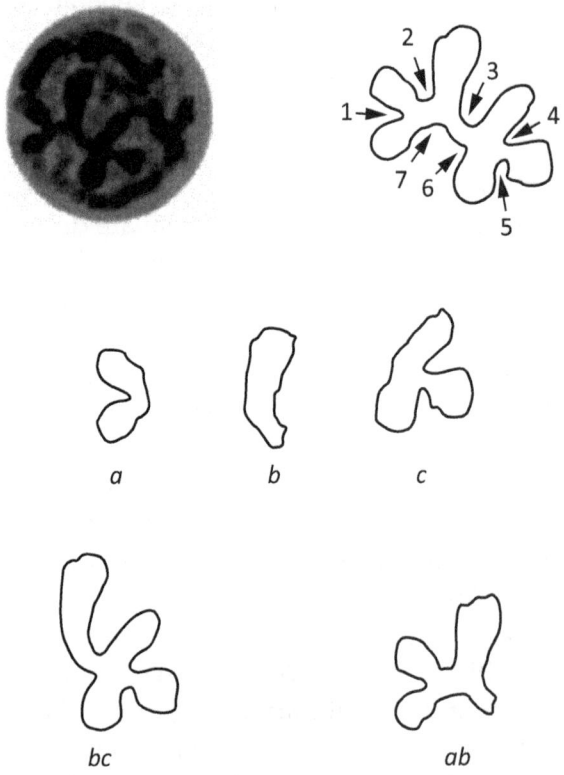

Source: Schyns and Rodet (1997).

or one conjunctive feature, the participants were asked to circle the components of other, new Martian cells. In this second phase of the experiment, the conjunctive features to which they were pre-exposed were circled as if they were elementary features, suggesting that the nature of the viewing experience in the first part of the experiment triggered "the development of new features that changed the perceptual appearance (the perceptual analysis) of stimuli" (Schyns & Rodet, 1997, p. 695).

In some cases, stimulus imprinting is known to reflect adaptive changes in specific cortical areas. Weinberger (1995) reviewed evidence for such changes in the auditory cortex. For example, rats that had received conditioning to an auditory tone showed modifications in the receptive fields in auditory cortical areas such that the tuning of the fields shifted to the frequency of the conditioned tones. In the visual domain, T. Yang and Maunsell (2004) found that cells in macaque visual area V4 (which contains neurons specific to orientation) were affected by training in an orientation discrimination task. Yang and Maunsell trained adult macaque monkeys to discriminate a narrow range of orientations at a specific retinal location of one eye. Compared to neurons corresponding to the untrained hemisphere, the V4 neurons whose receptive fields overlapped the trained location showed stronger responses and narrower orientation tuning curves, with the greatest changes being seen for neurons with preferred orientations close to the trained range of orientations. Studies such as this one combine with behavioral evidence to give us insights into the plasticity of the brain.

Differentiation

Perceptual learning can, roughly, be described as learning to tell stimuli apart. Not surprisingly, then, much of the literature on perceptual learning has focused on how percepts become increasingly differentiated. The term differentiation was coined by J. J. Gibson and Gibson (1955) to refer to how perceptual ability develops. They describe differentiation as "progressive elaboration of qualities, features, and dimensions of variation" (p. 34) by which the number of properties of objects increases. As more properties can be distinguished, it becomes possible to respond to aspects of differences between stimuli that we previously could not discriminate. Like other forms of perceptual learning, differentiation may occur for entire stimuli (e.g., identical twins) or parts of stimuli (e.g., the saturation of a color). It occurs as a direct result of exposure to stimuli, although, as we shall discuss ahead, it may be facilitated by attaching different labels or performing different responses to the stimuli to be learned.

Differentiation has been shown to develop in perceptual tasks ranging from simple discrimination to complex classification. In simple tasks, such as judging whether two lines are aligned relative to each other (i.e., whether the line is broken into two parts, known as vernier acuity), performance improves with training to the point of "hyperacuity": The degree of resolution that develops is finer even than that of individual photoreceptors (e.g., Poggio, Fahle, & Edelman, 1992). This hyperacuity is specific to the stimuli used during practice. In a typical paradigm, the practiced stimuli are presented in one or a narrow range of orientations. After extensive practice, transfer performance with a range of orientations is tested. That transfer occurs only for orientations close to the practiced orientations suggests that the effect takes place within the visual cortex (area V1) and not at higher processing levels (Spang, Grimsen, Herzog, & Fahle, 2010). After all, the receptive fields of neurons beyond the visual cortex are sensitive to a broader range of orientations than that for which transfer is found.

Multidimensional stimulus information can be decomposed into dimensions such as size, color, and shape, each of which can be attended to with little difficulty (Garner, 1974). But *integral stimulus dimensions*, such as those making up color (hue, lightness, and saturation), are processed holistically and difficult to decompose perceptually (see Kemler Nelson, 1993). Yet, differentiation can occur even for these integral dimensions. Using a training-transfer paradigm with integral stimulus sets of morphed faces that could be described mathematically along two dimensions, Goldstone and Steyvers (2001; see Figure 2.3) showed that participants learned not only the primary dimension that was diagnostic during training but also the irrelevant dimension. In a comparison of alternative models, M. Jones and Goldstone (2012) found evidence that the differentiated dimensions were indeed orthogonal in Euclidean space (i.e., had independent effects on performance), like separable dimensions are without the differentiation training.

Much of the evidence for differentiation comes from research on memory for faces—in particular, the own-race bias. The *own-race bias* is that own-race faces are better remembered than are faces of another, less familiar race. This phenomenon has been found in a range of cultural and racial groups (Kassin, Ellsworth, & Smith, 1989). The effect is "in our heads" and not in the faces to be judged, as no differences in physiognomic variability have been documented (e.g., A. G. Goldstein, 1979). There is general agreement that perceptual learning is at least one determinant of this effect (e.g., Hugenberg, Young, Bernstein, & Sacco, 2010), possibly because cues used for discriminating own-race faces are not useful for remembering other-race faces (Meissner & Brigham, 2001). One source of evidence for the perceptual-learning view is that experience with other races decreases the own-race bias with regard to those races with which one has experience (Chiroro & Valentine, 1995). Similarly, no advantage for one's own race is evident when the pictures

Figure 2.3 The stimuli used by Goldstone and Steyvers (2001). The horizontal dimension, Dimension A, is "the proportion of Face 1 relative to Face 2" dimension and the vertical dimension, Dimension B, might be called the "The proportion of Face 3 relative to Face 4" dimension. The two dimensions were orthogonal in that the proportion of Face 1 relative to Face 2 was independent of the proportion of Face 3 relative to Face 4. Each face consisted of equal proportions of the horizontal and vertical dimensions.

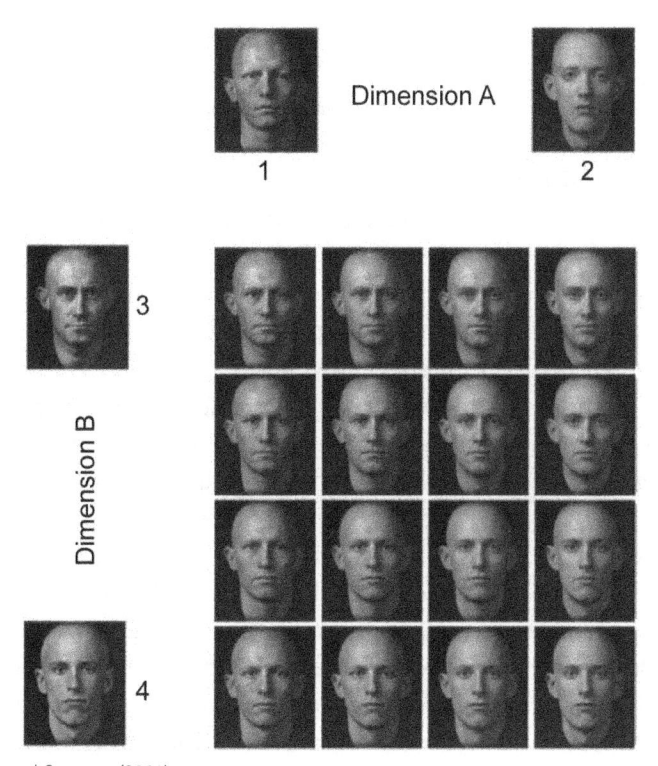

Source: Goldstone and Steyvers (2001).

are of people from another country, whose physical features are likely different from those with which one is familiar even when the people are of one's own race (Chiroro, Tredoux, Radaelli, & Meissner, 2008).

There are practical implications of the own-race bias, especially as regards to eyewitness testimony in courts of law (Brigham, Bennett, Meissner, & Mitchell, 2007). Poorer performance in identifying other-race faces implies not only that some people will not be remembered but also that other people will be misremembered. This has implications for eyewitness testimony because eyewitnesses will be more likely to misidentify a suspect of another race than one of the same race as having committed a crime. This led the New Jersey Supreme Court to rule that instructions to jurors warning them of the potential for misidentification of other-race persons may be given (*State v. Cromedy*, 1999).

At least one model of recognition memory includes a mechanism by which differentiation occurs (McClelland & Chappell, 1998). According to this model, features of stimuli are stored in memory and these features and their associated probabilities are updated each time the individual encounters the particular stimulus. As the evidence that a particular pattern of stimulus input produces a given pattern of activation in memory increases, so does the psychological sense of familiarity. Because the increase in the strength of a representation is accompanied by a decrease in the likelihood of responding to a novel, unrelated stimulus, familiarity, as McClelland and Chappell conclude, breeds differentiation.

More evidence that perceptual learning consists of developing the ability to differentiate features comes from the success of training that stresses learning relevant, distinctive features versus holistic properties of stimuli. An early demonstration of this was provided by Gagné and J. J. Gibson (J. J. Gibson, 1947), who were concerned with the practical problem of training cadets to distinguish between types of aircraft. In describing this problem, Gibson states, "It was . . . assumed that recognition training is essentially a kind of perceptual learning in which visual shapes not at the outset distinctive become capable of producing differential reactions" (p. 120). Gagné and J. J. Gibson contrasted a "total-form" instruction that emphasized the total form of each plane with a "feature" instruction that emphasized a set of distinctive features for each plane to be learned and encouraged students to focus on those features. At the end of a 30-hour training period, cadets who received the feature instruction performed better on a recognition test than did cadets who received the total-form instruction. Moreover, cadets in the total-form group asked their instructors for information regarding the features that could be used to distinguish similar planes, suggesting that search for distinctive features is a natural mode of learning.

Perceptual Unitization

Whereas developing sensitivity to particular features is a powerful learning mechanism, sometimes improvements in discrimination will depend on doing just the opposite. That is, learning may depend on *unitizing* features that were previously processed independently. Unitization has been defined as the "construction of single functional units that can be triggered when a complex configuration arises" (Goldstone, 1998, p. 602).

LaBerge (1973) provided a demonstration of how unitization of feature combinations can facilitate responding. He used as stimuli familiar letters (bdpq) or unfamiliar letter-like forms. When observers in his experiment had seen one of the letter-like stimuli in the same trial, they were just as fast to judge whether two letter-like stimuli were the same or different as they were to make such a judgment for letters. However, when they were not "cued" by presenting a letter-like stimulus at the beginning, they were better at making same-different judgments for the familiar letter stimuli than for the unfamiliar letter-like stimuli. LaBerge interpreted his findings in terms of a hierarchical model in which features are analyzed and then integrated into compound stimulus codes. Familiar stimuli are automatically integrated but unfamiliar stimuli are not. Because attention is required for feature integration of unfamiliar stimuli, more time is required to form the compound stimulus codes needed to process them. LaBerge showed further that with practice, as familiarity was gained with the initially unfamiliar letter-like forms, the difference in reaction time to letters and letter-like forms disappeared, suggesting that the letter-like forms had become unitized.

If unitization is a general process, it should occur for any sets of visual features. Shiffrin and Lightfoot (1997) examined the processes involved in transforming sets of elementary visual features into unitary characters using a visual search task in which a target character (e.g., the right character in the top row of Figure 2.4) was searched for in circular arrays of one to eight novel characters (composed of line segments for which no single feature could be used to identify the target; see Figure 2.4). Searching for a target

Figure 2.4 The novel stimuli used by Shiffrin and Lightfoot (1997). One visual search condition used the characters in just one of these rows. In a given row, each feature (i.e., internal line segment) occurs in exactly two characters, and every pair of characters shares exactly one feature. This repetition of features forces observers to search for a conjunction of features—no one feature can be used to identify a target.

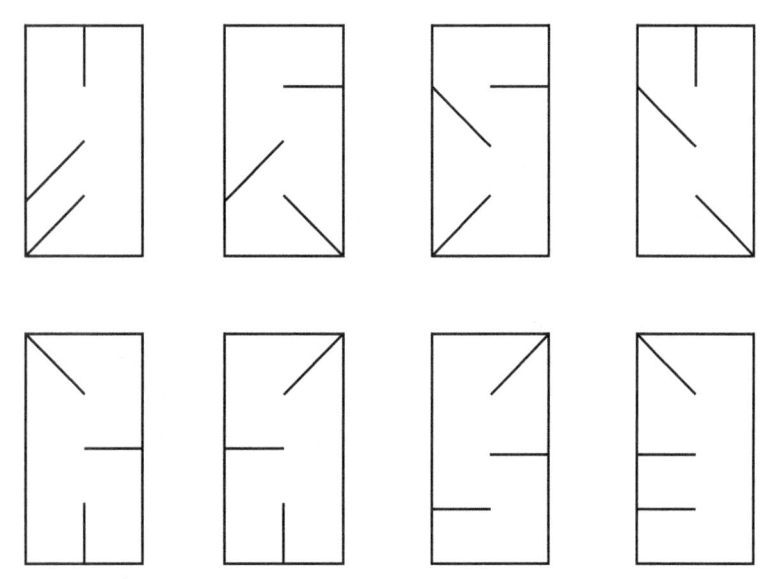

Source: Shiffrin and Lightfoot (1997).

among novel characters should be much slower than searching sets of familiar characters (e.g., looking for a letter target among other letter distractors) initially, but extensive practice should cause the novel stimuli to become unitized, thus speeding up the comparison process. Indeed, performance was slow and inaccurate initially, but improved with practice until it was—after more than 20,000 trials—comparable to that typically shown for familiar stimuli. Transfer to a new set of the novel stimuli was poor, suggesting that learning was specific to the trained stimuli. Shiffrin and Lightfoot concluded on the basis of these and other findings that the changes with practice were due to a unitization process that allowed holistic exposure to stimulus features.

Whereas some authors, such as Shiffrin and Lightfoot (1997), argue that unitization occurs only when task requirements are such that performance will benefit from the new units, others (e.g., McLaren & Mackintosh, 2000) have suggested that it can occur solely as a consequence of exposure to stimulus features, regardless of whether those features serve a functional purpose. Welham and Wills (2011) tested this prediction of the model proposed by McLaren and Mackintosh using a categorization task. In their first experiment, participants learned to categorize stimulus squares composed of 256 smaller squares, each of which could be black or white. The stimuli could be categorized on the basis of one of two configurations of elements that could occur in any quadrant of the display. Because these configurations completely predicted one category or the other, they should be unitized. Initially, people found it difficult to tell the different stimuli apart. Even when the configuration defining category membership was not easily discernible (see Figure 2.5), however, similarity ratings made after the training phase of the experiment were higher for pairs of stimuli that shared the critical configuration. The second experiment tested the prediction that features must serve a functional purpose in order to be unitized. In this experiment, the same stimuli used in Experiment 1 were used, but the stimuli were simply rated according to how attractive they were during the training phase. Similarity judgments made after training again suggested that unitization had occurred, even though it was not required for the attractiveness-rating task. A final experiment showed that the proportion of time that the eyes dwelled on the critical configurations increased over training blocks regardless of whether categorization of attractiveness judgments were made, suggesting that unitization increased the salience of the configurations regardless of its functional value.

Compelling evidence for unitization comes from how we process words. Every introductory psychology text has an example of the Stroop effect (Stroop, 1935), in which the naming of ink colors is disrupted when the

Figure 2.5 Stimuli such as those used in the "nonobvious configuration" conditions of Welham and Wills's (2011) experiments. Each training stimulus (top row) contained one of two category-defining configurations, such as that shown in the box on the right, in one of four locations. The rest of the stimulus comprised trial-unique noise.

Source: Welham and Wills (2011).

forms spell conflicting color names. This effect is often interpreted as evidence for the automatic processing of words even when it is not advantageous to do so. Other evidence for word unitization comes from studies that examine the effects of context on letter identification or text processing.

The first of these context effects, the *word-superiority effect*, is that identification accuracy for a single letter is higher when the letter is presented in the context of a word than when it is presented singly, even though more letters must be processed in the first case. For example, Reicher (1969) found people were better at identifying which of two letters had been briefly presented (and then masked) when the critical letter was presented as one of the letters in a word (e.g., choose between "d" and "p" after seeing the word "dark" as opposed to "park") than when it was presented in a jumbled up word (e.g., "dkra") or alone, but in the same spatial position on the screen (e.g., "d__"). That is, performance was better with the word context than without it. Letters also are identified more accurately in pseudowords ("legal" [pronounceable] nonwords like "darl" and "parl") than in illegal letter strings (like "dkra"), although this *pseudoword-superiority effect* is smaller than the word-superiority effect. The difference in magnitude of the word- and pseudoword- superiority effects is attributed to familiarity with specific words, whereas the pseudoword-superiority effect itself is attributed to familiarity with the language's orthographic structure (Grossi, Murphy, & Boggan, 2009).

Both the word- and pseudoword-superiority effects are reflected in components of the ERP (Coch & Mitra, 2010). For example, orthographic regularity affects the P150 component and lexicality (word vs. nonword) affects the

N200 component. The amplitudes of the later N300 and N400 components also depend on whether word or pseudowords (as opposed to orthographically irregular nonwords) are presented as stimuli.

By its nature, reading of text emphasizes word units over letter units: Skilled readers read words, not letters. When text is being read, word units can be expected to dominate letter units, so that identification of particular letters is actually inferior in the word context. Evidence for a *word-inferiority*, or *missing-letter effect*, has been found when passages are read for comprehension, as opposed to reading single words just for identification. For example, if you try to mark all the instances of the letter *t* while reading a text passage at normal speed, you will miss proportionately more occurrences of *t* in the word "the" than in the other words of the passage. This missing-letter effect has been attributed to unitization of very frequent words (Healy, 1994). The idea is that text analysis is a hierarchical process, and once a word is identified, processing at the "letter" level is terminated. Letters are missed most often when they are in familiar, unitized words, because it is those words that will often be identified quickly and automatically. Another view of the missing-letter effect is that words such as "the" serve mainly as structural cues used early in sentence processing; after they have served that purpose, they are then overshadowed as the later processing focuses on meaning (Koriat & Greenberg, 1994).

Advocates of the two accounts combined their views in the guidance–organization (GO) model (Greenberg, Healy, Koriat, & Kreiner, 2004). The GO model has five sources that contribute to letter-detection errors while reading text. The first two are perceptual: (a) unitization of function words due to their familiarity, and (b) identification of those words while they are still in the parafovea and have not yet been fixated directly. Another source is (c) contextual constraints, for which the predictability of function words in the sentence context also facilitates their identification in the parafovea. The remaining two sources are post-perceptual: (d) precedence for information relating to the sentence's structure in text processing, and (e) use of structure words identified in the parafovea to direct fixations preferentially to words with content information. In the model, unitization processes facilitate the parafoveal identification of function words, which operate as cues to the structural organization of the sentence, and the analysis of the organization of the sentence guides attention to content words, thus enabling understanding of the sentence's meaning.

According to the GO model, function words can support extraction of sentence structure only if they are identified swiftly, which is the case for high-frequency function words. Thus, the model predicts more missed letters for function words than content words only when the words are of high frequency. Roy-Charland and Saint-Aubin (2006) confirmed this prediction when they dissociated word frequency from word class. Another implication of the GO model is that processing is mediated by eye movements. Gaze duration should be positively correlated with letter detection since letter processing is more likely when the word is in foveal vision. Roy-Charland, Saint-Aubin, Klein, and Lawrence (2007) found that the model's predictions regarding eye movements were largely confirmed. But predictions about letter-detection latencies were not, although the authors suggested that those results could be accommodated by removing an assumption that processing at the letter and word levels is independent.

Reading is a task in which most of us are proficient, if not expert. Expertise in other tasks also may lead to unitization. One way that this has been demonstrated is with the so-called inversion effect. The inversion effect is that it is harder to recognize previously presented stimuli when they are rotated 180 degrees than when they are presented upright—especially if the stimuli are familiar. This finding was first demonstrated for faces (Yin, 1969), for which it is obtained most strongly and reliably (see Tanaka & Gauthier, 1997), but it also can be found for a range of stimuli for which expertise has been acquired. For example, Diamond and Carey (1986) found that dog breeders and judges showed an inversion effect for photographs of individual dogs of the same breed, whereas non–dog experts did not, and Rossion and Curran (2010) found that car experts showed a significant correlation between the level of expertise, as measured by an objective task, and the size of the inversion effect for car pictures.

Facilitating the Development of Perceptual Skill

Depending on the nature of perceptual skill, changes may occur in how neurons are tuned in visual cortex, how the output from low-level visual processing is weighted at the decision state at which response selection occurs, how categories are represented, or how relations between stimuli are processed (e.g., Sasaki, Náñez, & Watanabe, 2012). In fact, Watanabe and Sasaki (2015) have proposed a dual-process theory of visual perceptual learning according to which feature-based learning occurs as early as the primary visual cortex, whereas task-based learning specific to the particular task that is practiced occurs later in the visual information-processing streams. Given that there are different mechanisms of perceptual learning, training experiences must be matched to the type of information to be learned in order to maximize learning. Observing how different training regimes influence skill acquisition also can lead to new theoretical insights.

Studies of simple perceptual tasks such as discriminating the waveforms of different gratings (images containing a regular pattern of light and dark bands) and motion discrimination (perceiving the direction of motion of a subset of moving dots in a random-dot background) show that learning can affect very early levels of perceptual processing (Karni & Bertini, 1997), although the transfer of such perceptual learning is limited. In fact, it has been proposed that the acquisition of perceptual skill occurs at the earliest level of the stream for processing the sensory information in which the relevant stimulus parameter can be represented (Karni, 1996). According to this view, for example, learning to identify the presence of a small target texture of one orientation against a background texture of identical elements with a different orientation should occur in the visual cortex (V1) because it is the earliest level of the visual system that contains neurons sensitive to orientation.

Some aspects of perceptual learning occur without explicit feedback (e.g., Fahle & Edelman, 1993; Schyns & Rodet, 1997), but perceptual training is a necessity in other contexts. For example, when learners of a second language must learn to distinguish between phonemes that are not distinguished in the native language, such as when native Japanese speakers must distinguish between /r/ and /l/, feedback aids learning. Additional factors that facilitate learning to differentiate /l/ and /r/ are presenting the sounds in a word context and providing variability in the stimulus set by having the learner listen to words produced by many different speakers (Lively, Logan, & Pisoni, 1993).

The complexity of the environment can seem overwhelming when learning to distinguish new stimuli, such as in immersion learning of a foreign language, but as pointed out by Lively et al. (see also Nishi & Kewley-Port, 2007), it can be better to include a broad set of stimuli during training even at the risk of making the learning environment more complex. A similar issue is whether it is better to start training by making relatively complex discriminations or simpler ones. To address this question, Pellegrino, Doane, Fischer, and Alderton (1991) used random polygons as stimuli, with one group of observers making easy discriminations (i.e., distinguishing between very different polygons) and another group performing more difficult discriminations (distinguishing between more similar polygons). Reaction times were initially positively related to the complexity of the two forms that were being judged. The "difficult context" group showed a greater initial effect of stimulus complexity, suggesting that the difficult context forced the observers to process the stimuli in greater detail. Moreover, the effects of practice were much larger for the difficult context group than for the easy context group. By the eighth session of practice, the difficult context group showed mean reaction times similar to those of the easy context group and exhibited less of an effect of stimulus complexity. This latter finding suggests that the more detailed processing required for the difficult context group resulted in the learning of more precise representations of the forms. Performance in a transfer test provided additional evidence to support this interpretation. When tested with the complete set of polygons, the difficult context group showed no disruption in performance but the easy context group did.

Other studies have obtained results indicating that for other perceptual-learning tasks it is better to use a progressive training schedule. B. A. Church, Mercado, Wisniewski, and Liu (2013) had participants learn to discriminate a 1-second section of a bird song from ones that were speeded up by 20%, 30%, 50%, and 70%. On a subsequent test requiring the 1-second stimulus to be discriminated from ones speeded up by 10%, 20%, or 40%, participants who received blocks of training trials proceeding from easy (70%) to hard (20%) performed better than those who received the blocks in a hard-to-easy progression or random order. The benefit extended to the transfer durations as well as to the 20% duration that had been experienced in the original training. The general point illustrated by the Pellegrino et al. (1991) and B. A. Church et al. (2013) studies, that the context in which a task is practiced determines what is learned, is one that recurs throughout the book.

Stimulus complexity also influences how beneficial training will be. Sowden, Davies, and Roling (2000), studying whether improved sensitivity in detecting basic features could be a basis for improvement in reading X-ray images, found that novices improved over 4 days of training in a task of detecting dots in X-ray images, but showed no transfer to reversed contrast images when these images were simple. When more complex images were used, transfer (although not perfect) did occur. Airport security screening of luggage with X-ray images is a task similar to that of reading X-ray images. Koller, Drury, and Schwaninger (2009) evaluated the benefit of training with X-Ray Tutor (XRT), a training program that starts with easy views of threat devices (e.g., guns, knives, improvised explosive devices) and progresses at an individualized rate to more difficult views and complex images with superimposed objects. Screening performance of air traffic security personnel with on-the-job experience who received 6 months of training with XRT led to significantly better performance than a group who did not receive this additional training during the same period, particularly on recognition of threat targets. Brunstein and Gonzalez (2011) showed that the efficacy of such training might be increased by using a more diverse context in which relatively few exemplars of relatively many categories of threat items are seen during training.

Labeling features has been shown to be a powerful tool for facilitating learning. At a wine-tasting party, it is not uncommon for at least one person to find little difference among the various vintages. After much additional exposure to a variety of wines and learning to label the characteristics that distinguish among them, that same individual may become a connoisseur, pointing out subtle differences between wines of different regions or years (e.g., Parr, Heatherbell, & White, 2002).

A cross-sectional study by Zucco, Carassai, Baroni, and Stevenson (2011) illustrates the development of the connoisseur. As noted by Zucco et al., several types of learning are involved in acquiring wine expertise. Olfactory perceptual learning should occur implicitly as a function of being exposed to various vintages, whereas more cognitive learning (including the names of the component odors and schemas that represent the features defining each specific type of wine) occurs explicitly. Zucco et al. compared the performance of four groups of wine drinkers (casual wine drinkers, second-year students receiving wine training, third-year trainees, and professional sommeliers) on olfactory-judgment tasks. The latter three groups performed better than the casual drinkers on a wine recognition test, but the trainee groups actually did worse than the casual drinkers on identification of wine-relevant odors (i.e., odors commonly identified in wine). Second-year students were no better at naming component odors in describing the wines than were casual drinkers. The third-year students generated more descriptors than either of these two groups and the sommeliers even more. The finding that people with relatively little training outperform casual drinkers in discriminating between different wines suggests that olfactory discrimination occurs relatively quickly. The fact that differences in labeling different aspects of wine continued to improve as a function of training and experience is consistent with the idea that the more cognitive skills involved in wine tasting take longer to develop.

The importance of labeling in perceptual learning was more directly illustrated by Desor and Beauchamp (1974) in a study examining the effect of experience on the identification of odors. People were given extensive training with a set of 32 natural odors, such as those of molasses, a musty book, or ivy, until all of the odors were identified correctly in two consecutive sessions. Five days after this initial training, each of the 32 odors was presented three times in random order to be identified again. Whereas initially many errors were made, all of the individuals who received the training achieved the criterion of perfect discrimination and continued to show this level of performance after the 5-day retention interval. This finding is remarkable and a good demonstration of the power of labeling as it had been argued previously that the capacity of the olfactory channel, as estimated from the number of odors that could be identified without error, was relatively low (e.g., Engen & Pfaffman, 1960).

In the Desor and Beauchamp (1974) study, the accuracy with which odors could be identified (i.e., labeled) improved with practice. However, the question remains of whether performance of a task for which labeling is not required would also benefit from practice. One way to answer this question is with a relative discrimination task in which two stimuli are compared on each trial and classified as "same" or "different." Rabin (1988) examined the influence of experience on the relative discriminability of seven odor stimuli in an experiment in which three types of prior experience with olfactory stimuli were given to different groups of observers. One group was trained to label the target stimuli, another group performed a profiling task in which each odor in the target set was rated on a list of adjectives, and a third was trained to label a set of seven other odors. The latter group was considered a control group, as was a fourth group that received no pretraining. Discrimination performance was measured using a two-interval, *same-different* task. The participant sniffed an odor from one jar and then another odor from a second jar, and responded as to whether the two odors were the same or different. The group who learned to label the seven test stimuli was more sensitive at discriminating the stimuli than was the group who profiled the stimuli, and both of these experimental groups were more sensitive than the two control groups, which did not differ in performance.

One difference between prior experience labeling stimuli versus profiling them is that labeling requires discriminations to be made between stimuli, whereas profiling does not. It is likely this difference that accounts for the greater benefit arising from labeling than profiling when the criterion task is one in which relative discriminations must be made. Because labeling forces observers to attend to those features of a stimulus that make it distinctive and unique, it enables increased accuracy of discrimination.

Simply labeling features leads to better performance in many domains. Labeling has been used as the core of instructions for a difficult perceptual task: determining the sex of day-old chicks. Sexing chicks is a commercially important skill that takes many months to acquire (Lunn, 1948). To the untrained eye, the sex organs of male and female chicks appear identical, and many backyard chicken farmers have been disappointed when the chicks they bought, hoping for layers, turned out to be roosters. Commercial chick sexers can, after training and much experience, classify up to 1,000 chicks an hour with over 98% accuracy. Although manual skill in handling the chicks is necessary to reach such levels of performance, enhanced visual (and in rare cases, tactual) discrimination of the sex organs is primarily responsible for the improved ability to perform the job (Lunn, 1948).

Biederman and Shiffrar (1987) demonstrated how training to detect features can improve performance in the chick sexing task. With the help of an expert chick sexer, they determined that the critical region used to distinguish male and female chicks is a region called the bead. For males, the bead is usually convex, whereas for females it is usually concave or flat. Biederman and Shiffrar developed instructional materials that showed schematic diagrams of the beads for males and females, characterizing them as "round or fullish like a ball or watermelon" or "pointed, like an upside down pine tree, or flattish," respectively. When given these instructions, the performance of naïve observers at classifying pictures of rare and difficult chick genitalia increased from just above chance to the level achieved by a group of experts. This example illustrates the practical importance of understanding the basis for perceptual skill: In capitalizing on the natural learning mode of identifying and learning distinctive features, a highly effective training method was found.

Labeling is not always beneficial, as illustrated by a phenomenon known as *verbal overshadowing* (Chin & Schooler, 2008). When people are required to generate a verbal description of complex stimuli, such as faces, the description often interferes with their performance on a subsequent recognition test. That is, the requirement to verbalize seems to overshadow perceptual discrimination. Melcher and Schooler (1996) had non-wine drinkers, untrained wine drinkers, and trained wine experts taste a glass of red wine and, after engaging in verbal description of the wine or in an unrelated nonverbal task, try to identify the wine among three alternatives. Neither non-wine drinkers (who have little perceptual or conceptual knowledge about wines) nor the wine experts (who have considerable knowledge of both types) showed verbal overshadowing. However, the untrained wine drinkers did. Melcher and Schooler attributed this pattern of results to the fact that perceptual skill in discriminating wines precedes development of the skill of describing and labeling wines. Note that this interpretation is consistent with Zucco et al.'s (2011) hypothesis that for complex sensory experiences, perceptual learning precedes learning to apply verbal labels.

Melcher and Schooler's (1996) findings are correlational: They did not directly manipulate levels of wine expertise. To overcome this limitation, Melcher and Schooler (2004) conducted a similar study involving recognition of stimuli that are familiar to most people but for which they are not skilled at distinguishing: mushrooms. Participants received either no training, perceptual training (mushroom categorization), or conceptual (verbal) training (a lecture) before describing or simply viewing a mushroom. Performance on a recognition test was worse for people who described the mushroom before the recognition test for those in the perceptual-training group, but not for the no-training or conceptual-training groups. These results are consistent with the finding that perceptual skill in tasting wines can be overshadowed by describing the characteristics of wine and are in agreement with the general view that verbal information can interfere with perceptual processing. However, another account of these findings and similar ones is that verbalization causes a more general shift in processing or reliance on a more conservative criterion on the subsequent test (Chin & Schooler, 2008).

Visual Search

Visual search is an important part of everyday life and a key component of many jobs, including that of the airport security screener, described earlier, who searches images of the contents of luggage for threat devices. On any particular day we may search for a particular book among other books, a favorite compact disc in a stand, a dime in a handful of change, or a bike in a bicycle rack. Numerous variables affect how quickly and accurately each search is accomplished. More formally, visual search tasks have been a staple in cognitive psychology since early days of the field (e.g., Neisser, 1963), and of considerable research in perceptual learning—such as that of Shiffrin and Lightfoot (1997) discussed earlier in this chapter.

In a visual search task, observers search for one or more target stimuli among other, distractor, stimuli. The task may involve detecting whether a target is present or identifying which of two or more targets is present. If display duration or visibility is limited, the dependent measure of most interest is usually response accuracy, whereas if there are no such limitations, the primary interest is usually reaction time. Typical findings are that performance deteriorates as the number of distractors (or, *set size*) increases, and that, for a given set size, search times are longer when there is no target in the display than when there is.

Many factors influence the magnitude of the set-size effect (Eckstein, 2011). One such factor is retinal eccentricity: Increasing the size of the set affects performance more when the items are more spread out across the visual field (e.g., Carrasco, Evert, Chang, & Katz, 1995). Visual crowding and clutter can also slow visual search (e.g., Rosenholtz, Li, & Nakano, 2007; Wertheim, Hooge, Krikke, & Johnson, 2006). Another critical factor is similarity (Duncan & Humphreys, 1989). Not only does increased similarity of the targets to the distractors increase search difficulty, but so does increased dissimilarity between the distractors. Salience is also important: Both overt eye movements and covert attention shifts tend to be made to more salient objects or regions of a display before less salient ones (Itti & Koch, 2000). Finally, uncertainty about virtually any property of the target typically reduces search performance (Eckstein, 2011).

Treisman and Gelade (1980) were the first to show that if a target can be distinguished from distractors on the basis of a single feature (e.g., orientation), detection performance is relatively unaffected by the number of distractors in the display. For example, the task of detecting a vertical *T* in a field of oblique *T*s (see Figure 2.6, left) is easy regardless of the number of distractors. However, if a target is defined by a conjunction of features (e.g., orientation and form), performance is a decreasing function of the number of distractors. Consider the difficult task of detecting a vertical T in a field of oblique *T*s and vertical *L*s (see Figure 2.6, right). In this case, reaction time increases dramatically as the display size increases.

These results and other findings led Treisman and Gelade (1980) to develop the *feature-integration theory* of attention, which has been very influential in the area of visual search. According to this theory, individual features are processed preattentively in separate "feature maps," but the integration of features required to detect conjunctive targets requires attention. In this view, the detection of distinctive features is the result of parallel processing of the display elements, whereas detection of a conjunction of features requires serial search of individual display locations because attention can be directed to only one location at a time. In Treisman and Gelade's model, the set-size effect is due to the limited nature of the attentional processes that are required to integrate the features that make up conjunctive targets. When the search can be conducted preattentively on the basis of single features, thus bypassing this limited-capacity process, no set-size effects are predicted. Although feature-integration theory has been the subject of considerable debate (e.g., see Wolfe, Cave, & Franzel, 1989, who showed that search for targets defined by conjunctions of three features was less difficult than search for targets defined by conjunctions of only two features), the distinction between easy, *feature search*, and more difficult, *conjunctive search* is still made.

Figure 2.6 Feature (left) and conjunctive (right) search displays.

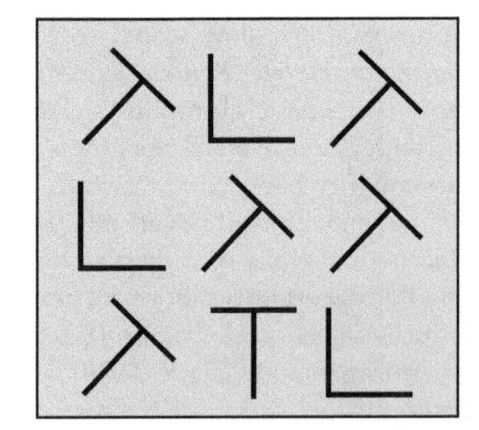

Another major factor determining the ease of search is practice. In one of the earliest of the contemporary studies of visual search, Neisser, Novick, and Lazar (1963) had participants scan lists of 50 strings (items) of six alphanumeric characters each to locate a target. In different blocks of scans conducted on each of 27 days the target in a list could be one of 1, 5, or 10 symbols. In the first testing session, search for 5 or 10 possible targets took more than twice as long (over 1.2 seconds per item) as search for a single possible target (0.6 seconds per item). Performance improved with practice, and by session 12 there was little difference between the three conditions. By session 27 the search time for all conditions was approximately 0.15 seconds per item.

Subsequent research established that elimination of set-size effects with practice, as in Neisser et al.'s (1963) study, occurs mainly when there is designation of particular stimuli as targets and others as distractors. When the mapping of stimuli to targets and distractors is consistent, such that a target on one trial is never a distractor on a different trial, search becomes, with practice, much more efficient than if the role of a stimulus varies between that of target and that of distractor (e.g., Shiffrin & Schneider, 1977). In fact, the ease with which consistently mapped targets can be found after extensive practice led to the idea that performance can be automatized, such that it is no longer subject to capacity limitations such as that underlying the set-size effect. Automatic processing will be discussed at more length in Chapter 4.

As Eckstein (2011, p. 8), notes, "Uncertainty regarding the spatial position of a target is at the core of what makes visual search difficult." He identified two statistical regularities of which people are able to take advantage to reduce this uncertainty. The first of these is target probabilities varying across locations. When the target is more likely to occur in some subset of locations than in others, performance is better at those locations. For example, Geng and Behrmann (2002) had participants indicate whether the target L or F was present in an array of distractor letters (T and E). The stimuli were displayed in a grid of six columns and three rows. In one condition the target occurred on one side of the screen with 80% probability and the other side with 20% probability. Even though the participants were not told of this relationship and most reported having no awareness of it when asked at the end of the session, they identified targets in the more probable side faster than those in the less probable side.

Some authors have suggested that the benefit for targets on the more probable side is due to short-term repetition benefits rather than to learning of the relations (e.g., Walthew & Gilchrist, 2006). However, Druker and Anderson (2010) obtained evidence that differences in spatial probability can in fact be learned. They reported results of two experiments using probability distributions that were continuous across the display, which allowed presentation of stimuli at high probability locations while minimizing spatial repetitions. Despite removing the benefit of short-term spatial repetition, performance was better at the high probability locations than at the lower probability ones.

The second regularity that can reduce the effects of spatial uncertainty is context, or contextual cueing. In the earliest study of contextual cuing, by Chun and Jiang (1998), observers had to indicate whether a target "T" stimulus, among distractor "L" shapes, was rotated 90° to the left or right. Unknown to the participants, within each trial block half of the trials consisted of 12 configurations of letters that were repeated in all blocks, whereas the other half of the trials consisted of 12 newly generated configurations. Performance was better for those trials on which the configuration repeated compared to those for which it was new. Thus, participants learned to use the context to "cue" the location at which the target was likely to be. The main point is that people learn regularities in displays across trials that benefit visual search, even when not told of those regularities.

Procedural Learning

The idea that the operations performed on stimuli while executing a task have an enduring effect on subsequent performance is referred to as *procedural learning*. Procedural learning theorists stress that stimuli are not remembered independently of the operations performed on them (e.g., Kolers & Roediger, 1984). Instead, learning is presumed to depend on the processing required during task performance. Evidence for such a procedural view has come from studies of reading.

In literate adults, reading is a highly overlearned skill requiring coordinated processes of perception, cognition, and action. Letter and word shapes must be recognized, eye movements must be controlled to select relevant text, and the meaning of the passage must be extracted. Because of its substantial perceptual component, reading would seem a natural choice for the study of perceptual skill acquisition. However, the degree of overlearning present in the adult population leaves little room for change within the context of an experiment.

To isolate the perceptual aspect of the reading process, an approach is needed for which the words and their associated meanings, as well as the syntax, remain familiar, but the perceptual characteristics are novel. Kolers (1975) adopted such an approach in his use of geometrically inverted text (see Figure 2.7). In one experiment, participants read 160 pages of inverted text over a 2-month period. As might be expected from looking at the text

Figure 2.7 Inverted text such as that used by Kolers (1975).

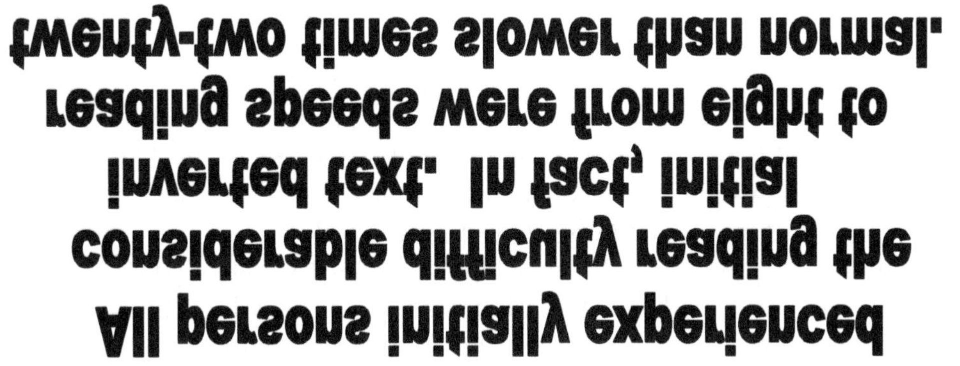

twenty-two times slower than normal.
reading speeds were from 8 to 22 times
inverted text. In fact, initial
considerable difficulty reading the
All persons initially experienced

in Figure 2.7, all persons initially experienced considerable difficulty reading the inverted text. In fact, initial reading speeds were from 8 to 22 times slower than normal. With practice, this initial difficulty was largely overcome. Learning followed the familiar power function, and by the end of the experiment the average rate of reading the inverted text was only slightly slower than a normal reading rate.

When the participants were retested more than a year later, the reading speed for previously unseen pages was much less than the initial reading speed had been, and reading speed was even faster for the pages that had been read a year or more earlier (Kolers, 1976). The savings in reading speed for the previously read pages relative to new pages apparently was due to experience with specific graphemic patterns. For example, Masson (1986) found that transfer of word identification skill for inverted text occurred only when the transfer words had the same letters as the practice words. Placing the locus of improvement at graphical pattern analysis suggests that reading inverted text is primarily a perceptual skill. The differential performance on old and new passages illustrates the specificity of the skill that has been learned. Kolers's results for the reading of transformed text are consistent with the procedural view of learning (Kolers & Roediger, 1984), according to which the way that symbols are manipulated during acquisition forms the basis for their retention, such that performance at a later time depends on the similarity of procedures in acquisition and test.

Adaptive Perception

Some authors have argued that there is a close relation between perception and action, and that perception adapts as a function of the task that is to be performed. Chopin and Mamassian (2010) examined this issue for *bistable perception*, in which two possible interpretations of a physical stimulus are perceived in alternation (e.g., the two orientations of a Necker cube or the famous duck/rabbit ambiguous figure). Their main concern was whether an interpretation that was required for success in one task would be perceived more often than would the other interpretation. Participants viewed Gabor patches (sine-wave gratings filtered through a normal probability distribution) presented in one orientation (e.g., left-tilted) to one eye and in the other orientation (right-tilted) to the other eye such that one orientation must dominate to achieve a stable percept. A search task that required localizing a Gabor patch presented at lower contrast than the other patches in the display was performed in alternation with a task in which the perceived orientation of the patches was reported. The target for the search task was presented to one eye only and thus had a stable orientation. On half of the blocks (Blocks 2 and 3 out of four blocks) the target always had the same orientation. The critical finding was that the orientation of the search target was also the first orientation perceived when bistable stimuli were presented in Blocks 2 and 3. This bias was also present in the fourth block, even though the orientation of the search target was random in that block, leading Chopin and Mamassian (2010, p. 1892) to conclude,

> We believe that the observed effect (i.e., first-percept bias) on bistability dynamics reflects long-lasting learning resulting from the visual search task. The visual system learns implicitly the probability of being rewarded in the search task when one of the two rivalrous interpretations is perceived. The more useful a percept is, the more the visual system makes it dominant at the first perceptual decision.

Learning may not be necessary for some stimuli to receive preferential processing. Some researchers have argued that evolutionary adaptation is responsible for faster identification of threatening stimuli, such as angry faces (e.g., Gerritsen, Frischen, Blake, Smilek, & Eastwood, 2008) and snakes and spiders (e.g., Öhman, Flykt, & Esteves, 2001). It has also been shown that the performance advantage for threatening stimuli (e.g., spiders) as compared to neutral stimuli (e.g., beetles) is greater for lethal spiders than for nonlethal spiders, especially when the spiders are shown on a picture of a hand rather than on a background such as a plant (Sulikowski, 2012). Thus, behavior seems to be sensitive to the implied level of threat and context in which the threat occurs. Evolutionary views of behavior suggest that gender differences relating to adaptation should be found in some cases. Stoet (2011) tested an implication of the hunter/gatherer model, according to which female cognition has evolutionarily adapted to gathering, by comparing the performance of females and males on a standard visual search task and on one that involved "gathering" fruits or letters displayed on a screen. The males performed better on both tasks, showing no evidence of the hypothesized advantage for females at searching and gathering.

According to the *action-specific perception* view (Proffitt, 2008; Witt, 2011) spatial perception is the result of adaptation: Perception of spatial relations is relative to a person's abilities to carry out intended actions and thus is influenced not only by the visual environment but also by the perceiver's body and his or her intended purpose. An example of the type of evidence provided for this view is Witt and Proffitt's (2005) finding, for softball players who had just completed a game, of a positive correlation between batting average in the games and the size of a circle they selected as best matching the size of the softball. That is, the ball was judged as being bigger if the batter had been able to hit it. Similarly, Witt, Linkenauger, Bakdash, and Proffitt (2008) found that golfers who putted well estimated the hole to be larger than those who did not. As yet another example, Witt and Sugovic (2013) showed that when participants attempted to catch a virtual fish by releasing a virtual net in a virtual reality environment, they released the net earlier when the net was small rather than large (consistent with perceiving the fish to be moving faster in the former case) and explicitly rated the fish speed to be higher.

Action-specific influences on perception seem to depend on visual attention being directed toward the target. For instance, Cañal-Bruland, Zhu, van der Kamp, and Masters (2011) showed that when visual feedback was eliminated in a golf-putting task, with only verbal feedback as to success or failure provided, there was no relation between performance and judgments of hole size. Likewise, when the hole was visible but participants had to putt the ball through a gap between two markers for it to go in the hole, there was no correlation of hole-size judgments with performance.

More problematic for the action-specific perception view is A. D. Cooper, Sterling, Bacon, and Bridgeman's (2012) argument that perception was confounded with memory in the work that was taken as support for action-specific perception. A. D. Cooper et al. dissociated perception and memory in an experiment in which participants threw marbles into various sized holes and estimated the hole sizes haptically or verbally. These estimates were made before the throw (with the hole visible), after the throw with the hole visible, or after the throw with the hole not visible (the memory condition). Throwing success was correlated with judged hole size in the memory condition, but not in the other conditions, leading the authors to conclude that memory, rather than perception, is action-specific. These and other challenges to aspects of the studies on action-specific perception (e.g., Durgin et al., 2009; Woods, Philbeck, & Danoff, 2009) suggest that caution be exercised in accepting that proposal based on current evidence.

Summary

In this chapter, we have illustrated how people become skilled at making perceptual distinctions. With practice, perceptual judgments come to be made faster and more accurately. The mechanisms of perceptual learning may involve attention weighting of individual stimulus dimensions, stimulus imprinting that forms new "detectors," differentiation of distinctive features, or unitization of features that results in more efficient processing of stimuli composed of more than one feature. For any specific perceptual learning phenomenon, there is often debate as to which of these types of mechanisms is responsible for the learning, and how early or late in the sensory system the learning is occurring.

Perceptual learning can occur incidentally in some tasks, without intention to learn or feedback. However, in other cases training with explicit feedback is required. Training to detect features is often beneficial to later performance, and progressive training for complex stimuli has been shown to be beneficial. Conceptual learning, such as that involved in learning to assign categories or labels to stimuli, may develop separately from learning to distinguish stimuli perceptually. Although labels are often helpful, they may "overshadow" the perceptual features and hinder learning in some cases.

In visual search tasks, performance typically decreases as set size increases. However, the amount of decrease is affected by numerous factors relating to the ease with which a target stimulus can be discriminated from distractors. There are two modes for perceptual processing and task performance, one that requires attentional resources and one that bypasses them. It is widely held that simple, featural discriminations can be made preattentively, whereas search for more complex stimuli requires attentional control. With practice, set-size effects decrease, and search for even complex targets seems to proceed relatively automatically.

Another theme explored in this chapter is that the procedures performed on stimuli determine the degree and nature of learning that will occur. Whereas both procedures and specific stimuli can be learned, in many cases the learning of one will be dependent on the learning of the other. In general, retention will be high when the procedures in effect during learning are reinstated at the time of retrieval.

Some researchers have argued that perceptual processing is a biological adaptation, which means that it is adapted to perform tasks that were important to survival during evolution of the species. Evolutionary arguments have taken the form that certain stimuli of adaptive significance are easier to detect as targets during visual search. More recently, such arguments have been used as part of the action-specific perception approach, according to which properties of the environment, the organism, and the action to be carried out interact to determine perception. Although considerable evidence consistent with this approach has been reported, both logical and empirical issues remain to be resolved if it is to be widely accepted.

3

Response Selection and Motor Skill

Extensive research in sport domains has shown that adult experts exhibit superior response selection performance (tactical decision making) as well as superior motor skill execution.

S. L. McPherson and J. N. Vickers (2004, p. 274)

In the 1988 Summer Olympic Games at Seoul, the decision in the final boxing match of the middle lightweight division went against the fighter who had landed nearly three times as many punches as his opponent in a seemingly one-sided fight. One consequence of this apparent "bad decision" was the introduction of a computerized scoring system, prior to the 1992 Games at Barcelona, that was intended to be more objective than the system that was then in use. This system, which was still in effect with only minor modifications for the 2012 Games in London, uses five judges, each of whom is equipped with an electronic box used to record responses. In each match, one boxer wears red and the other blue. If a judge detects a blow landed by the red boxer, a red button on the response box is to be pressed. Similarly, a blue button is to be pressed if the blue boxer lands a blow. For a point to be scored, three of the five judges must record a blow within a one-second interval. The boxer who receives the most points wins the match.

Despite the computerized scoring system, there was again a controversial match in the 1992 games, for which each judge recorded more blows for one boxer, but his opponent received more points and won the match. The discrepancy between the judges' individual scores and the point totals likely was a consequence of the restricted time interval during which responses from at least three judges had to be recorded. In the aftermath of this event, an international boxing official attributed the failure of the scoring system to the judges' slow speed of responding. According to him, "It's the reaction problem that is the problem we have. The machine could work provided people who press the buttons do it instantaneously" (quoted in Schuyler, 1992).

Unfortunately, it is well known that people do not have the capability to respond instantaneously. In addition to the time needed for the difficult perceptual discriminations required of judges, time is needed to select and execute the appropriate responses. The need to process and respond to several blows in quick succession makes selecting and executing the responses even more difficult than it would be if events were processed one at a time. These factors, along with natural variability in response times between individuals and the fact that judges tend to have a conservative criterion for recording a blow, make it likely that many responses by well-intentioned, trained judges will fall outside of the one-second interval allowed by the scoring system. Similar problems with scoring arose in the 2012 Games, for which the author of a blog entry titled "Olympic Boxing: Controversies Highlight the Failures of Scoring System" noted, "Many blame the computerised scoring, which requires the five judges to press a button within a second for a punch to score," emphasizing that one outspoken commentator said that he "would like to smash the scoring consoles with a hammer" (McClintock, 2012). Perhaps not too surprisingly, the computerized scoring system was replaced as of June 1, 2013, with a 10-point judging system (*Sports Illustrated*, 2013).

Most skills require responses more complicated than button presses, and in these tasks execution of precisely timed and organized movements (or, *motor control*) is essential. For example, in a task familiar to most of us, bicycling, the motor system is involved in the act of pedaling to generate power, the maintenance of balance, and steering. Motor acts must be coordinated not only with each other but also with continually changing sensory input as the cyclist perceives and responds to changes in the environment. Rapid adjustments in posture must be made in reaction to potholes and other variations in the road surface, and obstacles must be avoided. When riding a bicycle in a crowded place, such as a college campus, these adjustments require precise timing and anticipation to avoid collision with other vehicles or pedestrians. This example illustrates the major features of motor skill: the linking of receptor and effector functions; precise timing of movements and anticipation of motor requirements and consequences; and graded variations in the amount, direction, and duration of responses. Since even the most complex motor tasks require selection of the appropriate response ("early" cognitive representations of action) as well as physical movement execution ("late" motor processes; Hommel, Müsseler, Aschersleben, & Prinz, 2001), we begin this chapter by talking about the factors influencing response selection and the development of response-selection skill.

Response-Selection Skill

In all but the simplest task environments, appropriate responses have to be selected based on the information present in the environment. The processes of response selection are usually investigated in reaction-time tasks for which the alternative stimuli are readily discriminable and the motor requirements are minimal. This is because the major concern is not with the time course or accuracy of stimulus identification or response execution, but with the time to determine which response is to be made to the stimulus. As choice-reaction tasks are practiced, reaction times become progressively shorter, with group means typically following a power law. In fact, of the many variables that affect choice-reaction time, the one with the greatest effect is the amount of practice on the task (Rabbitt, 1989), and in relatively simple tasks, the process most affected by practice is response selection (Teichner & Krebs, 1974; Welford, 1976).

Pashler and Baylis (1991a) illustrated this last point in a study in which people practiced assigning symbolic stimuli (letters, digits, or nonalphanumeric characters) to categories by pressing one of three response keys. After the task had been practiced, either the perceptual, response-selection, or response-execution requirements were changed in a transfer condition. New stimuli added to practiced categories were responded to just as quickly as were the already practiced items, arguing against a perceptual basis for the practice effect; if the speedup had been wholly perceptual, it would have been restricted to the original stimuli. A response-execution basis for the improvement with practice was ruled out by showing little effect on performance of transferring from using the right hand to make the responses to using the left hand, or vice versa. That is, when the response-selection rules (e.g., "hit right key for numbers") remained the same, transfer performance was good even though different fingers were used to respond. But when the stimulus categories were reassigned to the response keys (e.g., when the rule "hit right key for numbers" was changed to "hit left key for numbers"), there was no benefit of prior practice.

The speed and accuracy with which responses can be selected—and the degree to which performance will improve with practice—are affected by a number of variables. These variables include the speed-accuracy criterion adopted by the performer, the number of stimulus and response alternatives, and the assignment of stimuli to responses.

Speed-Accuracy Trade-Off

The speed and accuracy of responding to a stimulus are closely linked. You can select a response quickly at the expense of accuracy (i.e., making incorrect responses with higher probability) or more slowly to attain higher accuracy. This linkage is called the speed-accuracy trade-off, with the trade-off being that a person can emphasize one to the detriment of the other. Figure 3.1 illustrates the function, which shows that as more time is taken to respond, accuracy improves. The function is S-shaped, which means that only very small changes in accuracy with changes in reaction time occur when responding is relatively slow or relatively fast. That is, when you have already slowed down responding to maximize accuracy, further slowing will lead to only small increases in accuracy, and when you are performing very quickly, at the expense of making many errors, at a certain point the error rate will cease to go up (i.e., one will be at chance accuracy already). Between these extremes, speed or accuracy may be emphasized at the cost of the other.

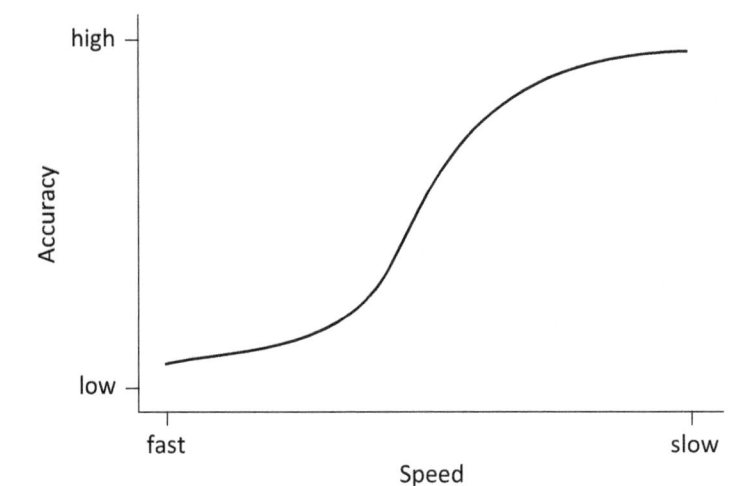

Figure 3.1 A speed-accuracy trade-off function.

In any experiment, thus, the possibility must be considered that differences in reaction time or accuracy between experimental conditions are attributable to speed-accuracy trade-offs. If faster responses are accompanied by higher error rates, then a speed-accuracy trade-off is implicated, which may imply that the factors being manipulated do not affect the efficiency of response-selection or some other process, but response strategy. It has even been suggested that a chief benefit of practice is to enable one to identify the optimal setting on the speed-accuracy function where speed is maximized without undue sacrifices in accuracy (e.g., Rabbitt, 1989).

One way to take both reaction time and accuracy into account is to apply a mathematical model to performance. An advantage of modeling can be that not only mean or median reaction times can be compared, but also predictions can be made about the entire distribution of reaction times. In *sequential sampling models*, for example, a noisy stimulus representation is sampled sequentially until enough information accumulates toward one of the response alternatives to reach a threshold, at which point that response is selected and executed (Van Zandt & Townsend, 2012). Such models include a variety of parameters that reflect different component psychological processes, including the rate at which information accumulates and any bias that may be present toward making one response or another. Speed-accuracy trade-off is typically modeled by setting the thresholds for individual response alternatives higher or lower, thus influencing the time to reach a threshold and the probability that the threshold reached will be that for an incorrect response. For skill acquisition, models can be fit to performance changes that occur with practice at a task, potentially providing a better understanding of the effect of practice on the component processes (Dutilh, Vandekerckhove, Tuerlinckx, & Wagenmakers, 2009).

Dutilh, Krypotos, and Wagenmakers (2011) applied a model of this type to data from an experiment in which participants performed a lexical-decision task (responding with keypresses to indicate whether a letter string was a word or a nonword). In the experiment, alternating blocks of trials contained letter strings that the participants had seen previously or that were new. Fitting the model to the data showed that several components were affected by practice, some in a stimulus-specific manner (i.e., only for blocks using previously seen stimuli) and some more generally (i.e., for all blocks). For trials on which the letter string was a word, an increase in accumulation rate was evident only for previously seen stimuli, suggesting a benefit due to experiencing the specific words in the experimental context. For trials on which the letter string was a nonword, an increase in accumulation rate was apparent for both new and previously seen strings, suggesting acquisition of a general skill at deciding that a letter string is in fact not a word.

Set-Size Effects and Uncertainty

One feature of response selection is that its duration lengthens as uncertainty about which stimulus will occur and which response will be required increases. This general rule was documented by Hick (1952) and Hyman (1953), who established that reaction time (RT) increases as a linear function of the logarithm of set size (n, the number of stimulus-response alternatives)—a relation known as the Hick-Hyman law:

$$RT = a + b\log_2(n),$$

where the intercept, a, of the function reflects the time attributable to perceptual and motor factors and the slope, b, reflects how much RT increases with each increase in set size.

Although uncertainty can be reduced by decreasing set size, it also can be reduced by cuing a subset of stimuli and responses ahead of the stimulus onset (Leonard, 1958) or making some stimuli and responses more likely than others (Hick, 1952). Thus, more generally, the Hick-Hyman law states that it is the *information* extracted from the stimulus to select the response (defined as reduction in uncertainty) that determines reaction time. Note that speed-accuracy trade-off is consistent with this general form of the law because the amount of information extracted from the stimulus is less when the speed-accuracy criterion is set to emphasize speed rather than accuracy.

Although the Hick-Hyman law holds across a range of situations, the slope of the function, b, depends on several factors, one being amount of practice. Practice largely eliminates set-size effects (Mowbray & Rhoades, 1959; Seibel, 1963). The virtual disappearance after practice of set-size effects, which are localized primarily at the response-selection stage, is one of the most convincing pieces of evidence that practice has a large influence on response-selection processes.

The Hick-Hyman law provides a good description of the relation between uncertainty and reaction time, but it does not provide an explanation of this relation. One model that has been proposed to explain the Hick-Hyman law is a sequential sampling model for which increasing the number of stimuli is assumed to increase the number of responses for which a threshold could be erroneously reached, resulting in an error. To keep a low error rate, as is typically desired in a reaction time study, you need to adjust the thresholds upward, allowing for a longer time processing the stimulus (Usher & McClelland, 2001). Another model (D. W. Schneider & Anderson, 2011) is based on the idea that the slowing of responses with increasing alternatives is due to a combination of associative interference while retrieving the assigned response from declarative memory and savings when the stimulus and response repeat. Savings occur on repetition trials—which are more common when the set-size is small—due to being able to bypass the normal retrieval process because the response to make to the stimulus is already in an active state. Associative interference, on the other hand, increases as the number of alternatives increases. This memory-based model accounts for the influence of practice on the set-size effect mainly through a reduction in time to retrieve the assigned response as this process becomes more automatic.

Stimulus-Response Compatibility Effects
Most users of laptop and desktop computers are used to scrolling through content by moving downward on the scrollbar to move the display upward on the screen, and vice versa, the mapping used by Microsoft Windows and most versions of Apple's Mac OS X operating systems. Beginning with the Mac OS X Lion version (OS X 10.7) in 2011, though, Apple switched the default value to a "natural" scrolling direction, intended to mimic what one does when swiping the touch screen of a smartphone or tablet computer. With this mapping, the content moves in the direction of the swiping or mouse movement: Downward movement produces downward scrolling, and upward movement produces upward scrolling. This change prompted an outcry from many users, who posted comments such as "Lion is unusable in this awful scrolling condition" and "Even though my brain can get adjusted to the new scrolling, my hand refuses to do so," and a flurry of dialogue on the Web about how to switch back to the old setting. Although positive assessments can be found—for example, "It took me only a few seconds to get used to moving in reverse and I have since found it very intuitive and you could argue that this is how scrolling should have always behaved" (Moylan, 2011; the prior statements are comments on the source article)—the issue of how to map scrolling direction highlights the need for establishing compatibility between the spatial representations for stimuli and responses, and the consequences of those responses (Chen & Proctor, 2013).

There are two types of relations between stimuli and responses that affect performance (Kornblum, Hasbroucq, & Osman, 1990). First, some stimulus sets have a natural correspondence with certain response sets. For example, visually displayed digits and spoken digit names naturally correspond by virtue of our extended experience with reading digits, whereas visually displayed digits and names of geometric shapes do not. *Set-level compatibility* is said to be high in the former case and low in the latter. When set-level compatibility is high, selection of the response corresponding to the stimulus is relatively fast (Alluisi & Muller, 1958).

Given that there is some degree of correspondence or similarity between the stimulus and response sets (i.e., if there is set-level compatibility), *element-level compatibility* effects may occur. That is, for a given pairing of stimulus and response sets, some mappings of stimuli and responses in the sets will produce faster and more accurate responses than will other mappings. For example, if the task is to say a digit name in response to a visually presented digit, the reaction time to name the digit (e.g., say "nine" in response to seeing the digit 9) will be faster than the time to say an arbitrarily assigned digit name (e.g., saying "five" in response to seeing the digit 9). When the accuracy and speed of performance in a choice-reaction task depend on the relation between the specific stimulus and response sets that are used and the way in which the members of the stimulus set are assigned to the responses, *stimulus-response compatibility* effects are said to occur. Because compatibility effects get larger with increasing number of alternatives, the slope of the Hick-Hyman function is smaller when the stimulus and response relations are highly compatible than when they are not.

Compatibility effects have been studied most widely using stimulus and response sets for which spatial location is the distinguishing feature of the elements in the sets. Fitts and Seeger (1953) established the existence of set-level compatibility effects with spatial stimulus and response sets, finding that responses were faster and more accurate when multiple stimulus locations were arranged in a way that corresponded with the spatial layout of the response panel than when they were not. Fitts and Deininger (1954) went on to explore element-level compatibility effects. In one condition, a panel with response buttons arranged in a circle was paired with a circular display of lights (see Figure 3.2). Responding was much faster when each light location in the display was assigned to the button at the corresponding location on the response panel (top panel) than when random pairings of lights to buttons were used (bottom panel). Performance was also considerably better when all stimuli were mapped to the mirror opposite response locations (middle panel) than with the random pairings, suggesting that general rules can be applied when there is a consistent relation between stimuli and responses.

Many subsequent researchers have used simpler versions of the spatial compatibility task with just two or four stimuli and responses used in order to isolate the critical factors influencing performance. Even in the basic task of responding to a stimulus in a right or left location by pressing a response key with the right or left hand, responding is faster when the left response is assigned to the left stimulus and the right response to the right stimulus than when the assignment is reversed. This is also the case when the hands

Figure 3.2 Maximum (spatially compatible), mirrored, and random (spatially incompatible) mappings of eight stimulus locations (circles) to eight response locations (arrows), configured in circular arrangements. Each arrow specifies the direction a stylus on the response board was to be moved in response to the stimulus.

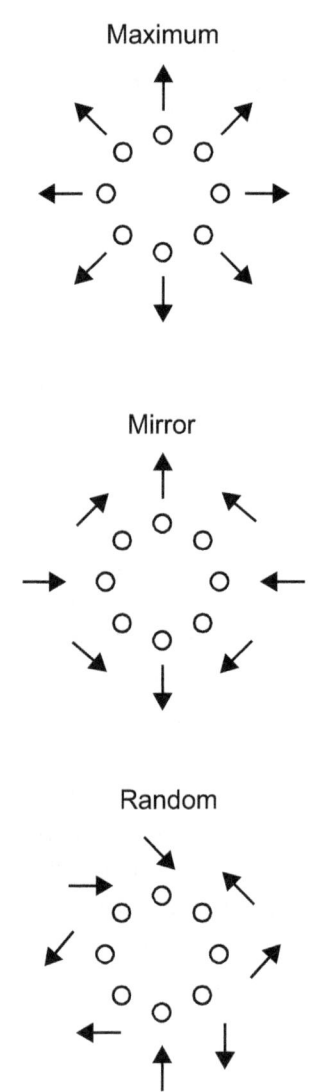

Maximum

Mirror

Random

Adapted from Fitts and Deininger (1954).

are crossed, so that the right hand operates the left key and the left hand the right key (e.g., Anzola, Bertoloni, Buchtel, & Rizzolatti, 1977), suggesting that it is the spatial representations (codes) of the stimuli and responses that must correspond and not, for example, the cerebral hemisphere in which the information is processed. More important, spatial compatibility effects are functions of response goals: When response keys are operated by hand-held sticks that are crossed, so that the right hand to the right operates the left key, and vice versa, correspondence of the key locations and stimulus locations yields the best performance (L. Riggio, Gawryszewski, & Umiltà, 1986). Coding accounts of spatial compatibility effects propose that the response assigned to a stimulus can be retrieved more quickly when the stimulus code corresponds to the response code than when it does not (Wallace, 1971). Even for a task as simple as pressing one of two keys to one of two possible stimuli for which each individual practices only a single mapping, the compatibility effect remains at about 50% of its initial size after more than 2,000 trials (Dutta & Proctor, 1992).

The finding that stimulus-response compatibility effects are not eliminated with practice (see also Fitts & Seeger, 1953) suggests that there are limits on how efficient response selection can become. An initial incompatibility restricts the level of performance that can ultimately be attained. This persistence of compatibility effects may reflect information-processing constraints that have evolved as a result of the spatial relations within the environment with which we interact. Alternatively, the persistence could be due to the fact that any task-specific procedures acquired from practice must be derived from the task representations on which initial performance is based. According to this interpretation, if the initial representations do not allow efficient translation, there are limits in the extent to which performance can improve.

As noted, precuing a subset of possible alternatives reduces reaction times through reducing uncertainty. However, not all precues are equally effective and the processes involved in selecting and preparing the cued subset of stimuli and responses are affected by spatial compatibility in much the same way as is the selection of the actual response. When the task is to press a key corresponding to a linear array of four stimulus locations mapped compatibly to keypress responses made with the middle and index fingers of each hand (see Figure 3.3), for example, precuing the two leftmost or two rightmost locations is more effective than precuing any other pair (J. Miller, 1982; Reeve & Proctor, 1984). This advantage is most evident when the interval between onset of the precue and the stimulus to respond is less than 1 s, with all pairs of cued locations benefiting to a similar extent when the interval is longer (Reeve & Proctor, 1984).

Practice with the task for several hundred trials leads to elimination of the advantage for the left-right precue pairs over the others, with all precue combinations showing similar benefits even at the shorter intervals (Cauraugh & Horrell, 1989; Proctor & Reeve, 1988). The probable reason why this difference goes away quickly with practice, whereas other SRC effects do not, is that all of the precue subsets are spatially compatible, even though some are initially more difficult to determine than others. As found for the

Figure 3.3 Stimulus displays for each precue condition in the spatial-precuing task, with the correct response corresponding to the location of the single plus sign in the third row.

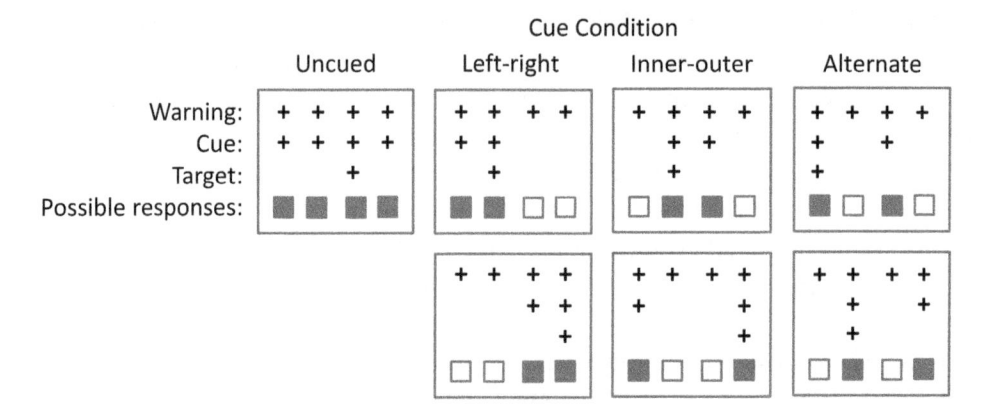

learning of perceptual procedures (see Chapter 2), the changes that occur with practice for the respective precue conditions are relatively durable, in that they are retained for at least 1 week (Proctor, Reeve, Weeks, Dornier, & Van Zandt, 1991). It has been argued that the left-right precuing advantage is due to the correspondence of the leftmost and rightmost halves of the stimulus displays with the natural left and right groupings of the response arrangement. This correspondence enables selection of those cued responses to be fast, automatic, and effortless (Adam, Hommel, & Umiltà, 2003). Elimination of this advantage with practice suggests that selection of other pairs of cued responses becomes automatic as well.

To this point, we have been discussing the influence on performance of the mapping of relevant stimulus information to responses. However, compatibility effects also occur when stimuli vary on a dimension that is irrelevant to the task. The effect of irrelevant spatial information on performance is called the Simon effect (J. R. Simon, 1990). In the Simon task, typically two stimuli are assigned to two responses, such as a left and a right keypress. The observer's task is to respond to the identity of the stimuli, ignoring where they are presented. Typically, the two stimuli, say, a red square assigned to a left key and a green square assigned to a right key, will be presented equal numbers of times on the right and on the left of the display. Even though stimulus location is task-irrelevant, reaction times are faster when stimulus and response locations are compatible. The Simon effect is typically attributed to automatic activation of the corresponding response produced rapidly at stimulus onset, which is then followed by activation of the assigned response by a slower, intentional process (e.g., Hommel, 1993). Additional time is required when the two sources of response activation are in conflict.

Like stimulus-response compatibility effects in general, the Simon effect is resistant to practice, showing an initial decrease followed by an effect that does not diminish with further practice (Prinz, Aschersleben, Hommel, & Vogt, 1995; Proctor & Lu, 1999). However, a small amount of practice (fewer than 100 trials) with a spatially incompatible mapping can reverse the effect not only when the Simon task is performed shortly thereafter but also a week later (Tagliabue, Zorzi, Umiltà, & Bassignani, 2000; Vu, Proctor, & Urcuioli, 2003). Thus, the "short-term" stimulus-response associations acquired from engaging in a specific task may continue to influence responding long after the task has changed.

Finally, you may have noticed that the scrolling example given at the beginning of this section actually involved compatibility between the response, or action, and the effect that it produced on the computer display. Kunde (2001) coined the term "response-effect compatibility" for such effects. He reported an experiment in which participants responded to one of four possible, centered color stimuli with an assigned keypress from a row of four, which lit one outline box from a row of four on the screen. Even though the lighting of the assigned box occurred after the key was pressed, responses were faster when the response-effect mapping was spatially compatible than when it was not. Elsner and Hommel (2001) showed that when each response produces a distinct effect, bidirectional associations are acquired that can then influence response selection. Their participants performed a set of trials in which they freely selected a left or right keypress to make, when signaled, with one keypress followed by a low pitch tone and the other with a high pitch tone. When the tones were later used as stimuli in a two-choice-reaction task, responses were faster when each tone was assigned to the response that had previously produced it than when the assignment was opposite. These and similar results have been attributed to response selection being based on anticipated sensory consequences, in at least some circumstances, and there is currently debate over whether the response-effect associations are acquired and activated automatically or only when intended.

Sequential Effects

As mentioned in the description of D. W. Schneider and Anderson's (2011) model of the Hick-Hyman law, when a stimulus is repeated on consecutive trials, response time to the second presentation is typically faster than if a different stimulus is presented (Kornblum, 1973). Such *repetition effects* have been attributed to the process of response selection because they interact with both set size (Kornblum, 1975) and stimulus-response compatibility (Bertelson, 1963; Kornblum, 1969). The fact that the effects of compatibility and set size are reduced on repetition trials suggests that response selection is facilitated on those trials, or even bypassed altogether (Pashler & Baylis, 1991b).

Results consistent with the bypass proposal are that the benefits of repetition are greater the larger the stimulus set size (Kornblum, 1973; Rabbitt & Vyas, 1979) and that the benefits are reduced with practice. In other words, the benefits of facilitating response-selection are greater for situations in which response selection should take longer. The relation between repetition and practice effects is, however, still far from understood. Evidence that there may be a close link between the two is that the nature of the repetition benefit changes with practice. Initially, the major component of the repetition effect is that of specific stimulus repetition, consistent with response selection being bypassed through retrieval of the prior stimulus-response episode. With practice, though, the repetition effect becomes largely a function of repetition of a stimulus from the same category as the preceding one (Rabbitt, 1968; Rabbitt & Vyas, 1979), implying that its basis now is in the categorization procedures involved in response selection.

Motor Learning

Many skills require "the integration of well-adjusted muscular performances" (Pear, 1948, p. 92)—that is, motor control. An extreme example of such skill was displayed on June 23, 2013, when Nik Wallenda completed a nearly 23-minute walk on a tightrope wire across the Grand Canyon. The walk, performed without a harness or safety net, was difficult even for an accomplished aerialist like Wallenda because of the high winds in the canyon. Consistent with the emphasis on specificity of practice in this book, Wallenda oriented his training toward the conditions under which he would have to perform:

> Wallenda previously said he was prepared for the various conditions he would face.
> "I've trained very, very hard in my hometown of Sarasota, Fla.," he said. "I've trained during tropical storm Andrea with wind gusts of 52 miles per hour in a torrential downpour. I've trained with my wind machines, 91-mile-an-hour winds last week on the wires."
> Wallenda also has trained to deal with the nuances of the wire itself. . . . "It has a life of its own," Wallenda said about the wire. "It's important that I change my rhythms because I can build a frequency into this cable that will become larger and larger, and I have to slow down, speed up and adjust my step sizes."
>
> (Stump, 2013)

Although most of us will never accomplish feats of motor control like those of Nik Wallenda, we learn and perform many highly skilled motor acts throughout our lifetimes.

From the perspective of the three-stage model of information processing introduced in Chapter 1, a response must be selected before it is executed. From this perspective, the factors that influence motor learning are often considered somewhat independently of the factors that influence perception or response selection. However, although a skilled pianist, surgeon, or tightrope walker must execute complex motor actions rapidly, efficiently, and with little error, these actions clearly depend on skilled perceiving and selection of action goals.

Conditions that promote the acquisition and retention of motor skills have been the subject of research for more than a century. Much of this research has focused on relatively simple laboratory tasks that allow isolation of the various factors that might promote skill learning. Although some consideration will be given to real-world skills in this chapter, our main goal is to convey what is known about motor learning from basic research on motor skill.

Motor learning has been studied from two different perspectives. One, the *motor-programming* view, continues along similar lines to the information-processing explanations offered for response selection, emphasizing central action plans (programs) that organize and control movements. The other, the *dynamical systems* perspective, stresses the role played by the mechanical properties of the body in the execution of movements. Research on motor learning has been conducted from both of these perspectives relatively independently in the recent past. Although the perspectives are often presented as in opposition, it is also possible to view their contributions as complementary (Anson, Elliott, & Davids, 2005).

Motor-Programming Perspective

The motor-programming view has been prominent since the late 1960s (Keele, 1968), and it continues to be influential today (Vimercati, Galli, Rigoldi, Ancillao, & Albertini, 2013). It is exemplified by Schmidt's (1975) *schema theory*, according to which movements are controlled by central representations or plans called generalized *motor programs*. Each program is presumed to cover an entire class of movements, such as a kicking action, which is characterized by relatively constant ("invariant") features such as sequence and timing. Like a computer program, the motor program has parameters for which values must be specified to execute a specific movement from a given class (e.g., kicking a football with certain force and speed with the right leg).

These parameter values are provided by schemas that develop with practice, allowing the performer to execute the movements within the class with increasing speed and accuracy. *Recall* and *recognition* schemas are thought to play a role in learning. The recall schema specifies the initial parameter values for generating the intended movement, whereas the recognition schema serves as a referent against which sensory feedback from task performance can be compared. For slow positioning movements, mismatches between the feedback resulting from performance and that expected by the recognition schema lead to modifications of the movement as it is being made. For both fast and slow movements, comparison of feedback to the recognition schema allows learning to occur through revisions of the recall and recognition schemas.

According to schema theory, when a movement is executed with a motor program, four types of information contribute to schema refinement: (a) environmental conditions prior to the movement; (b) parameter values assigned to the program; (c) knowledge of the correctness of the outcome; and (d) sensory consequences of the movement. Because the improvement of schemas depends on the information associated with the execution of particular instances of schemas, schema theory predicts that the schemas for a movement class will be learned better if a person performs a variety of movements within the class, rather than practicing just one specific movement repeatedly. Also, knowledge of the outcome of the movements is deemed to be essential to efficient learning.

Although all the details of schema theory are not still widely accepted, it is the basis for much of our current understanding of how knowledge of results and practice schedules influence acquisition, retention, and transfer of motor skill (C. H. Shea & Wulf, 2005). Also, the distinction between motor programs and their parameters, which is central to the theory, is still made in many motor skills studies.

Dynamical Systems Approach

The dynamical systems approach is based on the idea that much if not all of the regularity found in skilled movements can be explained in terms of physical characteristics of the body, governed by laws of physics, chemistry, and physiology (Latash, 2012). A movement pattern emerges as a consequence of constraints placed on it by the body structure, the physical environment, and the rules and goals of the task that is to be performed (Hu & Newell, 2011; K. M. Newell, 1986). The approach puts less emphasis on central action plans than does the motor-programming approach, and more emphasis on functional synergies between muscles, joints, and the force producing mechanisms of the nervous system. These synergies, often called *coordinative structures*, are considered to be flexible and able to adapt quickly to conditions to allow groups of muscles to execute intended actions (Kelso, Tuller, Vatikiotis-Bateson, & Fowler, 1984; Saltzman & Munhall, 1992)—for example, controlling balance (Chvatal, Torres-Oviedo, Safavynia, & Ting, 2011). The main hypothesis of the dynamical systems approach is that the central nervous system achieves coordinated action by means of these coordinative structures assembled from abstract, functionally specific equations of motion, or dynamics.

The architecture of a dynamic action system can be represented by a set of equations that determines the range of movement forms that the system can exhibit. To execute a particular class of movement, an appropriate set of parameters must be assembled to constrain the architecture to produce the task-specific, multiple-degree-of-freedom ensemble that acts as a coordinative structure. The system architecture and parameter specifications establish the boundary conditions for performance, with moment-to-moment performance described in terms of the states of the system. That is, instead of relying on a motor program to explain the guidance of movement, control of a movement is described as occurring online in response to the immediate environmental conditions. Kelso and his colleagues (e.g., Zanone & Kelso, 1992) have used the term *intrinsic dynamics* to refer to these constraints, which reflect the preexisting capacities that a person brings to a new task, and the term *behavioral information* to refer to the movement pattern that is to be performed in the task. From the dynamical systems perspective, intrinsic dynamics should be reflected in the spontaneous patterns of coordination adopted in a specific situation. Movement patterns in tasks for which the behavioral information is consistent with the intrinsic dynamics will be stable, whereas tasks for which the behavioral information conflicts with the intrinsic dynamics should be difficult and may shift to more stable movement patterns.

These predictions have been verified in tasks requiring coordinated bimanual rhythmic movements (Kelso, 1984). When the index fingers of the respective hands are to be repeatedly flexed and extended in time with a metronome, most people will spontaneously move the fingers in phase with respect to the required muscle movements (flexing and extending the fingers together) or 180° out of phase (or anti-phase, flexing one while extending the other). When instructed to try to maintain one of these coordination patterns, the in-phase pattern is more stable than the out-of-phase pattern (i.e., it shows less variability and is easier to maintain as the metronome speeds up). At high movement frequencies, the anti-phase coordination pattern will break down and shift to the in-phase pattern (i.e., a phase transition occurs). The intrinsic dynamics for these coordinative movements are classified as *bistable*, with, in dynamical systems terminology, attractors at 0° (in-phase) and 180° (anti-phase).

The intrinsic dynamics of the action system serve as the foundation of coordination on which learning of the control requirements for a specific task must be based. Although the system may be bistable initially, it is possible with practice to learn new attractors. Zanone and Kelso (1992) had people practice moving the left finger to lag in phase by 90° behind the right finger. Note that this phase relation is intermediate to the in-phase (0°) and anti-phase (180°) patterns that are stable attractors at low movement frequencies. With practice, the mean relative phasing progressively approached the required phasing of 90°. Moreover, when phasings of 60° to 105° were subsequently required, they were attracted toward 90°. These data suggest that the 90° relative phasing became a new attractor as a consequence of the practice with it.

Although the bistable 0° and 180° attractors are evident initially for most participants, some individuals also show a 90° attractor initially—that is, a *tristable* pattern. Kostrubiec, Zanone, Fuchs, and Kelso (2012) presented evidence that the learning of a 135° intermediate pattern for this tristable group is different from the learning of a new 90° attractor that occurs for bistable participants (see Figure 3.4). Rather than forming a new attractor at 135°, the previous 90° attractor shifts toward 135°. Consequently, Kostrubiec et al. proposed that learning in these tasks can occur through two distinct mechanisms, one that establishes a new attractor and another that shifts a preexisting attractor toward the learned phase relation.

Problems of Movement Control

Broadly speaking, making any movement requires that the motor system solve three problems: (a) Narrow down the possible number of ways of making the movement, (b) make movements in the right order, and (c) integrate perceptual and motor information (Rosenbaum, 2002). The first of these problems is called the *degrees-of-freedom* problem. Due to our anatomical structure, many ways exist for realizing virtually any movement goal. Even a simple action, like reaching to turn on a computer, can follow a number of different trajectories, restricted only by the possible movements of the joints involved. The dimensions of movement (e.g., horizontal, vertical, rotation) allowed by those joints are called degrees of freedom. In general, the more complex the movement, the more degrees of freedom there are available. The problem, as framed by Bernstein (1967), is how to eliminate redundant degrees of freedom. Bernstein (1996) concluded that this was accomplished early in motor learning by freezing degrees of freedom (e.g., locking the knees to learn a slalom "skiing" task; Vereijken, van Emmerik,

Figure 3.4 Row A shows the root mean square error (RMSE) in maintaining the relative phase of finger movements (bars) for participants with bistable (left column) and tristable (right column) dynamics (illustrated by the wavy lines above the bars). Row B shows, as a function of practice, the reduction in absolute error (AE) of the relative phase (left column) and the standard deviation (SD) of the relative phase. Note that only the 90°-Bistable group shows a reduction in SD with practice, which implies that they learned a new attractor (labeled bifurcation) but the 90°-Bistable group did not (labeled shift). Row C shows the RMSE in performance and the dynamics after practicing the task. Both groups now show a tristable pattern of attractors.

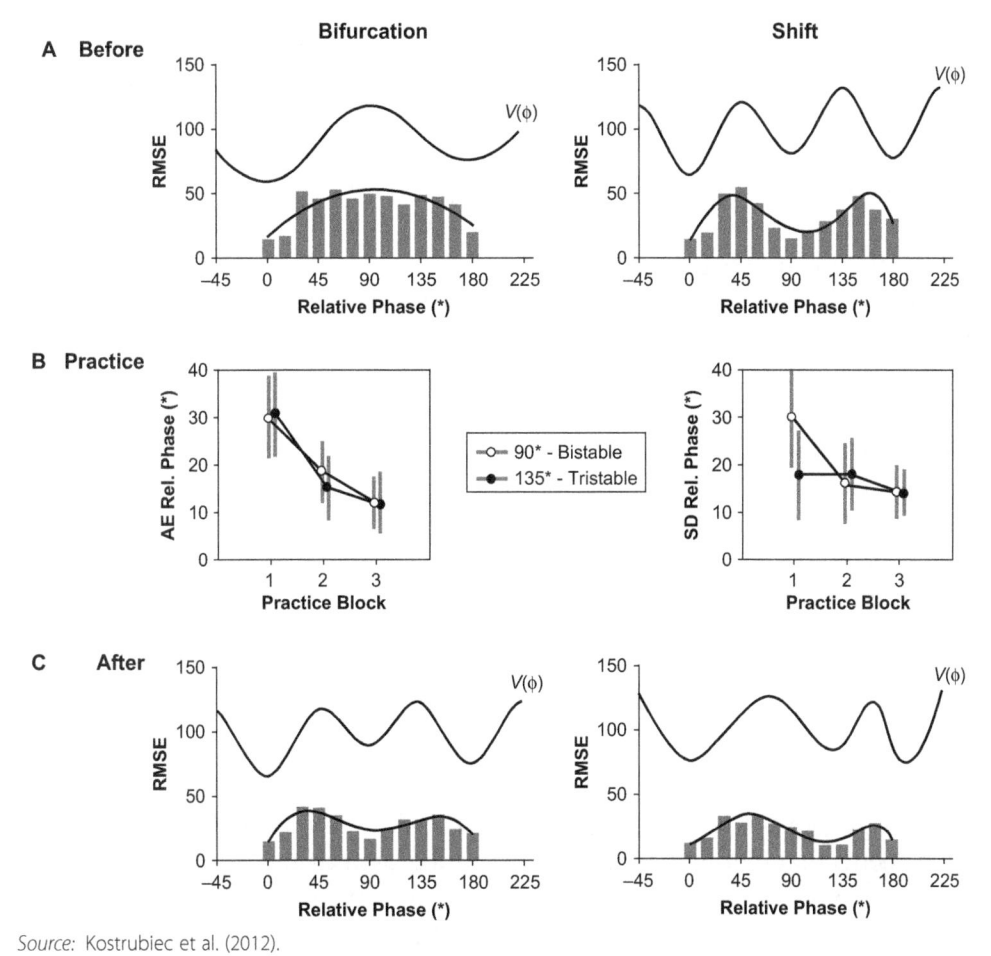

Source: Kostrubiec et al. (2012).

Whiting, & Newell, 1992), then gradually freeing them up as the task is practiced, and ultimately learning to use external physical forces to assist in execution of the motor skill.

Following Bernstein's framing of the movement degrees of freedom as being a problem, many solutions to the problem have been offered that rely on optimization of some cost function in arriving at a unique solution for the movement trajectory (see Prilutsky & Zatsiorsky, 2002). Latash (2010,

2012) has taken a different view: Rather than treating the degrees of freedom for movement as requiring a unique solution, he views degrees of freedom as providing an abundance of alternate ways for accomplishing the same task under various conditions. Families of solutions that solve the task are activated through motor synergy, "a neural organization that ensures co-variation among elemental variables (along time or across repetitive attempts at a task) that stabilizes the value or time profile of the performance variable" (Latash, 2010, p. 643). This synergy ensures that elemental variables covary in such a way as to minimize variance of the performance variable under dynamically changing conditions. In this view, practicing a motor task leads to (a) the elaboration of strong synergies that stabilize critical aspects of performance, and (b) the eventual incorporation of other task constraints into performance, such as minimizing fatigue, which has the effect of "loosening" the synergies (Latash, 2010).

The second problem is that of serial order. Many skills, such as playing musical instruments, require the organization of sequences of discrete movements. The serial order problem concerns how the timing and ordering of the movement elements in the sequences are controlled. A simple hypothesis is that movements are organized as *linear chains* in which the sensory feedback produced by one response initiates the next one in the sequence. But Lashley (1951) emphasized that this account is not feasible because the same motor elements enter into nearly all acts in many different orders and permutations. He proposed that some higher-order control elements must be involved to select the proper movement in any specific context. The idea that control of serial order occurs by hierarchical plans, or motor programs, has been supported by studies that require learning of movement sequences that can be broken into subgroups. In such studies, the number of levels in the hierarchy between one movement and the next predicts the time taken between responses (e.g., Povel & Collard, 1982; see Figure 3.5).

It seems that hierarchical plans are formed by making changes in the plan for the immediately completed movement sequence so that the movement sequence that is to be performed next is distinguished from it (Rosenbaum, Cohen, Jax, Weiss, & van der Wel, 2007). Evidence for this principle includes a sequential effect called the "parameter remapping effect" (Rosenbaum, Weber, Hazelett, & Hindorff, 1986). In Rosenbaum et al.'s (1986) study, participants made more errors when tapping the sequence MMIiiMIi (where capital letters indicate the right hand, lowercase letters indicate the left hand, and the letters m and i indicate the middle and index fingers, respectively) than when tapping the sequence MIiimmIIM. The apparent reason for the greater difficulty of tapping the former sequence is that because the number of taps made by each finger changes in the former sequence but not the latter, remapping of

Figure 3.5 A hierarchical decision tree for the sequence {1 2 1 2 2 3 2 3} (top) and the predicted pattern of response latencies derived from the number of nodes to be traversed (bottom).

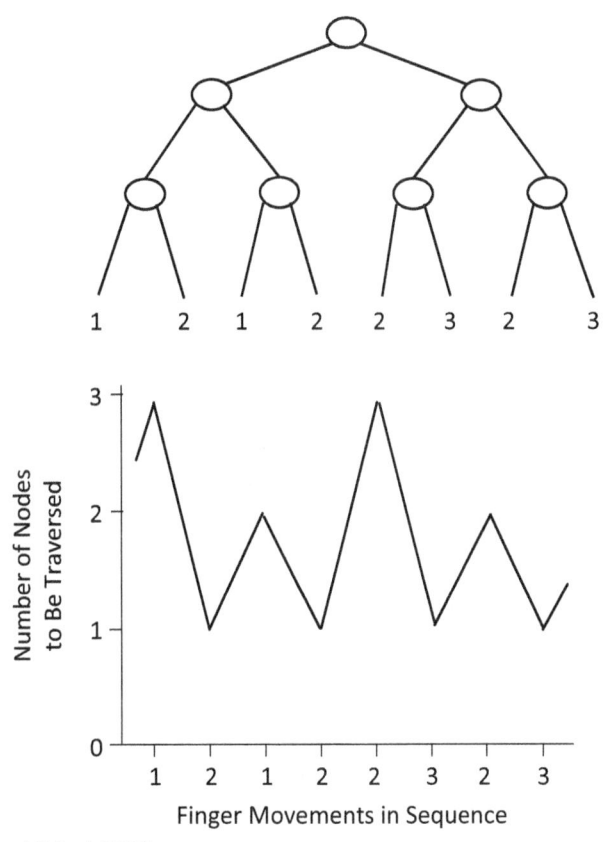

Adapted from Povel and Collard (1982).

the "number-of-taps" parameter is needed only in the first case. Other evidence for hierarchical plans comes from an effect called "hand path priming" (Jax & Rosenbaum, 2007). Jax and Rosenbaum had people move a stick figure representation of their arm on a display between a central location and one of 12 circularly arranged target locations. On some trials an obstacle (which had to be avoided) was in the path between the two. When the preceding trial contained an obstacle, the movement trajectory on the next trial without an obstacle was more circular than needed, as if the person was avoiding an obstacle. This outcome was evident regardless of the relation of the new target location to the preceding one, suggesting that the same spatiotemporal movement plan was being used from one trial to the next, and that new parameters were being supplied to execute the required movement.

The third problem, that of perceptual-motor integration, has two aspects: How does perception influence movement, and how does movement affect perception? Movement does not occur in a perceptual vacuum but is dependent on perceptual information. Before a movement can be initiated, the relevant aspects of the environment must be perceived. The characteristics of the environment and the behavioral intentions of the actor together determine which movements will be appropriate. For example, if one's intent is to grasp an object, the trajectory that the movement takes will be a function of the position of the object to be grasped, the current position of the limb to be moved, and the points at which the object will be grasped (Voudouris, Brenner, Schot, & Smeets, 2010). Moreover, the movements of the fingers and hand also are determined by perceived properties of the to-be-grasped object, such as its size and estimated weight (Jeannerod & Marteniuk, 1992), as well as the intended action (Herbort & Butz, 2010). Perception comes into play at many points in the grasping process, as well as in the execution of other actions. In addition to visual information, sensory input from receptors in the muscles, tendons, joints, and skin plays an important role in the guidance of action.

Factors Influencing Motor Skill Acquisition

Many factors influence the acquisition of motor skill, including motivation, fatigue, practice schedules, and feedback. Factors that produce the relatively permanent changes in behavior characteristic of learning need to be distinguished from those that produce only temporary changes in performance (Schmidt & Lee, 2011). Because any changes in performance observed during the training period (the acquisition phase) could be either temporary or more permanent, it is necessary to include retention tests, in which performance is tested at a later time, or transfer tests, in which performance under altered conditions is evaluated, to determine unambiguously if the variables of interest have an effect on learning. Of the many factors that can be considered in studies of motor learning, methods of feedback and practice schedules, which have both temporary and more permanent influences on performance, have received the most attention.

Feedback

As discussed, movement-related sensory information plays an integral role in the learning and performance of motor skills. A performer continually receives information through the senses about the positions of the limbs, the locations of objects in the environment, body posture, and so on. Information may also be available regarding success in attaining the desired goal. A distinction can be made between the intrinsic feedback inherent in producing a response and extrinsic, or augmented, feedback that adds to the intrinsic feedback (Schmidt & Lee, 2011).

Intrinsic Feedback

There are several sources of intrinsic feedback: proprioception from mechanoreceptors in the muscles, joints, and skin that provide information about movement, pressure, and position; vision; and to a much lesser extent, audition. Also, the vestibular sense, which consists of receptors in the inner ear that respond to movement and changes in position of the head, is important for maintaining posture and balance.

One issue of concern for skill acquisition is whether use of intrinsic feedback changes with practice. Most skill acquisition frameworks, such as Fitts's taxonomy described in Chapter 1, presume that performance becomes automatized as a function of skill and, hence, becomes less reliant on feedback. If so, there should be a shift from closed-loop control, which relies on sensory feedback, to open-loop control, which does not, with practice. For some types of tasks, such a shift may occur. One early study to find evidence supporting this shift was Pew's (1966) study in which participants had to try to maintain the position of a cursor at the center of a screen by alternately pressing a left or right key, each of which produced an acceleration of the cursor in the corresponding direction. Response patterns suggested that participants used visual feedback about cursor movement to perform the task initially, but in later sessions shifted to an open-loop strategy of rhythmically pressing the alternative response keys. In many other motor tasks, however, performance was better with than without vision even after much practice and suffered when the visual information was later removed. Proteau and Cournoyer (1990) had individuals practice moving a stylus rapidly to a target for 150 trials under conditions of full vision, vision of the handheld stylus and the target, or vision of the target only. Performance was best with full vision, although that for persons who could see the stylus and target approached the performance of the full-vision group late in practice. When visual information was eliminated in a transfer test, the groups with full vision and the stylus-plus-target visible performed worse than the target-only group, suggesting that visual feedback was still essential for persons who practiced with detailed visual information available to them.

For complex visuo-motor transformations, the type of visual feedback provided during practice can influence the precision of the internal model that is acquired. This is illustrated by a study by Sülzenbrück and Heuer (2011), in which people operated a virtual tool, for which the cursor on a screen represented the tool tip, by moving a pen on a digitizing tablet. Only the screen was visible, ensuring that the movements of the cursor were attended to. The task was to move the cursor from a start position to a target at one of eight locations quickly and accurately—that is, following the shortest path possible. Notably, the hand had to move in a curved path for the cursor to move in a straight line to the target location. During practice, persons who received continuous visual feedback showed little deviation from linear movement of the cursor, but they did take longer to execute the movement than did those who received only feedback about the final position of the cursor or the final position plus trajectory. In transfer tests without visual feedback, the group that had practiced with continuous visual feedback showed larger errors than did the other two groups. Sülzenbrück and Heuer concluded that more accurate internal models were acquired when visual feedback was available only at the end of the action rather than continuously, presumably because it caused the performers to rely less on closed-loop control.

Extrinsic Feedback

It is possible to learn at least some skills solely on the basis of intrinsic feedback, but learning usually is more efficient when extrinsic (or augmented) feedback is provided, as in the case of the conditions of the previous example in which visual feedback was provided after completing the movement. This feedback can be in the form of knowledge of results (KR), as in the final position of the cursor relative to the target, or knowledge of performance (KP), as in the trajectory showing how the movement to the target was executed. In most laboratory tasks augmented feedback is usually provided after a response has been completed, but in more complex skills it can be provided coexisting with execution of the task (Sigrist, Rauter, Riener, & Wolf, 2013). KR not only can provide information on which learning can be based but also can have motivational influences (Wulf, Shea, & Lewthwaite, 2010).

Because KR benefits learning, it is reasonable to assume that the more KR that is provided, the better learning will be. But this is not the case. Winstein and Schmidt (1990) found that learning to perform a complex movement was at least as good when KR was provided at random 33% of the time as when it was provided on 100% of the learning trials. Wulf and Schmidt (1989) showed similar results for learning a class of movements, each movement of which had the same relative timing structure (same order of sub-movements) but different absolute timing (timing of the sub-movements). That is, reduced KR benefited learning of an entire action class governed by a single generalized motor program. Providing KR to an observer watching someone else perform a task also yields better learning when it is given on only 33% of trials rather than 100%, and this benefit for reduced KR continues when the observer subsequently engages in a series of trials performing the task (Badets & Blandin, 2004).

Another way in which KR can be provided is through a summary of performance, in the form of a graph, at the end of a set of trials. That reducing the frequency of KR benefits learning suggests that summary KR may be more effective than KR provided for each individual trial. Lavery (1962) found support for this proposition in a study of tasks for which a steel ball (which was out of sight of the performer) was to be driven a specified distance (e.g., 20 inches) by pulling and releasing a plunger (as in pinball) or striking the end of a rod with a rubber hammer. A summary graph presented after each 20 trials, which provided qualitative KR (direction of error) or quantitative KR (direction and magnitude of error) for each trial, yielded better retention than did either type of KR provided immediately after each trial, even though performance during acquisition was worse with the summary graph than with immediate KR. This finding was later confirmed in a simple ballistic-timing task (Schmidt, Young, Swinnen, & Shapiro, 1989).

Schmidt and colleagues proposed a *guidance* hypothesis to explain why 100% KR does not produce better learning than less KR or summary KR. According to this hypothesis, the information provided by the KR guides the performer toward the performance goal. Immediate performance benefits from this guidance, but the performer may rely too heavily on the guidance if it is provided every trial and be at a disadvantage when it is removed. Support of the guidance hypothesis was obtained for a bimanual coordination task in which circular movements were to be made with each hand, 90° out of phase, in time with metronome pulses (Maslovat, Brunke, Chua, & Franks, 2009). Performance of participants who received continuous visual feedback of the movements on a computer screen deteriorated when the feedback was removed, but that of participants who received only discrete feedback at each metronome pulse did not.

A final point to note about feedback schedules is that it is beneficial in many circumstances to allow the learner to self-regulate the trials on which KR is received (e.g., Chiviacowsky, Wulf, Laroque de Medeiros, & Kaefer, 2008). Advantages of this type of self-regulated feedback include making the learner more active and motivated, causing him to devote greater effort to learning the task. It also allows the learner to use the feedback to provide information about specific aspects of performance, such as the effectiveness of a strategy change (Wulf et al., 2010).

Another issue regarding the timing of KR is when it should be given relative to the end of task performance. It has long been recognized that it takes time to process extrinsic feedback (Salmoni, Schmidt, & Walter, 1984), but time is also needed to process intrinsic feedback (Swinnen, Schmidt,

Nicholson, & Shapiro, 1990). If KR is provided too soon after performance of a task, it can disrupt processing of intrinsic feedback, leading to a failure to develop the internal representation, or recognition schema, necessary for detection of error as a movement is being executed. Swinnen (1990) obtained evidence for the view that active information processing occurs in the interval between task completion and KR by interpolating a secondary, attention-demanding task, which required estimating the time taken by the experimenter to execute a movement, in the intervals before and after KR. This interpolated task interfered with learning, as evidenced by poorer performance on a no-KR retention test, and the interference was greater when the task was performed before KR delay rather than after KR. Swinnen suggested that the interpolated task likely required development of a recognition schema to serve as a referent for evaluating the experimenter's movements, and this requirement could have interfered specifically with the development of such a recognition schema for the performer's movement task.

Feedback provided at task completion works well for tasks that require single degree-of-freedom movements or scaling of a single general movement pattern (K. M. Newell, 1991). However, for the multiple degrees-of-freedom tasks that are more characteristic of behaviors in natural situations, KR is less effective. In these cases, knowledge of performance, with respect to the forces applied during performance (kinetic feedback) or the temporal and spatial properties of the movement that was executed (kinematic feedback), is needed to provide information not just about the outcome but also about the dynamics of the movement used to produce the outcome. Whereas KR provides no information about what aspects of the movement contributed to successful performance, knowledge of performance can provide such information and direct the performer's attention to those aspects that are critical to performance (Young & Schmidt, 1992).

English (1942) reported anecdotal evidence for the efficacy of kinetic feedback from a study of the instruction of military recruits in rifle shooting that had been conducted in the 1920s. It was determined that a central factor in successful shooting was the "trigger squeeze"; so, a rifle was modified to provide feedback about trigger pressure by building a fluid-filled tube into the stock. When the trigger was squeezed, a change in the level of the liquid occurred corresponding to the force of the squeeze. A recruit could thus receive direct feedback about whether a proper squeeze had been applied. English described the results obtained when this feedback was used during training as excellent, noting, "men given up as hopeless by their officers and non-commissioned officers showed rapid improvement in a large percentage of cases" (p. 4).

English (1942) went on to stress that the success of the training was due to the recruit acquiring "a local kinesthetic insight into what he is required to do. . . . [and that] sound instruction must first discover the particular kind and locus of the insight required for each sort of situation" (p. 5). These points have been emphasized by K. M. Newell and Walter (1981), who advocated the use of performance feedback. In most cases, the task criterion specifies what information the feedback must provide to be effective. For example, providing a graph showing the force-time history for isometric task performance (i.e., the force exerted throughout a trial as a function of time) benefits the production of a particular force-time relation but not that of a particular peak force (K. M. Newell, Sparrow, & Quinn, 1985). The feedback regarding force-time history is not beneficial in the latter case because the time course of the forces exerted is not relevant to the task goal of producing a specified peak force.

Schedules of Practice

In addition to the type and schedule of feedback, the scheduling of the practice trials can affect the acquisition of motor skill. The most-studied practice variables are the spacing of trials and whether variations of a task are practiced in a blocked (only trials of one type practiced together) or randomized (different movements practiced within a block of trials) manner.

Distribution of practice has a long history of research in the study of motor learning (J. A. Adams, 1987). Many studies show that massed practice results in considerably poorer performance during acquisition than does distributed practice, but the effects on learning are less clear. Lee and Genovese (1988) conducted a meta-analysis of the literature that showed that massed practice does result in poorer learning than distributed practice, although the effect is smaller on retention tests than during acquisition. This meta-analysis was based on continuous (e.g., tracking) tasks. In at least some cases, when the task is discrete (e.g., turning pegs in a pegboard; Carron, 1969), no difference between massed and distributed practice during acquisition and an advantage for massed practice on a retention test has been found. To determine whether distribution of practice operates differently for discrete and continuous tasks, Lee and Genovese (1989) compared learning of discrete and continuous versions of the same task. Their results verified that massed practice was beneficial for learning the discrete version of the task but detrimental for learning the continuous version. Lee and Genovese suggested that the differences likely reflect the occurrence of different types of information processing during the interval between trials for discrete versus continuous tasks.

When different tasks or task variations must be learned, the tasks can be practiced in blocks of one task at a time or with the tasks randomly intermixed. Blocked versus random practice has been shown to be a factor influencing learning and performance, and its effect extends to non-motor domains. Contemporary interest in this variable dates from a study by J. B. Shea and Morgan (1979). During the acquisition phase of their study, three tasks were performed in which the right hand was used to knock down three of six barriers in a specific order. The three tasks were practiced one at a time in distinct blocks of trials or randomly intermixed. The blocked-practice group performed the tasks much faster than the random-practice group during acquisition. However, when tested after a retention interval of 10 minutes or 10 days, the blocked-practice group performed much more slowly in the condition in which the trials were randomly intermixed, and the random-practice group was faster for both the blocked and random conditions. The random-practice group also showed broader transfer to new versions of the task.

This general pattern of results, that blocked presentation improves performance during acquisition but retards learning, has been replicated in many laboratory situations, although it is less consistently found in more complex tasks learned outside of the lab (Merbah & Meulemans, 2011). Both the disadvantage for random practice during acquisition and its advantage for retention and transfer have been treated as due to the changes in context in blocked versus random practice, or *contextual interference*. According to this view, contextual interference is greater when changes in the experimental context occur from trial to trial. Shea and Morgan provided an elaboration account, proposing that the advantage for random presentation in their study resulted from the use of multiple processing strategies. Lee and Magill (1983) proposed as an alternative that random-practice conditions are effective because information from previous executions of the task is forgotten, and effort must be devoted to "reconstructing" the action plan. Both the elaboration and reconstruction accounts attribute the contextual interference effect to the random-practice schedule requiring more cognitive activity than does the blocked one.

Despite the prevalence of contextual interference effects in laboratory tasks, the literature on more complex real-world sports skills is mixed (Merbah & Meulemans, 2011), with, according to one review (Barreiros, Figueiredo, & Godinho, 2007), only 43% of field studies showing a transfer benefit for random over blocked practice. This suggests that the contextual interference effect is relatively weak in more complex tasks. One possible reason why a blocked-practice schedule may be as effective as a randomized one for complex motor tasks is that these tasks intrinsically induce deep-level cognitive processing. In fact, the added cognitive demands of a random-practice schedule may even overload the performer (Albaret & Thon, 1998). More important for real-world skills seems to be focus of attention. Instructions to focus attention on the goal of the action rather than on the movements required to execute it have consistently been found to yield better performance than instructions to focus on the movements themselves (Wulf, 2013). Attending to the action effect is presumed to promote reliance on automatic processes for motor control, whereas attending to the movements is presumed to interfere with those automatic processes that typically would control and coordinate the movements.

Our discussion of practice schedules to this point has focused mainly on physical practice. However, when combined with physical practice, mental practice can also be beneficial (Driskell, Copper, & Moran, 1994), as can observational learning in which a model is viewed performing the task (Ashford, Bennett, & Davids, 2006; Wulf et al., 2010). Mental imaging seems to affect learning much like vision, in that mentally imaging the visual feedback on trials produces specificity of practice results similar to those described earlier for actual visual feedback (Krigolson, Van Gyn, Tremblay, & Heath, 2006). Likewise, observational learning is affected in much the same way as physical practice by variables including relative feedback frequency (as mentioned earlier) and schedules of practice (Wolpert, Diederichsen, & Flanagan, 2011).

One issue that arises is where to place mental practice or observational learning relative to physical learning in a training schedule. Mental practice has been shown to be beneficial both early and late in practice (Driskell et al., 1994). A recent study by Ellenbuerger, Boutin, Blandin, Shea, and Panzer (2012) found that performing observational practice in the first of two sessions followed by physical practice in the second session was effective, whereas having the physical practice session first was not. The authors attributed this benefit of early observational practice to its allowing the movement sequence to be coded spatially, with subsequent physical practice providing the opportunity for additional motor codes to be developed.

Summary

Most skills require selection of alternative responses, or actions, and execution of precisely timed and organized movements is often essential. The time for response selection is affected by many factors, including the number of possible stimulus-response alternatives and the compatibility between stimulus and response. The benefit of maintaining high compatibility increases as the number of alternatives increases, mainly because the additional processing time required for response selection when the relation is incompatible increases greatly. Response selection benefits from practice, particularly when the number of stimulus-response alternatives is large, and not only is the benefit of practice less for a compatible mapping than for a less compatible one, but also a benefit for the compatible relation typically endures throughout a considerable amount of practice. Another factor that can reduce response-selection time is repetition of the stimulus and response from the preceding trial. Early in practice this repetition benefit is mainly due to bypassing the normal response-selection processes, whereas later in practice it may be due in part to the response-selection processes being more efficient.

Motor learning, or improvement in the execution of motor actions, has been the subject of considerable research. Three problems of concern in the study of motor control, those of degrees of freedom, serial order, and perceptual-motor integration, have guided much of this research. Several solutions to these problems, and how the performance changes with practice, have been proposed from two approaches, the motor-programming perspective and the dynamical systems perspective. The former emphasizes central plans for action, whereas the latter stresses the mechanical properties of the body. The majority of studies conducted on motor learning have been guided by the motor-programming perspective. Many of the studies on practice and feedback schedules have arisen from issues regarding the role and nature of motor programs. Among the more salient findings are that control of movements continues to rely on intrinsic feedback after extensive practice and that the schedules of practice and extrinsic feedback that support good performance during acquisition often do not result in the best learning. The dynamical systems perspective focuses on coordination of movements and emphasizes the properties of the motor system in particular contexts. The dynamical systems perspective has been shown to provide some fresh insights into the execution of coordinated movements and the acquisition of motor skill, and it will continue to play a prominent role in the future.

4

Attention and Skill

It has been known for a long time that paying "too much attention" to one's actions can disrupt performance, particularly if the skill is well practiced. . . . Perhaps even more interestingly, new research shows that the learning of new motor skills also suffers when we direct attention to the coordination of our movements.

G. Wulf (2007, p. vii)

Attention is integral to skill. Learning new material or skills requires attending to the right information—and ignoring wrong or irrelevant information—and an essential part of many skills is learning to allocate attention appropriately to the right information at the right time or to share attention across tasks or sources of information. At the same time, the role of attention might change as skill is acquired and some components are automatized. For example, most of us are so practiced at the task of driving that we are not aware of steering, braking, or changing gears as necessary—or, at times, even of the route that we are driving—while attending to both traffic and road conditions (but not billboards or noise coming from the backseat). The role of attention in skill acquisition and skilled performance is so important that no account of skill can be complete without a consideration of attention processes. In this chapter, we focus on the role of attention in the development of skill and on the development of attentional skill itself.

Conceptualizing Attention

One of the most often cited quotes in the literature on attention (from William James's [1890] monograph) begins "Everyone knows what attention is." The quote is popular for its eloquence, with its mention of the focalization and concentration of consciousness, but often used ironically simply because there are so many different conceptualizations of attention. Definitions of attention differ in their details, but most definitions include the idea of the dedication of a limited-capacity process or resource that is responsible for the selection of a subset of stimuli for further processing (A. Johnson & Proctor, 2004). Because our capacity to process information is limited, attending to the wrong information (and, hence, failing to attend to relevant information) can result in poor learning or performance. For example, listening to a conversation that is occurring nearby, instead of attending to a lecturer, is likely to result in embarrassment if you are called on to answer a question and in poor performance if the unattended material appears on an exam. The ability to control attention is also limited, such that it is often difficult to keep attention focused on just the pertinent information. To characterize and predict performance in all but the simplest situations, it is thus necessary to have an understanding of the role and nature of attention.

Attentional Bottlenecks

One of the most basic questions in the study of attention is whether attention can best be described as a resource that can be allocated at will to any of a number of processing activities or a limited-capacity processing bottleneck. Models that conceptualize attention as a bottleneck differ as to where in the stream of information processing selection is assumed to occur, and in whether this locus of selection is a structural, immutable property of the cognitive system or is under strategic control. In *early-selection theories* (e.g., Broadbent, 1958; Gaspelin, Ruthruff, & Jung, 2014), a selective filter is assumed to operate on sensory features of stimuli. Sensory representations of all presented stimuli are briefly activated, but only a stimulus allowed further processing by the selective filter will be identified, and all others will be lost. *Late-selection* theories, on the other hand, assume that any filtering of messages occurs relatively late in the processing sequence. For example, Deutsch and Deutsch (1963) and D. A. Norman (1968) proposed late-selection models according to which all stimuli are identified when their corresponding representations in memory are activated, with only those items that are deemed to be pertinent receiving further processing.

Whether selection occurs early or late has been a hotly debated topic in the study of attention, and neither theoretical approach can fully account for attentional selection. It has become clear that attention is needed for object recognition (e.g., Lachter, Forster, & Ruthruff, 2004; Yantis & Johnston, 1990), although when perceptual processing demands are low, attention may spill over from targets to distractors such that they, also, are recognized (Lavie, 1995). Perhaps more important than the debate about whether attentional selection occurs early or late in processing is the question of why attentional selection is necessary. As was discussed in Chapter 2, perceptual skill depends to a large extent on learning to attend to the appropriate features of stimuli. Neurobiological research has illustrated that a need for perceptual selectivity appears to arise during the processing of virtually any visual information when that information reaches the extrastriate cortex, a region of the brain dedicated to processing complex visual information. The receptive fields of neurons in the extrastriate cortex cover larger regions of the visual field than do the receptive fields of those in earlier processing regions (e.g., Desimone & Gross, 1979; Gatass, Sousa, & Gross, 1988; Hubel & Wiesel, 1968; A. T. Smith, Singh, Williams, & Greenlee, 2001), and often include representations of multiple objects. Thus, the information contained in a single neural signal is ambiguous (Reynolds, Chelazzi, & Desimone, 1999), and in order to achieve disambiguated representations, visual objects must compete for control of neural responses.

Stimuli in the visual field compete for attention, and the competition between stimuli is biased by the intentions, goals, or expectations of the observer (Desimone & Duncan, 1995). Competitive interactions occur that modulate the signals corresponding to the objects within a set of shared receptive fields (Ghose & Maunsell, 2008; Reynolds & Desimone, 2003; Womelsdorf, Anton-Erxleben, & Treue, 2008) and allow one object to dominate a given neuron's response train, effectively shrinking the neuron's receptive field around the attended stimulus (Moran & Desimone, 1985; Reynolds et al., 1999), thus sharpening our perception. Biased competition and the limitations on processing that such competitive processing imposes appear to be needed for the disambiguation of neural signals.

Attentional Resources

Many researchers view attention as a limited resource available to (and possibly needed for) all processing stages. In this view, two tasks can be performed together without decrement so long as the total amount of attentional capacity required does not exceed the available supply. If the capacity is exceeded, at least one task will suffer. The availability of resources depends on factors such as the arousal level of the performer, and performance at a given time depends both on the effort the performer exerts and the strategies followed for allocating attention (Kahneman, 1973). Resource models make the assumption that attention is under the person's control and can be removed from one task and devoted to the other in varying degrees. In fact, the ability to flexibly allocate attention across tasks is an important component of many skills, and the training of attentional allocation and prioritization strategies can have a strong and long-lasting influence on performance (Gopher, Brickner, & Navon, 1982).

As illustrated in Figure 4.1, attention allocation across two tasks can be represented as a performance operating characteristic (POC; D. A. Norman & Bobrow, 1975). To construct a POC, performers are instructed to allocate respectively more attention to one or the other of two tasks across different task conditions. Performance on Task A is represented on the vertical axis and performance on Task B on the horizontal axis. The point representing the intersection of single-task performance on the two tasks (Point P in Figure 4.1) serves as a referent for the measurement of the efficiency of dual-task performance. The more successfully the two tasks can be performed together, the closer plotted performance will be to Point P. However, even if one task is strongly emphasized over the other, performance is typically worse in the dual-task context than in the single-task context. This *cost of concurrence* may be due to such things as distraction by the secondary task (due to an inability to allocate sufficient attention to the primary task) and the need to coordinate the two tasks. A POC curve is obtained by biasing

Figure 4.1 A hypothetical POC curve. Point P represents single-task performance on Tasks A and B. Point a shows performance on both tasks when Task A is emphasized, Point b represents equal emphasis, and Point c represents an emphasis on Task B. The cost of concurrence is the difference between performing a task alone and performing it with another task, even when it receives full emphasis.

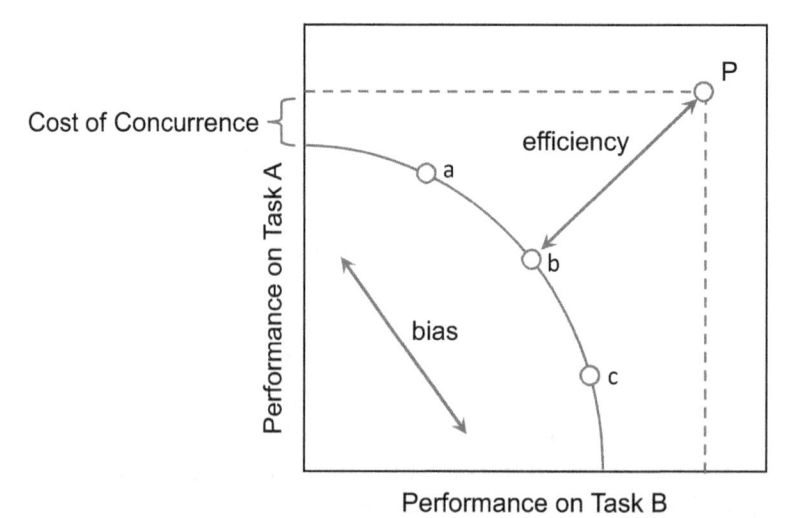

the performer to emphasize one task over the other in different blocks of trials. Performance is then plotted as a function of the allocation strategy to derive a curve that reflects the degree to which resources can be traded off between the two tasks.

Dual-task performance has been shown to benefit more from such training under variable-emphasis settings (e.g., Task 1 priority of 25, 50, or 75%—and corresponding Task 2 priority of 75, 50, and 25%) than from training without emphasis instructions or with only one priority (e.g., 50%; see, e.g., Gopher, 1993; Kramer, Larish, & Strayer, 1995). The better performance of those who train under variable emphases seems to stem from an improved ability to detect changes and adjust efforts to cope with changing task demands. When emphases are shifted, different components of the task become more salient, and these salient features may contribute to more complete and complex representations of the task (Boot et al., 2010). Gopher, Weil, and Siegel (1989) suggest that variable-emphasis training may also force participants to explore different strategies of performance, thus allowing them to overcome any limitations in performance due to initial adaptation of non-optimal strategies.

Variable-emphasis training leads to faster learning of the task at hand, and may lead to more transfer as well. Gopher, Weil, Bareket, and Caspi (1988; see also Gopher, Weil, & Bareket, 1994) showed that Israeli Air Force cadets who received variable-emphasis training with the Space Fortress game (a complex video game developed by cognitive psychologists in the 1980s as a research tool to study training strategies; Mané & Donchin, 1989) while undergoing flight training were more likely to complete the program than were cadets who did not receive the training. Similarly, Kramer et al. (1995) showed that participants who received variable-emphasis training while performing simultaneous gauge monitoring and arithmetic tasks showed more transfer to a novel scheduling/memory task than participants who merely practiced the gauge monitoring/arithmetic task.

Transfer following variable-emphasis training was further studied by Boot et al. (2010) using the Space Fortress game. They examined transfer to a range of basic and complex cognitive and perceptual-motor tasks after training on the Space Fortress game with or without variable emphasis. Variable-emphasis training led to a performance advantage only for those tasks that closely resembled one component of the Space Fortress game—and not to tasks designed to measure attentional control in general—leading the authors to conclude that variable-practice benefits are specific to the tasks practiced. M. W. Voss et al. (2012) also compared the effects of full- and variable-emphasis training on learning the Space Fortress game. Not only did they find that variable-emphasis trainees showed more improvement in the game, but also they used fMRI to show that variable-emphasis training resulted in the development of changes in brain network interaction reflective of more flexible skill learning and retrieval than did full-emphasis training. The variable-priority training advantage was associated with changes in connectivity with the declarative learning system (involving the hippocampus), whereas full-priority training seemed to strengthen links within the procedural learning system (involving the basal ganglia and primary motor areas). Moreover, the increased connectivity between the fronto-parietal networks (which have been linked to attention and working-memory capacity) and declarative systems observed in the variable-priority trainees was associated with the amount of learning evidenced. Voss et al. suggest that the enhanced gains seen with variable-emphasis training as compared to full-emphasis training may be due to the flexibility that comes with the declarative knowledge that seems to develop when priorities are changed. Whereas full-priority practice seems to affect neural networks that acquire and implement stimulus-response representations, variable-priority practice affects neural networks involved in higher-order relationships between goals and actions (Kantak, Sullivan, Fisher, Knowlton, & Winstein, 2010).

The Psychological Refractory Period Effect

The cost of concurrence that is generally found when two tasks are performed together suggests that there may be hardwired limitations in performing multiple tasks at the same time. In fact, although we will discuss some remarkable feats of time-sharing in this chapter, a large body of research suggests that the process of response selection (see Chapter 3) can be considered a bottleneck in human information processing. Evidence in support of this inference has been obtained in a dual-task paradigm in which stimuli for two different tasks, each of which requires a response, are presented in rapid succession. The main finding in such a situation is that reaction time to the second stimulus is slowed relative to when that stimulus is presented alone, and this slowing becomes greater as the interval between the two stimuli decreases. This effect is called the *psychological refractory period* (PRP) effect (M. C. Smith, 1967; Telford, 1931).

The most widely accepted theory of the PRP effect assigns it to a bottleneck in the response-selection stage (e.g., Leonhard, 2011; J. Miller & Durst, 2015; see Figure 4.2). By this account, the selection of two responses cannot occur in parallel: Selection of the second response must wait until selection of the first response is finished (Pashler, 1984; Welford, 1952). Any processing that precedes response selection can occur in parallel, even while the first response is being selected. This information must, however, be held in store until the response-selection mechanism becomes available.

Figure 4.2 Response-selection bottleneck in dual-task performance. Perception can be carried out in parallel with other processes, but response-selection can be performed for only one task at a time. Thus, Task 2 response selection is delayed until Task 1 response selection is finished.

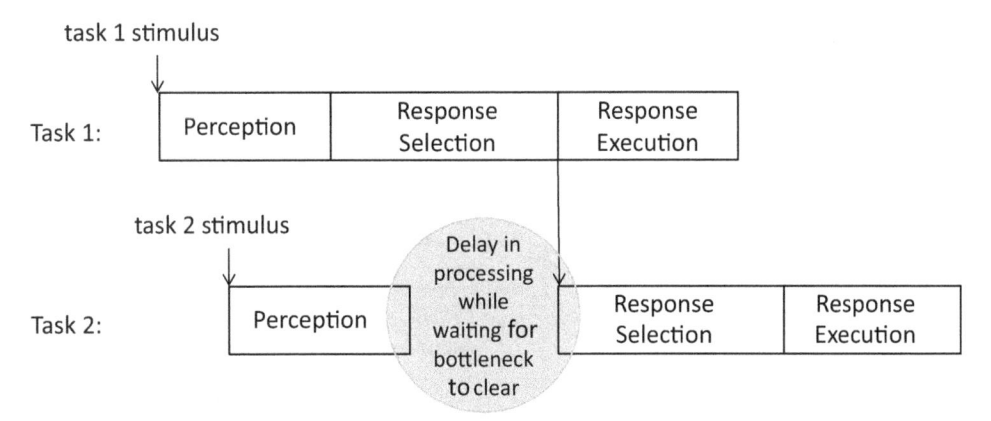

```
task 1 stimulus
      ↓
Task 1:  [ Perception | Response Selection | Response Execution ]

      task 2 stimulus
            ↓         (Delay in processing while waiting for bottleneck to clear)
Task 2:     [ Perception | ... | Response Selection | Response Execution ]
```

Because stimulus information is stored until the response-selection bottleneck is free, increasing the difficulty of perceptual identification of the Task 2 stimulus will have visible effects on reaction time only if the extra time needed for identification exceeds that needed for selection of the first response. That is, the effect of increasing the difficulty of Task 2 stimulus identification should be underadditive with that of reducing the interval between the two stimuli (Pashler, 1984; see Figure 4.3, right panel), such that the shorter the interval (and thus, the longer the wait before the response-selection bottleneck is cleared), the smaller the effect of increasing Task 2 stimulus identification difficulty.

Another implication of a response-selection bottleneck is that effects due to processes that occur after the bottleneck should not depend on the interval between the onsets of the two stimuli. Indeed, manipulations of response-selection (Figure 4.3, left panel) and response-execution difficulty have similar effects regardless of the interval between the two stimuli (McCann & Johnston, 1992; Van Selst & Jolicoeur, 1997). However, changes in Task 1 response-execution demands have been shown to affect Task 2 reaction times in a way that suggests that response execution is also subject to a bottleneck (De Jong, 1993; Jentzsch, Leuthold, & Ulrich, 2007).

An alternative depiction of the response-selection bottleneck is as a need to access working memory (e.g., to retrieve the response mapping or consolidate information; Koch & Rumiati, 2006) or a problem state (see Chapter 1). According to the problem-state hypothesis (Borst, Taatgen, & Van Rijn, 2010), bottlenecks in processing arise when a problem state (an intermediate representation of the current state of a task that is directly accessible to consciousness) must be accessed during task performance. Although the

Figure 4.3 Hypothetical data showing the effects of manipulating the difficulty of Task 2 response selection (left panel) and perceptual discrimination (right panel).

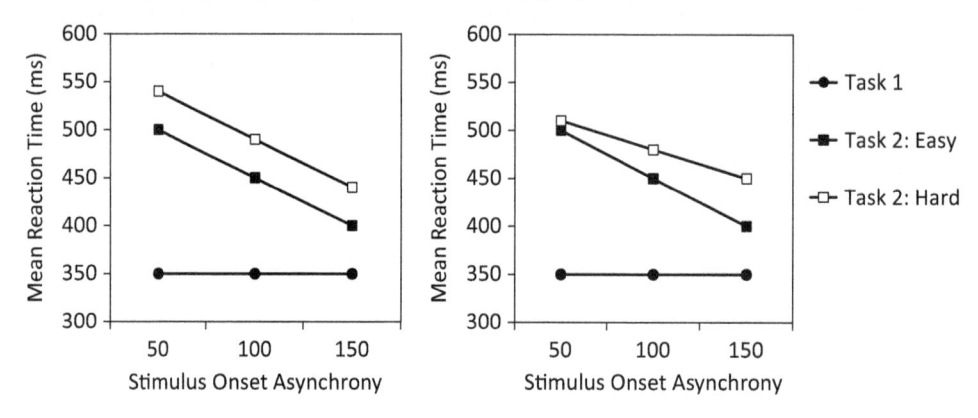

evidence for a true, structural bottleneck in performance is compelling, it has also been argued that the essential aspects of dual-task performance can be captured by a theoretical framework in which multiple tasks are executed concurrently and information processing (including response selection) occurs in parallel (Kieras, Meyer, Ballas, & Lauber, 2000; Meyer & Kieras, 1999). Meyer and Kieras's *executive-process interactive control* (EPIC) framework assumes that there are no structural limits to attentional capacity. Instead, executive control ("how people schedule tasks, allocate perceptual-motor resources, and coordinate task processes"; Kieras et al., 2000, p. 681) is used to give priority to one task, deferring the other. Yet another view of attentional limitations in information processing suggests that the capacity to perform response selection is limited but not all-or-none. According to this capacity-sharing view, the limited-capacity resources required for response selection can be allocated to Task 1 and Task 2 in graded amounts (e.g., Navon & Miller, 2002).

If the PRP effect is due to a structural bottleneck that is "hardwired" in the processing system, it should not be amenable to the effects of practice. Indeed, the PRP effect does seem to persist despite extended practice (e.g., Gottsdanker & Stelmach, 1971; Ruthruff, Van Selst, Johnston, & Remington, 2006; Van Selst, Ruthruff, & Johnston, 1999), although at a somewhat reduced level (Thomson, Danis, & Watter, 2015), suggesting that the bottleneck in response selection cannot be bypassed even when the joint tasks are practiced extensively. In some instances, however, nearly perfect time-sharing can be achieved. For example, Schumacher et al. (2001) combined a visual–manual task, in which the position of a circle was responded to with a spatially corresponding response and a tone of low, intermediate, or high pitch was responded to with the vocal response "one," "two," or "three," respectively.

Importantly, the two tasks were given equal priority (i.e., responses could be made in either order) so any interference effects could not be attributed to strategic effects resulting from the instruction to perform one task before the other. A typical PRP effect was found early in the practice period, but the effect was virtually eliminated by practice.

Specificity of Interference and Multiple Resources

According to resource models in which attention is characterized as a single, general purpose resource, if one task is performed concurrently with either of two other tasks that are of equal difficulty, the total attentional demands should be equivalent for the two dual-task situations and, hence, performance of the task should be the same in the two situations. However, numerous studies have shown that the ability to time-share two tasks depends not only on the difficulty of the tasks but also on their composition. For example, it is easier to monitor a screen for visual targets while listening to an auditorily presented message than it is to perform the monitoring task while reading, even when both the words to be read and the visual targets are within the field of view. Unitary resource models have been maintained in the face of such findings by allowing not only for interference due to attentional resource limitations but also for *structural interference* that occurs when tasks involve the same perceptual modality or response mechanism. Structural interference is invoked to explain such findings as that performance of two concurrent monitoring tasks tends to be worse when the stimuli for the tasks use the same perceptual modality rather than different modalities (e.g., Treisman & Davies, 1973).

Another way of explaining asymmetries in interference between tasks is to assume that specialized attentional resources are associated with different modalities or processes (Navon & Gopher, 1979; D. A. Norman & Bobrow, 1975). According to *multiple-resource accounts*, the degree of interference that will be observed when two tasks are performed together depends on the extent to which the same or different resources are required by the tasks (Wickens, 1984). Much evidence points to the existence of different processing resources for spatial and verbal processing, and the benefits of multimodal processing have become evident in a variety of domains (see, e.g., Sarter, 2007).

Tsang and Wickens (1988) obtained results consistent with the multiple-resource view when they combined a primary tracking task with secondary tasks that used either visual or verbal stimuli and manual or speech responses. In general, time-sharing performance with the tracking task was more efficient when the secondary task required speech responses rather than manual responses. Moreover, graded resource allocation as task difficulty was increased was observed only when the secondary task required manual responses, and this ability to allocate resources efficiently improved with practice. The fact that graded allocation was found only for manual responses suggests that a common resource is used in both the tracking and manual response tasks, but not when tracking is combined with the verbal response task. When two tasks tap the same resources, as for tracking and manual response tasks, strategic control of task performance plays a greater role than when the tasks tap different resources.

A relatively new theory of multiple-task performance, the *threaded cognition theory* (Salvucci & Taatgen, 2008), combines resource and bottleneck views of attention. According to this framework, which is embedded in the ACT-R cognitive architecture (J. R. Anderson et al., 2004; see Chapter 1), multiple-task interference occurs when demands are made on the same resources. The model includes perceptual, motor, and cognitive resources, with the latter being divided into declarative and procedural memory resources. The procedural resource takes the form of ACT-R production rules in which both the conditions and actions utilize buffers for information transfer. Interference occurs when a module being tested by a production is "busy" or when its buffer is full. When two or more new tasks must be combined for the first time, interference arises not because an executive process can attend to only one task at a time but because both tasks make nearly continuous demands on declarative memory. Cognition is "threaded" in the sense that a set of goals, each associated with its own thread of goal-related processing across available resources, can be actively maintained. The assumption that multiple goals can be actively maintained (which is not a general characteristic of ACT-R) enables task demands to be flexibly combined or separated simply by demanding resources when needed and releasing them when finished. When two or more rules are waiting for one resource, the thread that has been inactive for the longest is given access to the resource. Bottlenecks in performance can thus arise both because individual resources are limited and because their use is serial. The limitation that only one production rule can fire at a time further acts as a central bottleneck in performance.

Attention and Automaticity

Most models of skill acquisition emphasize the role that attention plays in learning new skills or even suggest that the limits of attention determine the rate at which a new task can be performed. At the same time, many models contain the assumption that attentional resources are freed up as skill develops and that some aspects of skill may become automatized, needing no resources at all. A characteristic of skilled performance, according to these models, is that attentional limitations are to some extent overcome as components of the task become automatized. Thus, although attention clearly plays a role in acquiring skill, many researchers have suggested that attention may not be necessary at all once a skill has been learned.

The traditional view of attentive processing (or "controlled" processing; R. C. Atkinson & Shiffrin, 1968) is that it is relatively slow, requires effort, and involves consciousness of one's actions. Skill development is described as a gradual (or abrupt) freeing of resources and shift to a capacity-free, stimulus-driven mode of performance that is not dependent on conscious control. Posner and Snyder (1975) described automatic processes as those that may occur "without intention, without any conscious awareness and without interference with other mental activity" (p. 81).

A fundamental question with regards to automatic and attentive processing is whether they are qualitatively distinct modes of processing. In a landmark series of studies, W. Schneider and Shiffrin (1977; Shiffrin & Schneider, 1977) found support for the idea that there are two different modes of processing and that controlled processing gives way to automatic processing if only enough practice of the appropriate sort is given. They used tasks in which observers were to search a series of briefly presented displays for one or more targets held in memory. In the *consistent-mapping* conditions, items that were targets on one trial (e.g., letters) could never serve as distractors on other trials. In the *varied-mapping* conditions, on the other hand, targets and distractors were drawn from the same set, such that items defined as targets on some trials could be designated as distractors on other trials. Both groups became faster and more accurate as they practiced the task, but after extensive practice the performance of the consistent-mapping group no longer depended on the number of elements in the search task, whereas that of the varied-mapping group did. Note that the independence of set size and search time suggests that processing was of "unlimited capacity"—one of the hallmarks of automaticity.

If automatic processing develops for consistently mapped tasks, performance should not suffer when an additional task must also be performed (so long as there is no structural interference). That is, if one of two tasks is automatic, such that it does not require any attentional resources, it should be possible to perform the two tasks simultaneously with little or no cost, even if they initially required a common resource. This has been shown to be the case in a variety of contexts, such as when skilled pianists play sight-read music (a task that should be highly automatized for them) without trouble when required to perform the unfamiliar task of shadowing auditorily presented words at the same time (Allport, Antonis, & Reynolds, 1972). On the basis of findings such as this one and additional studies showing surprisingly good time-sharing performance after extensive training, Spelke, Hirst, and Neisser (1976) concluded,

> Although individual strategies may have their own limitations, there are no obvious, general limits to attentional skills. Studies of attention which use unpracticed subjects, and infer mechanisms and limitations from their performance, will inevitably underestimate human capacities. Indeed, people's ability to develop skills in specialized situations is so great that it may never be possible to define general limits on cognitive capacity. (p. 229)

The view that controlled and automatic processing are qualitatively distinct has, to some extent, fallen out of favor. Within the realm of visual search, where Shiffrin and Schneider (1977) carried out their influential work supporting the dichotomy, researchers now tend speak about the efficiency of search, rather than pre-attentive and attentive search, and the role of attention in processing remains present across search types (e.g., Palmer, Fencsik, Flusberg, Horowitz, & Wolfe, 2011). Likewise, although the Stroop effect, in which a conflicting color word interferes with identification of the physical color in which the word or another stimulus is displayed, has been attributed to automaticity of word reading, evidence indicates that visual attention must be directed to the word for the "automatic" processing of its meaning to occur (e.g., Cho, Choi, & Proctor, 2012).

Rather than considering automaticity a form of processing, Neumann (1987) argues automaticity arises when all the information for performing a task is present in the input information (stimulus information available in the environment) or in long-term memory. Similarly, and in contrast to accounts of skill that posit a declarative phase followed by an autonomous phase in which attentional and memory demands are greatly reduced (see Chapter 1), Logan's (1988, 1990) *instance theory of automaticity suggests that the memory demands of performance do not qualitatively change as a function of skill*—at least not once the basic instructions have been mastered. Within the instance theory, the development of automaticity is described as a shift from a dependence on general algorithms for producing solutions to problems that do not rely on previous experience to a reliance on the retrieval of performance episodes. These episodes are the instances of instance theory, and they contain information that was attended to at the time of stimulus presentation as well as information about the response that was made. Memory plays a critical role in this model in which skilled, automatic performance entails a shift from algorithm-based performance to memory-based performance.

The instance theory of automaticity rests on several assumptions, the most important of which is that each time an object or event is encountered, it is encoded, stored, and retrieved. This is assumed to occur separately on every encounter, or *instance*. Performance speedup as a function of practice is predicted on the basis of the statistical properties of the distribution of retrieval times for instances: As the number of instances increases, the minimum time to retrieve an instance decreases. In this sense, automaticity can be seen as an example of implicit memory (enhanced performance on a memory task due to previous experience but without conscious recall) where the benefits of a single exposure are compounded over many exposures (Logan, 2005). As a result of experience, and of paying attention to the right things at the right time, a collection of instances builds up and gradually comes to dominate performance over the early dependence on algorithms. Consistent with the power law of practice (see Chapter 1), instance theory predicts that changes in performance will follow a power function. Moreover, because memory retrieval is fast, automatized tasks will show little interference with other tasks (Logan, 2005).

According to the proposition that "attention drives both the acquisition of automaticity and the expression of automaticity in skilled performance" (Logan & Compton, 1998, p. 114), selected information enters into the instances that come to drive performance, but ignored information does not. Moreover, if attention is not paid to the right cues, associations dependent on those cues will not be retrieved (Logan & Etherton, 1994). The dependence of memory on attention means that knowing (or learning) what to attend to is a critical component in the development of skill. On the other hand, learning *not* to attend to irrelevant information also is of importance for skill acquisition. One hypothesis about how learning to ignore irrelevant information contributes to performance changes with practice is the *information reduction hypothesis* (Haider & Frensch, 1996). According to this hypothesis, performance improvements can be attributed to learning to distinguish task-relevant information from task-redundant (and, therefore, task-irrelevant) information and then learning to ignore the task-irrelevant information. Knowing what to attend to will increase the chance that the right events are experienced such that useful instances are created, and the allocation of attention at encoding and retrieval will determine to a large extent both the nature of what is learned and the influence of previous experiences on performance in the present.

Another way in which learning not to attend to specific kinds of information may contribute to skilled performance is in motor learning. When we become skilled in sports and other predominantly motor skills, many aspects of movement become automatized (see Chapter 3). It has been suggested that paying attention to how actions are carried out can interfere with the automatic execution of action plans and lead to the breakdown of skilled performance (e.g., Masters, 1992). The effects of focusing on one's movements versus on the goal one is trying to accomplish are captured in the *constrained action hypothesis* (Wulf, 2007; Wulf, Shea, & Park, 2001). According to this hypothesis, when individuals focus their attention internally, on the movements they are making, they will tend to exercise conscious control over the coordination of movements that might otherwise be executed automatically. In contrast, if they adopt an external focus, focusing on the goal of the movement or the outcome they wish to achieve, conscious interference in the control of movement will be reduced. A study by Kal, van der Kamp, and Houdijk (2013), in which participants performed a leg flexion and extension task with an external or internal focus, provided evidence consistent with the constrained action hypothesis. Movement duration was shorter, and the movements were executed more fluently, with an external focus of attention than with an internal focus. Furthermore, only the internal focus condition showed interference with performance of a concurrent cognitive task, implying that little conscious attention was required for the external focus condition.

Attentional Skill

As discussed in the previous section, the role of attention may change as skill is acquired. In fact, many complex tasks can be performed only because some task components have become automatized, thus freeing up resources for other components. In many tasks, thus, it is essential to know not only what to attend to but also how to attend. That is, a principal aspect of skilled performance is skilled attending. Skilled attending is evident in visual search. As people gain experience with a visual search task, scanning patterns (the movements of the eyes to objects in the display) may tend to repeat and adapt to the task environment, thus increasing search efficiency (Myers & Gray, 2010). Complex, dynamic tasks often require performers to divide attention and processing resources among competing, dynamically changing stimuli or task demands for which priorities must be established and trade-offs made. Whether we are aware of attentional investments and can improve our ability to control and allocate attentional resources are important questions for understanding the acquisition of skill.

Attentional limitations are perhaps nowhere more evident than in situations in which attention must be divided across multiple tasks. In fact, a common way to measure the attentional demands (or mental workload) of one task (designated the primary task) is to pair it with a second task (designated the secondary task) and examine concurrent performance of the two tasks (Kerr, 1973). Most often, the performer is instructed to emphasize the primary task, letting secondary task performance suffer if there is any conflict. Relative performance of the secondary task under various conditions is taken to reflect the processing resources required by the primary task under those conditions.

When two or more tasks are performed together, instructions can emphasize giving equal weighting to both tasks, or the relative weightings assigned to the respective tasks can be varied systematically (as would be the case when constructing a POC, as described in an earlier section). Many real-world tasks require one to bias the relative emphasis given to one task over another, such as when attention is diverted from driving a car to answering a mobile telephone. Sudden changes in driving conditions can affect the quality of the conversation while driving and, more critically, talking on the phone has been shown to affect driving behavior (Strayer, Watson, & Drews, 2011). Trading off attention between two tasks, or *time-sharing*, is a skill that can be learned (Damos & Wickens, 1980) and that is predictive of performance in complex tasks (e.g., Kahneman, Ben-Ishai, & Lotan, 1973).

Time-Sharing Skill

Perfect time-sharing (the ability to perform two tasks concurrently as efficiently as performing the more difficult task in isolation) represents the apex of time-sharing skill. Many of us would like to think that time-sharing is perfect when we are required to perform one task (e.g., answering the question of a friend or colleague) while performing a task that has our priority (e.g., playing a computer game or texting an acquaintance) so that we can go on performing our initial task while dealing with the interruption. In fact, time-sharing is limited by the structure of the individual tasks and the way in which they are practiced. Response execution and perceptual demands limit the efficiency of time-sharing, and, as discussed in an earlier section of this chapter, bottlenecks in performance may limit performance even after much practice. The conditions of practice must also be optimized to achieve maximum time-sharing. Strategies to improve time-sharing include learning to grade the allocation of resources across tasks and optimizing the switching of attention between tasks or information sources. The development of efficient time-sharing has also been shown to depend on the provision of augmented feedback, in which details of the nature of the performance are given regarding the effects of time-sharing on each of the shared tasks (e.g., Gopher et al., 1982). Time-sharing will seldom be optimal simply because the component tasks have been practiced; learning to coordinate two tasks is necessary for time-sharing skill to develop (Oberauer & Kliegl, 2004).

The view that attention control is a skill suggests that the ability to allocate attention, or time-sharing ability, may differ across individuals. As might be expected given that most complex, real-world tasks require selective attending to different information sources, time-sharing ability has been shown to be a good predictor of success in many tasks. One time-sharing test of selective attention requires listening to lists of words and digits presented dichotically and writing down any digits detected in the relevant ear (Gopher, 1982). Lists are divided into two parts: before and after a switch of the relevant ear. A brief high- or low-pitched tone designates whether the right or left ear is relevant for the first part of each list, and another brief tone designates the right or left ear as relevant for the remainder of the list. The number of errors (reports of a digit from the wrong ear) in the second part of the list has been found to be diagnostic of future complex task performance, correlating negatively with successful completion of flight school and positively with the accident rate of bus drivers. Because errors of selective attention in the second half of the list were most diagnostic, it seems that the ability to switch attention from one source to the other when required is a critical component of attentional skill.

Enhancing Attention through Training

A growing body of work (reviewed in Bavelier, Green, Pouget, & Schrater, 2012) suggests that the attentional skills used in playing complex action video games might be generalizable to a wide range of basic attentional or perceptual tasks (see also Chapter 8). For example, Bavelier and her colleagues have shown that playing "first-person shooter" action video games may improve performance in basic attentional tasks, such as the flanker task, the attentional blink task (detecting two targets presented in rapid serial visual presentation), and an enumeration task (Green & Bavelier, 2003). Their general conclusion is that people who habitually play action video games spread attention more widely in time and space than non-gamers, and that video games may even teach people to quickly master new tasks (Bavelier et al., 2012). Others (e.g., Durlach, Kring, & Bowens, 2009; Rosser et al., 2007) have argued that video games can help develop skills that are integral to expertise in high-performance environments. However, some attempts to replicate findings of attentional enhancement have failed (e.g., Murphy & Spencer, 2009; see Boot, Blakely, & Simons, 2011, for a critical meta-analysis of improved cognition after video-gaming), and whether video-game training transfers broadly to enhance basic cognitive abilities is still debated.

Meta-analyses of 72 quasi-experimental (correlational) and 46 experimental studies conducted by Powers, Brooks, Aldrich, Palladino, and Alfieri (2013) do suggest that the effects of video-game training on information-processing ability are robust. Motor skills tended to show the greatest benefits in the experimental studies, whereas auditory and visual processing showed the greatest benefits in the quasi-experimental studies. Notably, effect sizes were small or nonexistent for executive function—a finding that is consistent with recent reviews documenting the ineffectiveness of training programs designed to enhance working memory (Melby-Lervåg & Hulme, 2013; Shipstead, Redick, & Engle, 2012). Several factors moderated the results in Powers et al.'s analyses, but one moderator that had no effect was time spent on training: In true experiments, effect sizes were similar whether participants spent more or less than 10 hours playing the video game before transferring to the criterion tasks, suggesting that learners quickly adapt to the demands of games and may not need extensive practice to benefit from them. As Powers et al. point out, the jury is still out regarding the benefits of video-game training. In some cases, at least, there is evidence for positive transfer to attentional tasks, but in other cases the benefits found in correlational studies (in which habitual players are compared to non-players) seem to be exaggerated due to self-selection or other issues (e.g., a "Hawthorne" effect in which players know they have been selected for an experiment because of their playing and thus try harder on experimental tasks).

Another way in which attention might be trained is with neurofeedback. Neurofeedback, a form of biofeedback in which one's brain activity is made visible to the participant by measuring the electroencephalogram and relating the relevant measure (e.g., alpha rhythm) to a visual display object (e.g., a ball that bounces higher as alpha synchronizes), has been used to treat children with attention-deficit/hyperactivity disorder (ADHD) since the 1970s (e.g., Lubar & Shouse, 1976). The goal of neurofeedback is typically to help the individual to learn to modify brain rhythms in order to improve attentional processing. Children with ADHD show spectral abnormalities in the EEG, such as increased frontal theta amplitude and decreased alpha and beta oscillations, in comparison to non-ADHD children (Clarke, Barry, McCarthy, & Selikowitz, 1998). Lubar, Swartwood, Swartwood, and O'Donnell (1995) showed that training children to increase the amplitude of the upper alpha rhythm (12–15 Hz; also referred to as the sensorimotor rhythm) and the lower beta rhythm (15–18 Hz) can enhance sustained attention and alleviate the symptoms of ADHD. In fact, neurofeedback training of the sensorimotor and lower beta rhythm has been shown to be as effective as methylphenidate (a psycho-stimulant commonly used to treat ADHD; Fuchs, Birbaumer, Lutzenberg, Gruzelier, & Kaiser, 2003).

Neurofeedback training has also been shown to improve attention (e.g., Egner & Gruzelier, 2004), memory (Vernon et al., 2003), and other cognitive processes in non-clinical populations. For example, Hanslmayr, Sauseng, Doppelmayr, Schabus, and Klimesch (2005) found that participants who were successful in learning to increase their alpha response during neurofeedback training improved performance on a mental rotation task.

Intelligence and Cognitive Control

In an earlier section of this chapter we discussed how time-sharing ability is related to performance in complex tasks. In fact, many studies have shown that the ability to divide attention between two tasks is related to general intelligence. It has even been argued that some dual tasks could be used as replacements for intelligence quotient (IQ) tests (Stankov, 1983). For example, Ben-Shakhar and Sheffer (2001) found that dual-task performance was more predictive of a general measure of cognitive performance (the Israeli college entrance exam) than was single-task performance. However, the superiority of dual-task performance measures was found only early in practice, suggesting that, at least for the tasks used in this study, the ability to allocate attention across the two tasks was quickly automated. Thus, it appears to be the ability to flexibly allocate attention in novel situations that is indicative of intelligence.

The ability to hold sets of instructions active in working in memory—a key function of cognitive control—has also been related to intelligence. In fact, tests that require keeping different instructions in mind, such as crossing out all occurrences of the letter "t" and circling all occurrences of the letter "e," are included in some intelligence test batteries. In such a task, alternate sets of instructions must be applied when task conditions demand it. People of relatively low intelligence have more difficulty initiating shifts of attention from one stimulus or stimulus dimension to another when the shifting rules have to be maintained in memory (Duncan, Emslie, Williams, Johnson, & Freer, 1996), suggesting that the particular aspect of attention that best describes general intelligence is attentional control exercised by the frontal lobes. Duncan et al. measured general intelligence (g) using standard tests of fluid intelligence, and then examined the relation between g and a phenomenon called goal neglect. Goal neglect is commonly seen in patients who have suffered injury to the frontal lobes. It can perhaps best be described as the failure to carry out a task requirement even though the instruction to do so has been understood. For example, Luria (1980) described a frontal-lobe patient who, instead of following the instruction to squeeze her hand when a light went on, failed to act but said, "I must squeeze!"

Duncan et al. studied goal neglect using a visual analogue of the dichotic listening task described earlier (Gopher, 1982; Gopher & Kahneman, 1971). Letter or digit pairs were presented one at a time in a display, and the task was to read the letters from only one side of the display. A trial began with the instruction to read either the left or right letters; after 10 pairs of stimuli a symbol was presented that indicated which side was relevant for the last three pairs. Goal neglect—failing to switch sides when that was required—was found to be inversely related to g in this task in both older and younger adults, although the relation was stronger for people of relatively low intelligence.

Intelligence has also been related to controlled processing, in general. Recall that controlled processing (R. C. Atkinson & Shiffrin, 1968) is defined as being relatively slow, requiring effort, and involving consciousness of one's actions, whereas automatic processing is often described as a capacity-free, stimulus-driven mode of performance that is not dependent on conscious control. One study that suggests that the ability to exercise controlled attention is related to intelligence was carried out by Tuholski, Engle, and Baylis (2001), who tested people of relatively low or high intelligence in a counting task. They used counting as the task because small numbers of objects can be recognized automatically in a process called subitizing. Most people can accurately subitize three to four items, and Tuholski et al. (2001) found that low- and high-intelligence individuals were equally able to subitize items when there were no distractors present in a display. In contrast, counting more than four items (which presumably depends on controlled processing to keep track of which items have already been counted) was performed better by high- than by low-intelligence individuals. When distractors that differed from the targets on the basis of a conjunction of features (e.g., counting red circles in a display with red square and green circle distractors), even small numbers of items had to be counted, rather than automatically subitized, as indicated by the fact that reaction times increased as a function of the number of items to be counted. In this case (when conjunction distractors required that targets be processed in a controlled manner) high-intelligence individuals outperformed those of lower intelligence even in the subitizing range of one to three items. The simplicity of the counting task lends strength to the argument that fundamental processes are at the core of differences in intelligence. The relation of controlled, but not automatic, processing to intelligence is also consistent with the finding that performance early in practice in attention-demanding tasks is more highly correlated with intelligence than is performance later in practice.

Mind Wandering and Executive Attention

As will be discussed in more detail in Chapter 8, individual differences in the ability to control attention are related to working-memory capacity and to other abilities, such as reading comprehension. One important factor in attentional control is staying on task by reducing the occurrence of task-unrelated thought (TUT) or mind wandering while engaged in activities such as reading texts. Mind wandering is defined as a shift of attention away from the stimuli or mental representations associated with the task at hand to the consideration of TUTs (e.g., Smallwood, Obonsawin, & Heim, 2003). Mind wandering is common. Most of us will remember the last time we daydreamed during a lecture or found ourselves making plans for the evening instead of concentrating on the road on the trip home. In fact, researchers estimate that people spend as much as 30%–50% of their time mind wandering (e.g., Kane et al., 2007; Killingsworth & Gilbert, 2010; McVay & Kane, 2009).

Not surprisingly, TUTs have been associated with disruptions to primary task performance. According to one view (McVay & Kane, 2009), unintended mind wandering can be seen as a lapse in attentional control. According to this Control Failures x Concerns view, TUTs reflect failures to properly maintain task goals, and the current concerns of the individual (e.g., what to cook for dinner) or environmental cues (e.g., a rumbling stomach) are assumed to automatically generate TUTs when an individual fails to maintain the current task goal (e.g., reading the text). Another view is that both task-related and task-unrelated thoughts compete for limited executive resources (Smallwood & Schooler, 2006). According to this executive-resource hypothesis, mind wandering should occur more frequently when the task is easy rather than hard because when the primary task is difficult and resource demanding, few resources are available for mind wandering to occur. Indeed, such a relationship between task difficulty and mind wandering is usually found (but see Feng, D'Mello, & Graesser, 2013).

The frequency with which TUTs occur is generally measured using thought probes in which the ongoing task is briefly interrupted and the person is asked to classify the content of his or her immediately preceding thoughts as being either on- or off-task. Significant negative correlations are generally found between task performance and individual differences in TUT rates (e.g., McVay & Kane, 2009; Smallwood et al., 2003). Moreover, moment-to-moment variations in task performance are related to mind wandering such that the likelihood of error is greater after an episode of TUT than after task-related thought (e.g., McVay & Kane, 2009; J. W. Schooler, Reichle, & Halpern, 2004).

There is still some debate about the underlying mechanisms of mind wandering, although it does seem clear that central executive resources are involved (Baird, Smallwood, & Schooler, 2011). Another factor involved in the occurrence of mind wandering is metacognition. Internal "self-talk" is negatively related to mind wandering (Bastian, Schooler, & Sackur, 2012). In fact, engaging in an activity that occupies the phonological loop (and, presumably, the ability to talk to oneself), reading out loud, results in significantly more mind wandering than does silent reading (Franklin, Mooneyham, Baird, & Schooler, 2014). Finally, it should be noted that even though mind wandering is typically detrimental to the task at hand, it may also provide benefits associated with freeing the mind from the immediate environment, such as focusing on plans for the future and allowing deliberation for complicated decisions (Smallwood & Andrews-Hanna, 2013).

Implicit Learning

When we need to learn how to perform a complex task, such as installing a new piece of hardware on the computer, we read the instructions or, better yet, find someone who can show us how to perform the task. We have a specific objective in mind and do our best to pay attention to the relevant pieces of information. In the process of meeting these task objectives, complex relationships that are incidental to the objectives may be learned as well. Performance will typically benefit from this incidental learning as long as the learned relations hold, but may be disrupted when they are altered. For example, most people learn through repetition to dial their home telephone number, or that of a close friend, rapidly and effortlessly. Yet, requiring that an additional digit (e.g., 9) be entered first to connect to an outside line may disrupt dialing of the phone number. This disruption can be attributed to the change of context instituted by the requirement to dial the extra digit. This change of context appears to interrupt the smooth, seemingly unconscious action of dialing a familiar number, even though the practiced number itself is unchanged.

Learning without intention—and without conscious awareness of what is being learned—is often called *implicit learning*. A hallmark of implicit learning is that learners often are not aware of any performance improvements and cannot state what they have learned. Asking about the role of awareness in learning is tantamount to asking about the role of consciousness in learning. Therefore, studying implicit learning may tell us something about the nature of consciousness itself, in addition to the role of experience in learning and the nature of mental representations. If learning occurs without awareness—that is, if learners are unconscious of what they are learning—do they learn other things or form mental representations that are different than those acquired during intentional, conscious learning episodes?

In other words, what is implicit learning for and how might implicitly acquired knowledge function?

One of the most popular tasks for studying implicit learning is the serial reaction time task (SRT task) introduced by Nissen and Bullemer (1987). In this task keys are pressed according to the spatial location of targets, and sequences of stimuli are repeated within the blocks of trials (designating the four possible stimulus positions from left to right as A, B, C, and D, the repeating sequence used by Nissen & Bullemer was D-B-C-A-C-B-D-C-B-A). People who practiced this SRT task with the 10-element repeating sequence showed vastly more improvement in the task than those who practiced with a random presentation of stimuli, even though the participants were not informed that there was a repeating sequence or instructed to look for repetitions while performing the task.

Organizing and making sense of the environment are something that comes naturally to most of us, and, indeed, Nissen and Bullemer's (1987) participants did report noticing the sequence, making it impossible to separate intentional and incidental learning effects. In order to address the question of whether awareness was necessary for the performance benefit to occur, Nissen and Bullemer repeated the experiment with Korsakoff patients whose profound amnesia should prevent them from recognizing and recalling the material to which they had been exposed. As predicted, the Korsakoff patients reported no awareness of the repeating sequence but their performance showed a degree of learning of the sequence comparable to that of controls.

Since Nissen and Bullemer's (1987) study more than 1,000 papers have examined the nature of incidental learning. The key questions are (a) whether such learning can, indeed, occur without awareness, (b) whether attention is needed for incidental learning to occur, and (c) what mechanisms underlie incidental learning (see Goschke, 1997, and Schwarb & Schumacher, 2012, for reviews).

There is much disagreement as to whether learning can occur without awareness. Not all studies with amnesiacs have shown unimpaired sequence learning (Curran, Smith, DiFranco, & Daggy, 2001), and high correlations between explicit knowledge and performance (e.g., Perruchet & Amorim, 1992) challenge the view that learning can occur without awareness. In order to answer the question of whether learning can occur without awareness of what is being learned, it is necessary to separate out any explicit knowledge of the task. Whereas in early studies learners were simply asked whether they were aware of a sequence or to generate the sequence, more recent studies have relied on an adaptation of Jacoby's (1991) *process dissociation procedure* to determine whether unconscious knowledge contributes to performance improvements (Destrebecqz & Cleeremans, 2001). The procedure is based on the claim that if knowledge is conscious, it can be brought under intentional control, and if it is unconscious, it cannot. It is thus possible to suppress conscious knowledge, but not unconscious knowledge. According to this logic, asking participants to generate as much of the sequence as possible (in a so-called inclusion condition) amounts to asking them to express their conscious knowledge, and any unconscious knowledge they might have may aid them in the task. On the other hand, instructions to produce a sequence *unlike* the practiced one (as given in the "exclusion" condition) require participants to rely on explicit knowledge to exclude practiced elements; reproduction of sequence elements, or "intrusions" in the exclusion condition, can thus be taken as evidence of implicit knowledge of the sequence.

Using the process dissociation procedure, Destrebecqz and Cleeremans (2001) found evidence for implicit knowledge (above chance reproduction of sequence elements in the exclusion condition) when a sequence had been practiced with a 0-ms response-stimulus interval (which, they reasoned, would allow subjects no time to anticipate the upcoming stimulus and acquire explicit knowledge) but not when the response-stimulus interval was 250 ms. In another application of the process dissociation procedure, Goschke (1997) tested the hypothesis that implicit knowledge develops before explicit knowledge. He found evidence of implicit knowledge in the exclusion condition soon after performance differences emerged in sequenced versus random versions of an SRT task, but not later in task performance. Thus, whether one finds evidence of implicit knowledge will depend on the extent to which explicit knowledge has developed (see also Fu, Fu, & Dienes, 2008). Although such evidence for truly implicit knowledge is intriguing, it should be noted that both the assumptions of the process dissociation procedure and the findings of Destrebecqz and Cleeremans have been challenged (e.g., Wilkinson & Shanks, 2004), leaving the question of whether learning without awareness is possible a matter of debate.

Another issue that has been studied with the SRT task is the role of attention in learning the relations between elements in the task. If attention is needed for sequence learning, requiring that learners perform an attention-demanding secondary task while practicing the SRT task should impair learning. A. Cohen, Ivry, and Keele (1990) first showed attention-related learning impairments using sequences containing either unique associations, in which each stimulus uniquely specified the following (e.g., A always followed by C), ambiguous associations, such that A might be followed by C in one case and by D in another, or both. A. Cohen et al. found that ambiguous sequences were not learned under dual-task conditions but that unique associations were. They suggested that associations between adjacent items are learned automatically, via a process that does not require attention, and that a second process, which requires attention to operate, is needed to build hierarchical codes for associations that involve more than two items.

Both the empirical finding of the necessity of attention for the learning of ambiguous sequence elements and the two-process model of A. Cohen et al. have been challenged. For example, Frensch, Buchner, and Lin (1994) found that both simple and ambiguous sequences were learned under both single- and dual-task conditions. However, the amount of learning that took place was reduced when a distractor task was present, suggesting that sequence learning is modulated by attention. Cleeremans and McClelland (1991) presented a parallel distributed processing model that accounts for incidental learning of ambiguous sequences without recourse to hierarchical mechanisms. The model relies on the encoding of the temporal context of the most recent three elements of the sequence for the encoding of associations. Anticipation of the next element of the sequence provides the information that drives encoding of the temporal structure, and the mechanisms underlying sensitivity to temporal context operate in conjunction with short-term and short-lived priming effects.

An intriguing hypothesis, similar to the idea that prediction or anticipation is the basis for learning, is that it is the response-effect relationship (see Chapter 3) that is first implicitly learned and that this might provide the basis for the development of explicit knowledge. To test this hypothesis, Ziessler (1998) modified Nissen and Bullemer's (1987) SRT paradigm so that the location of the stimulus on a particular trial was determined by the response made on the previous trial. Rather than responding to the location of the stimulus, as in Nissen and Bullemer's task, participants in Ziessler's experiments responded to the identity of a target in the presence of distractors. The location of the target was thus not relevant for the response, but knowledge of the location could be used to speed up search and, accordingly, reaction times. Ziessler manipulated the predictability of the position of the following stimulus by varying whether all stimuli assigned to a certain key predicted the same position, and showed that performance improved more when the response made reliably predicted the position of the next stimulus than when it only sometimes did. Moreover, only when the response-stimulus associations were perfectly reliable was negative transfer to a condition in which target position was random found. Consistent with the hypothesis that the relation between responses and target positions was implicitly learned, none of the participants in Ziessler's study reported noticing anything predictable about the position of the targets.

Various accounts of the nature of learning without intention (see Abrahamse, Jiménez, Verwey, & Clegg, 2010, for a review) have proposed that learning is based on the relations between stimuli (e.g., Clegg, 2005; Stadler, 1989), the relations between stimulus-response associations (e.g., Schwarb & Schumacher, 2010), and the sequence of motor responses (e.g., Bischoff-Grethe, Goedert, Willingham, & Grafton, 2004; but see J. D. Cohen et al., 1990). When responses are made to the location of the stimulus it is impossible to say whether performance improvements depend on the learning of perceptual relations (the relation of one stimulus to the next), stimulus-response associations, or response relations (the relation of one response to the next). Willingham, Nissen, & Bullemer (1989) used a task in which the locations of the stimuli followed a predictable sequence, but in which responses were made to the color of the stimuli, rather than their locations to attempt to tease apart the possible loci of learning in the SRT task. By assessing performance during practice and in a transfer task in which locations were responded to, they concluded that sequences based on stimulus locations were not learned when responses were based on the color of the stimuli. When the task contained a predictable sequence of stimulus-response pairs, however, considerable learning occurred. Because the group who learned the sequence of stimulus color-response pairs showed no transfer to a task in which the responses followed the same sequence, but were made to location rather than color, Willingham et al. concluded that the locus of learning was in the stimulus-response associations. Schwarb and Schumacher (2010) found that keeping only the stimuli or the responses (and not the association between them) constant in practice and transfer conditions disrupted sequence learning, which they interpreted as evidence that stimulus-response associations are learned in the SRT task. In a 2012 paper, Schwarb and Schumacher concluded that the stimulus-response association account provides a unifying framework for interpreting serial learning results.

Although the SRT task may not seem very interesting in and of itself, the proper sequencing of ordered stimuli and responses is an important part of many skills. For example, a skilled pianist must play the notes in a piece of music in the correct order, with proper timing and stress. Tasks such as comprehending speech and typing text also are serial in nature, and good performance depends on knowledge about the constraints on serial order inherent in particular tasks that restrict the set of possible events at any point in the sequence (Gentner, Larochelle, & Grudin, 1988; G. A. Miller & Isard, 1963). Sensitivity to sequential constraints may be a fundamental characteristic of human cognition.

Summary

Attention plays an integral role in selecting and becoming aware of information, in learning new information, and in integrating new information with existing knowledge. Although some skills may be learned implicitly, without conscious intention, gaining skill in most tasks involves learning to select relevant information and learning to cope with the demands of multiple aspects of task performance. Most tasks are affected by attentional limitations. Depending on the task, these limitations may manifest early or late in processing, and whether attentional limitations are fundamentally early or late is still debated.

Whether a particular task or task component can be performed well depends on the nature of the tasks to be performed, the level of skill attained in each component task, and the relative amount of attention allocated to the respective tasks. In complex tasks, dividing attention between different components of a task while learning it can be an efficient way of learning the task and can lead to the development of flexible performance strategies. Extensive, consistent practice can lead to the automatization of performance, enabling more efficient performance and resistance to dual-task interference.

Basic attentional abilities predict performance of more complex tasks, and attentional skill can be developed. However, there is much debate about the extent to which different kinds of practice will lead to transfer of attentional skill. Some studies show that practicing certain complex tasks will improve attentional skill and that this skill will transfer to a wide range of tasks, but others suggest that transfer will be limited to similar tasks. It may be possible to improve attentional abilities directly, by means of neurofeedback. In the new field of neuroergonomics (for a review see A. Johnson & Proctor, 2013), neuroscience techniques are being applied to select people with superior attentional skill and train and support attention. New developments in the study of attention are paving the way for a better understanding of skill.

5

Cognitive Skill and Instruction

Humans have the remarkable ability to acquire almost any skill given suitable instructions and practice.

N. A. Taatgen, D. Huss, D. Dickison, & J. R. Anderson (2008, p. 548)

The skill with which tasks can be learned and problems solved determines in part how successful we are in a given job or occupation, as well as the ease with which the hazards of everyday life are negotiated. Some problems, such as deciding on the purchase of a car or making a career choice, never seem to get any easier to solve. But many others, such as determining which statistical analysis is appropriate for a given type of data or selecting an appropriate fishing lure to use for the prevailing conditions, clearly benefit from repeated problem-solving episodes. Most problem solving depends on knowledge of facts as well as knowledge of techniques. The development of problem-solving skill will thus depend on how efficiently knowledge is conveyed and how factual knowledge is integrated with techniques to operate on that knowledge (Healy & Bourne, 2012).

Cognitive skill acquisition follows many of the principles that hold for other types of skills. Like other skills, cognitive skill proceeds through three phases (J. R. Anderson, 1982; Fitts, 1964; see Chapter 1). During the first, declarative or cognitive phase, learners seek to acquire domain knowledge by reading, discussion, and other activities, without yet trying to apply the knowledge. The intermediate, associative phase begins when learners start to try to solve problems, either on their own or with the help of worked examples. Because domain knowledge is seldom perfectly and completely understood at this phase, the learner will have to, in the course of problem solving, correct missing and incorrect domain knowledge. Experience in problem solving also leads to the acquisition of heuristic knowledge, or guidelines for solving particular problems. Once the knowledge base is complete and problems can be solved without conceptual errors, learners enter the autonomous phase, during which they continue to improve in speed and accuracy as a function of practice, even though their understanding of the domain and their basic approach to solving problems remain unchanged.

Problem-Solving Skill

Early problem-solving research focused primarily on relatively simple, puzzle-like tasks, or so-called *knowledge-lean* problems, that are well-defined and can be solved on the basis of task instructions and general reasoning skills. For example, in the Tower of Hanoi puzzle (see Figure 5.1) the problem is how to move the stack of disks from Peg A to Peg C in as few moves as possible (i.e., 2^N-1 moves, which would be seven moves for the three-disk version), moving only one disk at a time and never placing a larger disk on a smaller one. Tasks of this type have been used to evaluate how people represent problems and search for solutions. Of course, most problems are not solved in relative isolation from prior knowledge, and not all problems have single correct answers. Whenever a task deviates from the routine, general or task-specific problem-solving skills are needed. Often, uncertainty associated with the outcomes of specific actions further complicates the

Figure 5.1 The Tower of Hanoi. The goal is to move the three disks from Peg A to Peg C in as few moves as possible, moving only one disk at a time and never putting a larger disk on top of a smaller disk.

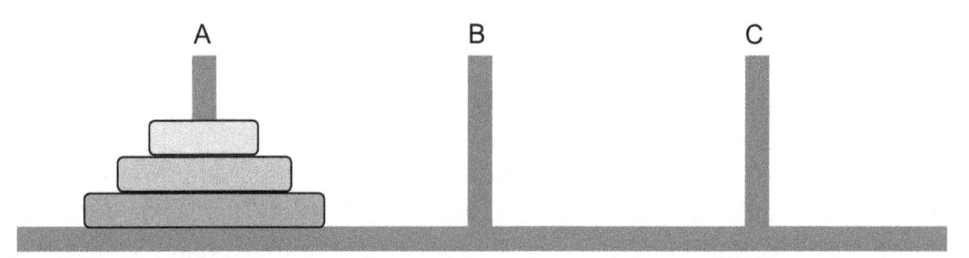

problem-solving task. Such ill-defined, *knowledge rich* problems draw on the problem solver's knowledge about a specific domain.

The Problem Space

When faced with a novel problem, whether it is knowledge-lean or knowledge-rich, we first have to understand it and to determine which options are available for solving the problem. A. Newell and Simon (1972) introduced a view of problem solving based on the concept of the *problem space*. They regarded the human problem solver as an information-processing system (see Chapter 1) in which a central processor receives sensory information, operates on a memory composed of symbol structures, and produces actions, and they sought to understand human problem solving by producing accurate analyses of the tasks to be performed and descriptions of the mechanisms involved in solving problems. The problem space consists of a description of possible *problem states* and *operators* for moving from one problem state to another. For example, in the game of chess the problem states are the various configurations of pieces on the game board and the operators are the legal moves for each piece.

During problem solving a sequence of operators is applied (or a *path* taken) to successive states. Specific problems bring with them *constraints* on the paths that may be taken. In the game of chess, constraints are placed on the ways in which each chess piece can be moved, and higher-order constraints, such as "protect the center," may also be applied. A problem in a problem space thus may be defined in terms of an initial state, a goal state, and any path constraints. To solve the problem, a path must be found that moves from the initial state to the goal state while satisfying the path constraints. Going back to the Tower of Hanoi puzzle illustrated in Figure 5.1, the states are the 27 allowable configurations of the disks on the pegs, the initial state is the configuration with the stack on peg A, and the goal state is the configuration with the stack on peg C. The path constraints are that only one disk can be moved at a time and that a larger disk cannot be placed on top of a smaller one. One operator is the action of moving a disk from one peg to another, and another is the recognition of the configuration of disks as an acceptable state.

The problem-space hypothesis identifies two processes, *understanding* and *search*, as being crucial in problem solving (VanLehn, 1989). "Understanding" consists of generating the problem space from information that is provided about the problem and inferences that are derived from that information. Essentially, the problem space is a mental representation of the problem to be solved. For many problems, task instructions, background knowledge, and previous experience with the same or similar tasks have a significant impact on this representation. Because the knowledge and experience that people bring to a problem-solving task vary, even the same task instructions may not result in all individuals adopting the same problem space. If the problem is misunderstood by an individual, its representation may be incorrect and solution difficulties will be likely to occur. Although a suitable problem space is crucial to problem solving, it does not ensure that a correct solution will be found. The problem space often is complex, with many possible paths to take, most of which will not lead to a solution. "Search" is needed to find an appropriate solution path within the problem space. The likelihood of a successful solution depends on the specific search strategies used.

If human information-processing capacity were unlimited, it would be possible to consider simultaneously the entire set of problem states and the relations between them. But processing capacity is limited such that, according to some theorists, only one problem-space operator can be applied and only a limited number of states considered at a time (e.g., A. Newell, 1980). So, strategies for searching the problem space are an important part of problem solving. Search through the problem space involves applying operators and considering the resulting states. More exactly, search proceeds by (a) selecting a state and then an operator; (b) applying the operator to the present state, thereby producing a new state; and (c) deciding whether to move into the new state and whether the goal state has been achieved. If the goal has not been achieved, this general procedure is repeated. For all but the most trivial problems, successful search will depend on some strategy for evaluating progress toward the goal and selecting the next move within the problem space.

Methods for guiding problem solution were initially described by researchers in artificial intelligence (see Table 5.1). The use of these methods by human problem solvers has been documented in a variety of situations. The methods are independent of any specific problem domain and thus are applicable to many different problem types. However, by themselves they are not very powerful and, hence, are called *weak methods*. One of the most widely discussed strategies is *means-ends analysis*, which proceeds by attempting to select and apply operators that will reduce the difference between the current state and the goal state. Means-ends analysis has an advantage over *hill-climbing*, in which the best possible solution is not known but steps toward a goal are taken if they improve some evaluation function. Because the current state is not compared to the best possible outcome when using a hill-climbing algorithm, it is possible that a problem-solving episode will end when a local maximum (the best alternative at one point in the problem-solving space) is found rather than proceeding until the best possible outcome is reached.

TABLE 5.1 Methods for Guiding Problem Solution

Generate and Test: Generate in any way possible a sequence of candidate steps, while testing each one to determine if it is the desired state.
Heuristic Search: Apply heuristics to guide the selection of operators and states, while remembering which states have been visited and which operators tried.
Hill Climbing: Apply operators to the current state, and select the one that produces a new state that gives an improved evaluation of the objective function.
Means-Ends Analysis: Compare the present state to the desired state and evaluate the difference. Select an operator to apply that leads to a new state that is closer to the goal state.
Operator Subgoaling: If no operator can be applied to the present state, create a subgoal to find a state in which an operator can be applied, and then proceed using heuristic search or means-ends analysis.
Planning: Simplify the present state by selecting a subset of information to process. Solve the simplified problem, and then use what is remembered of the solution path to solve the complete problem.

Many problems can be solved most efficiently by the creation of *subgoals*. Although useful subgoals can sometimes be identified at the outset of problem solving, they may not be readily apparent. Anzai (1987) developed a theory called *learning by doing* that specifies how subgoals are identified and learned through experience at solving problems of a given type. For example, when using a weak method, such as means-ends analysis, the problem solver may find that moving from one state to another greatly reduces the difference between the current state and the goal state. The new state would then be identified as a "good" state, and in future problem solving a subgoal would be set to achieve this state. Experience with a variety of complex problems of a given type leads to the acquisition of a hierarchy of subgoals for solving such problems.

Even though it is convenient to separate search strategies from problem understanding in the analysis of problem solving, search and understanding interact. The search process itself may uncover information that affects understanding of the problem and, hence, modifies the problem space. The interplay between search and understanding is particularly important when the problem to be solved is ill-defined. In the ill-defined problems typically encountered in everyday life, uncertainty often exists regarding one or more components of the problem space. For these problems, steps must be taken to refine and elaborate the problem-state representations and to seek information from memory or other sources to provide appropriate operators and necessary constraints. Furthermore, some problems require that processes of induction be invoked to create and modify knowledge structures. Not only is additional information necessary to develop the initial problem space for ill-defined problems, but also a restructuring of the problem space during the course of solving the problem may be required. More recent formulations of the problem-solving process attempt to capture dynamic interactions with the external environment and the memory stores of the problem solver (e.g., J. R. Anderson et al., 2004; see Chapter 1).

Metacognitive Skill

One characteristic of skilled problem solvers is that they are better able to monitor their own cognitive processing than are less-skilled problem solvers. These metacognitive skills apply to the (a) selection of problem representations and search strategies; (b) planning of the next move in executing a problem-solving strategy; (c) monitoring of progress toward the goal state as the strategy is executed; and (d) evaluation and, if necessary, revision of the strategy (R. J. Sternberg, 1988). Not only do good problem solvers monitor and evaluate the efficiency of their actions more than do poor problem solvers (Gick & Holyoak, 1980), but also they are able to state rules that describe their actions.

The fact that good problem solvers are better able to verbalize rules than are poor problem solvers has led some researchers to ask whether training problem solvers to verbalize condition-action rules will facilitate learning and transfer. Ahlum-Heath and Di Vesta (1986) tested this hypothesis using the Tower of Hanoi puzzle. Their subjects practiced a two-, three-, four-, or five-disk puzzle with or without the requirement to verbalize a condition-action rule (e.g., "if this disk is moved from peg x to peg y, then these conditions, effects, or subgoals will be achieved") prior to each move, before attempting a six-disk version of the puzzle. When tested on the six-disk puzzle, people who had been required to verbalize rules during practice outperformed those who had not been required to do so.

The benefit of verbalization is most likely that it makes the problem solver more aware of the task structure. By emphasizing consequences of actions, the requirement to verbalize encourages consideration and evaluation of the effectiveness of each particular move toward achievement of the goal. This, in turn, encourages the development of the metacognitive skill needed to evaluate the validity of planned transformations of the problem states, thus allowing more efficient selection of actions. Focusing on the effectiveness of actions in attaining the task goal should also facilitate the identification of subgoals that can then be incorporated into the representation of the target problem. Thus, verbalization of performance rules may influence both the representation of the problem and search of the problem space.

Verbalizations in the form of explanations to oneself (i.e., inferences about examples that go beyond the presented information), or *self-explanations*, facilitate the integration of new information into existing knowledge when studying worked-out examples in problem-solving tasks (Chi, Bassok, Lewis, Reimann, & Glaser, 1989) and in learning declarative knowledge from explanatory texts (Chi, de Leeuw, Chiu, & LaVancher, 1994). Some people are more likely to engage in self-explaining than are others, and these people tend to learn more from declarative texts than those who engage in less self-explaining. Training in self-explanation can improve learning dramatically (Bielaczyc, Pirolli, & Brown, 1995), although the benefits of training in self-explanation may be restricted to the initial stages of acquisition of knowledge and not to increased fluency in problem solving (Pirolli & Recker, 1994). Moreover, simply requiring people to explain leads to better learning of concepts, even without providing extensive training in explaining processes (Nokes-Malach, VanLehn, Belenky, Lichtenstein, & Cox, 2013).

Explaining one's actions to another—even when that other is a novice in the domain being explored—can lead to better solutions for complex problems. When working on a design problem, for example ("design a grill with a removable coal pan and a grid tray that can be fixed at an appropriate height above the coals"), people who explained their choices to a naïve bystander (in fact, the experimenter) suggested more alternatives, gave more additional explanations of functions, and made more corrections than people who performed a filler task before reevaluating their design (Wetzstein & Hacker, 2004). Engaging in explanations, evaluations, and justifications of design solutions appears to encourage analytic thinking. Reflective verbalization may also focus attention on aspects of the design that were not previously considered. That is, participants might redefine the problem space, allowing new thinking patterns and problem solutions to emerge. More specifically, participants who engaged in explanation more frequently switched between sketching and conceptual thinking. This more flexible, multimodal way of working may facilitate moving between different levels of abstraction in designing.

Generating explanations appears to facilitate performance in a number of ways. Important points seem to be that self-explaining (a) is constructive, and that newly constructed declarative or procedural knowledge can then be directly applied in transfer tests; (b) encourages the integration of new knowledge with previous knowledge, whereas simply summarizing new information, rather than explaining it, does not require this integration and is unlikely to lead to similar performance benefits; and (c) encourages the construction of accurate mental models of the processes to be explained by making inconsistencies in the model apparent, with the result that the model can be refined (Chi et al., 1989, 1994).

Self-explaining has proven advantages, but has a major disadvantage as an instructional tool. Namely, it depends on the motivation of the learner to engage in self-explanation or on the availability of a tutor to ensure that self-explanation takes place. An interesting question is thus whether providing explanations during problem solving will achieve the same benefits as self-explanation.

Learning from Examples

Many textbooks present worked examples as a way of conveying knowledge or teaching skills. The example-based learning that is assumed to occur from studying worked problems has been extensively investigated within the framework of cognitive load theory (Paas & Ayres, 2014; van Gog, Paas, & Sweller, 2010). One of the most influential theories in the fields of educational psychology and instructional design (Ozcinar, 2009), cognitive load theory (Paas, van Gog, & Sweller, 2010; Sweller, 1988; Sweller, van Merriënboer, & Paas, 1998; van Merriënboer & Sweller, 2005) is based on how learners incorporate new knowledge into schemas. Cognitive load theory was developed for the domain of learning of complex cognitive tasks, and is based on the assumption that learners tend to be overwhelmed by the number of "interactive information elements" that require simultaneous processing before meaningful learning can commence. A basic tenet of cognitive load theory is that instructions can control the excessively high load imposed by complex tasks, thus making it possible for the learner to devote limited cognitive resources to the material to be learned. The relatively "guided" instructional procedures advocated by cognitive load theorists have proven to be more effective—at least for novice students—than the relatively unguided instructional procedures used by advocates of discovery or inquiry learning.

A primary aim of cognitive load theory–based instruction is to ensure that learners' working memory is not overloaded by the information presented. According to cognitive load theory, three types of cognitive load will at any given time impose demands on the learner. *Intrinsic load* is the load associated with the complexity of the material to be learned, expressed in terms of *element interactivity* (the number of elements that need to be processed simultaneously by the learner; Sweller & Chandler, 1994). *Germane load* refers to the working-memory resources required to process the element interactivity that constitutes intrinsic cognitive load, and *extraneous load* is any load caused by suboptimal instructional design. Extraneous load diverts the learner away from schema acquisition and uses up working-memory resources that would otherwise be devoted to learning (Sweller et al., 1998). Intrinsic and extraneous cognitive load are assumed to be additive: Any increase in extraneous cognitive load reduces the working-memory resources that can be devoted to intrinsic cognitive load and hence reduces germane cognitive load. Similarly, reducing extraneous cognitive load frees cognitive resources for processing intrinsic to the task and thus increases germane cognitive load.

When the material to be learned is difficult or complex, intrinsic cognitive load is high, and it is important to decrease extraneous cognitive load to prevent overload. According to cognitive load theorists, the best way to do this is by presenting the material to be learned in an optimal way (see Sweller et al., 1998; van Merriënboer & Sweller, 2005). If intrinsic load exceeds working-memory–processing capacity, it can be necessary to restructure the problem domain to allow the simultaneous processing of all interactive information elements (i.e., to optimize germane cognitive load). Techniques for restructuring material to be learned, such as part-whole training, in which a subset of the information elements and interactions between them is practiced before adding all relevant elements and interactions (e.g., van Merriënboer, Kester, & Paas, 2006), have been adapted from the literature on training (see Chapter 10). Germane load can also be increased by presenting a variety of learning tasks (e.g., Paas & van Merriënboer, 1994) or by asking learners to engage in self-explanation (e.g., Chi et al., 1994). Perhaps the best-known and most-studied instructional method inspired by cognitive load theory is the use of worked examples. Studying worked examples rather than solving conventional problems reduces extraneous load because the problems are presented in such a way that learners can devote all available working-memory capacity to studying the worked-out solution and constructing a schema for solving similar problems (e.g., Paas & van Gog, 2006).

Example-based learning experiences generally consist of instruction in which concepts and principles of a domain are introduced, the study of worked examples that illustrate these concepts and principles, and practice in solving problems. Worked examples normally consist of three components: the formulation of the problem, the solution steps, and the final solution. Example-based learning has been shown to be more effective than learning by solving problems alone, particularly at early phases of cognitive skill acquisition (e.g., R. K. Atkinson, Derry, Renkl, & Wortham, 2000; W. M. Carroll, 1994). The benefits of example-based learning can be explained in terms of reduction of cognitive load (e.g., Sweller, 2005; Sweller et al., 1998). When first confronted with a problem, learners new to the knowledge domain are dependent on weak methods, such as means-ends analysis. These methods are assumed to put high demands on limited-capacity memory resources and seldom lead to the construction of problem-solving schemas that will support transfer (e.g., Renkl, Mandl, & Gruber, 1996; Sweller & Chandler, 1994). Providing worked examples reduces the time spent on irrelevant search and directs the learner's attention to the relevant problem, thus supporting learners in constructing problem-solving schemas.

To benefit from worked examples, learners must actively look for underlying principles. However, learners may have difficulties correctly explaining the principles underlying worked examples because of a lack of understanding (e.g., Berthold, Eysink, & Renkl, 2009; Renkl, 2002) or because they assume that they comprehend the problem when actually their understanding is incomplete. It has been suggested that providing instructional explanations along with examples might help learners to detect inconsistencies in their own understanding, thereby preventing them from falling victim to an "illusion of understanding" that might inhibit further learning (e.g., Chi et al., 1994). A meta-analysis of studies in which the effects of instructional explanations were studied suggests that providing learners with instructional explanations improves immediate performance but the benefits do not transfer to other problem types (Wittwer & Renkl, 2010). Moreover, instructional explanations show no benefit as compared to self-explanations. Asking learners to engage in self-explanatory activities appears to be the most effective means of maximizing transfer.

Learning and Remembering

Human beings have a remarkable ability to learn by doing and to solve novel problems. However, in most domains good performance depends on acquiring knowledge through instruction and study, and on restructuring that knowledge to accommodate new learning.

Acquiring Knowledge

Ask a native English speaker why it is better to say, "She is continuing to get funding for her research" rather than "She is continuing getting funding for her research," and he will likely say he doesn't know why—it just is so. When we learn a language we internalize a large set of rules that govern which utterances are allowable and which are not. Even when the stimuli and the rules for combining them are arbitrary, we are able to learn to distinguish "grammatical" from "ungrammatical" sequences (see Reber, 1989, and Pothos, 2007, for reviews). Such arbitrary rule sets, or *artificial grammars*, have been used to study the acquisition of knowledge. An example of an artificial grammar is shown in Figure 5.2. Grammatical strings are generated by proceeding from left to right along any path from an initial state (start) to the end state (output). At first, it is difficult to find any regularities in a set of grammatical strings produced by this grammar, such as in the set

Figure 5.2 An artificial grammar. The arrows are traversed from "start" to "output" to create grammatical strings made up of the letters at each traversed node. The five basic strings of the grammar, with the loops or recursions in brackets, are: [P[V]], PT[V]], T[V], T[X]S, and T[X][V].

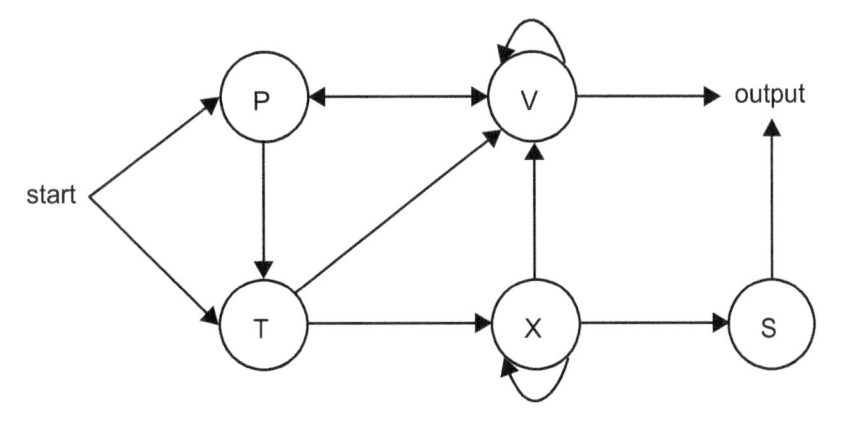

{PVVXXS, TXXVPV, TXS, PTXVV}, but a set of strings that follows a grammar is, indeed, easier to memorize than are random letter strings (Reber, 1967). Not only do people exposed to grammatical strings more easily remember the strings, but also they are able to classify new strings as grammatical or ungrammatical with reasonable accuracy, despite often being unable to state any rules verbally. It has even been shown that grammar learning transfers to new stimulus sets (Mathews et al., 1989; Reber, 1989), indicating that the structure of the grammar is learned independently from the elements to which it is applied.

The acquisition of the ability to classify strings as grammatical or ungrammatical simply by remembering strings of letters illustrates that declarative knowledge about objects and relations among them is often accompanied by procedural knowledge of how to perform acts on that knowledge (Bitan & Karni, 2004). However, instructing learners to look for regularities in the stimuli to be memorized can actually impede learning (Reber, 1976) when the relations to be learned are not salient (Reber, Kassin, Lewis, & Cantor, 1980), unless attention is directed to the relevant aspects of the stimuli in some way (Nokes & Ash, 2009) or immediate feedback is provided after grammaticality judgments are made (Opitz & Hofman, 2015). Participants in Opitz and Hofman's study who received explicit learning instructions coupled with feedback after grammaticality judgments showed more evidence of rule-based knowledge in a final test of grammaticality than did participants who learned the grammar implicitly, but even implicit learners showed evidence of rule learning after extensive practice. This led Opitz and Hofman to conclude that learning occurs by both similarity-based and rule-based mechanisms, and that the latter can occur either through explicit testing of rules or through a more passive abstraction process.

The fact that explicit instructions to look for regularities among the strings to be memorized impair learning unless the regularities are salient suggests that a passive mode of learning is more beneficial for learning. Similar conclusions have been reached about learning to control dynamic systems, such as simulated city transportation systems, in which the amount charged for parking a car and the time interval between buses are manipulated to control city revenue (Broadbent, 1977), or a sugar production factory with the goal of maintaining a specified level of sugar output (Berry & Broadbent, 1984; Dienes & Fahey, 1998). Performance at controlling such systems improves with practice, but declarative knowledge—as measured by post-performance questionnaires—tends not to be correlated with performance improvement (Rostami, Hadi Hosseini, Takahashi, Sugiura, & Kawashima, 2009). On the other hand, providing information about the system tends to improve the ability of people to answer questions about it, while having little if any impact on performance (Berry & Broadbent, 1984; Broadbent, Fitzgerald, & Broadbent, 1986). The dissociation of the effect of instructions regarding system dynamics on system control and questionnaire performance, as well as the statistical independence of the two measures of learning, suggests that there are two alternative modes of learning system control.

Berry and Broadbent (1988) and Hayes and Broadbent (1988) proposed that the two modes of learning to control dynamic systems can be characterized as *unselective* and *selective*. The unselective mode is thought to involve the passive aggregation of information pertinent to contingencies between all environmental variables. It operates outside of awareness and is thus not accessible as verbalizable knowledge. The lack of awareness and nonverbal nature of this learning characterize it as implicit. The selective mode involves actively attending to only a few variables and forming a representation of the relations among the variables that can be explicitly verbalized.

Selective learning is explicit, and can be triggered by instructing learners to search for the rules governing the behavior of the system. As with grammar learning, such instructions facilitate performance when the task is based on salient relationships for which hypotheses can be developed and tested but can have a detrimental effect when the task is based on non-salient relationships. More evidence that searching for non-salient relations can be counterproductive is that less transfer is seen from one control task with a non-salient rule to another when a hint to use what was learned in the first system when performing the task in the second is given than when no hint is given (Berry & Broadbent, 1988). Berry and Broadbent suggested that the negative impact of the hint might be due to its causing adoption of the selective mode of processing, which is less effective for these non-salient systems, rather than the unselective mode, which would normally be used.

Because the selective mode of learning is proposed to rely on attentional resources, it should be hindered by the requirement to perform a secondary, attention-demanding task. In contrast, an extra attentional load should not hinder learning in the unselective mode, because unselective learning is presumed not to require attention. Indeed, performing a secondary task of generating letters has been found to interfere with performance in a system with non-salient relations (i.e., in the selective mode) but not with performance in a system with salient relations (using the unselective mode; Hayes & Broadbent, 1988). A final source of evidence that implicit learning occurs during dynamic system control is that learning in the unselective mode appears to require active performance of the control task and not just observation (Berry, 1991), whereas observational learning has been found to occur when relations are salient. In sum, the research on system control suggests two distinct modes of learning similar to those implicated by the research on grammar learning. An unselective mode produces the best learning when the control relations are non-salient, whereas a selective mode is best when the control relations are salient.

Second Language Learning

Language learning—in particular, second language acquisition—is a particularly interesting task domain for several reasons. First, although small children acquire complex language skills seemingly without effort (although it takes years before they master the peculiarities and even the regularities of their mother tongue), adult learners of a second language may struggle for years to acquire even a rudimentary mastery of the new language. Second, language seems a perfect example of a task domain where the rules are complex to the degree that explicit mastery of them is beyond the ability of many learners. One of the key questions in second language acquisition is thus whether some types of knowledge are better acquired implicitly, rather than explicitly.

Much of the research on second language learning concentrates on the role of explicit and implicit learning processes and explicit and implicit knowledge. It is generally accepted that explicit and implicit knowledge both play a role in the acquisition of a second language, and that the two types of knowledge are dissociable (e.g., Hulstijn & de Graaff, 1994). Opinions differ according to how the two types of knowledge interact. One view is that explicit learning consists of the development of pattern recognizers that are then "tuned" by implicit learning processes during subsequent language processing (e.g., N. C. Ellis, 2005): Once a construction has been consolidated in the form of explicit memories for a number of high-frequency and prototypical exemplars, implicit learning can occur on every subsequent usage of the construction. According to this view, languages are learned through active use by these processes of tuning as long as comprehension and production are fluent. When communication breaks down, explicit processes of searching for meaning are triggered.

Usage-based theories of language acquisition emphasize implicit learning of constructions while engaging in communication (Krashen, 1982, 1994). According to these theories, linguistic competence emerges from the abstraction of regularities. The relative probabilities of the mappings between aspects of form and interpretation are noted implicitly, and generalizations emerge as memorized utterances are used in schematic linguistic constructions. Not all aspects of language can be acquired implicitly, however. Explicit instruction, defined as "the use of instructional strategies to draw the students' attention to or focus on form and/or structure" (Terrell, 1991, p. 53), is needed when the cues that must be learned are of low-salience, such that the learner is unlikely to notice the cue, and to explicitly link the cue and its interpretation. Explicit instruction is effective for many aspects of language-related knowledge (e.g., R. Ellis, 2001; Norris & Ortega, 2000; Spada, 1997).

Some types of knowledge and language abilities might benefit more from instruction than others, however, and whether explicit instruction is more effective than implicit learning may depend on the knowledge to be learned. For example, it has been argued that more difficult rules are by nature too complex to be successfully taught and thus are better learned implicitly by embedding them in opportunities for meaning-based practice (Krashen, 1994). The opposite has also been argued: that simple rules are best learned under implicit conditions and that at least some complex rules are best learned with explicit teaching (Hulstijn & de Graaff, 1994). Explicit teaching is argued to be necessary with difficult rules or features because the elements to be learned are difficult to notice in naturally occurring input. In such a case, a relatively implicit method such as *recasting*, in which a teacher rephrases the utterance of a learner, preserving the original meaning, but correcting the error or errors that were present in the original utterance, may be less effective than explaining why the utterance was in error (R. Ellis, Loewen, & Erlam, 2006).

Much research (reviewed in Norris & Ortega, 2000; Spada & Tomita, 2010) has supported the view that easy rules are better learned with explicit instruction than under implicit conditions. However, most tests of acquired knowledge have been declarative, knowledge-based tests rather than more implicit tests of fluency or spontaneous speech. On the basis of a meta-analysis of the effects of implicit versus explicit instruction on the acquisition of simple and complex knowledge, Spada and Tomita concluded that explicit instruction benefited the acquisition of both simple and complex features, but that the effects of implicit instruction were confined to complex features. The effects of explicit instruction on implicit knowledge and processing remain unclear (Doughty, 2004), but focusing attention on relevant form-meaning connections appears to set the stage for further learning.

Schemas for Remembering

New information is not learned by rote, but is interpreted in terms of what is already familiar. This point was made as early as 1932 by Bartlett, who had people read stories and then retell them repeatedly. He noticed that retellings of the stories were very similar to the first retelling—and in some aspects less similar to the original story. That is, people misremembered certain elements of the stories, and, having done so, tended to stick to the new story. Bartlett interpreted this tendency to modify the stories as evidence for the constructive nature of memory. He introduced the term "schema" for the knowledge structures that incorporate to-be-remembered knowledge and past experiences.

The fact that schemas play a role in remembering may seem encouraging for those who hope to enrich knowledge representations. It should be possible to present information in such a way that inconsistencies in prior schemas are revealed and connections with new information are reinforced. However, as will be discussed at more length in Chapter 7, inconsistencies in knowledge structures may persist even when error feedback is given. In Bartlett's (1932) study, the original story was presented only once, so it is perhaps not surprising that deviations from the original study were repeated. However, even when the original story is repeated after each retelling, errors persist and little new information is learned (Kay, 1955). In fact, Fritz, Morris, Bjork, Gelman, and Wickens (2000) showed that the same errors and omissions were repeated across a variety of presentation-test conditions, even when the errors and omissions were made explicit to the learner. Fritz et al. contrasted this so-called failure-of-further-learning effect with the steady acquisition rates typically seen in list-learning experiments (e.g., Battig, 1962). The main difference between the learning contexts is that coherent texts are learned in the former case, and lists of more-or-less unrelated stimuli in the latter. It seems that coherent texts afford the formation of schemas, and that these schemas are resistant to change. In this sense, the failure-of-further-learning effect resembles the finding that naïve theories of natural phenomena are persistent in the face of scientific instruction.

Another situation in which the mental representations constructed by learners influence later performance is when learning to use a device without instructions. Most of us are too impatient—or cocky—to read the instruction manual when we start using a new device, whether it is a telephone or a navigation device. Instead, we start using the device, and, in so doing, develop and test hypotheses about how it works. If not all relationships are salient, the hypotheses that develop about the nature of the relationships among the variables are likely to be erroneous because they are based on inadequate information. Consequently, effort must be devoted to testing and revising erroneous hypotheses, and this activity detracts from the task that is to be performed. Explicit learning can be facilitated by providing the learner with an appropriate mental model or by increasing the salience of the pertinent relations (Kieras & Bovair, 1984).

Learning to operate a device depends on a mental model of the inner working of the device, called a *device model*, as well as on an understanding of how particular actions map onto operation of the device. Learning to use a device can be facilitated by instructions that provide an appropriate device model at the outset, even when that model is based on a far-fetched analogy (e.g., the new television remote control is analogous to the control panel for a "phaser bank" on the Starship Enterprise and the "switch" button fires the phaser). Model-based instructions that capture the pertinent underlying relations have been shown to be more beneficial than learning device functions by rote and to lead to more transfer to other devices (Payne, Squibb, & Howes, 1990). Kieras and Bovair (1984) proposed that the benefit from a device model derives from its being used to infer how to operate the device. They showed that using a device model led to more correct inferences about the underlying procedures than did learning by rote. Moreover, verbal protocols showed that people instructed in the use of a device model explain their actions entirely in terms of the model, whereas those who learn by rote explained their actions in terms of superficial relations among indicators and controls. Thus, a device model appears to be helpful because it enables specific inferences about the operating procedures.

Learning by Analogy

Whether learning by examples or from expository text, the most important issue in the acquisition of cognitive skill is the amount of transfer that occurs from one situation to another. Much research has focused on *analogical transfer*, or the use of what has been learned in the course of problem solving to solve novel problems. When two problems have a similar underlying structure (i.e., when they share related problem spaces or mental models), the solution of one of the problems can sometimes guide the solution of the other. That is, a mental model that is applicable to a studied "source" problem can provide the necessary basis for a mental model that will help solve a related "target" problem. The potential value of an appropriate mental model is illustrated by the following example. If asked to predict the trajectory of a ball that is injected with some force into a coiled tube, many people predict that the ball will follow a curved trajectory even after leaving the tube (Kaiser, McCloskey, & Proffitt, 1986; see Figure 5.3). However, if the same question is asked regarding pressurized water traveling through a coiled hose, most people correctly predict that the trajectory of the water upon leaving the hose will be straight. If an individual is first presented with the hose problem and then asked to predict the trajectory in the ball problem, correct solution of the ball problem is more likely—provided that the similarity between the two problems is noted (Kaiser, Jonides, & Alexander, 1986).

The study of transfer from source to target problems has resulted in detailed descriptions of the process of solving problems by analogy (Holland, Holyoak, Nisbett, & Thagard, 1986). The first step in solving problems by analogy is to construct mental representations of the source and target problems. Because the relation between the two problems may not be obvious, the next step is to detect similarities between the two and to select the source as a potentially relevant analogue. The third step is the mapping of corresponding elements of the problems—that is, determining which elements play similar roles in the source and target problems. The final step is to adapt the mapping to generate rules that can be applied to the target problem to reach the parallel solution.

Merely presenting a similar problem does not ensure that transfer will occur. Several researchers have shown that instructions or hints must be given for analogies to be useful in solving subsequent problems. Gick and

Figure 5.3 The predicted (left) and actual (right) trajectory of a ball rolling out of a coiled hose.

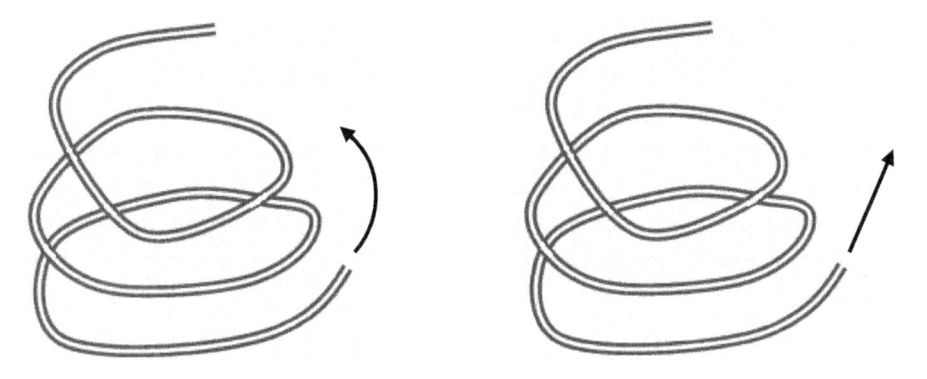

Holyoak (1980) came to this conclusion in studies in which the radiation problem (Duncker, 1945) was used to study possible transfer to other problems. In this problem, the task is to use a ray to destroy a tumor without destroying healthy tissue. To complicate matters, when the ray is of sufficient intensity to destroy the tumor, healthy tissue will also be destroyed. The solution, which is typically difficult to achieve, is to use many smaller rays, any one of which is not sufficiently strong to destroy healthy tissue, that converge at the site of the tumor. The cumulative effect of the rays at the tumor will be sufficient to destroy it, with the healthy tissue left intact at the other locations through which the rays pass (this same principle is embodied in the "Gamma Knife," a method of radiosurgical treatment that focuses gamma radiation from up to 201 radioactive cobalt sources on a tumor or other anomaly in the brain).

A situation analogous to the radiation problem is that of a general who is confronted with the problem of needing to capture a fortress at the center of a country. Hearing a story about the general capturing the fortress by dividing his troops into small groups that converge simultaneously on the fortress from multiple roads improves the solution rate for the radiation problem greatly, but only when a hint to use the story is given. The tendency to use a source problem as an analogue only when a hint is provided emphasizes the importance of looking for similarities between the source and target problems.

One factor that may restrict recognition of the underlying similarity between analogous problems is differences in the surface features of the problems. For example, in the foregoing radiation problem, surface features include a patient, a tumor, rays, and a doctor, whereas in the analogous, military problem, the corresponding surface features are a country, a fortress, troops, and a general. There is little similarity between the surface features of these two problems, so it is not surprising that people have difficulty recognizing that the military problem is analogous to the radiation problem. Consistent with the hypothesis that differences in surface features impede recognition of analogies, studies have shown that when spontaneous recognition of an analogue does occur, it is likely to be based on the similarity of the superficial features (Ross, 1987).

For analogues that have dissimilar surface features, spontaneous recognition is more likely to occur if the problem solver disregards the surface features and focuses on underlying similarities. Problem solvers can be led to focus on different aspects of the problems by wording target problems to emphasize their underlying similarity to source problems (Catrambone & Holyoak, 1989) or by writing the problems using generic relational words rather than concrete, domain-specific terms (Clement, Mawby, & Giles, 1994).

Another way of helping problem solvers to look beyond the surface is to expose them to two source problems and ask them to describe similarities between the two source problems (Gick & Holyoak, 1983). This procedure evidently encourages the development of an abstract schema that is common to the solutions of the problems and can be applied to the analogous target problem. Comparing two unsolved problems at the time of test can also promote retrieval of a single previously studied analogue, even when the solution to the additional problem is not known (Kurtz & Loewenstein, 2007). The problem solver must engage in active processes of comparison for the benefit to occur—performance on two test problems solved consecutively is no better than when the problems are solved in isolation. The benefit of comparing two problems at the time of test is greater for participants who read a prior analogous story than for those who did not, suggesting that problem comparison facilitates analogical retrieval, not just problem solving in general.

An essential factor in learning from any example is how learners refer to the examples. Novick and Holyoak (1991) studied how people learn from analogy by collecting verbal protocols while problem solvers noted similarities between two source problems. The protocols were then classified as indicating poor, intermediate, or good internal schemas on the basis of how many solution steps they contained. The quality of the schemas was positively correlated with target-problem performance, which suggests that schema extraction is a prerequisite for good transfer performance. In fact, schema extraction is sometimes regarded as a fifth step in analogical problem solving. The importance of abstracting general principles is also highlighted by comparing how good and poor learners learn from examples. Poor learners tend to rely heavily on problem solving by analogy as a general learning principle, referring to an example as soon as they notice that it may be relevant and copying as much of the solution as possible. On the other hand, good learners tend to refer to examples only when they reach an impasse in solving a problem. That is, good learners try to solve problems by themselves, whereas poor learners prefer to copy an example. The dependency of poor learners on specific aspects of examples is reflected in what they can report about their solutions. Whereas good learners try to verbalize abstract general solution methods, poor learners tend to simply paraphrase the solutions (Pirolli & Recker, 1994).

Novick and Holyoak's finding that the quality of schemas positively correlates with target-problem performance fits well with the model of analogical transfer outlined by Holland et al. (1986). Furthermore, the finding suggests that adaptation of the solution of the source problem to the target problem is a major locus of transfer difficulty in analogical problem solving.

Successful application of the source problem is not guaranteed even when the mapping of elements from that problem to the target problem is known by the problem solver.

The Einstellung (Mental-Set) Effect

Problem solving is one of the few tasks in which evidence for negative transfer is observed. For example, in the classic "water jar" problem studied by Luchins (1942), people who had used the same method to solve five problems involving pouring water between jars with different capacities to reach a desired end state (e.g., using jars with a capacity of 3, 5, and 8 cups, distribute 8 cups of water equally between the 5-cup and 8-cup jar) then persisted in using this method for problems that could have been solved using a simpler, more direct method (e.g., using jars with a capacity of 2, 4, and 8 cups, distribute 8 cups of water equally between the 4-cup and 8-cup jar). Similarity of superficial features between source and target problems may also lead to negative transfer that hinders solution of the target problem when the principles underlying the problems are not the same. There are numerous other demonstrations of *einstellung*, or inappropriate maintenance of a specific problem set, in problem-solving tasks (e.g., McKelvie, 1985). Set effects reflect transfer of previously learned procedures on the basis of surface similarity to task variations for which the procedures are either inefficient or inappropriate.

A phenomenon closely related to einstellung effects is that of functional fixedness, first reported by Maier (1930) and Duncker (1945). This phenomenon refers to the inability to use an object (e.g., a screwdriver) in a novel way (e.g., as a pendulum weight for a string) to solve a problem (e.g., tying together two hanging strings that are too far apart to be grabbed simultaneously). Functional fixedness decreases as the time that has elapsed since the object was used in the conventional manner increases (Adamson & Taylor, 1954) and is negatively correlated with the ability to overcome einstellung in water jug problems (Adamson & Taylor, 1954; McKelvie, 1984), suggesting that it also reflects inappropriate transfer of prior procedures to the novel task.

Einstellung may reflect a pervasive cognitive bias to ignore evidence against currently held hypotheses. Bilalić, McLeod, and Gobet (2010) describe how chess players shown game boards depicting a situation in which a familiar sequence of moves will lead to mate in five moves (the "smothered-mate" sequence) quickly discover how to accomplish this sequence, but fail to find an alternative, less common means of achieving mate in just three moves. Players did not fail to find the three-move solution because of its difficulty: When one player on the board was moved to make the smothered-mate sequence impossible, the three-move sequence was readily found. Instead, as revealed by measurements of eye movements, players who had found the smothered-mate solution simply kept going back over the same pieces and moves instead of actively searching the whole chess board. Perhaps the most interesting thing about these studies is that the players purport to be looking for alternative solutions. Thus, even though the players consciously thought that they were looking for new evidence, the eye movement data indicated that the previously activated problem solution prevented any other alternatives from becoming active.

Facilitating the Acquisition of Cognitive Skill

A characteristic of how people approach learning is that they want to get started fast, which often leads them to omit critical steps, and neglect to plan tasks or predict the outcomes of their explorations. They also prefer not to follow procedures, often reason from inference even when the similarity to the current situation is only superficial, and, finally, are often poor at recognizing, diagnosing, and recovering from errors (J. M. Carroll, 1997). Carroll has argued extensively that training environments should: (a) Allow users to get started fast and permit them to think and improvise; (b) embed information in real tasks; (c) relate new information to what people already know; and (d) support error recognition and recovery. In other words, good instruction should enable active learning while providing enough support to keep learners involved in useful tasks.

Like performance in many simpler tasks, efficient problem solution requires the use of appropriate strategies and selective access of relevant knowledge from past experience. Problem solving also resembles other task domains in that it obeys the power law of practice (see Chapter 1). The power law will generally hold for total time to perform a problem, total number of steps needed to solve complex problems, and time per step in problems ranging from alphabet arithmetic (in which letters are assigned numbers corresponding to their place in the alphabet; Logan & Klapp, 1991) to justifying geometry-like proofs developed from an artificial postulate set (Neves & Anderson, 1981).

As discussed in earlier chapters, various hypotheses have been offered to account for changes in speed and accuracy with practice. These hypotheses differ in whether they attribute the major changes in skilled performance to decreases in the time needed to retrieve previous problem-solving episodes (Logan, 1988), to execute component procedures (J. R. Anderson, 1982), or to restructure procedural components through compilation or chunking (A.

Newell & Rosenbloom, 1981; Taatgen & Lee, 2003). Theories of improvements with practice also differ in whether processing is assumed to become automatic such that it does not draw on working memory and hence imposes no processing load. However, most theories share the assumption that memory load is reduced because retrieval is faster or that restructuring, by which working-memory load is reduced through combining disparate components so that they can be processed as a unit, has occurred.

An early study of the relative contributions of component processing speedup and restructuring (Carlson, Sullivan, & Schneider, 1989) suggested that the memory demands of performing the task of predicting the output of logic gates (see Figure 5.4) did not change as a function of practice. The relative difficulty of solving different types of logic gate problems stayed the same across many (1,200) trials of practice, as did the effect of a memory

Figure 5.4 Three of the basic logic gates (*AND, OR,* and *INVERTER*; top) and a simple, faulty logic circuit (bottom). A gate is tested by requesting its output (e.g., the bottom left "AND" gate has an input of [1,1] and should thus have an output of "1"; if the test gives an output of "0," the gate is faulty. The problem to be solved is to find the faulty gate in as few tests as possible.

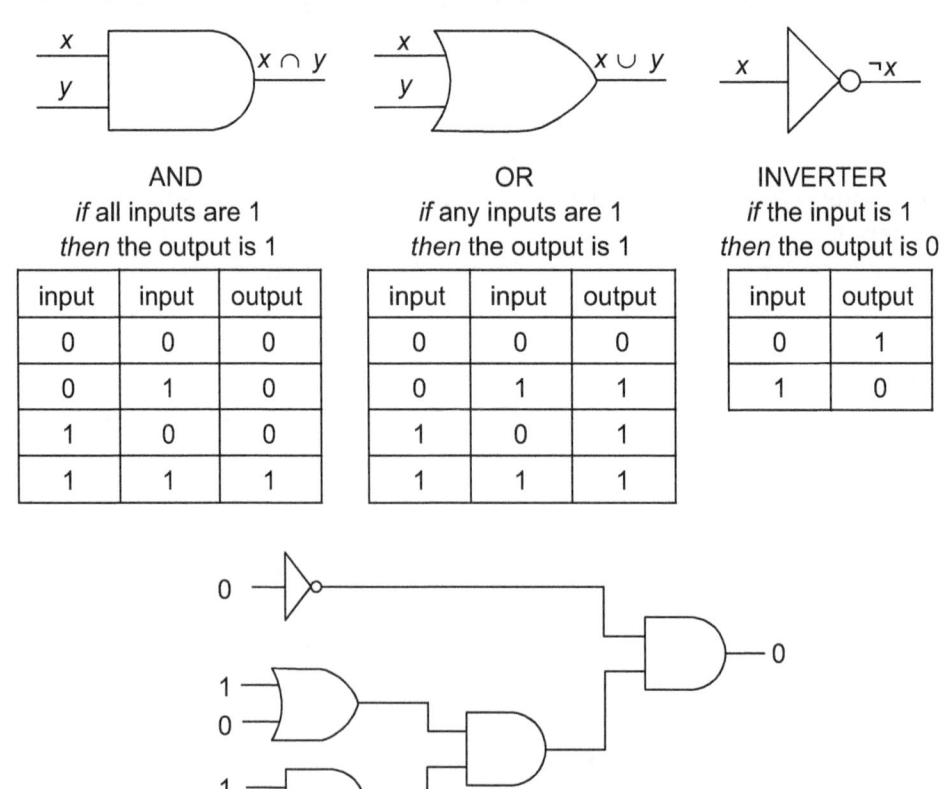

AND
if all inputs are 1
then the output is 1

input	input	output
0	0	0
0	1	0
1	0	0
1	1	1

OR
if any inputs are 1
then the output is 1

input	input	output
0	0	0
0	1	1
1	0	1
1	1	1

INVERTER
if the input is 1
then the output is 0

input	output
0	1
1	0

load: In all cases, simply holding an item in memory did not affect performance, but having to access the memory set to use an item held in memory for solving the logic problem did.

Although Carlson et al. (1989) found no evidence for a qualitative change in the way that people solve problems as they become practiced, more complex problems with hierarchies and subgoals have shown evidence of change. When logic gates are combined to build electronic circuits there are many ways in which the circuit might fail. The job of the electronics troubleshooter is to identify the failed gate. This task is so complex that the troubleshooter must (a) apply problem-solving operators (e.g., requesting information about the present output of a gate and the correct output), (b) use strategies for searching the problem space, and (c) find sequences of operators that will satisfy intermediate subgoals. The number of moves required to solve the problem is a measure of the efficiency of the search strategies used, and the time per move is a measure of the efficiency with which an operator is executed. Carlson, Khoo, Yaure, and Schneider (1990) found that performance on both of these measures improved rapidly early in practice but showed little additional benefit from more extended practice. Thus, learning apparently occurred at both the operator and search levels but only for the first 50 or so problems. Some evidence that subgoals for determining the current state of individual gates were formed and strengthened throughout the experiment was found, suggesting that practice can produce both restructuring of component steps, as suggested by A. Newell and Rosenbloom (1981), and speedup of component processes, as proposed by J. R. Anderson (1982).

Structuring Practice
In Chapter 3 we discussed the relative benefits of mixing versus blocking task variations on the learning of motor skills (for a more detailed review, see Magill & Hall, 1990). For motor skills, practice of different variations of a task in distinct blocks often produces better performance during acquisition than does randomized practice of the task variations, but poorer performance on subsequent retention and transfer tests. The difference in retention indicates that learning is better with randomized practice schedules than with blocked schedules. This better learning is attributed to more elaborate processing that is brought about by the requirement to reconstruct action plans in working memory as the context changes from trial to trial under the randomized schedule (e.g., Wright & Shea, 1991).

Carlson and Yaure (1990) demonstrated that the contextual interference effect is also obtained when learning logic problems of the type used in Carlson et al.'s earlier studies. In their study, participants received practice with four types of logic gates (AND, OR, NAND [in which the output is 0 if all inputs are 1], and NOR [in which the output is 0 if one or more inputs are 1]), either in distinct blocks for each type of gate or with the gates randomly intermixed. The participants then were transferred to a condition in which they solved problems made up of sequences of the practiced logic gates. Performance during practice was better with the blocked schedule than with the randomized schedule, but performance on the subsequent problems was better for those people who had practiced with the randomized schedule. This benefit of randomized practice persisted for 90–100 problems, the maximum number tested. On the basis of these data and a subsequent experiment, Carlson and Yaure suggested that the need to assemble the appropriate problem elements in working memory on each trial when conditions are randomized in practice leads to the development of procedures for reinstating the conditions of the problem. When conditions are blocked, there is no need to assemble elements for each trial and procedures for accomplishing this are not developed. Thus, not only is the contextual interference effect found in both motor learning and problem solving, but also the explanations provided for it are similar.

Spacing Practice Trials

Spacing versus massing trials of a given type is another variable which can be manipulated to improve learning. Spacing practice trials leads, in general, to better performance during the acquisition phase of learning motor skills, but the benefits of spacing versus massing practice trials on retention of motor skills are less clear. In the case of cognitive skills, distributing practice trials across time produces clear benefits on retention (see Cepeda, Vul, Rohrer, Wixted, & Pashler, 2008, for an overview). Even when only two repetitions of to-be-learned facts, word associations, or other materials are presented, a temporal gap between the first presentation of the items and the review leads to better retention than studying the items twice in the first place. One well-known aspect of the spacing effect is that the optimal time between presentations of the material to be learned depends on the retention interval (see Figure 5.5). In general, the longer the information must be retained, the longer the gap that will lead to optimal retention. However, the ratio of optimal gap to test delay decreases as test delay increases. For example, as demonstrated by Cepeda et al., the optimal gap for learning a particular stimulus set (obscure facts) was about 20%–40% of the delay (i.e., about 2 days) for a 1-week test delay and about 5%–10% (about 1 month) for a test delay of a year.

Although it is not clear what mechanisms of memory or learning underlie the spacing effect, it seems likely that massing study leads to unrealistically high levels of confidence in one's mastery of the material (Schmidt & Bjork,

Figure 5.5 The relation between test delay (retention interval) and the optimal gap (time between presentations of study material) plotted as the logarithm of gap and test delay. The open circles represent the studies in Cepeda, Pashler, Vul, Wixted, and Rohrer's (2006) meta-analysis. The dashed line shows the best-fit power regression line.

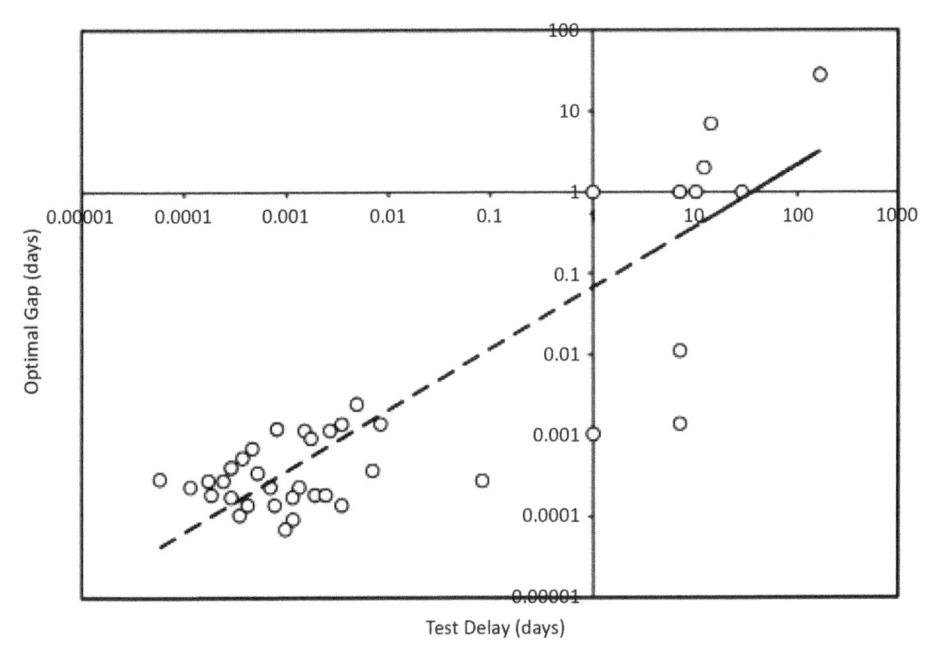

Source: Cepeda, Coburn, Rohrer, Wixted, Mozer, and Pashler (2009).

1992). Given the dependence of the optimal spacing on the retention interval, it is not possible to give absolute guidelines for optimally learning material. The main points are that spreading out the time available for study across time is better than massing it, and, because accuracy at test increases steeply as the gap increases and then declines much more gradually (Cepeda et al., 2006), an interval that is longer than optimal is to be preferred over an interval that is too short.

The Testing Effect

Feedback is critical for learning, and performance on tests is one of the most important sources of feedback in the cognitive domain. In fact, testing enhances later retention of many sorts of material more than does additional study of that material (Roediger & Karpicke, 2006). Testing thus not only assesses knowledge but also changes that knowledge, making it more accessible at a later point in time. Testing has positive effects on learning even when the correct answers are not given. Thus, the so-called *testing effect* seems to rest on the act of trying to retrieve information, rather than simply looking it up during a study episode. Controlled laboratory experiments have shown that testing has effects beyond those of requiring that learners spread out their studying to prepare for tests or giving feedback that can guide study of poorly learned material. The retrieval practice engendered by taking a test in and of itself often enhances learning and long-term retention (Jang, Pashler, & Huber, 2014; Lehman, Smith, & Karpicke, 2014).

Tulving (1967) provided the groundwork for experimental study of the testing effect by comparing the effectiveness of different study-test schedules on the learning of lists of words. The number of trials spent on the task was the same for all of his subjects, but one group alternated between study (in which the lists were viewed) and test (in which subjects simply recalled as many words as possible) trials, one group received three times as many study as test trials, and one group received three times as many test as study trials. Instead of the expected advantage for the group receiving the most study time, Tulving found essentially no differences in learning across the groups. Tulving's study shows that testing can replace study time without disadvantage; when long-term retention is tested, substituting testing for study trials often leads to better performance than studying alone.

Roediger and Karpicke (2006) describe work in which they used word lists and a procedure similar to that of Tulving's to replicate his finding of no difference between "study" and "test" groups in an initial learning session. However, in a delayed test given 1 week after the initial study/test learning session, learners who received more tests (and therefore less study time) clearly outperformed the group who received repeated study trials. In a study using obscure facts as stimuli, testing the facts using cued-recall (with feedback) led to better performance on tests given 5 minutes or 1, 2, 7, 14, or 42 days later than did an additional study presentation (Carpenter, Pashler, Wixted, & Vul, 2008). Power-function fits to the data from the latter study showed that testing increased the degree of learning in comparison with restudying and reduced the rate of forgetting.

The testing effect has been shown to generalize to classroom environments, at least at the university level (McDaniel, Anderson, Derbish, & Morrisette, 2007). McDaniel et al. showed that material tested with weekly quizzes containing multiple-choice and short-answer questions was better learned than material for which additional reading was provided. Moreover, short-answer quizzes were more beneficial than multiple-choice quizzes, suggesting that recall tests are more beneficial than recognition tests for subsequent memory performance. The benefits of testing have been demonstrated for a range of to-be-remembered materials (see Pashler, Rohrer, Cepeda, & Carpenter, 2007; Roediger & Karpicke, 2006).

One consequence of testing knowledge is that students will, especially when the tests contain multiple-choice items, tend to guess when they are unsure of the answer. It is possible that guessing—and even reading the lures on multiple-choice items—will lead to the creation of "false knowledge." That is, students may recognize on a later test information that they have created or seen as lures and mistake their feelings of recognition for actual knowledge. Such a negative testing effect was reported by Roediger and Marsh (2005) on a general knowledge test given after students had taken a multiple-choice test. Students who read more multiple-choice lures showed a smaller benefit of prior testing and were more likely to produce multiple-choice lures as incorrect answers on the final test than were those who saw fewer lures in the prior test. However, other researchers have found that even forced guessing did not impair learning, even when initial guesses were wrong and feedback was delayed (Kang, McDaniel, & Pashler, 2011).

Feedback

As in motor learning, feedback has an important role in the acquisition of knowledge and cognitive skill. Despite the danger that providing immediate feedback may lead students to "think they knew it all along" (Schmidt & Bjork, 1992), providing immediate, informative feedback has been shown to speed learning and improve retention. For example, Pashler, Cepeda, Wixted, and Rohrer (2005) found that foreign language vocabulary learning (learning of Luganda–English word pairs) was far better when learners were provided with correct answers immediately after making mistakes. Providing feedback after correct answers had little impact on learning in Pashler et al.'s study, even when learners had low confidence in their responses (but see Fazio, Huelser, Johnson, & Marsh, 2010, for evidence that the retention of low-confidence correct answers may be facilitated by feedback). For some types of knowledge, it may be better to delay feedback rather than giving feedback immediately. In a task in which the locations of cities on a map had to be learned, Guzmán-Muñoz and Johnson (2008) showed that providing immediate feedback after each city was placed on the map led to better performance during training, but poorer performance on immediate and delayed retention tests than did providing feedback only after all cities had been placed on the map. Detailed analyses of the relational knowledge learned in the map-learning task suggested that delaying the feedback gave learners the chance to look for relations between the items to be learned.

Overlearning

According to the power law of practice, performance will continue to speed up indefinitely as a task is practiced. In terms of cognitive skills, this speedup is well-accounted for by Logan's instance theory of automaticity (see Chapter 4), which posits that the speed of memory retrieval decreases as the number of instances—or problem-solving episodes—increases. This way of thinking suggests that *overlearning*—that is, continued practice after the attainment of error-free performance—will produce learning benefits.

Early studies (e.g., Krueger, 1929) suggested that overlearning might be an efficient means of improving retention. Krueger found that 50% overlearning (i.e., studying lists of words to be learned for an additional number of trials equal to half the number required to be able to perfectly reproduce the list) increased retention at intervals ranging from 2 to 28 days, with relatively more benefit at the longer intervals. Increasing overlearning to 100%, however, showed little, if any, additional benefit. Driskell, Willis, and Copper (1992) reported a meta-analysis on the effects of overlearning, and concluded that overlearning is beneficial for retention, although the benefits depend on the material to be learned, the amount of overlearning, and the retention interval. Contrary to what Krueger reported, Driskell et al. concluded that more overlearning leads to better retention, but that the effects of overlearning dissipate as the delay is increased. They reported that the benefit in performance gained from overlearning is, in general, reduced by 50% after just 3 weeks and suggest that refresher training is needed to prevent any effects of overlearning from disappearing within 5 to 6 weeks. One possible disadvantage of overlearning is that practice is typically massed, thus precluding any benefit of spacing. Providing refresher training is one way of overcoming this drawback, but, as argued by Pashler et al. (2007), the transience of any benefits of overlearning at the time of initial learning of material suggests that "overlearning appears to be inefficient almost to the point of wasting time" (p. 190).

Another way of examining the possible benefits of overlearning is to examine transfer, defined as the time saved in learning a transfer task because of prior practice with a learning task, divided by the time spent learning a training task (see Chapter 1). Because practice affects individual procedures or items of knowledge rather than a skill as a whole (VanLehn, 1996), speedup as a function of practice may be seen for some subskills in a transfer task and not for others. Transfer may be limited when learners change strategies for solving problems during practice. For example, in a given task (e.g., learning the multiplication tables), a shift from strategy A (repeated addition) to strategy B (retrieval from memory) may occur as a function of practice, whereas practice on the criterion, transfer task (e.g., solving word problems) might result in a shift to a different strategy (e.g., adding together hundreds, tens, etc.). If the amount of training is modest, only strategy A will be affected, and transfer will occur. However, if practice is extensive enough to cause a strategy shift, transfer will be suboptimal because the new strategy adopted in the training task does not overlap with the transfer task. That is, as the training time is increased beyond the amount of time that will produce benefits from practice with strategy A, the transfer ratio (time saved on the transfer task/time spent on learning task) will decrease. Overlearning the practice task may thus fail to save any time on the transfer task.

User Models and Intelligent Tutors

As discussed earlier in the chapter, the study of problem-solving behavior is historically tied to the study of computer algorithms for solving problems. In this section we describe how computer models of individual learners can be used to tailor instruction. *User models* are computer models of the knowledge or problem-solving processes of a computer user (van Rijn, Johnson, & Taatgen, 2011). User models may also be used to determine the interests of the user, as when a website collects user information so that the advertisements displayed on the site can be tailored to the user. Many user models are created solely to understand how problems are solved or how knowledge is acquired, but an important application of user models is to incorporate them in teaching applications to create *intelligent tutors* (e.g., Groen & Atkinson, 1966; Sleeman & Brown, 1982). Intelligent tutors use information about the learner to modify the presentation of information so that learning proceeds more efficiently. Information about the student may be gained directly by testing the learner's knowledge, or it may be gained more indirectly, through examining the interactions of the learner with the tutor. Just as a good human tutor attempts to adapt instructional material to the needs of the student, intelligent tutors guide learning and adapt navigational paths to facilitate learner control of knowledge acquisition. When deficiencies of knowledge are revealed, the tutor can provide remedial help by means of new examples or repeated explanation. The quality of this remedial help will depend on how well the tutor understands the learner—that is, on the quality of the user model—as well as on the strategies available for tailoring information to the student.

Once a user model has been developed by ascertaining what learners know, what they are trying to accomplish, and what specific help they might need, modeling techniques and reasoning strategies incorporated into the instructional system are applied to allow it to maintain an up-to-date understanding of the student and his or her learning activity. The model of the student can be used to adapt the learning system to the user by such means as creating problem sets that reflect the interests and weaknesses (or strengths) of the student, or phasing out assistance in finding solutions to problems at the appropriate time.

Probably the most successful and influential approach to student modeling is the *model-tracing method* (e.g., J. R. Anderson, Boyle, & Reiser, 1985; Heffernan, Koedinger, & Razzaq, 2008). In this technique, knowledge is represented in terms of productions (see Chapter 1). A "generic" student model contains all the productions an expert problem solver possesses within the problem domain and may also contain a library of "buggy" productions that embody common student mistakes. The expert model and buggy productions form the knowledge base used by the tutor to diagnose student performance. Each step taken by the student is compared to the output of the productions that the generic model would execute under the same circumstances in order to distinguish between valid procedures and actions based on errors or misconceptions. Other student-modeling techniques include using imprecise pattern-matching algorithms that operate on separate semantic and structural knowledge representations (e.g., Hawkes & Derry, 1996), model-tracing based on declarative knowledge (e.g., Pavlik & Anderson, 2008), and models based on Bayes's theorem (e.g., Conati, Gertner, & VanLehn, 2002).

Summary

Most people spend much of their lives acquiring knowledge. A general rule of thumb is that the more effort is put into knowledge acquisition, the more will be learned. Reconstruction of knowledge—whether through self-explanation, testing, or relearning with spaced practice—is key to learning. Awareness of learning or problem-solving strategies, or metacognition, is associated with skilled performance and may benefit learning by making learners more aware of task structure. However, when the task structure is not transparent or made salient, actively looking for regularities may actually hurt performance.

Learning in many domains appears to rely on both explicit and implicit processes and knowledge. In addition to learning relations that are necessary to meet the objectives of the tasks that we perform, we also learn much that is incidental to the tasks. Complex covariations in the environment can be detected and learned in the absence of the intention to do so. Moreover, this learning can affect performance even when the learned relations cannot be described verbally, and explicitly looking for explanations may interfere with the implicit learning on which many aspects of performance seem to be based.

Many principles and concepts discussed in earlier chapters, such as the power law of practice and the identical elements model of transfer, apply to cognitive skills as well. Problem-solving performance improves with practice, as does performance at almost any task. This improvement seems to involve both speedup in the execution of component processes and restructuring of the procedures that are used. The question of whether skill acquisition in problem solving and other cognitive domains shares underlying mechanisms with the acquisition of perceptual and motor skills is an important one. The finding of commonalities allows the development of widely applicable general theories of skill acquisition. Thus, although learning depends in important ways on the type of material to be learned, the general findings of power-law improvement with practice, restructuring of knowledge, and the effects of testing and practice schedules have important implications for how we view skill and develop training and instruction.

6

Expertise

The very best performers in a domain seem to possess a level of skill that is qualitatively different from that of individuals with extended experience within the same domain.

W. R. Boot and K. A. Ericsson (2013, p. 143)

The focus of this book is on skilled performance and training, but most of the studies discussed so far have examined the changes in performance that occur as people gain experience in tasks conducted in the laboratory over relatively short periods of time. We have seen how the high degree of control that such studies afford makes it possible to characterize many of the specific changes that occur as skill is acquired, and that most skills involve progressing through an initial declarative stage that requires considerable attentional effort and working-memory capacity to a procedural stage in which task performance is relatively automatic. Even after the procedural stage has been attained, however, performance may continue to improve due to experiencing particular problems repeatedly (J. R. Anderson, Fincham, & Douglass, 1997), possibly because the procedures relating the conditions and the corresponding actions associated with them increase in strength (e.g., Gonzalez, Lerch, & Lebiere, 2003). Alternatively, the improvement may occur because the encounters with specific problems are stored as separate "instances"

(Logan, 1988), with the time required to retrieve an instance decreasing as the number of instances increases.

But practice alone may not be enough to develop expertise. That is, although virtually anyone's performance will improve with practice, not everyone will achieve the status of "expert" in the practiced domain. Moreover, not all types of tasks benefit equally from simply practicing them. In this chapter we explore the characteristics of expertise and examine how expertise develops in different domains. In doing so we explore the intriguing question of whether experts are born or made. Excellence in many fields, such as performance music and sports, seems to be reserved for people who possess innate talent. Yet some researchers have argued that—given the basic physical prerequisites—anyone who devotes the necessary hours of considered practice can become an expert in virtually any field. We will come back to the issue of whether all individuals can benefit equally from practice in a later section of this chapter. A more basic question is, perhaps, whether all types of skill benefit equally from extended practice.

The Investigation of Expertise

To obtain a complete picture of skill, it is necessary to study how the knowledge and strategies possessed by experts are acquired and in what ways they differ from those of novices. The investigation of expertise typically proceeds in three steps (Ericsson & Smith, 1991), which can be clearly illustrated within the domain of chess, a convenient domain in which to study expertise because of the existence of detailed records of expert performance and an accurate scale that can be used to rank players according to their skill. The first step is to *identify the characteristics of superior performance in the domain of interest*. This is often accomplished by developing laboratory tasks representative of the required skill and having both experts and novices perform the tasks under controlled conditions. In the study of chess expertise, tasks such as selecting the best next move to make for a particular game configuration have been used (de Groot, 1946/1978; Saariluoma, 1984).

The second step is to *conduct a detailed analysis of the expert's performance in order to infer the nature of the cognitive processes involved*. The cognitive processes of chess experts have been inferred by comparing their performance to that of novices on variations of the tasks that have been identified as capturing superior performance. Measurements that have been used include: the time to select the best move, patterns of eye movements made while examining the board, and verbal protocols of the process of evaluating alternative moves. Chess masters rapidly perceive a given game configuration as a whole, with possible moves effortlessly retrieved as part of this process (de Groot, 1946/1978), in contrast to less expert players, who do not have the ability to recognize such patterns. However, chess masters apparently need time to search and plan ahead because when they are placed under speed stress (e.g., when playing "rapid" chess, for which all moves for a player must be made within a total time of 25–30 minutes, or rapid "blindfold" chess, for which, additionally, the board is not visible), they make more errors than when playing regular, slow chess (Chabris & Hearst, 2003). Surprisingly, the additional cognitive load of the blindfolded version of rapid chess does not lead to any more errors than the sighted version, suggesting that visual imagery may play a major role in chess skill (Hearst & Knott, 2008).

The final step in investigating expertise is to *develop an account of the expert's knowledge structures and processes.* Such an account should provide insight into the nature of the expert's knowledge structures, as well as into the experiences and training that enable the development of expertise. Models of the knowledge structures and processes of chess experts have been developed based on inferred characteristics of their expertise. One of the most cited models is that of Chase and Simon (1973), which is based on the concept of chunking. According to this model, experience with chess results in the ability to recognize increasingly larger groupings of game pieces (i.e., more complete problem states). This culminates in the chess master's ability to recognize chunks of sufficient size to allow the entire game configuration to be apprehended as a whole, bypassing limits of attention capacity, working memory, and long-term retrieval (Feltovich, Prietula, & Ericsson, 2006). Other accounts focus more on "thinking ahead" as one, and possibly the most significant, component of chess skill (Holding, 1985).

In the remainder of this chapter, we consider a range of methods for assessing the knowledge of experts in a variety of domains and characteristics of expert performance and its acquisition. The properties of expert performance are then illustrated for three specific skills, which are primarily perceptual, cognitive, and motoric, respectively.

Understanding Expert Knowledge

Many techniques have been developed to analyze knowledge organization and problem-solving strategies. These techniques can be classified as *direct* or *indirect* on the basis of whether the expert is consciously aware of the knowledge that is being elicited (Olson & Biolsi, 1991). Direct techniques require that the knowledge or relations between items that the expert must report are consciously available to the expert. Most often, open or structured interviews, concurrent or retrospective "think aloud" verbal protocols, or card-sorting classification tasks are used to elicit consciously accessed knowledge. However, because one characteristic of the development of expertise in a domain is that much information processing becomes automatized and, hence, not readily accessible to conscious awareness, indirect techniques utilize some other task, such as making similarity judgments for items or recalling lists of domain items, to infer the structure of the expert's knowledge. Various analysis methods can be applied to the data obtained with direct or indirect methods to refine the representation of the expert's knowledge.

For example, *hierarchical card sorting* (Chi, 2006) is a commonly used direct technique. In this classification task, investigators assume that the expert's knowledge is stored in hierarchies, and have the goal of revealing these hierarchies to uncover the structure of the expert's knowledge. First, the expert is given a stack of cards, each card of which contains an item of domain knowledge. She then sorts the cards into categories. A knowledge hierarchy is determined by having the expert re-sort the categories into subcategories until no further meaningful subdivision is possible. A method, such as the Pathfinder algorithm (Schvaneveldt, 1990), is then applied to analyze the hierarchical card-sorting results and to aid in their interpretation. If using the Pathfinder algorithm, for example, one would start with a network in which all of the concepts sorted by the expert were connected to each other, and, after applying the algorithm, would be left with a network in which only those concepts that are deemed to be most strongly related to each other (i.e., are within the same subcategory) are connected (see Figure 6.1). Reducing the number of links in the network in this way reveals

Figure 6.1 A matrix of proximity ratings (with 1 being most proximal) and the Pathfinder network derived from them. For example, the link between *A* and *C* is assigned a proximity rating of 3 and the links between *A* and *B* and between *B* and *C*, values of 1. Because the direct path from *A* to *C* has a higher weight than the indirect path from *A* to *B* to *C*, the direct link from *A* to *C* will not be in the final Pathfinder network, whereas the links from *A* to *B* and from *B* to *C* will.

	A	B	C	D
A	0	1	3	4
B	1	0	1	2
C	3	1	0	5
D	4	2	5	0

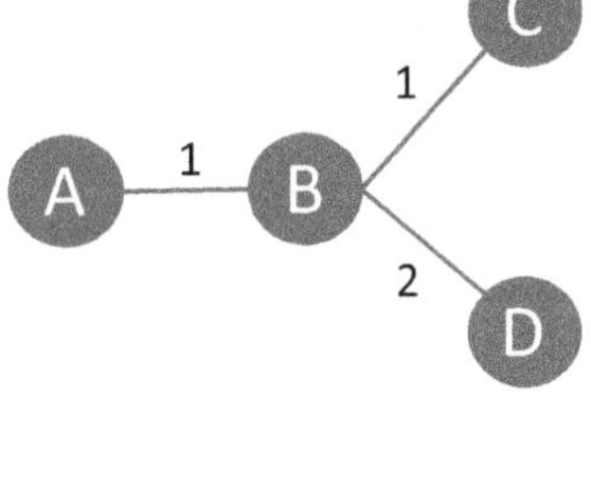

relationships among items. The algorithm can be applied likewise to a matrix of distances between concepts derived from judgments of similarity between pairs of items.

As an example, Wouters, van der Spek, and van Oostendorp (2011) used a Pathfinder analysis to evaluate learning from a serious computer game, "Code Red: Triage," which was developed to train players to evaluate the relative urgency of medical care needed for patients following a disaster. Wouters et al. analyzed the knowledge structures of experts at triage and of novices who lacked medical knowledge and experience both prior to playing the game and afterward. The Pathfinder algorithm was applied to participants' ratings of the relatedness of pairs of concepts from the triage domain to derive the knowledge representations. The network for the experts, shown in Figure 6.2, is characterized by the concepts being highly interconnected (i.e., most concepts are linked to at least two other concepts, with "classify victim," "pulse," and "blood circulation" having the most links). In contrast, prior to playing the game, the novices' averaged knowledge structure showed mainly isolated concepts with links to only a single other concept (see Figure 6.3, left). After playing the game, the novices' knowledge showed more

Figure 6.2 Network of triage concepts for experts found by Wouters et al. (2011).

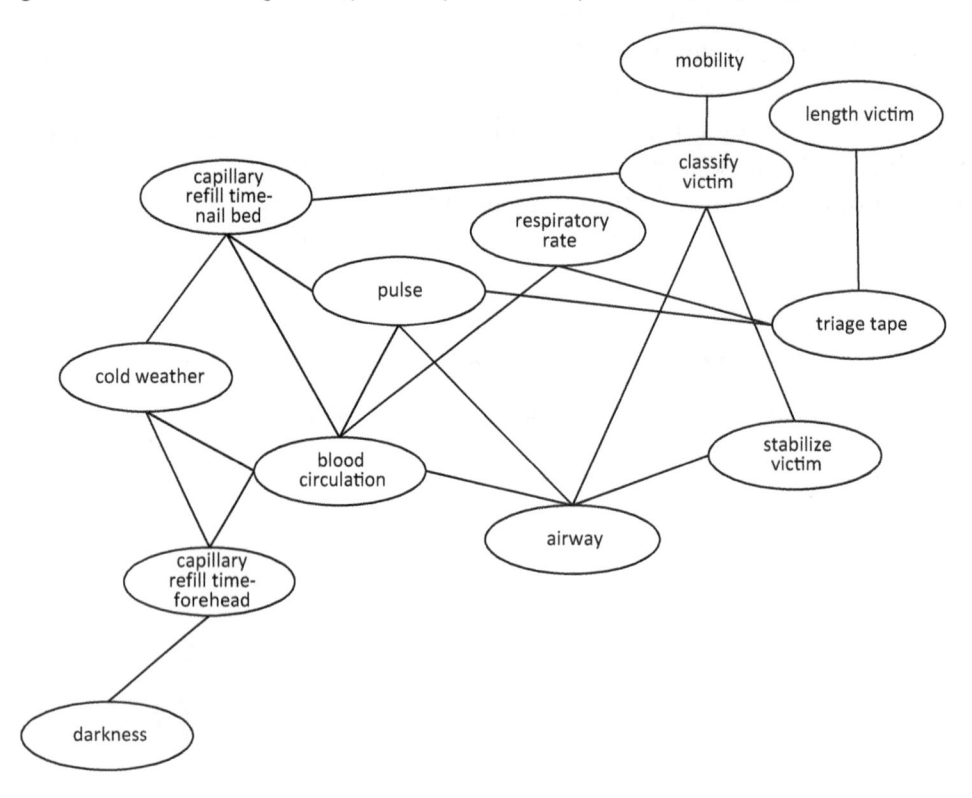

Figure 6.3 Networks of triage concepts for novices before (left network) and after (right network) training found by Wouters et al. (2011).

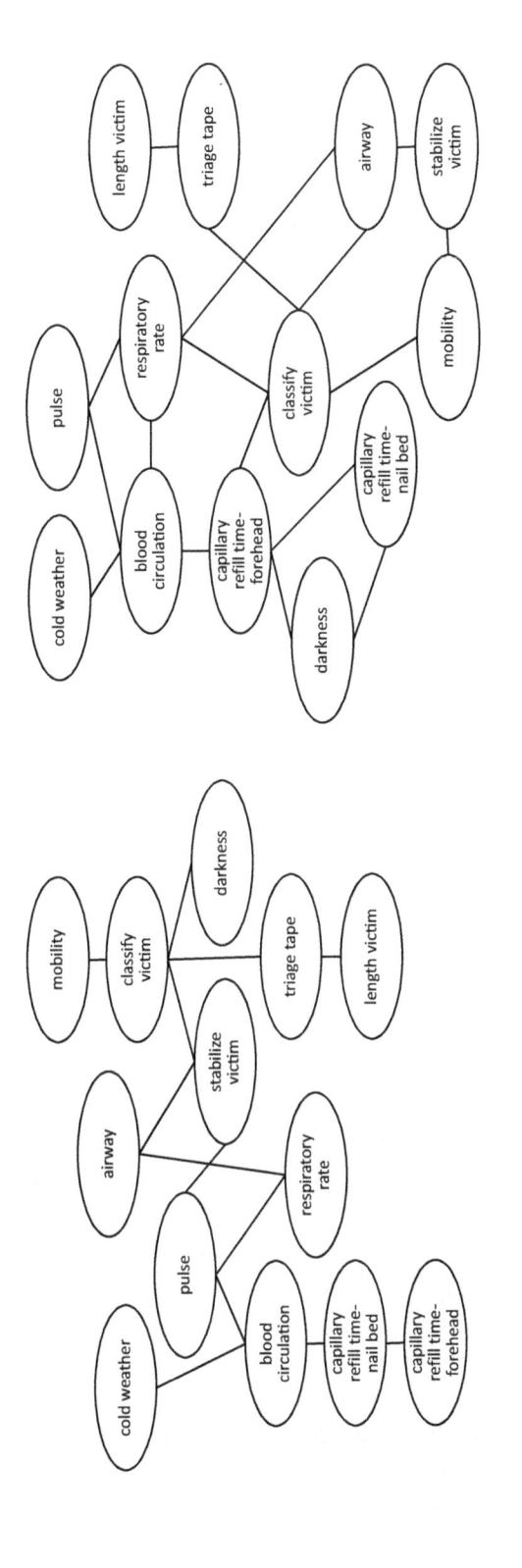

structure (i.e., most concepts were connected to at least two others; see Figure 6.3, right), although the structure differed from that of the experts.

Pathfinder networks have also been shown to be useful for evaluating current knowledge in other educational contexts, and even as an aid to cognition (see Chapter 5). This was illustrated by Trumpower and Sarwar (2010), who assessed high school physics students' conceptual knowledge of a recently completed unit on work, energy, and power by developing a Pathfinder network for each student. Each student was then shown his own network and asked to compare it to a referent network, with the goal of identifying inaccuracies in his knowledge and reflecting on them. Afterwards, when assessed again, the students' networks more closely approximated the referent, indicating improved understanding of the concepts.

Acquisition of Expert Performance

Perhaps the most enduring question in the study of expertise is whether the expert has superior innate ability, or if expertise is simply a result of extensive practice. Without question, differences in innate abilities play a role (e.g., R. W. Howard, 2009; Plomin, Shakeshaft, McMillan, & Trzaskowski, 2014). However, most studies of experts have found that the special characteristics that define expertise in a particular domain do not transfer broadly outside of that domain. That is, expertise is specific to the particular domain. If some innate ability were the basis for this expertise, it should show up in other domains as well. That it does not suggests that the superiority of experts is largely a result of practice and experience (Ericsson et al., 1993; Ericsson, Roring, & Nandagopal, 2007).

At what point does practice have extraordinary effects? Immediate continuation of practice beyond the point at which participants initially demonstrate learning (through correct recall or attaining a performance criterion) is known as *overlearning* (see Chapter 5). Overlearning can benefit both physical (perceptual-motor) and cognitive (verbal memory) task performance, although, as shown in the meta-analysis by Driskell, Willis, and Copper (1992), the benefits of overlearning tend to be smaller for perceptual-motor tasks than for verbal memory tasks. However, the benefit of overlearning is relatively durable for physical tasks (lasting across retention intervals of weeks), whereas for cognitive tasks it tends to decline or even disappear in a matter of weeks. In fact, overlearning has been found to substantially enhance recall of material such as geography facts in a delayed test given after 1 week, but the benefit of overlearning declined substantially thereafter (Rohrer, Taylor, Pashler, Wixted, & Cepeda, 2005). Thus, although overlearning cognitive materials produces some benefit, the evidence indicates that distributing the practice across time—for as little as 2 days (Rohrer, 2009; see Chapter 5)—is much more beneficial, particularly for long-term retention.

Most studies of overlearning have focused only on the retention of particular knowledge or skills in laboratory tasks, rather than on the development of expertise in a meaningful domain. A gulf exists between easily learned laboratory skills, such as responding quickly to a target letter in an array, and the skills shown by elite performers in the arts, sciences, and sports. The complex tasks required of these performers, as well as of experts in many other real-life domains, must be practiced for months or even years for proficiency to develop. Can the development of expertise be seen as extreme overlearning? For example, it has been suggested that in the game of chess 9 to 10 years of intensive practice is the minimum needed to achieve the highest rating of Grandmaster (H. A. Simon & Chase, 1973). To the extent that the 10-year rule holds, experts are made, not born, and overlearning does play an important role in the development of expertise. Although exceptions to this 10-year rule for chess have been noted (Hambrick et al., 2014), the rule seems to hold in general for a variety of other cognitive and physical skills (Ericsson, Krampe, & Tesch-Romer, 1993; Kaufman & Kaufman, 2007).

Three phases in the development of expertise have been identified (Bloom, 1985; Ericsson et al., 1993). As shown in Figure 6.4, the initial phase begins with an individual's introduction to the domain activities and is

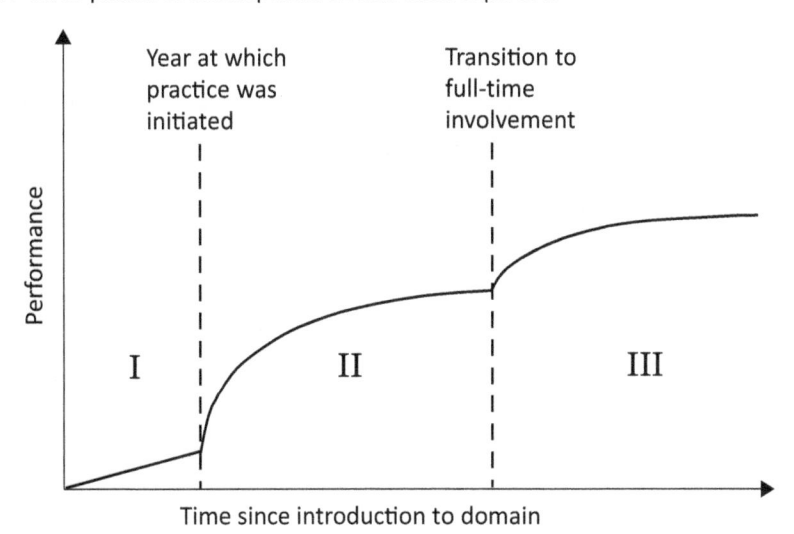

Figure 6.4 Three phases of development toward adult expertise.

Adapted from Bloom (1985).

characterized by relatively slow progress. That phase ends, and the second begins, when formalized instruction and deliberate practice—which involve activities specially intended to improve the level of current performance—are undertaken. This phase continues for an extended period of time, ending when the individual decides to make a full-time commitment toward improving performance in the domain. The final phase that follows this commitment is characterized by even more intensive practice than during the second phase.

The theory of deliberate practice proposed by Ericsson and colleagues (Ericsson, 2006; Ericsson et al., 1993; Ericsson et al., 2007) traces the development of expertise through these three stages. The primary assumption underlying the framework is that a person's level of performance is a monotonically increasing function of the amount of time that the person has engaged in *deliberate practice*. Many elite performers begin practicing at an early age, as in the case of high-wire walker Nik Wallenda, described in Chapter 3, often with the encouragement of a parent who helps to maintain a regular practice schedule. The amount of deliberate practice in which the individual engages will tend to increase once a personal commitment to excel in the domain is made.

Ericsson et al. (1993) obtained support for their theory of deliberate practice in a study of violinists. They examined violin students in a music academy who were classified into the categories of "the best violinists," "good violinists," and "music teachers," in order of decreasing skill. The category of skill in which a violinist fell was predictable from estimates of the total amount of deliberate practice in which the person had engaged during his or her life. Similar findings have been obtained for chess (Charness, Tuffiash, Krampe, Reingold, & Vasyukova, 2005) and typing (Keith & Ericsson, 2007), among other domains, lending support to Ericsson et al.'s conclusion: "Across many domains of expertise, a remarkably consistent pattern emerges: The best individuals start practice at earlier ages and maintain a higher level of daily practice" (p. 392).

Deliberate practice is presumed by Ericsson et al. (1993, 2007) to be effortful and not intrinsically enjoyable. Hence, the primary motivation for engaging in it is to improve performance. A recent study of expert and intermediate-level Gaelic football players (Gaelic football is an Irish sport) showed evidence consistent with this view of deliberate practice (Coughlan, Williams, McRobert, & Ford, 2014). The expert players chose to practice mainly the one of two kick types at which they were less skilled (and thus could improve the most), whereas the intermediate group chose to practice mainly the kick type at which they were more skilled. The experts not only chose the more challenging kick to practice but also rated their practice as more effortful and less enjoyable than did the intermediate-level players.

Most of us have made the casual observation that certain individuals have better abilities than other individuals in specific domains. In fact, the perception that a young child is "gifted" is what usually leads parents to start the costly rounds of instruction and deliberate practice that are necessary for a person to become highly skilled. However, Ericsson and colleagues (1993, 2007) maintain that a "perceived" ability is not necessarily a true ability, but that the perception of ability leads to deliberate practice, which then leads the person to perform better than his or her cohorts, thus reinforcing the perception that the individual is gifted. They recently stated, "Even the well-known fact that allegedly more 'talented' children improve faster in the beginning of their music development appears to be in large part due to the fact that these children spend more time in practice each week" (Ericsson et al., 2007, p. 35).

Many skills researchers have not taken as extreme a position as Ericsson and colleagues on the overriding influence of deliberate practice on development of expertise, as was evident in the commentaries published in the same journal issue as Ericsson et al.'s 2007 article. Indeed, Hambrick et al. (2014) emphasize that when studies of chess and music experts are examined closely, the amount of deliberate practice fails to account for much of the variance in performance. They conclude that deliberate practice is not sufficient to become an expert and that other factors—including a possible critical period early in life, intelligence, and personality —contribute to the development of expertise as well.

General Characteristics of Experts

Given that all skills are acquired through extensive training and practice, one might surmise that although the specific skills of experts in different domains differ, experts will exhibit certain general characteristics that distinguish their performance from that of novices. In fact, experts from a variety of domains do display several common characteristics (Chi, 2006; Glaser & Chi, 1988). One of the most widely discussed of these characteristics is that experts can readily perceive complex, meaningful patterns within their domain. For example, as mentioned earlier, the ability to perceive complex patterns, as demonstrated by superior memory for briefly presented midgame configurations of pieces, is one of the most robust characteristics distinguishing chess masters from less accomplished players (de Groot, 1946/1978; H. A. Simon & Chase, 1973). This superior memory ability has been interpreted as indicating that the experts encode domain information into larger meaningful chunks. Novices are presumed to have to encode the configurations in more numerous, smaller chunks, thus overloading working memory, because they lack the knowledge base necessary to encode larger chunks. Consistent with this interpretation, the memory performance of chess experts decreases to that of nonexperts when the configurations to be recalled are made up of randomly placed chess pieces. The excellent memory for chess positions demonstrated by chess masters illustrates another characteristic of experts, which is superior short-term and long-term retention for domain information. In the case of chess, experts have a large knowledge base of previous games into which new information can be integrated.

Because an expert has practiced extensively to acquire a particular skill, many of the basic components of the skill have become automatized. This frees up attentional resources for other aspects of the task, such as planning strategy. An example of this feature of skill can be found in a study of university-level ice hockey players conducted by Leavitt (1979). As a primary task, the players were required to skate as quickly as possible through a slalom course of pylons. Time to complete the course was measured when the primary task was performed alone or along with one or both of two secondary tasks, "stickhandling" a puck and identifying geometric forms shown on a screen located at the end of the arena. The secondary tasks had little effect on the skating times of the skilled hockey players but substantially slowed those of novice players. It should be noted, however, that sizable interference is still obtained for experts when the primary and secondary tasks are more structurally similar (e.g., dribbling a soccer ball while running a slalom course [M. D. Smith & Chamberlin, 1992] or performing a visuospatial secondary task while making judgments about visually displayed arrangements of chess pieces [Saariluoma, 1992]) and, hence, overlap to a greater degree in terms of the required processing resources.

The ability of experts to effortlessly recognize meaning in the information with which they are provided allows them to represent problems at a deeper, more principled level than can novices. As discussed earlier, problem representations can be inferred by having experts and novices classify problems by sorting them into groups. It has been shown, for example, that physics experts sort problems into categories according to fundamental principles, whereas novices sort the same problems according to the objects that are featured in the problems (Chi, Feltovich, & Glaser, 1981). Physics experts are also better able to generate solution plans before attempting to solve a problem (Priest & Lindsay, 1992). Because they are able to find appropriate problem representations and solution plans, experts spend a greater percentage of problem-solving time thinking about a problem before they begin to work on it than do novices. They may use this time to form a mental model of the situation that allows inferences to be drawn; or for ill-defined problems, constraints may be added to reduce the search space (J. F. Voss & Post, 1988). Associated with taking the time to gain conceptual understanding is a greater tendency to monitor one's progress toward the goal. Experts are more likely to recognize their own deficiencies or limitations and to evaluate their own performance.

Expertise in Three Specific Domains

Three task domains in which the characteristics of expertise have been studied extensively are diagnosing medical images, computer programming, and typing. Although the first two rely heavily on knowledge, the diagnosis of medical images has a large perceptual component, whereas computer programming is mainly a cognitive task, and typing has a significant motor component. Examining these three tasks in detail thus allows us to determine how expertise develops in the perceptual, cognitive, and (for a rather basic task) motor domains.

Interpreting Medical Images

Medical imaging plays a role in many medical specialties, and 40% of all hospital procedures are image-based (Beam, Krupinski, Kundel, Sickles, & Wagner, 2006). Most imaging research has been conducted in radiology (Krupinski, 2010), for which, as noted, diagnosis from images is a complex and difficult skill with a large perceptual component. It is not purely a perceptual skill, though, because diagnosis also requires analysis, or interpretation, of the medical image, a cognitive process that relies on formal knowledge of medicine and the integration of different sources of information (Krupinski, 2010). In B. P. Wood's (1999) words, "Radiologists believe that the expertise of the interpreter lies in a vast experience of seeing many thousands of radiologic patterns and synthesizing them into a coherent, organized, and searchable mental matrix of diagnostic meaning and pathologic features" (p. 1). Because training is relatively standardized for radiologists (after general training as medical doctors, they spend several years in residency reading X-ray pictures to diagnose medical problems), it is easy to find novices and experts in the domain and to know the nature and degree of their previous experience.

Early studies of radiological expertise emphasized the perceptual component of the skill by using tasks that involved detection of critical visual features in X-ray pictures. For example, Kundel and Nodine (1975) showed radiologists a series of 10 abnormal and 10 normal chest X-ray films for 200 ms each and, later, for an unlimited viewing time. In the "brief exposure" condition, approximately 70% of the radiologists' responses were correct (an abnormality was correctly identified or the picture was correctly classified as normal). This relatively high accuracy with brief exposures is in agreement with estimates that a trained radiologist will fixate on a significant anomaly within 0.5 seconds of viewing an image (Donovan & Manning, 2006) and with fMRI evidence that the cortical activations of the radiologist to the abnormalities are similar to those for naming animals—a highly automatic process (Melo et al., 2011). There is also some evidence to suggest that some of the learning of expert radiologists occurs early in the visual system: Expert radiologists showed greater sensitivity at detecting low contrast dots in an X-ray image than did novice student participants (Sowden, Davies, & Roling, 2000).

In Kundel and Nodine's (1975) study, detection was even better with unlimited viewing of the images. Thus, radiologists can often identify deviations from a normal X-ray picture in a single glance, but perform more accurately when there is sufficient time to search the picture. These findings led Kundel and Nodine to propose that radiologists use a two-step process for detecting potential target areas in which an initial global percept guides subsequent search for visual features. An expert's scan path of possible critical features is more efficient than those of less-skilled persons because the initial global percept encompasses more of the visual field and the visual pattern can be compared efficiently with the expert's schema, acquired from years of experience (Reingold & Sheridan, 2011). This point is illustrated by findings such as those of Kundel and LaFollette (1972), who recorded eye movements of untrained laypersons, medical students, radiology residents, and staff radiologists as they viewed normal and abnormal chest X-ray pictures. The radiologists scanned broad areas of the pictures, whereas the untrained people tended to restrict fixations to localized regions in the centers of the pictures. The global search pattern characteristic of the radiologist apparently depends on the knowledge of anatomy and pathology learned in medical school, since the residents and staff radiologists showed little difference in search patterns.

In agreement with the deduction that knowing where to look is important, it has been shown that novices read chest X-rays more accurately when each image is viewed with an overlay of the search pattern of an expert prior to their making a decision (Litchfield, Ball, Donovan, Manning, & Crawford, 2010). That the radiologists' knowledge influences the detection process is also evident in their detecting more target abnormalities that are important (e.g., ones indicative of cancer) than those that are not as important (Nakashima et al., 2015).

The skill of diagnosing with X-ray pictures involves cognitive, interpretive processes in addition to perceptual processes, so to assess skill in reading the pictures adequately, tasks that involve both of these processes are required. In one study emphasizing the cognitive evaluation component of skill in diagnosing X-ray pictures, Lesgold et al. (1988) collected concurrent verbal protocols from three groups (experienced staff radiologists, third- and fourth-year residents, and first- and second-year residents) as they examined X-ray films, and then recorded their oral diagnoses of the problem. Lesgold et al. also required the radiologists to substantiate their diagnoses by drawing the outlines of the relevant anatomy and areas of concern on an overlay of the X-ray picture. In a second phase of the experiment, the radiologists were told to draw the outlines of the features in the region of the X-ray picture known by the experimenters to be critical to the diagnosis. Following this, the radiologists rendered diagnoses again.

There were three main parts to the analysis of the data collected with this procedure: analysis of the verbal protocols that preceded the initial diagnosis, evaluation of the drawings done on the X-rays, and comparison of the first and second diagnoses. For the purpose of comparison, the protocols from each group were analyzed into *findings* (statements of observed properties of the film) and *relationships* (reasoning paths connecting findings; see Figure 6.5).

The performance of staff radiologists differed significantly from that of both groups of residents on all measures. Staff radiologists identified more findings, more causes of abnormalities, and more effects (outcomes of abnormal events) than did the residents. Perhaps most importantly, experts exhibited longer chains of reasoning—their findings were clustered and interconnected (see Figure 6.5). The staff radiologists appeared to do more inferential reasoning and developed more coherent models of the patient than did the two groups of residents, who did not differ on any of the measures. The protocols of all the residents were relatively fragmented and seemed to focus mainly on superficial features.

The differences between the staff and resident radiologists evidenced in the protocols were substantiated by differences in their drawings. Staff radiologists were able to make subtler distinctions in the X-ray films. Lesgold et al. (1988) reached the conclusion, similar to that drawn by Kundel and Nodine (1975), that experts' perceptions were apparently guided by schemas of patient anatomy and disease history that were tuned to the specific cases being evaluated. The experts were also better able to decouple the features in the film from their mental models of the patient's anatomy when that was required due to ambiguities in the film. In short, they used their schemas of patients' anatomy and medical history, along with their knowledge of how the films were made, to guide perception. The novice radiologists were

158 ◆ Expertise

Figure 6.5 An analyzed protocol from a Lesgold et al. (1988) listing of all findings (A through M) and reasoning paths, and illustrating the relations between the findings (in the rectangle at the bottom). Findings with one or more reasoning links between them form a reasoning *chain*. A *cluster* is a set of findings with a path from each set member to every other set member, ignoring direction. A *cause* is the origin of a reasoning link and an *effect* is the termination.

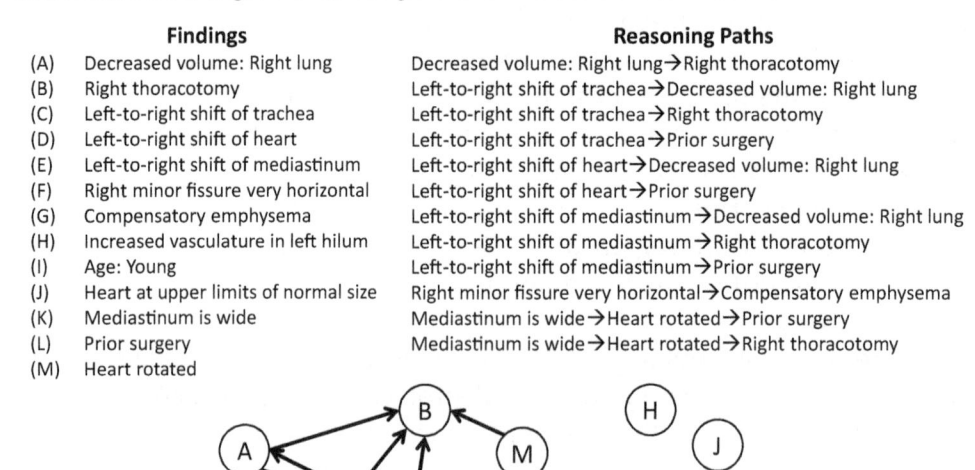

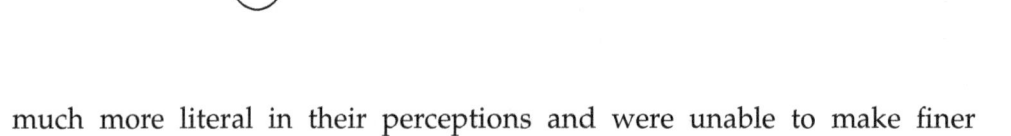

	Findings	Reasoning Paths
(A)	Decreased volume: Right lung	Decreased volume: Right lung→Right thoracotomy
(B)	Right thoracotomy	Left-to-right shift of trachea→Decreased volume: Right lung
(C)	Left-to-right shift of trachea	Left-to-right shift of trachea→Right thoracotomy
(D)	Left-to-right shift of heart	Left-to-right shift of trachea→Prior surgery
(E)	Left-to-right shift of mediastinum	Left-to-right shift of heart→Decreased volume: Right lung
(F)	Right minor fissure very horizontal	Left-to-right shift of heart→Prior surgery
(G)	Compensatory emphysema	Left-to-right shift of mediastinum→Decreased volume: Right lung
(H)	Increased vasculature in left hilum	Left-to-right shift of mediastinum→Right thoracotomy
(I)	Age: Young	Left-to-right shift of mediastinum→Prior surgery
(J)	Heart at upper limits of normal size	Right minor fissure very horizontal→Compensatory emphysema
(K)	Mediastinum is wide	Mediastinum is wide→Heart rotated→Prior surgery
(L)	Prior surgery	Mediastinum is wide→Heart rotated→Right thoracotomy
(M)	Heart rotated	

much more literal in their perceptions and were unable to make finer distinctions.

Lesgold et al. (1988) characterized the behavior of expert radiologists as consisting of building a mental representation of the patient and refining a schema for interpreting the X-ray picture. The major difference between expert and less expert radiologists is the manner in which schemas are invoked and refined. Schemas are triggered quickly by the expert, who works efficiently to reach a stage where an appropriate general schema is in control. The expert performs tests on the schema to confirm that it is the appropriate one and modifies it as required to accommodate new data. Less expert radiologists may fail to invoke a schema completely, to test the schema appropriately, or to complete the diagnosis process.

In summary, acquiring expertise in diagnosing X-ray pictures consists in part of developing global search strategies, acquired early in training, which can guide detection of potential target areas. Schemas of increasing refinement develop with more extended experience through processes of generalization and discrimination.

Computer Software Design and Programming

Software design and programming is a more purely cognitive skill than is reading and interpreting X-ray pictures. The domain is composed of the distinct tasks of requirement analysis and software design, programming and program comprehension, and testing and debugging (Sonnentag, Niessen, & Volmer, 2006). Also, because much design and programming occurs within teams, skills for cooperating and communicating with team members are essential.

The requirements analysis and design process requires identification of the goals that the new software system is to meet, and then arriving at a design that satisfies the requirements. Just as physics experts spend a relatively large proportion of their problem-solving time understanding the problem, expert software designers spend more time clarifying the requirements at the outset than do less experienced designers (Batra & Davis, 1992). Experts also decompose the design problem into more small subproblems than do novices, using a top-down, breadth-first decomposition strategy (Sonnentag et al., 2006).

The programmer must understand the goals of the resulting software design and implement them in a syntactically and logically correct computer program. An expert will typically have many years' experience writing programs to meet a variety of objectives and will know several programming languages. Programmers describe their progression as they developed expertise as being one in which qualitative changes in their abilities occurred (R. L. Campbell, Brown, & Di Bello, 1992). They report initially relying on a cookbook approach, but later developing an intuitive grasp of how to approach programming problems. A study by Arisholm and Sjøberg (2004) illustrates one type of difference between experts and novices. They noted that in object-oriented programming, like in Java, it is considered better to use a delegated control style, in which control is distributed among a number of classes of attributes and methods, than to use a centralized control style, because a program using the delegated style is easier to modify. Participants with different levels of expertise performed multiple modification tasks on Java programs that utilized a delegated or centralized control style. The expert programmers required less time to modify the software with a delegated control style than that with a centralized control style. In contrast, less experienced programmers had difficulty understanding the delegated control style and performed much better with the centralized control style. An implication of this finding is that less-skilled persons may find the programs developed by more skilled persons difficult to modify.

Research on programming expertise has revealed some of the other changes in processing associated with the acquisition of programming skill.

As is characteristic of experts in general, programming experts are able to remember more from a brief exposure of a program than are novices, primarily because they organize the information into larger chunks. Programmers generally show superior memory for normal programs and not for ones for which the order of the lines has been scrambled (Barfield, 1986; McKeithen, Reitman, Reuter, & Hirtle, 1981; Schneiderman, 1976). Also, for a group of professional software designers, a latent-path analysis (which reveals underlying causal links between variables) provided evidence that the influence of working-memory capacity and programming experience on programming skill was mediated by the amount of declarative programming knowledge possessed by the different designers (Bergersen & Gustafsson, 2011).

Expert programmers organize their knowledge by the meaning of the programming statements, as shown by a study of McKeithen et al. (1981). They had novices and experts study a list of reserved words from a programming language (ALGOL W), performing free recall of the list for many times after an initial criterion of correct recall twice in a row was met. An ordered-tree algorithm developed by Reitman and Reuter (1980) was then used to identify chunks in the recall orders by searching for items that were always recalled together. The algorithm produced ordered trees that captured the chunk structure of the list representations. Experts produced a greater number of chunks than novices, and these chunks appeared to be based on different organizing principles. As illustrated in Figure 6.6a, novices tended to organize their recall by common language principles or orthography. For example, all the words that start with *S* were recalled together. In contrast, the experts organized their recall by the ALGOL W–specific meaning of the words. For example, the chunks *if-then-else* and *while-do*, shown in the tree in Figure 6.6b, are commonly used programming statements.

How specific to a particular programming language is the knowledge organization of experts? Petre (1991) suggested that programmers approach tasks in an abstract, goal-dependent way that is independent of any specific programming language. The programmer's abstract knowledge can be characterized as consisting of programming plans and rules of programming discourse (Soloway, Adelson, & Ehrlich, 1988). *Programming plans* are the stereotypic action sequences used in nearly all programs, such as looping through a sequence of instructions. The *rules of programming discourse* (e.g., variable names should reflect function) govern the composition of programming plans to create the program needed to solve the task at hand. One question is whether there is any difference in how experts in object-oriented programming compare to those in more common, procedural-oriented programming. Corritore and Wiedenbeck (1999) had experts in C and C++ study functionally equivalent forms of a program in procedural

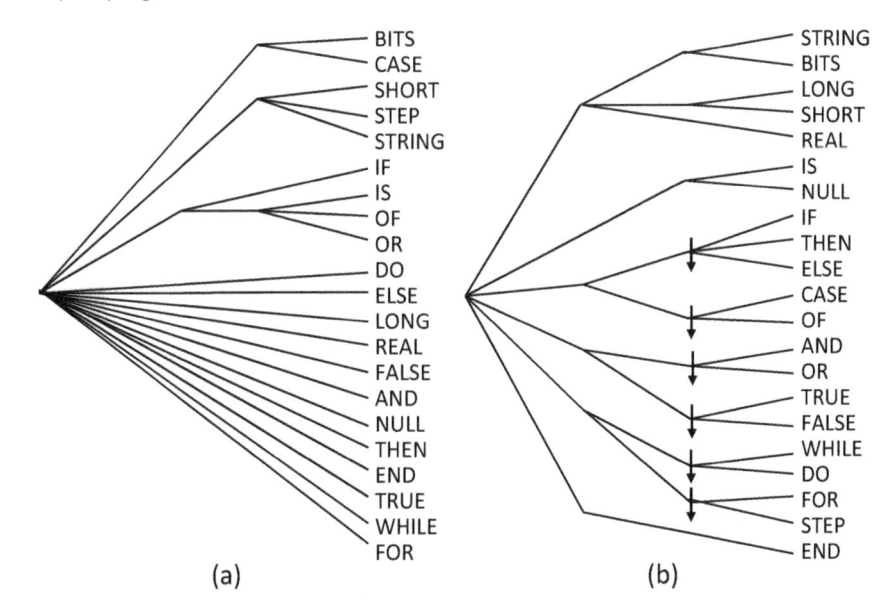

Figure 6.6 Ordered trees for recall of ALGOL W words derived from recall order of (a) a novice and (b) an expert programmer.

```
(a)                              (b)
  BITS                             STRING
  CASE                             BITS
  SHORT                            LONG
  STEP                             SHORT
  STRING                           REAL
  IF                               IS
  IS                               NULL
  OF                               IF
  OR                               THEN
  DO                               ELSE
  ELSE                             CASE
  LONG                             OF
  REAL                             AND
  FALSE                            OR
  AND                              TRUE
  NULL                             FALSE
  THEN                             WHILE
  END                              DO
  TRUE                             FOR
  WHILE                            STEP
  FOR                              END
```

Adapted from McKeithen et al. (1981).

C and object-oriented C++, respectively, and then answer questions about them. The object-oriented experts' knowledge of the program was predominantly domain-based initially, with little detailed program information, whereas the procedural experts' knowledge was more balanced between the two. However, after making modifications to the program, the knowledge representation of the object-oriented programmers resembled that of the procedural programmers, leading Corritore and Wiedenbeck to conclude that, in general, "expert programmers build a mixed mental representation of a larger program, which includes detailed program knowledge as well as domain-based knowledge" (p. 61).

If experts differ from novices in having programming plans and rules of programming discourse, then violations of this knowledge structure should interfere with the performance of experts but have little influence on the performance of novices. To test this hypothesis, Soloway and Ehrlich (1984) evaluated expert and novice programmers' comprehension of programs that differed only in whether a rule of programming discourse was violated. The experimental design required the participant to complete a blank line in each of eight programs, four of which violated a discourse rule and four of which did not. All of the programs were executable; that is, the violations were only against convention and were not incorrect ways of performing the task. The most important finding was that experts performed better than novices only when the programs were consistent with the rules of programming discourse. Moreover, when an incorrect answer to a program that violated discourse rules was given, it tended to be an answer that would have been correct if discourse rules had been followed.

For testing and debugging, errors in the programs need to be identified and removed. This requires that strategies and tactics be adopted that go beyond knowledge of the programming language itself (Romero, Du Boulay, Cox, Lutz, & Bryant, 2007). Experts adopt a more conceptually driven approach than novices in testing for errors (Krems, 1995), and they test more for inconsistency (Teasly, Leventhal, Mynatt, & Rohlman, 1994). Experts also require less time to debug a program (Vessey, 1986). Moreover, the strategies used by programmers to debug are distinct from those used by end users of programs, like spreadsheets, for which they need to program certain operations (Grigoreanu et al., 2012).

On the whole, then, the picture that emerges of expertise in software design and programming is consistent with the characteristics mentioned at the outset of the chapter. The knowledge structures lead to better, and qualitatively different, performance on memory tests, and actions are guided in part by a deeper understanding of the critical factors.

Expert Typing

The skills of diagnosing X-ray pictures and computer programming are largely independent of motor processes. However, many skills involve a significant motor component, and skill has traditionally been defined in terms of fluent motor performance. Expertise in most motor skills is difficult to study because of the complexity of performance and the associated difficulty of analyzing it in meaningful units. These problems can be circumvented to some extent in the study of typing. Realistic typing tasks can be carried out in the laboratory, and typing performance can be analyzed in terms of its component parts. Measures such as the latency to execute responses and the types of errors made can provide precise information about the nature of skilled typing. Moreover, because many people type, large populations of typists at various levels of skill are readily available.

Much research has been based on transcription typing, in which a typist enters displayed text using a keyboard (Wu & Liu, 2008). The typist must perceptually encode a chunk of text that is to be typed and then decompose this chunk into discrete characters that are translated into movement specifications. The contributions of the perceptual and cognitive aspects of typing can be dissociated from those of the motor processes involved in the execution of the finger movements, and the coordination of the perceptual, cognitive, and motor processes that is necessary for skilled typing can be examined.

Transcription used to be the most common form of typing, with the typist (often a secretary) entering handwritten or dictated text. But with the increasing use of computers for word processing, transcription is now estimated to make up less than 10% of the typing that is done, with composition of text being much more prevalent (Logan & Crump, 2011). Both involve language, but whereas transcription requires comprehension, composition involves mainly language generation.

Typing expertise seems to be determined largely by the amount of deliberate practice. Keith and Ericsson (2007) assessed the abilities of typists with several years of experience and conducted semi-structured interviews with them on their typing experience. They found that measures of perceptual speed and motor abilities were not significantly related to performance, but amount of typing since first becoming familiar with the keyboard was. More important, in agreement with the deliberate practice hypothesis, the best performing typists were those who had attended a typing class in the past and reported adopting the goal of typing quickly during their everyday typing tasks.

Empirical phenomena. Salthouse (1986) enumerated 29 phenomena of transcription typing (see Figure 6.7), which involve primarily (a) the way in which text is perceived and comprehended while typing, (b) the manner in which the characters to be typed are held in memory, (c) the nature of response selection and execution, and (d) the characteristics of skill and expertise. Since Salthouse described typing, several other phenomena have been noted, three involving eye movements (Wu & Liu, 2008), resulting in a total of 34 phenomena that theories of typing (e.g., John, 1996; Wu & Liu, 2008) must attempt to take into account.

With regard to text perception and comprehension, typing is faster if the text is composed of words rather than random letters, but no additional speed is gained when the words are organized into meaningful text. As might be expected from the absence of additional gain for meaningful text over random words, comprehension of text, as measured by subsequent retention tests, is usually poor. Evidence that the text about to be typed is held in memory comes from studies that show reduction in speed of typing when looking ahead is limited by controlling the amount of text that can be previewed at a given moment.

Most of the errors that occur in typing fall into four categories. A *substitution error* occurs when an incorrect character is inserted in place of the correct character. Some substitution errors, such as striking the key adjacent to the one intended, can be attributed to errors in execution. However, most seem to be response-selection errors for which an incorrect response is selected, but then the selected response is executed "correctly." When a

Figure 6.7 The Salthouse 29 and a Venn diagram showing the processes and performance characteristics to which they relate. The numbers in the diagram correspond to the numbered regularities. Numbers 30–34 are from Wu and Liu (2008).

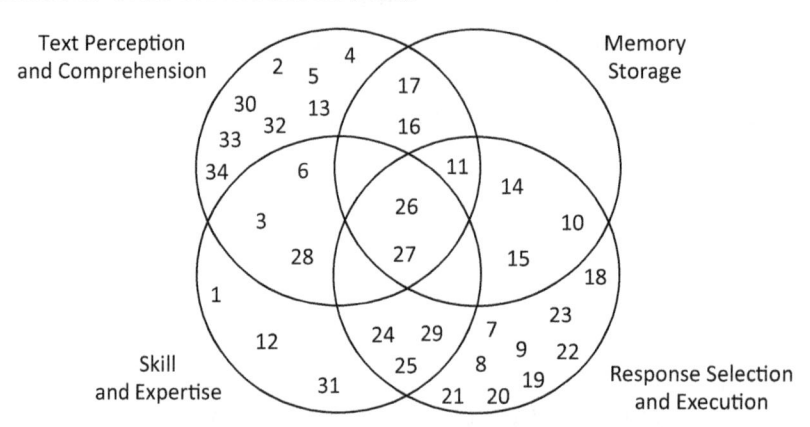

1. Faster than choice reaction time
2. Slower than reading
3. Skill/comprehension independence
4. Word-order independence
5. Slower with random letter order
6. Slower with restricted preview
7. Faster alternate-hand keystrokes
8. Faster frequent letter pairs
9. Word-length independence on interkey interval
10. Word initiation effect (first keystroke 20% slower)
11. Specific preceding letter context counts
12. Dual-task independence for highly skilled typists
13. Copy span size: 13.2 characters
14. Stopping span size 1-2 keystrokes
15. Eye-hand span size (moderate typists): 3-8 characters
16. Eye-hand span size less as meaning decreases
17. Replacement span size: ≈ 3 characters
18. 40-70% process detectable errors detected
19. Substitution errors mostly adjacent-key errors
20. Intrusion errors mostly short interkey intervals
21. Omission errors followed by long intervals
22. Transposition errors mostly cross-hand errors
23. 2-finger digraphs improve faster than 1-finger digraphs
24. Tapping faster with typing skill
25. Decrease of variability with skill
26. Increase of eye-hand span with skill
27. Increase of replacement span with skill
28. Moderate increase of copy span with skill
29. Increase of stopping span with typing speed
30. Detection span (the number of characters intervening between the one currently being typed and a unique character to be detected) is about 8
31. Learning curve follows power law of practice
32. Gaze duration per character decreases with enlarging of preview window size
33. Mean saccade size is about 4 characters
34. Fixation duration is around 400 ms

substitution error is made, it is more likely that the correct letter will be replaced with one of higher frequency than with one of lower frequency (Grudin, 1983). For example, substituting the more frequently occurring letter *D* for the less frequently occurring letter *K* occurs approximately twice as often as substituting *K* for *D*. An *intrusion error* is one in which an extra letter is typed. These errors seem to occur primarily in response execution as a consequence of imprecisely positioning the finger on the correct key to be typed so that the adjacent key is pressed as well.

Another error in response execution is the *omission error*, in which a character is left out. In many cases, the interval between the keystroke preceding the omission and that following it is roughly twice the normal interval for successive strokes, suggesting that the omission was due to insufficient force in typing the omitted letter. A *transposition error* involves reversing the order of two adjacent characters. Such errors primarily occur when the successive keystrokes involve fingers from different hands, which has led some researchers to suggest that transposition errors arise when advance preparation of a keypress inadvertently leads to it being executed out of sequence. The reason why this is more likely to occur across hands rather than for two fingers on the same hand is that it is easier to prepare the second of two finger movements in advance when it is not made by the same hand as the first of the movements.

Regularities in the performance of typists as they become skilled include greater speed, reduced variability, and more efficient procedures for preparing and holding items to be typed. Expert typists can type at speeds of up to 200 words per minute, and even average typists are fast enough that the intervals between successive keystrokes (mean = 177 ms in a study by Salthouse, 1984) are less than the reaction time in a two-choice-reaction task. Measured rates of repetitive tapping, using either the same finger or alternating between hands, are greater for skilled than unskilled typists, implying that at least part of experts' skill resides in motor processes.

In addition to looking at the speed of typing, we can look at the variability of the intervals between strokes. Interstroke variability refers to variations in intervals between different keystrokes and across different contexts, whereas intrastroke variability refers to variations in intervals across different instances of the same keystroke in the same context. Both types are negatively correlated with skill: as skill increases, variability decreases (Salthouse, 1984).

Another change that occurs with skill is in the efficiency with which letter digraphs typed with two different fingers on the same hand (e.g., *st*) or two fingers on different hands (e.g., *pr*) are executed. Response latencies for both of these types of digraphs show relatively greater improvement with increasing skill than do digraphs typed with the same finger on the same hand (e.g., *tr*). This finding indicates that skilled typists learn to overlap the execution of successive keystroke movements performed by different fingers. More generally, the faster tapping rates, decreases in variability, and differential speedup in typing digraphs indicate that a major part of skilled typing is the precise, highly coordinated control of the keypress movements. Additionally, the decreases in variability indicate improved synchronization of all of the component processes involved in transcription typing.

Because the speed at which keypress responses can be selected and executed improves as skill at typing is acquired, there is a need for the information on which these processes operate to be available at correspondingly increasing rates. The availability of information for response execution can be measured in part by the *eye-hand span*, which is the number of letters of forthcoming text that must be available to the typist if performance is to be optimal. The size of preview at which performance ceases to improve further is larger with increased skill. However, the maximum size of the eye-hand span is just seven characters, presumably because this is the maximum number that can be held in working memory at any one time. Other span measures also indicate that the skilled typist operates with larger chunks of information than does the less-skilled typist. The *replacement span* is how far in advance of the current keystroke the typist commits to a particular character (Salthouse & Saults, 1987). It is found by changing the test display to replace critical target letters at varying distances from the letter currently being typed and determining whether the target letter or its replacement is typed. Experts show a larger replacement span than nonexperts, indicating greater preparation for forthcoming keystrokes. As a result of this greater preparation, the *stopping span*, which is the number of keystrokes executed after a signal to stop, is also larger for expert typists.

A hierarchical control theory of typing. Some aspects of skilled typing are explicit and reportable, whereas others are not. This distinction is reflected in models of typing, which frequently assume that skilled typing is controlled hierarchically (e.g., John, 1996). One theory of this type that has received considerable empirical support is Logan and Crump's (2011) two-loop theory (see Figure 6.8). Their theory distinguishes two control loops, which they call the outer loop and the inner loop. The outer loop operates at the level of the words that are to be typed, and its contents are explicit and reportable (i.e., the typist is aware of the words he intends to type). In contrast, the inner loop comprises the keystrokes involved in typing those words, and its processes are implicit (i.e., the typist is not aware of exactly how the keystrokes are being executed). The theory does not account for how the skill of hierarchical typing control is acquired, in part because it is unclear how typing is built onto preexisting language skills (Logan & Crump, 2011).

Evidence to support the distinction between the two loops in skilled typing comes from analyzing response times. Logan (2003) had touch typists perform a variant of the Simon task (see Chapter 2) in which a four- or five-letter word, which was to be typed as quickly as possible, was presented to the left or right of fixation. For words typed entirely with fingers from a single hand, reaction time between word onset and the first keystroke showed a Simon effect (the initial keystroke was faster when the word's location corresponded with the hand used to type the letters than when it did not), but the intervals between the remaining keypresses did not. This result suggests that location correspondence operates at the outer-loop level, at which the word to be typed is determined, but not at the inner-loop level involved in the execution of the component letters. However, the Simon effect was larger for words typed entirely with a single hand than for words for which the first letter was typed with one hand and the remaining letters with the

Figure 6.8 (A) Depiction of Crump and Logan's two-loop theory of skilled typing, with (B) the contributions of each loop to reaction time (RT) and interkeystroke interval (IKSI) when typing a displayed word.

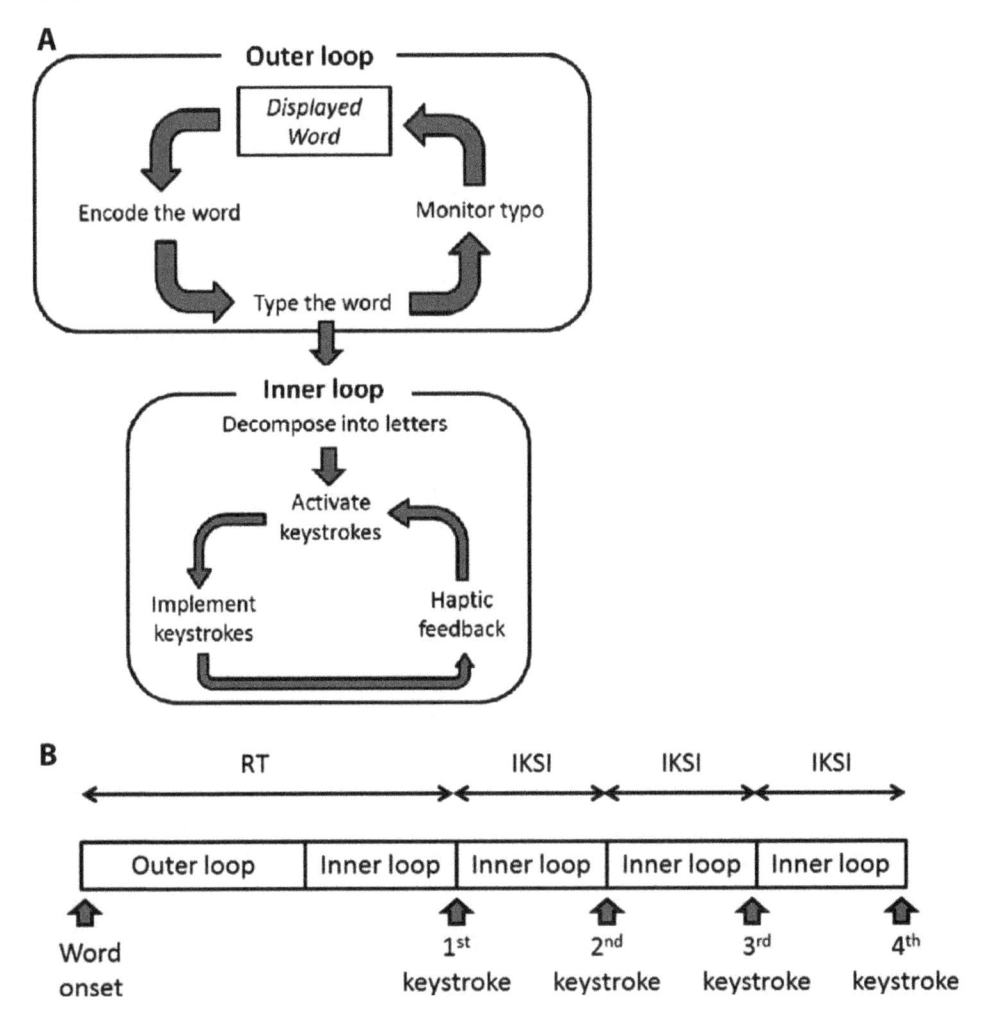

other, which implies that the locations of the respective letters were activated in parallel. These results were confirmed with the lateralized readiness potential (LRP), an indicator of selection of the right or left hand. The LRP was larger when all letters were to be typed with the same hand than when the hand for the first letter differed from that for the remaining letters (Logan, Miller, & Strayer, 2011).

Two other propositions of the theory are that the outer loop does not have access to how the inner loop executes keystrokes and that the types of feedback on which the respective loops rely are different. Support for the former proposition is conveyed by findings such as that typing is disrupted if one is instructed to type just the letters assigned to a single hand (Logan & Crump, 2009) and that typists show poor explicit knowledge of the locations of keys on the keyboard (Liu, Crump, & Logan, 2010). The activation by letters of their corresponding keypresses may be partly automatic for skilled typists (Rieger, 2004). But the psychological refractory period effect (see Chapter 3) for two vocal responses to a tone presented for the second of two tasks increases with increasing number of letters in the word when Task 1 is a typing task, which implies that selection at the level of individual letters is still a processing bottleneck (Yamaguchi, Logan, & Li, 2013).

With regard to feedback, the outer loop relies mainly on the appearance of characters on the computer's display screen while typing (Logan & Crump, 2010), whereas the inner loop relies more on tactual feedback from the keyboard. If the keyboard is modified to remove tactual feedback, performance decreases greatly (Crump & Logan, 2010), which should come as no surprise to anyone who has tried to type on a virtual keyboard on a tablet computer. Elimination of visual feedback also impairs performance, though. If the typed letters are not "echoed" on the display screen, reaction time to initiate typing of the word is increased; if the hands are not visible, the time between each keystroke increases (K. M. Snyder, Logan, & Yamaguchi, 2015). These results have been interpreted as due to application of strategies by the outer loop to the inner loop when visual feedback is absent to keep error rate low and allow the outer loop to monitor performance.

Other models of expert typing have been proposed (e.g., John, 1996; Rumelhart & Norman, 1982), some of which are successful in capturing the 32 phenomena listed in Figure 6.7 (e.g., Wu & Liu, 2008). Although none of the models gives a satisfactory account of how expert typists become highly skilled, they provide insights into the extreme ability of the information-processing system to coordinate and control behavior. Despite this ability, the performance of skilled typists still seems to be subject to many of the information-processing limitations that influence performance of less highly overlearned tasks.

Skilled Memory Theory

One of the most salient characteristics of experts is improved memory for information within the domain of expertise. Consequently, much effort has been devoted to determining the characteristics of skilled memory. As already noted from studies comparing experts to novices, the expert can encode domain-specific information more rapidly and efficiently than the novice, but does not show a more general ability to do so for information that is outside of the specific domain of expertise. Chase and Ericsson (1982) investigated the acquisition of efficient encoding and retrieval strategies and developed a descriptive theory of skilled memory. In their study, a participant, SF, practiced a digit span task for 2 years. The basic procedure involved listening to a sequence of digits spoken at a rate of 1 per second and then recalling the digits in the same order. If all digits were recalled correctly, the length of the next list was increased by a digit, and if they were not all recalled correctly, the length was decreased by a digit.

SF had a memory span of 7 digits for the lists presented during the first 4 hours of the experiment—a value that is typical of untrained individuals. SF's digit span remained under 10 digits throughout the first 4 days of practice but then increased on the fifth day to more than 10 digits. This increase could be attributed to the development by SF of a new mnemonic strategy. SF, who was a long-distance runner, used his knowledge of running times as a mnemonic aid. For example, he might encode the sequence 4003911 as 4 minutes, 39 and 11/100 seconds, and remember it as a good time for a mile. From the fifth day onward, he expanded this scheme of encoding digit groups in terms of running times and also added other categories, such as years and ages, for digit groups that could not be encoded as running times. His performance continued to improve across the 2 years of practice, reaching 82 digits by the end of the experiment.

Chase and Ericsson's (1982) investigation of memory span expertise identified three characteristics of skilled memory additional to those described earlier. First, they attributed the ability of SF to remember so many digits to the development of a rich system of retrieval cues that enabled rapid access to the stored information. Second, although the digit span task often is thought of as an indicator of working-memory capacity, Chase and Ericsson concluded that the superior performance of SF was possible because long-term memory was used as well. Several findings, such as the fact that requiring recitation of the alphabet between list presentation and recall (which should disrupt working memory) interfered with recall only of the last few digits, suggest that SF encoded a durable representation in long-term memory. Finally, after 2 years of training, memory span was still increasing for SF, leading Chase and Ericsson to conclude that the speed and efficiency of encoding continue to improve as the expert practices.

The Chase and Ericsson (1982) study examined memory skill for a task with no intrinsic meaning. That is, the material by itself provided no cues or context for remembering. Thus, the participant in that study had to bring additional knowledge to bear to structure the information. In contrast to the knowledge-lean material used by Chase and Ericsson, most material that must be remembered in real life has much more inherent meaning and structure. We might wonder if skilled memory for more structured material also requires an external mnemonic scheme.

Ericsson and Polson (1988) explored the generality of the skilled memory theory developed in the context of the digit span task by seeing whether the same characteristics held for someone with exceptional memory. The participant in their study was JC, a waiter who could remember up to 20 dinner orders without using pencil and paper. A method was devised to capture the elements of the task performed at work, while providing some experimental control. In this task, three, five, or eight pictures of people were laid out to depict customers at a table. After studying the pictures, JC requested the order of one person, which was read to him by an experimenter. When JC indicated that he was ready to hear the next order, the experimenter read the order for the next person in sequence clockwise. At any point in this progression, JC could ask to review the items in the current order or any of the preceding orders. Each order consisted of four items: a meat entree; a cooking temperature for the meat; a salad dressing; a starch. After all of the customer orders had been presented, JC was instructed to recall the items in any sequence.

The major results of the experiment were as follows. Rather than encoding each customer order as a unit, JC encoded the items from up to four orders in groups. JC's memory structure could be characterized as a matrix, with one dimension being the category of the menu item and the other being the customer order associated with the person who made it. He used several mnemonic strategies to associate and remember the items within groups of orders. For example, the temperatures of the meat were remembered pictorially, with the degree to which the meat was cooked coded as the ordinate of a graph and each order arranged on the abscissa. In contrast, salad dressings were remembered by coding only their first letters. Thus, the sequence thousand island, bleu cheese, thousand island, and oil and vinegar was coded as T-B-T-O.

Each time that a new order was presented, JC had to recall the previously encoded items and integrate them with the new items. Thus, he had to choose the category of item that he wished to encode and to rehearse the new item along with the previously encoded ones in that category before choosing the next category. The need to rehearse the items within a category simultaneously is most likely responsible for the grouping of the items into blocks of four. By encoding the orders in terms of the categories of the items, JC was able to use the category labels as a retrieval cue for the individual items.

Does JC's skill at remembering fit the framework of skilled memory theory? For the most part, it does. First, JC encoded the presented information efficiently and with the use of patterns. Existing semantic knowledge was brought to bear by JC in such ways as coding whether the starch selected was the starch usually served with a particular entree and encoding cooking temperatures in terms of an ordinal scale. JC encoded items within chunks of four to five items, presumably reflecting the limits of working memory. Second, JC encoded items with their category labels and used these labels for later retrieval. Third, JC used long-term memory to encode and retrieve the information, as indicated by the fact that he could recall many of the orders that he had taken at work earlier in the day. Fourth, the speed of encoding certainly was improved as a function of practice, even though JC was already highly practiced at remembering dinner orders.

To account for immediate recall of the memory experts exceeding the working-memory span, Ericsson and Kintsch (1995) proposed a mechanism that they called *long-term working memory*. Information in long-term working memory is stored in a form that is more stable than that in "short-term" working memory. Access to the information is maintained, though, by way of retrieval cues in short-term working memory.

Although Ericsson and Kintsch emphasized organizational knowledge, there is evidence that the expert's knowledge also benefits item-specific knowledge that makes individual items more distinct. Rawson and Van Overschelde (2008) tested students who were high or low in knowledge of American football, having them process lists of football words and cooking words from each of several categories (football: team names, penalties, positions, player names; cooking: entree names, spices, utensils, cooking techniques). Different groups of students sorted each word into the categories (intended to encourage organizational processing), rated each word for pleasantness (intended to promote item-specific processing), or both categorized and rated each word. On an unexpected free recall test, the football "experts" who both categorized and rated each word recalled the most football words, but showed no advantage for cooking words. People with low football knowledge showed no advantage of having categorized or rated the words. Other measures also indicated that those high in football knowledge benefited from item-specific processing as well as organizational processing on words within their domain of expertise. Thus, an expert's knowledge is advantageous to memory in multiple ways.

Summary

The nature of experts' knowledge and the ways in which this knowledge is acquired and brought to bear on specific problems within domains of expertise have been the subject of considerable research. Expertise typically is acquired through many years of intensive, deliberate practice in a particular domain, with 10 years typically given as the minimum time for expert levels of performance to be achieved. Accounts of expertise in terms of deliberate practice and experience have received more support and attention than accounts based on innate differences—to the extent that statements such as "experts are trained, not born" (W. Schneider, 1989, p. 10) are not uncommon. While deliberate practice seems to be necessary for expertise to develop, it does not seem to be sufficient.

The knowledge and strategies that an expert uses in performance of a task can be evaluated, and compared to those of novices using numerous direct and indirect techniques that have been developed for that purpose. Although some characteristics of expertise are specific to particular domains, many characteristics are found for experts in a range of domains. The expert develops (a) knowledge structures that enable her or him to encode information in large meaningful chunks, (b) strategies that enable efficient coordination of the various components of task performance, and (c) metacognitive abilities that allow evaluation of progress. Typically, procedures used by the expert are restricted to the particular domain of expertise and cannot be applied to other knowledge bases.

In addition to chess, three domains in which expertise has been investigated extensively are radiology, software design and programming, and typing. These three domains illustrate how an expert's knowledge and skills can influence information processing to yield superior performance. Across domains, the memory benefits that arise from knowledge make events more distinctive.

7

Why Errors Occur and Their Contributions to Learning

Learning from mistakes is easier said than done.

A. C. Edmondson (2004, p. 66)

Many people view errors, or mistakes, as events that should never have happened. An initial reaction to an error may be to cover one's tracks in order to hide the fact that one was made. Denial is another frequent reaction. For example, if you hear the honking of an angry motorist, your first reaction might be, "It wasn't me!" Further reflection may lead you to question whether you really had, for example, signaled before turning, and considering whether you had made this error might make you more conscious of signaling in the future. In other words, errors can provide valuable feedback about one's performance or skill level, providing a basis for learning to occur. The view that "we learn from our mistakes" can be contrasted with the view that mistakes detract from learning and that training environments should be designed to prevent errors from occurring. In this chapter we explore why errors occur and how they contribute to learning.

Errors and Action Control

In the human factors/ergonomics literature, a distinction is often made between two types of errors, *mistakes* and *slips of action*. Mistakes are considered to result from errors of deliberation (i.e., actions that are taken deliberately, but that are based on an incorrect assessment of the situation) and slips of action to result from so-called automatic behavior or the failure to maintain action goals (Reason, 2013). In contrast to mistakes, slips are more likely to arise when some aspects of performance are automatized. Take the example of intending to do one thing but doing something else instead, such as opening a new package of tea with the intention of filling the empty tea canister, but instead pouring the package of tea leaves into the waiting teapot. This is a case in which the correct action was performed (that of pouring), but the object of the action (the teapot) was the inappropriate one. Reason (1979) argued that such errors arise when well-learned behaviors are performed more or less automatically, without conscious mediation or monitoring. In other words, slips of action occur because of the way skilled action is organized and automated.

Reason's ideas about slips of action are based on the notion that many behaviors can be performed in an open-loop manner—that is, without feedback—just by "running" the appropriate motor program (see Chapter 3). Because open-loop performance by definition is performance without feedback or conscious monitoring, a motor program can "hijack" behavior when action goals are not consciously maintained. Slips of action are thus most likely to occur during the automatic execution of highly practiced, routine actions or during lapses of attention. Action slips can, in fact, be described as failures of attention, with slips occurring either because the wrong action plan is maintained or because attention is switched to the wrong elements of a plan or aspects of the environment. The failures of attention that result in slips may have everyday causes, such as sleepiness or distraction, but more long-term disruptive thoughts, such as those following a natural disaster such as an earthquake, have also been shown to be associated with slips (Helton, Head, & Kemp, 2011).

Slips occur often, as most of us can attest to. In one study (Reason, 1979), 35 people were found to commit over 400 unintended acts in just 2 weeks. These acts can be characterized by the type of information-processing error made. For instance, putting the lid to the jam pot on the sugar canister can be classified as a failure of discrimination, whereas unwrapping a candy bar and then throwing the candy in the wastebasket while keeping the wrapper is an example transposing two elements of an action sequence. Many errors seem to be due to a failure to test or monitor the progress of an action, such as in the famous example reported by William James (1890/1950) of going into the bedroom to change for dinner and, instead, putting on pajamas and going to bed. This so-called capture error illustrates the interaction between control and motor programs. James's action was "captured" by the context of the bedroom, and the presumably dominant program of getting ready for bed was activated. Going back to the tea problem, it seems that the recently deactivated, but generally more common, plan for filling the teapot superseded the newer, less common plan of filling the tea canister.

Initiating and Maintaining Action Plans
The occurrence of action slips may reveal something about how intentions are represented and acted upon. Whereas Reason (1979) explained slips in terms of failures to control motor programs, D. A. Norman (1981) suggested that they can be explained in terms of schemas that embody the procedural knowledge needed for carrying out an act. Recall from Chapter 3 that schemas are generalized procedures for carrying out actions that embody both motor programs and rules for selecting between specific versions of motor programs. According to Norman, any complicated act requires a number of schemas, arranged in a particular control structure. Correct performance requires that the right schemas be activated at the right time and with the right information. This view of action control as moving from control based on intention to schema triggering as a function of skill is consistent with theories of skill acquisition that hypothesize a reduced role of attention with increasing skill. Performance becomes automatic in that well-learned schemas are ready to be executed whenever the appropriate set of conditions enables their selection. The idea that attention is not involved in much skilled performance is also supported by the fact that deliberate control of skilled performance can lead to deterioration of that performance (see Chapter 4; Beilock, Carr, MacMahon, & Starkes, 2002), and is in agreement with Neumann's (1987) view of automaticity, according to which processing is automatic when all aspects or parameters of an action are specified in long-term memory or are directly available in the environment. Only when there is insufficient information to perform an action are attentional mechanisms needed for parameter specification. It is the application of attention that gives rise to conscious awareness of action and that can cause interference with other actions.

According to D. A. Norman (1981, p. 3), "For a slip to be started, yet caught, means that there must exist some monitoring mechanism of behavior—a mechanism that is separate from that responsible for the selection and execution of the act." D. A. Norman and Shallice (1986) suggested that the basic mechanism of action control is *contention scheduling*—a more or less passive process that emerges naturally as a result of the way schemas are learned and performed. The contention-scheduling system directly activates and orders action schemas that are linked to each other via inhibitory or excitatory connections. A schema is triggered for execution when environmental conditions match the triggering conditions incorporated in the schema. Action slips such as capture errors occur when intentions are not actively maintained and schemas become activated simply because their triggering conditions are present in the environment. Table 7.1 gives an overview of the other types of action slips that can occur when schemas are erroneously activated or triggered.

Schemas are triggered whenever their activation exceeds a threshold, whether this activation comes from contention scheduling, the activation of other schemas, or environmental conditions (see Figure 7.1). Whenever a less familiar version of an action sequence must be performed in place of a more familiar one, or when no schema exists for performing an action, top-down mechanisms are needed for schema activation and action control. In Norman and Shallice's model, top-down control of action is performed by the *supervisory attention system* (SAS). The SAS is presumed to directly activate

TABLE 7.1 Classification of Action Slips Due to Erroneous Activation or Triggering of Schemas

Slips that arise from faulty activation of schemas
Unintentional activation (activation of schemas not part of a current action plan)
• *Capture errors*: Capture of control by a better learned but currently inappropriate schema
• *Data-driven activation*: Schemas inappropriately triggered by outside events
• *Associative activation*: Activation by another, currently active schema
Loss of activation
• Forgetting an intention (but continuing to perform the action)
• Misordering the components of an action sequence
• Skipping steps in an action sequence
• Repeating steps in an action sequence
Slips due to faulty triggering of schemas
False triggering: Correct schema triggered at inappropriate time
• Spoonerisms: Reversal of event components
• Blends: Combinations of components from two competing schemas
• Thoughts leading to actions: Triggering of schemas meant only to be thought, not executed
• Premature triggering
Failure to trigger: When an active schema never gets invoked because
• Action is preempted by competing schemas
• There is insufficient activation as a result of forgetting or initial activation is too low
• Trigger condition does not match due to insufficient or faulty specification

Figure 7.1 A schematic view of action scheduling as proposed by D. A. Norman and Shallice (1986).

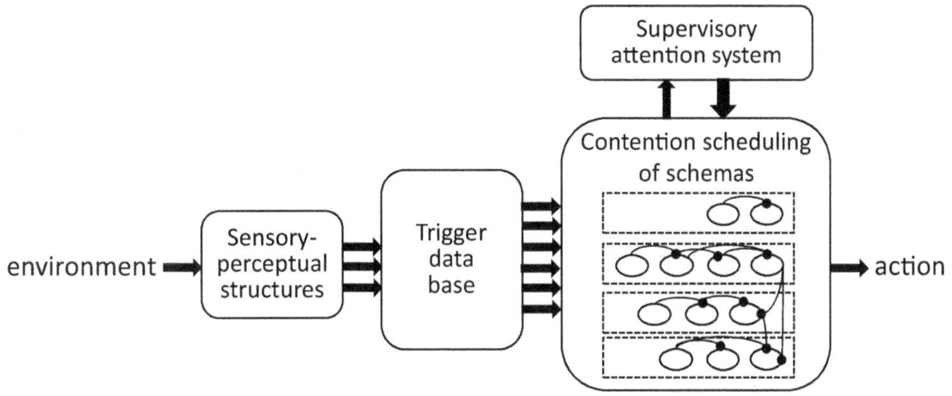

or inhibit schemas, but not to select them: Control always proceeds through the process of contention scheduling, with the SAS biasing selection by inhibiting some schemas and activating others. The control exercised by the SAS can be viewed as "attention." When attentional activation by the SAS is withdrawn, the activation value of the schema will decrease to the value determined by the other sorts of activational input. Absent-mindedness, such as forgetting why you entered a room or what you are looking for, results from a failure to keep the SAS engaged in the face of competing schemas. The SAS is also needed to resist habitual or tempting actions, as when intending to nurse a beer while waiting for a friend or to overcome reluctance to perform an action or to overcome a bad habit. In the first case, lapses of attention might lead to the beer being drunk "before you know it"; in the second, continued application of attention can eventually result in the learning of new schemas for actions that initially were difficult to perform.

One way to prevent slips from occurring is to redesign the human-machine interface. For example, most automatic teller machines in the United States were originally designed to first give the cash asked for in a cash transaction, and only then to return the bank card of the user. Since the goal of the transaction is to "get money," many people fail to retrieve the card because the goal of the transaction is no longer active. To discourage this *post-completion error*, it has been argued that the machines should be redesigned so that the card has to be removed before the cash is dispensed (Sun, 2007). When redesign is not feasible, training aimed at increasing the relevance of the error-prone action to the main task goal may reduce errors. In the area of human-computer action, a common slip is the "device initialization error." Such an error is said to have occurred when a skilled user of a device forgets to perform some initialization action, such as positioning the cursor in a text entry box before typing in a password, or failing to press the "insert" key on the computer keyboard when moving between overwriting old text and inserting new text. These errors are not the result of not knowing how to perform the action. In fact, they generally occur while well-learned procedures are being executed, and appear to occur because computer users are focused on subsequent data entry steps—which are, after all, the goal of the action—when they should first attend to initialization. Hiltz, Back, and Blandford (2010) showed that modifying training to connect execution of a step that is commonly omitted to the task goal can significantly reduce error rates for that step.

Effects of Making Errors on Learning

As will be discussed in a later section of this chapter, error seems to play a very important role in classical and instrumental conditioning. The question of whether errors are beneficial to more complicated forms of learning has been a matter of some debate. Whereas some researchers focus on the advantages of learning by exploration, in which learners are given the freedom to explore the task environment and to make mistakes, others suggest that error-free learning environments may lead to more efficient learning. Another issue is that whereas errors may call one's attention to opportunities for learning, attention is also required for processing error information. Errors can thus lead to a slowing in performance as time is taken to figure out what went wrong or to make an effort to consciously recall task requirements, and the surprise associated with the occurrence of an error may interrupt the processing of features of the task that are necessary for the recovery or continuation of the task. For example, having to read a feedback display could distract an operator from monitoring displays that are necessary to maintain situation awareness in a dynamic environment. On the one hand, thus, learning in an environment where mistakes can be made allows learners to test hypotheses and to learn to cope with mistakes. On the other hand, recovering from mistakes takes time, and mistakes, once made, may be learned and repeated.

In Chapter 5 we discussed research demonstrating that the "learning by discovery" in which people tend to engage can be relatively inefficient because many of the options that are tried out are inappropriate and result in time being devoted to correcting mistakes rather than to learning basic functions. For example, J. M. Carroll and Carrithers (1984) found that novice users of a word processor made many mistakes in trying to learn to perform simple tasks, and that most of the mistakes were the result of attempting to carry out unneeded, more advanced commands. In contrast, learners who used a "training wheels" word processor interface created by disabling unneeded menu choices, commands, and function keys in order to block errors learned to complete simple tasks more quickly than those using the unmodified word processor—and performed better on a comprehension posttest. The major advantage of the simplified interface seemed to be that users spent more time performing criterion tasks and less time recovering from errors.

Whether people benefit from the opportunity to discover relations on their own may depend on the complexity of the task environment. Studies that have shown a benefit for allowing people to make errors have tended to use fairly constrained tasks, such as copying a specific PowerPoint slide after receiving instruction on component actions (e.g., Keith & Frese, 2005). Keith and Frese suggest that the benefit of allowing errors during training can be attributed to the metacognitive processing and conscious control of emotions that accompany a strategy of learning from errors (see also Chapter 10). Likewise, people who learned definitions of unfamiliar English words or translations into another language under conditions that required generating responses before receiving feedback (which led to many errors), versus reading the words and their definitions/translations, or choosing answers from provided alternatives and receiving feedback (which resulted in fewer errors), performed better on a later memory test (Potts & Shanks, 2014). Not surprisingly, self-reports of learning showed little awareness that the condition with many errors resulted in the best learning, most likely because of the additional difficulty it imposed on learners during the acquisition phase of the task.

Learning from Errors

In some theories of learning, errors are the critical events that trigger learning episodes, or "salient, unexpected events that can motivate further learning" (Ivancic & Hesketh, 2000, p. 1967). A detected error gives the performer feedback that performance was less than optimal and should trigger a search for the conditions that led to the mistake. But once errors are made, how do we keep from making them again? And what are the cognitive mechanisms that enable people to detect and correct their own errors while learning?

Failed expectations may trigger a process by which explanation patterns are adapted to unexpected situations (a process that has been referred to as "tweaking"; Schank, 1986). In the realm of complex, cognitive skills, learning from errors can be described as constraining overly general knowledge structures (Ohlsson, 1996). Domain-specific declarative knowledge allows the detection of errors as learners detect a conflict between what they believe ought to be true and what they perceive to be the case. Errors are detected when the result achieved by performing an action does not match up with the learner's expectations; they are recognized via particular features or patterns of features that indicate incorrect actions in the particular task environment. It may seem paradoxical that learners are presumed to detect errors with the help of prior, domain-specific knowledge. We can ask why the particular action leading to the error was performed if the learner has enough knowledge to recognize the action as incorrect. Ohlsson describes the dissociation between task execution (action) and outcome monitoring (evaluation) in terms of declarative and procedural knowledge (see Chapter 1). Whereas procedural knowledge is assumed to generate and organize action, declarative knowledge supports explanation, inference, and prediction. In Ohlsson's production-system model of learning from performance errors, declarative knowledge has a prescriptive rather than descriptive function. Being prescriptive, it can be compared with task outcomes to judge their success. Action and judgment are thus presumed to rely on two distinct knowledge bases: the declarative knowledge required to judge performance and the practical (procedural) knowledge required to perform. Because action and judgment draw on separate knowledge bases, learners often perform actions that they themselves recognize as erroneous as soon as the outcomes become evident.

Errors signal faults in underlying practical knowledge and a need to specialize that knowledge. According to Ohlsson's (1996) theory of learning from errors, errors result when a general rule is applied to an exception. Thus, the acquisition of correct knowledge in itself does not suffice to correct an error. It is necessary to specialize the rules in question by incorporating into them more information about the task environment. As in ACT-R (J. R. Anderson et al., 2004; see Chapter 1), learning results in increasingly specialized conditions and, as a consequence, the rule will be activated in fewer and fewer situations. Errors are corrected by specializing faulty knowledge structures so that they become active only in situations in which they are appropriate. Correcting errors thus implies improving future action by removing faults (incomplete specifications) in the underlying practical knowledge. If people are to learn from their errors by revising rules, they must carry out the processes of blame assignment and error attribution (see Figure 7.2). Blame assignment involves identifying the incorrect action and hence the faulty rule. Error attribution involves identifying the features of the situation that interacted with the action to produce the undesirable outcome. A learning episode thus consists of the cycle of blame assignment, error attribution, and rule revision or, in other words, in identifying the point where things went wrong, and identifying some feature that can be used to modify the description of the situation so that the incorrect action will not be repeated.

Figure 7.2 The functional breakdown of learning from errors according to Ohlsson's (1996) model of learning from performance errors.

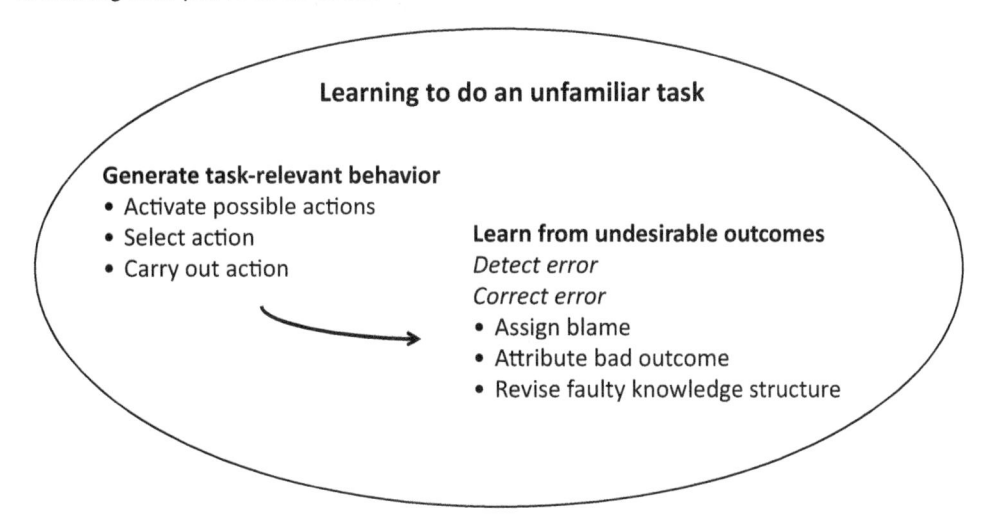

Learning to do an unfamiliar task

Generate task-relevant behavior
- Activate possible actions
- Select action
- Carry out action

Learn from undesirable outcomes
Detect error
Correct error
- Assign blame
- Attribute bad outcome
- Revise faulty knowledge structure

Learning from Post-Event Reviews

Detecting potential failures and adapting to new conditions that necessitate revision of old and successful routines, or integration of old and new routines, require that learners understand when and why these routines work and under what conditions they do not. In many situations, individuals or teams must be able to respond flexibly to new situations, revising their understanding of situations and their response strategies when new events are detected (Weick, Sutcliffe, & Obstfeld, 1999). Learning from experience depends on comparing actual to desired outcomes, and on identifying factors that narrow the difference. Failures are in many cases more salient than successes and may be better motivators for drawing lessons from experience. Errors are particularly useful for highlighting areas of misunderstanding or suboptimal performance and act as triggers to reflect on one's understanding of the domain. In the area of problem solving, specific aspects of mental models may be refuted by errors, triggering a search for new boundary conditions (e.g., Ohlsson, 1996).

Debriefing, or after-event review, has been shown to improve team performance by encouraging team members to reflect on successes and failures. Debriefing is best described as a systematic process by which observations and interpretations of team processes and performance are shared (Vashdi, Bamberger, Erez, & Weiss-Meilik, 2007). In a debriefing session, an operation or mission, such as an Air Force sortie or a surgical operation, is analyzed with respect to task requirements and objectives. Assumptions or processes that may have limited effectiveness are discussed, and means of applying the lessons learned to future operations are determined. The debriefing often is led by a facilitator, who is trained to conduct effective debriefings, but team-led debriefings without a facilitator can also be effective, as long as there is some structure to them (Eddy, Tannenbaum, & Mathieu, 2013).

Debriefing is a standard procedure in many military operations (e.g., S. Ellis & Davidi, 2005), and is becoming more common in surgical teams (Bethune, Sasirekha, Sahu, Cawthorn, & Pullyblank, 2011). Debriefings have been shown to highlight potential problems, improve team culture, and lead to organizational change. Engaging in debriefing can enhance team learning by facilitating the acquisition of and reflection upon the feedback generated by actions. Debriefing can encourage reflexivity, by which teams work to identify problems and resolve them in order to improve performance. Reflexive teams are assumed to think proactively, challenging the appropriateness of team and organizational objectives and the assumptions that underlie them (Vashdi et al., 2007).

In many settings, such as in some hospitals, debriefings take place only after negative outcomes—despite recommendations to conduct debriefings after each surgery, mission, or other complex team performance (e.g., Neily et al., 2010). Much can be learned from after-event review of successful as well as unsuccessful performance (S. Ellis & Davidi, 2005; S. Ellis, Mendel, & Nir, 2006). After a successful event, the most effective review is one that focuses on the identification of incorrect actions. In this case, individuals or teams learn to identify whether successful performance is a result of their own ability or effort, or whether luck played a role. In terms of training, learning from successes is necessary whenever the cost of errors is unacceptably high. S. Ellis and Davidi proposed that the logic of the after-event review is that learners who want to improve their performance after successful performance will need to focus on the "internal logic of their plans (prior mental models) and on the potential misfits between the existing mental model and the conditions under which performance was executed" (S. Ellis & Davidi, 2005, p. 859).

The after-event review, as described by S. Ellis and Davidi, is a debriefing procedure that is meant to optimize learning by encouraging cognitive elaboration of experiential data through processes of self-explanation, data verification, and feedback. Self-explanation is construed as an active process of gathering, analyzing, and integrating data about how behaviors were carried out. Generating explanations for actions should facilitate the construction of "if-then" rules that improve subsequent performance and encourage the integration of newly learned material with existing knowledge (Chi et al., 1994). The process of data verification is intended to help decision makers evaluate past actions and outcomes in such a way that biases in decision making, such as the confirmation bias (bias toward seeking information that is consistent with hypothesis) and hindsight bias (bias toward overestimating the likelihood of events after they have occurred), are overcome. In the after-event review, decision makers are confronted with other people's perceptions of the events under review and the critical decisions leading up to them. Confrontation with other points of views should help individuals process information that is inconsistent with a priori hypotheses (thus overcoming the confirmation bias) and cause them to evaluate past decisions in the light of the context in which they were made—rather than in the context of whether the desired outcome was achieved—thus encouraging objective evaluation of decision quality rather than associating positive outcomes with good decisions. Feedback given in after-event reviews focuses on both product and process to help participants modify or restructure in memory domain knowledge or tactics or to improve metacognitive knowledge. The focus of the review is not so much on the provision of feedback as on the process of searching for that feedback through what S. Ellis and Davidi refer to as "guided self-explanation."

After-event reviews of successful missions have been shown to be effective in the laboratory (R. Ellis et al., 2006) and in the context of learning military ground navigation skills (S. Ellis & Davidi, 2005). Because the Israeli military requires after-event review of failures, S. Ellis and Davidi compared a condition in which only failures were reviewed with a condition in which both failures and successes were reviewed. Soldiers were debriefed after a "mission" in which several points along a route had to be found. In the success-and-failure condition, soldiers were first asked to identify the positive and negative aspects of the mission and then were asked to recount decisions that led to either successful performance or failure. Lastly, they were asked to indicate aspects of the navigation exercise that should be altered or retained. In the failures-only condition, only negative aspects of the mission were discussed, and only points needing improvement were noted. The effects of the debriefing were evaluated by converting the statements made during debriefing into *cognitive cause maps* (Weick & Bougon, 1986). These maps, which are intended to reflect learners' mental models of successes or failures, consist of nodes representing constructs, and arrows between nodes representing subjects' beliefs about causal relationships between particular groups of constructs. For example, a soldier's statement that he selected the wrong route because he did not have enough time to study the day before relates the construct "study" with the construct "performance" via the belief that study time improves performance. The number of constructs and beliefs in the cognitive cause maps was greater for the successes-and-failures group than for the failures-only group (see Figure 7.3),

Figure 7.3 Cognitive cause maps for a failed mission from (a) a group who reflected only on factors leading to failure and (b) a group who considered both factors leading to success and failure (b).

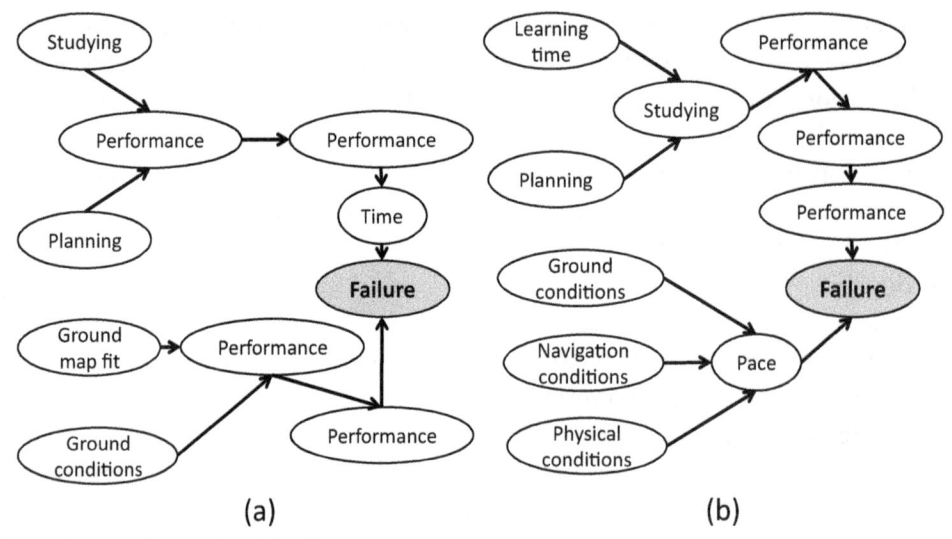

(a)

(b)

Adapted from S. Ellis and Davidi (2005).

suggesting that the former group did indeed form a richer mental model of the task. Moreover, the complexity of the maps of the successes-and-failures group increased across training trials, whereas that of the failures-only group showed little change. For both groups, the maps of failed events were more complex than the maps of successful events, suggesting that including failure situations in training may lead to more complex task representations.

Performance Monitoring

To benefit from a mistake, we must realize that we have made one. Detecting mistakes thus requires the ability to monitor the progress or results of actions. In the previous section we discussed how learning complex tasks depends on being able to determine why a mistake was made and how the mistake can be avoided in the future. Such learning depends on recognizing situations that led to mistakes and remembering how mistakes can be avoided and thus can be assumed to depend heavily on processes of memory. Memory resources are required to detect mistakes, to review the events that may have led to them, to retrieve appropriate actions, and to reject any inappropriate actions that may be automatically retrieved in a given situation.

Most tasks are forgiving in the sense that small lapses do not result in serious consequences. However, if performance is to improve or even remain at an acceptable level, it can be necessary to monitor performance for even small lapses that might lower the optimality of performance. The challenge in these cases is to find the best way of directing a performer's attention to his or her mistakes so that smooth, integrated performance develops. An important finding in perceptual-motor learning is that it is not necessary—and may indeed be harmful—to give a performer feedback on every trial of a task (see Chapter 3). In fact, decreasing the percentage of trials on which knowledge of results is provided across a training period can lead to better learning.

Skilled performance is generally described as being relatively fast and error-free, but under some circumstances, more skilled performers may actually be more error-prone than less-skilled performers. The very speed and automaticity of behavior might result in a failure to notice mistakes. For example, B. G. Bell, Gardner, and Woltz (1997) found that more successful trainees (as measured by response time) made more undetected errors in a transfer session when a cognitive task was learned under speed emphasis and the transfer session emphasized accuracy. Fluency in a task may bring with it an increased chance of making undetected errors.

This finding conflicts to some extent with Rabbitt and Browes's (see Rabbitt, 1990) finding that performers can detect risky performance in perceptual-motor tasks—that is, people can not only detect their errors but also detect when they run a high risk of making an error by responding too quickly. It may be that an emphasis on speed during training leads to greater acceptance of risky behavior and a reduced tendency to monitor errors. This finding could have important implications for the design of training programs. For example, some driving schools now use driving simulators for training. Because the consequences of a mistake in a simulator are obviously less serious than the consequences of a mistake on the road, care will need to be taken to design driving scenarios that encourage learners to adopt the correct strategy.

Responses are generally slower after an error trial than after a correct one. This *post-error slowing* is a common finding in many choice-reaction tasks and is most often interpreted in terms of a change in the threshold for making a response or in terms of post-error processing. Evidence for an electrophysiological correlate of performance monitoring was first found in two independent studies (Falkenstein, Hohnsbein, & Hoormann, 1991; Gehring, Coles, Meyer, & Donchin, 1990) in which EEG was measured while people made speeded responses in so-called *conflict tasks* in which it was necessary to overcome habitual response tendencies in order to make a correct response. The negative electrical potential that peaks 50–100 ms after an error has been made was named the *error-related negativity* (ERN; Gehring et al., 1990; see Figure 7.4) by one of the groups who discovered it, and the *error negativity* (Ne; Falkenstein et al., 1991) by the other.

Figure 7.4 EEG components (CRN and ERN) related to performance monitoring.

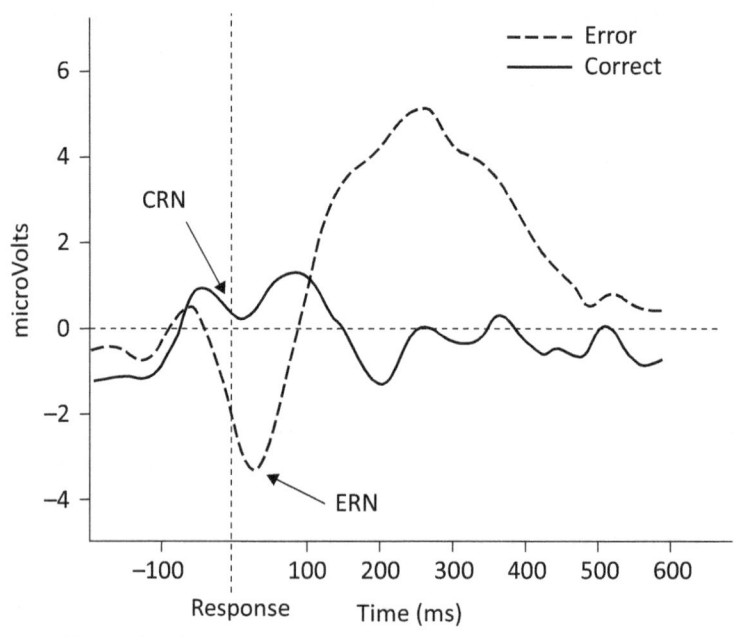

From A. Johnson and Proctor (2013).

Initially, the ERN was described as a "mismatch signal" that occurs when representations of the actual response and the required response are not the same (Gehring, Goss, Coles, & Meyer, 1993). Findings of negativity similar to the ERN after correct responses, however, suggest that the ERN may reflect the comparison of the actual and required responses rather than the outcome of this comparison process (Falkenstein, Hohnsbein, & Hoormann, 1996; Vidal, Hasbroucq, Grapperon, & Bonnet, 2000). This ERN-like, correct-related negativity (CRN; see Figure 7.4) is smaller than the ERN and more pronounced on high-conflict correct trials, on which a small amount of electromyographic activity is observed in the muscles that would be used to make the incorrect response (Vidal et al., 2000). Such "partial" errors are characterized by longer RTs than those for correct trials and are marked with negative waves of similar latency and scalp topography as the full-error trials on which the incorrect response is actually made. Independent component analysis, a technique that allows the separation of brain sources contributing to scalp-recorded EEG, has suggested that the ERN and CRN share a common generator in the brain, in the anterior cingulate cortex (ACC; Gentsch, Ullsperger, & Ullsperger, 2009; Roger, Bénar, Vidal, Hasbroucq, & Burle, 2010). Findings of negativity similar to the ERN after a correct response suggest that both signals reflect the activity of a single action-monitoring system that is activated by conflict trials, whether the response is incorrect or correct.

Error detection also may allow the performer to execute processes that correct the error (Crump & Logan, 2013). For example, upon getting visual feedback that an incorrect key was pressed, a typist may correct the error before proceeding. Crump and Logan found that when correction was allowed, skilled typists typically made the correction and then proceeded to type at their normal speed. Only when the option of correcting the error was unavailable did they slow their typing following an error. These results suggest that, at least for typists, inhibition of a tendency to correct the erroneous response may be the source of the post-error slowing.

The first "proof of concept" applications have been developed to show the potential of performance monitoring based on error- or feedback-related processing (A. Johnson & Proctor, 2013). As the brain systems underlying the lapses in control that result in error become better understood it will be increasingly important to study individual differences in conflict monitoring and feedback processing and to determine the best possible interventions for overcoming the lapses that lead to error.

Prediction Error and Learning

Errors act as warning signals to engage conscious control in order to keep us on task, and adaptive behavior, in general, depends on the ability to learn from feedback and to use this learning to predict future events. For example, any major purchase may be followed by pleasure or by buyer's remorse. Decision-making behavior, such as choosing which new television to purchase, will be influenced by predictions of the pleasure (e.g., the excitement of owning a home theater) or regret (e.g., possible dissatisfaction with the sound quality of the speakers) that the purchase will bring, and future decision making will likely be influenced by the actual outcome. In fact, ideomotor theories of learning and performance consider anticipation of consequences to be fundamental to action selection and learning (Hommel, 2013; Shin, Proctor, & Capaldi, 2010). According to ideomotor theories, the perceptual consequences of actions—including emotional reactions—become associated with those actions. Subsequently, anticipation of the consequences (e.g., anticipation of the pleasure to be gained or the feeling associated with the movement itself) will come to control selection, initiation, and possibly execution of action (Eder, Rothermund, De Houwer, & Hommel, 2015). More generally, adaptive behavior is based on determining those cues that will lead to positive events or are predictive of painful or aversive events. Being able to predict impending harm is critical for survival, be that potential source of harm a burner on the stove-top or unattended luggage at a train station.

Prediction error, often referred to as *surprise*, is a driving force for learning because it signals when it is necessary to update predictions (Schultz, Dayan, & Montague, 1997; Shanks, 1995). Prediction has been studied extensively in conditioning experiments using animals and humans (Garrison, Erdeniz, & Done, 2013), where, according to some theories, the difference between expectations and outcomes drives learning. The two major aspects of most accounts of prediction learning are thus the predictions themselves (the "values") and the error in those predictions. For example, in the Rescorla-Wagner model of learning (Rescorla & Wagner, 1972) the prediction-error signal is the discrepancy between an outcome and its prediction, and this signal proportionally increases (or decreases) the subsequent prediction generated by a conditioned stimulus (CS). The prediction-error signal thus drives learning by specifying how the predictions should change. The basic principle of the model is that the size of the trial-specific prediction error—that is, the degree of surprise incurred by an event—determines the change in strength of the relationship between two stimuli or between a stimulus and response.

There is still debate about the nature of the neural systems underlying learning to associate cues with positive and negative events (i.e., the neural mechanisms underlying appetitive and aversive conditioning). However, a growing body of research suggests that both systems are sensitive to prediction error, and that learning involves shifting the analysis of prediction error from the onset of the outcome to the onset of the CS (Sutton & Barto, 1990). According to this *temporal difference* approach, learning can be described as a function of the prediction error, which is computed as the difference between the actual outcome and the difference in values that are predicted on successive trials.

The temporal difference model has been shown to provide a good fit to a range of conditioning data and has been used as the basis for determining the neural underpinnings of conditioning. For example, in a study in which dopaminergic cells were measured while training a monkey to associate a stimulus with the reward of juice, Schultz (1998) found that the firing rate of the cells increased when the juice was given early in training. As predicted by the temporal difference model, as training progressed, this increase in firing rate occurred progressively earlier, until it occurred upon presentation of the earliest reliable stimulus for the reward. Moreover, once the animal was fully trained, the cells no longer showed an increase in firing rate for the juice itself.

When there is uncertainty about the correct response in a particular situation—such as in probabilistic-learning tasks in which trial-and-error responses are made to learn which choices are associated with the highest reward—the correctness of an action cannot be judged by the person performing the task and external feedback is necessary to evaluate response outcomes. In such cases, a negative electrical potential called the feedback-related negativity (FRN; see Figure 7.5) occurs approximately 200–350 ms after the feedback is presented (Miltner, Braun, & Coles, 1997; see, for a review, Nieuwenhuis, Holroyd, Mol, & Coles, 2004). Evidence consistent with the idea that the FRN is a neural signal related to learning includes that negative performance feedback (e.g., monetary loss) elicits an FRN of greater amplitude than does positive feedback (e.g., monetary gain), and as learning progresses and expectations regarding task-reward contingencies associated with particular choices begin to develop, FRN amplitude after expected outcomes decreases relative to when the outcome is unexpected (Holroyd, Larsen, & Cohen, 2004).

In most conditioning studies, the learned associations have been relevant for behavior either because they were linked to rewards or punishment (e.g., O'Doherty et al., 2003; Seymour et al., 2004) or because learners received feedback on their performance (e.g., Fletcher et al., 2001; Turner et al., 2004). Much of the learning that occurs in everyday life, however, occurs without intention or conscious recognition of outcomes (see Chapters 4 and 6). Like explicit associative learning, such incidental learning of stimulus-stimulus associations has been linked to trial-by-trial activity

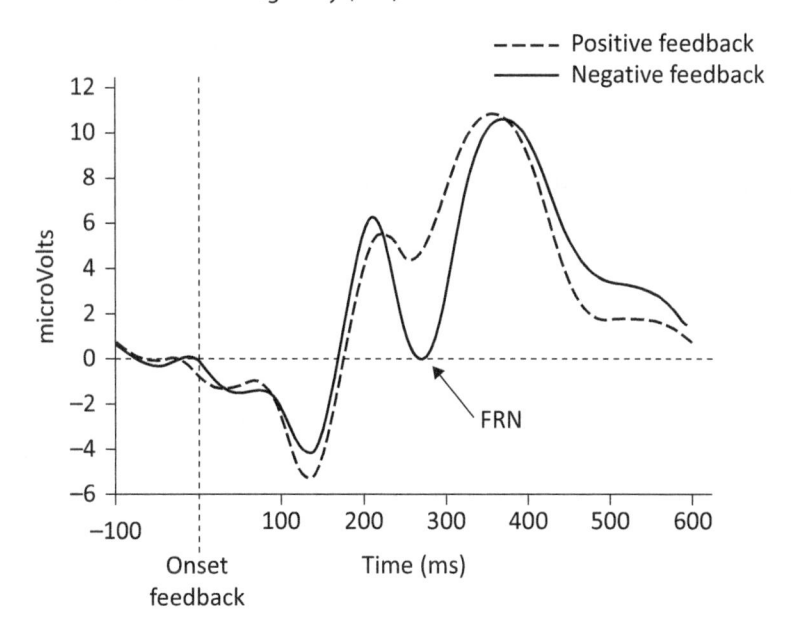

Figure 7.5 The feedback-related negativity (FRN).

that reflects prediction errors. Den Ouden, Friston, Daw, McIntosh, and Stephan (2009) used a design in which a target-detection task was performed while two visual or auditory stimuli unrelated to the target-detection task were presented. The relation between the two stimuli was manipulated so that learning of associations that are irrelevant for current behavioral goals could be studied. When one CS (e.g., a visual stimulus) could be predicted from the other (e.g., an auditory stimulus), learning-related changes in BOLD (blood oxygen level–dependent) responses in the primary visual cortex and putamen occurred that were consistent with estimates of prediction error obtained from the Rescorla-Wagner model. Learning occurred even though there was no need to process either CS. In keeping with a prediction-error account, according to which surprising events signal the need for learning in order to update predictions (e.g., Schultz & Dickinson, 2000; Shanks, 1995), the brain should concentrate resources on representing surprising sensory events. Brain regions encoding prediction errors during learning should show increasing activation on trials in which the outcome was unexpected according to any learned contingencies, and, if anything, decreasing activation on trials in which the outcome was expected. Indeed, both V1 and the putamen showed an increased response when an expected visual stimulus was omitted or when an unexpected visual stimulus was presented. Moreover, responses to predicted stimuli, for which prediction error would become increasingly smaller, diminished across the learning period. Consistent with a proposed role of the right dorsolateral prefrontal cortex (DLPFC) in prediction (or error) processing (Fletcher et al., 2001), the right DLPFC became increasingly active as a function of learning when a visual stimulus was predicted as compared to when it was not.

Repeating Errors Made during Training

Imagine that in trying to find the house of a friend for the first time you make a wrong turn at an intersection. If you fail to engage in deliberate processing of the cues that led you to make the wrong turn (perhaps because you are busy trying to figure out how to get back on track), you may repeat your mistake the next time you are faced with the same intersection. After all, the intersection will seem familiar, and you might remember having made the turn before without remembering that it did not bring you any closer to your goal. Such events suggest that episodic memories (memories specific to one occasion) are not all-or-none in composition: Actions can be remembered independently of their consequences.

Mistakes are an unavoidable aspect of learning in many domains, even in simple tasks, such as learning lists of words. In many verbal learning studies, for example, participants are initially presented with lists of words that are too long to be remembered faultlessly, and the list is presented repeatedly until the learner can repeat the items in the correct order without making mistakes. Learning in such a situation can be described as a process of remembering new associations and unlearning incorrect ones (e.g., Kay, 1951; Lansdale & How, 1996). In general, list learning improves with practice as mistakes are weeded out and omissions are corrected. However, as discussed in Chapter 5 and first documented by Bartlett (1932), when textual materials are to be learned, a failure-of-further-learning effect may occur. Repeatedly presenting passages of text—and repeatedly testing learners on their ability to reproduce those texts—leads to little learning beyond the first presentation (Fritz et al., 2000; Kay, 1955). In fact, each subsequent reproduction of the text may tend to be more like the previous reproduction and less like the original passage, even when the original passage is repeated, as learners tend to repeat the same correct items and make the same errors week after week (Kay, 1955).

Mistakes made early in practice can influence the course of perceptual-motor learning as well. Once an incorrect response has been made, it may be remembered and repeated again even when feedback regarding the accuracy of responses is provided (e.g., Holding, 1970). Thus, although mistakes can provide valuable feedback about performance, they may also negatively influence the acquisition of new information or skills when the mistakes themselves are "learned." For example, most of us have experienced making a mistake such as clicking on the wrong button on a computer interface and, then, even though the mistake was noticed, repeating the same action at the next opportunity. The dynamic nature of our interactions with the world means that we need to learn from our errors and recover quickly from them, but the same adaptability of the system that allows us to learn from errors can make us more susceptible to making errors. In other words, having made an error once may result in changes to the system that lead us to make the error again.

The propensity to repeat errors is perhaps most evident in language use, which, according to some, is best described as a dynamic system that is tuned to process recent input, and thus shares many mechanisms with language acquisition (e.g., Bock & Griffin, 2000; Dell, Reed, Adams, & Meyer, 2000). This property of language allows us to adapt our speech to the listener or the situation, and to learn new words or speech patterns on-the-fly. A downside of this plasticity is that making a language-production error may increase the likelihood of making that same error again. In other words, the error itself may be learned. For example, it has been shown that having had a tip-of-the-tongue (TOT) experience for a word once makes it more likely that a tip-of-the-tongue state will result when trying to recall the word again—even if one received help retrieving the word the first time (Warriner & Humphreys, 2008). Warriner and Humphreys elicited TOT states by giving definitions of words and asking speakers to respond as to whether they knew a word, did not know it, or knew it but just could not recall it. If speakers indicated being in a TOT state, they were told to keep thinking about the word and trying to retrieve it for either 10 or 30 seconds before being told the correct answer. The amount of time spent trying to retrieve the word was thus the amount of time the speaker was in the error state. When tested on the same words 2 days later, speakers were not only more likely to block on words they were not able to remember the first time than on the other words used in the experiment, but also more likely to have a tip-of-the-tongue experience for words they had tried to retrieve for 30 seconds than for words that they had tried to retrieve for only 10 seconds. It seems that making an error once effectively reinforces that erroneous state, in this case an incomplete or incorrect mapping from the abstract word form (or lemma) to the phonological form of the word (assuming a spreading activation model of spoken word production in which activation proceeds from a nonverbal concept to an abstract word (or lemma), and then to a phonological form for the word and the learning of the mapping between lemma and phonological form is accomplished by adjusting connection weights between representations at each level, in response to experience; e.g., Dell, 1986; Levelt, Roelofs, & Meyer, 1999).

K. R. Humphreys, Menzies, and Lake (2010) showed that speakers who make a phonological speech error once (e.g., saying "flute fries" when trying to say "fruit flies") are more likely to make that same error again. During a learning phase, these errors were elicited using a paradigm in which speakers read word pairs silently, but were told that they should be prepared to read the word pair aloud whenever a signal to do so was given. Speakers were biased to make errors on some trials by preceding the word pair to be read aloud with a number of word pairs in which the initial consonants were reversed. For example, "fruit flies" might be preceded by "flip frappe," "flays frame," and "flop frays." When the same word pair on which speakers made an error was presented again later, speakers were four times more likely to repeat that error than to make an error to a word pair they had read correctly during the study phase. However, the tendency to repeat one's errors lasted for only 5 to 10 minutes, and only when the first and second presentation of the word pairs occurred within the same experimental session.

Although the effects of making errors found by K. R. Humphreys et al. (2010) were short-lived, error production can have longer-lived effects. Lafond, Tremblay, and Parmentier (2010; see also Couture, Lafond, & Tremblay, 2008) demonstrated this for the Hebb repetition effect (Hebb, 1961), which refers to the finding that lists of stimuli repeated in a sequential recall task are remembered better than would be expected on the basis of practice effects alone. In a typical paradigm, lists of words or other visual or auditory stimuli are presented one at a time, and the learner's task is to remember the stimuli in the order in which they were presented. Most lists are presented only once during a session, but a few, critical lists are repeatedly periodically. Better performance on the repeated lists is called the Hebb repetition effect. It has been suggested that the effect is due to implicit learning, and much work has focused on determining the boundary conditions for its occurrence (e.g., Oberauer & Meyer, 2009; Parmentier, Maybery, Huitson, & Jones, 2008).

Couture et al. (2008) hypothesized that some failures to find the Hebb repetition effect may not be due to a lack of sequence learning, but instead to error learning that offsets any positive effects of learning correct responses. They hypothesized that implicit learning takes place even under conditions that seem to suppress the Hebb repetition effect and suggested that the probability of a given response increases with the number of prior occurrences of that response regardless of whether the response was produced in error. This point was also made by McClelland (2001) with regard to why adults may find it difficult to learn how to distinguish speech sounds that are not contrasted in their native language. McClelland also made the more general point that associative learning may result in responses being strengthened regardless of whether they are correct, and that this strengthening leads to failures to benefit from practice whenever erroneous responses are routinely elicited. The best-known description of associative learning is Hebb's rule. Formulated to explain associative learning, it suggests that the mechanisms of synaptic modification will reflect whatever pattern was elicited by the input. Experimental work suggests that the stronger the elicited activation, the stronger the effect will be and the longer it will last. Hebbian learning implies an increase in the probability that a subsequent, similar input will produce the same activation, and repeated association will increase the efficiency with which outputs are elicited.

In a serial recall task, such as that used in the Hebb repetition paradigm, error responses include recalling the correct item in the wrong serial position (transpositions), recalling an item that was not part of the sequence (intrusions), or recalling an item in the serial position occupied by the item in the preceding (but not the current) sequence (protrusions). Protrusion errors, in particular, show that associations from preceding trials can influence recall in the current trial (see, e.g., Estes, 1991). Usually, items to be produced in a serial recall task are scored as correct only when they are recalled in the same serial position in which they were initially presented. In order to explore the hypothesis that erroneous responses are learned, Couture et al. adopted a scoring procedure used by Estes to examine errors as well as correct responses as a function of repetitions. Their method avoids the bias that there will be an increase in error repetitions each time an error is made simply because the chance of a repetition of an error goes up when the pool of erroneous responses is greater. To avoid this bias, they analyzed response probabilities, taking into account the number of times a particular response had been made in preceding trials. Learning was thus not measured as a function of the number of previous presentations of the list, but rather as a function of the responses made across successive repetitions of the list. As shown in Figure 7.6, they found that people learned from both their correct and incorrect responses.

Evidence of the learning of errors has the important theoretical consequence that it suggests learning from repetitions of a sequence is not exclusively due to the cumulative traces of the correct sequence stored in memory, but that the traces in memory include the responses made to the stimuli—

Figure 7.6 Mean learning slopes and probability of recalling an item as a function of the number of times an item was previously recalled for the experimental data of Couture et al. (2008). The slope for correct responses is the average learning slope for nine correct responses (one for each serial position in the serial learning task used). The slope for errors is the average learning slope for the 16 errors studied.

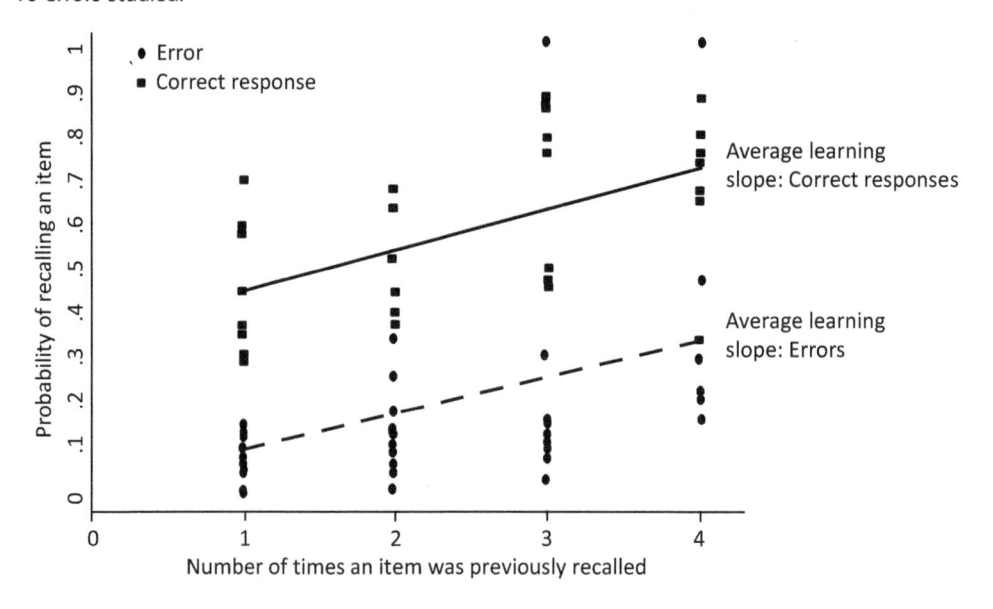

regardless of whether these were correct. In other words, a response becomes more probable as a function of the number of times that it has been produced. Lafond et al. (2010) found that the probability of producing a given response increased as a function of the number of times the same response had previously been made regardless of whether that response was in error. Evidence of error learning across repeated sequences was found such that error probabilities associated with individual responses increased across the number of past occurrences. No evidence of such learning was found across "filler" lists that were not repeated during the experiment and for which no response learning would be expected because the correct responses varied from one list to another.

Even skills learned to the point of automaticity may be subject to the interfering effects of learned errors (Lansdale & How, 1996). Errors that are learned during training and repeated at test or transfer are conceptually similar to capture errors, in which a more familiar action is executed mistakenly because a lapse of attention allows the common elements in the present circumstances (requiring a different action) to direct performance. Both the errors made by skilled performers and capture errors reflect lapses of attention; in the first case attention has been withdrawn from the task as a function of practice and in the second case the goal of behavior is not kept active when it should be. Both errors reflect sampling from memory that goes uncensored by the attention mechanisms needed to reject inappropriate actions. The propensity of people to repeat actions (even when they are errors) emphasizes the importance of designing computer and other interfaces so that errors are unlikely to occur.

A typical view of perceptual-motor learning is that the beginner's initial attempts to perform a task are based on verbally encoded instructions or tips for performance (see Chapter 1). Novice performance is often characterized as hypothesis testing, as the instructed actions are attempted and their outcomes evaluated. For example, a ping-pong player might formulate a rule by testing various task-related hypotheses. The first rule might involve how hard to hit the ball—hard enough to get it over the net but not so hard as to miss the table altogether. Later rules might relate the angle of the racket to the topspin of the ball or how to time particular strokes relative to the position of the ball. In most cases, the novice will have to rely primarily on visual, auditory, proprioceptive, or other sensory feedback to evaluate outcomes and to determine the correctness of hypotheses. In other cases a trainer or opponent will be present to give feedback both on outcomes and on the way in which actions are carried out. Regardless of the source of the feedback, hypothesis testing is assumed to lead to a set of declarative rules that can guide performance. Continued application of these rules leads to proceduralization, such that the rules no longer need to be retrieved, and performance is no longer dependent on declarative control.

It has been suggested that rather than growing out of declarative knowledge, procedural knowledge can develop alongside declarative knowledge. This idea was put forward by Berry and Broadbent (1988), who introduced the concept of selective (looking for cues, testing hypotheses) and unselective (implicit) learning. They found that the expression of declarative knowledge, presumed to result from selective learning, depends on the availability of working memory, whereas the application of procedural memory, presumed to result from unselective learning, does not. This view contrasts with the widely held assumption that a procedural stage of skill follows a declarative stage, and that performance in the procedural stage is based on procedures created from declarative knowledge. This contrast was discussed in Chapter 5 in the context of implicit and explicit memory. The key issue is whether perceptual-motor learning can occur without declarative mediation.

Masters (1992) demonstrated that motor learning (golf putting) could occur while working-memory resources were tied up—thus preventing engagement in hypothesis testing and presumably forcing people to engage in what Broadbent termed unselective processing—although performance was not as good as that achieved when the task was learned without a memory-demanding task. Moreover, structuring training to prevent errors from occurring, which also is hypothesized to encourage the use of implicit, unselective learning processes, leads to a relative insusceptibility to performance breakdown under conditions of distraction (Maxwell, Masters, Kerr, & Weedon, 2001). If learning occurs without a memory-demanding task, not only do learners report more explicit knowledge, but also they show a larger performance decrement when the learned task must be performed along with a secondary task.

If hypothesis testing is dependent on feedback, eliminating feedback should lead to a different mode of learning. According to Maxwell, Masters, and Eves (2003), eliminating feedback such that performers cannot distinguish correct actions from incorrect ones will lead people to encode all actions, regardless of their outcomes. Such learning is procedural in the sense that it will be difficult to verbalize because no corresponding declarative knowledge has been generated. They compared the performance of people who learned a golf-putting task under normal conditions (full auditory and visual feedback) with that of people who were unable to see or hear the result of hitting the ball during training. Both groups performed a visual search task between trials to prevent a focus on proprioceptive and tactile feedback. After a learning period, both groups performed a set of trials with full feedback, and a transfer task in which a secondary, tone-counting task was performed while putting. Although the limited feedback group seemed to have learned essentially nothing based on their performance in the full-feedback trials, they improved substantially across the transfer phase. In contrast, the group who practiced with full feedback showed worse performance in the dual-task condition. In a final experiment, Maxwell et al. showed more evidence of procedural learning without feedback in the form of similar changes in kinematic data for full- and reduced-feedback groups. However, as is the case with feedback in general, if performers come to rely on working memory during learning, their performance will suffer when working-memory resources are depleted by another task. Structuring training to prevent errors might lead to the development of more robust procedures for performing a task.

According to Maxwell et al. (2003), when errors are detected by comparing movement outcomes to desired goals, explicit hypotheses are generated in order to subsequently adjust movements in order to increase the chances of success. This results in conscious attention to movements. Successful performance is less likely to be followed by such explicit adjustment and control of movements. Cognitive demand (or processing) following error trials is assumed to be higher than following successful trials.

If the commission of errors triggers an explicit processing mode, the extra cognitive load associated with this processing should be most apparent in the movement preparation phase because hypothesis testing is more likely to occur during this period rather than during the execution of the movement itself. However, Masters and Maxwell's *theory of reinvestment* predicts that following an error, performers are likely to increase conscious control of their movements in order to correct performance (e.g., Masters and Maxwell, 2008; Wulf & Prinz, 2001) by eliminating past errors. Lam, Masters, and Maxwell (2010) used the probe-reaction time paradigm—in which cognitive load is "probed" by presenting a signal requiring a response at different stages of task execution and reaction time to the probe signal is measured—to determine whether cognitive demands were higher in both the pre-movement phase and during movements in post-error trials than in trials following successful performance. In their experiment, people with no prior golfing experience practiced putting a golf ball. Cognitive demand was assessed by simple verbal reaction time to an auditory tone (the probe signal). Preparation was defined as the period of time between placing the putter behind the ball and initiating the backswing. Execution was defined as the entire movement, beginning with initiation of the backswing and end of the forward swing. Probe signals were presented during the preparation phase on approximately one-third of the trials and during movement execution on approximately one-third of the trials. Performance on the golf-putting task improved across practice, and did not depend on whether a probe signal was presented during the trial. The probe-signal reaction time was higher on trials following performance errors than on trials following successful putts, consistent with the hypothesis that more cognitive effort was involved with putts following errors than successes. Probe-signal reaction times during movement preparation were longer than those during movement execution, suggesting that some process other than a focus on movement is involved. Participants spent more time preparing movements after an error had been made; this was especially evident for preparation time.

The fact that probe-signal reaction times were also elevated during movement execution on post-error trials suggests that performers devote more resources to monitor and control their movements and outcomes after errors have been made. The theory of reinvestment (Masters & Maxwell, 2008) claims that performers attempt to consciously control behavior when they perceive a need to avoid potential failures. Errors are an important cue that future performance may suffer. However, left to their own devices, many performers will use this cue to engage in just the sort of conscious, controlled processing that is likely to disrupt skilled movement (Beilock et al., 2002).

Attentional factors associated with error recovery have led researchers to examine the benefits—and costs—of making errors in learning new skills. As demonstrated by the sometimes disastrous effects of witnesses being encouraged to speculate and try harder to remember during interrogation, errors can have lasting effects on performance. People asked to imagine that something may have happened and then asked to remember what actually happened are more likely to falsely remember an event than people who never engaged in bringing the event to mind (e.g., Ost, Vrij, Costall, & Bull, 2002). Similarly, as discussed earlier in this chapter, simply having made an error can lead to an increase in the chance of making an error again. This problem is particularly pronounced in amnesiacs. In a trial-and-error learning situation, healthy people show some tendency to repeat erroneous responses, once made, but this tendency is much more pronounced in amnesiacs. Relative to an errorless learning condition, in which they are told the correct response on the first trials (e.g., in a word-stem completion task, the experimenter might say, "I'm thinking of a word that starts with QU and that word is QUOTE"), amnesiacs take much longer to learn a given response when they are first given a chance to supply their own response (e.g., when they are allowed to guess what the word might be) and guess incorrectly, even when the correct answer is written down by the participant in both cases (Baddeley & Wilson, 1994). The relatively poor performance of amnesic persons in such an errorful learning condition suggests that declarative, explicit memory may play a major role in the elimination of learning errors. Memory is needed not only to retrieve correct answers but also to reject incorrect ones.

The link between memory and erroneous responses is such that errors made during learning can be used to predict what will be forgotten. In some cognitive tasks, such as learning sequences of words or objects, forgetting consists of "remembering" mistakes, in that an error made during training is substituted for a correct response. This idea forms the basis for one model of forgetting (Lansdale & How, 1996). In this model, the results of a sequence-learning experiment were captured with a Markov model in which representations of correct sequential relationships coexist with memory traces containing incorrect information about the same elements of the sequence. Forgetting is described largely in terms of remembering the mistakes made during the acquisition phase of the experiment: With time there is an increasing inability to discriminate correct representations in memory from erroneous ones, which results in erroneous information being retrieved more often as time goes by. Memory for having made an error is better when controlled, overt acknowledgment of having made an error occurs (Rabbitt, 1990). What remains to be determined is how we can enhance the probability that a given retrieved action or option is recognized as an error.

As Lansdale and How (1996) put it, "There is a trade-off between the advantages of allowing trainees or subjects to make errors ('we learn from our mistakes') and the danger that, in so doing, we both change the nature of their memory and reinforce the likelihood of the errors recurring" (p. 355). To err is human, and to repeat our errors is also human. The challenge is to use errors to advantage in training programs while ensuring that they do not become a fixed feature of skilled performance.

Error Orientation

There are individual differences in how often people make errors and in how they deal with errors when they have been made. For example, some people make many more slips of actions than others, and the propensity to make these slips has been related to capture of attention by irrelevant stimuli (Larson & Perry, 1999). People also differ in how they view errors and how they deal with them once they have occurred. The Error Orientation Questionnaire (EOQ; Rybowiak, Garst, Frese, & Batinic, 1999) was developed to measure attitudes to errors and coping with errors in work environments. The EOQ consists of eight scales (error competence, learning from errors, error risk taking, error strain, error anticipation, covering up errors, error communication, and thinking about errors) that, together, give an indication of how individuals view and cope with errors. The questionnaire is designed to be used in organizations as one measure of organizational culture. Like the individuals who work there, organizations can be characterized by the extent to which errors are viewed as events that must be prevented at all costs versus as opportunities for learning. Since total error prevention is an unobtainable goal, an error-averse organizational culture can negatively impact production (Marsick & Watkins, 2003). Workers will be less prone to take risks, and thus will be less creative, and will be less able to deal with errors when they do occur. The EOQ can be used to give an indication of how different groups within an organization view error, and whether interventions are necessary to create a climate in which constructive processes of learning from failures will be engaged in.

Summary

Performance errors reveal much about the state of a learner's understanding of a task or domain. In Chapter 5, we described how such information could be used to deliver better instruction. In this chapter, the focus was on the theoretical importance of errors and the importance of error feedback in learning.

Errors arise for different reasons. Some errors tell us something about how action is organized. Slips of action, for example, are an inescapable part of human performance, reflecting as they do the automatization of many aspects of performance. They reflect the roles of attention and intention in organizing behavior much as theories of skill emphasize the shift from controlled to automatic processing as skill develops.

Whether it is beneficial to make errors during learning depends on the task. In some simple tasks, error is an efficient signal for learning. Prediction error, or surprise when outcomes do not match predictions, is an important driving force in learning. Tasks such as simple office tasks may also benefit from being learned under conditions where errors can be made, but only if the task is not too complex.

A downside of learning from errors is that the errors themselves may be learned and repeated. Moreover, errors can disrupt ongoing action or even trigger a switch to a more controlled, inefficient processing mode than is appropriate to the situation.

A number of electrophysiological markers of pre- and post-error states have been identified. Theories of performance monitoring have been developed that provide the basis for predicting when errors are likely to occur and how they will be dealt with. The pervasiveness of errors makes it imperative that an appropriate strategy for dealing with errors in learning situations be considered.

8

Individual Differences in Skill Acquisition and Maintenance

In order to study the acquisition of complex skills, it is a good research strategy to have a theory of individual differences.

N. A. Taatgen (2002, p. 103)

Individuals differ in many ways, including that some persons seem to acquire knowledge and skills more easily than others. This is evident in the improvements in performance time that occur as a result of practice, which follow a power function that has achieved the status of a law: The power law of practice (see Chapter 1). Some individuals show a steeper learning curve than others. Of theoretical note, close inspection of individual learning curves suggests that the "power law" may be a misnomer since, as you may recollect, Heathcote, Brown, and Mewhort (2000) provided evidence that learning curves for individuals are better fit by exponential functions. More recently, R. W. Howard (2014) reported that the improvement with practice across years for most chess players was fit best by a quadratic function, although the change for the best players conformed to a power function. Whether individual performance is better fit by a power, exponential, or quadratic function may seem like a minor detail. The general point, though, is important: Focusing on group performance to the exclusion of individual performance may lead to incorrect conclusions about the nature of skill acquisition and skilled performance.

The role of individual differences may be especially pronounced for complex or well-practiced tasks, such as chess. According to Jensen (2006, p. x) the increasing importance of individual differences with increases in task complexity and practice can be captured in two laws of individual differences:

1. Individual differences in learning and performance *increase* as task complexity increases,
2. Individual differences in performance *increase* with continuing practice and experience, unless the task itself imposes an artificially low ceiling on proficiency.

Perhaps most notably, individual differences have been the focus of a great deal of applied research on the selection of personnel for training. Especially in the military, there is considerable interest in the selection of individuals for appropriate jobs and specializations (Schmitt, 2012). Although the focus of concern tends to be on inter-individual differences, or differences between people (i.e., selecting the right person for the right job), it is also important not to ignore short-term intra-individual variability, which may itself differ across individuals (Wang, Hamaker, & Bergeman, 2012). For example, not only does mean response time in a task increase with age, but also variability within individuals does (i.e., the response time from one time to the next varies more widely). Mella, Fagot, Lecerf, and de Ribaupierre (2015) found a correlation between intra-individual variability in response time and unspeeded measures of working-memory capacity, suggesting that the two are linked, particularly in older adults. Studying individual difference variables may lead to a better understanding of specific skills and of skill in general. The determination of those individual characteristics that enable someone to become skilled at a task points to factors important for performance of that task.

In this chapter, we provide a brief introduction to the study of individual differences and discuss some frameworks that have been offered to account for the relation between skill and individual difference variables. Emphasis is given to theories that address the interaction between stages of skill acquisition and cognitive and perceptual-motor abilities. As an example of the interplay between the study of skill and the determination of individual differences, we take a look at the research on reading skill. Finally, we consider a specific individual difference variable, aging, and its impact on skill acquisition and performance.

Intelligence and Aptitudes

Francis Galton (1869, 1883) was one of the first researchers to pursue the notion that, through testing, one could discover the innate "intellectual capacity" of individuals. In his search for the characteristics that made some humans more fit for survival than others, Galton used performance on simple sensory and motor tests and various physiological indices as measures of mental ability. Galton, influenced by the work of his cousin, Charles Darwin, concluded that mental abilities were largely inherited, as emphasized by the title of his 1869 book, *Hereditary Genius*. This idea has been upheld by subsequent research, which indicates that heritability accounts for 30% of general intelligence differences in early childhood, increasing to as much as 70%–80% for such differences in adults (Deary, Penke, & Johnson, 2010). Furthermore, findings of moderate stability in intelligence in a group of individuals born in Scotland in 1921 as measured at 11 and 90 years of age (Deary, Pattie, & Starr, 2013) also suggest a role for genetics in determining intellectual ability. A recent, large-scale study (including more than 100,000 persons) linked a genetic locus with educational attainment (Trampush et al., 2015), thus further establishing the genetic basis of cognitive ability.

James McKeen Cattell (1890) extended the research begun by Galton in his own testing of the "fundamental sensory discrimination abilities" underlying differences in intellectual ability. Cattell and Galton both included measures of reaction time on basic perceptual-motor tasks in their test batteries, but found little relation between reaction time and measures of cognitive intelligence (occupational status in Galton's case and general intelligence for Cattell and his students). Later studies, however, showed that the failures to find a relationship were due mainly to measurement problems and that reaction time on basic tasks with minimal cognitive demands is highly correlated with performance on intelligence tests (Jensen, 2006), such as when responses are made with compatible spatial stimulus-response mappings (Nissan, Liewald, & Deary, 2013).

Binet (1905), a pioneer in the development of the field of intelligence testing, focused on cognitive tasks involving comprehension, reasoning, and judgment, rather than on perceptual-motor tasks. He selected verbal and practical tasks that were performed successfully more often by older than younger children and by "bright" than "dim" children of the same chronological age. These tasks were presumed to reflect the cognitive abilities relevant to educational settings. Binet helped to develop the first numerical scale for intelligence, the Binet-Simon scale, based on overall performance on a variety of such tasks. Binet's (Binet & Henri, 1895) "worksamples of life performance" (Cronbach, 1970/1990, p. 199) correlated with success in school and provided the basis for theories of general intelligence and ability.

The relative success of Binet's testing movement influenced Spearman (1904, 1927), who developed *two-factor theory*, which states that performance on any mental test is attributable to a general ability factor, *g*, along with more specific group factors (e.g., visual-spatial and verbal abilities) and abilities particular to the test. Two-factor theory and the conception of *g* have had a lasting influence on testing and individual differences research, with Deary (2012a) stating, "Spearman's *g* is one of the most replicated results in psychology (Carroll, 1993)" (p. 146). However, the conception of general intelligence has been, and continues to be, hotly debated (see Deary, 2012b). As an alternative, some researchers have favored "many-factor" theories in which there is no *g* factor (Thurstone, 1935). However, in a review of relevant studies, J. B. Carroll (1993) concluded that evidence still supported a *g* factor, as well as a distinction between crystalized intelligence—an ability to access and use knowledge and skills—and fluid intelligence—an ability to reason and think about novel problems, unrelated to knowledge (first proposed by R. B. Cattell, 1943). More recent evidence has suggested that a theory that includes *g* but that distinguishes verbal, perceptual, and image rotation abilities as a second hierarchical level provides a better fit to data than does the model with fluid vs. crystalized intelligence as the second dimension (W. Johnson & Bouchard, 2005; Major, Johnson, & Deary, 2012).

Intelligence and ability tests continue to be developed and studied because of the need to classify people and as part of the search for general psychological theories of human intelligence. Ability tests have been useful for highlighting subgroups of strengths and weaknesses of individuals and for matching the characteristics of applicants with the demands of jobs (see, e.g., Scherbaum & Goldstein, 2015; Scherbaum et al., 2012). They have also been used to evaluate the contribution of specific abilities to more complex performance, as described ahead.

Cognitive and Neural Correlates Approaches

Aptitude can be defined generally as "any characteristic of trainees that determines their ability to profit from instruction, including abilities, skills, knowledge, and even previous achievement (Cronbach & Snow, 1977)" (Tannenbaum & Yukl, 1992, p. 416). An aptitude can be cognitive or physical. General intelligence, spatial ability, quantitative skill, and psychomotor ability all have been treated as general aptitudes. According to Ackerman and Kyllonen (1991), the important questions to ask are: "How do we define an aptitude?" "How are aptitudes related to each other?" "What are the relationships between aptitudes and success in skill development?"

A common method for determining the nature of aptitudes is the *cognitive correlates* approach (Fleishman & Quaintance, 1984), which is used to determine the relationships between aptitudes, abilities, and task performance. The general procedure is to compare similarities and differences between high- and low-ability individuals on a variety of tasks. For example, Hunt (1978) first divided people into groups of high and low verbal ability based on their performance in verbal aptitude tests, and then tested these groups on basic cognitive tasks, such as choice-reaction time. After testing, he determined which of the basic tasks correlated most highly with the global verbal ability measure. Among other things, the time to decode (i.e., to recognize) highly overlearned information (e.g., the letter *A*) was correlated with verbal ability, whereas the time to retrieve facts presented recently in the experimental context was not. On the basis of these findings, Hunt concluded that people with high verbal ability can decode verbal stimuli faster than can people of low verbal ability.

The goal of research such as Hunt's (1978) is to obtain a better understanding of the general ability of interest, but critics of this approach (e.g., J. B. Carroll, 1993) have argued that it is of little use because the aspect of the general test with which the experimental tasks are correlated cannot be determined. For example, a correlation between performance in a choice-reaction task and a test of verbal ability could reflect only the fact that tests of verbal ability are speeded. Thus, the correlation may reveal nothing concerning the ability of interest, but only something about the testing situation.

Despite this general concern, the cognitive correlates approach has been successful in adding to our knowledge of many skills. For example, performance on working-memory tasks is positively correlated with performance on intelligence tests (Ackerman, Beier, & Boyle, 2005). Conway and Kovacs (2013) analyzed the correlations between various working-memory tasks and intelligence tests, and concluded that the correlation is more specifically mainly that of the executive-control component of working memory with the fluid reasoning component of intelligence. In other words, people who perform better at more complex working-memory tasks with a large cognitive control component perform better specifically on tests that would be classified as measuring fluid intelligence. In a more applied example, Barron and Rose (2013) identified two components of ability, those of spatial orientation and perceptual speed, that were correlated with performance of candidates in a U.S. Air Force pilot training program.

An avenue of research extending the cognitive correlates approach to neural correlates was begun by Haier et al. (1988). Using the technique of positron emission tomography, whereby the brain's glucose use (and, by extension, its activity) is measured during performance of relatively brief tasks, Haier et al. found that individuals with a relatively high intelligence quotient (IQ, as measured by general intelligence tests) metabolized less glucose than individuals with lower IQ while solving problems. This finding suggests that efficient processing at a physiological level is correlated with intelligence—that is, that the brains of people with higher intelligence use less energy than those of people with lower intelligence to solve the same problems. This proposed relation is called the neural efficiency hypothesis (Brancucci, 2012).

Neubauer and Fink (2009) reviewed evidence from brain imaging and other methods for the neural efficiency hypothesis and concluded that the situation is more complex than depicted originally. Although many studies have shown the inverse relation between amount of brain activation and IQ, several moderating factors are important, including the person's sex, task complexity and difficulty, state of learning, and the distinction between frontal and parietal cortical areas. One of the more interesting findings is that men and women show different patterns of activation as a function of type of task. Men show the inverse relation between brain activation and intelligence for visual-spatial tasks and women do not, but women show the inverse relation for verbal or affective tasks and men do not (Jaušovec & Jaušovec, 2008; Neubauer, Fink, & Schrausser, 2002).

With regard to task difficulty, results consistent with the neural efficiency hypothesis have been obtained with tasks of low or medium difficulty but not ones of high difficulty, where there tends to be a reversal (Neubauer et al., 1999). However, Toffanin, Johnson, De Jong, and Martens (2007) found no evidence of differences in brain activation for low- and high-IQ participants in a sentence-picture verification task when use of a verbal or visual strategy was controlled. The predicted relation was confirmed, though, for a personal decision-making task that is quite different from the problems on intelligence tests (Di Domenico, Rodrigo, Ayaz, Fournier, & Ruocco, 2015), indicating that it seems to be a general property of individual differences in cognition. Neubauer and Fink (2009) propose that at high difficulty levels, less capable individuals decide that they cannot perform the task well and devote less effort to it. The decrease in brain activation from a pretest to a posttest performed after training has been found to be greater for persons with high IQ than for persons with lower IQ (Haier et al., 1992; Neubauer et al., 2004), suggesting that the gain in efficiency from practice is also a function of intelligence. Finally, the decrease in activation with higher levels of intelligence occurs mainly for the dorso-lateral prefrontal cortex and the parietal lobes (Jaušovec & Jaušovec, 2004), two of the primary brain regions whose size is correlated with intelligence (Brancucci, 2012; Deary et al., 2010; Jung & Haier, 2007).

Cognitive Components Approach

An alternative approach to understanding individual differences in information-processing capabilities is to analyze a task in terms of its processing stages, and then to estimate an individual's performance at each of these stages. Measures of performance at individual stages are then correlated with measures of overall task success so as to determine the relative contribution of each stage to success in the task. This approach, sometimes called the *cognitive components* approach (Ackerman & Kyllonen, 1991), was developed by Robert Sternberg (1979). To use the cognitive components method, the investigator must have (a) a good understanding of the processing stages involved in performance of a task and (b) a procedure that allows performance at each stage to be estimated.

Sternberg's (1979) componential theory of human intelligence satisfies the first objective. It begins by distinguishing *composite tasks*, the complete tasks for which abilities are studied, from *subtasks* into which the tasks can be decomposed. Three components represent the basic abilities of the performers of the tasks (Sternberg, 2011). *Metacomponents* are the executive-control processes that regulate the processes of planning, monitoring progress, and deciding on alternative courses of action. *Information-processing* or *performance components* are the more basic processes involved in making comparisons between stimuli, selecting and initiating a response, and so on. *Knowledge-acquisition components* are those components involved in learning declarative knowledge and problem-solving strategies.

Sternberg (1977) applied the cognitive components approach to a variety of composite tasks, including analogy and classification problems of the form shown in Figure 8.1, by precuing different parts of the analogy or problem in advance. The analogies examined by Sternberg were of the form $A:B::C:D_1,D_2$, where A, B, C, and D_i are terms, ":" means "is to" and "::" means "as", and D_1 or D_2 is to be chosen as the answer. A specific analogy of this type is BASKETBALL:LEBRON JAMES :: BASEBALL: (a) ALBERT PUJOLS, (b) WILL FERRELL. Sternberg identified six processing components that pertain to the terms in an analogy problem (see Figure 8.1), the four major components of which are: *encoding*, in which attributes of each term in the problem are identified; *inference*, in which the rule relating A to B is discovered; *mapping*, in which a rule that maps the domain of the source analogue onto the target is determined; and *application*, in which a plausible answer D' is generated and evaluated against the alternatives D_1 and D_2. He was able to isolate these components by examining performance on subtasks in which 0, 1, 2, or 3 of the terms were precued prior to presentation of the complete problem (see Figure 8.1, precue boxes). Participants processed the precued information before indicating with a button press that they were ready to proceed,

Figure 8.1 Sternberg's conception of intelligence, showing some possible tasks, subtasks, components, and metacomponents. The variety of subtasks illustrates Sternberg's precuing procedure, and the six processing components are those proposed by Sternberg to be involved in solving analogy problems. A, B, C, and D correspond to the terms in the analogy.

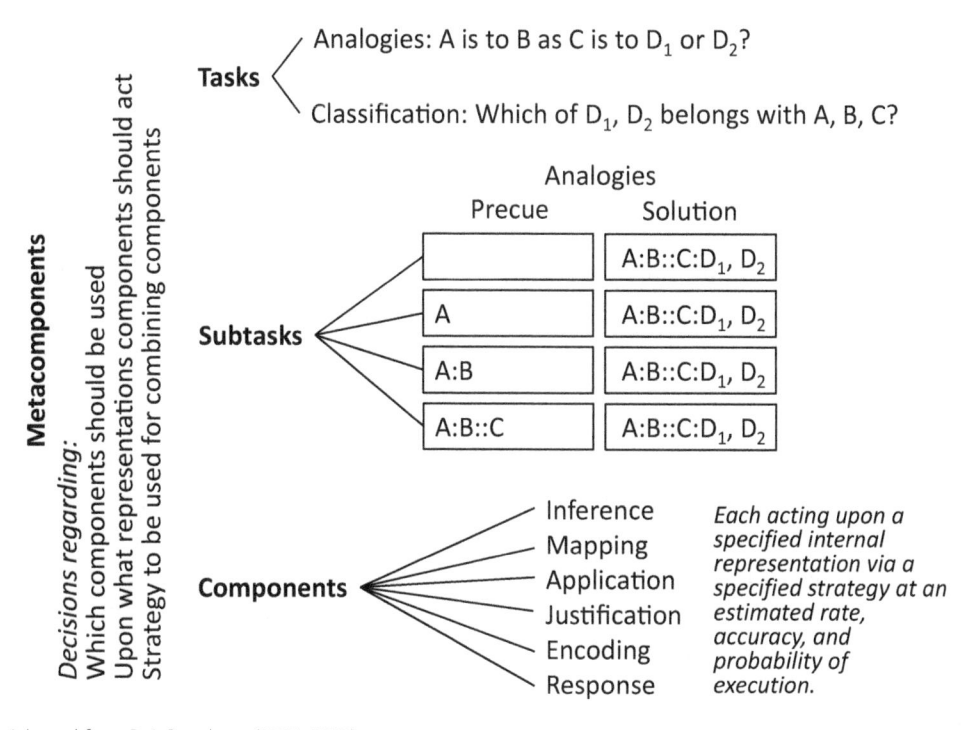

Tasks:
- Analogies: A is to B as C is to D_1 or D_2?
- Classification: Which of D_1, D_2 belongs with A, B, C?

Subtasks (Analogies):

Precue	Solution
	A:B::C:D_1, D_2
A	A:B::C:D_1, D_2
A:B	A:B::C:D_1, D_2
A:B::C	A:B::C:D_1, D_2

Components:
- Inference
- Mapping
- Application
- Justification
- Encoding
- Response

Each acting upon a specified internal representation via a specified strategy at an estimated rate, accuracy, and probability of execution.

Metacomponents — Decisions regarding:
- Which components should be used
- Upon what representations components should act
- Strategy to be used for combining components

Adapted from R. J. Sternberg (1977, 1979).

allowing the time to perform the second part of the trial to be influenced only by the component processes that remained to be performed. For example, if A:B was precued, A and B could be identified and the rule relating them inferred, meaning that those processes would not contribute to the response time in the second part, when the complete problem was presented. Detailed analyses of the results allowed determination of which of several specific models of these components best fit the data.

General reasoning ability, as measured by a standardized test, correlated with several aspects of component performance. Specifically, reasoning ability was most highly correlated with the speed of the preparation and response components: Individuals with high reasoning ability tended to perform these information-processing components faster than individuals with low reasoning ability. Reasoning ability was also found to be correlated with the relative time spent in encoding, with people of high reasoning ability spending relatively more time encoding the terms than people of low reasoning ability. Sternberg (1979) interpreted this finding as indicating that better reasoners adopt a strategy of obtaining good encodings before engaging in the attribute-comparison processes, much as experts in a domain develop better representations of a problem before proceeding toward solution (see Chapter 5). From this example of solving analogies, it should be apparent that the cognitive components approach provides a more detailed analysis of abilities than does the cognitive correlates approach.

The componential subtheory is one part of Sternberg's (2011) theory of successful intelligence, "according to which intelligence is the ability to achieve success in life, given one's personal standards, within one's sociocultural context" (Sternberg, 1999, pp. 292–293). The second part is the triarchic theory of intelligence, according to which analytical reasoning of the type emphasized by the componential subtheory is only one of three aspects of intelligence. The second aspect, creative intelligence, refers to skills related to creative thinking that go beyond what intelligence tests typically measure, whereas the third aspect, practical intelligence, involves application of the components to practical problems in everyday life. The final part of the theory of successful intelligence is the extent to which a person is able to capitalize on her strengths and compensate for weaknesses.

Sternberg and colleagues have advocated that students be taught the analytic, creative, and practical aspects of intelligent problem solving in the context of solutions that will be useful to achieve success in life (e.g., Sternberg, Grigorenko, & Zhang, 2008). Performance on an assessment battery based on the theory of successful intelligence has been shown to predict the academic performance of 4th through 6th grade students relatively well in the year following administration of the battery (Mandelman, Barbot, & Grigorenko, 2015). The battery predicted 32% of the overall grade for English and of the improvement in grades during the year for science.

Aptitude-Treatment Interactions

Individuals bring with them to any training task characteristics that determine their ability to benefit from instruction, and extensive research has been conducted on how these aptitudes interact with learning environments (Cronbach & Snow, 1977). Aptitudes can be divided into three categories: cognitive (intellectual), conative (volitional), and affective (personality; Ackerman & Kyllonen, 1991). Although most of the research relevant to skill acquisition has concerned cognitive variables, significant relations between performance and conative and affective aptitudes also have been found (Kupermintz, 2002). As Ackerman (2013) puts it,

> "Talent" . . . is the individual's current standing on various dimensions of individual differences (e.g., cognitive, affective, conative).

These traits arise through a complex interaction of genetics and environment, but once developed, are relatively stable and important determinants of future behaviors and skill development. (p. 12)

Whenever two or more treatments have differential impact on individuals varying on some trait, an *aptitude-treatment interaction* is said to exist. An example is the finding that students who test low in memory-strategy skills (the ability to structure and organize story content for retrieval from long-term memory) show a benefit on comprehension and transfer of presenting explanatory text for a picture auditorily rather than visually (supposedly reducing visual processing demands), whereas those who test high do not (Seufert, Schütze, & Brünken, 2009). Two aptitude-treatment interactions relevant to skill acquisition have received considerable attention. The first of these, the influence of high versus low structure in learning environments on learning of high- versus low-ability learners, concerns general cognitive aptitude. Figure 8.2 shows the nature of this interaction. High-ability learners tend to perform better in learning environments with low structure (e.g., independent readings, discovery learning) rather than high structure (e.g., lecture and drill), whereas low-ability learners tend to do the opposite. High vs. low structure also interacts with the conative/affective aptitude of achievement motivation. Individuals who seek achievement independently, with a low level of anxiety, perform best in low-structure

Figure 8.2 The aptitude-treatment interaction between ability level and learning environment structure.

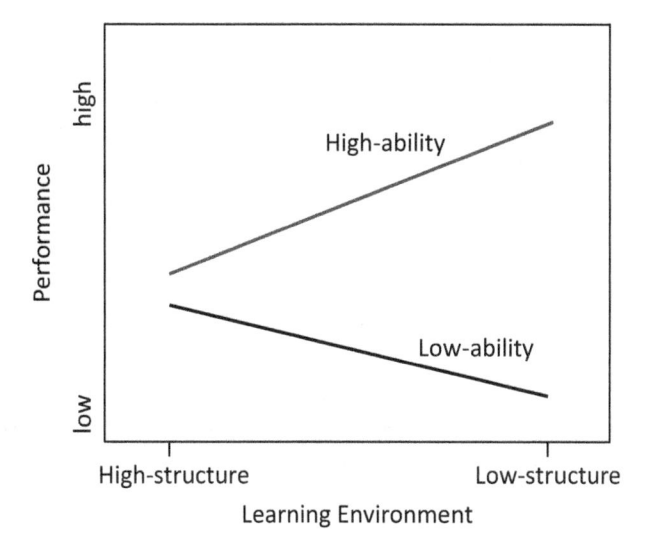

environments, whereas individuals who are oriented toward achievement via conformance (i.e., having high levels of anxiety) perform better in high-structure environments.

Another aptitude-treatment interaction involves high versus low cognitive ability and part-whole training strategies (see Chapter 5). Recall that in part-whole training, individual task components are first introduced in isolation, before the whole task is trained. Low-ability individuals may receive more benefit from such a strategy because, in essence, they have more to learn. Foss, Fabiani, Mané, and Donchin (1989) performed an analysis of performance of the Space Fortress game (which you may recall from Chapter 4) that indicated that low-ability individuals are deficient in basic skills and employ less effective strategies. Part-whole training should be useful in remediating basic skills so that a better foundation for skill acquisition will be in place. As emphasized in Chapter 10, the success of such a strategy will depend on a thorough task analysis so that necessary skills are defined.

Task Analysis Based on Individual Difference Variables

Some researchers have argued that human abilities are not a good basis for determining job requirements or training procedures because of problems of identification and definition of these abilities (see Patrick, 1992). However, other researchers have persisted in developing taxonomies of abilities to be used for just these purposes. A pioneer in the development of ability taxonomies was R. M. Gagné, whose book, *The Conditions of Learning* (1985), went through four editions. Gagné, who was explicitly concerned with the problem of training, argued for the concept of varieties of learning and the determination of the conditions that promote them. An attractive aspect of Gagné's formulation is its emphasis on the process of learning—in which existing knowledge, skills, habits, and actions are modified. The five categories of learning capabilities, outlined in Table 8.1, are intellectual skill, cognitive strategy, verbal information, attitude, and motor skill. The third column of the table gives the conditions necessary for each capability to develop. Gagné stressed that each capability defines its own set of learning objectives, and that conditions for learning depend on the type of skill to be developed.

Another prominent abilities researcher is E. A. Fleishman, whose *ability requirements* approach, along with most other taxonomies of human performance, is described by Fleishman and Quaintance (1984). Fleishman's work in identifying human abilities depended on extensive factor-analytic studies.

TABLE 8.1 Gagné's Categories of Learned Capabilities

Capability	Description	Conditions	Example
Intellectual Skill	Learning and elaboration of discriminations, concepts, and rules	Not improved by practice or context but by learning of prerequisite skills	Predicting behavior of an individual based on classification of its type
Cognitive Strategy	Internal skills that govern behavior when attempting to learn new material or in thinking and reasoning	Refined by practice in learning, remembering, defining, and solving problems	Using analogy to solve a novel problem
Verbal Information	Learning facts, principles, generalizations, and bodies of knowledge	Acquired via the presentation of material within an organized, meaningful context	Stating Fitts's three stages of skill acquisition
Attitude	Preference to engage in a specified activity	Not learned by practice or modified by context, but may be modified by observing a role model	Deciding to become a psychology major
Motor Skills	Performing organized motor acts	Learned with practice over long periods of time	Playing tennis

(Adapted from Gagné & Briggs, 1974)

Factor analysis is a family of techniques for identifying the number and nature of factors present in a collection of data. Fleishman's basic procedure was to give extensive training on a complex task and to administer a battery of tests for reference. Measures taken at different levels of learning on the criterion task and scores from the battery of reference tests are then intercorrelated, and the resulting matrix factor analyzed. The results of the factor analysis are taken to represent the percentage of variance accounted for by each factor as a function of stage of practice on the criterion task. As a direct outcome of his research program, Fleishman and his colleagues identified numerous psychomotor and physical proficiency factors that underlie the performance of tasks (see Table 8.2). Fleishman (1978) described his work in classifying elements of human behavior as

> laboratory research in which tasks are specifically designed or selected to test certain hypothesis about the organisation of abilities in a certain range of tasks. The experimental battery of tasks is administered to several hundred subjects, and the correlation patterns examined. Subsequent studies tend to introduce task variations aimed at sharpening or limiting our ability factor definitions. (p. 1009)

TABLE 8.2 Psychomotor and Physical Proficiency Factors Resulting from Fleishman's Factor-Analytic Studies

Factor	Description	Example
Psychomotor Factors		
Control Precision	Fine, highly controlled muscular movements performed to adjust the position of a control mechanism	Steer aircraft via joystick movements
Multilimb Coordination	Coordinate the movements of a number of limbs simultaneously	Operate a back hoe
Response Orientation	Rapid recognition of the direction of a visual stimulus, and the initiation of an appropriate response	Flip switch in response to onset of light
Reaction Time	Speed of reaction to simple stimulus (does not include choice between alternatives)	Press key when tone is heard
Speed of Arm Movement	Speed of gross, discrete arm movement with minimal regard to accuracy	Rapidly move series of controls
Rate Control	Time continuous, anticipatory motor adjustments to reflect changes in track stimulus	Keep a cursor on a moving track
Manual Dexterity	Skillful manipulation of large objects under conditions of speed stress	Use hand tools to assemble engine
Finger Dexterity	Skillful, controlled finger movements	Fit nuts on bolts
Arm-HandSteadiness	Precise arm-hand positioning in which strength and speed requirements are minimized	Perform retinal surgery
Wrist-Finger Speed	Rapid pendular (back and forth) or rotary wrist movements with little demand for accuracy	Tapping test
Aiming	Accurate, restricted hand movements requiring precise eye-hand coordination	Using correction fluid to alter a document
Physical Proficiency Factors		
Extent Flexibility	Extend or stretch body	Twist to touch targeton wall
Dynamic Flexibility	Speed and flexibility of rapid trunk or limb movements	Perform sequence of precise large muscle movements
Explosive Strength	Mobilization of energy for burst of effort	Perform long jump

Factor	Description	Example
Static Strength	Exert maximum strength against fairly immovable objects	Lift heavy object
Dynamic Strength	Exert muscular force repeatedly or continuously	Scale a wall
Trunk Strength	Dynamic strength particular to trunk muscles	Perform sit-ups
Gross Body Coordination	Perform simultaneous movements involving the entire body	Perform the tango
Gross Body Equilibrium	Maintain or regain body balance	Walk a balance beam
Stamina	Exert sustained physical effort involving the cardiovascular system	Run a mile as quickly as possible

(Adapted from Fleishman & Quaintance, 1984)

A usual (but not universal) finding is that the number of factors with significant loadings decreases from early to late in practice, and the nature of the factors also changes. In tasks with significant motor components, the shift seen with training is from early factor loadings on perceptual abilities to later loadings on motor abilities (see Chapter 3). For example, using four-choice-reaction as a criterion task and a test battery that included both printed and motor tests, Fleishman and Hempel (1954) found that two cognitive and perceptual factors, spatial relations and verbal, accounted for most of the variance early in training. After an appreciable amount of training, two motor factors, reaction time and rate of movement, accounted for a large amount of the variance, with some additional loading on spatial relations.

Dynamic Accounts of Abilities and Skill

Ackerman's Modified Radex Model

Skill development is by nature dynamic, and empirical work by Fleishman and others made it clear that the contribution of different abilities to performance changes as skill develops. Ackerman (1988) created a theory of the determinants of individual differences in performance based on the three-phase account of skill acquisition (e.g., Fitts & Posner, 1967; see Chapter 1), and a so-called radex model of individual differences in ability that illustrates the relation between task complexity and human abilities (Marshalek, Lohman, & Snow, 1983; see Figure 8.3). As shown in Figure 8.3,

Figure 8.3 The radex model of Marshalek et al. (1983). The dependency of performance on general intelligence increases as a positive function of complexity.

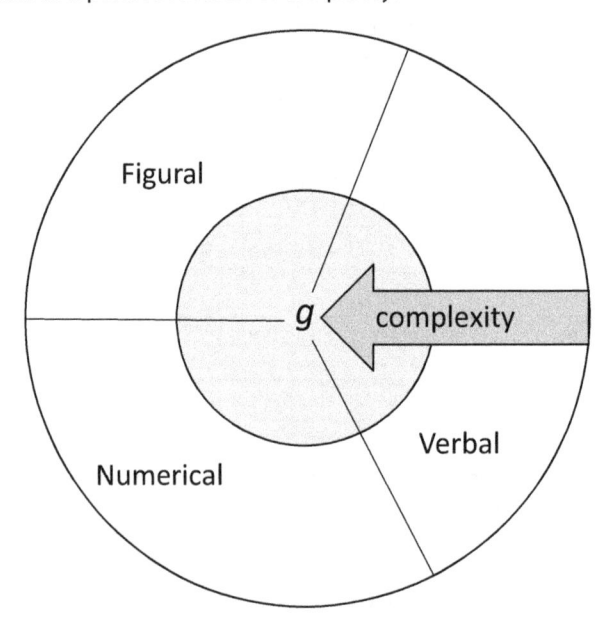

the radex model is composed of general intellectual ability (g), and *figural*, *numerical*, and *verbal* abilities, each of which can be decomposed into component abilities. For example, the verbal ability factor might include vocabulary, reading comprehension, and associational fluency. The arrow in the figure shows that as the complexity of the task or material being tested increases, so does the covariation of performance with tests of general intellectual ability. As complexity decreases, measures have more in common with one of the groups of more specific abilities. The third dimension in the radex model (in addition to complexity and type of ability) is speed of processing, which can contribute to performance across the phases of skill acquisition. The theory describes the relation of ability classes to phases of skill acquisition and can be used to predict the association between individual differences in ability and individual differences in performance across levels of skill.

In the initial, declarative phase of skill acquisition, substantial demands are made on cognitive abilities such as memory, reasoning, and knowledge retrieval. Because initial performance often depends on background knowledge and general spatial, verbal, and numeric abilities, general and broad content abilities should be predictive of individual differences in the declarative phase of skill acquisition. Figure 8.4 shows that the declarative phase of skill acquisition is associated with the general abilities shown at the top of the cylinder.

Figure 8.4 Ackerman's modified radex model of abilities and skill. As skill (speed) increases, reliance on general abilities decreases and the importance of psychomotor ability increases.

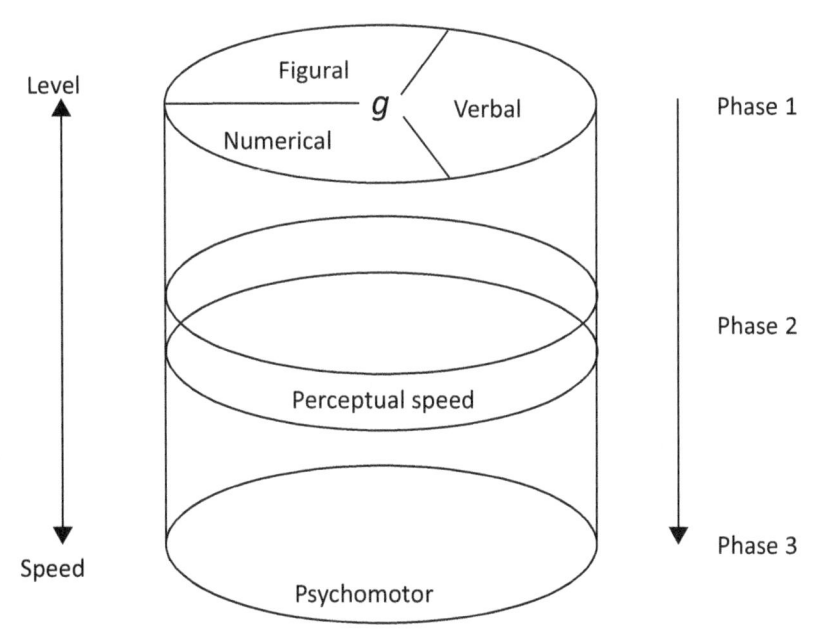

Performance in the second, associative phase of skill acquisition, wherein learners develop streamlined productions or rules for performance, depends more upon task-specific associations and less on general, declarative knowledge. As speed and efficiency of performance develop, the learner becomes less dependent on conscious mediation and the dependency of performance on general abilities is reduced. Moving down the cylinder in Figure 8.4, along the speed dimension, we see that Phase 2 performance is predicted to rely more heavily on perceptual speed ability than does initial performance.

In the final, autonomous phase of skill acquisition, procedures have become automatized and performance is fluent and relatively free of attentional demands. Declarative knowledge is now relatively unimportant and not consciously accessed. As can be seen in Figure 8.4, in this phase psychomotor ability becomes a more important determinant of performance.

Figure 8.5 provides a different graphical summary of the roles of general ability, perceptual speed, and psychomotor ability in the performance of a perceptual-motor task. The three functions illustrate the dynamic nature of the determinants of individual differences in skilled performance. An examination of the functions reveals that an answer to the question, "What are the most important determinants of performance?" will depend on the stage

Figure 8.5 Ackerman's proposed functions underlying skilled performance.

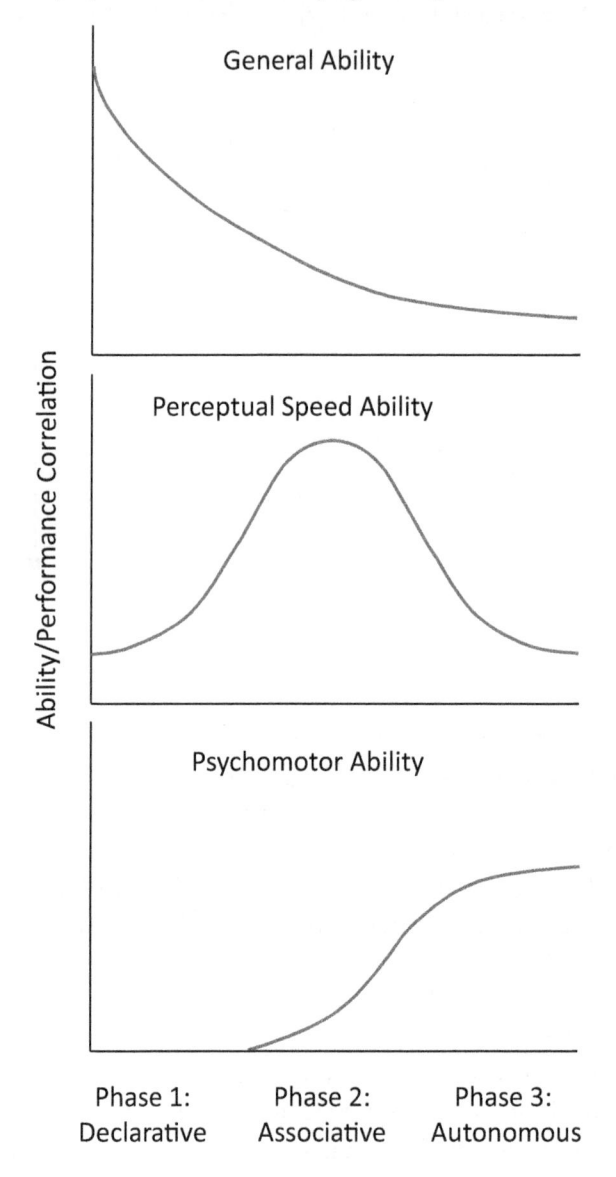

Y-axis: Ability/Performance Correlation

General Ability

Perceptual Speed Ability

Psychomotor Ability

Phase 1: Declarative   Phase 2: Associative   Phase 3: Autonomous

of skill development that is considered. Thus, a person high in general ability but low in psychomotor ability might initially perform better than a person with a different ability profile. For example, learning to use a new electrical gadget, such as an electronic planner with handwriting recognition capability, might initially depend more on the ability to understand the device's function and the instructions for its use. After the instructions have been mastered, the ability to enter information efficiently will become increasingly important. A person with hopeless handwriting, for example, might quickly figure out how to use the new planner, but be unable to develop proficiency because of this psychomotor limitation.

A prediction of the radex model is that the importance of particular individual differences may vary across different levels of skill. Ackerman (1992) investigated the ability determinants of individual differences with both traditional ability testing and skill-acquisition measures using a complex air traffic controller simulation task (TRACON), and found that individual differences across different levels of skill were predictable from the battery of ability measures. In the complex task used in the study, general ability was a substantial predictor of performance across skill levels. Interactions in ability and performance were observed that were consistent with the principles of skill acquisition and cognitive ability determinants outlined in Ackerman's earlier work, in that correlations between perceptual speed ability and skill were observed even at high practice levels. However, the correlations for general ability and skill increased over time, perhaps because the amount of novel information that had to be processed throughout task performance remained substantial. This conjecture was supported to some extent by later data showing that, in a less complex air traffic control task, the correlation with general ability decreased as participants became skilled at the task (Ackerman & Cianciolo, 2000). A more recent reanalysis of data from the TRACON task with what is called *latent growth curve modeling* provided evidence that a composite function of spatial-numerical ability for predicting differences in initial performance and perceptual speed for predicting the slope of the learning function accounted for approximately 30% of the individual differences in skill acquisition (Voelkle, Wittmann, & Ackerman, 2006).

Cognitive modeling using the ACT-R architecture (see Chapter 1) has also been used to test Ackerman's (1988) theory of the individual differences underlying performance at different stages of skill acquisition. Using data from Ackerman (1990), Taatgen (2002) argued that general intelligence can be modeled within ACT-R by a parameter controlling the amount of spreading activation in memory, and, thus, is related to working-memory capacity. Speed of knowledge compilation, manipulated with a parameter controlling proceduralization speed, corresponds to Ackerman's perceptual speed. Psychomotor speed is modeled by the time needed to make a keypress. As predicted by Ackerman, differences in the spread of activation parameter affected model performance the most at early stages of learning, differences in the speed of proceduralization had the most influence at intermediate stages of learning, and the role of the time needed for the model to make a keypress increased as a function of practice as the variability associated with the other factors decreased.

The goal of the ACT-R model was to capture the learning in this task by predicting the improvement in performance of participants at both a global level and the level of individual keystrokes. The task was to land planes in an air traffic control task. The use of specific runways is restricted by rules that relate to the kind of aircraft that is to be landed, whether the runway is short or long, and the present weather conditions. For example, a McDonnell Douglas DC-10 airliner can land on a short runway if the wind is less than 40 knots and there is no ice on the runway, which should lead to formation of the following production rule:

IF   The goal is to land a plane and a plane has been selected that can be landed on the short runway (match of goal buffer)
AND   you are currently looking at the short runway and it is not occupied (match of visual buffer)
AND   the right hand is not used at this moment (match of manual buffer)
THEN   note that we are moving to the short runway (change to goal buffer)
AND   push the arrow-down key (change to manual buffer)
AND   move attention to the weather information (change to visual buffer) . . .

Because this production rule and others like it are specific to the particular task, they must be acquired by practice with the task. For persons starting to learn the task, the model assumes that the instructions convey the task-specific knowledge about air traffic control required to perform the task, but that it is in declarative memory. This knowledge is not highly activated and must be interpreted by general production rules in order for the task to be executed.

The transition in performance from novice to expert is modeled by the process of production compilation (Taatgen & Anderson, 2002; see Chapter 1). New rules compete with the "parent" rules until they are established, after which they can provide a basis for even faster rules. After extensive practice, the rule set acquired by the model will perform like an expert. The model has been shown to predict increases in performance of the overall task and individual subtasks in Ackerman's (1988) experiments (see Taatgen & Lee, 2003).

Norman and Shallice's Levels of Action Control

An alternative account of skill acquisition is Norman and Shallice's (1986) *levels of action control*. This account describes the development of skill, given a consistent mapping of task components to responses, as a shift in the level of control exercised by the performer as a function of practice. Generally,

Norman and Shallice explain the shift in performance from early to late in practice in terms of the development of appropriate schemas for action control. Early in practice, performance depends on attentional control to coordinate many different *component* schemas for the execution of component tasks. In the associative phase of practice, so-called *source* schemas are developed that coordinate the selection and control of the component schemas. In the autonomous phase, source schemas themselves are triggered in a reflexive manner.

It follows from Norman and Shallice's account that performance on component tasks should be a better predictor of performance early in practice than later, before the component schemas have been organized (and, in a sense, subsumed) by the source schemas. Additionally, the nature of attentional demands changes as a function of practice. Early in practice, control is more qualitative in nature and serves the function of selecting appropriate strategies. In the associative phase, attentional control is required to coordinate the selection and execution of the source schemas. Thus, in this intermediate phase of skill development, the ability to allocate attention should be predictive of performance.

Matthews, Jones, and Chamberlain (1992) conducted a study to compare these predictions of Norman and Shallice's (1986) theory of individual differences and skill against those of Ackerman's (1988) modified radex model, which posits that skill development is characterized by a decreased reliance on general intelligence, a transient role for content abilities, and a final correlation of ability with perceptual-motor skill. They examined individual differences in performance of a simulated letter-sorting task for a group of untrained persons recruited from the community and a group of British Postal Service mail-coding operator trainees. To examine the relation of component abilities and skill, they tested the perceptual speed (using tasks ranging from letter matching to five-choice serial reaction), psychomotor ability (tapping speed), and general intelligence (digit span) of the participants in each group.

Based on Ackerman's (1988) account, Matthews et al. (1992) predicted that low-ability individuals, being slow in proceduralization, should show a larger correlation with digit span than with the other measures, since their performance should be at the cognitive phase, where general intelligence largely determines performance. High-ability individuals should proceduralize task knowledge more quickly and show higher correlations with the perceptual components. From Norman and Shallice's (1986) theory, Matthews et al. inferred that low-ability individuals' performance would depend more on component abilities—and should correlate more highly with these abilities—than should high-ability individuals' performance. Since the high-ability individuals should develop source schemas that require attentional control, the general personality measures of energetic arousal and extroversion, for which increasing values are associated with greater attentional resources, should be more highly correlated with performance for these persons.

Correlations computed between mail sorting skill and the various component measures showed that both the cognitive components and personality variables were associated with posttraining mail sorting performance, and that the correlations depended on the ability sample. For the Post Office sample, the only consistent predictor was the degree of extroversion: Extroverts within this sample were faster at coding mail and tended to be more accurate. For the general sample, the cognitive component measures were better predictors of performance. High speed and accuracy of mail coding were associated with better performance on both of the speeded component measures and digit recall. Comparisons between low- and high-ability individuals within the general sample showed a similar pattern: Extroversion was a better predictor of performance for the high-ability group, and the cognitive measures were more predictive for the low-ability group.

The interaction between ability group and predictive variables is consistent with Norman and Shallice's (1986) theory if variability in skill is associated with variability in executing component schemas for low-ability individuals and with variability in executing source schemas in high-ability individuals. It is more difficult to reconcile Ackerman's (1988) model with these results. Perceptual speed and general ability did not seem to trade off as good predictors of ability as a function of the skill level of the individuals. Matthews et al. (1992) suggested that the reason why Ackerman's model failed to account for these data, but performed well in other cases (e.g., Ackerman, 1988), is that the latter studies used "ability factors as predictors rather than discrete elementary cognitive tasks whose variation would reflect task-specific procedures or schemas as well as abilities" (p. 416). In other words, in complex tasks with many subcomponents, such as mail coding, measures of elementary component processes and executive control of performance may account for variance in performance additional to that predicted by psychometric ability measures.

Problems of Interpretation in Understanding the Relation between Abilities and Skill Level

The modified radex model of abilities and skills developed by Ackerman (1988, 1991) predicts that the dependencies between specific abilities and performance will vary as a function of the skill level of the performer. This model is one in a long history of the study of the nature of the relation between abilities and performance. As illustrated by the Matthews et al. (1992) study, the generality of models of this type is questionable. The major problem in validating such models and determining the relation between abilities and skill has been the difficulty of measuring both changes in skill and the association of abilities with performance. For example, Woodrow's (1946) conclusion that there is little shared variance between measures of general intellectual ability and measures of individual differences in learning is suspect because most of the research leading to this conclusion was based on the use of gain scores (i.e., the difference between initial and final performance scores) to measure learning. As Cronbach and Snow (1977) have pointed out, gain scores can be unreliable because the reliability of gain scores is a function of the reliabilities of the two scores from which they are derived. That is, gain scores have two sources of unreliability, and low correlations between tests and gain scores could be attributable to this unreliability.

Problems also exist with the other major technique used to determine the relation between skill acquisition and abilities, factor analysis. The goal of the approach, as described earlier, is to predict performance differences from ability measures. That is, we want measurements of some ability, x, to predict performance on some task, y. However, factor analysis is a technique in which all variables are treated alike—that is, in a nondirectional manner. Thus, factor analysis cannot properly be used to explain dependencies of performance on abilities. As Thurstone (1947) stated, "Whenever the investigator pivots his attention on one of the given variables which is central in importance and which is to be predicted by a set of independent variables, he is not talking about a factor problem" (p. 59). Furthermore, each factor is determined by both the measures of criterion task performance and the reference battery scores. Because the factors are partly derived from the criterion task performance, it is difficult to justify their use in predicting performance.

Evidence that these criticisms of factor analysis in the context of identifying relations between abilities and performance should be given credence comes from a study by J. A. Adams (1953). This study challenged Fleishman's generalization that the number of factors with significant loadings decreases from early to late in practice and shifts from verbal-cognitive to perceptual-motor loadings. Adams used Fleishman's procedure of administering both practice on a criterion task and a reference battery of tests. But, rather than employing factor analysis, Adams used the reference test scores as predictors in a regression equation. In multiple regression, the question asked is, "Do the independent variables (reference battery scores) predict the dependent variable (criterion task performance)?" As the criterion task, Adams used a test called the Complex Coordination Test. The reference battery he used contained 32 printed tests, 13 fine motor control tests (e.g., sticking pins in holes), and six more complex motor tests. Practice was given on the complex motor tests so that performance both early and late in practice could be compared with criterion task performance. The scores on the printed and motor tests, and the performance on the complex motor tasks both early and late in practice, were used as independent variables in a regression equation to predict both initial and final criterion task performance.

The percentage of the variance in the criterion task performance accounted for by the printed tests, simple motor tests, and early performance on the complex motor tests was less for final than for initial criterion task performance. This finding is consistent with earlier work showing decreasing correlations of reference test scores with criterion task performance as a function of practice. However, an examination of the contribution of each type of test to the prediction of criterion task performance revealed that the predictive ability of the printed tests was equal for initial and final criterion task performance. For both verbal and motor tests, some regression weights (a regression weight is an index of the ability to predict criterion performance from a specific predictor task value) increased, some stayed the same, and some decreased. That is, individual differences in complex motor performance as a function of practice could not be predicted on the basis of an orderly transition from reliance on verbal-cognitive to perceptual-motor ability. Moreover, when performance late in practice on the complex motor reference tasks was used in the regression equation, more of the variance in final criterion task performance than in initial criterion task performance was accounted for. This last finding lends optimism to the problem of predicting final performance on a criterion task, since it shows that increasing skill does not result in highly specific ability but can be predicted from the performance of a related skill.

To summarize, interpretations of abilities and their use in predicting performance across levels of skill are fraught with problems. Reanalyses of data using alternative statistical techniques (e.g., Ackerman's [1987] reanalysis of several studies conducted by Fleishman and his colleagues) may show quite different patterns of results and lead to a different set of conclusions. For example, although Fleishman and Quaintance (1984) concluded that task-specific factors are increasingly important determinants of performance with increasing practice, Ackerman's (1987) reanalysis of the data showed that, in some cases, task-specific abilities play a decreasing role in performance as skill increases.

It is encouraging to find evidence that general abilities can predict later performance and that skill is not entirely specific to particular task components. However, a complete evaluation of specific models intended to characterize the relation between ability and skill will depend on the development of better conceptions of abilities. J. A. Adams (1987) suggested that an approach whereby abilities are viewed as dynamic and developing (rather than static and not open to modification) may be more successful in describing determinants of individual differences in learning. From this perspective, measures of abilities should be taken at different levels of skill on predictor tasks, as well as at different levels of skill on the criterion task, to allow for the effects of practice on specific abilities. This conception of abilities as open to change brings into question the traditional distinction between abilities as enduring general traits limited in number and skill as the level of proficiency in a particular task. To quote J. A. Adams (1987), "Greater scientific advance can come from determining the fundamental nature of abilities than from assuming that abilities are existential entities that await discovery with a diligent application of factor analysis" (p. 57).

Individual Differences in Reading Skill

Perhaps because it is a skill fundamental to learning and education, reading ability has been extensively studied (Snowling & Hulme, 2005). Reading tasks, such as word naming and lexical decision (i.e., determining whether a letter string forms a word), are linked to more general tests of verbal ability, which is in itself correlated with a wide range of tasks. The study of individual differences in reading skill can lead to a better understanding of the components of verbal skill and the interrelationships among them (e.g., Butler, Jared, & Hains, 1984). Moreover, comparisons of readers from different skill levels can help identify the subskills that are necessary for efficient processing of verbal material, both when reading aloud and reading for comprehension.

With regard to reading aloud, a dual-route model has been widely accepted. One route, called lexical, involves accessing knowledge of spellings and pronunciations of a word in a mental lexicon. The other route, called nonlexical, allows the letter string to be "sounded out" through the use of rules that relate orthographic segments (e.g., syllables) to phonological segments. Evidence in support of the dual-route model includes that reaction times are longer to read aloud irregular words rather than regular words, suggesting competition between the two routes. In a review chapter, Coltheart (2005) concluded,

> Reading theorists have reached unanimity concerning the existence in the human reading system of two separate procedures for reading aloud—that is, dual routes from print to speech. One of these processing routes is usable only when the stimulus to be read is a real word; it cannot read nonwords. The other route can read all nonwords and regular words; there is still some dispute concerning how well it reads irregular words. (p. 23)

Current issues include which of several computational dual-route models, implemented in connectionist or rule-based frameworks, provides the best account of the detailed experimental results (Pritchard, Coltheart, Palethorpe, & Castles, 2012).

Two subskills relating to comprehension in which researchers have been interested are the abilities to use orthographic (word shape) and phonological (sound) information. Although some theories of reading state that the reader may access the meaning of a word directly on the basis of the recognition of a word shape or pattern of features without "sounding the word out" (e.g., Coltheart, 1978), other theories state that word recognition is based on a phonological code derived from the reader's knowledge of the correspondence between spelling and pronunciation (e.g., McCusker, Hillinger, & Bias, 1981). Again, though, a dual-route model of reading comprehension that allows meaning to be accessed directly via the visual pattern or indirectly by way of a mediating phonological code (e.g., Baron, 1977) seems most consistent with the evidence. Access of meaning by either of these routes is called *decoding*, and a study of young adults from 16 to 24 years of age confirms that decoding ability is the strongest correlate of reading skill (Braze, Tabor, Shankweiler, & Mencl, 2007).

One finding in support of a phonological route to comprehension is that people are more likely to classify a word falsely as a member of a designated category when the word is a homophone of a target category member (e.g., classify *break* as a car part) than when the word has spelling similar to a target (e.g., classify *brave* as a car part; Van Orden, 1987). If orthography were more important, the word most similar in spelling to the target word should more often be misclassified as a target. Jared and Seidenberg (1991) challenged this evidence of a stronger role for phonological information by showing that the effect was obtained only for words having a low frequency in the English language. Given that phonology plays a much greater role in the reading performance of less-skilled readers (M. J. Adams, 1990), Jared and Seidenberg suggest that the transition to skilled reading is marked by a shift from phonologically mediated to direct access of meaning.

Other evidence indicates the relative importance of orthographic information in skilled reading. For example, skilled readers are more sensitive to syllable boundaries than are less-skilled readers. This is illustrated by the finding that individuals who score high on vocabulary tests are less affected by word length when performing word naming or lexical-decision tasks than are low scorers (Butler & Hains, 1979). Those who score low on vocabulary tests perform these tasks more slowly as the words (or nonwords) become larger. What is the reason for this difference in ability to process word information quickly? At some stage of processing affected by word length, high-vocabulary readers are faster. It has been proposed that high-vocabulary readers are better able to use the redundancy present in the English language to make their classifications (Butler et al., 1984). However, Jackson and McClelland (1975, 1979) found that skilled readers are faster than nonskilled readers at any task requiring memory retrieval and suggested that the difference in speed depends on the complexity of the to-be-remembered memory code. Thus, differences in word naming and lexical decision could be due either to speed differences between low- and high-ability readers in retrieving orthographic information during word processing or to speed differences during lexical retrieval.

Butler et al. (1984) tested between these hypotheses by presenting low- and high-vocabulary readers with pseudowords varying in their approximation to English. For example, a zero-order approximation to English is a randomly ordered string of letters (e.g., kgtrjdi), whereas a fourth-order approximation is a pronounceable nonword (e.g., dinglect). Second-order approximations would lie between the two in terms of pronouncibility. After viewing the letter strings for a brief (60-ms) period, as many as possible of the letters that had been presented were to be reported. Butler et al. found that high-vocabulary individuals recalled more letters in the fourth-order approximation strings than did low-vocabulary individuals, but low-vocabulary individuals recalled more letters in the zero-order approximation strings. It seems that the high-vocabulary readers are more sensitive to the structure of the letter strings and better able to use redundancy when it is present. From this finding, Butler et al. concluded that individual differences in lexical-decision and naming tasks reflect differences in reading skill and the efficiency of letter sequence parsing prior to word recognition, rather than speed differences in lexical retrieval. In a second experiment, they found that skilled readers were more sensitive to syllabic structure than were nonskilled readers. Nonskilled readers, on the other hand, were more affected by characteristics of the presentation that were unrelated to word boundaries. A generalization from this research is that skilled readers process letter strings in a more holistic fashion than do nonskilled readers.

According to the lexical quality hypothesis, reading also depends on lexical representations of high quality, where lexical quality "refers to the extent to which the reader's knowledge of a given word represents the word's form and meaning constituents and knowledge of word use that combines meaning with pragmatic features" (Perfetti, 2007, p. 359). This knowledge includes detailed orthographic, phonological, and semantic representations. Braze et al. (2007), in their study of young adult readers, found that, as predicted by the lexical quality hypothesis, vocabulary knowledge contributed to reading ability in addition to the aforementioned contribution of decoding ability. They concluded, "there is appreciable evidence suggesting that both decoding skill and word knowledge are worthy targets of remediation efforts directed toward adult unskilled readers" (p. 240).

Another concern in reading skill is how working memory might be used in the comprehension of text. Masson and Miller (1983) noted that the ability to store and process information in working memory is positively related to scores on standardized reading comprehension tests and to long-term encoding and retrieval of explicitly presented information, as well as with the ability to integrate information for the purposes of making inferences. However, the ability to store information (without the requirement to process it) is not related to these abilities. Thus, the ability to coordinate storage and processing functions in working memory may be an important determinant of text processing skill. In the case of short-term memory (e.g., Carlson, Sullivan, & Schneider, 1989, see Chapter 5), storing and using information have different costs in terms of processing demand. In the case of reading, the ability to process information is more predictive of the cognitive ability to draw inferences.

The importance of taking processing demands into account has been demonstrated in reading from hypertext, as well as from traditional texts (Naumann, Richter, Christmann, & Groeben, 2008). A hypertext document contains pages that can be accessed via hyperlinks. As compared to conventional text, the organization is nonlinear. Hypertext has the potential benefit of allowing readers to easily access relevant material as needed, but new strategies are needed if this benefit is to be realized. Participants in Naumann et al.'s study received training on either of two learning strategies: cognitive, which involved organization and elaboration, and metacognitive, which involved planning and monitoring. Measures of working-memory capacity, a reading span test similar to the operation span test described in an earlier chapter, and reading skill, as assessed by a test of sentence-level reading comprehension efficiency, revealed aptitude-treatment interactions. Learning outcomes and quality of navigational behavior showed that, relative to a control group that was not taught specific strategies, participants with high working-memory capacity or reading skill benefited from either type of strategy training, whereas those with low working-memory capacity or reading skill showed a cost.

Skilled readers may process words more efficiently than do less-skilled readers. However, there is an alternative explanation for why some readers are less skilled. Not only is reading skill highly correlated with other verbal abilities such as listening comprehension, but also it is correlated with the ability to comprehend nonverbal picture stories (Gernsbacher, Varner, & Faust, 1990). This apparent overlap in ability to perform a range of tasks has led some researchers to suggest that all these behaviors depend on the same underlying mechanisms. Gernsbacher (1993) proposed that one such underlying mechanism is the ability to suppress unwanted or inappropriate mental representations. The basic idea is that when reading or performing other cognitive tasks much stored information may be activated automatically or retrieved unintentionally. That is, along with the appropriate representations, related but task-inappropriate representations are activated. To illustrate this, read the following sentence: "While placing her bet, she glanced at the spade held in her hand." Most likely, the sentence brought to mind the image of a playing card, perhaps the ace of spades. It is also possible that you thought of a different sort of spade—one used for digging the garden. Successful reading depends on the determination of the appropriate meaning of ambiguous words and the suppression of inappropriate meanings, just as successful execution of an action depends on selecting one motor plan and suppressing all others.

An array of experiments has been conducted that shows that less-skilled readers have more trouble suppressing inappropriate meanings than do skilled readers (Gernsbacher, 1993, 1997). For example, immediately after reading a sentence such as *He dug with the spade*, both skilled and unskilled readers have trouble determining whether the word *ace* fits into the sentence context relative to the time it takes to make the judgment after reading a sentence with an unambiguous word such as shovel. However, if they are asked to make such a judgment 1 second after reading the sentence, the unskilled readers have much more trouble rejecting the inappropriate word than do skilled readers (see Figure 8.6). This difference suggests that more skilled readers are better able to suppress irrelevant representations than are less-skilled readers. Similar differences are obtained for latencies to reject homophones (e.g., reject *patients* after reading the sentence *She treated the dog with great patience*), and words related to pictures that were to be ignored (Gernsbacher, 1993). Gernsbacher and colleagues have extended this research to multiple goals in narrative texts. One study showed that readers took longer to verify the original goal in a narrative after a new goal was

Figure 8.6 Estimated activation of the inappropriate meaning of an ambiguous word by skilled and unskilled comprehenders when tested immediately after the presentation of a sentence prime or after a 1-second delay.

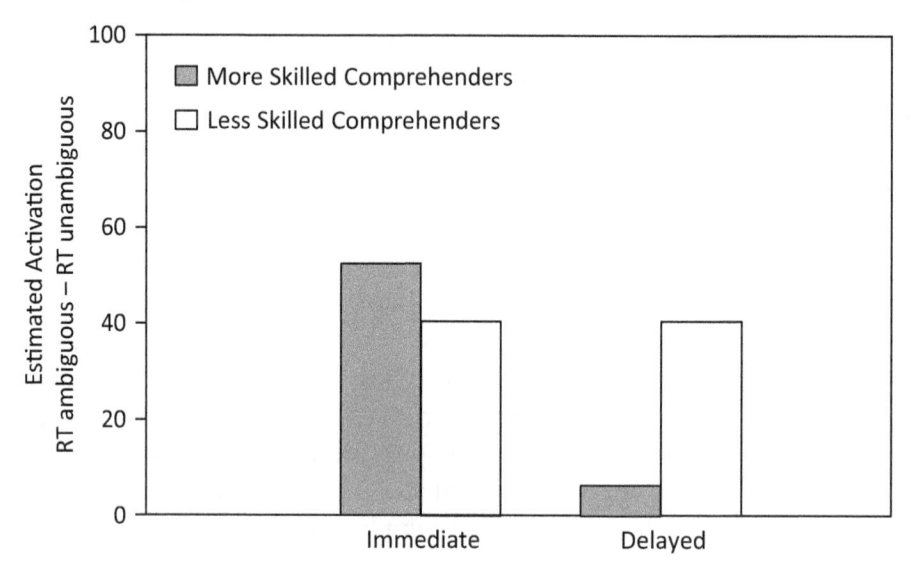

Adapted from Gernsbacher (1990).

introduced compared to when the new information was neutral (Linderholm et al., 2004).

The hypothesis that suppression of irrelevant or inappropriate information is a general cognitive function gains some support from the finding of individual differences in the ability to suppress information in different populations. For example, Connelly and Hasher (1993) found that elderly adults showed less suppression of distracting information than did young adults. However, whereas elderly adults showed less suppression of object information, they showed normal or above-average suppression of location information. This difference in suppression suggests that separate mechanisms of suppression might act on the neural systems that process object and location information.

An alternative possibility is that suppression in the reading tasks does not reflect a general inhibitory capability at all. McNamara and McDaniel (2004) presented evidence that Gernsbacher's suppression results could be explained better by a knowledge-based account in which greater activation of knowledge relevant to the material overpowers the inapplicable meanings. Specifically, they reported three experiments in which they dissociated knowledge from reading skill, and in all cases, the greater knowledge was associated with quicker suppression of conflicting meanings. Two of the experiments had participants respond to ambiguous words in baseball-related sentence contexts, and those participants with greater baseball knowledge were better at suppressing the irrelevant meaning of baseball-related words but not general-topic words. In their third experiment, again independent of reading skill, participants with greater general knowledge showed evidence of more quickly suppressing the irrelevant meaning of ambiguous words in general-topic sentences. The alternative viewpoint advocated by McNamara and McDaniel is that suppression comes about from greater activation of information associated with relevant meanings than from an active inhibition or irrelevant meanings.

As a final note, most studies have assumed that all skilled readers process information in a similar manner. However, individual differences between skilled readers have been found that conform to Perfetti's (2007) lexical quality hypothesis (Andrews, 2015), which emphasizes the flexibility and precision of lexical knowledge. Andrews and colleagues have used masked orthographical and morphological priming methods, in which a priming stimulus is displayed briefly (for approximately 50 ms), and then masked, prior to a target stimulus that requires a response. Because participants typically show little awareness of the prime, it is reasonable to attribute the priming effects to early lexical processes. By varying the relations of the primes to the target stimuli and the judgments that are to be made, they have identified two dimensions of difference among skilled readers. One is an overall proficiency dimension revealed in measures of spelling, vocabulary, and reading comprehension. The other is a factor relating to a discrepancy between vocabulary/reading on the one hand and spelling on the other. These factors basically influence the relative roles of facilitation and inhibition induced by the relation of the prime stimulus to the word to which a response is to be made.

Skill and Aging

Sooner or later, all of us will be faced with the prospect of changes in our abilities to perform certain tasks simply because of our ages. Some of the changes in our abilities will be due to physical deterioration, such as failing eyesight and loss of strength. But evidence is accumulating to indicate that changes in information-processing ability also occur, such as possible changes in inhibitory mechanisms as mentioned in the preceding section. In this section, we review what is known about changes in the ability to perform simple information-processing tasks and the implications of these changes for skill maintenance and acquisition.

One change that occurs in older adults is that the speed of information processing slows (Salthouse & Madden, 2008). This slowing of information processing not only may impact performance of tasks in which rapid responses are required, such as driving, but also may mediate differences in decision making that characterize older adults (Henninger, Madden, & Huettel, 2010). There is evidence to suggest that this general slowing is due to a loss of mass of white matter throughout the brain. Penke et al. (2010) conducted MRI scans of 132 healthy individuals of approximately 72 years age. Detailed analyses showed that individuals' scores on a general factor that captures the common variance in integrity across eight white matter tracts were correlated with a general factor of information-processing speed, with individual tracts showing no correlation beyond the variance explained by the common factor. These results imply that impaired cortical connectivity is a global process influencing various major tracts.

Given that a decrease in information speed is a significant deficit for older adults, a question is whether training can reduce the deficit. Evidence suggests that training that focuses specifically on cognitive speed of processing can be effective (M. L. Ellis, Edwards, Peterson, Roker, & Athilingam, 2014). Moreover, two recent reviews of the literature on action-based video games reached the conclusion that they can benefit processing speed, as well as aspects of attention (Bavelier et al., 2012; Toril, Reales, & Ballesteros, 2014). For example, Szelag and Skolimowska (2012) assigned healthy older adults to one of three groups. The temporal training group received 8 weeks of training on games requiring temporal information processing of auditory nonverbal material and nonsense syllables; the active control group received a comparable amount of training but on non-temporal computer games available in Windows XP; the passive control group received no training during the 8-week period. Various cognitive functions, including temporal information processing and some aspects of attention and short-term memory, were evaluated prior to and after training. Although both training groups showed improved temporal information processing, only the temporal training group evidenced better attention and memory performance, indicative of improved cognitive functioning.

A related issue is whether a physical training program, which improves physical fitness, can improve the cognitive functioning of older adults. On the basis of a meta-analysis of existing studies, Colcombe and Kramer (2003) concluded, "Fitness training increased performance 0.5 SD on average, regardless of the type of cognitive task, the training method, or participants' characteristics" (p. 128). They found that executive-control processes benefited more than other processes, though. As a recent example, Langlois et al. (2013) assigned frail older adults to a group that received exercise training three times a week for 12 weeks or to a control group that did not. The exercise group showed larger gains not only in tests of executive control but also in tests of processing speed and working memory.

In earlier chapters, we examined in some detail the operations and procedures that underlie performance of many tasks. For example, a problem solver must perceive the elements of the problem, construct a representation of the problem space, and, most likely, apply some heuristic strategy to reach a solution. Success may depend on the ability to detect similarities to other problems, to infer relationships, and to coordinate information in working memory. The consideration of complex tasks in terms of more basic abilities suggests that the ability to perform basic information-processing tasks should be predictive of more complex task performance. This reasoning underlies many attempts to understand aging processes by determining the relationship between age and the efficiency of elementary cognitive processes (e.g., Salthouse, 1985).

The general finding regarding the relationship between age and basic cognitive processing is that the two things are negatively related. That is, older persons generally perform less well on basic cognitive tests than do younger persons. One study demonstrating this negative relation was conducted by Salthouse, Kausler, and Saults (1988). Salthouse et al. administered a set of cognitive test batteries to groups of 129 and 233 adults who ranged from 20 to 79 years of age. Table 8.3 summarizes the results of correlating

TABLE 8.3 Summary Correlations between Tests of Elementary Cognitive Processes and Chronological Age

Age Correlation	Measure/Ability	Task Description
-0.55	Digit symbol speed/speed of information processing	Rate of determining whether symbols and digits match according to a specified code
-0.36	Number comparison speed/speed of information processing	Rate of determining whether two strings of digits are identical
-0.38	Verbal memory/Capacity for temporarily retaining information	Accuracy of recalling the identities of target letters from a matrix
-0.43	Spatial memory/capacity for temporarily retaining Information	Accuracy of recalling the location of target letters from a matrix
-0.34	Paired associates/efficiency in forming associations	Accuracy of recalling the response word associated with a stimulus word
-0.43	Geometric analogies/infer or abstract relationships	Accuracy of determining the truth or falsity of geometric Analogies

(Adapted from Salthouse, 1989)

chronological age with performance of the various tests administered. On several measures of ability, including speed of information processing (e.g., time to make a true-false decision), storage of information in memory (visual and spatial memory measures), and formation and recollection of simple associations (e.g., paired associates task), increased age was associated with poorer performance. The important question, then, is to what degree decreases in the efficiency or effectiveness of basic cognitive processing interfere with the acquisition and performance of skills.

The relationship between skill and aging is not as clear-cut as the relationship between aging and basic cognitive processing. Even though the supposed constituent elements of skill seem to degrade with age, skilled performance does not necessarily suffer (Salthouse, 1989). To examine the relation between aging and cognitive components of skill, it is necessary to first control for other factors (e.g., physical changes, initial skill proficiency). For example, Cappelletti, Didino, Stoianov, and Zorzi (2014) had younger and older adults perform a numerosity discrimination task that required judging which of two sets of items was more numerous and arithmetic tasks. Performance was unimpaired on the arithmetic tasks but impaired on the numerosity task. However, the authors provided evidence that the impairment in numerosity judgments was associated with suppressing incongruent information (e.g., the less numerous items being larger in size than the more numerous ones), and concluded that number skills are maintained in healthy older adults.

One approach to controlling for other factors has been termed the *Molar equivalence–Molecular decomposition* strategy (Salthouse, 1984). This strategy involves selecting individuals to have the same level of skill, and then analyzing the effects of age on the efficiency of the processes that are the components of that skill. Thus, the question that is asked concerns whether people of different ages rely on the efficiency of the same component processes when performance is at equivalent levels. The outcome of the limited amount of research that has been conducted using this strategy suggests that older individuals rely less on domain-related memory skills but are still able to achieve the same performance levels as younger persons. For example, in the domain of chess, Charness (1981) found that older players were less accurate in recalling meaningful game configurations (see Chapter 7) and had a different recall organization. Specifically, older players utilized a smaller number of chunks than did younger players. Older players were also faster at selecting a next move than were younger players. Analyses of players' protocols suggested that this was because fewer alternative moves were considered by the older players (perhaps because of memory limitations, but more likely due to a different criterion for move selection—namely, older players tended to select the first acceptable move). It is not clear whether the ability of older players to match that of younger players despite some lower basic cognitive abilities is due to compensation of deficient abilities by some other age-related or experience-based factor, or if it is due to a different task composition. That is, with experience, a skill may be encapsulated or compiled in such a way that it no longer directly depends on basic processes, but has a form that is automated or somehow independent of other abilities. It will be interesting to see more research on the intriguing possibility that skilled performance can become somehow independent of basic abilities.

The other important question regarding aging and skill is "How does aging affect the ability to acquire new skills?" Based on the finding that older persons are more limited in basic cognitive abilities, it might be expected that skill acquisition ability would also be limited. However, there is little evidence for this (Salthouse, 1989). The lack of evidence is in large part due to the paucity of studies of skill acquisition in older persons, but is also due to difficulties in controlling for experience-related factors. One study that examined the acquisition of a perceptual-motor skill found that the acquisition functions for young and old persons were about the same (Salthouse & Somberg, 1982). Older persons did not perform as well as younger persons either at the outset of the task or after 50 hours of practice, but the acquisition curves for both groups were similar. Somewhat earlier, Thorndike, Bregman, Tilton, and Woodward (1928) reported several studies showing a greater degree of improvement in older persons for tasks such as left-hand writing (using right-handed individuals) and learning Esperanto (an artificial language). These somewhat contradictory results are not resolved by any more recent studies, so the question of how aging affects skill acquisition remains an open one.

Summary

Psychologists have been interested in measuring individual differences since the 19th century, and this interest has led to the development of many different conceptions of human abilities. One of the most controversial areas in the study of individual differences is the extent to which an "ability to learn" exists separate from general ability. In fact, learning ability is often equated with intelligence. Apart from general intelligence, different abilities have been shown to correlate with task performance. Much research has been concerned with the extent to which measures of specific abilities can be used to predict performance early and late in practice. The research evidence on this question is mixed; the predictive ability of different measures seems to depend on the type of criterion task and the nature of the measures of component abilities.

The joint study of individual differences and skill acquisition can lead to new understanding of particular skills as the abilities that correlate with that skill are discovered. For example, in reading, the view that there is both phonologically mediated and direct access of lexical knowledge receives support from the finding that skilled readers are less sensitive to phonological information and more sensitive to orthographic information than are less-skilled readers. Although the efficiency of basic cognitive processes tends to decline with age, similar declines in skill are not always seen. Moreover, the ability to acquire new skills may or may not be limited by increasing age. Continued study of skill and aging is certainly warranted, both because of the need to understand age-related performance problems and to understand better the nature of skill. Apparent dissociations between basic cognitive abilities and level of skill suggest possible hypotheses regarding the building blocks of skill and the eventual structure of skilled behavior.

9

Situational Influences on Skilled Performance

Certainly, precise adjustment to a complex situation does depend on a great deal of automation in perception, judgement, and action control. But experts achieve the highest levels of performance by integrating or meshing cognitive and automatic processes closely.

W. Christensen, J. Sutton, & D. McIlwain (2015, p. 280)

Skills often have to be performed under extreme conditions. A skilled firefighter must make quick decisions and take appropriate actions while operating in extreme heat and under the stress imposed by the potential for loss of life and property. A pianist entering a competition must perform in front of a critical audience, with the knowledge that the performance is being evaluated in relation to that of other skilled pianists. And a basketball player may be placed in the situation of having to make a shot at a crucial point in a championship game. Whether the player executes the shot accurately may determine not only the outcome of the game but also whether the team wins the season championship. The stress imposed by situations such as these can alter performance dramatically.

A good example of someone who excelled in such critical or "clutch" situations is the former professional National Basketball Association player Michael Jordan. Jordan, who won six championships with the Chicago Bulls, in two runs of 3 successive years, was named Number 1 in a 2012 list, *The 25 Most Clutch Players in NBA Finals History*. The authors of the list, Diaz, Palladino, and Evans (2012), describe the reason why they placed Jordan at the top:

> Where do we start? Switching hands in mid-air against the Lakers in '91? Six straight threes [3-point shots] against the Blazers in '92? The pass to Paxson against the Suns in '93? Beating the Sonics on Father's Day in '96? The "Flu Game" against the Jazz in '97? Or "The Shot" against the Jazz in '98? How about never facing a Game 7 [of a 7-game championship series, for which 4 victories must be achieved to win the series] in six Finals appearances?

Any sports fan can probably think of many examples of the opposite case, in which an athlete was known for *not* performing well in crucial situations. What distinguishes a "clutch player" like Michael Jordan from a "choke artist"? This is one of the questions that has been of interest to researchers who study the effects of situational factors on skilled performance. The starting point for most contemporary research on performance-moderating factors is arousal or activation theory. *Arousal* as a construct was originally proposed as a unitary dimension of activation, varying from the low levels associated with sleeping to the extremely high levels associated with stressful situations. Arousal is presumed to govern the overall activation level, with the direction of behavior (i.e., the specific activity in which the person engages), which is determined by purposes and goals. The stress produced at high arousal levels is caused by stimuli that a person appraises as "stressors." It is characterized by subjective reports of a stressful experience, a non-specific increase in arousal, and the feedback that the brain receives from this response to stressors (Ursin & Eriksen, 2004).

Although variants of the construct of arousal were suggested as far back as the 1920s, the notion that there is a continuum of arousal reflecting the intensive aspect of behavior did not become widely accepted until the 1950s and 1960s (e.g., Duffy, 1962; Malmo, 1959). Its acceptance was based largely on the discovery that the reticular formation of the brain stem, which receives input from all of the senses and is connected to the cerebral cortex, produces a diffuse activation pattern in the electroencephalogram (Lindsley, 1951; Moruzzi & Magoun, 1949), with higher levels of activation presumably corresponding to higher levels of arousal. With regard to performance, the general idea behind arousal theory is that factors such as time of day, sleep deprivation, incentives, and drug use can be thought to exert their effects on performance by influencing the arousal level. It has become apparent that the concept of a unitary construct of arousal is an oversimplification and that at least two types of arousal, energetic and tense, can be distinguished by self-report questionnaires (Boehringer, Schwabe, & Schachinger, 2010; Thayer, 1989). Energetic arousal is an alertness dimension ranging from tired to energetic (i.e., the dimension most typically thought of with regard to arousal), whereas tense arousal is a mood dimension ranging from calm to highly anxious.

Arousal and Performance

The first work to be interpreted as evidence for a relationship between level of arousal and performance is that of Yerkes and Dodson (1908). They conducted a series of experiments in which mice had to avoid the darker of two boxes in a chamber and enter the lighter box. If a mouse entered the darker box, it received an electrical shock. Yerkes and Dodson conducted three experiments in which the difficulty of the discrimination to be learned was manipulated by varying the difference in brightness between the two boxes and different mice learned the discrimination under different intensities of shock. For the simplest discrimination, the rate of learning was an increasing function of the shock intensity. However, for the more difficult discriminations, learning was an inverted U-shaped function of intensity, being slower for high- and low-intensity shocks than for intermediate values. Moreover, the shock intensity associated with the fastest learning was less for the most difficult task than for the task of intermediate difficulty.

When the construct of arousal became popular in the 1950s and researchers collected additional data suggesting that the relation between arousal and performance might have an inverted U-shape (see, e.g., Hebb, 1955), Yerkes and Dodson's inverted U-shaped functions for shock intensity and learning were noted and generalized as functions relating arousal and performance. The generalization that performance is an inverted U-shaped function of arousal, and that the optimal arousal level is a decreasing function of task complexity, came to be called the *Yerkes-Dodson law* (see Figure 9.1). In terms of the Yerkes-Dodson law, one might conjecture that Michael Jordan's superior performance in playoff games was due to his having a lower baseline level of arousal than most people. According to this reasoning, the increase in arousal that accompanies big games moves his arousal level closer to the optimum rather than beyond the optimum.

The status and value of the Yerkes-Dodson law and the concept of arousal have been debated. Articles within the past 10 years claimed, "The robustness of the Yerkes-Dodson law is quite impressive" (Johnston, Moreno, Regas,

Figure 9.1 The Yerkes-Dodson law. Quality of performance is an inverted U-shaped function of arousal level, with the optimal arousal level being lower for complex tasks than for simple tasks.

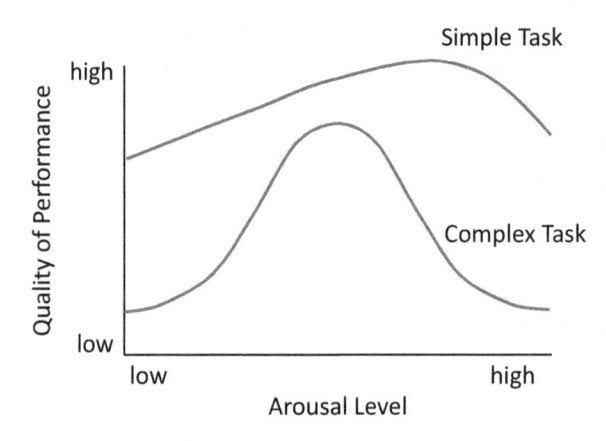

Tyler, & Foreyt, 2012, p. 677), and "The concept [of arousal] has been controversial, but seems to us to be necessary in physiological, psychological, and clinical science, in man and animals" (Ursin & Eriksen, 2004, p. 587). Consistent with these views, Spiekermann and Korunovska (2014) found that both performance on a creativity test and quality of information sharing with others varied as an inverted U-shaped function of computer interface complexity, which they interpreted in terms of the Yerkes-Dodson law.

In opposition are statements like "the Yerkes-Dodson law has served out its role in psychology and is no longer needed" (Christianson, 1992, p. 298) and the law is "an over-simplistic and fundamentally flawed proposition" (Hancock & Ganey, 2003, p. 5). To the extent it captures an important relation between arousal and performance, though, the Yerkes-Dodson law is just a description of that relation and not an explanation, and theoretical accounts are needed.

Theories Based on General Arousal and the Yerkes-Dodson Law

The cognitive activation theory (CAT) of stress (Ursin & Eriksen, 2004, 2010) is a comprehensive account of the physiological and behavioral consequences of stress that is built on the concept of general arousal. CAT places emphasis on learned expectancies of outcomes to actions taken in the presence of certain physical stimuli (potential stressors). These expectancies can be negative, neutral, or positive, with "coping" behaviors regarded as ones with positive outcome expectancies. Stress is produced when expectancies and the sensory information for the current situation mismatch, and results in the triggering of general activation that increases behavioral and psychological arousal. This activation is regarded in CAT as adaptive, in that it leads the person to try to determine solutions to remove the stress. Prolonged levels of high arousal are not considered to be good, though, and impose a health risk.

CAT focuses only on high arousal situations and does not have much to say about how the nature of information processing changes as a function of arousal level, except that a stressor draws the organism's attention to it. Two prominent accounts of the Yerkes-Dodson law, the cue-utilization hypothesis and the multiple-resources hypothesis, attribute the relation between arousal and performance to specific changes in information processing.

The cue-utilization hypothesis (Easterbrook, 1959) is one of the oldest and best-known accounts of the Yerkes-Dodson law. This hypothesis is based on the idea that the range of cues that a person can observe, maintain an orientation toward, respond to, or associate with responses changes as a function of arousal. According to Easterbrook, as arousal increases, the range of cues to which the person attends is reduced (i.e., attention narrows). The cue-utilization hypothesis accounts for the inverted U-shaped function by assuming that at low levels of arousal, both task-relevant (or central) and task-irrelevant (or peripheral) cues are utilized, and the task-irrelevant cues interfere with performance to some extent. As arousal increases, the peripheral or irrelevant cues are excluded from the range of cue utilization. Because the range is increasingly restricted to the task-relevant cues, performance improves. However, when the point is reached at which all of the remaining cues being utilized are task-relevant, any further increase in arousal will result in some relevant cues being excluded. Thus, performance will decline at high arousal levels. Assuming that difficult tasks have a higher proportion of task-relevant cues than do easy tasks, the fact that performance deteriorates at a lower level of arousal for complex tasks than for simple tasks is also explained.

Support for the cue-utilization hypothesis has come primarily from evidence for attentional narrowing (i.e., a restriction in the range of cues utilized) in dual-task contexts, such as those in which a tracking task for which the element to be tracked is presented centrally and stimuli for secondary tasks are presented peripherally. For example, when people performed 1-minute trials of a continuous tracking task, and at the same time had to turn out lights that occurred occasionally in the peripheral visual field or to respond to an occasional deflection of a pointer of a peripherally located dial, performance on the tracking task depended on whether a bonus was offered for high combined scores on the central tracking task and the peripheral tasks (Bahrick, Fitts, & Rankin, 1952). When the bonus could be earned, performance on the central tracking task improved, but performance on the peripheral tasks declined. Assuming that the influence of the bonus is to increase arousal, these results suggest that increasing arousal causes the range of cue utilization to be restricted to the central cues. Similar results have been obtained for shocks administered randomly during performance of the tracking task (Bacon, 1974) and for selection of stimuli from multi-letter displays under conditions of high temporal expectancy (for which arousal should be higher) versus low temporal expectancy (Sørensen, Vangkilde, & Bundesen, 2015). From an evolutionary perspective, and consistent with CAT's view that the stress response is adaptive (Ursin & Eriksen, 2010), the restriction of cues attended at high arousal levels may have been beneficial for tasks such as escaping from a predator (Hanoch & Vitouch, 2004).

The other explanation of the Yerkes-Dodson law is M. S. Humphreys and Revelle's (1984) *multiple-resources* account, which attributes the inverted U-shaped relation of arousal and performance to opposing effects of arousal on two distinct information-processing components. The first of these components is *sustained information transfer*, which encompasses all of the processes involved in identifying a stimulus and selecting and executing a response to it. Humphreys and Revelle liken this component to the concept of sustained attention and propose that the resources available for information transfer increase monotonically as a function of arousal level. The second component is *short-term memory*, which encompasses the processes required to retain and retrieve information in the short-term store. In contrast to sustained information transfer, the resources for short-term memory are presumed to decrease monotonically as arousal increases.

Humphreys and Revelle's (1984) multiple-resource model makes different predictions for the influence of arousal on performance as a function of the relative demands that a task places on information-transfer and short-term memory resources. For tasks with little or no short-term memory demands, such as choice reactions, vigilance (monitoring displays for signals that rarely occur), and letter cancellation, performance should be solely a function of the sustained information-transfer component and, hence, should be an increasing function of arousal. For tasks that have significant short-term memory demands as well, such as digit span and running memory tasks, performance should be a combination of the increasing and decreasing functions and, thus, an inverted U-shaped function of arousal (see Figure 9.2). Moreover, as the task demands for short-term memory resources increase relative to the demands for information-transfer resources, the arousal level at which optimal performance is obtained should decrease. Because complex tasks typically draw more on short-term memory resources than do simple tasks, the optimal arousal level for performing complex tasks should be less.

Figure 9.2 Humphreys and Revelle's multiple-resources model. The increasing function for information transfer and decreasing function for short-term memory combine to produce an inverted U-shaped function for performance of tasks in which both resources are demanded.

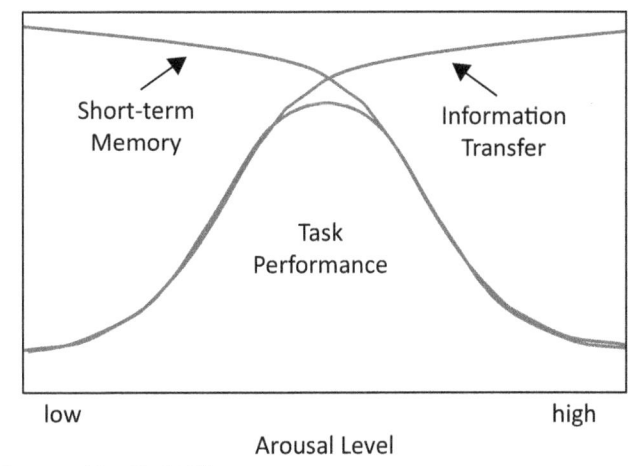

Source: M. S. Humphreys and Revelle (1984).

The explanations for the inverted U-shaped function proposed by Easterbrook (1959) and Humphreys and Revelle (1984) both attribute the function to two factors (irrelevant and relevant cues in the first case; information transfer and short-term memory in the second case) and assume that the primary limitation is on controlled information processing. This makes it difficult to test between the explanations. For example, the cue-utilization hypothesis has been tested by comparing performance decrements associated with arousal for single- and dual-task situations. Consistent with the view that a wider range of cues is relevant in the dual-task situation, decreases in performance are usually greater for dual-task performance than for single-task performance (e.g., Bacon, 1974). However, it can also be argued that the dual-task situation usually imposes a greater short-term memory load, which makes the results also consistent with Humphreys and Revelle's model. In fact, Bacon (1974) interpreted the greater decrement for dual- as compared to single-task performance as showing that whether peripheral cues can be excluded from processing is a function of short-term memory demands.

Arguments against "General Arousal" and the Yerkes-Dodson Law

The construct of arousal has come under severe criticism because at least one neural system in addition to the reticular activation system (i.e., the hypothalamic-limbic system involved in emotional arousal) contributes to arousal. Moreover, many of the criterion measures that are supposed to reflect arousal do not correlate highly with each other (Lacey, 1967; Neiss, 1988). Also, as is evident from the many explanations for the Yerkes-Dodson law, the law is essentially irrefutable (Neiss, 1988). There are many instances in the literature in which the inverted U-shaped function was not obtained, but for which additional ad hoc assumptions make the results appear consistent with the law. Neiss concluded that the Yerkes-Dodson law is correct only in the trivial sense that "subjects with incentive will outperform either those with none or those responding to a serious plausible threat" (p. 345), or in stronger terms, that "the motivated outperform the apathetic and terrified" (p. 355). Perhaps the most serious criticism that Neiss (1988) leveled against the Yerkes-Dodson law is that it obscures individual differences in performance under conditions in which threats or incentives are high, which Neiss regarded as the most salient feature of such situations. Specifically, with the exception of ad hoc conjectures of the type that we presented as a possible reason for why Michael Jordan performed well in championship games (that he may have a lower baseline arousal than other persons), the construct of arousal level itself does not provide much insight into why some individuals enter a facilitative state in threatening situations whereas others enter a debilitative state. Even in life-threatening situations, for which arousal should be extremely high, 12% to 25% of people show appropriately organized responses (Tyhurst, 1951), as the pilot Chesley Sullenberger did on January 15, 2009, when he safely landed US Airways Flight 1549 in the Hudson River after it had lost power in both engines while leaving LaGuardia Airport in New York.

Given that high arousal itself does not preclude successful performance of complex tasks, Neiss (1988) argued that perhaps cognitive and affective factors, as well as biological factors, should be considered to enable better understanding of individual differences in responding in high-stress situations. Constructs such as tense arousal (Thayer, 1989), as well as the CAT account of stress (Ursin & Eriksen, 2010), mentioned earlier, may be important for understanding the role of affective factors, and accounts such as the multiple-resources account of the Yerkes-Dodson law (Humphreys & Revelle, 1994) may help elucidate the effects of arousal on information processing.

Although the Yerkes-Dodson law is a simplification that does not adequately capture the complex, interactive effects that many variables have on performance, in many cases, though not always, performance is an inverted U-shaped function of such variables as drug use and incentives. The breakdown in performance that is often observed at high levels of these variables apparently reflects to a large extent processes involved in maintaining appropriate information in working memory and directing behavior toward the task being performed. Many of us seek to increase our arousal on a regular basis by engaging in sports or other exercise, and we may experience changes in our ability to perform cognitive tasks during and after engaging in exercise. However, whereas some people report increased mental acuity and clarity of thought, others report trouble concentrating, or difficulty making decisions following exercise. The effects of exercise-induced arousal on the performance of cognitive tasks have been the subject of considerable debate. A large body of literature on the topic (summarized in Brisswalter, Collardeau, & Arcelin, 2002; Tomporowski, 2003) points to conflicting findings. Individual differences in physical condition, intensity of exercise, and personality no doubt contribute to the diversity of the findings, but according to recent meta-analyses (Chang, Labban, Gapin, & Etnier, 2012; Lambourne & Tomporowski, 2010), it is possible to conclude that exercise has a small, positive effect on cognitive ability following exercise.

Lambourne and Tomporowski, who restricted their meta-analysis to college-age participants, found that this effect is moderated by type of exercise and type of cognitive task. For example, of the two types of exercise most commonly examined, cycling and running, cycling leads to larger positive effects, and the effects of exercise on memory tend to be larger than those on executive function or information-processing speed. It should also be noted that effect size was moderated by type of study: When a control group, rather than a pretest, posttest design was used, effect size tended to be smaller, probably because of confounds with practice effects in the latter designs. Chang et al., who included studies with children and elderly adults in their meta-analysis, found that exercise also benefits cognitive performance during exercise, although these benefits may be limited to individuals who are fit and may not apply in the first few minutes of an exercise period. Lambourne and Tomporowski noted that the link between acute exercise and memory storage and retrieval processes is of particular practical and theoretical interest because it may help explain why chronic exercise interventions that are made up of series of acute exercise bouts favorably impact executive function and memory processes in older adults (Colcombe & Kramer, 2003).

Circadian Rhythms

Most everyone is aware that personal performance is not of constant efficiency across the day, and that the time of day for which performance is optimal for one person may differ from that for another. For example, some of us are "morning" persons, who are able to accomplish work that requires considerable concentration (e.g., writing book chapters) more efficiently in the morning than in the afternoon or evening. However, others dislike working in the morning and prefer to perform demanding work later in the day. Cyclical influences on performance, such as time of day, have been investigated by researchers since the latter part of the 19th century (e.g., Lombard, 1887).

Human biological and performance rhythms can be described in terms of their period (length of time for completion of one cycle), amplitude (the range of oscillation during the cycle), and phase (the relative location, with respect to the maximum and minimum values, of the rhythm in time; Hockey, 1986). Rhythmic changes with a period of approximately 24 hours, which are of primary concern in the present chapter, are called *circadian rhythms*. Many physiological functions follow a circadian rhythm, with a distinction made between endogenous rhythms, those that result primarily from natural bodily functions, and exogenous rhythms, those that are a function primarily of external environmental cues. Both endogenous and exogenous rhythms have a natural periodicity of longer than 24 hours, but become entrained to 24-hour periods by time-giving cues (often called by their German name, *Zeitgebers*; Aschoff, 1954). The circadian timing of sleep is regulated by a system involving the suprachiasmatic nucleus (SCN), located in the anterior hypothalamus (Shirani & St. Louis, 2009). The SCN receives input from a variety of sources, the most important of which comes from specialized, non-vision-related retinal ganglion cells. These cells respond primarily to short-wavelength blue light, and it is the input from these cells that allows the SCN to become "entrained" to environmental light cues. Output from the SCN goes primarily to other areas of the hypothalamus, and indirectly to the pineal gland, which is the major source of melatonin, a hormone that helps to regulate the sleep-wake cycle.

Body Temperature and Performance

The most widely studied biological rhythm is body temperature. Temperature usually reaches a minimum around 5:00 a.m., and then increases throughout the day until about 10:00 p.m., at which time it starts to drop again (see Figure 9.3). It is regarded as endogenous because it will shift only slightly to a period of 25 hours when a person is isolated from time-giving cues. As with many physiological processes, the temperature rhythm deteriorates in older adults (Weinert & Waterhouse, 2007).

Like the results described by the Yerkes-Dodson law, diurnal variations in performance have often been interpreted in terms of changes along a dimension of arousal (most likely the energetic dimension), which the circadian rhythm for temperature is supposed to reflect. Kleitman and Jackson (1950) provided evidence for such a proposal by showing a parallel throughout the day between body temperature and performance efficiency for rapidly

Figure 9.3 Oral temperature and performance of visual search tasks, averaged across four separate studies, as a function of time of day.

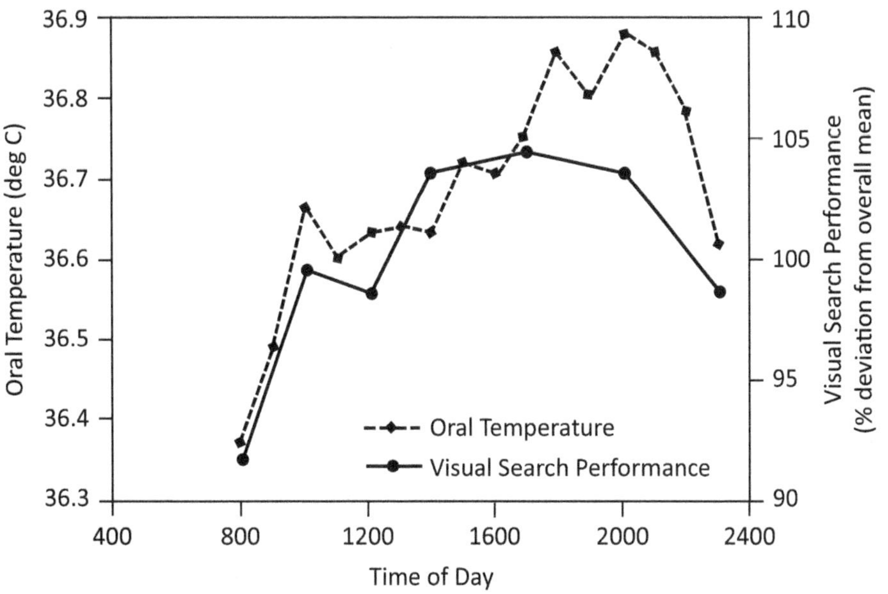

Adapted from Smith (1992).

naming series of color patches, making odd/even choice reactions regarding the number of lights illuminated, and operating a flight simulator under conditions that required vigilance and attention to many details. The parallel between body temperature and performance, illustrated in Figure 9.3, which shows performance as a function of time of day for visual search tasks, has been found for performance of many perceptual-motor tasks. Based on such findings, Kleitman (1938/1963) concluded that "most of the curves of performance can be brought into line with the known 24-hr body temperature curves" (p. 161).

Memory and Cognitive Tasks

The conclusion that temperature and performance were closely related (Kleitman, 1938/1963) turned out to be erroneous, in part because it was based largely on perceptual-motor tasks that required minimal cognitive effort and placed little demand on short-term memory. When tasks with significant short-term memory components are considered, such as verbal reasoning and mental arithmetic, performance typically is better in the morning than later in the day, peaking around midday (e.g., Folkard, 1975). Moreover, when memory for information is tested immediately, performance is usually best early in the morning and deteriorates progressively throughout the rest

Figure 9.4 Immediate memory performance as a function of time of day, with oral temperature shown by the dotted line.

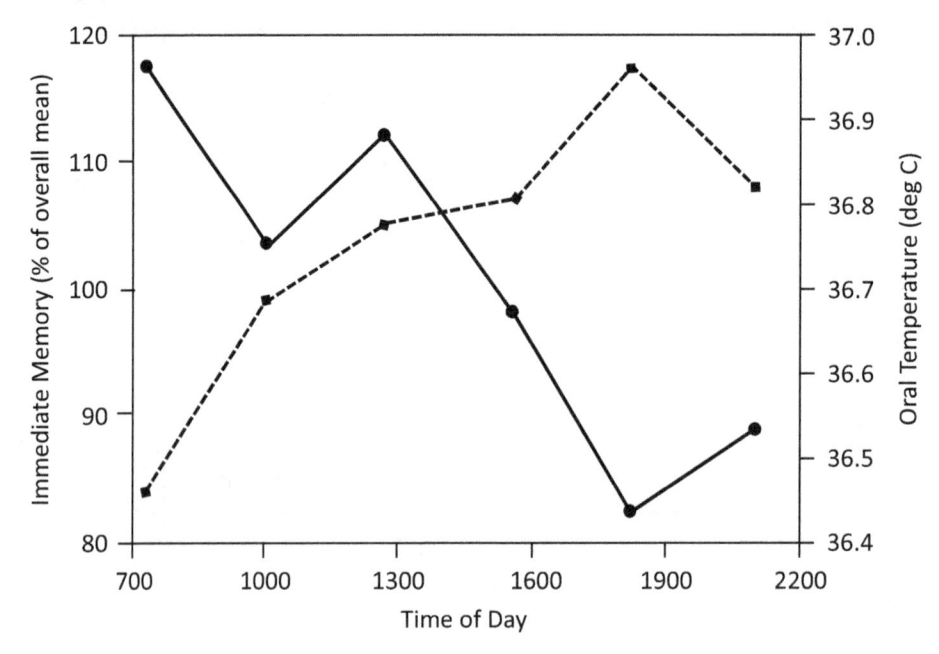

Adapted from Smith (1992).

of the day, such as when people read short articles and then immediately answer multiple-choice questions about the contents (Folkard & Monk, 1980; see Figure 9.4). Such data suggest that the peak performance for tasks varies from late in the day (for tasks with minimal short-term memory demands) to early in the day (for tasks with heavy short-term memory demands). If we assume that arousal increases throughout the day, we can account for such results in terms of Humphreys and Revelle's (1984) multiple-resources model. The implication is that information-transfer resources increase throughout the day, while short-term memory resources decrease.

The morning advantage for tasks with a substantial short-term memory component seems to be due at least in part to changes in cognitive strategy that occur during the day. For example, Folkard and Monk (1979) proposed that people have a tendency to engage in relatively more maintenance rehearsal (e.g., repeating words silently) in the morning and relatively more elaborative rehearsal (e.g., attempting to establish meaningful relations among items) in the afternoon. They tested whether this would be the case by having people attempt to recall lists of 15 items in the order in which they were presented. Performance was better in the morning for all except the last few items, which were equally well recalled in the morning and afternoon (i.e., the recency effect was unaffected by time of day). However, when an articulatory suppression task (counting repeatedly from one to ten at two digits per second in time with a metronome) had to be performed while the lists were presented, immediate recall performance decreased in the morning but was unaffected in the afternoon. That is, under conditions of articulatory suppression, the difference between morning and afternoon performances was eliminated. Since articulatory suppression typically is thought to prevent maintenance rehearsal, this finding suggests that the morning advantage can be attributed to a maintenance rehearsal strategy (see also Oakhill, 1988).

Because elaborative rehearsal is thought to be better than maintenance rehearsal for long-term retention, an evening advantage should be apparent for delayed recall. Indeed, Folkard and Monk (1980) obtained an evening advantage in experiments in which recall was delayed by several days. Moreover, other studies have found that people spend more time integrating text as they are reading in the afternoon than in the morning (Oakhill, 1988) and show better delayed recall of more important information in the evening, with text structure influencing evening recall but not morning recall (Marks & Folkard, 1988). Thus, whereas it may be best to perform tasks that benefit from maintenance rehearsal early in the day, learning of materials that requires elaborative rehearsal may be better later in the day.

Contemporary models attribute performance fluctuations as a function of time of day to at least two sources (Carrier & Monk, 2000): the number of hours since waking and the state of the circadian timing system (as indicated by body temperature and other physiological measures). Evidence consistent with this view comes from studies in which the normal sleep-wake cycle is suspended by not allowing sleep, so that only the latter of the two processes is isolated. Performance in a variety of tasks, including those involving memory, follows the temperature cycle closely in this case, being poorest when temperature is lowest (M. P. Johnson et al., 1992; Monk et al., 1997). These findings suggest that the different patterns for various tasks across the day that are often seen may be due to the first component, time since waking.

Speed-Accuracy Trade-Off

Even for perceptual-motor tasks that do not have significant short-term memory demands, performance does not always peak late in the day. One hypothesis is that the tendency for speed of perceptual-motor performance to peak late in the day, as well as the deviations from this pattern, might be accountable in terms of a strategy shift, in this case, from one emphasizing accuracy of responding early in the day to one emphasizing speed of responding later in the day (Monk & Leng, 1982). Evidence for this is that the increase in speed of responding that occurs as the day progresses is accomplished at least in part through the cost of being less accurate (i.e., people show a speed-accuracy trade-off; Monk & Leng; see also Craig & Condon, 1985). Monk and Leng noted that the peak performance speed for tasks in which poor accuracy has deleterious effects on performance, such as placing pegs in holes, occurs earlier in the day than the peak speed for tasks on which accuracy has little effect. This suggests that there is an increasing tendency to make disruptive errors later in the day.

The hypothesis that the differences in speed of responding across the day can be attributed to a strategy shift was evaluated by A. P. Smith (1991), who explicitly manipulated the speed-accuracy criterion during both early morning and early evening sessions. He reasoned that explicitly encouraging either high speed or high accuracy should eliminate any differences in performance due to such strategies. Participants in his study performed a self-paced serial reaction task in which they were to move their hand from a "home" plate to one of three target plates whenever one of three lights came on. Instructions emphasized either speed or accuracy, or were neutral. The instructions were effective in manipulating performance, but did not interact with time of day: Responding was faster and less accurate in the evening under all three conditions. Because the instructions to adopt specific strategies emphasizing speed or accuracy did not eliminate the difference between morning and evening performances, Smith concluded that the shift in speed-accuracy criterion that occurs across the day most likely is not due to intentional strategies.

Adaptation

Because the phases of the circadian rhythm cycle typically are set to coincide with an activity cycle of working during the day and sleeping at night, a change to a schedule that is inconsistent with the cycle can be disruptive. The "jet lag" that most people suffer, including fatigue and difficulty sleeping, when they fly to a locale in a new time zone is a good example of this disruption. If the shift in time is very great, as, for example, on a flight from Chicago to Paris, the body may be entering the normal nighttime phase during the day and vice versa, tending to make the person sleepy during the day and wakeful at night. Over a period of several days, roughly equal to two-thirds of the number of time zones crossed (Waterhouse, Reilly, Atkinson, & Edwards, 2007), the feeling of jet lag disappears. What this indicates is that the circadian rhythms adapt to the changes. This adaptation occurs because the new physical and social time cues entrain the rhythms and shift their periods.

Disruption and adaptation are evident in performance measures as well as in subjective experience and physiological measures. For example, people

Figure 9.5 Adaptation of the circadian rhythms for temperature and task performance after westward or eastward flights of 6-hour tranzonal displacement.

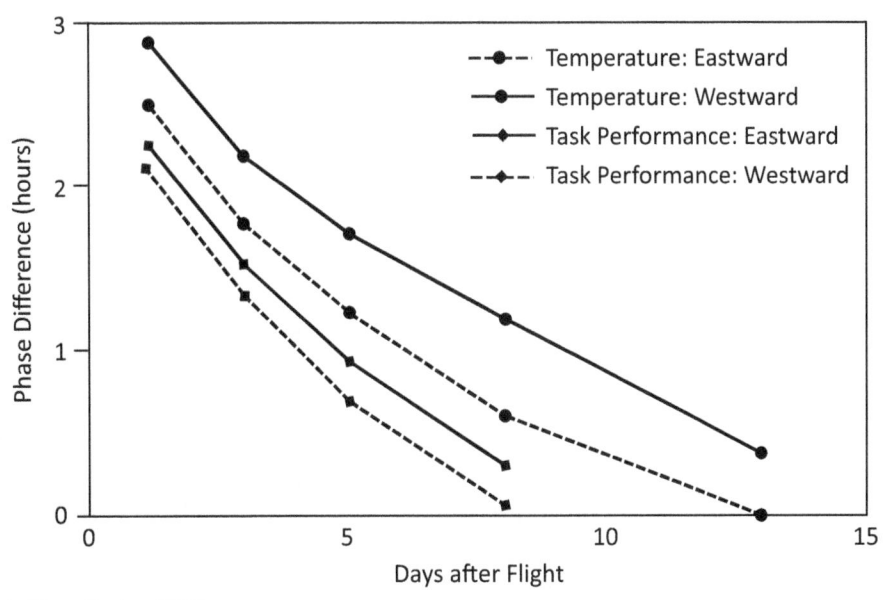

Adapted from Hockey (1986).

who performed symbol cancellation and addition tasks after eastward or westward tranzonal flights of 6-hour displacement showed gradual shifts in the phase of the circadian rhythm on both tasks that eventually coincided with the new time zone (see Figure 9.5; K. E. Klein, Wegman, & Hunt, 1972). Klein et al. also obtained the standard finding that adaptation of physiological rhythms, in this case temperature, occurs more rapidly for flights from east to west than from west to east. This asymmetry likely has its basis in the fact that the normal period is longer than 24 hours when time-giving cues are not present. Consequently, the adjustment necessary for a lengthened day (east-to-west flight) is more natural than the adjustment for a shortened day (west-to-east flight). Klein et al. found a similar pattern for performance of the symbol cancellation and addition tasks.

Jet lag is a particular concern for athletes who may have to travel across several time zones for competition. Their performance suffers from deficits associated with the mismatch of circadian rhythms with the new time zone (Reilly, 2009a), as would be expected. Highly trained athletes who travel from the U.S. to Asia or Europe, or vice versa, show disruptions to mood and loss of anaerobic power and dynamic strength (Hill, Hill, Fields, & Smith, 1993). A study of all major league baseball games in the U.S. found a disadvantage for the traveling team that was larger when the time change involved 3 hours (winning percentage of 39.4%) rather than 1 or 2 hours (winning percentages of 48.3% and 48.2%), with teams traveling from west to east being more likely to win than teams traveling from east to west (Winter, Hammond, Green, Zhang, & Bliwise, 2009). It has been recommended that athletes should arrive in the new country sufficiently far in advance for the circadian rhythms to adapt to the new time zone. Effects of jet lag can be minimized by controlling when to be exposed to light, avoiding long naps during the period of adjustment, and strategically using exercise (Reilly, 2009b).

Individual Differences
Individual differences have been found in the circadian rhythms for both biological and performance measures. Research such as that by Horne and Östberg (1976) using the Morningness-Eveningness Questionnaire (a 19-item multiple-choice questionnaire consisting of items such as "Approximately what time would you go to bed if you were entirely free to plan your evening?") has confirmed the notion that there is a distinction between morning types and evening types. Body temperature for those who prefer working in the morning runs higher in the morning and lower at night than that of the evening types. More importantly, major differences in performance across times of day occur on perceptual-motor tasks. For example, whereas evening types show the typical increase in performance speed throughout the day on a visual detection task, morning types show the reverse function (Horne, Brass, & Pettit, 1980). Given the propensity for young adults to want to stay up through much of the night, it is not too surprising that there is an increase toward morningness with increasing age, due in largest part to an inability to sleep late (Monk & Kupfer, 2007).

Sleep Deprivation and Fatigue

The diurnal changes in performance described in the previous section occur in people who are receiving a normal amount of sleep each night. Sleep following initial learning may be beneficial in consolidating or retaining what has been learned. As with other issues, this one is not simple to resolve. Cai and Rickard (2009) noted that previous studies suggesting that sleep was beneficial for consolidation of motor skills confounded circadian and homeostatic factors with the manipulation of sleep versus no-sleep. They controlled for those factors for a motor task in which a sequence of five keypresses was performed repetitively and found no benefit of sleep during the period after the initial acquisition trials. Somewhat contradictory results were reported by Robertson, Pascual-Leone, and Press (2012), who had participants perform a sequential reaction task with four fingers in which the sequence of stimuli and responses repeated every 12 trials. A group for which the sequence learning was implicit, in the sense that they were not told of a repeating sequence nor was there anything to signify it, showed no benefit of sleep, as in Cai and Rickard's study. However, a group that was told of the repeating sequence and had the start of a new sequence signaled by a change in color did show a benefit of sleep, implying that explicit skill learning benefits from sleep.

Skilled performance can additionally be affected by sleep deprivation. Students in college often pull "all-nighters" at the time of final examinations to learn material in preparation for exams. Although such a strategy may increase a student's knowledge of the material that is to be tested, the sleep-deprived state in which the exams are taken often has the undesired consequence of adversely affecting performance. The second author remembers as an undergraduate studying all night for two final exams the next day. At the second of the two finals, an English essay examination, his pen periodically drifted from the line on which he was writing as he fought to stay awake. As shall be seen, such intermittent lapses of attention are a major contributor to performance decrements associated with sleep deprivation.

A variety of tasks show impairment when performed after periods of sleep deprivation of 24 hours or longer (Dinges & Kribbs, 1991). Performance deficits will be more apparent on tasks that are of long duration than on short-duration tasks. This point is evident in a study by Dinges and Powell (1988), in which an auditory simple-reaction task was performed for 10-minute periods after a normal night's sleep or after 1 or 2 nights of sleep deprivation. Although some decrement in performance associated with sleep deprivation was evident in the first minute of testing, the decrement increased across the 10-minute period, particularly when the task was performed after 2 nights of sleep deprivation.

Why does performance deteriorate when a person is sleep-deprived? The most widely accepted explanation for the majority of the effect is the *lapse hypothesis*, first proposed by Williams, Lubin, and Goodnow (1959). According to this hypothesis, a sleep-deprived person periodically falls asleep for a few seconds, creating a lapse in information processing. These lapses are presumed to increase in frequency and duration with increasing sleep loss and increasing time on task. Williams et al. noted that in self-paced tasks the lapses show up primarily in longer reaction times. They found that in such tasks the variability, as well as the mean, of the reaction times increases as sleep deprivation increases. That is, although some reaction times are about as fast as in undeprived conditions, an increasing number of extremely slow reactions are mixed in. In experimenter-paced tasks, the lapses show up primarily in the accuracy of performance. In other words, experimenter pacing removes the option of maintaining accuracy by delaying responding, and so errors occur.

Although there is considerable evidence that lapses account for a significant part of the performance decrement due to sleep loss, there also seems to be a reduction in processing efficiency during the non-lapse periods (Kjellberg, 1977). One line of evidence to this effect is that the reaction times for the fastest responses, which should be reflecting performance between lapses, also show increases during sleep deprivation (Dinges & Kribbs, 1991). The findings of Dinges and Powell (1988), cited earlier to illustrate the role of time on task, also provide evidence of decreased efficiency during non-lapse periods. Even with the contribution of lapses removed, both an overall performance decrement and its increase as a function of time on task are still present.

Other factors, such as circadian rhythms, may moderate the effects of sleep deprivation (Tilley & Brown, 1992). Basically, the circadian rhythm for task performance can be superimposed onto the sleep-deprivation function. That is, a similar cycle will be apparent each day of sleep deprivation, but with a progressively lower mean. For example, Figure 9.6 shows performance

Figure 9.6 Subtraction rate as a function of time of day for a 5-minute, iterative, descending subtraction task during 36 hours without sleep. The performance profile on this task is one of linear decline superimposed on the circadian performance rhythm.

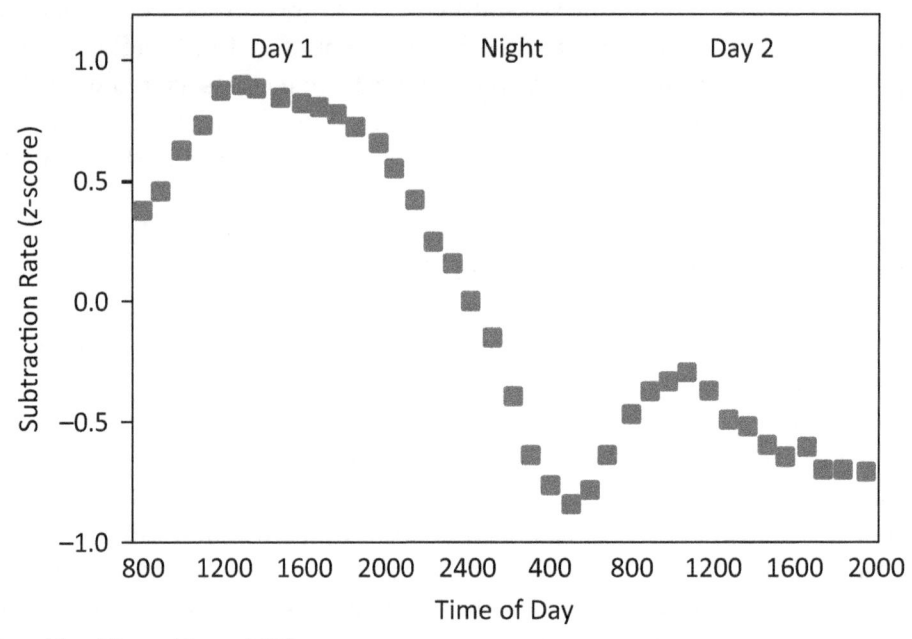

Adapted from Tilley and Brown (1992).

on a mental arithmetic task, for which the peak is typically around mid-morning, over a period of 2 days without sleep. The mid-morning peak is apparent on both days, but at a considerably lower level of performance on Day 2 than on Day 1. Another moderating variable is modest exercise, which tends to reduce the sleep-loss decrement when performed immediately prior to testing. Tilley and Bohle (1988) illustrated the apparent benefit of exercise in combating the harmful effects of sleep deprivation by testing high school students taking part in an all-night disco dancing marathon. Every 2 hours, each of eight students performed a simple reaction-time task for 20 minutes. For a control condition, performance was measured in a similar manner on another night in which the students were allowed to engage in activities with a minimum of physical activity, such as watching television and playing board games. Reaction times were significantly faster overall and less variable during the dancing marathon, with the difference being particularly pronounced for the late night hours in which performance is normally poorest. Tilley and Bohle concluded that the exercise provided by the dancing likely increased the arousal levels of the students, making them less drowsy and better able to concentrate, but you can probably think of other factors associated with dancing that might also have resulted in increased arousal!

Effects similar to those observed when a person is sleep-deprived can also be observed when the person is fatigued from continually engaging in an activity (Craig & Cooper, 1992). In particular, lapses of attention increase in frequency when a person is fatigued, much as they do under sleep deprivation (Bills, 1931). This results in occasional extremely long response times, which increase the variability of performance. These effects of fatigue are evident not only on the continued performance of the fatiguing task itself, but also on the performance of other tasks performed afterwards, as illustrated by two studies that examined pilots engaged in the fatiguing task of flying simulated or real aircraft. Drew (1979) studied the performance of pilots controlling a flight simulator over periods of 2 hours or longer. Control of the aircraft worsened by as much as 50% during the flight. Errors, particularly those involving timing, increased during the flight, and the pilots tolerated progressively larger deviations from target values for such things as airspeed. Lapses of attention were also evident in responses to changes in gauges. Not only did performance of the individual tasks decrease, but also the task as a whole lost its integrity and was perceived more in terms of its elements. That the fatigue that accumulates during a lengthy flight also has deleterious effects on tasks performed after completion of the flight was shown through experiments conducted on civilian air crews immediately upon return from a trip and after not having flown for 8 days (Welford, Brown, & Gabb, 1950). Performance at solving an electrical problem and at plotting location on a grid was impaired for the pilots who had just returned from trips, particularly for those whose flight routes were regarded as hard (e.g., routes for which there was little time on the ground between legs of the flight).

The discovery of retinal ganglion cells that are sensitive to blue light and convey this signal to SCN has set off a flurry of research to determine if blue light in the workplace can improve alertness, especially during shift work or periods of fatigue. Although some successes have been reported (Chellappa et al., 2011; Taillard et al., 2012), evidence to date is mixed. One problem is that whereas blue light may seem an attractive intervention because of its naturalness, in the environments in which it is most effective—namely, at night—it may be perceived as cold and artificial, or difficult to tolerate. For example, although Taillard et al. found that blue light exposure improved nighttime driving in young male drivers as much as did ingestion of caffeine (as compared to a caffeine-free placebo), more than 15% of the participants studied had to be dropped from the analysis because they could not tolerate the blue light while driving.

Stressful Physical Environments

As we just discussed, light is an environmental factor that can affect performance indirectly, through its influence on the sleep-wake cycle and alertness, but also directly, when low light levels or glare interfere with vision. Two other aspects of the environment that are considered to be stressful and deleterious to skilled performance are noise and extreme temperatures.

Effects of Noise
Noise is generally regarded as unwanted sound that has no direct bearing on the task at hand. In contemporary society, noise of varying magnitude and frequency composition is present in virtually every work and domestic setting. Loud noise levels can affect perception of auditory stimuli through masking of the signals and through temporary elevation of hearing thresholds (D. M. Jones, 1983). Our concern, however, is with whether noise exerts any effects above and beyond those associated with hearing in the performance of tasks that do not depend on auditory perception. Because noise is usually thought of as a stressor that increases arousal level, we would expect noise to have effects on performance that extend beyond its influence on auditory information processing.

Most tasks that tap basic information-processing functions show little effect of continuous noise (A. P. Smith & Jones, 1992). Sensory functions (e.g., visual accommodation), motor skills, and simple reaction times (when sufficient warning is provided) all show little impairment by noise. However, noise does seem to have a major influence on attentional control. For example, when multiple tasks are performed in noise, attentional narrowing of the type described by Easterbrook's cue-utilization hypothesis often occurs. Hockey (1970) found that when a central tracking task was paired with a peripheral light detection task (as in the task used by Bahrick et al., 1952), performance of the tracking task improved under noisy conditions relative to quiet conditions, whereas responses to the occasional light stimuli became slower.

Noise can also affect higher-order processes, such as the use of strategies (A. P. Smith & Jones, 1992). First, the strategies selected to perform a task may be different when noise is present versus when it is not. For memory tasks, noise leads to less use of elaborative rehearsal and more maintenance rehearsal (Daee & Wilding, 1977) and to relatively more emphasis in recall on local detail rather than global structure (A. P. Smith, 1985). Second, noise reinforces the use of a single, dominant strategy and leads to inflexibility in switching from one strategy to another when conditions change to make a new strategy more appropriate. When past experiences or instructions indicate an obvious strategy, this strategy will tend to be relied on more exclusively in noisy environments (e.g., Wilding, Mohindra, & Breen-Lewis, 1982). Third, noise reduces the efficiency of processes used to monitor behavior and change performance. One such process that we discussed in Chapter 3 is that of setting the speed-accuracy criterion in choice-reaction tasks. Recall that to perform efficiently, a criterion for responding must be set that leads to fast responding but minimal errors. Rabbitt (1979) has proposed that noise decreases the efficiency with which this criterion is determined and controlled.

People who live near a major highway or in the approach path of an airport may have sustained exposure to noise across many years. Continual exposure to noise may have effects other than those related to auditory perception and task performance (Stansfeld and Matheson (2003). One effect is simply annoyance, which may induce stress and resulting health consequences. Noise also can disturb sleep, causing an increase in the number of wakenings and the number of switches between sleep phases. Sleep disturbance is associated with increases in blood pressure and heart rate, as well as with less positive mood and impaired performance of cognitive tasks the next day.

Effects of Extreme Temperatures

Another physical stressor common to many work environments is extreme temperature. High temperature levels have been shown to produce only minor effects on performance of simple perceptual-motor tasks (J. D. Ramsey, 1983). As is the case under noise, attentional narrowing tends to occur under heat stress. For example, Bursill (1958) found that high ambient temperatures increased the number of misses of peripheral light stimuli that occurred during performance of a central tracking task. Consistent with the view that attentional focus narrows, this deleterious effect of heat was an increasing function of lateral eccentricity at which the stimuli were presented.

Heat seems to have two opposing effects on skilled performance. Mackworth (1961) found that more skilled performers on a physical push-pull task showed a greater decrement in performance from an increased heat load than did less-skilled performers. In contrast, skilled telegraph operators showed less of a decrement from heat than did less-skilled operators. The apparent resolution of these seemingly paradoxical findings is that the people who were performing better on the push-pull task were doing so because they were exerting more effort, and thus had a greater mental and physical load than those who were performing less well, whereas the mental load most likely is less for skilled telegraphers than for unskilled ones. In other words, the group with the most mental load to begin with showed the largest decrement when heat was increased.

Extreme cold can also affect performance. Skills requiring manual dexterity deteriorate when the skin temperature goes below approximately 20 degrees Celsius. Clark and Jones (1962) showed that the magnitude of a cold decrement of this type for the time to tie sets of knots remained relatively constant as skill at knot tying increased across 3 weeks of practice. Moreover, people who practiced for the first 2 weeks under warm conditions (hand skin temperature of 32 degrees Celsius) and then transferred to cold conditions (skin temperature of 7 degrees Celsius) in the last week performed worse in the cold than did those who practiced under the cold conditions or who alternated between warm and cold conditions on successive days. To explain these results, Clark and Jones proposed that the thermal conditions become part of the stimulus complex that controls the manual response or, in other words, that people learn to perform the task specifically with warm or cold hands. This proposal is consistent with the notion of procedural reinstatement (described more fully in the next chapter)—that subsequent retention and transfer are better when the test procedures match closely those that were required during initial practice (Healy & Bourne, 2012).

In addition to reducing physical dexterity, cold temperatures induce performance decrements on a variety of tasks for which dexterity is not a factor (Brooke & Ellis, 1992). One possibility for these decrements is that extreme cold is distracting and induces lapses of attention, much like drowsiness and fatigue. Another possibility is that arousal becomes sufficiently high that performance deteriorates. H. D. Ellis (1982) tested between these possibilities by measuring errors and lag trials (responses taking more than twice the normal reaction time) as a serial choice-reaction task was performed in which digits were classified as odd or even. The mean number of errors increased when the task was performed in the cold. However, the number of lag trials decreased, contrary to the outcome expected if the participants were becoming more distracted under cold conditions. Moreover, N. R. Ellis, Wilcock, and Zaman (1985) showed that these effects of cold on performance were much greater for a difficult eight-choice-reaction task than for an easier four-choice task. Thus, the deleterious effect of cold temperatures on performance does not seem to involve lapses of attention of the type that occurs when the performer is sleep-deprived or fatigued.

Drug Use and Performance

The effects of drug use on skilled performance are well known. If nothing else, the widespread incidence of automobile accidents while driving under the influence of alcohol attests to this fact. Many other drugs, both legal and illegal, medicinal and recreational, influence performance as well. For example, combining ecstasy (MDMA) with alcohol can be especially dangerous because the feelings of alertness caused by MDMA can make intoxicated individuals unaware of the impairing effects of drugs such as alcohol, thereby giving them the sense that it is safe to drive and creating a potentially serious risk to traffic safety (Veldstra et al., 2012). On the other hand, drugs are often used because they are believed to enhance performance. One drug, caffeine, has a long history of use as a performance enhancer, as will be discussed in more detail in the next section. Other drugs that were originally designed to alleviate symptoms associated with neuropsychological impairments are increasingly being used in an attempt to boost cognitive capacities. Drugs used to treat ADHD (attention-deficit/hyperactivity disorder), in particular, are being used by students hoping to improve concentration when cramming for exams (Babcock & Byrne, 2000), and other stimulants are used by long-haul truckers (da Silva, de Pinho, de Mello, de Bruin, & de Bruin, 2009) or by aircrew members on military missions (e.g., C. S. Ramsey, Werchan, Isdahl, Fischer, & Gibbons, 2008), and by high school and college students hoping to boost test scores (Babcock & Byrne, 2000). Another commonly used drug, modafinil, which promotes wakefulness, is used by people with disturbed sleeping patterns (e.g., due to jet lag, shiftwork, or sleep disorders), but also by people hoping to improve their ability to concentrate (Sahakian & Morein-Zamir, 2007). The promise of cognition-enhancing drugs is far-reaching: Drugs that target either the onset of long-term potentiation or memory consolidation are being developed to improve memory, and drugs targeting the dopamine and noradrenaline neurotransmitter systems may not only restore deficient executive function but also enhance normal executive function (Farah et al., 2004; although such improvements may be limited to low-performing individuals; R. Elliott et al., 1997; Mehta et al., 2000).

The fact that individuals vary in how they react to different drugs is a major concern with using drugs for performance enhancement. For example, the dopamine agonist bromocriptine enhances various executive functions for low-working memory-capacity individuals, but has a detrimental effect on the performance of high-working memory-capacity individuals (Kimberg, D'Esposito, & Farah, 1997). Variability in how people react to the same drugs makes specifying a general protocol for the use of drugs to enhance cognitive function difficult. Moreover, little is known about the long-term effects various drugs might have. Perhaps more fundamental is the question of whether performance enhancement of healthy human function—or neurocognitive enhancement, as it is also known—is a desirable goal.

Farah et al. (2004) summarize many of the arguments for and against neurocognitive enhancement. Major ethical and practical issues are: Who should decide whether performance-enhancing drugs will be administered and how the performance of people benefiting from enhancement should be evaluated? How can safety be ensured when intervening in a complex, not fully understood system? How can individuals be protected against coercion (explicit or implicit pressure to engage in neurocognitive enhancement either because of pressure from an employer who recognizes the benefits of a more attentive and less forgetful workforce or because of fears of competing against enhanced co-workers)? How can distributive justice be preserved when faced with cost and social barriers to neurocognitive enhancement, as there are for other benefits, such as health care and schooling? Finally, because modifying brains affects individuals, it is important to consider how neurocognitive enhancement affects our understanding of "what it means to be a person, to be healthy and whole, to do meaningful work, and to value human life in all its imperfection" (Farah et al., 2004, p. 424). It can be argued that the quest to improve on natural endowments brings with it the risk of "pathologizing" normal function. The widespread use of coffee attests to the capacity of individuals to become adapted to some kinds of enhancement and to how widespread societal acceptance of such enhancement can become.

Effects of Caffeine

Caffeine occurs naturally in coffee, tea, and chocolate, is added to many soft drinks, and is found in certain medications. It is a stimulant that can help prevent drowsiness and maintain alertness when engaging in activities such as studying late into the night or driving on a long trip. Caffeine produces an increase in activity of the central nervous system by blocking a naturally occurring modulator of neural activity called adenosine (S. H. Snyder, 1984). In humans, the peak blood levels of caffeine occur 15–45 minutes after ingestion, and the half-life is 5–6 hours (Lieberman, 1992).

As you might expect, ingestion of caffeine has been found to increase self-reported alertness and to reduce fatigue. Such effects have been obtained for doses as low as 64 mg (Lieberman, Wurtman, Emde, & Coviella, 1987), which is equivalent to a weak cup of coffee. Consistent with such self-reports, caffeine has also been shown to increase performance on tasks requiring vigilance. For example, Hauty and Payne (1955) demonstrated a beneficial effect of caffeine on monitoring performance in an aviation-training device, and Baker and Theologus (1972) showed that it enhanced performance on a visual monitoring task.

Caffeine is often used to increase alertness when driving. There is also evidence that it improves driving performance. Early evidence for this came from a study by Regina et al. (1974). Drivers who were moderate coffee drinkers performed two 90-minute driving periods in an automobile-driving simulator after ingesting 200 mg of caffeine or a placebo. The simulator, constructed around the chassis of a 1965 Rambler, presented a realistic driving situation that corresponded to driving along a straight, flat road in a rural environment at twilight. The driver interacted with a lead car by accelerating, decelerating, or braking in response to the lead car's actions. In addition, the high beam light periodically came on, requiring a response to shut it off. Performance of all aspects of the task was improved by caffeine. Response times to lead car accelerations and decelerations were substantially faster, as were those to the high beam signal. Moreover, substantially fewer of the high beam signals were missed. The results of the study thus seemed to confirm both the folklore belief that caffeine enhances driving performance and the implication from laboratory tasks that it should do so.

Even small amounts of caffeine may benefit performance. Lieberman, Wurtman, Emde, Roberts, and Coviella (1987) had people perform a vigilance task, in which they were to respond by pressing a key whenever a 330-ms tone occurred within a stream of 400-ms tones, for an hour after ingesting either a placebo or 32, 64, 128, or 256 mg of caffeine in capsule form. Even as little as 32 mg of caffeine, which is typically thought to be below the level at which behavioral effects will be observed, increased the number of target tones that were detected relative to the placebo without affecting false-alarm rates. Lieberman et al. similarly found reaction times to be reduced, without an accompanying increase in error rates, at all dosage levels for a four-choice-reaction task in which individuals responded to the location of a visual stimulus by pressing the corresponding key. This study suggests that even amounts of caffeine equivalent to those found in a 12-oz cola drink or a cup of tea may be sufficient to improve performance efficiency.

The effects of caffeine may not always be positive. Brunyé, Mahoney, Lieberman, and Taylor (2010) examined the effects of caffeine on attention using an attention task in which a target must be attended and distractors assigned to a competing response must be ignored (the ANT, designed to measure attentional orienting, alerting, and executive attention; Fan et al., 2005; Rueda et al., 2004). They found that doses of 100, 200, or 400 mg of caffeine tended to improve attentional function relative to no caffeine, but that maximal effects were reached with 200 mg caffeine. However, the benefits of caffeine on attention were restricted to the attentional functions of alerting and executive control. Attentional orienting was not benefited by caffeine consumption. This study illustrates the importance of understanding the dose-response relationships with regards to the drug being administered so that the appropriate amounts can be given for the person and context. It also illustrates the importance of understanding the task that will be performed. A detailed understanding of the components of the task may be necessary to design an appropriate performance plan.

Effects of Nicotine

Nicotine is present in tobacco and is most often ingested by smoking. When a puff of cigarette smoke is inhaled into the lungs, brain nicotine levels become high within 10 seconds and then decline rapidly (Wesnes & Parrott, 1992). Plasma levels of nicotine have a half-life of approximately 2 hours. Smokers typically show beneficial effects of nicotine on a range of performance measures. However, because nicotine is an addictive drug, these benefits may be only with respect to impaired performance for smokers deprived of nicotine and not with respect to the performance of nonsmokers. This point is illustrated by a study of Heimstra, Bancroft, and DeKock (1967) in which individuals were tested in a driving simulator for 6 hours. Smokers who were allowed to smoke performed throughout the period at a level comparable to that of nonsmokers. However, smokers who were not allowed to smoke performed significantly worse than either of the other two groups.

Effects of nicotine on the performance of other sustained vigilance tasks suggest that it may have a true facilitative effect. Wesnes and Warburton (1978) had smokers smoke either regular cigarettes or nicotine-free cigarettes at 20-minute intervals during both auditory and visual vigilance tasks. The decline in performance that usually occurs in the latter part of the vigil for nonsmokers was largely absent for the smokers who smoked the nicotine-containing cigarettes but not for those who smoked the placebo cigarettes.

Since nonsmokers would be expected to show a vigilance decrement, this outcome suggests that the benefit for the smokers who were allowed to smoke normal cigarettes was over and above any decrements in performance for the smokers who were deprived of nicotine. Wesnes and Warburton (1984) obtained similar results for nonsmokers when nicotine was administered in tablets, providing further evidence that nicotine has a facilitative effect relative to the baseline performance of nonsmokers.

Nicotine has also been found to influence performance on a range of other basic and complex tasks that require high levels of concentration. Wesnes and Parrott (1992) suggested that the general benefit of nicotine in such tasks is due to an increase in processing resources. However, this general benefit is not apparent on tasks involving short- or long-term retention of verbal materials, suggesting that if nicotine has any effect on learning and memory, that effect is negative. In terms of Humphreys and Revelle's (1984) model, the effects of nicotine would seem to be on the information-transfer resources and not the short-term memory resources.

Effects of Alcohol

Alcohol is a depressant that tends to have a relatively widespread deleterious effect on performance. Substantial individual differences exist in the relation of alcohol intake to peak blood alcohol level, the time at which this peak is reached, and the elimination rate. For example, Finnigan and Hammersley (1992) described a study in which 16 persons received an alcohol dose designed to achieve a peak blood alcohol level of 80 mg% (mg of alcohol per 100 ml of blood). Actual peak levels ranged from 47 to 81 mg%, with the peak occurring anywhere between 20 and 60 minutes after consuming the alcohol and the elimination rates varying from 4 to 40 mg% per hour. Moreover, there was little correlation between these three measures. Because of these substantial individual differences in the physiological effects of alcohol, the extent to which and the time at which alcohol affects performance can also be expected to vary widely across individuals.

Alcohol impairs performance in a variety of tasks, decreasing the accuracy of tracking, slowing decision making, reducing memory performance, and increasing body sway. The best explanation for the widespread effects of alcohol on performance is that it produces a general slowing in the speed of information processing. Whether the impairment shows up primarily in increased reaction times or in decreased accuracy is in part a function of whether the performer can detect that errors are being made. Maylor, Rabbitt, Sahgal, and Wright (1987) had people perform a serial choice-reaction task and a visual search task, with and without alcohol. For the choice-reaction task, alcohol produced slower reaction times for both correct and incorrect responses, but had virtually no effect on the error rate. In contrast, for the visual search task, alcohol decreased accuracy but had no effect on search speed. The crucial difference between the two tasks was that errors in the choice task involved overt responses that could be detected, whereas errors in the search task involved misses of targets and thus could not be detected. When performers were aware of having made errors, they apparently altered their speed/accuracy criteria to maintain their accuracy at the level that it would be if alcohol had not been consumed; when they were not aware of their errors, such an adjustment could not be made.

It is obvious from the inordinate numbers of automobile accidents associated with alcohol that people do not always adjust their speed-accuracy criteria to minimize errors even when errors are detectable. Other factors likely come into play, with one factor being beliefs about alcohol. McMillen and Wells-Parker (1987) found that persons who believed that they had ingested a moderate amount of alcohol prior to performing a simulated driving task (regardless of whether they had actually ingested alcohol) showed greater risk-taking behavior, as measured by time spent at high speed and number of cars passed. In a follow-up study, this pattern was found to hold only for individuals classified as high sensation seekers; low sensation seekers showed more cautious behavior when they thought that they had ingested alcohol (McMillen, Smith, & Wells-Parker, 1989). It should be apparent that the tendency of some individuals to take greater risks when consuming alcohol, along with the reduced rate of information processing, can have serious consequences.

At least three possible predictions have been suggested for how consumption of alcohol might interact with level of practice as skill is acquired. First, alcohol might have less of a disruptive effect on the performance of a highly practiced task than on a less well-practiced task. This proposal arises in part from attentional models in which processing becomes automatized and the role of attention decreases as performance becomes well-practiced (e.g., W. Schneider & Shiffrin, 1977). If automatic processes are less susceptible to disruption by alcohol, then the influence of alcohol on performance should be reduced at higher levels of practice. Although this argument is plausible, there is little support for it. For example, Maylor and Rabbitt (1988) had individuals perform word categorization and visual search tasks for several days. Alcohol impaired performance to a similar extent both early and late in practice and under both consistent-mapping conditions (which should promote the development of automaticity) and varied-mapping conditions (for which attentional demands should remain high). They obtained similar results for performance in a video game in which the task was to destroy a tank by dropping a bomb onto it from a plane moving horizontally across the screen (Maylor & Rabbitt, 1987) and for a dual task involving visual tracking and auditory detection (Maylor, Rabbitt, James, & Kerr, 1990).

A second possible effect of the interaction of alcohol and practice is on learning. Specifically, alcohol ingested prior to practice might be expected to slow the rate of learning. Maylor and Rabbitt's (1987, 1988) findings have also run counter to this possibility. They had people perform either the categorization task, the visual search task, or the bombing task for 4 days under the influence of alcohol and then for a fifth day without ingesting alcohol. Performances in the last session showed improvement and were similar to those of individuals who had performed without alcohol all along, suggesting that learning occurred to a similar extent regardless of whether alcohol had been consumed during the practice sessions.

Finally, another possibility is that alcohol may produce state-dependent learning, such that a task practiced while under the influence of alcohol will be performed better when it later must be performed under the influence than will a task that was initially practiced while not under the influence. Again, Maylor and Rabbitt (1987, 1988) found no support for this proposition. For the tasks described earlier, participants performed in a second session after having practiced either with or without alcohol in the first session. Those who had practiced previously under the influence of alcohol performed no better in the second session than did those who had not.

It has also been suggested that the disruptive effect of alcohol on performance is greater for tasks that require divided attention, such as driving, than for tasks that do not. Evidence to this effect was provided by Brewer and Sandow (1980), who conducted an investigation of metropolitan automobile accidents and found that drivers who were intoxicated were more likely than unintoxicated drivers to have been engaged in some activity at the time of an accident that was secondary to the driving task. However, there does not seem to be any unique deficit in the ability to divide attention that is associated with alcohol impairment. Maylor et al. (1990) had persons perform visual tracking and auditory tone-detection tasks in both single- and dual-task contexts. Although speed of responding for the detection task was influenced more by alcohol in the dual-task context, an analysis showed no effect of alcohol on relative divided-attention costs but did show a strong effect of practice. The absolute effect of alcohol in the dual-task context was not reduced with practice, even though the decrease in relative divided-attention costs with practice suggested decreasing attentional involvement. This outcome is consistent with the view that the effect of alcohol is not influenced by attentional requirements.

In short, the primary effect of alcohol seems to be to produce a decrease in the rate of information processing. This shows up as decrements in speed or accuracy of performance, or both, for virtually any task that is performed under the influence of alcohol. Because of the greater demands imposed by more complex tasks, the absolute amount of performance decrement is an increasing function of task complexity. However, alcohol does not seem to impair control processes, such as the ability to judge response speed and to coordinate dual tasks, so its effects are relatively independent of those induced by practice.

Summary

The central theme of this chapter is that the quality of human performance at any given level of skill is a function of many variables that influence stress and arousal. Performance of any task suffers if the performer's arousal level is too low. For many tasks, performance also deteriorates at high levels of arousal. There is not complete agreement regarding why this deterioration occurs, but the accounts focus primarily on a reduced capacity of processing resources and a reduced ability to control the allocation of these resources. These reductions are often accompanied by strategy changes. Moreover, the specific effects of the variables that induce different arousal levels are not equivalent.

Performance varies systematically throughout the day. The speed at which simple perceptual-motor tasks are performed typically increases from morning until late in the evening (as does body temperature), whereas immediate memory tasks usually show performance peaks early in the day. These two performance patterns are consistent with the hypothesis of the multiple-resources model that information-transfer resources increase, but short-term memory resources decrease, as arousal increases. However, these performance patterns reflect, at least in part, changes in speed-accuracy criteria and rehearsal strategies. Sleep deprivation and fatigue also exert effects on performance, to a large extent through lapses in processing that result in exceedingly long response times to or misses of target events.

Aspects of the physical environment, such as loud noise and extreme temperature, also affect the quality of performance. Noise not only interferes with the processing of auditory stimuli but also decreases attentional capacity and control of its allocation, which show up in inappropriate and less flexible selection of strategies for performing tasks. Extreme temperatures produce similar decreases in processing resources, with cold temperatures causing additional problems for performing tasks that require manual dexterity.

Drugs can have both positive and negative impacts on performance. Caffeine can offset the low levels of arousal that accompany sleep deprivation and fatigue, having a facilitative effect on the performance of tasks that require continuous monitoring of displays. Likewise, nicotine has a facilitative effect on the performance of many tasks, although this effect is at least in part due to its offsetting impairments in performance that occur for nicotine-deprived smokers. Finally, alcohol causes an across-the-board debilitative effect on performance that is best characterized as a reduction in the speed at which information is processed. Because self-monitoring skills are little affected, people who have consumed alcohol can slow their performance speed to maintain accuracy, if feedback is available.

Although much of the research in this chapter was conducted from the perspective of a unidimensional construct of arousal, virtually all researchers agree that this construct has deficiencies. A fuller understanding of how to optimize performance in various situations will emerge as the specific influences of various stressors and arousing variables, as well as the strategies used by individuals who perform well in the various situations, come to be better understood.

10

Designing Effective Training Systems

Without a knowledgeable and skillful workforce, organizations are likely to suffer. With that in mind, training in organizations should be of the utmost importance.
          E. Salas, K. A. Wilson, H. A. Priest, & J. W. Guthrie (2006, p. 503)

Throughout this book we have described techniques for training different types and components of skill. We have discussed factors influencing skill acquisition and have discussed the major models of how skill is acquired. In this chapter we argue that there is more to training than the application of techniques for acquiring skill. Effective training programs are built on an understanding of the task being trained for, the people being trained, and the environment in which the trained task will be performed. Not only will the quality of the design and delivery of the program influence training success, but so will the attitudes and the motivation of the trainees and the organizational context (Noe, 1986). The success of any training program will thus depend on gaining the support of trainees and the organization and on removing any barriers to implementing trained knowledge or skills. Given that motivation, ability, and organizational factors all play a role in the success of training programs, it is not surprising that training is an interdisciplinary research area, with contributions from the fields of cognitive and industrial/organizational psychology, human factors and ergonomics, instructional design, and human resource management.

Assessing Training Requirements

According to common wisdom, the first phase of training program development for specific skills should be needs assessment (I. L. Goldstein & Ford, 2002). Needs assessment involves determining what knowledge or skills are prerequisite to training activities and what the goals of the training should be. It should be viewed as an ongoing process in which the organization acts proactively, anticipating training needs and any barriers to implementing training. Needs assessment focuses on identifying specific problem areas in the organization and determining whether training is an appropriate solution to the problems.

For example, communication problems have been implicated as a factor in the breakdown of team performance in environments such as the operating theater (e.g., Awad et al., 2005). Training in communication skills can address this problem, but only if the problem is well understood and all parties receive the training needed and the opportunity to practice the learned skills. For example, training nurses to speak up when they perceive a potential error is unlikely to result in performance improvements if surgeons do not receive training in which they learn to listen to opposing viewpoints from others. Moreover, the success of communication training in reducing incidents in the operating theater will depend on an organizational culture that values error reporting. Communication training will have no impact on performance in situations in which communication is already adequate, illustrating the importance of a problem-based approach to identifying training needs. Other reasons for conducting needs assessments prior to implementing training programs are to collect data that can be used to evaluate the effectiveness of the training program and to perform a training cost-benefit analysis.

Whereas skills researchers are usually concerned with the individual performer of a task and with how skill can best be understood, the organization views skill as a means of accomplishing organizational goals. The focus of an organizational needs assessment is thus on discrepancies between employee skills and the skills required for effective job performance (see Figure 10.1): Needs assessment should reflect the goals of the organization (e.g., improving the safety climate in a hospital) and translate these goals into trainable skills (e.g., improving teamwork skills).

Figure 10.1 An overview of the steps to be taken in determining training needs.

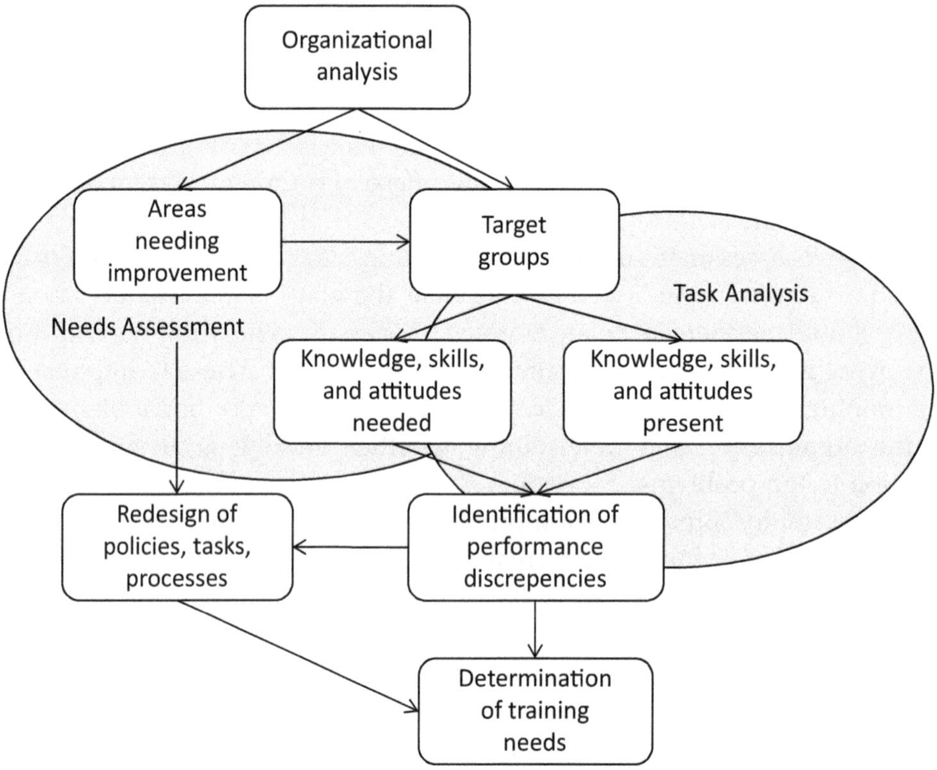

```
                    ┌──────────────┐
                    │ Organizational│
                    │   analysis   │
                    └──────────────┘
          ┌────────────┬───────────┐
          ▼            ▼           
    ┌──────────┐   ┌────────┐
    │  Areas   │   │ Target │
    │ needing  │──▶│ groups │         Task Analysis
    │improvement│   └────────┘
    └──────────┘
  Needs Assessment
              ┌─────────────┐   ┌─────────────┐
              │Knowledge,   │   │Knowledge,   │
              │skills, and  │   │skills, and  │
              │attitudes    │   │attitudes    │
              │needed       │   │present      │
              └─────────────┘   └─────────────┘
    ┌──────────┐       ┌──────────────┐
    │Redesign of│      │Identification│
    │policies, │◀─────│of performance│
    │tasks,     │      │discrepancies │
    │processes  │      └──────────────┘
    └──────────┘             │
                             ▼
                    ┌──────────────┐
                    │Determination │
                    │ of training  │
                    │    needs     │
                    └──────────────┘
```

The goal of the assessment is to identify problems that can be solved by training. Of course, needs assessment may also reveal policies, practices, or procedures that need to be changed in order to increase safety or efficiency (Brown, 2002). In such a case, a bottom-up training approach may not be sufficient to bring about organizational change, but new training needs may arise if policies or procedures are changed to address the situation.

Data for needs analysis can come from a variety of sources. The impetus for conducting a needs analysis may come from organizational data, such as turnover or absenteeism rate, employee grievances, customer complaints, quality control, or accident records (Aguinis & Kraiger, 2009). Specific training needs are, however, identified by means of *task analysis*. A task analysis consists of describing job requirements in such a way that the employee knowledge and skills needed to perform the job can be evaluated and training needs determined.

Most techniques for analyzing tasks focus on the description, analysis, and evaluation of the performance demands placed on the human by other aspects of the human-machine system within which tasks are performed. The focus of the analysis might be on decomposing tasks into their constituent information-processing requirements, such as perceptual, decisional, or motor components, or into the principles, rules, and goals contained in expert knowledge. Further distinctions may be made between automatic and controlled processes, and the allocation of attention may be described. For example, *principled task decomposition* (Frederiksen & White, 1989) involves breaking down a task into subtasks, specifying the information-processing requirements of each subtask, and describing the characteristics of experts in the task. Frederiksen and White used principled task decomposition to develop a training program for the Space Fortress game (Mané & Donchin, 1989; see Chapter 4) by first identifying the hierarchical relationships between skill and knowledge components that are involved in the transition from novice to expert performance in the game and then constructing training activities for the individual component processes as well as for their integration. Compared to a control group who simply played the Space Fortress game, people who were trained with the componential training for the same amount of time performed less well when they first played the game. However, the componential-training group quickly overtook the whole-game training group, suggesting that the specific knowledge and heuristics taught in the componential training had a beneficial effect on learning, although some initial integration of the learned skills was needed. The benefit of componential over whole-task practice may be partly due to the development of strategies by which attention can be more efficiently allocated to individual aspects of task performance.

When task analysis (and related techniques, such as cognitive work analysis; Vicente, 1999) is used not only to describe task components but also to uncover the knowledge and thought processes that underlie that performance (Roth, 2008), it is often referred to as *cognitive task analysis*. Such in-depth analyses of tasks allow the identification of points at which human error is likely to occur and can uncover opportunities to improve performance at both the individual and team levels.

Cognitive task analysis grew out of work such as that described in Chapters 1 and 6 in which knowledge elicitation techniques are applied to capture the knowledge and strategies of experts performing complex cognitive tasks. Methods for eliciting and representing expert knowledge such as "think aloud" protocols (Ericsson & Simon, 1980) and psychological scaling methods (Cooke, 1994; Cooke, Salas, Cannon-Bowers, & Stout, 2000) are used to uncover how expertise is represented (e.g., Hoffman, Aitken, & Duffield, 2009). Other methods, including structured interview techniques, critical incident analysis (for investigating actual incidents, accidents, or disasters;

Flanagan, 1954), and field observation of performance in actual environments or high-fidelity simulators (Woods, 1993), are used to study the performance of individuals and teams.

Cognitive task analysis has been most widely applied in complex environments, such as nuclear systems control rooms and military command centers. It has its roots in cognitive systems engineering (Hollnagel & Woods, 2005; Rasmussen, 1986) and naturalistic decision making (G. Klein, 1997). It rests on methods that are functional in that they specify the goals, constraints, and affordances (the qualities of objects that allow actions to be performed on them) that characterize the tasks that are carried out. One widely used method is the *critical decision method* (G. A. Klein, Calderwood, & MacGregor, 1989) in which questions are asked to elicit retrospective descriptions of past incidents. Several rounds of questioning or cognitive "walkthroughs" of the event are typically carried out in order understand the challenges experienced by the operator and the knowledge and cognitive strategies that were used to cope with the demands of the situation. Questions such as "If the decision was not the best one for the circumstances, what training, knowledge, or information could have helped to make it better?" are posed by the researcher to elicit rich descriptions of events.

A more formal way of representing the goals, means of achieving goals, and the constraints that define the boundaries of a domain is in terms of an *abstraction hierarchy* (Rasmussen, 1986; Vicente, 1999; Xu, 2007). Such a hierarchy provides a framework for determining which functions should be performed by people versus machines as well as which cognitive activities or limitations characterize performance. Structural constraints associated with equipment, resources, and so forth are combined with functional descriptions to provide goal-oriented descriptions of primary objectives and how these objectives can be realized. Lower-order physical properties detail how the goals can be executed, as well as the object properties that enable goal execution. The resulting "structural means-ends hierarchy" defines the work environment being acted upon.

The first step in conducting a cognitive task analysis is to determine the object to be described and the depth of analysis required, such as one aspect of an aircraft-automation system. The second step is to define the characteristics of the work environment, which in the example of an aircraft-automation system would include *physical constraints*, such as automation mode transition algorithms, and *intentional constraints*, such as the airlines' practices for automation and automation procedures associated with meeting those priorities while maintaining compliance with air traffic control. An abstraction hierarchy is developed by collecting domain knowledge (e.g., by reviewing pilot training materials and system manuals and by conducting interviews with pilots and flight deck designers). The abstraction hierarchy describes the functional purposes, such as "safety" and "on-time flights," at the top of the hierarchy; the abstract functions, or the global system values to be prioritized, minimized, or maximized (in order to satisfy the physical and intentional constraints); and the generalized functions, or processes that are executed or coordinated in support of higher-level purposes, such as those involved in switching from manual control to the automated mode.

Detailed abstraction hierarchies such as that constructed by Xu (2007) can be used to identify potential problems and needs for training for both routine and novel situations. Because the abstraction hierarchy represents the knowledge of the operator, it provides a framework to assess whether mental models are complete and effective for searching for solutions within the domain. Thus, hierarchies can be used for identifying training requirements. They also can be used for analyzing the mistakes made during training (see Figure 10.2). Based on findings that pilots' misconceptions and misuses of automation were more likely to occur at the levels of abstract and generalized functions rather than lower-order physical functions, Xu concluded that current training focusing on how the system functions rather than why it functions as it does is likely to lead to a limited repertoire of automation procedures, thus limiting the ability of pilots to deal with novel

Figure 10.2 The levels of the abstraction hierarchy (left column) and errors related to automation made during simulated flight in the study of Xu (2007).

	Abstraction Hierarchy	Simulator Study Data		
Functional properties	Functional purposes			
	Abstract functions	Failed to meet altitude constraints on descent due to unclear active target	Did not notice and correct loss of flight management computer altitude restriction due to runway change	Violated assigned airspeed on descent
	Generalized functions	Flew vertical navigation altitude instead of vertical navigation path in cruise after new cruise altitude updated	Delayed leaving an altitude after being requested to climb	Poorly managed airspeed restriction due to inefficient use of automation of speed target propagation across flight management computer cruise and descent pages
			Failed to start down at top of descent—started down late	
		Failed to detect the artificial vertical navigation while climbing	Failed to detect the artificial autothrottle transition while descending	Failed to detect the artificial vertical navigation transition while descending
Physical properties	Physical functions			
	Physical devices			

situations. This conclusion led to the suggestion that training be extended to include more information about the automation systems and the aircraft being controlled, and that it include new automation procedures. Xu's assessment is consistent with a recent study of 18 Boeing 747 pilots that showed that when the pilots were tested on scenarios on which they typically train, responses corresponded with accepted standards, whereas when novelty was added to the same events the responses often deviated from the standards (Croft, 2015).

Structuring Training

Because many skills are too complex to be learned all at once, training may be more effective when only certain aspects of a skill are learned at a time. Sometimes learning is facilitated by simplifying skills for training purposes, and other times it is better to break the skills into component parts and then to recombine these parts. As discussed in Chapter 4, having people put variable amounts of emphasis on task components during training can be an effective means of optimizing training. Importantly, automatic processing, as assessed by an apparent insensitivity to attentional resources or demands, can develop with learning when the right conditions are provided. The essential conditions seem to be the consistency of the discrimination and interpretation of the stimuli, and the stimulus-to-response mapping (W. Schneider & Fisk, 1982). The development of automaticity has been shown for a range of tasks. The idea that it depends more on the consistency of the stimulus-response mappings than on properties of the stimuli, such as perceptual salience, is supported by the finding that automaticity can develop when training is given on stimuli that have been divided into arbitrary classes (Shiffrin & Schneider, 1977).

Determining which method of training is likely to be the most effective requires a thorough understanding of the task to be trained. In general, part-task training, such as the componential-training method of Frederiksen and White (1989), has been shown to be an effective method of training difficult tasks or tasks with independent components (Holding, 1965; Wightman & Lintern, 1985). If successful performance depends on understanding interactions between the stimuli used for different aspects of the task, or if actions must be performed in parallel, another training method, *simplification*, may be more effective. Simplifying tasks when they are first practiced and then gradually increasing the difficulty of the task is a means of keeping the task intact so that trainees can learn how component processes interact or can be performed in parallel. When multiple task components must be carried out in parallel, the demands imposed by the need to recombine the separate skills may counteract any benefits of part-task training. In such a case, *integrative training*, in which the whole task is practiced but performers are instructed to emphasize certain of the skills, may lead to more robust skills than hierarchical or other part-task training methods (Fabiani et al., 1989). Training that emphasizes the development of automaticity in task components (Shebilske, Goettl, & Regian, 1999) can be used in conjunction with part-task training. Training for automaticity has been used successfully with air traffic controllers to promote automatic processing of perceptual information, such as the distances between aircraft and indications of maneuvers, such as the start of turns (W. Schneider, Vidulich, & Yeh, 1982).

Many methods of part-task training have been proposed. If a task consists of components with clear starting and stopping points, it can simply be segmented into the different components. *Backward chaining* involves practicing the last step in a segmented task first, with earlier components added later. Whether backward chaining will be more effective than *forward chaining*, in which segments are trained in order, starting with the first one, will depend on the type of feedback that is available for evaluating performance. If the task is complex and the initial steps are far removed from the goal, there might be a benefit for backward chaining because this begins by emphasizing the steps closest to the goal. When feedback from one component influences performance on the next, forward chaining might be more effective (Wightman & Lintern, 1985). The benefits of part-task training can be long-lasting. For example, Marmie and Healy (1995) showed that people who practiced either the whole task (searching for a target, sighting it, and firing) or, for several sessions, only the sighting and firing components of a simulated tank gunnery task performed equally well in whole-task retention sessions given immediately after training or 1 month later in overall performance (proportion of kills) and in time to identify the target, but the part-task training group, which was able to devote more resources to the sighting and firing components of the task during training, showed a long-lasting benefit in time to fire.

According to instance theories of learning, in which each learning experience is assumed to be encoded separately (see Chapter 4), transfer should occur between compatible tasks, where compatibility is defined as a condition in which "traces laid down in one task context can be used to support performance in another" (Logan & Compton, 1998, p. 119). Incompatible traces will be of no use and may even cause confusion if retrieved. This view is consistent with the long-standing identical elements view (see Chapter 1) that transfer will occur whenever elements in the practiced task are also present in the transfer task. A framework for conceptualizing when transfer will occur that considers both verbalizable, declarative and procedural or "how to" knowledge is the *procedural reinstatement principle* (Healy, Wohldmann, & Bourne, 2005). According to this principle, procedures are associated with facts during learning, and transfer is assumed to occur to the extent to which particular fact-procedure combinations can be used in the transfer context. Healy et al. summarize a variety of studies on the learning and retention of simple cognitive skills and conclude that retention will be the greatest when performance requires the procedures employed during training, when information received during training can be related to previous experience and can be retrieved directly, when trained information is made distinctive, and when refresher or practice opportunities are provided. In other words, both procedures and information provide the cues necessary for retrieving information.

The procedural reinstatement principle makes important predictions regarding the effectiveness of training. Namely, training can be expected to be effective only to the extent that the information linked to procedures during training is also so linked during transfer. For example, part-whole transfer will be expected only when the particular procedures practiced are linked to the same information during transfer. Whole-part transfer (practicing a whole task and then transferring to one part of that task), in particular, should be limited when a given procedure is linked to more information than in the part-task condition. Support for these predictions has been found in a range of tasks (see Healy et al., 2005, for an overview). For example, Healy et al. have shown limited part-whole task transfer (i.e., transfer from an x or y reversed condition to an x and y reversed condition) and no whole-part task transfer in a task requiring perceptual-motor coordination in moving a computer mouse for which either the x, y, or both components were reversed.

Simulator Training

Many tasks are so complex that training must be carried out in a high-fidelity simulator. Building high-fidelity simulators is expensive, so there is pressure on designers to include only those cues that lead to better transfer to the actual task. One approach to determining which aspects of the target environment need to be included in the training environment is to emphasize cue-response relations (Cormier, 1987), deciding which cues are necessary for the determination of responses. This approach has been used in designing simulators for training complex or dangerous tasks. If one can identify the relevant cue-response relations, only the cues that are necessary need be incorporated into the simulator. Unfortunately, determining these relations is not always easy. For example, it has been found that motion cues can lead to better performance in a flight simulator (e.g., Perry & Naish, 1964), but not to better transfer to actual flight (e.g., Jacobs & Roscoe, 1975). To understand this discrepancy, it is necessary to look at the type of motion cues presented. In general, the presence of disturbance motion cues (cues associated with outside influences) is more important for transfer of simulator training to actual flight. However, for relatively unstable, difficult-to-fly aircraft, maneuver cues (cues associated with control actions) can be important, especially for novices (de Winter, Dodou, & Mulder, 2012; Gawron, Bailey, & Lehman, 1995).

Team Training

When tasks are performed not by individuals working alone but by individuals working in teams, not only limitations in knowledge or skills but also poor performance of non-technical skills can lead to errors. Non-technical skills are the cognitive and interpersonal skills that complement an individual's technical or clinical knowledge and facilitate effective performance. Particular concerns in team performance are communication, stress recognition, and the coordination of team members' activities. Being a part of a team requires that one be able to predict other team members' behavior and be able to give and receive feedback and backup support (Salas et al., 2008). This level of involvement in team activities requires knowledge of what other team members are doing and of what they know. Salas and colleagues (e.g., Salas & Cannon-Bowers, 1997) refer to this knowledge as a *shared mental model*. They suggest that this knowledge allows team members to anticipate each other's actions and to maintain an accurate, up-to-date picture of the current situation (i.e., situation awareness).

A training strategy that is unique to team training and that focuses on building the ability to anticipate what team members will do is *cross-training*. In cross-training, team members receive information and training in the tasks of other team members. In addition to providing the team with backup knowledge should a team member be absent, cross-training may also contribute to the development of a shared mental model. Volpe, Cannon-Bowers, Salas, and Spector (1996; see also Gorman, Cooke, & Amazeen, 2010) showed that two-person teams who received cross-training used more efficient communication strategies and showed better task performance than teams not provided with this knowledge.

A challenge for teams, especially in complex environments, is to adapt to novel situations. In such a situation, stress may be high, and established protocols may not apply. Stachowski, Kaplan, and Waller (2009) found that better-performing teams faced with novel situations exhibited fewer systematic patterns of interaction, engaged in less complex interaction, and exhibited patterns that encompassed fewer behaviors (e.g., verbal statements), involved fewer actors, and incorporated less back-and-forth communication than did teams who performed less well. Specialized training, such as training team members to recognize high-stress conditions and adapt their behavior accordingly, has been found to improve performance in novel situations (Entin & Serfaty, 1999), as has a training method in which team roles are disrupted (e.g., by simulating failure of a communication channel), forcing team members to coordinate their actions in novel ways to achieve their objectives (Gorman et al., 2010). On the basis of a meta-analysis of over 90 tests of the effectiveness of various methods of team training, Salas et al. (2008) concluded that team training added value to training programs across a wide variety of settings. The most benefit was seen for team processes such as communication and coordination. Team training thus has the potential to aid in the formation of efficient and adaptive teams, who are capable of "shedding established patterns of interaction" (Stachowski et al., 2009, p. 6) and performing with economy of effort.

Crew Resource Management

One domain where the potential of team training to improve team performance and to increase safety has been demonstrated is aviation human factors (Edkins, 2002). It was within the area of aviation that crew resource management (CRM; for a review see O'Connor et al., 2008) was developed. A training intervention for improving team communication and effectiveness, CRM was inspired by a number of air disasters in which human error—in particular suboptimal communication—was identified as the major contributing factor. For example, in the Tenerife disaster in 1977 that cost the lives of 583 passengers and crew, poor communication combined with poor weather conditions and unusual circumstances to create the worst air disaster then on record. Analyses of the communication records of the KLM plane involved in the crash revealed that the copilot was not able to adequately express his concerns about whether clearance to take off had been given. The pilot and copilot seemed to be at cross-purposes; the pilot asked the copilot to ask for clearance, and the copilot radioed that they were "ready for takeoff" and "waiting for our ATC clearance." Air traffic control then gave route instructions; these instructions contained the word "takeoff"—but no explicit instruction that they were cleared for takeoff. The pilot interrupted the copilot's reading back of the instructions with the statement "we're going." This decision was the fatal one and could have been prevented if the copilot had been more assertive in relaying the tower's instructions and if the communication between the tower and cockpit had been less ambiguous. Many of the factors identified as having played a role in the accident's occurrence led to changes in procedures. Of these, the need to create a flatter hierarchy in the cockpit and the need to encourage decision making by mutual agreement are key components of CRM.

In addition to addressing communication and decision making, CRM training focuses on the skills involved in recognizing signs of stress and adapting performance to stressful situations, working as a team, and recognizing when human error is likely to occur and taking steps to prevent it. Usually conducted in a simulator (but sometimes just on the basis of videos of crew performance), CRM normally consists of role-playing as well as classroom instruction.

Crew resource management is directed at individuals in a unit or team context, and individual characteristics, such as prior knowledge of CRM and pretraining self-efficacy, as well as team characteristics, such as the size of the group and the degree of familiarity of team members with each other, can be expected to influence individual training outcomes. Training outcomes at the team level, such as better teamwork and team cohesion and decision making, will be further influenced by the organization climate and constraints, such as the support of the commander and opportunities for use of the skills. Transfer outcomes such as commitment to safety and improved crew morale at the individual level contribute to better mission planning at the team level, and, ultimately, to improved safety procedures and fewer incidents.

The success of CRM in improving aviation safety has led to its applications in other fields, most notably anesthesiology and surgical and emergency medical care. In a medical environment, such training often involves simulating or role-playing key moments, such as the patient handover (transfer of the patient from one set of carers to another) or debriefing after an operation or procedure. The main focuses of the training in medical settings are communication (debriefing, effective communication with patients when errors occur); improving error awareness and enhancing professionals' sense of responsibility for the reduction of error; teaching about the human-machine interface; teamwork and leadership, including decision making as a team and the importance of clarity of roles; shared mental models; and, finally, situational awareness (M. Gordon, Darbyshire, & Baker, 2012).

The goal of improving patient safety is often cited in the context of training, but often without concrete evidence or guidance of how to achieve advances in patient safety. In fact, in their systematic review of the literature of the training of non-technical skills in medical settings M. Gordon et al. (2012) note that whereas most of the reviewed studies report positive outcomes on learning, the outcomes reported in the studies tended to reflect immediate learning or reactions to the training itself, and few report any attempt to measure changes in patient safety outcomes. Thus, although there is evidence that non-technical skill training is valued within the medical profession, there is as yet little evidence, as stated by Gordon et al., that supports "the translation of knowledge, skills and attitudes into behaviour change and reductions in adverse events" (2012, p. 1051). This shortcoming is a serious one, especially for policy making.

The need to determine whether interventions such as CRM training result in measurable outcomes for safety has led to the development of so-called behavioral markers for non-technical skills. Behavioral markers are skills or behaviors described in such a way that they are directly observable (in the case of social skills) or can be inferred from communication (in the case of cognitive skills). For example, the NOTECHS (non-technical skills) system for assessing pilots' CRM skills (Flin et al., 2003) contains behavioral markers for four categories: cooperation, leadership and managerial skills, situation awareness, and decision making, each of which is further broken down into several elements (see Figure 10.3). For each of the elements within the categories, there are behavioral markers of both effective and ineffective behaviors.

Figure 10.3 The category-element-behavioral marker structure of the NOTECHS system. Typically, the examples of good and poor practice are used in a rating list for evaluating performance.

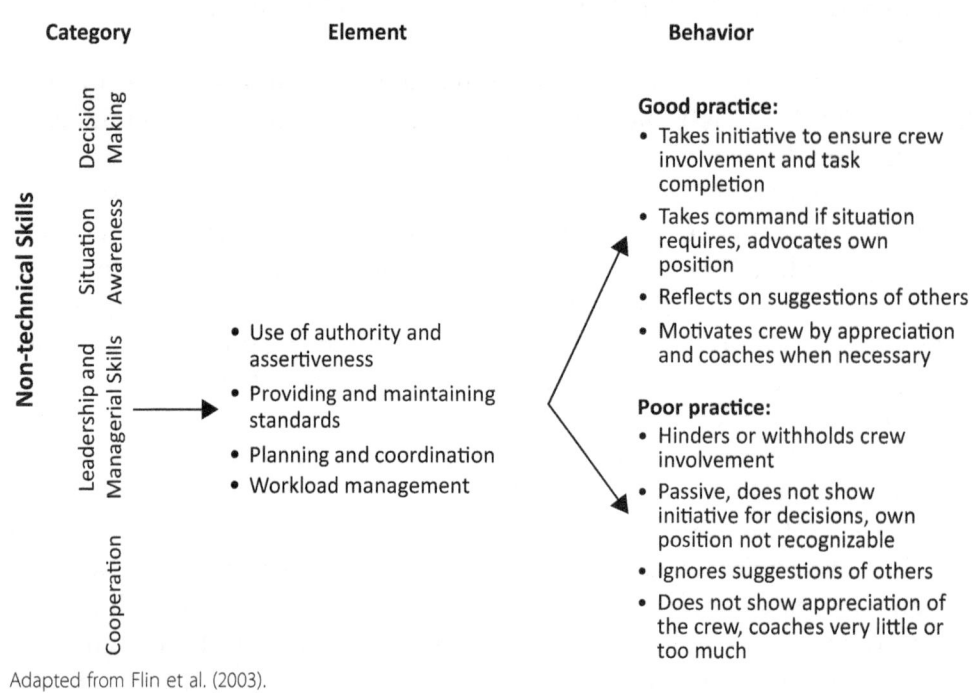

Category	Element	Behavior
Non-technical Skills: Decision Making, Situation Awareness, Leadership and Managerial Skills, Cooperation	• Use of authority and assertiveness • Providing and maintaining standards • Planning and coordination • Workload management	**Good practice:** • Takes initiative to ensure crew involvement and task completion • Takes command if situation requires, advocates own position • Reflects on suggestions of others • Motivates crew by appreciation and coaches when necessary **Poor practice:** • Hinders or withholds crew involvement • Passive, does not show initiative for decisions, own position not recognizable • Ignores suggestions of others • Does not show appreciation of the crew, coaches very little or too much

Adapted from Flin et al. (2003).

For example, "considering others" is an element of the category cooperation, which is a social skill. A behavioral marker of good practice for this element is "takes notice of the suggestions of other crew members even if s/he does not agree" and a behavioral marker of poor practice is "ignores suggestions of other crew members." Just as CRM training spread from aviation to medical and other contexts, so have the use and development of behavioral markers of non-technical skills. Behavioral marker systems have been developed for contexts ranging from anesthesiology (Fletcher, Flin, McGeorge, & Patey 2004) and emergency medicine (S. Cooper et al., 2010) to the officer of the deck at sea (O'Connor & Long, 2011).

Implementing and Evaluating Training in Organizations

The most important criterion for judging the success of a training program is the extent to which the skills learned during training transfer to the environment of interest (Baldwin & Ford, 1988). The major questions of interest thus concern how durable training effects are (i.e., whether they last beyond the training sessions) and how broad they are (i.e., whether the effects transfer to conditions different to those under which training occurred). New skills or knowledge will be useful to the organization only to the extent to which they can be used. Thus, work environments need to be structured so that the acquisition of skill is facilitated and so that environmental conditions do not interfere with performance of skills, once learned. Organizational support is also necessary for optimal transfer of trained skills.

Transfer Climate

Company investment in training can backfire if opportunities to use new knowledge or skills are not provided. Transfer climate refers to the actions of management that convey their support for the transfer of training, as well as the value that is placed on the successful transfer of training by the organization (Rouiller & Goldstein, 1993). An important aspect of transfer climate is that learned skills *can* be transferred. That is, there must be no barriers to transfer such as lack of equipment or opportunity. Building a positive transfer climate requires that employees be asked whether there are any barriers to transfer. Moreover, trainees should be encouraged to identify training outcomes that are valuable to the organization and successful implementation of these outcomes should be rewarded (Machin & Fogarty, 2004).

From the standpoint of an organization, skills training may have several functions in addition to providing the workers with the tools needed to perform their jobs. Facilitating learning is an obvious function of training.

A less obvious benefit of training might be to retain employees. Participation in training programs is often seen as a benefit by employees, and the skills they acquire can lead to improved opportunities within the organization. If training is seen as a benefit, and taking advantage of training opportunities is encouraged, the company culture may be enhanced. Training can also be used as an incentive for good performance or to send the message that an organization cares about its employees (Aguinis, 2009). Opportunities to learn skills that can lead to more desired positions within the organization can be used to encourage workers to master current tasks. When the organization takes such a view, it can create a continuous learning environment in which a directed and long-term effort to learn and apply knowledge and skills is valued and encouraged. If what is learned cannot be implemented, employees will question its value and, by extension, the commitment of the organization to employee development. For example, tuition reimbursement to earn a new degree may be offered as an employee incentive. While employees are engaged in educational activities, turnover is indeed reduced. Once new certificates or degrees have been earned, however, turnover has been found to increase if promotion to a position for which the new qualifications are necessary is not possible (Aguinis, 2009).

Continuous Learning
Continuous learning (or career-related continuous learning) is an individual-level phenomenon, as opposed to organizational learning or learning organizations (Argyris, 1998; London & Smither, 1999). Although immediate job performance may be enhanced by learning, the focus of continuous learning is on-the-job or career development. Continuous learning is self-initiated and discretionary. In contrast to mandatory training programs, employees who engage in continuous learning are proactive in choosing activities to engage in, and sustain this over time. Organizations support continuous learning by providing opportunities to engage in activities such as reading, discussing with colleagues, and accepting challenging job assignments, in addition to offering more formal activities. Employees thus develop competencies so as to be able to adapt to changing job requirements or employers (Gibb, 2001).

The changing nature of work and organizational developments put pressure on individuals to adapt to rapidly changing work environments, requiring that they update their knowledge and skills in order to maintain their places within the organizations and to remain competitive in their fields. Continuous knowledge development is essential for organizations facing global competition. Many organizations deal with rapid technological development by offering development programs to their employees with the hope that such development programs will keep employees' knowledge, skills, and abilities up-to-date, thus optimizing performance and enhancing the intellectual capital of an organization (Rowold & Kauffeld, 2009).

Continuous learning environments in which development programs are offered "on demand" are assumed to create employees who can be described as "knowing what, how, why—and caring" about their work. In addition to formal training (e.g., off-the-job, lecture-based, or computer-based training courses focusing on [1] task-related knowledge and skills, [2] methods, such as presentation, and problem-solving skills, and [3] social skills, such as communication and team training), informal activities may contribute to continuous learning (Rowold & Kauffeld, 2009). Informal learning opportunities that take place during regular work assignments include activities such as reading trade journals or discussing new ideas with colleagues.

Surprisingly, although employees' participation in development activities has been found to be related to their commitment to the organization and job satisfaction (e.g., Birdi, Allen, & Warr, 1997), relatively little research has addressed whether there is a relationship between continuous learning and the competencies needed for the job or whether informal development activities are equally efficient. In one large-scale study involving nearly 20 different companies, the efficacy of formal and informal professional training, methods (e.g., problem solving), and social training or learning-related activities was assessed by relating learning experience to work-related competencies, while controlling for time spent on the job (Rowold & Kauffeld, 2009). Of the formal activities, only methods training was found to lead to improvements, whereas all types of informal learning experience were found to be related to more professional, work-related method, or work-related social competencies. An important conclusion that can be drawn from this study is that formal training may quickly become obsolete, whereas informal on-the-job learning is likely to be more related to the actual needs of the worker for performing his or her work.

Trainee Characteristics

Self-Efficacy
In addition to the knowledge and skills possessed (and needed) by learners, it is important to consider their readiness and motivation to learn. The attitudes, expectations, and self-beliefs that learners bring to the training experience have been shown to be related to outcome measures and affective reactions to the training. The factor with the strongest relation to readiness to engage in training—and to training benefits—is self-efficacy (Colquitt,

LePine, & Noe 2000). Self-efficacy refers to individuals' belief that they can successfully perform a task (R. E. Wood & Bandura, 1989) and to how they deal with setbacks in goal-directed behavior (Locke & Latham 1990).

Self-efficacy is sometimes referred to as the "can do" of trainees' intention to learn and transfer, as opposed to the "will do" aspect of training instrumentality. Whereas trainees need to be confident in their abilities in order to be motivated to learn (i.e., they need high self-efficacy), they also need to believe that performing at a required level is related to outcomes they value (as reflected by high instrumentality; Chiaburu & Lindsay, 2008). Readiness to engage in training is fostered by demonstrating the value of training and lowering trainee anxiety about the training (see Table 10.1 for an overview of ways in which pretraining self-efficacy and training instrumentality may be enhanced). Transfer of training to the workplace requires motivation, a belief in the instrumentality of what has been learned, and proper organizational support.

Goal Orientation

Another important variable influencing trainee readiness and training success is the goal orientation of the learner. Learners with a performance orientation are motivated by doing well according to external indicators of success, such as grades or pay bonuses. Learners with a mastery orientation, on the other hand, seek to become proficient in a topic to the best of their ability. Stevens and Gist (1997) showed that goal orientation can be influenced. Specifically, Stevens and Gist showed that having learners engage in self-management—which emphasizes attention to steps to enhance skill use—encouraged learners to adopt mastery goals, whereas goal setting emphasizing the achievement of superior outcomes encouraged learners to adopt performance goals. This is important because mastery goals have been associated with a number of affective, motivational, and

TABLE 10.1 Methods for Increasing Pretraining Self-Efficacy and Training Instrumentality

Emphasize learning outcomes.
Make clear to trainees that the purpose of the training is to improve performance and not to uncover deficiencies.
Educate trainees about the purpose and content of the training before it takes place.
Optimize learning by providing trainees with practice using effective learning strategies, such as mnemonics.
Arrange for peers who have successfully completed the training to explain to trainees how the training has been useful to them.
Detail how what is learned during the training will be applied in the workplace and provide opportunities for practice.

cognitive benefits. Mastery-oriented individuals are more likely to view skills as acquirable and to interpret difficulty in learning or failure as evidence that they themselves need to exert more effort or change tactics. Performance-oriented individuals, on the other hand, may regard skills as fixed abilities and interpret task difficulty or failure as evidence of low ability. Goal orientation thus affects transfer performance: Mastery-oriented individuals will be more likely to focus on finding task strategies that may lead to success, whereas performance-oriented individuals may focus on evidence of their inadequacies, become angry or defensive, and withdraw from the task (Gist & Stevens, 1998). Mastery-oriented training led the learners in Stevens and Gist's study to engage in more skill-maintenance activities; these learners also planned to exert more effort and demonstrated more positive affect than did their counterparts who received performance-oriented training.

Transfer Motivation
Without transfer, the time, money, and resources put into increasing a person's abilities are wasted. Unfortunately, the low return on investment for training is a major concern. Sometimes the problem of poor transfer lies with the organization: Trainees may find little opportunity or support to apply what they have learned (Quiñones, 1997). Currently, most researchers agree that motivation is the major limiting factor for training transfer (Gegenfurtner, Veermans, Festner, & Gruber, 2009). Motivation to transfer is defined as the desire of the trainee to use the knowledge and skills learned in training on the job (Noe, 1986). It may be the only factor to mediate the effect of other antecedents on the transfer of training since opportunities to perform, while a necessary factor, are not sufficient to ensure that training will be applied at work.

Individual attitudes and attributes affect trainee motivation even before trainees attend a training program. Attitudes toward training, motivation to learn, personality traits, and work commitment are all factors that can determine motivation to transfer learning at work (e.g., Chiaburu & Lindsay, 2008; Rowold, 2007; Seyler, Holton, Bates, Burnett, & Carvalho, 1998). In addition, mastery goals (reflected in the wish to master a topic to the best of one's ability) induce more motivation to transfer than do performance goals (reflected in the wish to receive external recognition for one's performance; Mesmer-Magnus & Viswesvaran, 2007). Dimensions of work commitment that have been related to motivation to transfer include career commitment, organizational commitment, job involvement, and work ethic (Gegenfurtner et al., 2009), with transfer motivation being largely a function of organizational commitment and the transfer environment (Seyler et al., 1998).

Employees who report liking the training content also are more likely to show motivation to transfer.

How an organization presents a training program to its employees determines, in part, the extent to which a trainee will be motivated to transfer learning to the workplace. Pretraining interventions that promote favorable perceptions toward the program include providing realistic information about the training intervention prior to training and offering trainees the opportunity to provide input regarding the intervention (Holton, Bates, & Ruona, 2000; Russ-Eft, 2002). Framing the training in this way serves to communicate the company's expectations (Bates & Holton, 2004). An organizational culture that values the importance of learning at work has also been found to be positively related to trainees' transfer motivation (e.g., Bates & Holton, 2004). Transfer motivation will tend to be high when trainees understand that the organization expects them to use the training in the workplace and low when the prevailing climate is one of resistance to change. Other organizational culture factors likely to influence transfer motivation, but that have not been fully explored, include whether the culture is dominated by error prevention. An error-prevention culture may result in reluctance to apply new skills or procedures at work for fear of negative consequences (Gegenfurtner et al., 2009).

Transfer motivation is also shaped by the training itself, such as the nature of instruction (see Chapter 6), the conditions under which it is given, and any consequences that emerge during training. The evidence for a relation between success in learning and motivation to use this learning back on the job is, however, tenuous. It remains unclear whether transfer motivation predicts learning or whether learning predicts transfer motivation.

Transfer motivation can interact with performance self-efficacy, expectations, and training reactions (R. Smith, Jayasuriya, Caputi, & Hammer, 2008). The learning transfer system inventory (Holton et al., 2000) measures transfer effort-performance expectations by measuring the expectation that investing effort to use trained skills and knowledge at work will improve future job performance, and measures performance outcome expectations by measuring the expectation that increased job performance will lead to other outcomes that the trainee values. Both of these subscales have been related to trainees' transfer motivation (e.g., Bates & Holton, 2004; Kirwan & Birchall, 2006). Trainees' affective reactions and how they value the content and judge the utility of the program play a large role in determining if participants will be motivated to transfer learning to the workplace.

How trainees perceive the way in which the work environment facilitates or inhibits transfer will affect trainee motivation. Job characteristics and social support are perhaps the most important factors determining the transfer of newly learned skills. Job characteristics such as autonomy (Leitl & Zempel-Dohmen, 2006), workload, opportunity to perform (e.g., Bates & Holton, 2004), and situational constraints all affect transfer motivation. Many dimensions of social support, including supervisor support, peer support, supervisor sanctions, and performance coaching/feedback, have been linked to transfer motivation, but the effects are not always positive. First, there seems to be clear evidence of the facilitating effects of supervisor support on employees' transfer motivation (e.g., Bates & Holton, 2004; Devos et al., 2007; Kirwan & Birchall, 2006; Leitl & Zempel-Dohmen, 2006; Seyler et al., 1998). However, supervisor support does not necessarily lead to increased transfer motivation. Supportive supervisors may sometimes be seen as coercive, endangering the feeling of autonomy in applying training at work (Deelstra et al., 2003). In general, peer support is perceived as being more useful than supervisor support (Bates & Holton, 2004; Chiaburu & Marinova, 2005; Kirwan & Birchall, 2006); one factor in this may be the extent to which trainees identify with those giving them support (Pidd, 2004).

A recent review of training motivation (Gegenfurtner et al., 2009) reported only three studies that found a significant relation between training motivation and the subsequent use of what had been learned (Axtell, Maitlis, & Yearta., 1997; Chiaburu & Lindsay, 2008; Machin & Fogarty, 1997). It seems obvious that transfer motivation mediates transfer, but it is important to realize that high motivation is not a goal in and of itself. The failure to find significant effects of transfer motivation on actual transfer may be due to ceiling effects (if trainees are required to use new skills, little variability in the use of these skills will be apparent) or floor effects (if aspects of the organization prevent the new skills from being implemented, they will not be). A final consideration is that the measures of motivation that have been used in most studies are unidimensional, and transfer motivation may be a multidimensional construct. This consideration is leading to new models of transfer motivation (Gegenfurtner et al., 2009).

Evaluating Training Effectiveness

The organizational or societal value of training is increasingly being recognized. Human capital development is now recognized as important by such diverse economies or economic blocks as the European Union, regions of Oceania, and India (Aguinis & Kraiger, 2009), and the importance of training to society is reflected in national policies that encourage the design and delivery of training programs. Ideally, training should be evaluated with (a) comparison groups, (b) pretraining and posttraining measures of change,

(c) random assignment, (d) longitudinal measures, and (e) multiple measures of training outcomes. Although many aspects of training have been evaluated this way, experimental evaluation of training in the organization is not always possible (or even ethical, as it is difficult to justify withholding a training that is expected to provide benefits).

Of the many possible reasons to provide training to employees, maintaining or increasing competitiveness is an important one. The added value of training is hard to measure, but the results of a meta-analysis of over 1,100 effect sizes (Arthur, Bennett, Edens, & Bell, 2003) point to the positive effects of training on job-related behaviors and performance. How should training effectiveness be measured? For much of the 20th century, most evaluation focused only on the training itself. When transfer was evaluated (as it should be), evaluations tended to rely on self-reports of application of training to work performance. According to one widely used (and criticized) framework for evaluation (Kirkpatrick, 1976, 1994), evaluation should start with an assessment of whether trainees liked the training (i.e., reaction), and follow with assessments of learning, behavioral change (i.e., transfer), and results for the organization (e.g., reduced costs, improved quality). The major criticism of this approach is that it is presented as a hierarchy, leading many managers to concentrate on the first step without considering the purpose of the evaluation (Kraiger, 2002).

Training evaluation has as its purpose providing results that can be used to make decisions about the necessity and usefulness of training. If the primary purpose of offering training is to improve return on investment, employee satisfaction is not relevant. However, if training is seen as a way of improving the affect or motivation of employees, employee satisfaction with the training may be the most relevant outcome measure. Moreover, the decisions to be made about training may be formative or summative. How and when to evaluate training will depend on whether the purpose of the training is to improve training (as in formative decisions) as opposed to deciding whether to continue a training program. Formative questions include whether the trainer and training materials are effective, and whether trainees have the necessary prerequisite knowledge to benefit from the training. Summative questions include whether the training is still related to job requirements and whether the return justifies the investment.

A number of obstacles to evaluation have been identified. Evaluation is costly and requires some knowledge and skill. Many training departments may "want" to do more to evaluate training, but fail to do so because they do not know how or because there is no pressure from management to do it (Kirkpatrick, 1994). In fact, the most often reported reason for not conducting an evaluation of training is that management does not require it (Twitchell, Holton, & Trott, 2000), followed by cost and time constraints. Kraiger (2002) pointed out another reason that likely affects whether training is evaluated. This is the perception that there is "everything to lose and nothing to gain." This perception—which likely arises because of the diversity of reasons for offering training—can lead to a situation in which the quality of training suffers. An organization that advertises training as a job benefit simply does not want to hear that the training is inadequate. This attitude can lead to a situation in which training is not evaluated, and thus not improved.

Practical guidelines for improving evaluation center on the purpose of the evaluation (Kraiger, 2002). These include asking organizational stakeholders, including trainers, and managers how the results of the evaluation will be used, determining how evaluation outcomes have been used in the past, and making certain that the data collected is appropriate for the stated purpose of the evaluation. For example, if the evaluation will be used to update training content or delivery, course ratings should be supplemented by expert judgments of the training and may include the formation of an advisory panel. An evaluation of payoffs to the organization will focus on performance and transfer, and may be based on cost-benefit analysis, surveys, or supervisor ratings.

Maximizing the Benefits of Training

Of the general principles of skill acquisition discussed in this book, the most important are to ensure sufficient stimulus variability and to structure the conditions of practice to encourage elaborative processing and the development of automaticity. Another important factor is the appropriate use of feedback. Reducing feedback across the course of skill acquisition may encourage the development of self-regulatory skills that enhance the ability of the learner to generalize the skills beyond the training episode. A particularly effective source of feedback in many tasks is the errors made during performance (see Chapter 7). In *error management training* technique (Heimbeck, Frese, Sonnentag, & Keith, 2003; Keith & Frese, 2008), training situations are designed to elicit errors and learners are encouraged to view errors as valuable, informative feedback. According to Frese, Keith, and colleagues, error management training may aid learning because error recognition makes learners rethink their strategies and thus helps prevent the automatization of inefficient strategies.

Another advantage of error management training is that learners gain experience in dealing emotionally with errors. Because they are confronted with errors early on in training, they learn to exert control over their emotions in order to deal with them. Kanfer and colleagues (e.g., Kanfer, 1996; Kanfer & Ackerman, 1989) have pointed out that negative emotions can harm task performance, especially in early stages of learning, because they can divert attention away from the task and toward the self. Self-regulatory processes that reduce performance anxiety and other negative emotional reactions can be trained, and such emotional control processes are important for learning to occur (B. S. Bell & Kozlowski, 2002).

Because both metacognitive activities, such as reflecting on one's mistakes, and emotional control require conscious, cognitive processing, error management training can be expected to be most effective in situations in which sufficient time and resources are available to engage in these activities. This may explain why error management has proven to be most successful when structured tasks with clear objectives are used.

National Culture and Training

Interest in culture and training began out of recognition of the problems faced by employees sent abroad to work for their companies. Expatriates can be considered an important resource for creating and maintaining a company's competitive advantage, but there are also costs and risks associated with sending workers abroad. Not only do expatriates cost much more than they would at home, but also employees sent abroad may suffer reduced self-confidence or motivation. In fact, it has been estimated that up to 40% of employees sent abroad for a year or more return home early (Black & Mendenhall, 1990). Because of the costs to individuals, their families, and companies of failure to adjust to the new country, the adjustment of expatriates has become a major concern (Kraimer, Wayne, & Jaworski, 2001) and different training programs have been developed to increase psychological comfort and feelings of familiarity within the new environment. Most cross-cultural training programs are given in the home country in order to prepare employees for their future host country settings. A major goal of these pre-departure cross-cultural training programs is to enhance the adjustment of expatriates by developing their awareness (and acceptance) of differences and similarities in norms and behaviors between their home and host countries (Black & Mendenhall, 1990). Given the prevalence of cross-cultural training, there have been relatively few evaluations of its effectiveness. Studies that have evaluated the effectiveness of cross-cultural training show mixed results, leading Littrell, Salas, Hess, Paley, and Riedel (2006) to conclude that "many controversies continue to plague the literature with respect to the goals, content, effectiveness, and processes of cross-cultural training" (p. 356). This is not surprising in that the nature of the training, trainee characteristics, and cultural aspects of the training and transfer situations differ widely.

A variety of theoretical frameworks have been proposed to explain why cross-cultural training should facilitate the success of an overseas assignment. Programs based on social learning theory (Bandura, 1977) emphasize experience and the observation of others performing the behaviors. According to this view, cross-cultural training is viewed as a social learning process in which social skills are acquired through observation and practice. According to the dynamics of adjustment theory (A. T. Church, 1982) expatriate adjustment occurs across time, with the expatriate moving from optimistic to confused, to near complete adjustment, and expertise (i.e., adjustment is a U-shaped function of time). Many programs focus on reducing "culture shock." Critical to these programs is the idea that if expectations are met, higher levels of job satisfaction, commitment, adjustment, and performance will be achieved. On the other hand, unmet expectations may lead to job dissatisfaction and turnover. Cross-cultural training is thus focused on increasing the likelihood that expatriates will develop accurate expectations. Although widely referred to (e.g., Black & Mendenhall, 1990; Caligiuri, Phillips, Lazarova, Tarique, & Bürgi, 2001; A. T. Church, 1982), these theories have received few empirical tests.

One model of cross-cultural training that acknowledges that adjustment is a process, not a one-time event, is that of Selmer, Torbiörn, and de Leon (1998). Their training program is structured so as to correspond to the cycle of adaptation to a foreign environment. A consequence of a dynamic view of adjustment is that training should have a different impact at different phases of a foreign assignment, as the individual's receptiveness to the culture changes. Selmer et al. distinguish four phases of adjustment: the ethnocentric phase, the culture-shocked phase, the conformist phase, and the adjusted phase. Predeparture training material should include key information regarding local living conditions, and employees should receive details regarding the process of cross-cultural adjustment in order to prepare them for culture shock and the changes they will undergo as they adapt to the host environment. Post-arrival training should stress differences between the expatriate's home culture and the culture of the host country in order to build cultural awareness and lower ethnocentrism. After a few weeks, as culture shock sets in, training should focus on "learning how to learn" about the new environment. Finally, as the expatriate moves into the conformist phase, training experiences should allow the expatriate to interact with host nationals, and to receive feedback on the appropriateness of his or her behavior.

One factor making it difficult to establish a relationship between cross-cultural training and expatriate performance is that little is known about moderators of the relationships between cross-cultural training and expatriate performance (Black & Mendenhall, 1990; Morris & Robie, 2001). Factors that may moderate the relationship between cross-cultural training and expatriate performance include timing, duration, and content of the training, and family, job, organizational, and cultural attributes. Personality attributes, such as the Big Five personality trait "openness to experience," may also be related to cross-cultural training outcomes (Lievens, Harris, Van Keer, & Bisqueret, 2003). Performing a needs assessment to reveal strengths and weaknesses of individual employees can provide the basis for tailoring cross-cultural training to individual needs (Figure 10.1; Littrell et al.). At least one study has concluded that any effects of cross-cultural training are outweighed by the benefits of learning the language of the host country (Puck, Kittler, & Wright, 2008).

Multicultural training is intended to improve the ability of employees to interact with individuals from diverse cultural backgrounds by means of raising their cultural awareness. Members of multicultural teams, in particular, may benefit from cross-cultural training. Teams must make decisions in complex and uncertain situations (Burke, Priest, Wooten, DiazGranados, & Salas, 2009), and the lower levels of cohesion and trust in multicultural as opposed to same-culture teams can be problematic. Multicultural teams may also be especially susceptible to communication problems, such as misinterpretation and loss of communication, and the use of inappropriate stereotypes may further interfere with team processes (Burke et al., 2009; Salas, Burke, Wilson-Donnelly, & Fowlkes, 2004). Multicultural team training holds promise for preparing multicultural teams to interact effectively.

Differences in culture may affect not only how employees interact with each other but also how they react to the training itself. For example, cultural differences in trainees have led Helmreich, Merritt, and colleagues (e.g., Helmreich, Wilhelm, Klinect, & Merritt, 2001) to conclude that crew resource management training must be adapted to national culture in order to be effective. Dimensions of national culture (Hofstede & Hofstede, 2005) that may influence the effectiveness of training include *individualism/collectivism*, *power distance*, and *uncertainty avoidance*. Individualistic cultures (e.g., that of the United States and the Netherlands) place value on the freedom of the individual to pursue his or her own goals, whereas collectivistic cultures (e.g., that of Indonesia) emphasize the responsibility of the individual to fit in the group and to take responsibility for other group members. Power distance refers to the acceptance of idea that power is distributed unequally. People in high power-distance cultures tend to be afraid to say what they think or to be different from their superiors. Uncertainty avoidance is characterized as the extent to which the members of institutions and organizations within a society feel threatened by uncertain, unknown, ambiguous, or unstructured situations.

B. Yang, Wang, and Drewry (2009) outline a research agenda for investigating cultural factors in training. For example, they suggest that trainees from collectivistic cultures will be more positive about training and more motivated to engage in training activities when the benefits to the group or organization are made clear, whereas trainees from individualistic cultures will be more concerned with increasing their own competencies. They also suggest that trainees from cultures high in power distance will show a relative benefit for non-participatory training methods, such as presentations and lectures, whereas trainees from low power-distance cultures will be more likely to benefit from participative activities, such as role-playing. Another factor that may be affected by culture may be whether trainees will respond better to training given by an expert (as would be expected in a high power-distance culture) or a peer (which would be more valued in a low power-distance culture).

Summary

Many of the topics discussed throughout this book have implications for performance in real-world environments, especially the workplace. Most jobs require the execution of complex procedures integrating perceptual, cognitive, and motor processes, and the complexity of real-world environments puts demands on the individual to adapt to new circumstances. In this chapter, we considered how skills research can be applied to organizational training contexts.

Developing training procedures requires an understanding of training needs and task components, and thus should begin with task and job analysis. It is necessary to consider both the trainee and the task environment. A good understanding of the task is necessary to be able to take into account the factors that need to be considered in breaking down and recombining component tasks for training.

When people work in teams, non-technical skills such as communication and leadership skills are important determinants of performance. Team training has been shown to have added value to increase team members' functioning. In high-performance and stressful situations, crew resource management training has been shown to improve individual and team functioning.

Whether a training program has value for an organization will depend on the extent to which the benefits of training transfer to the organizational context. Trainee self-efficacy, goal orientation, and perceptions of training instrumentality affect motivation to transfer. The transfer climate within the organization will also influence transfer.

Research on cross-cultural training has until now focused on preparing employees for an expatriate assignment. Increasingly, interest is growing in how people of different cultures might react differently to training programs.

References

Abernethy, B., Schorer, J., Jackson, R. C., & Hagemann, N. (2012). Perceptual training methods compared: The relative efficacy of different approaches to enhancing sport-specific anticipation. *Journal of Experimental Psychology: Applied, 18*, 143–153.

Abrahamse, E., Jiménez, L., Verwey, W., & Clegg, B. (2010). Representing serial action and perception. *Psychonomic Bulletin & Review, 17*, 603–623.

Ackerman, P. L. (1987). Individual differences in skill learning: An integration of psychometric and information processing perspectives. *Psychological Bulletin, 10*, 3–27.

Ackerman, P. L. (1988). Components of individual differences during skill acquisition: Cognitive abilities and information processing. *Journal of Experimental Psychology: General, 117*, 288–318.

Ackerman, P. L. (1992). Predicting individual differences in complex skill acquisition: Dynamics of ability determinants. *Journal of Applied Psychology, 77*, 598–614.

Ackerman, P. L. (2013). Nonsense, common sense, and science of expert performance: Talent and individual differences. *Intelligence, 45*, 6–17.

Ackerman, P. L., Beier, M. E., & Boyle, M. O. (2005). Working memory and intelligence: The same or different constructs? *Psychological Bulletin, 131*, 30–60.

Ackerman, P. L., & Cianciolo, A. T. (2000). Cognitive, perceptual-speed, and psychomotor determinants of individual differences during skill acquisition. *Journal of Experimental Psychology: Applied, 6*, 259–290.

Ackerman, P. L., & Kyllonen, P. C. (1991). Trainee characteristics. In J. E. Morrison (Ed.), *Training for performance: Principles of applied human learning* (pp. 193–229). London: John Wiley & Sons.

Adam, J. J., Hommel, B., & Umiltà, C. (2003). Preparing for perception and action (I): The role of grouping in the response-cuing paradigm. *Cognitive Psychology, 46*, 302–358.

Adams, J. A. (1953). *The prediction of performance at advanced stages of training on a complex psychomotor task* (Res. Bull. No. 53–49). Lackland Air Force Base, TX: Perceptual and Motor Skills Research Laboratory, Human Resources Research Center.

Adams, J. A. (1987). Historical review and appraisal of research on the learning, retention, and transfer of human motor skills. *Psychological Bulletin, 101*, 41–74.

Adams, M. J. (1990). *Beginning to read: Thinking and learning about print*. Cambridge, MA: MIT Press.

Adamson, R. E., & Taylor, D. W. (1954). Functional fixedness as related to elapsed time and to set. *Journal of Experimental Psychology, 47*, 122–126.

Aguinis, H. (2009). *Performance management* (2nd ed.). Upper Saddle River, NJ: Prentice Hall.

Aguinis, H., & Kraiger, K. (2009). Benefits of training and development for individuals and teams, organizations, and society. *Annual Review of Psychology, 60*, 451–474.

Ahlum-Heath, M. E., & di Vesta, F. J. (1986). The effect of conscious controlled verbalization of a cognitive strategy on transfer in problem solving. *Memory & Cognition, 14*, 281–285.

Albaret, J. M., & Thon, B. (1998). Differential effects of task complexity on contextual interference in a drawing task. *Acta Psychologica, 100*, 9–24.

Allport, D., Antonis, B., & Reynolds, P. (1972). On the division of attention: A disproof of the single channel hypothesis. *Quarterly Journal of Experimental Psychology, 24*, 225–235.

Alluisi, E. A., & Muller, P. F., Jr. (1958). Verbal and motor responses to seven symbolic visual codes: A study in S-R compatibility. *Journal of Experimental Psychology, 55*, 247–254.

Anderson, J. R. (1982). Acquisition of cognitive skill. *Psychological Review, 89*, 369–406.

Anderson, J. R. (1993). *Rules of the mind*. Hillsdale, NJ: Lawrence Erlbaum.

Anderson, J. R. (2007). Using brain imaging to guide the development of a cognitive architecture. In W. D. Gray (Ed.), *Integrated models of cognitive systems* (pp. 49–62). New York: Oxford University Press.

Anderson, J. R., Bothell, D., Byrne, M. D., Douglass, S., Lebiere, C., & Qin, Y. (2004). An integrated theory of the mind. *Psychological Review, 111*, 1036–1060.

Anderson, J. R., Boyle, C., & Reiser, B. J. (1985). Intelligent tutoring systems. *Science, 228*, 456–462.

Anderson, J. R., Fincham, J. M., & Douglass, S. (1997). The role of examples and rules in the acquisition of a cognitive skill. *Journal of Experimental Psychology: Learning, Memory, and Cognition, 23*, 932–945.

Anderson, J. R., & Lebiere, C. (1998). *The atomic components of thought*. Mahwah, NJ: Lawrence Erlbaum.

Andrews, S. (2015). Individual differences among skilled readers: The role of lexical quality. In A. Pollatsek & R. Treiman (Eds.), *The Oxford handbook of reading* (pp. 129–148). New York: Oxford University Press.

Anson, G., Elliott, D., & Davids, K. (2005). Information processing and constraints-based views of skill acquisition: Divergent or complementary? *Motor Control, 9*, 217–241.

Anzai, Y. (1987). Doing, understanding, and learning in problem solving. In D. Klahr, P. Langley, & R. Neches (Eds.), *Production system models of learning and development* (pp. 55–97). Cambridge, MA: MIT Press.

Anzola, G. P., Bertoloni, G., Buchtel, H. A., & Rizzolatti, G. (1977). Spatial compatibility and anatomical factors in simple and choice reaction time. *Neuropsychologia, 15*, 295–302.

Argyris, C. (1998). Managers, workers, and organizations. *Society, 35*, 343–346.

Arisholm, E., & Sjøberg, D.I.K. (2004). Evaluating the effect of a delegated versus centralized control style on the maintainability of object-oriented software. *IEEE Transactions on Software Engineering, 30*, 521–534.

Arthur, W. J., Bennett, W. J., Edens, P., & Bell, S. T. (2003). Effectiveness of training in organizations: A meta-analysis of design and evaluation features. *Journal of Applied Psychology, 88*, 234–245.

Aschoff, J. (1954). Zeitgeber der tierischen tagesperiodik. *Naturwissenshaft, 41*, 40–56.

Ashford, D., Bennett, S. J., & Davids, K. (2006). Observational modeling effects for movement dynamics and movement outcome measures across differing task constraints: A meta-analysis. *Journal of Motor Behavior, 38*, 185–205.

Atkinson, R. C., & Shiffrin, R. M. (1968). Human memory: A proposed system and its control processes. In K. W. Spence & J. T. Spence (Eds.), *The psychology of learning and motivation: Advances in research and theory* (Vol. 2, pp. 89–195). New York: Academic Press.

Atkinson, R. K., Derry, S. J., Renkl, A., & Wortham, D. (2000). Learning from examples: Instructional principles from the worked examples research. *Review of Educational Research, 70*, 181–214.

Awad, S. S., Shawn, P. F., Bellows, C., Albo, D., Green-Rashad, B., De la Garza, M., & Berger, D. H. (2005). Bridging the communication gap in the operating room with medical team training. *American Journal of Surgery, 190*, 770–774.

Axtell, C. M., Maitlis, S., & Yearta, S. (1997). Predicting immediate and longer-term transfer of training. *Personnel Review, 26*, 201–213.

Babcock, Q., & Byrne, T. (2000). Student perceptions of methylphenidate abuse at a public liberal arts college. *Journal of American College Health, 49*, 143–145.

Bacon, S. J. (1974). Arousal and the range of cue utilization. *Journal of Experimental Psychology, 102*, 81–87.

Baddeley, A., & Wilson, B. A. (1994). When implicit learning fails: Amnesia and the problem of error elimination. *Neuropsychologia, 32*, 53–68.

Badets, A., & Blandin, Y. (2004). The role of knowledge of results frequency in learning through observation. *Journal of Motor Behavior, 36*, 62–70.

Bahrick, H. P., Fitts, P. M., & Rankin, R. E. (1952). Effect of incentives upon reactions to peripheral stimuli. *Journal of Experimental Psychology, 44*, 400–406.

Baird, B., Smallwood, J., & Schooler, J. W. (2011). Back to the future: Autobiographical planning and the functionality of mind-wandering. *Consciousness and Cognition, 20*, 1604–1611.

Baker, W. J., & Theologus, G. C. (1972). Effects of caffeine on visual monitoring. *Journal of Applied Psychology, 56*, 422–427.

Baldwin, T. T., & Ford, J. (1988). Transfer of training: A review and directions for future research. *Personnel Psychology, 41*, 63–105.

Bancino, R., & Zevalkink, C. (2007). Soft skills: The new curriculum for hard-core technical professionals. *Techniques, 82*(5), 20–22.

Bandura, A. (1977). *Social learning theory*. Englewood Cliffs, NJ: Prentice Hall.

Barfield, W. (1986). Expert-novice differences for software: Implications for problem-solving and knowledge acquisition. *Behaviour and Information Technology, 5*, 15–29.

Baron, J. (1977). Mechanisms for pronouncing printed words: use and acquisition. In D. LaBerge & S. J. Samuels (Eds.), *Basic processes in reading: Perception and comprehension* (pp. 175–216). Hillsdale, NJ: Lawrence Erlbaum.

Barreiros, J., Figueiredo, T., & Godinho, M. (2007). The contextual interference effect in applied settings. *European Physical Education Review, 13*, 195–208.

Barron, L. G., & Rose, M. R. (2013). Relative validity of distinct spatial abilities: An example with implications for diversity. *International Journal of Selection and Assessment, 21*, 400–406.

Barrows, H. S., & Tamblyn, R. (1980). *Problem-based learning: An approach to medical education*. New York: Springer.

Bartlett, F. (1932). *Remembering: A study in experimental and social psychology*. New York: Cambridge University Press.

Bastian, M., Schooler, J. W., & Sackur, J. (2012). Mind-wandering and the little voice of meta-consciousness. Poster presented at the *Summer Institute on the Evolution and Functions of Consciousness*. Montreal, Canada.

Bates, R. A., & Holton, E. F. (2004). Linking workplace literacy skills and transfer system perceptions. *Human Resource Development Quarterly, 15*, 153–170.

Batra, D., & Davis, J. G. (1992). Conceptual data modeling in database design: Similarities and differences between expert and novice designers. *International Journal of Man-Machine Studies, 37*, 83–101.

Battig, W. F. (1962). Paired-associate learning under simultaneous repetition and nonrepetition conditions. *Journal of Experimental Psychology, 64*, 87–93.

Bavelier, D., Green, C., Pouget, A., & Schrater, P. (2012). Brain plasticity through the life span: Learning to learn and action video games. *Annual Review of Neuroscience, 35*, 391–416.

Beale, J. M., & Keil, F. C. (1995). Categorical effects in the perception of faces. *Cognition, 57*, 217–219.

Beam, C. A., Krupinski, E. A., Kundel, H. L., Sickles, E. A., & Wagner, R. F. (2006). The place of medical image perception in 21st-century health care. *Journal of the American College of Radiology, 3*, 409–412.

Beier, M. E., & Oswald, F. L. (2012). Is cognitive ability a liability? A critique and future research agenda on skilled performance. *Journal of Experimental Psychology: Applied, 18*, 331–345.

Beilock, S. L., Carr, T. H., MacMahon, C., & Starkes, J. L. (2002). When paying attention becomes counterproductive: Impact of divided versus skill-focused attention on novice and experienced performance of sensorimotor skills. *Journal of Experimental Psychology: Applied, 8*, 6–16.

Bell, B. G., Gardner, M. K., & Woltz, D. J. (1997). Individual differences in undetected errors in skilled performance. *Learning and Individual Differences, 9*, 43–61.

Bell, B. S., & Kozlowski, S. J. (2002). Adaptive guidance: Enhancing self-regulation, knowledge, and performance in technology-based training. *Personnel Psychology, 55*, 267–306.

Ben-Shakhar, G., & Sheffer, L. (2001). The relationship between the ability to divide attention and standard measures of general cognitive abilities. *Intelligence, 29*, 293–306.

Bergersen, G., & Gustafsson, J. (2011). Programming skill, knowledge, and working memory among professional software developers from an investment theory perspective. *Journal of Individual Differences, 32*, 201–209.

Bernstein, N. A. (1967). *The co-ordination and regulation of movements*. Oxford, UK: Pergamon Press.

Bernstein, N. A. (1996). On dexterity and its development. In M. L. Latash & M. T. Turvey (Eds.), *Dexterity and its development* (pp. 1–244). Mahwah, NJ: Lawrence Erlbaum.

Berry, D. C. (1991). The role of action in implicit learning. *Quarterly Journal of Experimental Psychology, 43A*, 881–906.

Berry, D. C., & Broadbent, D. E. (1984). On the relationship between task performance and associated verbalizable knowledge. *Quarterly Journal of Experimental Psychology, 36A*, 209–231.

Berry, D. C., & Broadbent, D. E. (1988). Interactive tasks and the implicit-explicit distinction. *British Journal of Psychology, 79*, 251–272.

Bertelson, P. (1963). S-R relationships and reaction times to new versus repeated signals in a serial task. *Journal of Experimental Psychology, 65,* 478–484.

Berthold, K., Eysink, T. S., & Renkl, A. (2009). Assisting self-explanation prompts are more effective than open prompts when learning with multiple representations. *Instructional Science, 37,* 345–363.

Bethune, R., Sasirekha, G., Sahu, A., Cawthorn, S., & Pullyblank, A. (2011). Use of briefings and debriefings as a tool in improving team work, efficiency, and communication in the operating theatre. *Postgraduate Medical Journal, 87,* 331–334. doi:10.1136/pgmj.2009.095802

Biederman, I., & Shiffrar, M. M. (1987). Sexing day-old chicks: A case study and expert systems analysis of a difficult perceptual-learning task. *Journal of Experimental Psychology: Learning, Memory, and Cognition, 13,* 640–645.

Bielaczyc, K., Pirolli, P. L., & Brown, A. L. (1995). Training in self-explanation and self-regulation strategies: Investigating the effects of knowledge acquisition activities on problem solving. *Cognition and Instruction, 13,* 221–252.

Bilalić, M., McLeod, P., & Gobet, F. (2010). The mechanism of the Einstellung (set) effect: A pervasive source of cognitive bias. *Current Directions in Psychological Science, 19,* 111–115.

Bills, A. G. (1931). A new principle of mental fatigue. *American Journal of Psychology, 43,* 230–245.

Binet, A. (1905). New methods for the diagnosis of the intellectual level of subnormals. *L'Annee Psychologique, 12,* 191–244. Transl. by E. S. Kite, 1916, in *The development of intelligence in children.* Vineland, NJ: Publ. Training School Vineland.

Binet, A., & Henri, V. (1895). La psychologie individuelle. *L'Anee Psychologique, 2*(81), 411–465.

Birdi, K., Allen, C., & Warr, P. (1997). Correlates and perceived outcomes of four types of employee development activity. *Journal of Applied Psychology, 82,* 845–857.

Birrer, D. D., & Morgan, G. G. (2010). Psychological skills training as a way to enhance an athlete's performance in high-intensity sports. *Scandinavian Journal of Medicine & Science in Sports, 20*(Suppl. 2), 78–87.

Bischoff-Grethe, A., Goedert, K., Willingham, D., & Grafton, S. (2004). Neural substrates of response-based sequence learning using fMRI. *Journal of Cognitive Neuroscience, 16,* 127–138.

Bitan, T. T., & Karni, A. A. (2004). Procedural and declarative knowledge of word recognition and letter decoding in reading an artificial script. *Cognitive Brain Research, 19,* 229–243.

Black, J., & Mendenhall, M. (1990). Cross-cultural training effectiveness: A review and a theoretical framework for future research. *Academy of Management Review, 15*(1), 113–136.

Bloom, B. S. (1985). Generalizations about talent development. In B. S. Bloom (Ed.), *Developing talent in young people* (pp. 507–549). New York: Ballantine Books.

Bock, K., & Griffin, Z. M. (2000). The persistence of structural priming: Transient activation or implicit learning? *Journal of Experimental Psychology: General, 129,* 177–192.

Boehringer, A., Schwabe, L., & Schachinger, H. (2010). A combination of high stress-induced tense and energetic arousal compensates for impairing effects of stress on memory retrieval in men. *Stress: The International Journal on the Biology of Stress, 13,* 444–453.

Boot, W. R., Basak, C., Erickson, K. I., Neider, M., Simons, D. J., Fabiani, M., ... Kramer, A. F. (2010). Transfer of skill engendered by complex task training under conditions of variable priority. *Acta Psychologica, 135*, 349–357.

Boot, W. R., Blakely, D. P., & Simons, D. J. (2011). Do action video games improve perception and cognition? *Frontiers in Psychology, 2*, 226.

Boot, W. R., & Ericsson, K. A. (2013). Expertise. In J. D. Lee, A. Kirlik, J. D. Lee, & A. Kirlik (Eds.), *The Oxford handbook of cognitive engineering* (pp. 143–158). New York: Oxford University Press.

Borst, J. P., Taatgen, N. A., & van Rijn, H. (2010). The problem state: A cognitive bottleneck in multitasking. *Journal of Experimental Psychology: Learning, Memory, and Cognition, 36*, 363–382.

Brancucci, A. (2012). Neural correlates of cognitive ability. *Journal of Neuroscience Research, 90*, 1299–1309.

Braze, D., Tabor, W., Shankweiler, D. P., & Mencl, W. (2007). Speaking up for vocabulary: Reading skill differences in young adults. *Journal of Learning Disabilities, 40*, 226–243.

Brewer, N., & Sandow, B. (1980). Alcohol effects on driver performance under conditions of divided attention. *Ergonomics, 23*, 185–190.

Briggs, B. (2013). High stress in high heels: Asiana Air flight crew praised for timely response. *U.S. News on NBCNEWS.com.* Downloaded from http://www.nbcnews.com/travel/high-stress-high-heels-asiana-air-flight-crew-praised-timely-6C10574503

Brigham, J. C., Bennett, L., Meissner, C. A., & Mitchell, T. L. (2007). The influence of race on eyewitness memory. In R. L. Lindsay, D. F. Ross, J. Read, & M. P. Toglia (Eds.), *The handbook of eyewitness psychology, Vol. II: Memory for people* (pp. 257–281). Mahwah, NJ: Lawrence Erlbaum.

Brisswalter, J. B., Collardeau, M., & Arcelin, R. (2002). Effects of acute physical exercise characteristics on cognitive performance. *Sports Medicine, 32*, 555–566.

Broadbent, D. E. (1958). *Perception and communication.* Oxford, UK: Pergamon.

Broadbent, D. E. (1977). Levels, hierarchies, and the locus of control. *Quarterly Journal of Experimental Psychology, 29*, 181–201.

Broadbent, D. E., Fitzgerald, P., & Broadbent, M.H.P. (1986). Implicit and explicit knowledge in the control of complex systems. *British Journal of Psychology, 77*, 33–50.

Brooke, S., & Ellis, H. (1992). Cold. In A. P. Smith & D. M. Jones (Eds.), *Handbook of human performance, Vol. 1: The physical environment* (pp. 105–130). San Diego: Academic Press.

Brown, J. (2002). Training needs assessment: A must for developing an effective training program. *Public Personnel Management, 31*, 569–578.

Brunstein, A., & Gonzalez, C. (2011). Preparing for novelty with diverse training. *Applied Cognitive Psychology, 25*, 682–691.

Brunyé, T. T., Mahoney, C. R., Lieberman, H. R., & Taylor, H. A. (2010). Caffeine modulates attention network function. *Brain & Cognition, 72*, 181–188.

Bryan, W. L., & Harter, N. (1897). Studies in the physiology and psychology of the telegraphic language. *Psychological Review, 4*, 27–53.

Bryan, W. L., & Harter, N. (1899). Studies on the telegraphic language: The acquisition of a hierarchy of habits. *Psychological Review, 6*, 345–375.

Burke, C., Priest, H. A., Wooten, S., DiazGranados, D., & Salas, E. (2009). Understanding the cognitive processes in adaptive multicultural teams: A framework. In E. Salas, G. F. Goodwin, & C. Burke (Eds.), *Team effectiveness in complex organizations: Cross-disciplinary perspectives and approaches* (pp. 209–240). New York: Routledge.

Burns, M. I., Baylor, C. R., Morris, M. A., McNalley, T. E., & Yorkston, K. M. (2012). Training healthcare providers in patient–provider communication: What speech-language pathology and medical education can learn from one another. *Aphasiology, 26*, 673–688.

Bursill, A. E. (1958). The restriction of peripheral vision during exposure to hot and humid conditions. *Quarterly Journal of Experimental Psychology, 10*, 113–129.

Busemeyer, J. R., & Diederich, A. (2010). *Cognitive modeling*. Thousand Oaks, CA: SAGE.

Butler, B. E., & Hains, S. (1979). Individual differences in word recognition. *Memory & Cognition, 7*, 68–76.

Butler, B. E., Jared, D., & Hains, S. (1984). Reading skill and the use of orthographic knowledge by mature readers. *Psychological Research, 46*, 337–353.

Byrne, M. D., & Anderson, J. R. (2001). Serial modules in parallel: The psychological refractory period and perfect time-sharing. *Psychological Review, 108*, 847–869.

Cabeza, R., & Nyberg, L. (2000). Imaging cognition II: An empirical review of 275 PET and fMRI studies. *Journal of Cognitive Neuroscience, 12*, 1–47.

Cai, D. J., & Rickard, T. C. (2009). Reconsidering the role of sleep for motor memory. *Behavioral Neuroscience, 123*, 1153–1157.

Caligiuri, P., Phillips, J., Lazarova, M., Tarique, I., & Bürgi, P. (2001). The theory of met expectations applied to expatriate adjustment: The role of cross-cultural training. *International Journal of Human Resource Management, 12*, 357–372.

Campbell, J.I.D., Fuchs-Lacelle, S., & Phenix, T. L. (2006). Identical elements model of arithmetic memory: Extension to addition and subtraction. *Memory & Cognition, 34*, 633–647.

Campbell, R. L., Brown, N. R., & Di Bello, L. A. (1992). The programmer's burden: Developing expertise in programming. In R. R. Hoffman (Ed.), *The psychology of expertise* (pp. 269–294). New York: Springer-Verlag.

Cañal-Bruland, R., Zhu, F. F., van der Kamp, J., & Masters, R. W. (2011). Target-directed visual attention is a prerequisite for action-specific perception. *Acta Psychologica, 136*, 285–289.

Cappelletti, M., Didino, D., Stoianov, I., & Zorzi, M. (2014). Number skills are maintained in healthy ageing. *Cognitive Psychology, 69*, 25–45.

Carlson, R. A., Khoo, B. H., Yaure, R. G., & Schneider, W. (1990). Acquisition of a problem-solving skill: Levels of organization and use of working memory. *Journal of Experimental Psychology: General, 119*, 193–214.

Carlson, R. A., Sullivan, M. A., & Schneider, W. (1989). Practice and working memory effects in building procedural skill. *Journal of Experimental Psychology: Learning, Memory, and Cognition, 15*, 517–526.

Carlson, R. A., & Yaure, R. G. (1990). Practice schedules and the use of component skills in problem solving. *Journal of Experimental Psychology: Learning, Memory, and Cognition, 16*, 484–496.

Carpenter, S., Pashler, H., Wixted, J., & Vul, E. (2008). The effects of tests on learning and forgetting. *Memory & Cognition, 36*, 438–448.

Carrasco, M., Evert, D. L., Chang, I., & Katz, S. M. (1995). The eccentricity effect: Target eccentricity affects performance on conjunction searches. *Perception & Psychophysics, 57*, 1241–1261.

Carrier, J., & Monk, T. (2000). Circadian rhythms of performance: New trends. *Chronobiology International: The Journal of Biological & Medical Rhythm Research, 17*, 719–732.

Carroll, J. B. (1993). *Human mental abilities: A survey of factor analytic studies.* New York: Cambridge University Press.

Carroll, J. M. (1997). Toward minimalist training: Supporting the sense-making activities of computer users. In M. A. Quiñones & A. Ehrenstein (Eds.), *Training for a rapidly changing workplace: Applications of psychological research* (pp. 303–328). Washington, DC: American Psychological Association.

Carroll, J. M., & Carrithers, C. (1984). Blocking learner error states in a training-wheels system. *Human Factors, 26*, 377–389.

Carroll, W. M. (1994). Using worked examples as an instructional support in the algebra classroom. *Journal of Educational Psychology, 86*, 360–367.

Carron, A. V. (1969). Performance and learning in a discrete motor task under massed vs. distributed practice. *Research Quarterly, 40*, 481–489.

Catrambone, R., & Holyoak, K. J. (1989). Overcoming contextual limitations on problem-solving transfer. *Journal of Experimental Psychology: Learning, Memory, and Cognition, 15*, 1147–1156.

Cattell, J. M. (1890). Mental tests and measurements. *Mind, 15*, 373–381.

Cattell, R. B. (1943). The measurement of adult intelligence. *Psychological Bulletin, 40*, 153–193.

Cauraugh, J. H., & Horrell, J. F. (1989). Advanced preparation of discrete finger responses: Nonmotoric evidence. *Acta Psychologica, 72*, 117–138.

Cepeda, N. J., Coburn, N., Rohrer, D., Wixted, J. T., Mozer, M. C., & Pashler, H. (2009). Optimizing distributed practice: Theoretical analysis and practical implications. *Experimental Psychology, 56*, 236–246.

Cepeda, N. J., Pashler, H., Vul, E., Wixted, J. T., & Rohrer, D. (2006). Distributed practice in verbal recall tasks: A review and quantitative synthesis. *Psychological Bulletin, 132*, 354–380.

Cepeda, N. J., Vul, E., Rohrer, D., Wixted, J. T., & Pashler, H. (2008). Spacing effects in learning: A temporal ridgeline of optimal retention. *Psychological Science, 19*, 1095–1102.

Chabris, C. F., & Hearst, E. S. (2003). Visualization, pattern recognition, and forward search: Effects of playing speed and sight of the position on grandmaster chess errors. *Cognitive Science, 27*, 637–648.

Chang, Y. K., Labban, J. D., Gapin, J. I., & Etnier, J. L. (2012). The effects of acute exercise on cognitive performance: A meta-analysis. *Brain Research, 1453*, 87–101.

Charness, N. (1981). Aging and skilled problem solving. *Journal of Experimental Psychology: General, 110*, 21–38.

Charness, N., Tuffiash, M., Krampe, R., Reingold, E., & Vasyukova, E. (2005). The role of deliberate practice in chess expertise. *Applied Cognitive Psychology, 19*, 151–165.

Chase, W. G., & Ericsson, K. A. (1982). Skill and working memory. In G. H. Bower (Ed.), *The psychology of learning and motivation* (Vol. 16, pp. 1–58). New York: Academic Press.

Chase, W. G., & Simon, H. A. (1973). Perception in chess. *Cognitive Psychology, 4*, 55–81.

Chellappa, S. L., Steiner, R., Blattner, P., Oelhafen, P., Götz, T., & Cajochen, C. (2011). Non-visual effects of light on melatonin, alertness and cognitive performance: Can blue-enriched light keep us alert? *Plos ONE, 6*(1), ArtID: e16429. doi:10.1371/journal.pone.0016429

Chen, J., & Proctor, R. W. (2013). Response–effect compatibility defines the natural scrolling direction. *Human Factors, 55*, 1112–1129.

Chi, M.T.H. (2006). Laboratory methods for assessing experts' and novices' knowledge. In K. A. Ericsson, N. Charness, P. J. Feltovich, & R. R. Hoffman (Eds.), *The Cambridge handbook of expertise and human performance* (pp. 167–184). New York: Cambridge University Press.

Chi, M.T.H., Bassok, M., Lewis, M. W., & Reimann, P., & Glaser, R. (1989). Self-explanations: How students study and use examples in learning to solve problems. *Cognitive Science, 13*, 145–182.

Chi, M.T.H., de Leeuw, N., Chiu, M. H., & Lavancher, C. (1994). Eliciting self-explanations improves understanding. *Cognitive Science, 18*, 439–477.

Chi, M.T.H., Feltovich, P. J., & Glaser, R. (1981). Categorization and representation of physics problems by experts and novices. *Cognitive Science, 5*, 121–152.

Chiaburu, D. S., & Lindsay, D. R. (2008). Can do or will do? The importance of self-efficacy and instrumentality for training transfer. *Human Resource Development International, 11*, 199–206.

Chiaburu, D. S., & Marinova, S. V. (2005). What predicts skill transfer? An exploratory study of goal orientation, training self-efficacy and organizational supports. *International Journal of Training and Development, 9*, 110–123.

Chin, J. M., & Schooler, J. W. (2008). Why do words hurt? Content, process, and criterion shift accounts of verbal overshadowing. *European Journal of Cognitive Psychology, 20*, 396–413.

Chiroro, P. M., Tredoux, C. G., Radaelli, S., & Meissner, C. A. (2008). Recognizing faces across continents: The effect of within-race variations on the own-race bias in face recognition. *Psychonomic Bulletin & Review, 15*, 1089–1092.

Chiroro, P., & Valentine, T. (1995). An investigation of the contact hypothesis of the own-race bias in face recognition. *Quarterly Journal of Experimental Psychology, 48A*, 879–894.

Chiviacowsky, S., Wulf, G., Laroque de Medeiros, F., & Kaefer, A. (2008). Learning benefits of self-controlled knowledge of results in 10-year-old children. *Research Quarterly for Exercise and Sport, 79*, 405–10.

Cho, Y. S., Choi, J. M., & Proctor, R. W. (2012). Likelihood of attending to the color word modulates Stroop interference. *Attention, Perception, & Psychophysics, 74*, 416–429.

Chopin, A., & Mamassian, P. (2010). Task usefulness affects perception of rivalrous images. *Psychological Science, 21*, 1886–1893.

Christensen, W., Sutton, J., & McIlwain, D. (2015). Putting pressure on theories of choking: Towards an expanded perspective on breakdown in skilled performance. *Phenomenology and the Cognitive Sciences, 14*, 253–293.

Christianson, S.-A. (1992). Emotional stress and eyewitness memory: A critical review. *Psychological Bulletin, 112*, 284–309.

Chun, M. M., & Jiang, Y. (1998). Contextual cueing: Implicit learning and memory of visual context guides spatial attention. *Cognitive Psychology, 36*, 28–71.

Church, A. T. (1982). Sojourner adjustment. *Psychological Bulletin, 91*, 540–572.

Church, B. A., Mercado, E., Wisniewski, M. G., & Liu, E. H. (2013). Temporal dynamics in auditory perceptual learning: Impact of sequencing and incidental learning. *Journal of Experimental Psychology: Learning, Memory, and Cognition, 39*, 270–276.

Chvatal, S. A., Torres-Oviedo, G., Safavynia, S. A., & Ting, L. H. (2011). Common muscle synergies for control of center of mass and force in nonstepping and stepping postural behaviors. *Journal of Neurophysiology, 106*, 999–1015.

Clark, R. E., & Jones, C. E. (1962). Manual performance during cold exposure as a function of practice level and the thermal conditions of training. *Journal of Applied Psychology, 46*, 276–280.

Clarke, A. R., Barry, R. J., McCarthy, R., & Selikowitz, M. (1998). EEG analysis in attention-deficit/hyperactivity disorder: A comparative study of two subtypes. *Psychiatry Research, 81*, 19–29.

Cleeremans, A. (1993). *Mechanisms of implicit learning: Connectionist models of sequence processing*. Cambridge, MA: MIT Press.

Cleeremans, A., & McClelland, J. (1991). Learning the structure of event sequences. *Journal of Experimental Psychology: General, 120*, 235–253.

Clegg, B. (2005). Stimulus-specific sequence representation in serial reaction time tasks. *Quarterly Journal of Experimental Psychology A: Human Experimental Psychology, 58*(A), 1087–1101.

Clement, C. A., Mawby, R., & Giles, D. E. (1994). The effects of manifest relational similarity on analog retrieval. *Journal of Memory and Language, 33*, 396–420.

Coch, D., & Mitra, P. (2010). Word and pseudoword superiority effects reflected in the ERP waveform. *Brain Research, 1329*, 159–174.

Cohen, A., Ivry, R. I., & Keele, S. W. (1990). Attention and structure in sequence learning. *Journal of Experimental Psychology: Learning, Memory, and Cognition, 16*, 17–30.

Cohen, J. D., Dunbar, K., & McClelland, J. L. (1990). On the control of automatic processes: A parallel distributed processing account of the Stroop effect. *Psychological Review, 97*, 332–361.

Colcombe, S. J., & Kramer, A. F., 2003. Fitness effects on the cognitive function of older adults: A meta-analytic study. *Psychological Science, 14*, 125–130.

Colquitt, J. A., LePine, J. A., & Noe, R. A. (2000). Toward an integrative theory of training motivation: A meta-analytic path analysis of 20 years of research. *Journal of Applied Psychology, 85*, 678–707.

Coltheart, M. (1978). Lexical access in simple reading tasks. In G. Underwood (Ed.), *Strategies of information processing* (pp. 151–216). San Diego, CA: Academic Press.

Coltheart, M. (2005). Modeling reading: The dual-route approach. In M. J. Snowling & C. Hulme (Eds.), *The science of reading: A handbook* (pp. 7–23). Malden, MA: Blackwell.

Conati, C., Gertner, A., & VanLehn, K. (2002). Using Bayesian networks to manage uncertainty in student modeling. *User Modeling and User-Adapted Interaction, 12*, 371–417.

Connelly, S. L., & Hasher, L. (1993). Aging and the inhibition of spatial location. *Journal of Experimental Psychology: Human Perception and Performance, 19*, 1238–1250.

Conway, A.R.A., & Kovacs, K. (2013). Individual differences in intelligence and working memory: A review of latent variable models. In B. H. Ross (Ed.), *The psychology of learning and motivation* (Vol. 58, pp. 233–270). San Diego, CA: Academic Press.

Cooke, N. J. (1994). Varieties of knowledge elicitation techniques. *International Journal of Human-Computer Studies, 41*, 801–849.

Cooke, N. J., Salas, E., Cannon-Bowers, J. A., & Stout, R. (2000). Measuring team knowledge. *Human Factors, 42*, 151–173.

Cooper, A. D., Sterling, C. P., Bacon, M. P., & Bridgeman, B. (2012). Does action affect perception or memory? *Vision Research, 62*, 235–240.

Cooper, S., Cant, R., Porter, J., Sellick, K., Somers, G., Kinsman, L., & Nestel, D. (2010). Rating medical emergency teamwork performance: Development of the Team Emergency Assessment Measure (TEAM). *Resuscitation, 81*, 446–452.

Cormier, S. M. (1987). The structural processes underlying transfer of training. In S. M. Cormier & J. D. Hagman (Eds.), *Transfer of learning: Contemporary research and applications* (pp. 151–181). San Diego, CA: Academic Press.

Corritore, C. L., & Wiedenbeck, S. (1999). Mental representations of expert procedural and object-oriented programmers in a software maintenance task. *International Journal of Human-Computer Studies, 50*, 61–83.

Corver, S. C., & Aneziris, O. N. (2015). The impact of controller support tools in enroute air traffic control on cognitive error modes: A comparative analysis in two operational environments. *Safety Science, 71*(Pt A), 2–15.

Coughlan, E. K., Williams, A., McRobert, A. P., & Ford, P. R. (2014). How experts practice: A novel test of deliberate practice theory. *Journal of Experimental Psychology: Learning, Memory, and Cognition, 40*, 449–458.

Couture, M., Lafond, D., & Tremblay, S. (2008). Learning correct responses and errors in the Hebb repetition effect: Two faces of the same coin. *Journal of Experimental Psychology: Learning, Memory, and Cognition, 34*, 524–532.

Craig, A., & Condon, R. (1985). Speed-accuracy trade-off and time of day. *Acta Psychologica, 58*, 115–122.

Craig, A., & Cooper, R. E. (1992). Symptoms of acute and chronic fatigue. In A. P. Smith & D. M. Jones (Eds.), *Handbook of human performance* (Vol. 3, pp. 289–339). London: Academic Press.

Craik, K.J.W. (1948). Theory of the human operator in control systems: II. Man as an element in a control system. *British Journal of Psychology, 38*, 142–148.

Croft, J. (2015). NASA tackles memorized pilot training: Retooling simulator training to truly test the element of surprise. *Aviation Week & Space Technology*, January 26, 177(2), 60.

Cronbach, L. J. (1970/1990). *Essentials of psychological testing* (3rd ed.). New York: Harper and Row.

Cronbach, L. J., & Snow, R. E. (1977). *Aptitudes and instructional methods: A handbook for research on interactions*. New York: Irvington Publishers.

Cross, K. P. (1981). *Adults as learners*. San Francisco: Jossey-Bass.

Crump, M.J.C., & Logan, G. D. (2010). Warning, this keyboard will de-construct: The role of the keyboard in skilled typewriting. *Psychonomic Bulletin & Review, 17*, 394–399.

Crump, M.J.C., & Logan, G. D. (2013). Prevention and correction in post-error performance: An ounce of prevention, a pound of cure. *Journal of Experimental Psychology: General, 142*, 692–709.

Curran, T., Smith, M., DiFranco, J., & Daggy, A. (2001). Structural influences on implicit and explicit sequence learning. In *The psychology of learning and motivation: Advances in research and theory* (Vol. 40, pp. 147–182). San Diego, CA: Academic Press.

Daee, S., & Wilding, J. (1977). Effects of high intensity white noise on short-term memory for position in a list and sequence. *British Journal of Psychology, 68*, 335–349.

Damos, D. L., & Wickens, C. D. (1980). The identification and transfer of timesharing skills. *Acta Psychologica, 46*, 15–39.

da Silva, F. Jr., de Pinho, R., de Mello, M., de Bruin, V., & de Bruin, P. (2009). Risk factors for depression in truck drivers. *Social Psychiatry and Psychiatric Epidemiology, 44*, 125–129.

de Groot, A. (1978). *Thought and choice in chess*. The Hague: Mouton. (Original published 1946)

De Jong, R. (1993). Multiple bottlenecks in overlapping task performance. *Journal of Experimental Psychology: Human Perception and Performance, 19*, 965–980.

de Winter, J. F., Dodou, D., & Mulder, M. (2012). Training effectiveness of whole body flight simulator motion: A comprehensive meta-analysis. *International Journal of Aviation Psychology, 22*, 164–183.

Deary, I. J. (2012a). 125 years of intelligence in *The American Journal of Psychology*. *American Journal of Psychology, 125*, 145–154.

Deary, I. J. (2012b). Intelligence. *Annual Review of Psychology, 63*, 453–482.

Deary, I. J., Pattie, A., & Starr, J. M. (2013). The stability of intelligence from age 11 to age 90 years: The Lothian Birth Cohort of 1921. *Psychological Science, 24*, 2361–2368.

Deary, I. J., Penke, L., & Johnson, W. (2010). The neuroscience of human intelligence differences. *Nature Reviews Neuroscience, 11*, 201–211.

Deelstra, J. T., Peeters, M. C., Schaufeli, W. B., Stroebe, W., Zijlstra, F. R., & Van Doornen, L. P. (2003). Receiving instrumental support at work: When help is not welcome. *Journal of Applied Psychology, 88*, 324–331.

Dell, G. S. (1986). A spreading-activation of retrieval in sentence production. *Psychological Review, 93*, 283–321.

Dell, G. S., Reed, K. D., Adams, D. R., & Meyer, A. S. (2000). Speech errors, phonotactic constraints, and implicit learning: A study of the role of experience in language production. *Journal of Experimental Psychology: Learning, Memory, and Cognition, 26*, 1355–1367.

den Ouden, H. M., Friston, K. J., Daw, N. D., McIntosh, A. R., & Stephan, K. E. (2009). A dual role for prediction error in associative learning. *Cerebral Cortex, 19*, 1175–1185.

Derbinsky, N., & Laird, J. E. (2013). Effective and efficient forgetting of learned knowledge in Soar's working and procedural memories. *Cognitive Systems Research, 24*, 104–113.

Desimone, R., & Duncan, J. (1995). Neural mechanisms of selective visual attention. *Annual Review of Neuroscience, 18*, 193–222.

Desimone, R., & Gross, C. G. (1979). Visual areas in the temporal cortex of the macaque. *Brain Research, 178*, 363–380.

Desor, J. A., & Beauchamp, G. K. (1974). The human capacity to transmit olfactory information. *Perception & Psychophysics, 16*, 551–556.

Destrebecqz, A., & Cleeremans, A. (2001). Can sequence learning be implicit? New evidence with the process dissociation procedure. *Psychonomic Bulletin & Review, 8*, 343–350.

Deutsch, J. A., & Deutsch, D. (1963). Attention: Some theoretical considerations. *Psychological Review, 70*, 80–90.

Devos, C., Dumay, X., Bonami, M., Bates, R., & Holton, E. I. (2007). The Learning Transfer System Inventory (LTSI) translated into French: Internal structure and predictive validity. *International Journal of Training and Development, 11*, 181–199.

Di Domenico, S. I., Rodrigo, A. H., Ayaz, H., Fournier, M. A., & Ruocco, A. C. (2015). Decision-making conflict and the neural efficiency hypothesis of intelligence: A functional near-infrared spectroscopy investigation. *Neuroimage, 109*, 307–317.

Diamond, R., & Carey, S. (1986). Why faces are and are not special: An effect of expertise. *Journal or Experimental Psychology: General, 115*, 107–117.

Diaz, A., Palladino, P., & Evans, S. (2012). The 25 most clutch players in NBA finals history. *Complex Sports*, June 15. Downloaded June 29, 2013, from http://www.complex.com/sports/2012/06/the-25-most-clutch-players-in-nba-finals-history/clutch-finals-1

Dienes, Z., & Fahey, R. (1998). The role of implicit memory in controlling a dynamic system. *Quarterly Journal of Experimental Psychology A: Human Experimental Psychology, 51A*(3), 593–614.

Dinges, D. F., & Kribbs, N. B. (1991). Performing while sleepy: Effects of experimentally-induced sleepiness. In T. H. Monk (Ed.), *Sleep, sleepiness, and performance* (pp. 97–128). New York: John Wiley.

Dinges, D. F., & Powell, J. W. (1988). Sleepiness is more than lapsing. *Sleep Research, 17*, 84.

Donchin, E., & Coles, M.G.H. (1988). Is the P300 component a manifestation of context updating? *Behavioral and Brain Sciences, 11*, 357–374.

Donders, F. C. (1868). Die Schnelligkeit psychischer Prozesse. *Archiv für Anatomie und Physiologie* und wissenschaftliche Medizin, 657–681. [On the speed of mental processes. In W. G. Koster (Ed. & Trans.) (1969). *Attention and performance II* (pp. 412–431). Amsterdam: North-Holland.]

Donovan, T., & Manning, D. J. (2006). Successful reporting by nonmedical practitioners, such as radiographers, will always be task-specific and limited in scope. *Radiography, 12*, 7–12.

Dosher, B. A., & Lu, Z. L. (1999). Mechanisms of perceptual learning. *Vision Research, 39*, 3197–3221.

Doughty, C. J. (2004). Effects of instruction on learning a second language: A critique of instructed SLA research. In B. VanPatten, J. Williams, S. Rott, & M. Overstreet (Eds.), *Form-meaning connections in second language acquisition* (pp. 181–202). Mahwah, NJ: Lawrence Erlbaum.

Drew, G. C. (1979). An experimental study of mental fatigue. Reprinted in E. J. Dearnaley & P. B. Warr (Eds.), *Aircrew stress in wartime operations* (pp. 135–177). New York: Academic Press. (Original published 1940)

Driskell, J. E., Copper, C., & Moran, A. (1994). Does mental practice enhance performance? *Journal of Applied Psychology, 79*, 481–492.

Driskell, J. E., Willis, R. P., & Copper, C. (1992). Effect of overlearning on retention. *Journal of Applied Psychology, 77*, 615–622.

Druker, M., & Anderson, B. (2010). Spatial probability aids visual stimulus discrimination. *Frontiers in Human Neuroscience, 4*(63), 1–10.
Duffy, E. (1962). *Activation and behavior.* New York: John Wiley.
Duncan, J., Emslie, H., Williams, P., Johnson, R., & Freer, C. (1996). Intelligence and the frontal lobe: The organization of goal-directed behavior. *Cognitive Psychology, 30,* 257–303.
Duncan, J., & Humphreys, G. W. (1989). Visual search and stimulus similarity. *Psychological Review, 96,* 433–458.
Duncker, K. (1945). On problem solving. *Psychological Monographs, 58* (no. 270).
Dunning, D. L., & Holmes, J. (2014). Does working memory training promote the use of strategies on untrained working memory tasks? *Memory & Cognition, 42,* 854–862.
Durgin, F. H., Baird, J. A., Greenburg, M., Russell, R., Shaughnessy, K., & Waymouth, S. (2009). Who is being deceived? The experimental demands of wearing a backpack. *Psychonomic Bulletin & Review, 16,* 964–969.
Durlach, P. J., Kring, J. P., & Bowens, L. D. (2009). Effects of action video game experience on change detection. *Military Psychology, 21,* 24–39.
Durso, F. T., & Manning, C. A. (2008). Air traffic control. In P. R. DeLucia (Ed.), *Reviews of human factors and ergonomics* (Vol. 4, pp. 195–244). Santa Monica, CA: Human Factors and Ergonomics Society.
Dutilh, G., Krypotos, A., & Wagenmakers, E. (2011). Task-related versus stimulus-specific practice: A diffusion model account. *Experimental Psychology, 58,* 434–442.
Dutilh, G., Vandekerckhove, J., Tuerlinckx, F., & Wagenmakers, E. (2009). A diffusion model decomposition of the practice effect. *Psychonomic Bulletin & Review, 16,* 1026–1036.
Dutta, A., & Proctor, R. W. (1992). Persistence of stimulus-response compatibility effects with extended practice. *Journal of Experimental Psychology: Learning, Memory, and Cognition, 18,* 801–809.
Easterbrook, J. A. (1959). The effect of emotion on cue utilization and the organization of behavior. *Psychological Review, 66,* 183–201.
Ebbinghaus, H. (1885/1964). *Memory: A contribution to experimental psychology.* H. A. Rugler & C. E. Bussenius (Transl.). New York: Dover.
Eckstein, M. P. (2011). Visual search: A retrospective. *Journal of Vision, 11,* 1–36.
Eddy, E. R., Tannenbaum, S. I., & Mathieu, J. E. (2013). Helping teams to help themselves: Comparing two team-led debriefing methods. *Personnel Psychology, 66,* 975–1008.
Eder, A. B., Rothermund, K., De Houwer, J., & Hommel, B. (2015). Directive and incentive functions of affective action consequences: An ideomotor approach. *Psychological Research, 79,* 630–649.
Edkins, G. D. (2002). A review of the benefits of aviation human factors training. *Human Factors and Aerospace Safety, 2,* 201–216.
Edmondson, A. C. (2004). Learning from mistakes is easier said than done: Group and organizational influences on the detection and correction of human error. *Journal of Applied Behavioral Science, 40,* 66–90.
Egner, T., & Gruzelier, J. H. (2004). EEG biofeedback of low beta band components: Frequency-specific effects on variables of attention and event-related brain potentials. *Clinical Neurophysiology, 115,* 131–139.

Eimas, P. D., Siqueland, E. R., Jusczyk, P., & Vigorito, G. (1971). Speech perception in infants. *Science, 171*, 303–306.

Eimer, M. (1996). The N2pc as an indicator of attentional selectivity. *Electroencephalography and Clinical Neurophysiology, 99*, 225–234.

Ellenbuerger, T., Boutin, A., Blandin, Y., Shea, C. H., & Panzer, S. (2012). Scheduling observational and physical practice: Influence on the coding of simple motor sequences. *Quarterly Journal of Experimental Psychology, 65*, 1260–1273.

Elliott, D., Helsen, W. F., & Chua, R. (2001). A century later: Woodworth's (1899) two-component model of goal-directed aiming. *Psychological Bulletin, 127*, 42–57.

Elliott, R., Sahakian, B., Matthews, K., Bannerjea, A., Rimmer, J., & Robbins, T. W. (1997). Effects of methylphenidate on spatial working memory and planning in healthy young adults. *Psychopharmacology, 131*, 196–206.

Ellis, H. D. (1982). The effects of cold on the performance of serial choice reaction time and various discrete tasks. *Human Factors, 24*, 589–598.

Ellis, M. L., Edwards, J. D., Peterson, L., Roker, R., & Athilingam, P. (2014). Effects of cognitive speed of processing training among older adults with heart failure. *Journal of Aging and Health, 26*, 600–615.

Ellis, N. C. (2005). At the interface: Dynamic interactions of explicit and implicit language knowledge. *Studies in Second Language Acquisition, 27*, 305–352.

Ellis, N. R., Wilcock, S. E., & Zaman, S. A. (1985). Cold and performance: The effects of information load, analgesics, and the rate of cooling. *Aviation, Space, and Environmental Medicine, 61*, 399–405.

Ellis, R. (2001). Introduction: Investigating form-focused instruction. *Language Learning, 51*(Suppl 1), 1–46.

Ellis, R., Loewen, S., & Erlam, R. (2006). Implicit and explicit corrective feedback and the acquisition of L2 grammar. *Studies in Second Language Acquisition, 28*, 339–368.

Ellis, S., & Davidi, I. (2005). After-event reviews: Drawing lessons from successful and failed experience. *Journal of Applied Psychology, 90*, 857–871.

Ellis, S., Mendel, R., & Nir, M. (2006). Learning from successful and failed experience: The moderating role of kind of after-event review. *Journal of Applied Psychology, 91*, 669–680.

Elsner, B., & Hommel, B. (2001). Effect anticipation and action control. *Journal of Experimental Psychology: Human Perception and Performance, 27*, 229–240.

Elstein, A. S., Shulman, L. S., & Sprafka, S. A. (1978). *Medical problem solving: An analysis of clinical reasoning*. Cambridge, MA: Harvard University Press.

Engen, T., & Pfaffman, C. (1960). Absolute judgment of odor quality. *Journal of Experimental Psychology, 59*, 214–219.

English, H. B. (1942). How psychology can facilitate military training: A concrete example. *Journal of Applied Psychology, 26*, 3–7.

Entin, E. E., & Serfaty, D. (1999). Adaptive team coordination. *Human Factors, 41*, 312–325.

Ericsson, K. A. (2006). The influence of experience and deliberate practice on the development of superior expert performance. In K. A. Ericsson, N. Charness, P. J. Feltovich, & R. R. Hoffman (Eds.), *The Cambridge handbook of expertise and human performance* (pp. 685–706). New York: Cambridge University Press.

Ericsson, K. A., & Kintsch, W. (1995). Long-term working memory. *Psychological Review, 102,* 211–245.

Ericsson, K. A., Krampe, R. Th., & Tesch-Romer, C. (1993). The role of deliberate practice in the acquisition of expert performance. *Psychological Review, 100,* 363–406.

Ericsson, K. A., & Polson, P. G. (1988). A cognitive analysis of exceptional memory for restaurant orders. In M.T.H. Chi, R. Glaser, & M. J. Farr (Eds.), *The nature of expertise* (pp. 23–70). Hillsdale, NJ: Erlbaum.

Ericsson, K., Roring, R. W., & Nandagopal, K. (2007). Giftedness and evidence for reproducibly superior performance: An account based on the expert performance framework. *High Ability Studies, 18,* 3–56.

Ericsson, K. A., & Simon, H. A. (1980). Verbal reports as data. *Psychological Review, 87,* 215–251.

Ericsson, K. A., & Simon, H. A. (1993). *Protocol analysis.* Cambridge, MA: MIT Press.

Ericsson, K. A., & Smith, J. (1991). Prospects and limits of the empirical study of expertise: An introduction. In K. A. Ericsson & J. Smith (Eds.), *Toward a general theory of expertise: Prospects and limits* (pp. 1–38). New York: Cambridge University Press.

Estes, W. K. (1991). On types of item coding and sources of recall in short-term memory. In W. E. Hockley & S. Lewandowski (Eds.), *Relating theory and data: Essays on human memory in honor of Bennet B. Murdock* (pp. 155–173). Hillsdale, NJ: Lawrence Erlbaum.

Fabiani, M., Buckley, J., Gratton, G., Coles, M.G.H., Donchin, E., & Logie, R. (1989). The training of complex task performance. *Acta Psychologica, 71,* 259–299.

Fahle, M., & Edelman, S. (1993). Long-term learning in Vernier acuity: Effects of stimulus orientation, range and of feedback. *Vision Research, 33,* 397–412.

Falkenstein, M., Hohnsbein, J., & Hoormann, J. (1991). Effects of crossmodal divided attention on late ERP components. II. Error processing in choice reaction tasks. *Electroencephalography and Clinical Neurophysiology, 78,* 447–455.

Falkenstein, M., Hohnsbein, J., & Hoormann, J. (1996). Differential processing of motor errors. In C. Ogura, Y. Koga, & M. Shimokochi (Eds.), *Recent advances in event-related brain potential research* (pp. 579–585). Amsterdam: Elsevier.

Fan, J., McCandliss, B. D., Fossella, J., Flombaum, J. I., & Posner, M. I. (2005). The activation of attentional networks. *Neuroimage, 26,* 471–479.

Farah, M. J., Illes, J., Cook-Deegan, R., Gardner, H., Kandel, E., King, P., . . . Wolpe, P. (2004). Neurocognitive enhancement: What can we do and what should we do? *Nature Reviews Neuroscience, 5,* 421–425.

Fazio, L. K., Huelser, B. J., Johnson, A., & Marsh, E. J. (2010). Receiving right/wrong feedback: Consequences for learning. *Memory, 18,* 335–350.

Feltovich, P. J., Prietula, M. J., & Ericsson, K. A. (2006). Studies of expertise from psychological perspectives. In K. A. Ericsson, N. Charness, P. J. Feltovich, & R. R. Hoffman (Eds.), *The Cambridge handbook of expertise and human performance* (pp. 41–67). Cambridge: Cambridge University Press.

Feng, S., D'Mello, S., & Graesser, A. C. (2013). Mind wandering while reading easy and difficult texts. *Psychonomic Bulletin & Review, 20,* 586–592.

Finnigan, F., & Hammersley, R. (1992). The effects of alcohol on performance. In A. P. Smith & D. M. Jones (Eds.), *Handbook of human performance, Vol. 2: Health and performance* (pp. 73–126). San Diego: Academic Press.

Fitts, P. M. (1962/1990). Factors in complex skill training. In R. Glaser (Ed.), *Training research and education* (pp. 177–197). Pittsburgh, PA: University of Pittsburgh Press. [Reprinted in M. Venturino (Ed.), *Selected readings in human factors* (pp. 275–295). Santa Monica, CA: Human Factors Society.]

Fitts, P. M. (1964). Perceptual-motor skill learning. In A. W. Melton (Ed.), *Categories of human learning* (pp. 243–285). New York: Academic Press.

Fitts, P. M., & Deininger, R. L. (1954). S-R compatibility: Correspondence among paired elements within stimulus and response codes. *Journal of Experimental Psychology, 48*, 483–492.

Fitts, P. M., & Posner, M. I. (1967). *Human performance*. Belmont, CA: Brooks/Cole.

Fitts, P. M., & Seeger, C. M. (1953). S-R compatibility: Spatial characteristics of stimulus and response codes. *Journal of Experimental Psychology, 46*, 199–210.

Flanagan, J. C. (1954). The critical incident technique. *Psychological Bulletin, 51*, 327–358.

Fleishman, E. A. (1978). Relating individual differences to the dimensions of human tasks. *Ergonomics, 21*, 1007–1019.

Fleishman, E. A., & Hempel, W. E., Jr. (1954). Changes in factor structure of a complex psychomotor test as a function of practice. *Psychometrika, 19*, 239–252.

Fleishman, E. A., & Quaintance, M. K. (1984). *Taxonomies of human performance: The description of human tasks*. Orlando, FL: Academic Press.

Fletcher, G., Flin, R., McGeorge, P., & Patey, R. (2004). Rating non-technical skills: Developing a behavioural marker system for use in anaesthesia. *Cognition, Technology, and Work, 6*, 165–171.

Fletcher, P. C., Anderson, J. M., Shanks, D. R., Honey, R. R., Carpenter, T. A., Donovan, T. T., . . . Bullmore, E. T. (2001). Responses of human frontal cortex to surprising events are predicted by formal associative learning theory. *Nature Neuroscience, 4*, 1043–1047.

Flin, R., Martin, L., Goeters, K., Hörmann, H., Amalberti, R., Valot, C., & Nijhuis, H. (2003). Development of the NOTECHS (non-technical skills) system for assessing pilots' CRM skills. *Human Factors and Aerospace Safety, 3*, 97–119.

Folkard, S. (1975). Diurnal variation in logical reasoning. *British Journal of Psychology, 66*, 1–8.

Folkard, S., & Monk, T. H. (1979). Time of day and processing strategy in free recall. *Quarterly Journal of Experimental Psychology, 31*, 461–475.

Folkard, S., & Monk, T. H. (1980). Circadian rhythms in human memory. *British Journal of Psychology, 71*, 295–307.

Folstein, J. R., & Van Petten, C. (2008). Influence of cognitive control and mismatch on the N2 component of the ERP: A review. *Psychophysiology, 45*, 152–170.

Foss, M. A., Fabiani, M., Mané, A. M., & Donchin, E. (1989). Unsupervised practice: The performance of the control group. *Acta Psychologica, 71*, 23–51.

Franklin, M. S., Mooneyham, B. W., Baird, B., & Schooler, J. W. (2014). Thinking one thing, saying another: The behavioral correlates of mind-wandering while reading aloud. *Psychonomic Bulletin & Review, 21*, 205–210.

Frederiksen, J. R., & White, B. Y. (1989). An approach to training based upon principled task decomposition. *Acta Psychologica, 71*, 89–146.

Frensch, P. A., Buchner, A., & Lin, J. (1994). Implicit learning of unique and ambiguous serial transitions in the presence and absence of a distractor task. *Journal of Experimental Psychology: Learning, Memory, and Cognition, 20*, 567–584.

Fritz, C. O., Morris, P. E., Bjork, R. A., Gelman, R., & Wickens, T. D. (2000). When further learning fails: Stability and change following repeated presentation of text. *British Journal of Psychology, 91*, 493–511.

Fu, Q., Fu, X., & Dienes, Z. (2008). Implicit sequence learning and conscious awareness. *Consciousness and Cognition: An International Journal, 17,* 185–202.

Fuchs, T., Birbaumer, N., Lutzenberger, W., Gruzelier, J. H., & Kaiser, J. (2003). Neurofeedback treatment for attention-deficit/hyperactivity disorder in children: A comparison with methylphenidate. *Applied Psychophysiology and Biofeedback, 28,* 1–12.

Gagné, R. M. (1985). *The conditions of learning and theory of instruction* (4th ed.). New York: Holt, Rinehart, and Winston.

Gagné, R. M., & Briggs, L. J. (1974). *Principles of instructional design.* New York: Holt, Rinehart & Winston.

Galton, F. (1869). *Hereditary genius: An inquiry into its laws and consequences.* New York: Macmillan.

Galton, F. (1883). *Inquiry into human faculty and its development.* New York: Macmillan.

Gao, Z., Yin, J., Xu, H., Shui, R., & Shen, M. (2011). Tracking object number or information load in visual working memory: Revisiting the cognitive implication of contralateral delay activity. *Biological Psychology, 87,* 296–302.

Garner, W. R. (1974). *The processing of information and structure.* New York: John Wiley.

Garrison, J., Erdeniz, B., & Done, J. (2013). Prediction error in reinforcement learning: A meta-analysis of neuroimaging studies. *Neuroscience and Biobehavioral Reviews, 37,* 1297–1310.

Gaspelin, N., Ruthruff, E., & Jung, K. (2014). Slippage theory and the flanker paradigm: An early-selection account of selective attention failures. *Journal of Experimental Psychology: Human Perception and Performance, 40,* 1257–1273.

Gatass, R., Sousa, A.P.B., & Gross, C. G. (1988). Visuotopic organization and extent of V3 and V4 of the macaque. *Journal of Neuroscience, 8,* 1831–1845.

Gawron, V., Bailey, R., & Lehman, E. (1995). Lessons learned in applying simulators to crewstation evaluation. *International Journal of Aviation Psychology, 5,* 277–290.

Gegenfurtner, A., Veermans, K., Festner, D., & Gruber, H. (2009). Motivation to transfer training: An integrative literature review. *Human Resource Development Review, 8,* 403–423.

Gehring, W. J., Coles, M.G.H., Meyer, D. E., & Donchin, E. (1990). The error-related negativity: An event-related brain potential accompanying errors. *Psychophysiology, 27,* S34.

Gehring, W. J., Goss, B., Coles, M. G., & Meyer, D. E. (1993). A neural system for error detection and compensation. *Psychological Science, 4,* 385–390.

Geng, J. J., & Behrmann, M. (2002). Probability cuing of target location facilitates visual search implicitly in normal participants and patients with hemispatial neglect. *Psychological Science, 13,* 520–525.

Gentner, D. R., Larochelle, S., & Grudin, J. (1988). Lexical, sublexical, and peripheral effects in skilled typewriting. *Cognitive Psychology, 20,* 524–548.

Gentsch, A., Ullsperger, P., & Ullsperger, M. (2009). Dissociable medial frontal negativities from a common monitoring system for self- and externally caused failure of goal achievement. *Neuroimage, 47,* 2023–2030.

Gernsbacher, M. A. (1993). Less skilled readers have less efficient suppression mechanisms. *Psychological Science, 4,* 294–298.

Gernsbacher, M. A., Varner, K. R., & Faust, M. (1990). Investigating differences in general comprehension skill. *Journal of Experimental Psychology: Learning, Memory, and Cognition, 12,* 430–445.

Gerritsen, C., Frischen, A., Blake, A., Smilek, D., & Eastwood, J. D. (2008). Visual search is not blind to emotion. *Perception & Psychophysics, 70,* 1047–1059.

Ghose, G. M., & Maunsell, J.H.R. (2008). Spatial summation can explain the attentional modulations of neuronal responses to multiple stimuli in area V4. *Journal of Neuroscience, 28,* 5115–5126.

Gibb, S. (2001). The state of human resource management evidence from employees' views of HRM systems and staff. *Employee Relations, 23,* 318–336.

Gibson, E. J. (1969). *Principles of perceptual learning and development.* New York: Appleton-Century-Crofts.

Gibson, J. J. (Ed.) (1947). *Motion picture testing and research.* Army Air Forces Aviation Psychology Program Research Reports, Report No. 7. Washington, DC: U.S. Government Printing Office.

Gibson, J. J., & Gibson, E. J. (1955). Perceptual learning: Differentiation or enrichment? *Psychological Review, 62,* 32–41.

Gick, M. L., & Holyoak, K. J. (1980). Analogical problem solving. *Cognitive Psychology, 12,* 306–355.

Gick, M. L., & Holyoak, K. J. (1983). Schema induction and analogical transfer. *Cognitive Psychology, 15,* 1–38.

Gist, M. E., & Stevens, C. (1998). Effects of practice conditions and supplemental training method on cognitive learning and interpersonal skill generalization. *Organizational Behavior and Human Decision Processes, 75,* 142–169.

Glaser, R., & Chi, M.T.H. (1988). Overview. In M.T.H. Chi, R. Glaser, & M. J. Farr (Eds.), *The nature of expertise* (pp. xv–xxviii). Hillsdale, NJ: Lawrence Erlbaum.

Goldstein, A. G. (1979). Race-related variation of facial features: Anthropometric data I. *Bulletin of the Psychonomic Society, 13,* 187–190.

Goldstein, I. L., & Ford, J. (2002). *Training in organizations: Needs assessment, development, and evaluation* (4th ed.). Belmont, CA: Wadsworth/Thomson Learning.

Goldstone, R. L. (1998). Perceptual learning. *Annual Review of Psychology, 49,* 585–612.

Goldstone, R. L., de Leeuw, J. R., & Landy, D. H. (2015). Fitting perception in and to cognition. *Cognition, 135,* 24–29.

Goldstone, R. L., & Hendrickson, A. T. (2010). Categorical perception. *Wiley Interdisciplinary Reviews: Cognitive Science, 1,* 69–78.

Goldstone, R. L., Lippa, Y., & Shiffrin, R. M. (2001). Altering object representations through category learning. *Cognition, 78,* 27–43.

Goldstone, R. L., Schyns, P. G., & Medin, D. L. (1997). Learning to bridge between perception and cognition. In R. L. Goldstone, D. L. Medin, & P. G. Schyns (Eds.), *Perceptual learning, Vol. 36: The psychology of learning and motivation* (pp. 1–14). San Diego, CA: Academic Press.

Goldstone, R. L., & Steyvers, M. (2001). The sensitization and differentiation of dimensions during category learning. *Journal of Experimental Psychology: General, 130,* 116–139.

Gonzalez, C., Lerch, J. F., & Lebiere, C. (2003). Instance-based learning in dynamic decision making. *Cognitive Science, 27,* 591–635.

Gopher, D. (1982). A selective attention test as a predictor of success in flight training. *Human Factors, 24,* 173–183.

Gopher, D. (1993). The skill of attention control: Acquisition and execution of attention strategies. In D. E. Meyer & S. Kornblum (Eds.), *Attention and performance XIV* (pp. 299–322). Cambridge, MA: MIT Press.

Gopher, D., Brickner, M., & Navon, D. (1982). Different difficulty manipulations interact differently with task emphasis: Evidence for multiple resources. *Journal of Experimental Psychology: Human Perception and Performance, 8*, 146–157.

Gopher, D., & Kahneman, D. (1971). Individual differences in attention and the prediction of flight criteria. *Perceptual and Motor Skills, 33*, 1335–1342.

Gopher, D., Weil, M., & Bareket, T. (1994). Transfer of skill from a computer game trainer to flight. *Human Factors, 36*, 387–405.

Gopher, D., Weil, M., Bareket, T., & Caspi, S. (1988). Fidelity of task structure as a guiding principle in the development of skill trainers based upon complex computer games. *Proceedings of the 32nd Annual Meeting of the Human Factors Society* (pp. 1266–1270). Anaheim, CA: Human Factors and Ergonomics Society.

Gopher, D., Weil, M., & Siegel, D. (1989). Practice under changing priorities: An approach to training of complex skills. *Acta Psychologica, 71*, 147–177.

Gordon, M., Darbyshire, D., & Baker, P. (2012). Non-technical skills training to enhance patient safety: A systematic review. *Medical Education, 46*, 1042–1054.

Gordon, T. G., Coovert, M. D., & Elliott, L. R. (2012). Integrating cognitive task analysis and verbal protocol analysis: A typology for describing jobs. In M. A. Wilson, W. R. Bennett, S. G. Gibson, & G. M. Alliger (Eds.), *The handbook of work analysis: Methods, systems, applications and science of work measurement in organizations* (pp. 625–640). New York: Routledge.

Gorman, J. C., Cooke, N. J., & Amazeen, P. G. (2010). Training adaptive teams. *Human Factors, 52*, 295–307.

Goschke, T. (1997). Implicit learning and unconscious knowledge: Mental representation, computational mechanisms, and brain structures. In K. Lamberts & D. Shanks (Eds.), *Knowledge, concepts, and categories* (pp. 247–334). Cambridge, MA: MIT Press.

Gottsdanker, R., & Stelmach, G. E. (1971). The persistence of psychological refractoriness. *Journal of Motor Behavior, 3*, 301–312.

Green, C. S., & Bavelier, D. (2003). Action video game modifies visual selective attention. *Nature, 423*, 534–537.

Greenberg, S. N., Healy, A. F., Koriat, A., & Kreiner, H. (2004). The GO model: A reconsideration of the role of structural units in guiding and organizing text on line. *Psychonomic Bulletin & Review, 11*, 428–433.

Grigoreanu, V., Burnett, M., Wiedenbeck, S., Cao, J., Rector, K., & Kwan, I. (2012). End-user debugging strategies: A sense making perspective. *ACM Transactions on Computer-Human Interaction, 19*, 5:1–5:28.

Groen, G. J., & Atkinson, R. C. (1966). Models for optimizing the learning process. *Psychological Bulletin, 66*, 309–320.

Grossi, G., Murphy, J., & Boggan, J. (2009). Word and pseudoword superiority effects in Italian-English bilinguals. *Bilingualism: Language and Cognition, 12*, 113–120.

Grudin, J. T. (1983). Error patterns in novice and skilled transcription typing. In W. E. Cooper (Ed.), *Cognitive aspects of skilled typewriting* (pp. 121–143). New York: Springer.

Guzmán-Muñoz, F. J., & Johnson, A. (2008). Error feedback and the acquisition of geographical representations. *Applied Cognitive Psychology, 22*, 979–995.

Haider, H., & Frensch, P. A. (1996). The role of information reduction in skill acquisition. *Cognitive Psychology, 30*, 304–337.

Haider, H., & Frensch, P. A. (2002). Why aggregated learning follows the power law of practice when individual learning does not: Comment on Rickard (1997, 1999), Delaney et al. (1998), and Palmieri (1999). *Journal of Experimental Psychology: Learning, Memory, and Cognition, 28,* 392–406.

Haier, R. J., Siegel, B. V., MacLachlan, A., Soderling, E., Lottenberg, S., & Buchsbaum, M. S. (1992). Regional glucose metabolic changes after learning a complex visuospatial/motor task: A positron emission tomographic study. *Brain Research, 570,* 134–143.

Haier, R. J., Siegel, B. V., Nuechterlein, K. H., Hazlett, E., Wu, J. C., Paek, J., . . . Buchsbaum, M. S. (1988). Cortical glucose metabolic rate correlates of abstract reasoning and attention studied with positron emission tomography. *Intelligence, 12,* 199–217.

Hambrick, D. Z., Oswald, F. L., Altmann, E. M., Meinz, E. J., Gobet, F., & Campitelli, G. (2014). Deliberate practice: Is that all it takes to become an expert? *Intelligence, 45,* 34–45.

Hancock, P. A., & Ganey, H. C. N. (2003). From the inverted-U to the extended-U: The evolution of a law of psychology. *Journal of Human Performance in Extreme Environments, 7,* 5–14.

Hanoch, Y., & Vitouch, O. (2004). When less is more: Information, emotional arousal and the ecological reframing of the Yerkes-Dodson Law. *Theory & Psychology, 14,* 427–452.

Hanslmayr, S., Sauseng, P., Doppelmayr, M., Schabus, M., & Klimesch, W. (2005). Increasing individual upper alpha power by neurofeedback improves cognitive performance in human subjects. *Applied Psychophysiology and Biofeedback, 30,* 1–10.

Harrison, T. L., Shipstead, Z., Hicks, K. L., Hambrick, D. Z., Redick, T. S., & Engle, R. W. (2013). Working memory training may increase working memory capacity but not fluid intelligence. *Psychological Science, 24,* 2409–2419.

Hauty, G. T., & Payne, R. B. (1955). Mitigation of work decrement. *Journal of Experimental Psychology, 49,* 60–67.

Hawkes, L. W., & Derry, S. J. (1996). Advances in local student modeling using informal fuzzy reasoning. *International Journal of Human-Computer Studies, 45,* 697–722.

Hayes, N. E., & Broadbent, D. E. (1988). Two modes of learning for interactive tasks. *Cognition, 28,* 249–276.

Healy, A. F. (1994). Letter detection: A window to unitization and other cognitive processes in reading text. *Psychonomic Bulletin & Review, 1,* 333–344.

Healy, A. F., & Bourne, L. E., Jr. (Eds.) (2012). *Training cognition: Optimizing efficiency, durability, and generalizability.* New York: Psychology Press.

Healy, A. F., Wohldmann, E. L., & Bourne, L. E., Jr. (2005). The procedural reinstatement principle: Studies on training, retention, and transfer. In A. F. Healy (Ed.), *Experimental cognitive psychology and its applications* (pp. 59–71). Washington, DC: American Psychological Association.

Hearst, E. S., & Knott, J. (2008). *Blindfold chess: History, psychology, techniques, champions, world records, and important games.* Jefferson, NC: McFarland.

Heathcote, A., Brown, S., & Mewhort, D. K. (2000). The power law repealed: The case for an exponential law of practice. *Psychonomic Bulletin & Review, 7,* 185–207.

Hebb, D. O. (1955). Drives and the C. N. S. (conceptual nervous system). *Psychological Review, 62,* 243–254.

Hebb, D. O. (1961). Distinctive features of learning in the higher animal. In J. F. Delafresnaye (Ed.), *Brain mechanisms and learning* (pp. 37–46). Oxford, UK: Blackwell.

Heffernan, N. T., Koedinger, K. R., & Razzaq, L. (2008). Expanding the model-tracing architecture: A 3rd generation intelligent tutor for algebra symbolization. *International Journal of Artificial Intelligence in Education, 18*, 153–178.

Heimbeck, D., Frese, M., Sonnentag, S., & Keith, N. (2003). Integrating errors into the training process: The function of error management instructions and the role of goal orientation. *Personnel Psychology, 56*, 333–361.

Heimstra, N. W., Bancroft, N. R., & DeKock, A. R. (1967). Effects of smoking upon sustained performance in a simulated driving task. *Annals of the New York Academy of Science, 142*, 295–307.

Helmreich, R. L., Merritt, A. C., & Wilhelm, J. A. (1999). The evolution of crew resource management training in commercial aviation. *International Journal of Aviation Psychology, 9*, 19–32.

Helmreich, R. L., Wilhelm, J. A., Klinect, J. R., & Merritt, A. C. (2001). Culture, error, and crew resource management. In E. Salas, C. A. Bowers, & E. Edens (Eds.), *Improving teamwork in organizations: Applications of resource management training* (pp. 305–331). Mahwah, NJ: Lawrence Erlbaum.

Helton, W. S., Head, J., & Kemp, S. (2011). Natural disaster induced cognitive disruption: Impacts on action slips. *Consciousness and Cognition: An International Journal, 20*, 1732–1737.

Henninger, D. E., Madden, D. J., & Huettel, S. A. (2010). Processing speed and memory mediate age-related differences in decision making. *Psychology and Aging, 25*, 262–270.

Herbort, O., & Butz, M. V. (2010). Planning and control of hand orientation in grasping movements. *Experimental Brain Research, 202*, 867–878.

Hick, W. E. (1952). On the rate of gain of information. *Quarterly Journal of Experimental Psychology, 4*, 11–26.

Hilgard, E. R. (1964). Introduction to Dover edition. In H. Ebbinghaus (Ed.) (H. A. Rugler & C. E. Bussenius, Trans.), *Memory: A contribution to experimental psychology* (pp. vii–x). New York: Dover.

Hill, D. W., Hill, C. M., Fields, K. L., & Smith, J. C. (1993). Effects of jet lag on factors related to sport performance. *Canadian Journal of Applied Physiology, 18*, 91–103.

Hiltz, K., Back, J., & Blandford, A. (2010). The roles of conceptual device models and user goals in avoiding device initialization errors. *Interacting with Computers, 22*, 363–374.

Hockey, G.R.J. (1970). Signal probability and spatial location as possible bases for increased selectivity in noise. *Quarterly Journal of Experimental Psychology, 22*, 37–42.

Hockey, G.R.J. (1986). Changes in operator efficiency as a function of environmental stress, fatigue, and circadian rhythms. In K. R. Boff, L. Kaufman, & J. P. Thomas (Eds.), *Handbook of human perception and performance, Vol. II: Cognitive processes and performance* (pp. 44–1 to 44–49). New York: John Wiley.

Hoffman, K. A., Aitken, L. M., & Duffield, C. (2009). A comparison of novice and expert nurses' cue collection during clinical decision-making: Verbal protocol analysis. *International Journal of Nursing Studies, 46*, 1335–1344.

Hofstede, G., & Hofstede, G. J. (2005). *Cultures and organizations: Software of the mind* (2nd ed.) New York: McGraw-Hill.
Holding, D. H. (1965). *Principles of training*. Oxford, UK: Pergamon Press.
Holding, D. H. (1970). Repeated errors in motor learning. *Ergonomics, 13*, 727–734.
Holding, D. H. (1985). *The psychology of chess skill*. Hillsdale, NJ: Erlbaum.
Holland, J. H., Holyoak, K. J., Nisbett, R. E., & Thagard, P. R. (1986). *Induction*. Cambridge, MA: MIT Press.
Hollnagel, E., & Woods, D. D. (2005). *Joint cognitive systems: Foundations of cognitive systems engineering*. Boca Raton, FL: CRC Press.
Holroyd, C. B., Larsen, J. T., & Cohen, J. D. (2004). Context dependence of the event-related brain potential associated with reward and punishment. *Psychophysiology, 41*, 245–253.
Holton, E. F., Bates, R. A., & Ruona, W. E. (2000). Development of a generalized learning transfer system inventory. *Human Resource Development Quarterly, 11*, 333–360.
Hommel, B. (1993). The relationship between stimulus processing and response selection in the Simon task: Evidence for a temporal overlap. *Psychological Research, 55*, 280–290.
Hommel, B. (2013). Ideomotor action control: On the perceptual grounding of voluntary actions and agents. In W. Prinz, M. Beisert, & A. Herwig (Eds.), *Action science: Foundations of an emerging discipline* (pp. 113–136). Cambridge, MA: MIT Press.
Hommel, B., Müsseler, J., Aschersleben, G., & Prinz, W. (2001). The theory of event coding (TEC): A framework for perception and action planning. *Behavioral and Brain Sciences, 24*, 849–937.
Horne, J. A., Brass, C. G., & Pettit, A. N. (1980). Circadian performance differences between morning and evening "types." *Ergonomics, 23*, 29–36.
Horne, J. A., & Ostberg, O. (1976). A self-assessment questionnaire to determine morningness-eveningness in human circadian rhythms. *International Journal of Chronobiology, 4*, 97–110.
Houghton, G. (Ed.) (2005). *Connectionist models in cognitive psychology*. New York: Psychology Press.
Howard, R. W. (2009). Individual differences in expertise development over decades in a complex intellectual domain. *Memory & Cognition, 37*, 194–209.
Howard, R. W. (2014). Learning curves in highly skilled chess players: A test of the generality of the power law of practice. *Acta Psychologica, 151*, 16–23.
Hu, X., & Newell, K. M. (2011). Modeling constraints to redundancy in bimanual force coordination. *Journal of Neurophysiology, 105*, 2169–2180.
Hubel, D. H., & Wiesel, T. N. (1968). Receptive fields and functional architecture of monkey striate cortex. *Journal of Physiology, 195*, 215–243.
Hugenberg, K., Young, S. G., Bernstein, M. J., & Sacco, D. F. (2010). The categorization-individuation model: An integrative account of the other-race recognition deficit. *Psychological Review, 117*, 1168–1187.
Hulstijn, J. H., & de Graaff, R. (1994). Under what conditions does explicit knowledge of a second language facilitate the acquisition of implicit knowledge? A research proposal. *AILA Review, 11*, 97–112.
Hummel, J. E., & Holyoak, K. J. (2003). A symbolic-connectionist theory of relational inference and generalization. *Psychological Review, 110*, 220–264.

Humphreys, K. R., Menzies, H., & Lake, J. K. (2010). Repeated speech errors: Evidence for learning. *Cognition, 117*, 151–165.

Humphreys, M. S., & Revelle, W. (1984). Personality, motivation, and performance: A theory of the relationship between individual differences and information processing. *Psychological Review, 91*, 153–184.

Hunt, E. B. (1978). Mechanics of verbal ability. *Psychological Review, 85*, 109–130.

Hyman, R. (1953). Stimulus information as a determinant of reaction time. *Journal of Experimental Psychology, 45*, 188–196.

Itti, L., & Koch, C. (2000). A saliency-based search mechanism for overt and covert shifts of visual attention. *Vision Research, 40*, 1489–1506.

Ivancic, K., & Hesketh, B. (2000). Learning from errors in a driving simulation: Effects on driving skill and self-confidence. *Ergonomics, 43*, 1966–1984.

Jackson, M. D., & McClelland, J. L. (1975). Sensory and cognitive determinants of reading speed. *Journal of Verbal Learning and Verbal Behavior, 14*, 565–574.

Jackson, M. D., & McClelland, J. L. (1979). Processing determinants of reading speed. *Journal of Experimental Psychology: General, 108*, 151–181.

Jacobs, R. S., & Roscoe, S. N. (1975). Simulator cockpit motion and the transfer of initial flight training. *Proceedings of the Human Factors Society 19th Annual Meeting* (pp. 218–226). Santa Monica, CA: Human Factors Society.

Jacoby, L. (1991). A process dissociation framework: Separating automatic from intentional uses of memory. *Journal of Memory and Language, 30*, 513–541.

James, W. (1890/1950). *The principles of psychology*. New York: Dover.

Jang, Y., Pashler, H., & Huber, D. E. (2014). Manipulations of choice familiarity in multiple-choice testing support a retrieval practice account of the testing effect. *Journal of Educational Psychology, 106*, 435–447.

Jared, D., & Seidenberg, M. S. (1991). Does word identification proceed from spelling to sound to meaning? *Journal of Experimental Psychology: General, 120*, 358–394.

Jaušovec, N., & Jaušovec, K. (2004). Differences in induced brain activity during the performance of learning and working-memory tasks related to intelligence. *Brain and Cognition, 54*, 65–74.

Jaušovec, N., & Jaušovec, K. (2008). Spatial rotation and recognizing emotions: Gender related differences in brain activity. *Intelligence, 36*, 383–393.

Jax, S. A., & Rosenbaum, D. A. (2007). Hand path priming in manual obstacle avoidance: Evidence that the dorsal stream does not only control visually guided actions in real time. *Journal of Experimental Psychology: Human Perception and Performance, 33*, 425–441.

Jeannerod, M., & Marteniuk, R. G. (1992). Functional characteristics of prehension: From data to artificial neural networks. In L. Proteau & D. Elliott (Eds.), *Vision and motor control* (pp. 197–232). Amsterdam: North-Holland.

Jensen, A. R. (2006). *Clocking the mind: Mental chronometry and individual differences*. Amsterdam: Elsevier Science & Technology.

Jentzsch, I., Leuthold, H., & Ulrich, R. (2007). Decomposing sources of response slowing in the PRP paradigm. *Journal of Experimental Psychology: Human Perception and Performance, 33*, 610–626.

John, B. E. (1996). TYPIST: A theory of performance in skilled typing. *Human-Computer Interaction, 11*, 321–355.

Johnson, A. (2013). Procedural memory and skill acquisition. In A. F. Healy & R. W. Proctor (Eds.), *Handbook of psychology, Vol. 4: Experimental psychology* (2nd ed., pp. 495–520), I. B. Weiner (Ed.-in Chief). Hoboken, NJ: John Wiley.

Johnson, A., & Proctor, R. W. (2004). *Attention: Theory and practice*. Thousand Oaks, CA: SAGE.

Johnson, A., & Proctor, R. W. (Eds.) (2013). *Neuroergonomics: A cognitive neuroscience approach to human factors and ergonomics*. Basingstoke, UK: Palgrave Macmillan.

Johnson, M. P., Duffy, J. F., Dijk, D. J., Ronda, J. M., Dyal, C. M., & Czeizler, C. A. (1992). Short-term memory, alertness and performance: A reappraisal of their relationship to body temperature. *Journal of Sleep Research, 1*, 24–29.

Johnson, W., & Bouchard, T. J., Jr. (2005). The structure of human intelligence: It is verbal, perceptual, and image rotation (VPR), not fluid and crystallized. *Intelligence, 33*, 393–416.

Johnston, C. A., Moreno, J., Regas, K., Tyler, C., & Foreyt, J. P. (2012). The application of the Yerkes-Dodson law in a childhood weight management program: Examining weight dissatisfaction. *Journal of Pediatric Psychology, 37*, 674–679.

Jones, D. M. (1983). Noise. In R. Hockey (Ed.), *Stress and fatigue in human performance* (pp. 61–95). New York: John Wiley.

Jones, M., & Goldstone, R. L. (2012). The structure of integral dimensions: Contrasting topological and Cartesian representations. *Journal of Experimental Psychology: Human Perception and Performance*, 111–132.

Jung, R. E., & Haier, R. J. (2007). The parieto-frontal integration theory (P-FIT) of intelligence: Converging neuroimaging evidence. *Behavioral and Brain Sciences, 30*, 130–154.

Kahneman, D. (1973). *Attention and effort*. Englewood Cliffs, NJ: Prentice Hall.

Kahneman, D., Ben-Ishai, R., & Lotan, M. (1973). Relation of a test of attention to road accidents. *Journal of Applied Psychology, 58*, 113–115.

Kaiser, M. K., Jonides, J., & Alexander, J. (1986). Intuitive reasoning about abstract and familiar physics problems. *Memory & Cognition, 14*, 308–312.

Kaiser, M. K., McCloskey, M., & Proffitt, D. R. (1986). Development of intuitive theories of motion: Curvilinear motion in the absence of external forces. *Developmental Psychology, 22*, 67–71.

Kal, E. C., van der Kamp, J. J., & Houdijk, H. H. (2013). External attentional focus enhances movement automatization: A comprehensive test of the constrained action hypothesis. *Human Movement Science, 32*, 527–539.

Kane, M. J., Brown, L. H., McVay, J. C., Silvia, P. J., Myin-Germeys, I., & Kwapil, T. R. (2007). For whom the mind wanders, and when: An experience-sampling study of working memory and executive control in daily life. *Psychological Science, 18*, 614–621.

Kanfer, R. (1996). Learning from failure: It is not easy. *Psychological Inquiry, 7*, 50–53.

Kanfer, R., & Ackerman, P. L. (1989). Motivation and cognitive abilities: An integrative/aptitude-treatment interaction approach to skill acquisition. *Journal of Applied Psychology, 74*, 657–690.

Kang, S. K., McDaniel, M. A., & Pashler, H. (2011). Effects of testing on learning of functions. *Psychonomic Bulletin & Review, 18*, 998–1005.

Kantak, S. S. Sullivan, K. J. Fisher, B. E. Knowlton, B. J., & Winstein, C. J. (2010). Neural substrates of motor memory consolidation depend on practice structure. *Nature Neuroscience, 13*, 923–925.

Karni, A. (1996). The acquisition of perceptual and motor skills: A memory system in the adult human cortex. *Cognitive Brain Research, 5*, 39–48.

Karni, A., & Bertini, G. (1997). Learning perceptual skills: Behavioral probes into adult plasticity. *Current Opinion in Neurobiology, 7,* 530–535.

Kassin, S. M., Ellsworth, P. C., & Smith, V. L. (1989). The "general acceptance" of psychological research on eyewitness testimony: A survey of experts. *American Psychologist, 44,* 1089–1098.

Kaufman, S., & Kaufman, J. C. (2007). Ten years to expertise, many more to greatness: An investigation of modern writers. *Journal of Creative Behavior, 41,* 114–124.

Kay, H. (1951). Learning of a serial task by different age groups. *Quarterly Journal of Experimental Psychology, 3,* 166–183.

Kay, H. (1955). Learning and retaining verbal material. *British Journal of Psychology, 46,* 81–100.

Keele, S. W. (1968). Movement control in skilled motor performance. *Psychological Bulletin, 70,* 387–403.

Keith, N., & Ericsson, K. (2007). A deliberate practice account of typing proficiency in everyday typists. *Journal of Experimental Psychology: Applied, 13,* 135–145.

Keith, N., & Frese, M. (2005). Self-Regulation in error management training: Emotion control and metacognition as mediators of performance effects. *Journal of Applied Psychology, 90,* 677–691.

Keith, N., & Frese, M. (2008). Effectiveness of error management training: A meta-analysis. *Journal of Applied Psychology, 93,* 59–69.

Kellman, P. J., & Massey, C. M. (2013). Perceptual learning, cognition, and expertise. In B. J. Ross (Ed.), *The psychology of learning and motivation* (Vol. 58, pp. 117–165). San Diego, CA: Academic Press.

Kelso, J.A.S. (1984). Phase transitions and critical behavior in human bimanual coordination. *American Journal of Physiology: Regulatory, Integrative, and Comparative Physiology, 15,* R1000–R1004.

Kelso, J.A.S., Tuller, B., Vatikiotis-Bateson, E. E., & Fowler, C. A. (1984). Functionally specific articulatory cooperation following jaw perturbations during speech: Evidence for coordinative structures. *Journal of Experimental Psychology: Human Perception and Performance, 10,* 812–832.

Kemler Nelson, D. G. (1993). Processing integral dimensions: The whole view. *Journal of Experimental Psychology: Human Perception and Performance, 19,* 1105–1113.

Kerr, B. (1973). Processing demands during mental operations. *Memory & Cognition, 1,* 401–412.

Keyes, H. (2012). Categorical perception effects for facial identity in robustly represented familiar and self-faces: The role of configural and featural information. *Quarterly Journal of Experimental Psychology, 65,* 760–772.

Kieras, D. E., & Bovair, S. (1984). The role of a mental model in learning to operate a device. *Cognitive Science, 8,* 255–273.

Kieras, D. E., Meyer, D. E., Ballas, J. A., & Lauber, E. J. (2000). Modern computational perspectives on executive mental processes and cognitive control: Where to from here. In S. Monsell & J. Driver (Eds.), *Control of cognitive processes: Attention and performance XVIII* (pp. 681–712). Cambridge, MA: MIT Press.

Kikutani, M. M., Roberson, D. D., & Hanley, J. R. (2010). Categorical perception for unfamiliar faces: The effect of covert and overt face learning. *Psychological Science, 21,* 865–872.

Killingsworth, M. A., & Gilbert, D. T. (2010). A wandering mind is an unhappy mind. *Science, 330,* 932.

Kimberg, D. Y., D'Esposito, M., & Farah, M. J. (1997). Effects of bromocriptine on human subjects depend on working memory capacity. *Neuroreport, 8*, 3581–3585.

Kirkpatrick, D. L. (1976). Evaluation. In R. L. Craig (Ed.), *Training and development handbook* (pp. 301–319). New York: McGraw-Hill.

Kirkpatrick, D. L. (1994). *Evaluating training programs: The four levels*. San Francisco: Berrett-Koehler.

Kirwan, C., & Birchall, D. (2006). Transfer of learning from management development programmes: Testing the Holton model. *International Journal of Training and Development, 10*, 252–268.

Kjellberg, A. (1977). Sleep deprivation and some aspects of performance: II. Lapses and other attentional effects. *Waking and Sleeping, 1*, 145–148.

Klein, G. (1997). The current status of the naturalistic decision making framework. In R. Flin, E. Salas, M. Strub, & L. Martin (Eds.), *Decision making under stress: Emerging themes and applications*. Aldershot, UK: Ashgate.

Klein, G. A., Calderwood, R., & MacGregor, D. (1989). Critical decision method for eliciting knowledge. *IEEE Transactions on Systems, Man and Cybernetics, 19*, 462–472.

Klein, K. E., Wegman, H. M., & Hunt, B. I. (1972). Desynchronization of body temperature and performance circadian rhythm as a result of outgoing and homegoing transmeridian flights. *Aerospace Medicine, 43*, 119–132.

Kleitman, N. (1963). *Sleep and wakefulness* (rev. ed.). Chicago, IL: University of Chicago Press. (Original published 1938)

Kleitman, N., & Jackson, D. P. (1950). Body temperature and performance under different routines. *Journal of Applied Physiology, 3*, 309–328.

Knowles, M. (1984). *The adult learner: A neglected species* (3rd ed.). Houston, TX: Gulf Publishing.

Koch, I., & Rumiati, R. I. (2006). Task-set inertia and memory-consolidation bottleneck in dual tasks. *Psychological Research, 70*, 448–458.

Kolers, P. A. (1975). Memorial consequences of automatized encoding. *Journal of Experimental Psychology: Human Learning and Memory, 1*, 689–701.

Kolers, P. A. (1976). Reading a year later. *Journal of Experimental Psychology: Human Learning and Memory, 2*, 554–565.

Kolers, P. A., & Roediger, H. L., III. (1984). Procedures of mind. *Journal of Verbal Learning and Verbal Behavior, 23*, 425–449.

Koller, S. M., Drury, C. G., & Schwaninger, A. (2009). Change of search time and non-search time in x-ray baggage screening due to training. *Ergonomics, 52*, 644–656.

Koriat, A., & Greenberg, S. N. (1994). The extraction of phrase structure during reading: Evidence from letter detection errors. *Psychonomic Bulletin & Review, 1*, 345–356.

Kornblum, S. (1969). Sequential determinants of information processing in serial and discrete choice reaction time. *Psychological Review, 76*, 113–131.

Kornblum, S. (1973). Sequential effects in choice reaction time: A tutorial review. In S. Kornblum (Ed.), *Attention and performance IV* (pp. 259–288). New York: Academic Press.

Kornblum, S. (1975). An invariance in choice reaction time with varying numbers of alternatives and constant probability. In P. Rabbitt & S. Dornic (Eds.), *Attention and performance V* (pp. 366–382). San Diego, CA: Academic Press.

Kornblum, S., Hasbroucq, T., & Osman, A. (1990). Dimensional overlap: Cognitive basis for stimulus-response compatibility—A model and taxonomy. *Psychological Review, 97*, 253–270.

Kostrubiec, V., Zanone, P. G., Fuchs, A., & Kelso, J. A. S. (2012). Beyond the blank slate: Routes to learning new coordination patterns depend on the intrinsic dynamics of the learner—Experimental evidence and theoretical model. *Frontiers in Human Neuroscience, 6*, ArtID: 222. doi:10.3389/fnhum.2012.00222

Kraiger, K. (2002). Decision-based evaluation. In K. Kraiger (Ed.), *Creating, implementing, and maintaining effective training and development: State-of-the-art lessons for practice* (pp. 331–375). San Francisco, CA: Jossey-Bass.

Kraimer, M. L., Wayne, S. J., & Jaworski, R. A. (2001). Sources of support and expatriate performance: The mediating role of expatriate adjustment. *Personnel Psychology, 54*, 71–99.

Kramer, A. F., Larish, J. F., & Strayer, D. L. (1995). Training for attentional control in dual task settings: A comparison of young and old adults. *Journal of Experimental Psychology: Applied, 1*, 50–76.

Krashen, S. (1982). *Principles and practice in second language acquisition*. Oxford, UK: Pergamon.

Krashen, S. (1994). The input hypothesis and its rivals. In N. Ellis (Ed.), *Implicit and explicit learning of languages* (pp. 45–77). London: Academic Press.

Krems, J. F. (1995). Expert strategies in debugging: Experimental results and a computational model. In K. F. Wender, F. Schmalhofer, & H.-D. Boecker (Eds.), *Cognition and computer programming* (pp. 241–254). Norwood, NJ: Ablex.

Krigolson, O., Van Gyn, G., Tremblay, L., & Heath, M. (2006). Is there "feedback" during visual imagery? Evidence from a specificity of practice paradigm. *Canadian Journal of Experimental Psychology, 60*, 24–32.

Krueger, W. F. (1929). The effect of overlearning on retention. *Journal of Experimental Psychology, 12*, 71–78. doi:10.1037/h007203

Krupinski, E. A. (2010). Current perspectives in medical image perception. *Attention, Perception, & Psychophysics, 72*, 1205–1217.

Kruschke, J. K. (1992). ALCOVE: An exemplar-based connectionist model of category learning. *Psychological Review, 99*, 22–44.

Kunde, W. (2001). Response-effect compatibility in manual choice reaction tasks. *Journal of Experimental Psychology: Human Perception and Performance, 27*, 387–394.

Kundel, H. L., & LaFollette, P. S. (1972). Visual search patterns and experience with radiological images. *Radiology, 103*, 523–528.

Kundel, H. L., & Nodine, C. F. (1975). Interpreting chest radiographs without visual search. *Radiology, 116*, 527–532.

Kupermintz, H. (2002). Affective and conative factors as aptitude resources in high school science achievement. *Educational Assessment, 8*, 123–137.

Kurtz, K. J., & Loewenstein, J. (2007). Converging on a new role for analogy in problem solving and retrieval: When two problems are better than one. *Memory & Cognition, 35*, 334–341.

LaBerge, D. (1973). Attention and the measurement of perceptual learning. *Memory & Cognition, 1*, 268–276.

Lacey, J. I. (1967). Somatic response patterning and stress: Some revisions of activation theory. In M. H. Appley & R. Trumbull (Eds.), *Psychological stress* (pp. 14–42). New York: Appleton-Century-Crofts.

Lachter, J., Forster, K. I., & Ruthruff, E. (2004). Forty years after Broadbent: Still no identification without attention. *Psychological Review, 111,* 880–913.

Lafond, D., Tremblay, S., & Parmentier, F. (2010). The ubiquitous nature of the Hebb repetition effect: Error learning mistaken for the absence of sequence learning. *Journal of Experimental Psychology: Learning, Memory, and Cognition, 36,* 515–522.

Lagopoulos, J. (2007). Event-related potentials. *Acta Neuropsychiatrica, 19,* 256–257.

Laird, J. E. (2012). *The Soar cognitive architecture.* Cambridge: MIT Press.

Lam, W., Masters, R. W., & Maxwell, J. P. (2010). Cognitive demands of error processing associated with preparation and execution of a motor skill. *Consciousness and Cognition: An International Journal, 19,* 1058–1061.

Lambourne, K., & Tomporowski, P. (2010). The effect of exercise-induced arousal on cognitive task performance: A meta-regression analysis. *Brain Research, 1341,* 12–24.

Langlois, F., Vu, T. M., Chassé, K., Dupuis, G., Kergoat, M., & Bherer, L. (2013). Benefits of physical exercise training on cognition and quality of life in frail older adults. *Journals of Gerontology: Series B: Psychological Sciences and Social Sciences, 68B,* 400–404.

Lansdale, M., & How, T. T. (1996). An analysis of errors in the learning, overlearning, and forgetting of sequences. *Quarterly Journal of Experimental Psychology: Human Experimental Psychology, 49A,* 341–356.

Larson, G. E., & Perry, Z. A. (1999). Visual capture and human error. *Applied Cognitive Psychology, 13,* 227–236.

Lashley, K. S. (1951). The problem of serial order in behavior. In L. A. Jeffress (Ed.), *Cerebral mechanisms in behavior: The Hixon symposium* (pp. 112–131). New York: John Wiley.

Latash, M. L. (2010). Stages in learning motor synergies: A view based on the equilibrium-point hypothesis. *Human Movement Science, 29,* 642–654.

Latash, M. L. (2012). The bliss (not the problem) of motor abundance (not redundancy). *Experimental Brain Research, 217,* 1–5.

Lavery, J. J. (1962). Retention of simple motor skills as a function of type of knowledge of results. *Canadian Journal of Psychology, 16,* 300–311.

Lavie, N. (1995). Perceptual load as a necessary condition for selective attention. *Journal of Experimental Psychology: Human Perception and Performance, 21,* 451–468.

Leavitt, J. (1979). Cognitive demands of skating and stick handling in ice hockey. *Canadian Journal of Applied Sport Sciences, 4,* 46–55.

Leberman, S., McDonald, L., & Doyle, S. (2006). *The transfer of learning: Participants' perspectives of adult education and training.* Farnham, UK: Gower.

Lee, T. D., & Genovese, E. D. (1988). Distribution of practice in motor skill acquisition: Learning and performance effects reconsidered. *Research Quarterly for Exercise and Sport, 59,* 277–287.

Lee, T. D., & Genovese, E. D. (1989). Distribution of practice in motor skill acquisition: Different effects for discrete and continuous tasks. *Research Quarterly for Exercise and Sport, 60,* 59–65.

Lee, T. D., & Magill, R. A. (1983). The locus of contextual interference in motor-skill acquisition. *Journal of Experimental Psychology: Learning, Memory, and Cognition, 9*, 730–746.

Lee, T. D., & Swinnen, S. P. (1993). Three legacies of Bryan and Harter: Automaticity, variability and change in skilled performance. In J. L. Starkes, F. Allard, J. L. Starkes, & F. Allard (Eds.), *Cognitive issues in motor expertise* (pp. 295–315). Amsterdam: North-Holland.

Lee, Y., Turkeltaub, P., Granger, R., & Raizada, R. S. (2012). Categorical speech processing in Broca's area: An fMRI study using multivariate pattern-based analysis. *Journal of Neuroscience, 32*, 3942–3948.

Leech, R., Mareschal, D., & Cooper, R. P. (2008). Analogy as relational priming: A developmental and computational perspective on the origins of a complex cognitive skill. *Behavioral & Brain Sciences, 31*, 357–414.

Lehman, M., Smith, M. A., & Karpicke, J. D. (2014). Toward an episodic context account of retrieval-based learning: Dissociating retrieval practice and elaboration. *Journal of Experimental Psychology: Learning, Memory, and Cognition, 40*, 1787–1794.

Leitl, J., & Zempel-Dohmen, J. (2006). Die Bedeutung des Arbeitsumfelds für die Veränderung der Transfermotivation [The impact of work environment on the changing level of motivation to transfer]. *Zeitschrift für Arbeits- und Organisationspsychologie, 50*, 92–102.

Leonard, J. A. (1958). Advance information in sensorimotor skills. *Quarterly Journal of Experimental Psychology, 5*, 141–149.

Leonhard, T. (2011). Determinants of central processing order in psychological refractory period paradigms: Central arrival times, detection times, or preparation? *Quarterly Journal of Experimental Psychology, 64*, 2012–2043.

Lesgold, A., Rubinson, H., Feltovich, P., Glaser, R., Klopfer, D., & Wang, Y. (1988). Expertise in a complex skill: Diagnosing X-ray pictures. In M.T.H. Chi, R. Glaser, & M. J. Farr (Eds.), *The nature of expertise* (pp. 311–342). Hillsdale, NJ: Lawrence Erlbaum.

Levelt, W.J.M., Roelofs, A., & Meyer, A. S. (1999). A theory of lexical access in speech production. *Behavioral and Brain Sciences, 22*, 1–45.

Liberman, A. M., Harris, K., Hoffman, H. S., & Griffith, B. C. (1957). The discrimination of speech sounds within and across phoneme boundaries. *Journal of Experimental Psychology, 54*, 358–368.

Lieberman, H. R. (1992). Caffeine. In A. P. Smith & D. M. Jones (Eds.), *Handbook of human performance, Vol. 2: Health and performance* (pp. 49–72). San Diego: Academic Press.

Lieberman, H. R., Wurtman, R. J., Emde, G. G., & Coviella, I.L.G. (1987). The effects of caffeine and aspirin on mood and performance. *Journal of Clinical Psychopharmacology, 7*, 315–320.

Lieberman, H. R., Wurtman, R. J., Emde, G. G., Roberts, C., & Coviella, I.L.G. (1987). The effects of low doses of caffeine on human performance and mood. *Psychopharmacology, 92*, 308–312.

Lievens, F., Harris, M. M., Van Keer, E., & Bisqueret, C. (2003). Predicting cross-cultural training performance: The validity of personality, cognitive ability, and dimensions measured by an assessment center and a behavior description interview. *Journal of Applied Psychology, 88*, 476–489.

Linderholm, T., Gernsbacher, M. A., van den Broek, P., Neninde, L., Robertson, R. W., & Sundermier, B. (2004). Suppression of story character goals during reading. *Discourse Processes, 37,* 67–78.

Lindsley, D. B. (1951). Emotion. In S. S. Stevens (Ed.), *Handbook of experimental psychology* (pp. 473–516). New York: John Wiley.

Litchfield, D., Ball, L. J., Donovan, T., Manning, D. J., & Crawford, T. (2010). Viewing another person's eye movements improves identification of pulmonary nodules in chest x-ray inspection. *Journal of Experimental Psychology: Applied, 16,* 251–262.

Littrell, L. N., Salas, E., Hess, K. P., Paley, M., & Riedel, S. (2006). Expatriate preparation: A critical analysis of 25 years of cross-cultural training research. *Human Resource Development Review, 5,* 355–388.

Liu, X., Crump, M.J.C., & Logan, G. D. (2010). Do you know where your fingers have been? Explicit knowledge of the spatial layout of the keyboard in skilled typists. *Memory & Cognition, 38,* 474–484.

Lively, S. E., Logan, J. S., & Pisoni, D. B. (1993). Training Japanese listeners to identify English /r/ and /l/. II: The role of phonetic environment and talker variability in learning new perceptual categories. *Journal of the Acoustical Society of America, 94,* 1242–1255.

Livingston, K. R., Andrews, J. K., & Harnad, S. (1998). Categorical perception effects induced by category learning. *Journal of Experimental Psychology: Learning, Memory, and Cognition, 24,* 732–753.

Locke, E. A., & Latham, G. P. (1990). Work motivation and satisfaction: Light at the end of the tunnel. *Psychological Science, 1,* 240–246.

Logan, G. D. (1988). Toward an instance theory of automatization. *Psychological Review, 95,* 492–527.

Logan, G. D. (1990). Repetition priming and automaticity: Common underlying mechanisms? *Cognitive Psychology, 22,* 1–35.

Logan, G. D. (2003). Simon-type effects: Chronometric evidence for keypress schemata in typewriting. *Journal of Experimental Psychology: Human Perception and Performance, 29,* 741–757.

Logan, G. D. (2005). Attention, automaticity, and executive control. In A. F. Healy (Ed.), *Experimental cognitive psychology and its applications* (pp. 129–139). Washington, DC: American Psychological Association.

Logan, G. D., & Compton, B. J. (1998). Attention and automaticity. In R. D. Wright (Ed.), *Visual attention: Vancouver studies in cognitive science* (Vol. 8, pp. 108–131). New York: Oxford University Press.

Logan, G. D., & Crump, M.J.C. (2009). The left hand doesn't know what the right hand is doing: The disruptive effects of attention to the hands in skilled typewriting. *Psychological Science, 10,* 1296–1300.

Logan, G. D., & Crump, M.J.C. (2010). Cognitive illusions of authorship reveal hierarchical error detection in skilled typists. *Science, 330,* 683–686.

Logan, G. D., & Crump, M. C. (2011). Hierarchical control of cognitive processes: The case for skilled typewriting. In B. H. Ross (Ed.), *The psychology of learning and motivation: Advances in research and theory* (Vol. 54, pp. 1–27). San Diego, CA: Academic Press.

Logan, G. D., & Etherton, J. L. (1994). What is learned during automatization? The role of attention in constructing an instance. *Journal of Experimental Psychology: Learning, Memory, and Cognition, 20,* 1022–1050.

Logan, G. D., & Klapp, S. T. (1991). Automatizing alphabet arithmetic: I. Is extended practice necessary to produce automaticity? *Journal of Experimental Psychology: Learning, Memory, and Cognition, 17,* 179–195.

Logan, G. D., Miller, A., & Strayer, D. L. (2011). Electrophysiological evidence for parallel response selection in skilled typists. *Psychological Science, 22,* 54–56.

Logie, R., Baddeley, A., Mané, A., Donchin, E., & Sheptak, R. (1989). Working memory in the acquisition of complex cognitive skills. *Acta Psychologica, 71,* 53–87.

Lombard, W. P. (1887). The variants of the normal knee jerk and their relation to the activity of the central nervous system. *American Journal of Psychology, 1,* 5–71.

London, M., & Smither, J. W. (1999). Career-related continuous learning: Defining the construct and mapping the process. In G. R. Ferris (Ed.), *Research in human resources management* (Vol. 17, pp. 81–121). Stamford, CT: JAI Press.

Love, B. C., Medin, D. L., & Gureckis, T. M. (2004). SUSTAIN: A network model of category learning. *Psychological Review, 111,* 309–332.

Lubar, J. F., & Shouse, M. N. (1976). EEG and behavioral changes in a hyperkinetic child concurrent with training of the sensorimotor rhythm (SMR): A preliminary report. *Biofeedback and Self-Regulation, 1,* 293–306.

Lubar, J. F., Swartwood, M. O., Swartwood, J. N., & O'Donnell, P. H. (1995). Evaluation of the effectiveness of EEG neurofeedback training for ADHD in a clinical setting as measured by changes in T.O.V.A. scores, behavioral ratings, and WISC-R performance. *Biofeedback and Self-Regulation, 20,* 83–99.

Luchins, A. S. (1942). Mechanization in problem solving. *Psychological Monographs, 54*(6) (whole no. 248).

Lunn, J. H. (1948). Chick sexing. *American Scientist, 36,* 280–287.

Luque, D., López, F. J., Marco-Pallares, J., Càmara, E., & Rodríguez-Fornells, A. (2012). Feedback-related brain potential activity complies with basic assumptions of associative learning theory. *Journal of Cognitive Neuroscience, 24,* 794–808.

Luria, A. R. (1980). *Higher cortical functions in man* (2nd ed.). New York: Basic Books. (Original published 1966)

Lyans, C. K. (1914). The doctrine of formal discipline. *Pedagogical Seminary, 21,* 343–393.

Machin, M. A., & Fogarty, G. J. (1997). The effects of self-efficacy, motivation to transfer, and situational constraints on transfer intentions and transfer of training. *Performance Improvement Quarterly, 10,* 98–115.

Machin, M. A., & Fogarty, G. J. (2004). Assessing the antecedents of transfer intentions in a training context. *International Journal of Training and Development, 8,* 222–236.

Mackworth, N. H. (1961). Researches on the measurement of human performance. In H. W. Sinaiko (Ed.), *Selected papers on human factors in the design and use of control systems* (pp. 174–331). New York: Dover.

Magill, R. A., & Hall, K. G. (1990). A review of the contextual interference effect in motor skill acquisition. *Human Movement Science, 9,* 241–289.

Maier, N.R.F. (1930). Reasoning in humans. *Journal of Comparative Psychology, 10,* 115–143.

Major, J. T., Johnson, W., & Deary, I. J. (2012). Comparing models of intelligence in Project TALENT: The VPR model fits better than the CHC and extended Gf–Gc models. *Intelligence, 40,* 543–559.

Malmo, R. B. (1959). Activation: A neuropsychological dimension. *Psychological Review, 66,* 367–386.

Mandelman, S. D., Barbot, B., & Grigorenko, E. L. (2015). Predicting academic performance and trajectories from a measure of successful intelligence. *Learning and Individual Differences*, doi:10.1016/j.lindif.2015.02.003

Mané, A., & Donchin, E. (1989). The space fortress game. *Acta Psychologica, 71*, 17–22.

Marks, M., & Folkard, S. (1988). The effects of time of day on recall from expository text. In M. Gruneberg, P. Morris, & R., Sykes (Eds.), *Practical aspects of memory: Current research and issues* (pp. 471–476). New York: Wiley.

Marmie, W. R., & Healy, A. F. (1995). The long-term retention of a complex skill. In A. F. Healy & L. E. Bourne, Jr. (Eds.), *Learning and memory of knowledge and skills: Durability and specificity* (pp. 30–65). Thousand Oaks, CA: SAGE.

Marshalek, B., Lohman, D. F., & Snow, R. E. (1983). The complexity continuum in the radex and hierarchical models of intelligence. *Intelligence, 7*, 107–127.

Marsick, V. J., & Watkins, K. E. (2003). Demonstrating the value of an organization's learning culture: The dimensions of the learning organization questionnaire. *Advances in Developing Human Resources, 5*, 132–151.

Maslovat, D., Brunke, K. M., Chua, R., & Franks, I. M. (2009). Feedback effects on learning a novel bimanual coordination pattern: Support for the guidance hypothesis. *Journal of Motor Behavior, 41*, 45–54.

Masson, M. E. (1986). Identification of typographically transformed words: Instance-based skill acquisition. *Journal of Experimental Psychology: Learning, Memory, and Cognition, 12*, 479–488.

Masson, M. E., & Miller, J. A. (1983). Working memory and individual differences in comprehension and memory of text. *Journal of Educational Psychology, 75*, 314–318.

Masters, R.S.W. (1992). Knowledge, knerves and know-how: The role of explicit versus implicit knowledge in the breakdown of a complex motor skill under pressure. *British Journal of Psychology, 83*, 343–358.

Masters, R., & Maxwell, J. (2008). The theory of reinvestment. *International Review of Sport and Exercise Psychology, 1*, 160–183.

Mathews, R. C., Buss, R. R., Stanley, W. B., Blanchard-Fields, F., Cho, J. R., & Druhan, B. (1989). Role of implicit and explicit processes in learning from examples: A synergistic effect. *Journal of Experimental Psychology: Learning, Memory, and Cognition, 15*, 1083–1100.

Matsuka, T., & Corter, J. E. (2008). Observed attention allocation processes in category learning. *Quarterly Journal of Experimental Psychology, 61*, 1067–1097.

Matthews, G., Jones, D. M., & Chamberlain, A. G. (1992). Predictors of individual differences in mail-coding skills and their variation with ability level. *Journal of Applied Psychology, 77*, 406–418.

Maxwell, J. P., Masters, R.S.W., & Eves, F. F. (2003). The role of working memory in motor learning and performance. *Consciousness and Cognition, 12*, 376–402.

Maxwell, J. P., Masters, R.S.W., Kerr, E., & Weedon, E. (2001). The implicit benefit of learning without errors. *Quarterly Journal of Experimental Psychology, 54A*, 1049–1068.

Maylor, E. A., & Rabbitt, P.M.A. (1987). Effects of practice and alcohol on performance of a perceptual-motor task. *Quarterly Journal of Experimental Psychology, 39A*, 777–795.

Maylor, E. A., & Rabbitt, P.M.A. (1988). Amount of practice and degree of attentional control have no influence on the adverse effect of alcohol in word categorization and visual search tasks. *Perception & Psychophysics, 44*, 117–126.

Maylor, E. A., Rabbitt, P.M.A., James, G. H., & Kerr, S. A. (1990). Effects of alcohol and extended practice on divided-attention performance. *Perception & Psychophysics, 48*, 445–452.

Maylor, E. A., Rabbitt, P.M.A., Sahgal, A., & Wright, C. (1987). Effects of alcohol on speed and accuracy in choice reaction time and visual search. *Acta Psychologica, 65*, 147–163.

McCann, R. S., & Johnston, J. C. (1992). Locus of the single-channel bottleneck in dual-task interference. *Journal of Experimental Psychology: Human Perception and Performance, 18*, 471–484.

McClelland, J. L. (1979). On the time relations of mental processes: An examination of systems of processes in cascade. *Psychological Review, 86*, 287–330.

McClelland, J. L. (2001). Failures to learn and their remediation: A Hebbian account. In J. L. McClelland & R. S. Siegler (Eds.), *Mechanisms of cognitive development: Behavioral and neural approaches* (pp. 97–211). Mahwah, NJ: Erlbaum.

McClelland, J. L., & Chappell, M. (1998). Familiarity breeds differentiation: A subjective-likelihood approach to the effects of experience in recognition memory. *Psychological Review, 105*, 724–760.

McClelland, J. L., Rumelhart, D. E., & the PDP Research Group (1986). *Parallel distributed processing: Explorations in the microstructure of cognition, Vol. 1: Foundations.* Cambridge, MA: MIT Press.

McClintock, A. (2012, August 2). Olympic boxing: Controversies highlight the failures of scoring system. *The Guardian: Olympics 2012.* Downloaded September 19, 2012, from http://www.guardian.co.uk/sport/blog/2012/aug/02/olympic-boxing-controversies-failures-scoring-system

McCusker, L. X., Hillinger, M. L., & Bias, R. G. (1981). Phonological recoding and reading. *Psychological Bulletin, 89*, 217–245.

McDaniel, M. A., Anderson, J. L., Derbish, M. H., & Morrisette, N. (2007). Testing the testing effect in the classroom. *European Journal of Cognitive Psychology, 19*, 494–513.

McKeithen, K. B., Reitman, J. S., Reuter, H. H., & Hirtle, S. C. (1981). Knowledge organization and skill differences in computer programmers. *Cognitive Psychology, 13*, 307–325.

McKelvie, S. J. (1984). Relationship between set and functional fixedness: A replication. *Perceptual and Motor Skills, 58*, 996–998.

McKelvie, S. J. (1985). Einstellung: Still alive and well. *Journal of General Psychology, 112*, 313–315.

McLaren, I.P.L., & Mackintosh, N. J. (2000). An elemental model of associative learning: I. Latent inhibition and perceptual learning. *Animal Learning & Behavior, 28*, 211–246.

McMillen, D. L., Smith, S. M., & Wells-Parker, E. (1989). The effects of alcohol, expectancy, and sensation seeking on driving risk taking. *Addictive Behaviors, 14*, 477–483.

McMillen, D. L., & Wells-Parker, E. (1987). The effect of alcohol consumption on risk-taking while driving. *Addictive Behaviors, 12*, 241–247.

McNamara, D. S., & McDaniel, M. A. (2004). Suppressing irrelevant information: Knowledge activation or inhibition? *Journal of Experimental Psychology: Learning, Memory, and Cognition, 30*, 465–482.

McPherson, S. L., & Vickers, J. N. (2004). Cognitive control in motor expertise. *International Journal of Sport and Exercise Psychology, 2*, 274–300.

McVay, J. C., & Kane, M. J. (2009). Conducting the train of thought: Working memory capacity, goal neglect, and mind wandering in an executive-control task. *Journal of Experimental Psychology: Learning, Memory, and Cognition, 35*, 196–204.

Mehta, M., Owen, A. M., Sahakian, B., Mavaddat, N., Pickard, J., & Robbins, T. (2000). Methylphenidate enhances working memory by modulating discrete frontal and parietal lobe regions in the human brain. *Journal of Neuroscience, 20*, RC65.

Meissner, C. A., & Brigham, J. C. (2001). Thirty years of investigating the own-race bias in memory for faces: A meta-analytic review. *Psychology, Public Policy, and Law, 7*, 3–35.

Melby-Lervåg, M., & Hulme, C. (2013). Is working memory training effective? A meta-analytic review. *Developmental Psychology, 49*, 270–291.

Melcher, J. M., & Schooler, J. W. (1996). The misremembrance of wines past: Verbal and perceptual expertise differentially mediate verbal overshadowing of taste memory. *Journal of Memory and Language, 35*, 231–245.

Melcher, J. M., & Schooler, J. W. (2004). Perceptual and conceptual training mediate the verbal overshadowing effect in an unfamiliar domain. *Memory & Cognition, 32*, 618–631.

Mella, N., Fagot, D., Lecerf, T., & de Ribaupierre, A. (2015). Working memory and intraindividual variability in processing speed: A lifespan developmental and individual-differences study. *Memory & Cognition, 43*, 340–356.

Melo, M., Scarpin, D. J., Amaro, E. J., Passos, R. D., Sato, J. R., Friston, K. J., & Price, C. J. (2011). How doctors generate diagnostic hypotheses: A study of radiological diagnosis with functional magnetic resonance imaging. *Plos ONE, 6*(12), doi:10.1371/journal.pone.0028752

Merbah, S., & Meulemans, T. (2011). Learning a motor skill: Effects of blocked versus random practice: A review. *Psychologica Belgica, 51*, 15–48.

Mesmer-Magnus, J. R., & Viswesvaran, C. (2007). Inducing maximal versus typical learning through the provision of a pre-training goal orientation. *Human Performance, 20*, 205–222.

Meyer, D. E., & Kieras, D. E. (1999). Precis to a practical unified theory of cognition and action: Some lessons from EPIC computational models of human multiple-task performance. In D. Gopher & A. Koriat (Eds.), *Attention and performance XVII* (pp. 17–88). Cambridge, MA: MIT Press.

Miller, G. A., & Isard, S. (1963). Some perceptual consequences of linguistic rules. *Journal of Verbal Learning and Verbal Behavior, 2*, 217–228.

Miller, J. (1982). Discrete versus continuous models of human information processing: In search of partial output. *Journal of Experimental Psychology: Human Perception and Performance, 8*, 273–296.

Miller, J., & Durst, M. (2015, July 13). A Comparison of the psychological refractory period and prioritized processing paradigms: Can the response-selection bottleneck model explain them both? *Journal of Experimental Psychology: Human Perception and Performance, 41*(5), 1420–1441. Downloaded from http://dx.doi.org/10.1037/xhp0000103

Miltner, W.H.R., Braun, C. H., & Coles, M.G.H. (1997). Event-related brain potentials following incorrect feedback in a time-estimation task: Evidence for a "generic" neural system for error detection. *Journal of Cognitive Neuroscience, 9*, 788–798.

Monk, T. H., Buysse, D. J., Reynolds, C. F., Berga, S. L., Jarrett, D. B., Begley, A. E., & Kupfer, D. J. (1997). Circadian rhythms in human performance and mood under constant conditions. *Journal of Sleep Research, 6*, 9–18.

Monk, T. H., & Kupfer, D. J. (2007). Which aspects of morningness-eveningness change with age? *Journal of Biological Rhythms, 22*, 278–280.

Monk, T. H., & Leng, V. C. (1982). Time of day effects in simple repetitive tasks: Some possible mechanisms. *Acta Psychologica, 51*, 207–221.

Moran, J., & Desimone, R. (1985). Selective attention gates visual processing in the extrastriate cortex. *Science, 229*, 782–784.

Moreau, D., Clerc, J., Mansy-Dannay, A., & Guerrien, A. (2012). Enhancing spatial ability through sport practice: Evidence for an effect of motor training on mental rotation performance. *Journal of Individual Differences, 33*, 83–88.

Morris, M. A., & Robie, C. (2001). A meta-analysis of the effects of cross-cultural training on expatriate performance and adjustment. *International Journal of Training and Development, 5*, 112–125.

Moruzzi, G., & Magoun, E. W. (1949). Brain-stem reticular formation and activation of the EEG. *Electroencephalography and Clinical Neurophysiology, 1*, 455–473.

Mowbray, G. H., & Rhoades, M. V. (1959). On the reduction of choice reaction times with practice. *Quarterly Journal of Experimental Psychology, 11*, 16–23.

Moylan, C. (2011). How to reverse Lion's mouse scrolling back to Snow Leopard's. Posted in OS X on July 20. Downloaded on May 24, 2013, from http://www.mactrast.com/2011/07/how-to-reverse-lions-mouse-scrolling-back-to-snow-leopards/

Murphy, K., & Spencer, A. (2009). Playing video games does not make for better visual attention skills. *Journal of Articles in Support of the Null Hypothesis, 6*, 1–20.

Myers, C. W., & Gray, W. D. (2010). Visual scan adaptation during repeated visual search. *Journal of Vision, 10*, 4, doi:10.1167/10.8.4

Nakashima, R., Watanabe, C., Maeda, E., Yoshikawa, T., Matsuda, I., Miki, S., & Yokosawa, K. (2015). The effect of expert knowledge on medical search: Medical experts have specialized abilities for detecting serious lesions. *Psychological Research, 79*, 729–738.

National Transportation Safety Board. (2014). Crash of Asiana flight 214 accident report summary. Public meeting of June 24. Downloaded from http://www.ntsb.gov/news/events/2014/asiana214/abstract.html

Naumann, J., Richter, T., Christmann, U., & Groeben, N. (2008). Working memory capacity and reading skill moderate the effectiveness of strategy training in learning from hypertext. *Learning and Individual Differences, 18*, 197–213.

Navon, D., & Gopher, D. (1979). On the economy of the human-processing system. *Psychological Review, 86*, 214–255.

Navon, D., & Miller, J. (2002). Queuing or sharing? A critical evaluation of the single-bottleneck notion. *Cognitive Psychology, 44*, 193–251.

Neily, J., Mills, P. D., Young-Xu, Y., Carney, B. T., West, P., Berger, D. H., . . . Bagian, J. P. (2010). Association between implementation of a medical team training program and surgical mortality. *JAMA, 304*, 1693–1700.

Neiss, R. (1988). Reconceptualizing arousal: Psychobiological states in motor performance. *Psychological Bulletin, 103*, 345–366.

Neisser, U. (1963). Decision-time without reaction-time: Experiments in visual scanning. *American Journal of Psychology, 76*, 376–385.
Neisser, U., Novick, R., & Lazar, R. (1963). Searching for ten targets simultaneously. *Perceptual and Motor Skills, 17*, 955–961.
Neubauer, A. C., & Fink, A. (2009). Intelligence and neural efficiency. *Neuroscience and Biobehavioral Reviews, 33*, 1004–1023.
Neubauer, A. C., Fink, A., & Schrausser, D. G. (2002). Intelligence and neural efficiency: The influence of task content and sex on the brain-IQ relationship. *Intelligence, 30*, 515–536.
Neubauer, A. C., Grabner, R. H., Freudenthaler, H., Beckmann, J. F., & Guthke, J. (2004). Intelligence and individual differences in becoming neurally efficient. *Acta Psychologica, 116*, 55–74.
Neubauer, A. C., Sange, G., & Pfurtscheller, G. (1999). Psychometric intelligence and event-related desynchronisation during performance of a letter matching task. In G. Pfurtscheller & F. H. Lopes da Silva (Eds.), *Event-related desynchronization (ERD) and related oscillatory EEG-phenomena of the awake brain* (pp. 219–231). Amsterdam: Elsevier.
Neumann, O. (1987). Beyond capacity: A functional view of attention. In H. Heuer & A. F. Sanders (Eds.), *Perspectives on perception and action* (pp. 361–394). Hillsdale, NJ: Erlbaum.
Neves, D. M., & Anderson, J. R. (1981). Knowledge compilation: Mechanisms for the automatization of cognitive skills. In J. R. Anderson (Ed.), *Cognitive skills and their acquisition* (pp. 57–84). Hillsdale, NJ: Lawrence Erlbaum.
Newell, A. (1980). Reasoning, problem solving, and decision processes: The problem space as a fundamental category. In R. S. Nickerson (Ed.), *Attention and performance VIII* (pp. 693–718). Hillsdale, NJ: Lawrence Erlbaum.
Newell, A. (1990). *Unified theories of cognition*. Cambridge, MA: Harvard University Press.
Newell, A., & Rosenbloom, P. S. (1981). Mechanisms of skill acquisition and the law of practice. In J. R. Anderson (Ed.), *Cognitive skills and their acquisition* (pp. 1–55). Hillsdale, NJ: Lawrence Erlbaum.
Newell, A., & Simon, H. A. (1972). *Human problem solving*. Englewood Cliffs, NJ: Prentice Hall.
Newell, K. M. (1986). Constraints on the development of coordination. In M. G. Wade & H. T. A. Whiting (Eds.), *Motor development in children: Aspects of coordination and control* (pp. 341–360). Dordrecht, Germany: Martinus Nijhoff.
Newell, K. M. (1991). Motor skill acquisition. *Annual Review of Psychology, 42*, 213–237.
Newell, K. M., Sparrow, W. A., & Quinn, J. T., Jr. (1985). Kinetic information feedback for learning isometric tasks. *Journal of Human Movement Studies, 11*, 113–123.
Newell, K. M., & Walter, C. B. (1981). Kinematic and kinetic parameters as information feedback in motor skill acquisition. *Journal of Human Movement Studies, 7*, 235–254.
Nieuwenhuis, S., Holroyd, C. B., Mol, N., & Coles, M. G. (2004). Reinforcement-related brain potentials from medial frontal cortex: Origins and functional significance. *Neuroscience and Biobehavioral Reviews, 28*, 441–448.
Nishi, K., & Kewley-Port, D. (2007). Training Japanese listeners to perceive American English vowels: Influence of training sets. *Journal of Speech, Language, and Hearing Research, 50*, 1496–1509.

Nissan, J., Liewald, D., & Deary, I. J. (2013). Reaction time and intelligence: Comparing associations based on two response modes. *Intelligence, 41,* 622–630.

Nissen, M. J., & Bullemer, P. (1987). Attentional requirements of learning: Evidence from performance measures. *Cognitive Psychology, 19,* 1–32.

Noe, R. A. (1986). Trainees' attributes and attitudes: Neglected influences on training effectiveness. *Academy of Management Review, 11,* 736–749.

Nokes, T. J., & Ash, I. K. (2009). Investigating the role of instructional focus in incidental pattern learning. *Journal of General Psychology, 137,* 84–113.

Nokes-Malach, T. J., VanLehn, K., Belenky, D. M., Lichtenstein, M., & Cox, G. (2013). Coordinating principles and examples through analogy and self-explanation. *European Journal of Psychology of Education, 28,* 1237–1263.

Norman, D. A. (1968). Toward a theory of memory and attention. *Psychological Review, 75,* 522–536.

Norman, D. A. (1981). Categorization of action slips. *Psychological Review, 88,* 1–15.

Norman, D. A., & Bobrow, D. J. (1975). On data-limited and resource-limited processes. *Cognitive Psychology, 7,* 44–64.

Norman, D. A., & Shallice, T. (1986). Attention to action: Willed and automatic control of behavior. In R. J. Davidson, G. E. Schwartz, & D. Shapiro (Eds.), *Consciousness and self-regulation: Advances in research and theory* (Vol. 4, pp. 1–18). New York: Plenum Press.

Norman, G. R., & Schmidt, H. G. (1992). The psychological basis of problem-based learning: A review of the evidence. *Academic Medicine, 67,* 557–565.

Norris, J., & Ortega, L. (2000). Effectiveness of L2 instruction: A research synthesis and quantitative meta-analysis. *Language Learning, 50,* 417–528.

Nosofsky, R. M. (1986). Attention, similarity, and identification-categorization relationship. *Journal of Experimental Psychology: General, 115,* 39–57.

Nosofsky, R. M. (2011). The generalized context model: An exemplar model of classification. In E. M. Pothos & A. J. Wills (Eds.), *Formal approaches in categorization* (pp. 18–39). New York: Cambridge University Press.

Novick, L. R., & Holyoak, K. J. (1991). Mathematical problem solving by analogy. *Journal of Experimental Psychology: Learning, Memory, and Cognition, 17,* 398–415.

Oakhill, J. (1988). Effects of time of day on text memory and inference. In M. Gruneberg, P. Morris, & R, Sykes (Eds.), *Practical aspects of memory: Current research and issues* (pp. 465–470). New York: John Wiley.

Oberauer, K., & Kliegl, R. (2004). Simultaneous cognitive operations in working memory after dual-task practice. *Journal of Experimental Psychology: Human Perception and Performance, 30,* 689–707.

Oberauer, K., & Meyer, N. (2009). The contributions of encoding, retention, and recall to the Hebb effect. *Memory, 17,* 774–781.

O'Connor, P., Campbell, J., Newon, J., Melton, J., Salas, E., & Wilson, K. A. (2008). Crew resource management training effectiveness: A meta-analysis and some critical needs. *International Journal of Aviation Psychology, 18,* 353–368.

O'Connor, P., & Long, W. (2011). The development of a prototype behavioral marker system for US Navy officers of the deck. *Safety Science, 49,* 1381–1387.

O'Doherty, J. P., Dayan, P., Friston, K., Critchley, H., & Dolan, R. J. (2003). Temporal difference models and reward-related learning in the human brain. *Neuron, 38,* 329–337.

Ohlsson, S. (1996). Learning from performance errors. *Psychological Review, 103*, 241–262.

Öhman, A., Flykt, A., & Esteves, F. (2001). Emotion drives attention: Detecting the snake in the grass. *Journal of Experimental Psychology: General, 130*, 466–478.

Olson, J. R., & Biolsi, K. J. (1991). Techniques for representing expert knowledge. In K. A. Ericsson & J. Smith (Eds.), *Toward a general theory of expertise: Prospects and limits* (pp. 240–285). New York: Cambridge University Press.

Opitz, B., & Hofmann, J. (2015). Concurrence of rule- and similarity-based mechanisms in artificial grammar learning. *Cognitive Psychology, 77*, 77–99.

Ost, J., Vrij, A., Costall, A., & Bull, R. (2002). Crashing memories and reality monitoring: Distinguishing between perceptions, imaginations and "false memories." *Applied Cognitive Psychology, 16*, 125–134.

Owen, A. M., Hampshire, A., Grahn, J. A., Stenton, R., Dajani, S., Burns, A. S., . . . Ballard, C. G. (2010). Putting brain training to the test. *Nature, 465*(7299), 775–778.

Ozcinar, Z. (2009). The topic of instructional design in research journals: A citation analysis for the years 1980–2008. *Australasian Journal of Educational Technology, 25*, 559–580.

Paas, F., & Ayres, P. (2014). Cognitive load theory: A broader view on the role of memory in learning and education. *Educational Psychology Review, 26*, 191–195.

Paas, F., & van Gog, T. (2006). Optimising worked example instruction: Different ways to increase germane cognitive load. *Learning and Instruction, 16*, 87–91.

Paas, F., van Gog, T., & Sweller, J. (2010). Cognitive load theory: New conceptualizations, specifications, and integrated research perspectives. *Educational Psychology Review, 22*, 115–121.

Paas, F. C., & van Merriënboer, J. G. (1994). Instructional control of cognitive load in the training of complex cognitive tasks. *Educational Psychology Review, 6*, 351–371.

Palmer, E. M., Fencsik, D. E., Flusberg, S. J., Horowitz, T. S., & Wolfe, J. M. (2011). Signal detection evidence for limited capacity in visual search. *Attention, Perception, & Psychophysics, 73*, 2413–2424.

Parmentier, F.B.R., Maybery, M. T., Huitson, M., & Jones, D. M. (2008). The perceptual determinants of repetition learning in auditory space. *Journal of Memory and Language, 58*, 978–997.

Parr, W. V., Heatherbell, D., & White, K. G. (2002). Demystifying wine expertise: Olfactory threshold, perceptual skill and semantic memory in expert and novice wine judges. *Chemical Senses, 27*, 747–755.

Pashler, H. A. (1984). Processing stages in overlapping tasks: Evidence for a central bottleneck. *Journal of Experimental Psychology: Human Perception and Performance, 10*, 358–377.

Pashler, H., & Baylis, G. C. (1991a). Procedural learning: 1. Locus of practice effects in speeded choice tasks. *Journal of Experimental Psychology: Learning, Memory, and Cognition, 17*, 20–32.

Pashler, H., & Baylis, G. C. (1991b). Procedural learning: 2. Intertrial repetition effects in speeded-choice tasks. *Journal of Experimental Psychology: Learning, Memory, and Cognition, 17*, 33–48.

Pashler, H., Cepeda, N., Wixted, J., & Rohrer, D. (2005). When does feedback facilitate learning of words? *Journal of Experimental Psychology: Learning, Memory, and Cognition, 31,* 3–8.

Pashler, H., Rohrer, D., Cepeda, N. J., & Carpenter, S. K. (2007). Enhancing learning and retarding forgetting: Choices and consequences. *Psychonomic Bulletin & Review, 14,* 187–193.

Patrick, J. (1992). *Training: Research and practice.* London: Academic Press.

Pavlik, P. I., & Anderson, J. R. (2008). Using a model to compute the optimal schedule of practice. *Journal of Experimental Psychology: Applied, 14,* 101–117.

Payne, S. J., Squibb, H. R., & Howes, A. (1990). The nature of device models: The yoked state space hypothesis and some experiments with text editors. *Human-Computer Interaction, 5,* 415–444.

Pear, T. H. (1948). Professor Bartlett on skill. *Occupational Psychology, 22,* 92–93.

Pellegrino, J. W., Doane, S. M., Fischer, S. C., & Alderton, D. (1991). Stimulus complexity effects in visual comparisons: The effects of practice and learning context. *Journal of Experimental Psychology: Human Perception and Performance, 17,* 781–791.

Penke, L., Maniega, S., Murray, C., Gow, A. J., Hernández, M., Clayden, J. D., . . . Deary, I. J. (2010). A general factor of brain white matter integrity predicts information processing speed in healthy older people. *Journal of Neuroscience, 30,* 7569–7574.

Perfetti, C. (2007). Reading ability: Lexical quality to comprehension. *Scientific Studies of Reading, 11,* 357–383.

Perruchet, P., & Amorim, M. A. (1992). Conscious knowledge and changes in performance sequence learning: Evidence against dissociation. *Journal of Experimental Psychology: Learning, Memory, and Cognition, 18,* 785–800.

Perry, D. H., & Naish, J. M. (1964). Flight simulation for research. *Journal of the Royal Aeronautical Society, 68,* 645–662.

Petre, M. (1991). What experts want from programming languages. *Ergonomics, 34,* 1113–1127.

Pew, R. W. (1966). Acquisition of hierarchical control over the temporal organization of a skill. *Journal of Experimental Psychology, 71,* 764–771.

Pidd, K. (2004). The impact of workplace support and identity on training transfer: A case study of drug and alcohol safety training in Australia. *International Journal of Training and Development, 8,* 274–288.

Pirolli, P., & Recker, M. (1994). Learning strategies and transfer in the domain of programming. *Cognition and Instruction, 12,* 235–275.

Plomin, R., Shakeshaft, N. G., McMillan, A., & Trzaskowski, M. (2014). Nature, nurture, and expertise. *Intelligence, 45,* 46–55.

Poggio, T., & Edelman, S. (1990). A network that learns to recognize three-dimensional objects. *Nature, 343,* 263–266.

Poggio, T., Fahle, M., & Edelman, S. (1992). Fast perceptual learning in visual hyperacuity. *Science, 256,* 1018–1021.

Poldrack, R. A., Prabhakaran, V., Seger, C. A., & Gabrieli, J. E. (1999). Striatal activation during acquisition of a cognitive skill. *Neuropsychology, 13,* 564–574.

Polich, J. (1993). Cognitive brain potentials. *Current Directions in Psychological Science, 2*(6), 175–179.

Polich, J. (2007). Updating P300: An integrative theory of P3a and P3b. *Clinical Neurophysiology, 118*, 2128–2148.

Polich, J., & Kok, A. (1995). Cognitive and biological determinants of P300: An integrative review. *Biological Psychology, 41*, 103–146.

Posner, M. I., & Mitchell, R. F. (1967). Chronometric analysis of classification. *Psychological Review, 74*, 392–409.

Posner, M. I., & Snyder, C. R. R. (1975). Attention and cognitive control. In R. L. Solso (Ed.), *Information processing and cognition: The Loyola symposium* (pp. 55–85). Hillsdale, NJ: Lawrence Erlbaum.

Pothos, E. M. (2007). Theories of artificial grammar learning. *Psychological Bulletin, 133*, 227–244.

Potts, R., & Shanks, D. R. (2014). The benefit of generating errors during learning. *Journal of Experimental Psychology: General, 143*, 644–667.

Povel, D.-J., & Collard, R. (1982). Structural factors in patterned finger tapping. *Acta Psychologica, 52*, 107–123.

Powers, K. L., Brooks, P. J., Aldrich, N. J., Palladino, M. A., & Alfieri, L. (2013). Effects of video-game play on information processing: A meta-analytic investigation. *Psychonomic Bulletin & Review, 20*, 1055–1079.

Priest, A. G., & Lindsay, R. O. (1992). New light on novice-expert differences in physics problem solving. *British Journal of Psychology, 83*, 389–405.

Prilutsky, B. I., & Zatsiorsky, V. M. (2002). Optimization-based models of muscle coordination. *Exercise and Sport Sciences Reviews, 30*, 32–38.

Prinz, W., Aschersleben, G., Hommel, B., & Vogt, S. (1995). Handlungen als Ereignisse [Actions as events]. In D. Dörner & E. van der Meer (Eds.), *DasGedächtnis: Probleme, Trends, Perspektiven* (pp. 129–168). Göttingen: Hogrefe.

Pritchard, S. C., Coltheart, M., Palethorpe, S., & Castles, A. (2012). Nonword reading: Comparing dual-route cascaded and connectionist dual-process models with human data. *Journal of Experimental Psychology: Human Perception and Performance, 38*, 1268–1288.

Proctor, R. W., & Lu, C.-H. (1999). Processing irrelevant location information: Practice and transfer effects in choice-reaction tasks. *Memory & Cognition, 27*, 63–77.

Proctor, R. W., & Reeve, T. G. (1988). The acquisition of task-specific productions and modification of declarative representations in spatial-precuing tasks. *Journal of Experimental Psychology: General, 117*, 182–196.

Proctor, R. W., Reeve, T. G., Weeks, D. J., Dornier, L., & Van Zandt, T. (1991). Acquisition, retention, and transfer of response selection skill in choice reaction tasks. *Journal of Experimental Psychology: Learning, Memory, and Cognition, 17*, 497–506.

Proffitt, D. R. (2008). An action-specific approach to spatial perception. In R. L. Klatzky, B. MacWhinney, & M. Behrman (Eds.), *Embodiment, ego-space, and action* (pp. 179–202). New York: Psychology Press.

Proteau, L., & Cournoyer, J. (1990). Vision of the stylus in a manual aiming task. *Quarterly Journal of Experimental Psychology, 42A*, 811–828.

Puck, J. F., Kittler, M. G., & Wright, C. (2008). Does it really work? Re-assessing the impact of pre-departure cross-cultural training on expatriate adjustment. *International Journal of Human Resource Management, 19*, 2182–2197.

Quiñones, M. A. (1997). Contextual influences on training effectiveness. In M. A. Quiñones & A. Ehrenstein (Eds.), *Training for a rapidly changing workplace:*

Applications of psychological research (pp. 177–199). Washington, DC: American Psychological Association.

Rabbitt, P. M. A. (1968). Repetition effects and signal classification strategies in serial choice-response tasks. *Quarterly Journal of Experimental Psychology, 20*, 232–240.

Rabbitt, P. M. A. (1979). Current paradigms and models in human information processing. In V. S. Hamilton & D. Warburton (Eds.), *Human stress and cognition* (pp. 115–140). New York: John Wiley.

Rabbitt, P. M. A. (1989). Sequential reactions. In D. H. Holding (Ed.), *Human skills* (2nd ed., pp. 147–170). New York: John Wiley.

Rabbitt, P. M. A. (1990). Age, IQ and awareness, and recall of errors. *Ergonomics, 33*, 1291–1305.

Rabbitt, P. M. A., & Vyas, S. (1979). Signal recency effects can be distinguished from signal repetition effects in serial CRT tasks. *Canadian Journal of Psychology, 33*, 88–95.

Rabin, M. D. (1988). Experience facilitates olfactory quality discrimination. *Perception & Psychophysics, 44*, 532–540.

Rabipour, S., & Davidson, P. S. (2015). Do you believe in brain training? A questionnaire about expectations of computerised cognitive training. *Behavioural Brain Research, 295*, 64–70. doi:10.1016/j.bbr.2015.01.002

Rabipour, S., & Raz, A. (2012). Training the brain: Fact and fad in cognitive and behavioral remediation. *Brain and Cognition, 79*, 159–179.

Ramsey, C. S., Werchan, P. M., Isdahl, W. M., Fischer, J., & Gibbons, J. A. (2008). Acceleration tolerance at night with acute fatigue and stimulants. *Aviation, Space, and Environmental Medicine, 79*, 769–773.

Ramsey, J. D. (1983). Heat and cold. In R. Hockey (Ed.), *Stress and fatigue in human performance* (pp. 33–60). New York: John Wiley.

Rasmussen, J. (1986). *Information processing and human-machine interaction: An approach to cognitive engineering*. Amsterdam: North-Holland.

Rawson, K. A., & Van Overschelde, J. P. (2008). How does knowledge promote memory? The distinctiveness theory of skilled memory. *Journal of Memory and Language, 58*, 646–668.

Raymond, W. D., Healy, A. F., & Bourne, L. E., Jr. (2012). A new taxonomy for training. In A. F. Healy & L. E. Bourne, Jr. (Eds.), *Training cognition: Optimizing efficiency, durability, and generalizability* (pp. 156–181). New York: Psychology Press.

Reason, J. T. (1979). Actions not as planned: The price of automatization. In G. Underwood & R. Stevens (Eds.), *Aspects of consciousness* (pp. 67–89). London: Academic Press.

Reason, J. T. (2013). *A life in error: From little slips to big disasters*. Burlington, VT: Ashgate.

Reber, A. S. (1967). Implicit learning of artificial grammars. *Journal of Verbal Learning and Verbal Behavior, 77*, 317–327.

Reber, A. S. (1976). Implicit learning of synthetic languages: The role of instructional set. *Journal of Experimental Psychology: Human Learning and Memory, 2*, 88–94.

Reber, A. S. (1989). Implicit learning and tacit knowledge. *Journal of Experimental Psychology: General, 118*, 219–235.

Reber, A. S., Kassin, S. M., Lewis, S., & Cantor, G. W. (1980). On the relationship between implicit and explicit modes in the learning of a complex rule structure. *Journal of Experimental Psychology: Human Learning and Memory, 6*, 492–502.

Redick, T. S., Shipstead, Z., Wiemers, E. A., Melby-Lervåg, M., & Hulme, C. (2015). What's working in working memory training? An educational perspective. *Educational Psychology Review, 27*, 617–633. doi:10.1007/s10648–015–9314–6

Reeve, T. G., & Proctor, R. W. (1984). On the advance preparation of discrete finger responses. *Journal of Experimental Psychology: Human Perception and Performance, 10*, 541–553.

Regina, E. G., Smith, G. M., Keiper, C. G., & McKelvey, R. K. (1974). Effects of caffeine on alertness in simulated automobile driving. *Journal of Applied Psychology, 59*, 483–489.

Reicher, G. M. (1969). Perceptual recognition as a function of meaningfulness of stimulus material. *Journal of Experimental Psychology, 81*, 275–280.

Reilly, T. (2009a). The body clock and athletic performance. *Biological Rhythm Research, 40*, 37–44.

Reilly, T. (2009b). How can travelling athletes deal with jet-lag? *Kinesiology, 41*, 128–135.

Reingold, E. M., & Sheridan, H. (2011). Eye movements and visual expertise in chess and medicine. In S. P. Liversedge, I. D. Gilchrist, & S. Everling (Eds.), *Oxford handbook on eye movements* (pp. 528–550). Oxford: Oxford University Press.

Reitman, J. S., & Reuter, H. R. (1980). Organization revealed by recall orders and confirmed by pauses. *Cognitive Psychology, 12*, 554–581.

Renkl, A. (2002). Worked-out examples: Instructional explanations support learning by self-explanations. *Learning and Instruction, 12*, 529–556.

Renkl, A., Mandl, H., & Gruber, H. (1996). Inert knowledge: Analyses and remedies. *Educational Psychologist, 31*, 115–121.

Rescorla, R. A., & Wagner, A. D. (1972). A theory of Pavlovian conditioning; Variations in the effectiveness of reinforcement and nonreinforcement. In A. H. Black & W. F. Prokasy (Eds.), *Classical conditioning II* (pp. 64–99). New York: Appleton-Century-Crofts.

Reynolds, J. H., Chelazzi, L., & Desimone, R. (1999). Competitive mechanisms subserve attention in macaque areas V2 and V4. *Journal of Neuroscience, 19*, 1736–1753.

Reynolds, J. H., & Desimone, R. (2003). Interacting roles of attention and visual salience in V4. *Neuron, 37*, 853–863.

Rickard, T. C. (2005). A revised identical elements model of arithmetic fact representation. *Journal of Experimental Psychology: Learning, Memory, and Cognition, 31*, 250–257.

Rieger, M. (2004). Automatic keypress activation in skilled typing. *Journal of Experimental Psychology: Human Perception and Performance, 30*, 555–565.

Riggio, L., Gawryszewski, L. G., & Umiltà, C. (1986). What is crossed in crossed-hand effects? *Acta Psychologica, 62*, 89–100.

Riggio, R. E., & Tan, S. J. (2014). *Leader interpersonal and influence skills: The soft skills of leadership*. New York: Routledge.

Roberson, D., & Davidoff, J. (2000). The categorical perception of colors and facial expressions: The effect of verbal interference. *Memory & Cognition, 28*, 977–986.

Robertson, E. M., Pascual-Leone, A., & Press, D. Z. (2004). Awareness modifies the skill-learning benefits of sleep. *Current Biology, 14*, 208–212.

Roediger, H. L., & Karpicke, J. D. (2006). The power of testing memory: Basic research and implications for educational practice. *Perspectives on Psychological Science, 1,* 181–210.

Roediger, H. L., & Marsh, E. J. (2005). The positive and negative consequences of multiple-choice testing. *Journal of Experimental Psychology: Learning, Memory and Cognition, 31,* 1155–1159.

Roger, C., Bénar, C. G., Vidal, F., Hasbroucq, T., & Burle, B. (2010). Rostral cingulate zone and correct response monitoring: ICA and source localization evidences for the unicity of correct- and error-negativities. *Neuroimage, 51,* 391–403.

Rogers, C. R., & Freiberg, H. J. (1994). *Freedom to learn* (3rd ed.). Columbus, OH: Merrill/Macmillan.

Rohrer, D. (2009). Avoidance of overlearning characterises the spacing effect. *European Journal of Cognitive Psychology, 21,* 1001–1012.

Rohrer, D., Taylor, K., Pashler, H., Wixted, J. T., & Cepeda, N. J. (2005). The effect of overlearning on long-term retention. *Applied Cognitive Psychology, 19,* 361–374.

Rolls, E. T. (2008). Face processing in different brain areas, and critical band masking. *Journal of Neuropsychology, 2,* 325–360.

Romero, P., Du Boulay, B., Cox, R., Lutz, R., & Bryant, S. (2007). Debugging strategies and tactics in a multirepresentation software environment. *International Journal of Human-Computer Studies, 61,* 992–1009.

Roscoe, S. N. (1980). *Aviation psychology*. Ames: Iowa State University Press.

Rosenbaum, D. A. (2002). Motor control. In H. Pashler & S. Yantis (Eds.), *Stevens' handbook of experimental psychology, Vol. 1: Sensation and perception* (3rd ed., pp. 315–339). Hoboken, NJ: John Wiley.

Rosenbaum, D. A., Cohen, R. G., Jax, S. A., Weiss, D. J., & van der Wel, R. (2007). The problem of serial order in behavior: Lashley's legacy. *Human Movement Science, 26,* 525–554.

Rosenbaum, D. A., Weber, R. J., Hazelett, W. M., & Hindorff, V. (1986). The parameter remapping effect in human performance: Evidence from tongue twisters and finger fumblers. *Journal of Memory and Language, 25,* 710–725.

Rosenholtz, R., Li, Y., & Nakano, L. (2007). Measuring visual clutter. *Journal of Vision, 7*(2):17, 1–22.

Ross, B. H. (1987). This is like that: The use of earlier problems and the separation of similarity effects. *Journal of Experimental Psychology: Learning, Memory, and Cognition, 13,* 629–639.

Rosser, J. C., Jr., Lynch, P. J., Cuddihy, L., Gentile, D. A., Klonsky, J., & Merrell, R. (2007). The impact of video games on training surgeons in the 21st century. *Archives of Surgery, 142,* 181–186.

Rossion, B., & Curran, T. (2010). Visual expertise with pictures of cars correlates with RT magnitude of the car inversion effect. *Perception, 39,* 173–183.

Rostami, M., Hadi Hosseini, S. M., Takahashi, M., Sugiura, M., & Kawashima, R. (2009). Neural bases of goal-directed implicit learning. *Neuroimage, 48,* 303–310.

Roth, E. M. (2008). Uncovering the requirements of cognitive work. *Human Factors, 50,* 475–480.

Rouiller, J. Z., & Goldstein, I. L. (1993). The relationship between organizational transfer climate and positive transfer of training. *Human Resource Development Quarterly, 4,* 377–390.

Rowold, J. (2007). The impact of personality on training-related aspects of motivation: Test of a longitudinal model. *Human Resource Development Quarterly, 18*, 9–31.

Rowold, J., & Kauffeld, S. (2009). Effects of career-related continuous learning on competencies. *Personnel Review, 38*, 90–101.

Roy-Charland, A., & Saint-Aubin, J. (2006). The interaction of word frequency and word class: A test of the GO model's account of the missing-letter effect. *Quarterly Journal of Experimental Psychology, 59*, 38–45.

Roy-Charland, A., Saint-Aubin, J., Klein, R. M., & Lawrence, M. (2007). Eye movements as direct tests of the GO model for the missing-letter effect. *Perception & Psychophysics, 69*, 324–337.

Rueda, M. R., Fan, J., McCandliss, B. D., Halparin, J. D., Gruber, D. B., Lercari, L. P., & Posner, M. I. (2004). Development of attentional networks in childhood. *Neuropsychologia, 42*, 1029–1040.

Rumelhart, D. E., & Norman, D. A. (1982). Simulating a skilled typist: A study of skilled cognitive-motor performance. *Cognitive Science, 6*, 1–36.

Russ-Eft, D. (2002). A typology of training design and work environment factors affecting workplace learning and transfer. *Human Resource Development Review, 1*, 45–65.

Ruthruff, E., Van Selst, M., Johnston, J. C., & Remington, R. (2006). How does practice reduce dual-task interference: Integration, automatization, or just stage-shortening? *Psychological Research, 70*, 125–142.

Rybowiak, V., Garst, H., Frese, M., & Batinic, B. (1999). Error Orientation Questionnaire (EOQ): Reliability, validity, and different language equivalence. *Journal of Organizational Behavior, 20*, 527–547.

Saariluoma, P. (1984). *Coding problem spaces in chess: A psychological study.* Helsinki: Societas Scientarium Fennica.

Saariluoma, P. (1992). Visuospatial and articulatory interference in chess players' information intake. *Applied Cognitive Psychology, 6*, 77–89.

Sahakian, B., & Morein-Zamir, S. (2007). Professor's little helper. *Nature, 450*, 1157–1159.

Salas, E., Burke, C., Wilson-Donnelly, K. A., & Fowlkes, J. E. (2004). Promoting effective leadership within multicultural teams: An event-based approach. In D. V. Day, S. J. Zaccaro, & S. M. Halpin (Eds.), *Leader development for transforming organizations: Growing leaders for tomorrow* (pp. 293–323). Mahwah, NJ: Lawrence Erlbaum.

Salas, E., & Cannon-Bowers, J. A. (1997). Methods, tools, and strategies for team training. In M. A. Quiñones & A. Ehrenstein (Eds.), *Training for a rapidly changing workplace: Applications of psychological research* (pp. 249–279). Washington, DC: American Psychological Association.

Salas, E., DiazGranados, D., Klein, C., Burke, C., Stagl, K., Goodwin, G., & Halpin, S. (2008). Does team training improve team performance? A meta-analysis. *Human Factors, 50*, 903–933.

Salas, E., Wilson, K. A., Priest, H. A., & Guthrie, J. W. (2006). Design, delivery, and evaluation of training systems. In G. Salvendy (Ed.), *Handbook of human factors and ergonomics* (3rd ed., pp. 472–512). Hoboken, NJ: John Wiley.

Salmoni, A. W., Schmidt, R. A., & Walter, C. B. (1984). Knowledge of results and motor learning: A review and critical reappraisal. *Psychological Bulletin, 95*, 355–386.

Salthouse, T. A. (1984). Effects of age and skill in typing. *Journal of Experimental Psychology: General, 113*, 345–371.

Salthouse, T. A. (1985). *A theory of cognitive aging*. Amsterdam: North-Holland.

Salthouse, T. A. (1986). Perceptual, cognitive, and motoric aspects of transcription typing. *Psychological Bulletin, 99*, 303–319.

Salthouse, T. A. (1989). Aging and skilled performance. In A. M. Colley & J. R. Beech (Eds.), *Acquisition and performance of cognitive skills* (pp. 247–264). Chichester, UK: John Wiley.

Salthouse, T. A. (2006). Mental exercise and mental aging. *Perspectives on Psychological Science, 1*, 68–87.

Salthouse, T. A., Kausler, D. H., & Saults, J. S. (1988). Investigation of student status, background variables, and the feasibility of standard tasks in cognitive aging research. *Psychology and Aging, 3*, 29–37.

Salthouse, T. A., & Madden, D. J. (2008). Information processing speed and aging. In J. DeLuca & J. H. Kalmar (Eds.), *Information processing speed in clinical populations* (pp. 221–241). Philadelphia, PA: Taylor & Francis.

Salthouse, T. A., & Saults, J. S. (1987). Multiple spans in transcription typing. *Journal of Applied Psychology, 72*, 187–196.

Salthouse, T. A., & Somberg, B. L. (1982). Skilled performance: Effects of adult age and experience on elementary processes. *Journal of Experimental Psychology, General, 111*, 176–207.

Saltzman, E. L., & Munhall, K. G. (1992). Skill acquisition and development: The roles of state-, parameter-, and graph-dynamics. *Journal of Motor Behavior, 24*, 49–57.

Salvucci, D. D., & Taatgen, N. A. (2008). Threaded cognition: An integrated theory of concurrent multitasking. *Psychological Review, 115*, 101–130.

Sanders, A. F. (1998). *Elements of human performance*. Mahwah, NJ: Lawrence Erlbaum.

Sarter, N. (2007). Multiple-resource theory as a basis for multimodal interface design: Success stories, qualifications, and research needs. In A. F. Kramer, D. A. Wiegmann, & A. Kirlik (Eds.), *Attention: From theory to practice* (pp. 187–195). New York: Oxford University Press.

Sasaki, Y., Náñez, J., & Watanabe, T. (2012). Recent progress in perceptual learning research. *WIREs Cognitive Science, 3*, 293–299. doi:10.1002/wcs.1175

Sauter, D. A., LeGuen, O., & Haun, D. M. (2011). Categorical perception of emotional facial expressions does not require lexical categories. *Emotion, 11*, 1479–1483.

Schank, R. (1986). *Explanation patterns: Understanding mechanically and creatively*. Hillsdale, NJ: Lawrence Erlbaum.

Scherbaum, C. A., & Goldstein, H. W. (2015). Intelligence and the modern world of work. *Human Resource Management Review, 25*, 1–3.

Scherbaum, C. A., Goldstein, H. W., Yusko, K. P., Ryan, R., & Hanges, P. J. (2012). Intelligence 2.0: Reestablishing a research program on g in I-O psychology. *Industrial and Organizational Psychology: Perspectives on Science and Practice, 5*, 128–148.

Schmidt, R. A. (1975). A schema theory of discrete motor skill learning. *Psychological Review, 82*, 225–260.

Schmidt, R. A., & Bjork, R. A. (1992). New conceptualizations of practice: Common principles in three paradigms suggest new concepts for training. *Psychological Science, 3*, 207–217.

Schmidt, R. A., & Lee, T. D. (2011). *Motor control and learning: A behavioral emphasis* (5th ed.). Champaign, IL: Human Kinetics.

Schmidt, R. A., Young, D. E., Swinnen, S., & Shapiro, D. D. (1989). Summary knowledge of results for skill acquisition: Support for the guidance hypothesis. *Journal of Experimental Psychology: Learning, Memory, and Cognition, 15,* 352–359.

Schmitt, N. (Ed.) (2012). *The Oxford handbook of personnel assessment and selection.* New York: Oxford University Press.

Schneider, D. W., & Anderson, J. R. (2011). A memory-based model of Hick's law. *Cognitive Psychology, 62,* 193–222.

Schneider, W. (1989). *Getting smart quicker: Training more skills in less time.* Transcript of Science and Public Policy Seminar presented by the Federation of Behavioral, Psychological, and Cognitive Sciences, April 7, Washington, DC.

Schneider, W., & Fisk, A. D. (1982). Degree of consistent training: Improvements in search performance and automatic process development. *Perception & Psychophysics, 31,* 160–168.

Schneider, W., & Shiffrin, R. M. (1977). Controlled and automatic human information processing: I. Detection, search, and attention. *Psychological Review, 84,* 1–66.

Schneider, W., Vidulich, M., & Yeh, Y.-Y. (1982). Training spatial skills for air-traffic control. *Proceedings of the Human Factors Society 26th Annual Meeting* (pp. 10–14). Santa Monica, CA: Human Factors Society.

Schneiderman, B. (1976). Exploratory experiments in programmer behavior. *International Journal of Computer and Information Sciences, 5,* 123–143.

Schooler, C. (2007). Use it—And keep it, longer, probably: A reply to Salthouse (2006). *Perspectives on Psychological Science, 2,* 24–29.

Schooler, J. W., Reichle, E. D., & Halpern, D. V. (2004). Zoning out while reading: Evidence for dissociations between experience and metaconsciousness. In D. T. Levin (Ed.), *Thinking and seeing: Visual metacognition in adults and children* (pp. 203–226). Cambridge, MA: MIT Press.

Schultz, W. (1998). Predictive reward signal of dopamine neurons. *Journal of Neurophysiology, 80,* 1–27.

Schultz, W., Dayan, P., & Montague, P. R. (1997). A neural substrate of prediction and reward. *Science, 275,* 1593–1599.

Schultz, W., & Dickinson, A. (2000). Neuronal coding of prediction errors. *Annual Review of Neuroscience, 23,* 473–500.

Schumacher, E. H., Seymour, T. L., Glass, J. M., Fencsik, D. E., Lauber, E. J., Kieras, D. E., & Meyer, D. E. (2001). Virtually perfect time sharing in dual-task performance: Uncorking the central cognitive bottleneck. *Psychological Science, 12,* 101–108.

Schuyler, Jr., E. (1992). Problems with the scoring system contribute to Griffin's defeat. Associated Press wire story, August 2.

Schvaneveldt, R. W. (Ed.) (1990). *Pathfinder associative networks: Studies in knowledge organization.* Norwood, NJ: Ablex.

Schwarb, H., & Schumacher, E. H. (2010). Implicit sequence learning is represented by stimulus–response rules. *Memory & Cognition, 38,* 677–688.

Schwarb, H., & Schumacher, E. H. (2012). Generalized lessons about sequence learning from the study of the serial reaction time task. *Advances in Cognitive Psychology, 8,* 165–178.

Schyns, P. G., & Rodet, L. (1997). Categorization creates functional features. *Journal of Experimental Psychology: Learning, Memory, and Cognition, 23,* 681–696.

Seibel, R. (1963). Discrimination reaction time for a 1,023-alternative task. *Journal of Experimental Psychology, 66,* 215–226.

Seidenberg, M. S. (2005). Connectionist models of word reading. *Current Directions in Psychological Science, 14,* 238–242.

Selmer, J., Torbiörn, I., & de Leon, C. T. (1998). Sequential cross-cultural training for expatriate business managers: Pre-departure and post-arrival. *International Journal of Human Resource Management, 9,* 831–840.

Seufert, T., Schütze, M., & Brünken, R. (2009). Memory characteristics and modality in multimedia learning: An aptitude—Treatment—Interaction study. *Learning and Instruction, 19,* 28–42.

Seyler, D. L., Holton, E. F., Bates, R. A., Burnett, M. F., & Carvalho, M. A. (1998). Factors affecting motivation to transfer training. *International Journal of Training and Development, 2,* 2–16.

Seymour, B., O'Doherty, J. P., Dayan, P., Koltzenburg, M., Jones, A. K., Dolan, R. J., . . . Frackowiak, R. S. (2004). Temporal difference models describe higher-order learning in humans. *Nature, 429*(6992), 664–667.

Shallice, T. (1988). *From neuropsychology to mental structure.* New York: Cambridge University Press.

Shanks, D. R. (1995). Is human learning rational? *Quarterly Journal of Experimental Psychology: Human Experimental Psychology, 48A,* 257–279.

Shea, C. H., & Wulf, G. (2005). Schema theory: A critical appraisal and reevaluation. *Journal of Motor Behavior, 37,* 85–101.

Shea, J. B., & Morgan, R. L. (1979). Contextual interference effects on the acquisition, retention, and transfer of a motor skill. *Journal of Experimental Psychology: Learning, Memory, and Cognition, 5,* 179–187.

Shebilske, W. L., Goettl, B. P., & Regian, J. W. (1999). Executive control and automatic processes as complex skills develop in laboratory and applied settings. In D. Gopher & A. Koriat (Eds.), *Attention and performance XVII: Cognitive regulation of performance: Interaction of theory and application* (pp. 401–431). Cambridge, MA: MIT Press.

Shiffrin, R. M., & Lightfoot, N. (1997). Perceptual learning of alphanumeric-like characters. In R. L. Goldstone, D. L. Medin, & P. G. Schyns (Eds.), *Perceptual learning, Vol. 36: The psychology of learning and motivation* (pp. 45–81). San Diego, CA: Academic Press.

Shiffrin, R. M., & Schneider, W. (1977). Controlled and automatic human information processing: II. Perceptual learning, automatic attending, and a general theory. *Psychological Review, 84,* 127–190.

Shin, Y. K., Proctor, R. W., & Capaldi, E. J. (2010). A review of contemporary ideomotor theory. *Psychological Bulletin, 136,* 943–974.

Shipstead, Z., Redick, T. S., & Engle, R. W. (2012). Is working memory training effective? *Psychological Bulletin, 138,* 628–654.

Shirani, A., & St. Louis, E. K. (2009). Illuminating rationale and uses for light therapy. *Journal of Clinical Sleep Medicine, 5,* 155–163.

Sigrist, R., Rauter, G., Riener, R., & Wolf, P. (2013). Augmented visual, auditory, haptic, and multimodal feedback in motor learning: A review. *Psychonomic Bulletin & Review, 20,* 21–53.

Simon, H. A., & Chase, W. G. (1973). Skill in chess. *American Scientist, 61*, 394–403.
Simon, J. R. (1990). The effects of an irrelevant directional cue on human information processing. In R. W. Proctor & T. G. Reeve (Eds.), *Stimulus-response compatibility: An integrated perspective* (pp. 31–86). Amsterdam: North-Holland.
Sleeman, D., & Brown, J. S. (Eds.) (1982). *Intelligent tutoring systems.* London: Academic Press.
Smallwood, J., & Andrews-Hanna, J. (2013). Not all minds that wander are lost: The importance of a balanced perspective on the mind-wandering state. *Frontiers in Psychology, 4*, ArtID: 441.
Smallwood, J. M., Baracaia, S. F., Lowe, M., & Obonsawin, M. (2003). Task unrelated thought whilst encoding information. *Consciousness and Cognition, 12*, 452–484.
Smallwood, J., Obonsawin, M., & Heim, D. (2003). Task unrelated thought: The role of distributed processing. *Consciousness and Cognition, 12*, 169–189.
Smallwood, J., & Schooler, J. W. (2006). The restless mind. *Psychological Bulletin, 132*, 946–958.
Smith, A. P. (1985). The effects of noise on the processing of global shape and local detail. *Psychological Research, 47*, 103–108.
Smith, A. P. (1991). Strategy choice and time of day: An investigation of diurnal variation in speed and accuracy. In E. J. Lovesey (Ed.), *Contemporary ergonomics 1991* (pp. 44–48). London: Taylor and Francis.
Smith, A.P. (1992). Time of day and performance. In A.P. Smith & D.M. Jones (Eds.), *Handbook of human performance: Vol. 1. The physical environment* (pp. 1–28). San Diego: Academic Press.
Smith, A. P., & Jones, D. M. (1992). Noise and performance. In D. M. Jones & A. P. Smith (Eds.), *Handbook of human performance, Vol. 1: The physical environment* (pp. 1–28). San Diego: Academic Press.
Smith, A. T., Singh, K. D., Williams, A. L., & Greenlee, M. W. (2001). Estimating receptive field size from fMRI data in human striate and extrastriate visual cortex. *Cerebral Cortex, 11*, 1182–1190.
Smith, M. C. (1967). Theories of the psychological refractory period. *Psychological Bulletin, 67*, 202–213.
Smith, M. D., & Chamberlin, C. J. (1992). Effects of adding cognitively demanding tasks on soccer skill performance. *Perceptual and Motor Skills, 75*, 955–961.
Smith, R., Jayasuriya, R., Caputi, P., & Hammer, D. (2008). Exploring the role of goal theory in understanding training motivation. *International Journal of Training and Development, 12*, 54–72.
Smulders, F.T.Y., & Miller, J. O. (2011). The lateralized readiness potential. In S. Luck & E. Kappenman (Eds.), *Oxford handbook of event-related potential components* (pp. 209–229). New York, NY: Oxford University Press.
Snoddy, G. S. (1926). Learning and stability: A psychophysiological analysis of a case of motor learning with clinical applications. *Journal of Applied Psychology, 10*, 1–36.
Snowling, M. J., & Hulme, C. (Eds.) (2005). *The science of reading: A handbook.* Malden, MA: Blackwell.
Snyder, K. M., Logan, G. D., & Yamaguchi, M. (2015). Watch what you type: The role of visual feedback from the screen and hands in skilled typewriting. *Attention, Perception, & Psychophysics, 77*, 282–292.
Snyder, S. H. (1984). Adenosine as a mediator of the behavioral effects of xanthines. In P. B. Dews (Ed.), *Caffeine* (pp. 129–141). New York: Springer.

Soloway, E., Adelson, B., & Ehrlich, K. (1988). Knowledge and processes in the comprehension of computer programs. In M.T.H. Chi, R. Glaser, & M. J. Farr (Eds.), *The nature of expertise* (pp. 129–152). Hillsdale, NJ: Erlbaum.

Soloway, E., & Ehrlich, K. (1984). Empirical studies of programming knowledge. *IEEE Transactions on Software Engineering, SE-10*, 595–609.

Sonnentag, S., Niessen, C., & Volmer, J. (2006). Expertise in software design. In K. A. Ericsson, N. Charness, P. J. Feltovich, & R. R. Hoffman (Eds.), *The Cambridge handbook of expertise and human performance* (pp. 373–387). New York: Cambridge University Press.

Sørensen, T. A., Vangkilde, S., & Bundesen, C. (2015). Components of attention modulated by temporal expectation. *Journal of Experimental Psychology: Learning, Memory, and Cognition, 41*, 178–192.

Sowden, P. T., Davies, I.R.L., & Roling, P. (2000). Perceptual learning of the detection of features in X-ray images: A functional role for improvements in adults' visual sensitivity? *Journal of Experimental Psychology: Human Perception and Performance, 26*, 379–390.

Spada, N. (1997). Form-focused instruction and second language acquisition: A review of classroom and laboratory research. *Language Teaching, 30*, 73–87.

Spada, N., & Tomita, Y. (2010). Interactions between type of instruction and type of language feature: A meta-analysis. *Language Learning, 60*, 263–308.

Spang, K. K., Grimsen, C. C., Herzog, M. H., & Fahle, M. (2010). Orientation specificity of learning vernier discriminations. *Vision Research, 50*, 479–485.

Spearman, C. (1904). "General intelligence," objectively determined and measured. *American Journal of Psychology, 15*, 201–293.

Spearman, C. (1927). *The abilities of man*. New York: Macmillan.

Spelke, E., Hirst, W., & Neisser, U. (1976). Skills of divided attention. *Cognition, 4*, 215–230.

Spiekermann, S., & Korunovska, J. (2014). The importance of interface complexity and entropy for online information sharing. *Behaviour & Information Technology, 33*, 636–645.

Sports Illustrated. (2013). Boxing Association reveals changes to Olympic rules, scoring. Downloaded from http://www.si.com/mma/2013/03/23/boxing-changes

Stachowski, A. A., Kaplan, S. A., & Waller, M. J. (2009). The benefits of flexible team interaction during crises. *Journal of Applied Psychology, 94*, 1536–1543.

Stadler, M. A. (1989). On learning complex procedural knowledge. *Journal of Experimental Psychology: Learning, Memory, and Cognition, 15*, 1061–1069.

Stankov, L. (1983). Attention and intelligence. *Journal of Educational Psychology, 75*, 471–490.

Stansfeld, S. A., & Matheson, M. P. (2003). Noise pollution: non-auditory effects on health. *British Medical Bulletin, 68*, 243–257.

State v. Cromedy, 158 N.J. 112 (1999).

Sternberg, R. J. (1977). *Intelligence, information processing and analogical reasoning: The componential analysis of human abilities*. Hillsdale, NJ: Lawrence Erlbaum.

Sternberg, R. J. (1979). The nature of mental abilities. *American Psychologist, 34*, 214–230.

Sternberg, R. J. (1988). Intelligence. In R. J. Sternberg & E. E. Smith, *The psychology of human thought* (pp. 267–308). New York: Cambridge University Press.

Sternberg, R. J. (1999). The theory of successful intelligence. *Review of General Psychology, 3,* 292–316. doi:10.1037/1089-2680.3.4.292

Sternberg, R. J. (2011). The theory of successful intelligence. In R. J. Sternberg & S. Kaufman (Eds.), *The Cambridge handbook of intelligence* (pp. 504–527). New York: Cambridge University Press.

Sternberg, R. J., Grigorenko, E. L., & Zhang, L.-F. (2008). Styles of learning and thinking matter in instruction and assessment. *Perspectives on Psychological Science, 3,* 486–506.

Sternberg, S. (1969). The discovery of processing stages: Extensions of Donders' method. In W. G. Koster (Ed.), *Attention and performance II, Acta Psychologica, 30,* 276–315.

Stevens, C. K., & Gist, M. E. (1997). Effects of self-efficacy and goal orientation training on negotiation skill maintenance: What are the mechanisms? *Personnel Psychology, 50,* 955–978.

Stoet, G. (2011). Sex differences in search and gathering skills. *Evolution and Human Behavior, 32,* 416–422.

Strayer, D. L., Watson, J. M., & Drews, F. A. (2011). Cognitive distraction while multitasking in the automobile. In B. H. Ross (Ed.), *The psychology of learning and motivation: Advances in research and theory* (Vol. 54, pp. 29–58). San Diego, CA: Academic Press.

Stroop, J. R. (1935). Studies of interference in serial verbal reactions. *Journal of Experimental Psychology, 18,* 643–662.

Stump, S. (2013). He did it! Daredevil Nik Wallenda wire walks across the Grand Canyon. *Today News,* June 23. Downloaded from http://www.today.com/news/he-did-it-daredevil-nik-wallenda-wire-walks-across-grand-6C10411621

Sulikowski, D. (2012). Venom, speed, and caution: Effects on performance in a visual search task. *Evolution and Human Behavior, 33,* 365–377.

Sülzenbrück, S., & Heuer, H. (2011). Type of visual feedback during practice influences the precision of the acquired internal model of a complex visuo-motor transformation. *Ergonomics, 54,* 34–46.

Sun, C. (2007, Sept. 17). Do you leave your ATM card in the ATM? *TechRepublic.* Downloaded on February 15, 2011, from http://www.techrepublic.com/blog/helpdesk/do-you-leave-your-atm-card-in-the-atm/78

Sutton, R. S., & Barto, A. G. (1990). Time-derivative models of Pavlovian reinforcement. In M. Gabriel, & J. Moore (Eds.), *Learning and computational neuroscience: Foundations of adaptive networks* (pp. 497–537). Cambridge, MA: MIT Press.

Sweller, J. (1988). Cognitive load during problem solving: Effects on learning. *Cognitive Science, 12,* 257–285.

Sweller, J. (2005). The redundancy principle in multimedia learning. In R. E. Mayer (Ed.), *The Cambridge handbook of multimedia learning* (pp. 159–167). New York: Cambridge University Press.

Sweller, J., & Chandler, P. (1994). Why some material is difficult to learn. *Cognition and Instruction, 12,* 185–233.

Sweller, J., van Merriënboer, J. G., & Paas, F. C. (1998). Cognitive architecture and instructional design. *Educational Psychology Review, 10,* 251–296.

Swinnen, S. P. (1990). Interpolated activities during the knowledge-of-results delay and the post-knowledge-of-results interval: Effects on performance and learning. *Journal of Experimental Psychology: Learning, Memory, and Cognition, 16*, 692–705.

Swinnen, S. P., Schmidt, R. A., Nicholson, D. E., & Shapiro, D. C. (1990). Information feedback for skill acquisition: Instantaneous knowledge of results degrades learning. *Journal of Experimental Psychology: Learning, Memory, and Cognition, 16*, 706–716.

Szelag, E., & Skolimowska, J. (2012). Cognitive function in elderly can be ameliorated by training in temporal information processing. *Restorative Neurology and Neuroscience, 30*, 419–434.

Taatgen, N. A. (2002). A model of individual differences in skill acquisition in the Kanfer-Ackerman air traffic control task. *Cognitive Systems Research, 3*, 103–112.

Taatgen, N. A., & Anderson, J. R. (2002). Why do children learn to say "broke"? A model of the past tense without feedback. *Cognition, 86*, 123–155.

Taatgen, N. A., Huss, D., Dickison, D., & Anderson, J. R. (2008). The acquisition of robust and flexible cognitive skills. *Journal of Experimental Psychology: General, 137*, 548–565.

Taatgen, N. A., & Lee, F. J. (2003). Production compilation: Simple mechanism to model complex skill acquisition. *Human Factors, 45*, 61–76.

Taatgen, N. A., van Oploo, M., Braaksma, J., & Niemantsverdriet, J. (2003). How to construct a believable opponent using cognitive modeling in the game of Set. In F. Detje, D. Dörner, & H. Schaub (Eds.), *Proceedings of the Fifth International Conference on Cognitive Modeling* (pp. 201–206). Bamberg: Universitätsverlag Bamberg.

Tagliabue, M., Zorzi, M., Umiltà, C., & Bassignani, F. (2000). The role of LTM links and STM links in the Simon effect. *Journal of Experimental Psychology: Human Perception and Performance, 26*, 648–670.

Taillard, J., Capelli, A., Sagaspe, P., Anund, A., Akerstedt, T., & Philip, P. (2012). In-car nocturnal blue light exposure improves motorway driving: A randomized controlled trial. *Plos ONE, 7*(10), doi:10.1371/journal.pone.0046750

Tanaka, J., & Gauthier, I. (1997). Expertise in object and face recognition, In: R. L. Goldstone, D. L. Medin, & P. G. Schyns (Eds.), *Psychology of learning and motivation* (Vol. 36, pp. 83–125). San Diego, CA: Academic Press.

Tannenbaum, S. I., & Yukl, G. (1992). Training and development in work organizations. *Annual Review of Psychology, 43*, 399–441.

Teasly, B. E., Leventhal, L. M., Mynatt, C. R., & Rohlman, D. S. (1994). Why software testing is sometimes ineffective: Two applied studies of positive test strategy. *Journal of Applied Psychology, 79*, 142–155.

Teichner, W. H., & Krebs, M. J. (1974). Laws of visual choice reaction time. *Psychological Review, 81*, 75–98.

Telford, C. W. (1931). The refractory phase of voluntary and associative responses. *Journal of Experimental Psychology, 14*, 1–36.

Terrell, T. D. (1991). The role of grammar instruction in a communicative approach. *Modern Language Journal, 75*, 52–63.

Thayer, R. E. (1989). *The biopsychology of mood and arousal*. New York: Oxford University Press.

Thomson, S. J., Danis, L. K., & Watter, S. (2015). PRP training shows task1 response selection is the locus of the backward response compatibility effect. *Psychonomic Bulletin & Review, 22*, 212–218.

Thorndike, E. L., Bregman, E. O., Tilton, J. W., & Woodward, E. (1928). *Adult learning*. New York: Macmillan.

Thorndike, E. L., & Woodworth, R. S. (1901a). The influence of improvement in one mental function upon the efficiency of other functions. I. *Psychological Review, 8*, 247–261.

Thorndike, E. L., & Woodworth, R. S. (1901b). The influence of improvement in one mental function upon the efficiency of other functions. II. The estimation of magnitudes. *Psychological Review, 8*, 384–395.

Thorndike, E. L., & Woodworth, R. S. (1901c). The influence of improvement in one mental function upon the efficiency of other functions. III. Functions involving attention, observation, and discrimination. *Psychological Review, 8*, 553–564.

Thurstone, L. L. (1935). *The vectors of mind*. Chicago: University of Chicago Press.

Thurstone, L. L. (1947). *Multiple factor analysis*. Chicago: University of Chicago Press.

Tilley, A. J., & Bohle, P. (1988). Twisting the night away: The effects of all night disco dancing on reaction time. *Perceptual and Motor Skills, 66*, 107–112.

Tilley, A., & Brown, S. (1992). Sleep deprivation. In A. P. Smith & D. M. Jones (Eds.), *Handbook of human performance* (Vol. 3: State and Trait; pp. 237–259). San Diego, CA: Academic Press.

Toffanin, P., Johnson, A., de Jong, R., & Martens, S. (2007). Rethinking neural efficiency: Effects of controlling for strategy use. *Behavioral Neuroscience, 121*, 854–870.

Tomporowski, P. D. (2003). Effects of acute bouts of exercise on cognition. *Acta Psychologica, 112*, 297–324.

Toril, P., Reales, J. M., & Ballesteros, S. (2014). Video game training enhances cognition of older adults: A meta-analytic study. *Psychology and Aging, 29*, 706–716.

Townsend, J. T. (1974). Issues and models concerning the processing of a finite number of inputs. In B. H. Kantowitz (Ed.), *Human information processing: Tutorials in performance and cognition* (pp. 133–185). Hillsdale, NJ: Lawrence Erlbaum.

Trampush, J. W., Lencz, T., Knowles, E., Davies, G., Guha, S., Pe'er, I., . . . Malhotra, A. K. (2015). Independent evidence for an association between general cognitive ability and a genetic locus for educational attainment. *American Journal of Medical Genetics Part B: Neuropsychiatric Genetics, 168*, 363–373.

Treisman, A. M., & Davies, A. (1973). Divided attention to ear and eye. In S. Kornblum (Ed.), *Attention and performance IV* (pp. 101–117). New York: Academic Press.

Treisman, A. M., & Gelade, G. (1980). A feature-integration theory of attention. *Cognitive Psychology, 12*, 97–136.

Trumpower, D. L., & Sarwar, G. (2010). Effectiveness of structural feedback provided by Pathfinder networks. *Journal of Educational Computing Research, 43*, 7–24.

Tsang, P. S., & Wickens, C. D. (1988). The structural constraints and resource control of resource allocation. *Human Performance, 1*, 45–72.

Tuholski, S. W., Engle, R. W., & Baylis, G. C. (2001). Individual differences in working memory capacity and enumeration. *Memory & Cognition, 29*, 484–492.

Tulving, E. (1967). The effects of presentation and recall of material in free-recall learning. *Journal of Verbal Learning and Verbal Behavior, 6*, 175–184.

Turner, D. C., Aitken, M. F., Shanks, D. R., Sahakian, B. J., Robbins, T. W., Schwarzbauer, C., & Fletcher, P. C. (2004). The role of the lateral frontal cortex in causal associative learning: Exploring preventative and super-learning. *Cerebral Cortex, 14*, 872–880.

Twitchell, S., Holton, E. F., & Trott, J. W. (2000). Technical training evaluation practices in the United States. *Performance Improvement Quarterly, 13,* 84–109.

Tyhurst, J. S. (1951). Individual reactions to community disaster. *American Journal of Psychiatry, 107,* 764–769.

Ullman, S. (1989). Aligning pictorial descriptions: An approach to object recognition. *Cognition, 32,* 193–254.

Ursin, H., & Eriksen, H. R. (2004). The cognitive activation theory of stress. *Psychoneuroendocrinology, 29,* 567–592.

Ursin, H., & Eriksen, H. R. (2010). Cognitive activation theory of stress (CATS). *Neuroscience and Biobehavioral Reviews, 34,* 877–881.

Usher, M., & McClelland, J. L. (2001). The time course of perceptual choice: The leaky, competing accumulator model. *Psychological Review, 108,* 550–592.

van der Gijp, A., van der Schaaf, M. F., van der Schaaf, I. C., Huige, J. M., Ravesloot, C. J., van Schaik, J. J., & ten Cate, T. J. (2014). Interpretation of radiological images: Towards a framework of knowledge and skills. *Advances in Health Sciences Education, 19,* 565–580.

van Gog, T., Paas, F., & Sweller, J. (2010). Cognitive load theory: Advances in research on worked examples, animations, and cognitive load measurement. *Educational Psychology Review, 22,* 375–378.

van Merriënboer, J. G., Kester, L., & Paas, F. (2006). Teaching complex rather than simple tasks: Balancing intrinsic and germane load to enhance transfer of learning. *Applied Cognitive Psychology, 20,* 343–352.

van Merriënboer, J. G., & Sweller, J. (2005). Cognitive load theory and complex learning: Recent developments and future directions. *Educational Psychology Review, 17,* 147–177.

Van Orden, G. C. (1987). A ROWS is a ROSE: Spelling, sound, and reading. *Memory & Cognition, 15,* 181–198.

van Rijn, H., Johnson, A., & Taatgen, N. (2011). Cognitive user modeling. In R. W. Proctor & K.-P. L. Vu (Eds.), *Handbook of human factors in web design* (2nd ed., pp. 523–538). Boca Raton, FL: CRC Press.

Van Selst, M., & Jolicoeur, P. (1997). Decision and response in dual-task interference. *Cognitive Psychology, 33,* 266–307.

Van Selst, M., Ruthruff, E., & Johnston, J. C. (1999). Can practice eliminate the psychological refractory period effect? *Journal of Experimental Psychology: Human Perception and Performance, 25,* 1268–1283.

Van Zandt, T., & Townsend, J. T. (2012). Mathematical psychology. In H. Cooper (Ed.-in-Chief), *APA handbook of research methods in psychology, Vol 2: Research designs: Quantitative, qualitative, neuropsychological, and biological* (pp. 369–386). Washington, DC: American Psychological Association.

VanLehn, K. (1989). Problem solving and cognitive skill acquisition. In M. I. Posner (Ed.), *Foundations of cognitive science* (pp. 527–579). Cambridge, MA: MIT Press.

VanLehn, K. (1996). Cognitive skill acquisition. *Annual Review of Psychology, 47,* 513–539.

Vashdi, D. R., Bamberger, P. A., Erez, M., & Weiss-Meilik, A. (2007). Briefing-debriefing: Using a reflexive organizational learning model from the military to enhance the performance of surgical teams. *Human Resource Management, 46,* 115–142.

Veldstra, J. L., Brookhuis, K. A., de Waard, D., Molmans, B. W., Verstraete, A. G., Skopp, G., & Jantos, R. (2012). Effects of alcohol (BAC 0.5‰) and ecstasy

(MDMA 100 mg) on simulated driving performance and traffic safety. *Psychopharmacology, 222,* 377–390.

Vereijken, B., van Emmerik, R.E.A., Whiting, H.T.A., & Newell, K. M. (1992). Free(z)ing degrees of freedom in skill acquisition. *Journal of Motor Behavior, 24,* 133–142.

Verhave, T., & van Hoorn, W. (1987). The winds of doctrine: Ebbinghaus and his reputation in America. In D. Gorfein & R. Hoffman (Eds.), *Memory and learning: The Ebbinghaus centennial conference* (pp. 89–102). Hillsdale, NJ: Lawrence Erlbaum.

Vernon, D., Egner, T., Cooper, N., Compton, T., Neilands, C., Sheri, A., & Gruzelier, J. (2003). The effect of training distinct neurofeedback protocols on aspects of cognitive performance. *International Journal of Psychophysiology, 47,* 75–85.

Vessey, I. (1986). Expertise in debugging computer programs: An analysis of the content of verbal protocols. *IEEE Transactions on Systems, Man, and Cybernetics, 16,* 621–637.

Vicente, K. J. (1999). *Cognitive work analysis: Toward safe, productive, and healthy computer based work.* Mahwah, NJ: Lawrence Erlbaum.

Vidal, F., Hasbroucq, T., Grapperon, J., & Bonnet, M. (2000). Is the "error negativity" specific to errors? *Biological Psychology, 51,* 109–128.

Vimercati, S., Galli, M., Rigoldi, C., Ancillao, A., & Albertini, G. (2013). Motor strategies and motor programs during an arm tapping task in adults with Down Syndrome. *Experimental Brain Research, 225,* 333–338.

Voelkle, M. C., Wittmann, W. W., & Ackerman, P. L. (2006). Abilities and skill acquisition: A latent growth curve approach. *Learning and Individual Differences, 16,* 303–319.

Volpe, C. E., Cannon-Bowers, J. A., Salas, E., & Spector, P. E. (1996). The impact of cross-training on team functioning: An empirical investigation. *Human Factors, 38,* 87–100.

Voss, J. F., & Post, T. A. (1988). On the solving of ill-structured problems. In M.T.H. Chi, R. Glaser, & M. J. Farr (Eds.), *The nature of expertise* (pp. 261–285). Hillsdale, NJ: Lawrence Erlbaum.

Voss, M. W., Prakash, R., Erickson, K. I., Boot, W. R., Basak, C., Neider, M. B., . . . Kramer, A. F. (2012). Effects of training strategies implemented in a complex videogame on functional connectivity of attentional networks. *Neuroimage, 59,* 138–148.

Voudouris, D., Brenner, E., Schot, W. D., & Smeets, J. J. (2010). Does planning a different trajectory influence the choice of grasping points? *Experimental Brain Research, 206,* 15–24.

Vu, K.-P.L., Kiken, A., Chiappe, D., Strybel, T. Z., & Battiste, V. (2013). Application of part-whole training methods to evaluate when to introduce NextGen air traffic management tools to students. *American Journal of Psychology, 126,* 433–447.

Vu, K.-P.L., Proctor, R. W., & Urcuioli, P. (2003). Transfer effects of incompatible location-relevant mappings on a subsequent visual or auditory Simon task. *Memory & Cognition, 31,* 1146–1152.

Wallace, R. J. (1971). S-R compatibility and the idea of a response code. *Journal of Experimental Psychology, 88,* 354–360.

Walthew, C., & Gilchrist, I. D. (2006). Target location probability effects in visual search: An effect of sequential dependencies. *Journal of Experimental Psychology: Human Perception and Performance, 32,* 1294–1301.

Wang, L. P., Hamaker, E., & Bergeman, C. S. (2012). Investigating inter-individual differences in short-term intra-individual variability. *Psychological Methods, 17,* 567–581.

Wankel, C., & Stachowicz-Stanusch, A. (Eds.) (2011). *Management education for integrity ethically educating tomorrow's business leaders.* Bingley, UK: Emerald Group Publishing.

Warriner, A. B., & Humphreys, K. R. (2008). Learning to fail: Reoccurring tip-of-the-tongue states. *Quarterly Journal of Experimental Psychology, 61,* 535–542.

Watanabe, T., & Sasaki, Y. (2015). Perceptual learning: Toward a comprehensive theory. *Annual Review of Psychology, 66,* 197–221.

Waterhouse, J., Reilly, T., Atkinson, G., & Edwards, B. (2007). Jet lag: Trends and coping strategies. *The Lancet, 369,* 1117–1127.

Weick, K. E., & Bougon, M. (1986). Organizations as cognitive maps: Charting ways to success and failure. In H. P. Sims, Jr., D. A. Gioia, & Associates (Eds.), *The thinking organization* (pp. 102–135). San Francisco: Jossey-Bass.

Weick, K. E., Sutcliffe, K. M., & Obstfeld, D. (1999). Organizing for high reliability: Processes of collective mindfulness. In B. Staw & R. Sutton (Eds.), *Research in organizational behavior* (pp. 23–81). Greenwich, CT: JAI Press.

Weinberger, N. M. (1995). Dynamic regulation of receptive fields and maps in the adult sensory cortex. *Annual Review of Neuroscience, 18,*129–158.

Weinert, D., & Waterhouse, J. (2007). The circadian rhythm of core temperature: Effects of physical activity and aging. *Physiology & Behavior, 90,* 246–256.

Welford, A. T. (1952). The "psychological refractory period" and the timing of high-speed performance—a review and a theory. *British Journal of Psychology, 43,* 2–19.

Welford, A. T. (1976). *Skilled performance: Perceptual and motor skills.* Glenview, IL: Scott, Foresman.

Welford, A. T., Brown, R. A., & Gabb, J. E. (1950). Two experiments on fatigue as affecting skilled performance in civilian aircrew. *British Journal of Psychology, 40,* 195–211.

Welham, A. K., & Wills, A. J. (2011). Unitization, similarity, and overt attention in categorization and exposure. *Memory & Cognition, 39,* 1518–1533.

Wertheim, A. H., Hooge, I.T.C., Krikke, K., & Johnson, A. (2006). How important is lateral masking in visual search? *Experimental Brain Research, 170,* 387–402.

Wesnes, K. A., & Parrott, A. C. (1992). Smoking, nicotine, and human performance. In A. P. Smith & D. M. Jones (Eds.), *Handbook of human performance, Vol 2: Health and performance* (pp. 127–167). San Diego, CA: Academic Press.

Wesnes, K., & Warburton, D. M. (1978). The effects of cigarette smoking and nicotine tablets upon human attention. In R. E. Thornton (Ed.), *Smoking behaviour: Physiological and psychological influences* (pp. 131–147). London: Churchill Livingstone.

Wesnes, K., & Warburton, D. M. (1984). Effects of scopolamine and nicotine on human rapid information processing performance. *Psychopharmacology, 82,* 147–150.

Wetzstein, A., & Hacker, W. (2004). Reflective verbalization improves solutions—The effects of question-based reflection in design problem solving. *Applied Cognitive Psychology, 18,* 145–156.

Wickens, C. D. (1984). Processing resources in attention. In R. Parasuraman & D. R. Davies (Eds.), *Varieties of attention* (pp. 63–102). New York: Academic Press.

Wightman, D. C., & Lintern, G. (1985). Part-task training for tracking and manual control. *Human Factors, 27*, 267–283.

Wilding, J., Mohindra, N., & Breen-Lewis, K. (1982). Noise effects in free recall with different orienting tasks. *British Journal of Psychology, 73*, 479–486.

Wilkinson, L., & Shanks, D. (2004). Intentional control and implicit sequence learning. *Journal of Experimental Psychology: Learning, Memory, and Cognition, 30*, 354–369.

Williams, H. L., Lubin, A., & Goodnow, J. J. (1959). Impaired performance with acute sleep loss. *Psychological Monographs: General and Applied, 73*, 1–26.

Willingham, D. B., Nissen, M. J., & Bullemer, P. (1989). On the development of procedural knowledge. *Journal of Experimental Psychology: Learning, Memory, and Cognition, 15*, 1047–1060. doi:10.1037/0278-7393.15.6.1047

Winstein, C. J., & Schmidt, R. A. (1990). Reduced frequency of knowledge of results enhances motor skill learning. *Journal of Experimental Psychology: Learning, Memory, and Cognition, 16*, 677–691.

Winter, W. C., Hammond, W. R., Green, N. H., Zhang, Z., & Bliwise, D. L. (2009). Measuring circadian advantage in major league baseball: A 10-year retrospective study. *International Journal of Sports Physiology and Performance, 4*, 394–401.

Wisher, R. A., Sabol, M. A., & Kern, R. P. (1995). Modeling acquisition of an advanced skill: The case of Morse code copying. *Instructional Science, 23*, 381–403.

Witt, J. K. (2011). Action's effect on perception. *Current Directions in Psychological Science, 20*, 201–206.

Witt, J. K., Linkenauger, S. A., Bakdash, J. Z., & Proffitt, D. R. (2008). Putting to a bigger hole: Golf performance relates to perceived size. *Psychonomic Bulletin & Review, 15*, 581–585.

Witt, J. K., & Proffitt, D. R. (2005). See the ball, hit the ball: Apparent ball size is correlated with batting average. *Psychological Science, 16*, 937–938.

Witt, J. K., & Sugovic, M. (2013). Catching ease influences perceived speed: Evidence for action-specific effects from action-based measures. *Psychonomic Bulletin & Review, 20*, 1364–1370.

Wittwer, J., & Renkl, A. (2010). How effective are instructional explanations in example-based learning? A meta-analytic review. *Educational Psychology Review, 22*, 393–409.

Wixted, J. T., & Carpenter, S. K. (2007). The Wickelgren power law and the Ebbinghaus savings function. *Psychological Science, 18*, 133–134.

Wolfe, J. M., Cave, K. R., & Franzel, S. L. (1989). Guided search: An alternative to the feature integration model for visual search. *Journal of Experimental Psychology: Human Perception and Performance, 15*, 419–433.

Wolpert, D. M., Diederichsen, J., & Flanagan, R. (2011). Principles of sensorimotor learning. *Nature Reviews Neuroscience, 12*, 739–751.

Womelsdorf, T., Anton-Erxleben, K., & Treue, S. (2008). Receptive field shift and shrinkage in macaque area MT through attentional gain modulation. *Journal of Neuroscience, 28*, 8934–8944.

Wood, B. P. (1999). Visual expertise. *Radiology, 211*, 1–3.

Wood, R. E., & Bandura, A. (1989). Social-cognitive theory of organizational management. *Academy of Management Review, 14*, 361–384.

Woodrow, H. (1946). The ability to learn. *Psychological Review, 53*, 147–158.

Woods, A. J., Philbeck, J. W., & Danoff, J. V. (2009). The various "perceptions" of distance: An alternative view of how effort affects distance judgments. *Journal of Experimental Psychology: Human Perception and Performance, 35*, 1104–1117.

Woodworth, R. S. (1899). The accuracy of voluntary movement. *Psychological Review, 3* (Monograph Supplement), 1–119.

Wouters, P., van der Spek, E. D., & van Oostendorp, H. (2011). Measuring learning in serious games: A case study with structural assessment. *Educational Technology Research and Development, 59*, 741–763.

Wright, D. L., & Shea, C. H. (1991). Contextual dependencies in motor skills. *Memory & Cognition, 19*, 361–370.

Wu, C., & Liu, Y. (2008). Queuing network modeling of transcription typing. *ACM Transactions on Computer-Human Interaction, 15*, 1–45.

Wulf, G. (2007). *Attention and motor skill learning.* Champaign, IL: Human Kinetics.

Wulf, G. (2013). Attentional focus and motor learning: A review of 15 years. *International Review of Sport and Exercise Psychology, 6*, 77–104.

Wulf, G., & Prinz, W. (2001). Directing attention to movement effects enhances learning: A review. *Psychonomic Bulletin & Review, 8*, 648–660.

Wulf, G., & Schmidt, R. A. (1989). The learning of generalized motor programs: Reducing the relative frequency of knowledge of results enhances memory. *Journal of Experimental Psychology: Learning, Memory, and Cognition, 15*, 748–757.

Wulf, G., Shea, C. H., & Lewthwaite, R. (2010). Motor skill learning and performance: A review of influential factors. *Medical Education, 44*, 75–84.

Wulf, G., Shea, C. H., & Park, J. H. (2001). Attention in motor learning: Preferences for and advantages of an external focus. *Research Quarterly for Exercise and Sport, 72*, 335–344.

Xu, W. (2007). Identifying problems and generating recommendations for enhancing complex systems: Applying the abstraction hierarchy framework as an analytical tool. *Human Factors, 49*, 975–994.

Yamaguchi, M., Logan, G. D., & Li, V. (2013). Multiple bottlenecks in hierarchical control of action sequences: What does "response selection" select in skilled typewriting? *Journal of Experimental Psychology: Human Perception and Performance, 39*, 1059–1084.

Yang, B., Wang, Y., & Drewry, A. (2009). Does it matter where to conduct training? Accounting for cultural factors. *Human Resource Management Review, 19*, 324–333.

Yang, T., & Maunsell, J.H.R. (2004). The effect of perceptual learning on neuronal responses in monkey visual area V4. *Journal of Neuroscience, 24*, 1617–1626.

Yantis, S., & Johnston, J. C. (1990). On the locus of visual selection: Evidence from focused attention tasks. *Journal of Experimental Psychology: Human Perception and Performance, 16*, 135–149.

Yerkes, R. M., & Dodson, J. D. (1908). The relation of strength of stimulus to rapidity of habit formation. *Journal of Comparative Neurology and Psychology, 18*, 459–482.

Yin, R. K. (1969). Looking at upside-down faces. *Journal of Experimental Psychology, 81*, 141–145.

Young, D. E., & Schmidt, R. A. (1992). Augmented kinematic feedback for motor learning. *Journal of Motor Behavior, 24,* 261–273.

Zaepffel, M., & Brochier, T. (2012). Planning of visually guided reach-to-grasp movements: Inference from reaction time and contingent negative variation (CNV). *Psychophysiology, 49,* 17–30.

Zanone, P. G., & Kelso, J.A.S. (1992). Evolution of behavioral attractors with learning: Nonequilibrium phase transitions. *Journal of Experimental Psychology: Human Perception and Performance, 18,* 403–421.

Ziessler, M. (1998). Response-effect learning as a major component of implicit serial learning. *Journal of Experimental Psychology: Learning, Memory, and Cognition, 24,* 962–978.

Zucco, G. M., Carassai, A., Baroni, M. R., & Stevenson, R. J. (2011). Labeling, identification, and recognition of wine-relevant odorants in expert sommeliers, intermediates, and untrained wine drinkers. *Perception, 40,* 598–607.

Author Index

Abernethy, B. 27
Abrahamse, E. 111
Ackerman, P. L. 205–6, 208, 210, 215, 217–22, 224, 290
Adam, J. J. 68
Adams, D. R. 191
Adams, J. A. 83, 223–5
Adams, M. J. 226
Adamson, R. E. 132
Adelson, B. 160
Aguinis, H. 270, 282, 287
Ahlum-Heath, M. E. 118
Aitken, L. M. 271
Aitken, M. F. 189
Akerstedt, T. 256
Albaret, J. M. 85
Albertini, G. 71
Albo, D. 269
Alderton, D. 44
Aldrich, N. J. 103
Alexander, J. 129
Alfieri, L. 103
Allen, C. 283
Allport, D. 98
Alluisi, E. A. 64
Altmann, E. M. 151, 153
Amalberti, R. 280
Amaro, E. J. 156
Amazeen, P. G. 277–8
Amorim, M. A. 108
Ancillao, A. 71
Anderson, B. 51
Anderson, J. L. 138
Anderson, J. M. 189–90
Anderson, J. R. 20–2, 63, 69, 96, 113, 118, 133, 135, 142, 144, 180, 220
Andrews, J. K. 33
Andrews, S. 231
Andrews-Hanna, J. 107
Aneziris, O. N. 2
Anson, G. 71

Anton-Erxleben, K. 89
Antonis, B. 98
Anund, A. 256
Anzai, Y. 117
Anzola, G. P. 66
Arcelin, R. 245
Argyris, C. 282
Arisholm, E. 159
Arthur, W. J. 288
Aschersleben, G. 60, 69
Aschoff, J. 246
Ash, I. K. 123
Ashford, D. 85
Athilingam, P. 232
Atkinson, G. 250
Atkinson, R. C. 97, 105, 141
Atkinson, R. K. 121
Awad, S. S. 269
Axtell, C. M. 287
Ayaz, H. 207
Ayres, P. 120–1

Babcock, Q. 259
Back, J. 178
Bacon, M. P. 55
Bacon, S. J. 242–3
Baddeley, A. 16–17, 199
Badets, A. 81
Bagian, J. P. 182
Bahrick, H. P. 241, 257
Bailey, R. 277
Baird, B. 107
Baird, J. A. 56
Bakdash, J. Z. 55
Baker, P. 279–80
Baker, W. J. 261
Baldwin, T. T. 281
Ball, L. J. 156
Ballard, C. G. 10
Ballas, J. A. 94
Ballesteros, S. 232

Bamberger, P. A. 181–2
Bancino, R. 25
Bancroft, N. R. 262
Bandura, A. 284, 291
Bannerjea, A. 260
Baracaia, S. F. 106
Barbot, B. 210
Bareket, T. 91
Barfield, W. 160
Baron, J. 226
Baroni, M. R. 46, 48
Barreiros, J. 84
Barron, L. G. 206
Barrows, H. S. 26
Bartlett, F. 127, 191
Barto, A. G. 188
Basak, C. 91–2
Bassignani, F. 69
Bassok, M. 119
Bastian, M. 107
Bates, R. A. 285–7
Batinic, B. 199
Batra, D. 159
Battig, W. F. 127
Battiste, V. 2
Bavelier, D. 102, 232
Baylis, G. C. 60, 70, 105
Baylor, C. R. 26
Beale, J. M. 33
Beam, C. A. 155
Beauchamp, G. K. 46
Beckmann, J. F. 207
Begley, A. E. 249
Behrmann, M. 51
Beier, M. E. 3, 206
Beilock, S. L. 175, 198
Belenky, D. M. 119
Bell, B. G. 185
Bell, B. S. 290
Bell, S. T. 288
Bellows, C. 269
Bénar, C. G. 186
Ben-Ishai, R. 101
Bennett, L. 37
Bennett, S. J. 85
Bennett, W. J. 288
Ben-Shakhar, G. 104

Berga, S. L. 249
Bergeman, C. S. 203
Berger, D. H. 182, 269
Bergersen, G. 160
Bernstein, M. J. 36
Bernstein, N. A. 74–5
Berry, D. C. 124–5, 196
Bertelson, P. 69
Berthold, K. 122
Bertini, G. 44
Bertoloni, G. 66
Bethune, R. 182
Bherer, L. 232
Bias, R. G. 226
Biederman, I. 47–8
Bielaczyc, K. 119
Bilalić, M. 132
Bills, A. G. 255
Binet, A. 204–5
Biolsi, K. J. 146
Birbaumer, N. 103
Birchall, D. 286–7
Birdi, K. 283
Birrer, D. D. 27
Bischoff-Grethe, A. 111
Bisqueret, C. 292
Bitan, T. T. 123
Bjork, R. A. 127, 136, 139, 191
Black, J. 290–2
Blake, A. 54
Blakely, D. P. 102
Blanchard-Fields, F. 123
Blandford, A. 178
Blandin, Y. 81, 85
Blattner, P. 256
Bliwise, D. L. 252
Bloom, B. S. 151
Bobrow, D. J. 90, 95
Bock, K. 191
Boehringer, A. 239
Boggan, J. 41
Bohle, P. 255
Bonami, M. 287
Bonnet, M. 186
Boot, W. R. 91–2, 102, 144
Borst, J. P. 93
Bothell, D. 20

Bouchard, T.J., Jr. 205
Bougon, M. 183
Bourne, L. E., Jr. 3, 113, 258, 276
Boutin, A. 85
Bovair, S. 128
Bowens, L. D. 102
Boyle, C. 142
Boyle, M. O. 206
Braaksma, J. 32
Brancucci, A. 207
Brass, C. G. 252
Braun, C. H. 189
Braze, D. 226, 228
Breen-Lewis, K. 257
Bregman, E. O. 235
Brenner, E. 78
Brewer, N. 265
Brickner, M. 90
Bridgeman, B. 55
Briggs, B. 2
Briggs, L. J. 213
Brigham, J. C. 36–7
Brisswalter, J. B. 245
Broadbent, D. E. 88, 124–5, 196
Broadbent, M.H.P. 124
Brochier, T. 19
Brooke, S. 258
Brooks, P. J. 103
Brown, A. L. 119
Brown, J. 270
Brown, J. S. 141
Brown, L. H. 106
Brown, N. R. 159
Brown, R. A. 255
Brown, S. 8–9, 202, 254
Brunke, K. M. 81
Brünken, R. 211
Brunstein, A. 45
Brunyé, T. T. 262
Bryan, W. L. 5–7, 13
Bryant, S. 162
Buchner, A. 110
Buchsbaum, M. S. 206–7
Buchtel, H. A. 66
Buckley, J. 275
Bull, R. 198
Bullemer, P. 108, 110
Bullmore, E. T. 189–90

Bundesen, C. 242
Bürgi, P. 291
Burke, C. 292
Burle, B. 186
Burnett, M. 162
Burnett, M. F. 285
Burns, A. S. 10
Burns, M. I. 26
Bursill, A. E. 257
Busemeyer, J. R. 25
Buss, R. R. 123
Butler, B. E. 225–7
Butz, M. V. 78
Buysse, D. J. 249
Byrne, M. D. 20, 22
Byrne, T. 259

Cabeza, R. 19–20
Cai, D. J. 252–3
Cajochen, C. 256
Calderwood, R. 272
Caligiuri, P. 291
Càmara, E. 19
Campbell, J. 278
Campbell, J.I.D. 10–11
Campbell, R. L. 159
Campitelli, G. 151, 153
Cañal-Bruland, R. 55
Cannon-Bowers, J. A. 271, 277
Cant, R. 281
Cantor, G. W. 123
Cao, J. 162
Capaldi, E. J. 187
Capelli, A. 256
Cappelletti, M. 234
Caputi, P. 286
Carassai, A. 46, 48
Carey, S. 43
Carlson, R. A. 134–6, 228
Carney, B. T. 182
Carpenter, S. K. 5, 138
Carpenter, T. A. 189–90
Carr, T. H. 175, 198
Carrasco, M. 49
Carrier, J. 249
Carrithers, C. 178
Carroll, J. B. 205–6
Carroll, J. M. 133, 178

Carron, A. V. 83
Carvalho, M. A. 285
Caspi, S. 91
Castles, A. 226
Catrambone, R. 130
Cattell, J. M. 204
Cattell, R. B. 205
Cauraugh, J. H. 67
Cave, K. R. 50
Cawthorn, S. 182
Cepeda, N. J. 136–7, 138–9, 150
Chabris, C. F. 146
Chamberlain, A. G. 221–3
Chamberlin, C. J. 154
Chandler, P. 120–1
Chang, I. 49
Chang, Y. K. 245
Chappell, M. 38
Charness, N. 152, 234
Chase, W. G. 146, 153, 169
Chassé, K. 232
Chelazzi, L. 89
Chellappa, S. L. 256
Chen, J. 64
Chi, M.T.H. 119, 121–2, 147, 153–4
Chiaburu, D. S. 284–5, 287
Chiappe, D. 2
Chin, J. M. 48–9
Chiroro, P. M. 36–7
Chiu, M. H. 119, 121–2, 182
Chiviacowsky, S. 81
Cho, J. R. 123
Cho, Y. S. 98
Choi, J. M. 98
Chopin, A. 53–4
Christensen, W. 237
Christianson, S. A. 240
Christmann, U. 228
Chua, R. 11, 81
Chun, M. M. 52
Church, A. T. 291
Church, B. A. 45
Chvatal, S. A. 73
Cianciolo, A. T. 219
Clark, R. E. 258
Clayden, J. D. 232
Cleeremans, A. 5, 109–10
Clegg, B. 111

Clement, C. A. 130
Clerc, J. 27
Coburn, N. 137
Coch, D. 41
Cohen, A. 109
Cohen, J. D. 24–5, 111, 189
Cohen, R. G. 76
Colcombe, S. J. 232, 245
Coles, M. G. H. 19, 185–6, 189, 275
Collard, R. 76–7
Collardeau, M. 245
Colquitt, J. A. 283–4
Coltheart, M. 225
Compton, B. J. 99, 275
Compton, T. 104
Conati, C. 142
Condon, R. 250
Connelly, S. L. 230
Conway, A.R.A. 206
Cook-Deegan, R. 260
Cooke, N. J. 271, 277–8
Cooper, A. D. 55
Cooper, N. 104
Cooper, R. E. 255
Cooper, R. P. 24
Cooper, S. 281
Coovert, M. D. 17
Copper, C. 85, 140, 150
Cormier, S. M. 276
Corritore, C. L. 160–1
Corter, J. E. 31
Corver, S. C. 2
Costall, A. 198
Coughlan, E. K. 152
Cournoyer, J. 79
Couture, M. 193–52
Coviella, I.L.G. 261
Cox, G. 119
Cox, R. 162
Craig, A. 250, 255
Craik, K. J. W. 12
Crawford, T. 156
Critchley, H. 189
Croft, J. 274
Cronbach, L. J. 204–5, 210, 223
Cross, K. P. 26
Crump, M.J.C. 163, 166–8, 187
Cuddihy, L. 102

Curran, T. 43, 108
Czeizler, C. A. 249

Daee, S. 257
Daggy, A. 108
Dajani, S. 10
Damos, D. L. 101
Danis, L. K. 94
Danoff, J. V. 56
Darbyshire, D. 279–80
da Silva, F. Jr. 259
Davidi, I. 182–4
Davidoff, J. 33
Davids, K. 71, 85
Davidson, P. S. 10
Davies, A. 95
Davies, G. 204
Davies, I.R.L. 45, 156
Davis, J. G. 159
Daw, N. D. 190
Dayan, P. 188–9
Deary, I. J. 204–5, 207, 232
de Bruin, P. 259
de Bruin, V. 259
Deelstra, J. T. 287
de Graaff, R. 125–6
de Groot, A. 145–6, 153
De Houwer, J. 187
Deininger, R. L. 65–6
de Jong, R. 93, 207
DeKock, A. R. 262
De la Garza, M. 269
de Leeuw, J. R. 29
de Leeuw, N. 119, 121–2, 182
de Leon, C. T. 291
Dell, G. S. 191–2
de Mello, M. 259
den Ouden, H. M. 190
de Pinho, R. 259
Derbinsky, N. 20–1
Derbish, M. H. 138
de Ribaupierre, A. 203
Derry, S. J. 121, 142
Desimone, R. 89
Desor, J. A. 46
D'Esposito, M. 260
Destrebecqz, A. 109
Deutsch, D. 88

Deutsch, J. A. 88
Devos, C. 287
de Winter, J. F. 277
Diamond, R. 43
Diaz, A. 238
DiazGranados, D. 292
Di Bello, L. A. 159
Dickinson, A. 190
Dickison, D. 113
Didino, D. 234
Di Domenico, S. I. 207
Diederich, A. 25
Diederichsen, J. 85
Dienes, Z. 109, 124
DiFranco, J. 108
Dijk, D. J. 249
Dinges, D. F. 253–4
di Vesta, F. J. 118
D'Mello, S. 106
Doane, S. M. 44
Dodou, D. 277
Dodson, J. D. 239
Dolan, R. J. 189
Donchin, E. 16–17, 19, 91, 185, 212, 271, 275
Donders, F. C. 15
Done, J. 188
Donovan, T. T. 156, 189
Doppelmayr, M. 104
Dornier, L. 68
Dosher, B. A. 30
Doughty, C. J. 127
Douglass, S. 20, 144
Doyle, S. 11
Drew, G. C. 255
Drewry, A. 293
Drews, F. A. 101
Driskell, J. E. 85, 140, 150
Druhan, B. 123
Druker, M. 51
Drury, C. G. 45
Du Boulay, B. 162
Duffield, C. 271
Duffy, E. 238
Duffy, J. F. 249
Dumay, X. 287
Dunbar, K. 24–5, 111
Duncan, J. 49, 89, 104–5

Duncker, K. 130, 132
Dunning, D. L. 10
Dupuis, G. 232
Durgin, F. H. 56
Durlach, P. J. 102
Durso, F. T. 3
Durst, M. 92
Dutilh, G. 62
Dutta, A. 67
Dyal, C. M. 249

Easterbrook, J. A. 241, 243, 257
Eastwood, J. D. 54
Ebbinghaus, H. 4
Eckstein, M. P. 49, 51
Eddy, E. R. 182
Edelman, S. 33, 36, 44
Edens, P. 288
Eder, A. B. 187
Edkins, G. D. 278
Edmondson, A. C. 173
Edwards, B. 250
Edwards, J. D. 232
Egner, T. 104
Ehrlich, K. 160–1
Eimas, P. D. 33
Ellenbuerger, T. 85
Elliott, D. 11, 71
Elliott, L. R. 17
Elliott, R. 260
Ellis, H. 258
Ellis, H. D. 258
Ellis, M. L. 232
Ellis, N. C. 125
Ellis, N. R. 259
Ellis, R. 125–6, 183
Ellis, S. 182–4
Ellsworth, P. C. 36
Elsner, B. 69
Elstein, A. S. 26
Emde, G. G. 261
Emslie, H. 104–5
Engen, T. 46
Engle, R. W. 10, 103, 105
English, H. B. 82–3
Entin, E. E. 278
Erdeniz, B. 188
Erez, M. 181–2

Erickson, K. I. 91–2
Ericsson, K. A. 17, 144–6, 150–3, 163, 169–71, 271
Eriksen, H. R. 238, 240, 242, 244
Erlam, R. 126
Estes, W. K. 194
Esteves, F. 54
Etherton, J. L. 99
Etnier, J. L. 245
Evans, S. 238
Evert, D. L. 49
Eves, F. F. 196–7
Eysink, T. S. 122

Fabiani, M. 212, 275
Fagot, D. 203
Fahey, R. 124
Fahle, M. 36, 44
Falkenstein, M. 185–6
Fan, J. 262
Farah, M. J. 260
Faust, M. 229
Fazio, L. K. 139
Feltovich, P. J. 119, 146, 154, 157–8
Fencsik, D. E. 94, 98
Feng, S. 106
Festner, D. 285–7
Fields, K. L. 251
Figueiredo, T. 84
Fincham, J. M. 144
Fink, A. 207
Finnigan, F. 263
Fischer, S. C. 44
Fisher, B. E. 92
Fisk, A. D. 274
Fitts, P. M. 13–14, 22, 65–7, 79, 113, 213, 215, 241, 257
Fitzgerald, P. 124
Flanagan, J. C. 272
Flanagan, R. 85
Fleishman, E. A. 206, 212–15, 224
Fletcher, G. 281
Fletcher, P. C. 189–90
Flin, R. 280–1
Flombaum, J. I. 262
Flusberg, S. J. 98
Flykt, A. 54
Fogarty, G. J. 281, 287

Folkard, S. 247–9
Folstein, J. R. 18
Ford, J. 269, 281
Ford, P. R. 152
Foreyt, J. P. 239–40
Forster, K. I. 89
Foss, M. A. 212
Fossella, J. 262
Fournier, M. A. 207
Fowler, C. A. 73
Fowlkes, J. E. 292
Frackowiak, R. S. 189
Franklin, M. S. 107
Franks, I. M. 81
Franzel, S. L. 50
Frederiksen, J. R. 271, 274
Freer, C. 104–5
Freiberg, H. J. 26
Frensch, P. A. 8, 31, 99, 110
Frese, M. 179, 199, 289
Freudenthaler, H. 207
Frischen, A. 54
Friston, K. 156, 189–90
Fritz, C. O. 127, 191
Fu, Q. 109
Fu, X. 109
Fuchs, A. 74–5
Fuchs, T. 103
Fuchs-Lacelle, S. 10–11

Gabb, J. E. 255
Gabrieli, J. E. 20
Gagné, R. M. 38, 212–13
Galli, M. 71
Galton, F. 204
Ganey, H. C. N. 240
Gao, Z. 19
Gapin, J. I. 245
Gardner, H. 260
Gardner, M. K. 185
Garner, W. R. 36
Garrison, J. 188
Garst, H. 199
Gaspelin, N. 88
Gatass, R. 89
Gauthier, I. 43
Gawron, V. 277
Gawryszewski, L. G. 67

Gegenfurtner, A. 285–7
Gehring, W. J. 185–6
Gelade, G. 49–50
Gelman, R. 127, 191
Geng, J. J. 51
Genovese, E. D. 83
Gentile, D. A. 102
Gentner, D. R. 111
Gentsch, A. 186
Gernsbacher, M. A. 229–30
Gerritsen, C. 54
Gertner, A. 142
Ghose, G. M. 89
Gibb, S. 282
Gibson, E. J. 30, 35
Gibson, J. J. 35, 38
Gick, M. L. 118, 129–30, 131
Gilbert, D. T. R. 106
Gilchrist, I. D. 51
Giles, D. E. 130
Gist, M. E. 284–5
Glaser, R. 119, 153–4, 157–8
Glass, J. M. 94
Gobet, F. 132, 151, 153
Godinho, M. 84
Goedert, K. 111
Goeters, K. 280
Goettl, B. P. 275
Goldstein, A. G. 36
Goldstein, H. W. 205
Goldstein, I. L. 269, 281
Goldstone, R. L. 29–30, 32–3, 36–8
Gonzalez, C. 45, 144
Goodnow, J. J. 253
Goodwin, G. 292
Gopher, D. 90–1, 95, 101–2, 105
Gordon, M. 279–80
Gordon, T. R. 17
Gorman, J. C. 277–8
Goschke, T. 108–9
Goss, B. 186
Gottsdanker, R. 94
Götz, T. 256
Gow, A. J. 232
Grabner, R. H. 207
Graesser, A. C. 106
Grafton, S. 111

Grahn, J. A. 10
Granger, R. 32
Grapperon, J. 186
Gratton, G. 275
Gray, W. D. 100
Green, C. 102, 232
Green, N. H. 252
Greenberg, S. N. 42
Greenburg, M. 56
Greenlee, M. W. 89
Green-Rashad, B. 269
Griffin, Z. M. 191
Griffith, B. C. 32
Grigoreanu, V. 162
Grigorenko, E. L. 210
Grimsen, C. C. 36
Groeben, N. 228
Groen, G. J. 141
Gross, C. G. 89
Grossi, G. 41
Gruber, D. B. 262
Gruber, H. 121, 285–7
Grudin, J. T. 111, 164
Gruzelier, J. H. 103–4
Guerrien, A. 27
Guha, S. 204
Gureckis, T. M. 31
Gustafsson, J. 160
Guthke, J. 207
Guthrie, J. W. 268
Guzmán-Muñoz, F. J. 139

Hacker, W. 119
Hadi Hosseini, S. M. 124
Hagemann, N. 27
Haider, H. 8, 31, 99
Haier, R. J. 206–7
Hains, S. 225–7
Hall, K. G. 135
Halparin, J. D. 262
Halpern, D. V. 106
Halpin, S. 292
Hamaker, E. 203
Hambrick, D. Z. 10, 151, 153
Hammer, D. 286
Hammersley, R. 263
Hammond, W. R. 252
Hampshire, A. 10

Hancock, P. A. 240
Hanges, P. J. 205
Hanley, J. R. 33
Hanoch, Y. 242
Hanslmayr, S. 104
Harnad, S. 33
Harris, K. 32
Harris, M. M. 292
Harrison, T. L. 10
Harter, N. 5–7, 13
Hasbroucq, T. 64, 186
Hasher, L. 230
Haun, D. M. 32
Hauty, G. T. 261
Hawkes, L. W. 142
Hayes, N. E. 124–5
Hazelett, W. M. 76
Hazlett, E. 206
Head, J. 174
Healy, A. F. 3, 42, 113, 258, 275–6
Hearst, E. S. 146
Heath, M. 85
Heathcote, A. 8–9, 202
Heatherbell, D. 46
Hebb, D. O. 193, 239
Heffernan, N. T. 142
Heim, D. 106
Heimbeck, D. 289
Heimstra, N. W. 262
Helmreich, R. L. 26, 292
Helsen, W. F. 11
Helton, W. S. 174
Hempel, W. E., Jr. 215
Hendrickson, A. T. 32
Henninger, D. E. 232
Henri, V. 204
Herbort, O. 78
Hernández, M. 232
Herzog, M. H. 36
Hesketh, B. 179
Hess, K. P. 290, 292
Heuer, H. 79–80
Hicks, K. L. 10
Hilgard, E. R. 4
Hill, C. M. 251
Hill, D. W. 251
Hillinger, M. L. 226
Hiltz, K. 178

Hindorff, V. 76
Hirst, W. 98
Hirtle, S. C. 160–1
Hockey, G. R. J. 246, 251, 257
Hoffman, H. S. 32
Hoffman, K. A. 271
Hofman, J. 123
Hofstede, G. 292
Hofstede, G. J. 292
Hohnsbein, J. 185–6
Holding, D. H. 146, 191, 274
Holland, J. H. 129, 131
Hollnagel, E. 272
Holmes, J. 10
Holroyd, C. B. 189
Holton, E. F. 285–7, 289
Holyoak, K. J. 25, 118, 129–31
Hommel, B. 60, 68–9, 187
Honey, R. R. 189–90
Hooge, I.T.C. 49
Hoormann, J. 185–6
Hörmann, H. 280
Horne, J. A. 252
Horowitz, T. S. 98
Horrell, J. F. 67
Houdijk, H. H. 100
How, T. T. 191, 195, 199
Howard, R. W. 150, 202
Howes, A. 128
Hu, X. 72
Hubel, D. H. 89
Huber, D. E. 138
Huelser, B. J. 139
Huettel, S. A. 232
Hugenberg, K. 36
Huige, J. M. 3
Huitson, M. 193
Hulme, C. 10, 103, 225
Hulstijn, J. H. 125–6
Hummel, J. E. 25
Humphreys, G. W. 49
Humphreys, K. R. 192–3
Humphreys, M. S. 242–4, 248, 263
Hunt, B. I. 251
Hunt, E. B. 206
Huss, D. 113
Hyman, R. 63

Illes, J. 260
Isard, S. 111
Itti, L. 49
Ivancic, K. 179
Ivry, R. I. 109

Jackson, D. P. 246
Jackson, M. D. 22, 227
Jackson, R. C. 27
Jacobs, R. S. 277
Jacoby, L. 108
James, G. H. 265
James, W. 88, 175
Jang, Y. 138
Jared, D. 225–7
Jarrett, D. B. 249
Jaušovec, K. 207
Jaušovec, N. 207
Jaworski, R. A. 290
Jax, S. A. 76–7
Jayasuriya, R. 286
Jeannerod, M. 78
Jensen, A. R. 203–4
Jentzsch, I. 93
Jiang, Y. 52
Jiménez, L. 111
John, B. E. 163, 166, 168
Johnson, A. 2, 18, 49, 88, 112, 139, 141,
    186–7, 207
Johnson, M. P. 249
Johnson, R. 104–5
Johnson, W. 204–5, 232
Johnston, C. A. 239–40
Johnston, J. C. 89, 93–4
Jolicoeur, P. 93
Jones, A. K. 189
Jones, C. E. 258
Jones, D. M. 193, 221–3, 256–7
Jones, M. 36
Jonides, J. 129
Jung, K. 88
Jung, R. E. 207
Jusczyk, P. 33

Kaefer, A. 81
Kahneman, D. 30, 89, 101, 105
Kaiser, J. 103

Kaiser, M. K. 129
Kal, E. C. 100
Kandel, E. 260
Kane, M. J. 106
Kanfer, R. 290
Kang, S. K. 139
Kantak, S. S. 92
Kaplan, S. A. 277–8
Karni, A. 44, 123
Karpicke, J. D. 137–8
Kassin, S. M. 36, 122
Katz, S. M. 49
Kauffeld, S. 283
Kaufman, J. C. 151
Kaufman, S. 151
Kausler, D. H. 233
Kawashima, R. 124
Kay, H. 127, 191
Keele, S. W. 71, 109
Keil, F. C. 33
Keiper, C. G. 261
Keith, N. 152, 163, 179, 289
Kellman, P. J. 30
Kelso, J. A. S. 73–5
Kemler Nelson, D. G. 36
Kemp, S. 174
Kergoat, M. 232
Kern, R. P. 6
Kerr, B. 101
Kerr, E. 196
Kerr, S. A. 265
Kester, L. 121
Kewley-Port, D. 44
Keyes, H. 33
Khoo, B. H. 135
Kieras, D. E. 94, 128
Kiken, A. 2
Kikutani, M. M. 33
Killingsworth, M. A. 106
Kimberg, D. Y. 260
King, P. 260
Kinsman, L. 281
Kintsch, W. 171
Kirkpatrick, D. L. 288
Kirwan, C. 286–7
Kittler, M. G. 292
Kjellberg, A. 254

Klapp, S. T. 133
Klein, C. 292
Klein, G. A. 272
Klein, K. E. 251
Klein, R. M. 43
Kleitman, N. 246–7
Kliegl, R. 102
Klimesch, W. 104
Klinect, J. R. 292
Klonsky, J. 102
Klopfer, D. 157–8
Knott, J. 146
Knowles, E. 204
Knowles, M. 26
Knowlton, B. J. 92
Koch, C. 49
Koch, I. 93
Koedinger, K. R. 142
Kok, A. 19
Kolers, P. A. 52–3
Koller, S. M. 45
Koltzenburg, M. 189
Koriat, A. 42
Kornblum, S. 64, 69–70
Korunovska, J. 240
Kostrubiec, V. 74–5
Kovacs, K. 206
Kozlowski, S. J. 290
Kraiger, K. 270, 287–9
Kraimer, M. L. 290
Kramer, A. F. 91–2, 232, 245
Krampe, R. 151–3
Krashen, S. 126
Krebs, M. J. 60
Kreiner, H. 42
Krems, J. F. 162
Kribbs, N. B. 253–4
Krigolson, O. 85
Krikke, K. 49
Kring, J. P. 102
Krueger, W. F. 140
Krupinski, E. A. 4, 155
Kruschke, J. K. 31
Krypotos, A. 62
Kunde, W. 69
Kundel, H. L. 155–77
Kupermintz, H. 210

Kupfer, D. J. 249, 252
Kwan, I. 162
Kwapil, T. 106
Kyllonen, P. C. 205, 208, 210

Labban, J. D. 245
LaBerge, D. 38–9
Lacey, J. I. 244
Lachter, J. 89
LaFollette, P. S. 156
Lafond, D. 193–5
Lagopoulos, J. 18
Laird, J. E. 20–1
Lake, J. K. 192–3
Lam, W. 197
Lambourne, K. 245
Landy, D. H. 29
Langlois, F. 232
Lansdale, M. 191, 195, 199
Larish, J. F. 91
Larochelle, S. 111
Laroque de Medeiros, F. 81
Larsen, J. T. 189
Larson, G. E. 199
Lashley, K. S. 76
Latash, M. L. 72, 75–6
Latham, G. P. 284
Lauber, E. J. 94
Lavancher, C. 119, 121–2, 182
Lavery, J. J. 81
Lavie, N. 89
Lawrence, M. 43
Lazar, R. 51
Lazarova, M. 291
Leavitt, J. 154
Leberman, S. 11
Lebiere, C. 20–1, 144
Lecerf, T. 203
Lee, F. J. 23, 134, 220
Lee, T. D. 7, 78–9, 83–4
Lee, Y. 32
Leech, R. 24
LeGuen, O. 32
Lehman, E. 277
Lehman, M. 138
Leitl, J. 287
Lencz, T. 204
Leng, V. C. 249–50

Leonard, J. A. 63
Leonhard, T. 92
LePine, J. A. 283–4
Lercari, L. P. 262
Lerch, J. F. 144
Lesgold, A. 157–8
Leuthold, H. 93
Levelt, W. J. M. 192
Leventhal, L. M. 162
Lewis, M. W. 119
Lewis, S. 123
Lewthwaite, R. 80–1, 85
Li, V. 168
Li, Y. 49
Liberman, A. M. 32
Lichtenstein, M. 119
Lieberman, H. R. 261–2
Lievens, F. 292
Liewald, D. 204
Lightfoot, N. 39–40, 49
Lin, J. 110
Linderholm, T. 230
Lindsay, D. R. 284–5, 287
Lindsay, R. O. 154
Lindsley, D. B. 238
Linkenauger, S. A. 55
Lintern, G. 274–5
Lippa, Y. 33
Litchfield, D. 156
Littrell, L. N. 290–1, 292
Liu, E. H. 45
Liu, X. 168
Liu, Y. 162–4, 168
Lively, S. E. 44
Livingston, K. R. 33
Locke, E. A. 284
Loewen, S. 126
Logan, G. D. 98–9, 133, 139, 145, 163, 166–8, 187, 275
Logan, J. S. 44
Logie, R. 16–17, 275
Lohman, D. F. 215–16
Lombard, W. P. 246
London, M. 282
Long, W. 281
López, F. J. 19
Lotan, M. 101
Lottenberg, S. 207

Love, B. C. 31
Lowe, M. 106
Lu, C. H. 69
Lu, Z. L. 30
Lubar, J. F. 103
Lubin, A. 253
Luchins, A. S. 132
Lunn, J. H. 47
Luque, D. 19
Luria, A. R. 104
Lutz, R. 162
Lutzenberger, W. 103
Lyans, C. K. 1, 9
Lynch, P. J. 102

MacGregor, D. 272
Machin, M. A. 281, 287
Mackintosh, N. J. 40
Mackworth, N. H. 258
MacLachlan, A. 207
MacMahon, C. 175, 198
Madden, D. J. 231–2
Maeda, E. 156
Magill, R. A. 84, 135
Magoun, E. W. 238
Mahoney, C. R. 262
Maier, N.R.F. 132
Maitlis, S. 287
Major, J. T. 205
Malhotra, A. K. 204
Malmo, R. B. 238
Mamassian, P. 53–4
Mandelman, S. D. 210
Mandl, H. 121
Mané, A. 16–17, 91, 212, 271
Maniega, S. 232
Manning, C. A. 3
Manning, D. J. 156
Mansy-Dannay, A. 27
Marco-Pallares, J. 19
Mareschal, D. 24
Marinova, S. V. 287
Marks, M. 249
Marmie, W. R. 275
Marsh, E. J. 139
Marshalek, B. 215–16
Marsick, V. J. 200
Marteniuk, R. G. 78

Martens, S. 207
Martin, L. 280
Maslovat, D. 81
Massey, C. M. 30
Masson, M. E. 53, 228
Masters, R. W. 55, 100, 196–8
Matheson, M. P. 257
Mathews, R. C. 123
Mathieu, J. E. 182
Matsuda, I. 156
Matsuka, T. 31
Matthews, G. 221–3
Matthews, K. 260
Maunsell, J.H.R. 35, 89
Mavaddat, N. 260
Mawby, R. 130
Maxwell, J. P. 196–8
Maybery, M. T. 193
Maylor, E. A. 263–5
McCandliss, B. D. 262
McCann, R. S. 93
McClelland, J. L. 16, 24–5, 38, 63, 110–11, 193, 227
McClintock, A. 59
McCloskey, M. 129
McCusker, L. X. 226
McDaniel, M. A. 138–9, 230–1
McDonald, L. 11
McGeorge, P. 281
McIlwain, D. 237
McIntosh, A. R. 190
McKeithen, K. B. 160–1
McKelvey, R. K. 261
McKelvie, S. J. 132
McLaren, I.P.L. 40
McLeod, P. 132
McMillan, A. 150
McMillen, D. L. 264
McNalley, T. E. 26
McNamara, D. S. 230–1
McPherson, S. L. 58
McRobert, A. P. 152
McVay, J. C. 106
Medin, D. L. 30–1
Mehta, M. 260
Meinz, E. J. 151, 153
Meissner, C. A. 36–7
Melby-Lervåg, M. 10, 103

Melcher, J. M. 48
Mella, N. 203
Melo, M. 156
Melton, J. 278
Mencl, W. 226, 228
Mendel, R. 182
Mendenhall, M. 290–2
Menzies, H. 192–3
Merbah, S. 84
Mercado, E. 45
Merrell, R. 102
Merritt, A. C. 26, 292
Mesmer-Magnus, J. R. 285
Meulemans, T. 84
Mewhort, D. K. 8–9, 202
Meyer, A. S. 191–2
Meyer, D. E. 94, 185–6
Meyer, N. 193
Miki, S. 156
Miller, A. 167
Miller, G. A. 111
Miller, J. 67, 92, 94
Miller, J. A. 228
Mills, P. D. 182
Miltner, W.H.R. 189
Mitchell, R. F. 15
Mitchell, T. L. 37
Mitra, P. 41
Mohindra, N. 257
Mol, N. 189
Monk, T. H. 248–50, 252
Montague, P. R. 188
Mooneyham, B. W. 107
Moran, A. 85
Moreau, D. 27
Morein-Zamir, S. 259–60
Moreno, J. 239–40
Morgan, G. G. 27
Morgan, R. L. 84
Morris, M. A. 26, 292
Morris, P. E. 127, 191
Morrisette, N. 138
Moruzzi, G. 238
Mowbray, G. H. 63
Moylan, C. 64
Mozer, M. C. 137
Mulder, M. 277
Muller, P. F., Jr. 64

Munhall, K. G. 73
Murphy, J. 41
Murphy, K. 102
Murray, C. 232
Müsseler, J. 60
Myers, C. W. 100
Myin-Germeys, I. 106
Mynatt, C. R. 162

Naish, J. M. 277
Nakano, L. 49
Nakashima, R. 156
Nandagopal, K. 150, 152, 153
Náñez, J. 43
National Transportation Safety Board 1
Naumann, J. 228
Navon, D. 90, 94–5
Neider, M. 91–2
Neilands, C. 104
Neily, J. 182
Neiss, R. 244
Neisser, U. 49, 51, 98
Neninde, L. 230
Nestel, D. 281
Neubauer, A. C. 207
Neumann, O. 98, 175
Neves, D. M. 133
Newell, A. 8, 13, 20, 23, 115–16, 133–5
Newell, K. M. 72, 75, 82–3
Newon, J. 278
Nicholson, D. E. 82
Niemantsverdriet, J. 32
Niessen, C. 159
Nieuwenhuis, S. 189
Nijhuis, H. 280
Nir, M. 182
Nisbett, R. E. 129, 131
Nishi, K. 44
Nissan, J. 204
Nissen, M. J. 108, 110
Nodine, C. F. 155–7
Noe, R. A. 268, 283–5
Nokes, T. J. 123
Nokes-Malach, T. J. 119
Norman, D. A. 88, 90, 95, 168, 175–7, 220–2
Norman, G. R. 26

Norris, J. 126
Nosofsky, R. M. 31, 33
Novick, R. 51, 131
Nuechterlein, K. H. 206
Nyberg, L. 19–20

Oberauer, K. 102, 193
Obonsawin, M. 106
Obstfeld, D. 181, 183
O'Connor, P. 278, 281
O'Doherty, J. P. 189
O'Donnell, P. H. 103
Oelhafen, P. 256
Ohlsson, S. 179–81
Öhman, A. 54
Olson, J. R. 146
Opitz, B. 123
Ortega, L. 126
Osman, A. 64
Ost, J. 198
Ostberg, O. 252
Oswald, F. L. 3, 151, 153
Owen, A. M. 10, 260

Paas, F. C. 120–1
Paek, J. 206
Palethorpe, S. 226
Paley, M. 290, 292
Palladino, M. A. 103
Palladino, P. 238
Palmer, E. M. 98
Panzer, S. 85
Park, J. H. 100
Parmentier, F. 193, 195
Parrott, A. C. 262–3
Pascual-Leone, A. 252
Pashler, H. 60, 92–3, 136–40, 150
Passos, R. D. 156
Patey, R. 281
Patrick, J. 212
Pattie, A. 204
Pavlik, P. I. 142
Payne, R. B. 261
Payne, S. J. 128
PDP Research Group 24
Pear, T. H. 70
Pe'er, I. 204
Peeters, M. C. 287

Pellegrino, J. W. 44
Penke, L. 204, 232
Perfetti, C. 228, 231
Perruchet, P. 108
Perry, D. H. 277
Perry, Z. A. 199
Peterson, L. 232
Petre, M. 160
Pettit, A. N. 252
Pew, R. W. 79
Pfaffman, C. 46
Pfurtscheller, G. 207
Phenix, T. L. 10–11
Philbeck, J. W. 56
Philip, P. 256
Phillips, J. 291
Pickard, J. 260
Pidd, K. 287
Pirolli, P. L. 119, 131
Pisoni, D. B. 44
Plomin, R. 150
Poggio, T. 33, 36
Poldrack, R. A. 20
Polich, J. 18–19
Polson, P. G. 170
Porter, J. 281
Posner, M. I. 13, 15, 97, 215, 262
Post, T. A. 155
Pothos, E. M. 122
Potts, R. 179
Pouget, A. 102, 232
Povel, D. J. 76–7
Powell, J. W. 253–4
Powers, K. L. 103
Prabhakaran, V. 20
Prakash, R. 91–2
Press, D. Z. 252
Price, C. J. 156
Priest, A. G. 154
Priest, H. A. 268, 292
Prietula, M. J. 146
Prilutsky, B. I. 75
Prinz, W. 60, 69, 197
Pritchard, S. C. 226
Proctor, R. W. 18, 64, 67–9, 88, 98, 112, 186–7
Proffitt, D. R. 55, 129
Proteau, L. 79

Puck, J. F. 292
Pullyblank, A. 182

Qin, Y. 20
Quaintance, M. K. 206, 212–15, 224
Quinn, J. T., Jr. 83
Quiñones, M. A. 285

Rabbitt, P.M.A. 60, 62, 70, 185, 199, 257, 263–5
Rabin, M. D. 47
Rabipour, S. 10
Radaelli, S. 37
Raizada, R. S. 32
Ramsey, J. D. 257
Rankin, R. E. 241, 257
Rasmussen, J. 272
Rauter, G. 80
Ravesloot, C. J. 3
Rawson, K. A. 171
Raymond, W. D. 3
Raz, A. 10
Razzaq, L. 142
Reales, J. M. 232
Reason, J. T. 174–5
Reber, A. S. 122–3
Recker, M. 119, 131
Rector, K. 162
Redick, T. S. 10, 103
Reed, K. D. 191
Reeve, T. G. 67–8
Regas, K. 239–40
Regian, J. W. 275
Regina, E. G. 261
Reicher, G. M. 41
Reichle, E. D. 106
Reilly, T. 250–2
Reimann, P. 119
Reingold, E. M. 152, 156
Reiser, B. J. 142
Reitman, J. S. 160–1
Remington, R. 94
Renkl, A. 121–2
Rescorla, R. A. 188
Reuter, H. H. 160–1
Revelle, W. 242–4, 248, 263
Reynolds, C. F. 249

Reynolds, J. H. 89
Reynolds, P. 98
Rhoades, M. V. 63
Richter, T. 228
Rickard, T. C. 11, 252–3
Riedel, S. 290, 292
Riener, R. 80
Riggio, L. 67
Riggio, R. E. 25
Rigoldi, C. 71
Rimmer, J. 260
Rizzolatti, G. 66
Robbins, T. W. 189, 260
Roberson, D. 33
Roberts, C. 261
Robertson, E. M. 252
Robertson, R. W. 230
Robie, C. 292
Rodet, L. 34–5, 44
Rodrigo, A. H. 207
Rodríguez-Fornells, A. 19
Roediger, H. L., III. 52–3, 137–9
Roelofs, A. 192
Roger, C. 186
Rogers, C. R. 26
Rohlman, D. S. 162
Rohrer, D. 136–9, 150–1
Roker, R. 232
Roling, P. 45, 156
Rolls, E. T. 24
Romero, P. 162
Ronda, J. M. 249
Roring, R. W. 150, 152, 153
Roscoe, S. N. 26, 277
Rose, M. R. 206
Rosenbaum, D. A. 74, 76–7
Rosenbloom, P. S. 23, 134–5
Rosenholtz, R. 49
Ross, B. H. 130
Rosser, J. C., Jr. 102
Rossion, B. 43
Rostami, M. 124
Roth, E. M. 271
Rothermund, K. 187
Rouiller, J. Z. 281
Rowold, J. 283, 285
Roy-Charland, A. 42–3

Rubinson, H. 157–8
Rueda, M.R. 262
Rumelhart, D.E. 24, 168
Rumiati, R.I. 93
Ruocco, A.C. 207
Ruona, W.E. 286
Russ-Eft, D. 286
Russell, R. 56
Ruthruff, E. 88–9, 94
Ryan, R. 205
Rybowiak, V. 199

Saariluoma, P. 145, 154
Sabol, M.A. 6
Sacco, D.F. 36
Sackur, J. 107
Safavynia, S.A. 73
Sagaspe, P. 256
Sahakian, B.J. 189, 259–60
Sahgal, A. 263
Sahu, A. 182
Saint-Aubin, J. 42–3
St. Louis, E.K. 246
Salas, E. 268, 271, 277–8, 290, 292
Salthouse, T.A. 10, 163–6, 231, 233–6
Saltzman, E.L. 73
Salvucci, D.D. 96
Sanders, A.F. 16
Sandow, B. 265
Sange, G. 207
Sarter, N. 95
Sarwar, G. 150
Sasaki, Y. 30, 43
Sasirekha, G. 182
Sato, J.R. 156
Saults, J.S. 166, 233
Sauseng, P. 104
Sauter, D.A. 32
Scarpin, D.J. 156
Schabus, M. 104
Schachinger, H. 239
Schank, R. 179
Schaufeli, W.B. 287
Scherbaum, C.A. 205
Schmidt, H.G. 26
Schmidt, R.A. 71, 78–82, 136, 139
Schmitt, N. 203

Schneider, D.W. 63, 69
Schneider, W. 51, 97–8, 134–5, 172, 228, 264, 274–5
Schneiderman, B. 160
Schooler, C. 10
Schooler, J.W. 48–9, 106–7
Schorer, J. 27
Schot, W.D. 78
Schrater, P. 102, 232
Schrausser, D.G. 207
Schultz, W. 188, 190
Schumacher, E.H. 94, 108–11
Schütze, M. 211
Schuyler, Jr., E. 59
Schvaneveldt, R.W. 147
Schwabe, L. 239
Schwaninger, A. 45
Schwarb, H. 108–11
Schwarzbauer, C. 189
Schyns, P.G. 30, 34–5, 44
Seeger, C.M. 65, 67
Seger, C.A. 20
Seibel, R. 63
Seidenberg, M.S. 24, 226
Sellick, K. 281
Selmer, J. 291
Serfaty, D. 278
Seufert, T. 211
Seyler, D.L. 285
Seymour, B. 189
Seymour, T.L. 94
Shakeshaft, N.G. 150
Shallice, T. 20, 175–7, 220–2
Shanks, D.R. 109, 179, 188, 189–90
Shankweiler, D.P. 226, 228
Shapiro, D.C. 82
Shapiro, D.D. 81
Shaughnessy, K. 56
Shawn, P.F. 269
Shea, C.H. 72, 80–1, 85, 100, 135
Shea, J.B. 84
Shebilske, W.L. 275
Sheffer, L. 104
Shen, M. 19
Sheptak, R. 16–17
Sheri, A. 104
Sheridan, H. 156

Shiffrar, M. M. 47–8
Shiffrin, R. M. 33, 39–40, 49, 51, 97–8, 105, 264, 274
Shin, Y. K. 187
Shipstead, Z. 10, 103
Shirani, A. 246
Shouse, M. N. 103
Shui, R. 19
Shulman, L. S. 26
Sickles, E. A. 155
Siegel, B. V. 206–7
Siegel, D. 91
Sigrist, R. 80
Silvia, P. J. 106
Simon, H. A. 13, 17, 115, 146, 151, 153, 271
Simon, J. R. 68
Simons, D. J. 102
Singh, K. D. 89
Siqueland, E. R. 33
Sjøberg, D.I.K. 159
Skolimowska, J. 232
Sleeman, D. 141
Smallwood, J. 106–7
Smeets, J. J. 78
Smilek, D. 54
Smith, A. P. 247, 250, 256–7
Smith, A. T. 89
Smith, G. M. 261
Smith, J. 145
Smith, J. C. 251
Smith, M. 108
Smith, M. A. 138
Smith, M. C. 92
Smith, M. D. 154
Smith, R. 286
Smith, S. M. 264
Smith, V. L. 36
Smither, J. W. 282
Snoddy, G. S. 8
Snow, R. E. 205, 210, 215–16, 223
Snowling, M. J. 225
Snyder, C. R. R. 97
Snyder, K. M. 168
Snyder, S. H. 261
Soderling, E. 207
Soloway, E. 160–1
Somberg, B. L. 235

Somers, G. 281
Sonnentag, S. 159, 289
Sørensen, T. A. 242
Sousa, A.P.B. 89
Sowden, P. T. 45, 156
Spada, N. 126–7
Spang, K. K. 36
Sparrow, W. A. 83
Spearman, C. 205
Spector, P. E. 277
Spelke, E. 98
Spencer, A. 102
Spiekermann, S. 240
Sports Illustrated 59
Sprafka, S. A. 26
Squibb, H. R. 128
Stachowicz-Stanusch, A. 27
Stachowski, A. A. 277–8
Stadler, M. A. 111
Stagl, K. 292
Stankov, L. 104
Stanley, W. B. 123
Stansfeld, S. A. 257
Starkes, J. L. 175, 198
Starr, J. M. 204
State v. Cromedy 37
Steiner, R. 256
Stelmach, G. E. 94
Stenton, R. 10
Stephan, K. E. 190
Sterling, C. P. 55
Sternberg, R. J. 118, 208–10
Sternberg, S. 16
Stevens, C. K. 284–5
Stevenson, R. J. 46, 48
Steyvers, M. 36–7
Stoet, G. 54
Stoianov, I. 234
Stout, R. 271
Strayer, D. L. 91, 101, 167
Stroebe, W. 287
Stroop, J. R. 40
Strybel, T. Z. 2
Stump, S. 70
Sugiura, M. 124
Sugovic, M. 55
Sulikowski, D. 54
Sullivan, K. J. 92

Sullivan, M. A. 134, 228
Sülzenbrück, S. 79–80
Sun, C. 177
Sundermier, B. 230
Sutcliffe, K. M. 181, 183
Sutton, J. 237
Sutton, R. S. 188
Swartwood, J. N. 103
Swartwood, M. O. 103
Sweller, J. 120–1
Swinnen, S. P. 7, 81–2
Szelag, E. 232

Taatgen, N. A. 23, 32, 93, 96, 113, 134, 141, 202, 219–20
Tabor, W. 226, 228
Tagliabue, M. 69
Taillard, J. 256
Takahashi, M. 124
Tamblyn, R. 26
Tan, S. J. 25
Tanaka, J. 43
Tannenbaum, S. I. 182, 205
Tarique, I. 291
Taylor, D. W. 132
Taylor, H. A. 262
Taylor, K. 150
Teasly, B. E. 162
Teichner, W. H. 60
Telford, C. W. 92
ten Cate, T. J. 3
Terrell, T. D. 126
Tesch-Romer, C. 151–3
Thagard, P. R. 129, 131
Thayer, R. E. 239, 244
Theologus, G. C. 261
Thomson, S. J. 94
Thon, B. 85
Thorndike, E. L. 9–10, 235
Thurstone, L. L. 205, 223
Tilley, A. 254
Tilley, A. J. 255
Tilton, J. W. 235
Ting, L. H. 73
Toffanin, P. 207
Tomita, Y. 126–7
Tomporowski, P. 245
Torbiörn, I. 291

Toril, P. 232
Torres-Oviedo, G. 73
Townsend, J. T. 16, 62
Trampush, J. W. 204
Tredoux, C. G. 37
Treisman, A. M. 49–50, 95
Tremblay, L. 85
Tremblay, S. 193–5
Treue, S. 89
Trott, J. W. 289
Trumpower, D. L. 150
Trzaskowski, M. 150
Tsang, P. S. 95
Tuerlinckx, F. 62
Tuffiash, M. 152
Tuholski, S. W. 105
Tuller, B. 73
Tulving, E. 138
Turkeltaub, P. 32
Turner, D. C. 189
Twitchell, S. 289
Tyhurst, J. S. 244
Tyler, C. 239–40

Ullman, S. 33
Ullsperger, M. 186
Ullsperger, P. 186
Ulrich, R. 93
Umiltà, C. 67–9
Urcuioli, P. 69
Ursin, H. 238, 240, 242, 244
Usher, M. 63

Valentine, T. 36
Valot, C. 280
Vandekerckhove, J. 62
van den Broek, P. 230
van der Gijp, A. 3
van der Kamp, J. J. 55, 100
van der Schaaf, I. C. 3
van der Schaaf, M. F. 3
van der Spek, E. D. 148–9
van der Wel, R. 76
Van Doornen, L. P. 287
van Emmerik, R. E. A. 74–5
Vangkilde, S. 242
Van Gyn, G. 85
van Hoorn, W. 5

Van Keer, E. 292
VanLehn, K. 115, 119, 140, 142
van Merriënboer, J. G. 120–1
van Oostendorp, H. 148–9
van Oploo, M. 32
Van Orden, G. C. 226
Van Overschelde, J. P. 171
Van Petten, C. 18
van Rijn, H. 93, 141
van Schaik, J. J. 3
Van Selst, M. 93–4
Van Zandt, T. 62, 68
Varner, K. R. 229
Vashdi, D. R. 181–2
Vasyukova, E. 152
Vatikiotis-Bateson, E. E. 73
Veermans, K. 285–7
Veldstra, J. L. 259
Vereijken, B. 74–5
Verhave, T. 5
Vernon, D. 104
Verwey, W. 111
Vessey, I. 162
Vicente, K. J. 271–2
Vickers, J. N. 58
Vidal, F. 186
Vidulich, M. 275
Vigorito, G. 33
Vimercati, S. 71
Viswesvaran, C. 285
Vitouch, O. 242
Voelkle, M. C. 219
Vogt, S. 69
Volmer, J. 159
Volpe, C. E. 277
Voss, J. F. 155
Voss, M. W. 91–2
Voudouris, D. 78
Vrij, A. 198
Vu, K. P. L. 2, 69
Vu, T. M. 232
Vul, E. 136–8
Vyas, S. 70

Wagenmakers, E. 62
Wagner, A. D. 188
Wagner, R. F. 155
Wallace, R. J. 67

Waller, M. J. 277–8
Walter, C. B. 81, 83
Walthew, C. 51
Wang, L. P. 203
Wang, Y. 157–8, 293
Wankel, C. 27
Warburton, D. M. 262–3
Warr, P. 283
Warriner, A. B. 192
Watanabe, C. 156
Watanabe, T. 30, 43
Waterhouse, J. 246, 250
Watkins, K. E. 200
Watson, J. M. 101
Watter, S. 94
Waymouth, S. 56
Wayne, S. J. 290
Weber, R. J. 76
Weedon, E. 196
Weeks, D. J. 68
Wegman, H. M. 251
Weick, K. E. 181, 183
Weil, M. 91
Weinberger, N. M. 35
Weinert, D. 246
Weiss, D. J. 76
Weiss-Meilik, A. 181–2
Welford, A. T. 60, 92, 255
Welham, A. K. 40–1
Wells-Parker, E. 264
Wertheim, A. H. 49
Wesnes, K. A. 262–3
West, P. 182
Wetzstein, A. 119
White, B. Y. 271, 274
White, K. G. 46
Whiting, H. T. A. 74–5
Wickens, C. D. 95, 101
Wickens, T. D. 127, 191
Wiedenbeck, S. 160–2
Wiemers, E. A. 10
Wiesel, T. N. 89
Wightman, D. C. 274–5
Wilcock, S. E. 259
Wilding, J. 257
Wilhelm, J. A. 26, 292
Wilkinson, L. 109
Williams, A. 152

Williams, A. L. 89
Williams, H. L. 253
Williams, P. 104–5
Willingham, D. B. 111
Willis, R. P. 140, 150
Wills, A. J. 40–1
Wilson, B. A. 199
Wilson, K. A. 278
Wilson-Donnelly, K. A. 292
Winstein, C. J. 80, 92
Winter, W. C. 252
Wisher, R. A. 6
Wisniewski, M. G. 45
Witt, J. K. 55
Wittmann, W. W. 219
Wittwer, J. 122
Wixted, J. T. 5, 136–9, 150
Wohldmann, E. L. 276
Wolf, P. 80
Wolfe, J. M. 50, 98
Wolpe, P. 260
Wolpert, D. M. 85
Woltz, D. J. 185
Womelsdorf, T. 89
Wood, B. P. 155
Wood, R. E. 284
Woodrow, H. 223
Woods, A. J. 56
Woods, D. D. 272
Woodward, E. 235
Woodworth, R. S. 9–12
Wooten, S. 292
Wortham, D. 121
Wouters, P. 148–9
Wright, C. 263–92
Wright, D. L. 135
Wu, C. 162–4, 168
Wu, J. C. 206

Wulf, G. 72, 80–1, 85, 87, 100, 197
Wurtman, R. J. 261

Xu, H. 19
Xu, W. 272–4

Yamaguchi, M. 168
Yang, B. 293
Yang, T. 35
Yantis, S. 89
Yaure, R. G. 135–6
Yearta, S. 287
Yeh, Y. Y. 275
Yerkes, R. M. 239
Yin, J. 19
Yin, R. K. 43
Yokosawa, K. 156
Yorkston, K. M. 26
Yoshikawa, T. 156
Young, D. E. 81–2
Young, S. G. 36
Young-Xu, Y. 182
Yukl, G. 205
Yusko, K. P. 205

Zaepffel, M. 19
Zaman, S. A. 259
Zanone, P. G. 73–5
Zatsiorsky, V. M. 75
Zempel-Dohmen, J. 287
Zevalkink, C. 25
Zhang, L. F. 210
Zhang, Z. 252
Zhu, F. F. 55
Ziessler, M. 110
Zijlstra, F. R. 287
Zorzi, M. 69, 234
Zucco, G. M. 46, 48

Subject Index

action control 174–8; contention scheduling in 175–6; schema triggering in 176–7; supervisory attentional system in 176–7; *see also* motor control
ACT-R 20–2, 25, 180; in threaded cognition theory 96, 219–20
adaptive perception 53–5; action-specific perception view of 55–6
additive factors method 16
aging and skill 231–5; cognitive components of 233–5; general slowing in 231–2; training effects in 232–3
air traffic control 2–3, 219
alcohol 263–6; effects on information processing 263–4; skill level and 264–6
analogical learning and transfer 128–32; in problem solving 208–10
aptitude-treatment interactions 210–12, 228
arousal and performance 89, 238–45; cognitive activation theory of stress 240–1; criticisms of arousal construct 243–5; cue-utilization hypothesis 241–2; multiple-resources account 242–3, 263; Yerkes-Dodson Law 239–44
associative phase of skill 14, 114, 217, 221
attention: definition 88
attentional bottlenecks 88–9; early-selection theories 88; late-selection theories 88
attentional resources 89; unitary *vs.* multiple resource models 95–6; *see also* performance operating characteristic
attentional skill 100–1; and training 102–4; *see also* time-sharing skill
automaticity 25, 97–8, 175; instance theory of 98–9; and training 274–5
autonomous phase of skill 14, 22, 98, 114, 217, 221

bistable perception 53–4
brain plasticity 35
brain training 10

caffeine 260–2; attentional effects of 262
capture errors: and lapses of attention 175–6, 195
categorical perception 31–3
chess: expertise in 132–3, 145–6, 151–4, 202–3, 234
circadian rhythms 245–6; adaptation of 250–2; and arousal 246; body temperature and performance 246–7; effects on memory and cognition 247–9; individual differences in 252; and speed-accuracy trade-off 249–50
cognitive load theory 120–2; and example-based learning 121–2
cognitive skill acquisition: locus of 133–5; phases of 113–14; power law in 133
connectionist models 23–5
constrained action hypothesis 100
contextual interference effect 84, 135–36; *see also* variable practice
continuous learning 282–3
crew resource management 278–81; behavioral markers in 280–1

debriefing: case study 183–4; learning from 181; role of self-explanation in 182–3
declarative knowledge 22, 92, 119, 123–4, 126, 142, 179–80, 196, 208, 217
declarative phase of skill 22, 98, 216
deliberate practice 152–3, 163
discovery learning 178, 211
doctrine of formal discipline 9–11
drug use and performance 259–60

Einstellung (mental-set) effect 132–3
Error Orientation Questionnaire 199–200

error recovery 179, 198
errors made during learning: causes of 190–9; effects on learning 179–80
exemplar models 33
expertise: in computer programming 159–62; deliberate practice account of 152–3; in interpreting medical images 155–8; investigation of 145–50; phases in the development of 151–2; in typing 162–8
expert knowledge: direct and indirect methods for studying 146–50
experts: common characteristics of 153–4; memory ability of 153–4; problem solving in 154

failure-of-further-learning effect 127, 191
feedback in knowledge learning 139

goal orientation 284–5
grammar learning 122–4; implicit learning in 224–5; rule-based knowledge learning in 223
guidance hypothesis 81

Hebb repetition effect 193
Hebb's rule 193

implicit learning 107; locus of 110–11; role of attention in 109–10; role of awareness in 108–9
incidental learning 107, 189–90; see also implicit learning
individual differences in reading skill 225–31; and dual-route model 225–6; role of suppression of irrelevant information in 229–31; and working memory 228–9
individual differences in skill acquisition 203; evaluating models of 222–5; levels of action control account of 220–2; modified radex model of 215–19, 222
information-processing approach 12–13
information reduction hypothesis 99
instance theory of automaticity 98–9; and overlearning 139
instructional explanations and learning 122

intelligence and aptitudes 204–10; cognitive components approach to 208–10; cognitive correlates approach to 206; neural correlates approach to 206–7; two-factor theory of 205
intelligence and cognitive control 104–5

labeling features 45–8; and verbal overshadowing 48–9
learning curves 7–8
learning from examples 120–2
long-term working memory 171

medical diagnosis 3–4, 155–8
mental models 119, 128–9, 181, 273; cognitive cause maps of 183–4; for devices 128; in expertise 154, 157; shared 277
mental practice 85
metacognitive skill and problem solving 118–20; in expertise 172; and self explanations 118–20; and training 179, 183, 229–30, 290
mind wandering and executive attention 106–7
mistakes of action 174
motivation 120, 152, 211, 283, 285–7, 288
motor control, problems of: degrees of freedom 74–6; perceptual-motor integration 77–8; serial order 76–7
motor learning 70–1; dynamical systems perspective on 72–4; motor programming perspective on 71–2
motor skill 60; acquisition of 78; constrained action hypothesis of 100; intrinsic feedback in 79–80; knowledge of results in 80–2; schedules of practice in (see practice schedules)
multiple-task performance see psychological refractory period effect; time-sharing skill

needs assessment 269–70
neurofeedback 103–4
nicotine: effects on information processing 262–3
noise, effects on: attentional control 257; information processing 257; sleep 257

overlearning 139–40; and expertise 150–1
own-race bias and perceptual learning 36–7

Pathfinder algorithm 147–50
perceptual learning: definition 30; locus of 43–4; and training 38, 44–9; *see also* perceptual learning mechanisms
perceptual learning mechanisms: attention weighting 30–3; differentiation 35–8; perceptual unitization 38–43; stimulus imprinting 33–5
performance monitoring 184–7; EEG markers of 185–6; and post-error slowing 185
performance operating characteristic 90–1, 101
plateaus in learning 6
power law of practice 8–9, 25; individual differences in 202; and instance theory 99
practice schedules 83–5; blocked *vs.* randomized 84–5, 135–6; spacing of trials in 83
prediction error and learning 187–90; temporal difference approach to 188–90
probabilistic learning 188–9
problem solving: knowledge-lean problems 114; knowledge-rich problems 114–15; weak methods for 116–17
problem-space hypothesis 115–16
procedural knowledge 22, 119, 123, 175, 180, 196
procedural learning view 52–3; encouraging during training 196–8
procedural memory 21, 96, 196
procedural phase of skill 22
procedural reinstatement principle 275–6
psychological refractory period effect 92–5; effects of practice on 94–5; executive-process interactive control account of 94; response-selection bottleneck account of 92–3

psychophysiological measures 18–20; in neurofeedback; in probabilistic learning; related to performance monitoring 185–6

recognition memory and differentiation 38
response-selection skill 60–1

savings paradigm 4–5
schemas: in action control 175; in motor control 70–1; for remembering 127–8
second language learning 125–7
selective learning 124–5, 196
self-efficacy 283–4
sequential effects (repetition effects) 69–70
set-size effects and Hick-Hyman Law 63–4
Simon effect 68–9, 166
simulator training 276–7
skill: definition 2; historical overview 4–12; ways of studying 3
skill acquisition: common mechanisms in 2; information processing approach to 12–13; models of 20–5, 63, 99–100, 215–22; phases of 13–14, 144; quantifying 14–20
skilled attending 100
skilled memory theory 168–71
sleep deprivation: and circadian rhythm 254–5; effects of blue light on 256; effects on consolidation 252–3; effects on performance 253–5; lapse hypothesis and 253–4
slips of action 174–7, 199
SOAR 20–1
soft skills: and crew resource management 26; training of 25–6
speed-accuracy tradeoff 61–2; sequential sampling model of 62
sport training 27; and arousal 238
stimulus-response compatibility effects 64–9; effects of practice on 67, 69; element-level 65; precuing effects 67–8; response-effect compatibility 69; set-level 64; *see also* Simon effect
stress 25–6, 238, 240–2, 244, 277–9; environmental 256–9

subtractive method 15–16
system control learning: selective and unselective modes 124–5

task analysis 270–4; ability requirements approach to 212–15; cognitive 271–4; principled task decomposition method of 271
team training 277–8; cross training 277; shared mental model in 277
temperature extremes: effects on attention of 257–9; and skilled performance 258
template models 33
testing effect 137–9
theory of identical elements 10–11, 275
theory of reinvestment 197–8
time-sharing skill 101–2; structural interference in 95; test of selective attention 102; training of 101
training methods 274–6; part-task training 274–6; procedural-reinstatement principle 276
training programs: evaluation of 281, 287–9; maximizing benefits of 289–90; and national culture 290–3
transfer climate 281

transfer motivation 285–7
transfer paradigm 9–10, 78

unselective learning 196–7
user models 141–2; and intelligent tutors 141; and model-tracing method 142

variable-emphasis training 91–2
verbal protocol analysis 17; applications of 128, 131, 145, 147, 167–8, 271
visual search 49–52; adaptive 54–5; circadian effects on 247; contextual cuing in 52; effects of alcohol on 264–5; feature-integration theory of 50; feature *vs.* conjunctive 50; perceptual unitization in 39–40; practice effects in 97–8, 100; set-size effects in 49

word-inferiority effect 42
word-superiority effect 41–2
worked examples 120–2
working memory 12, 19–20, 93, 206, 219; in expertise 146, 154; training 10, 92, 103, 197

Yerkes-Dodson law 239–44